Monica,
All the best
James Kelleher

Path of Light
Volume II
The Domains of Life

Path of Light
Volume II

The Domains of Life

James Kelleher

AHIMSA
San Francisco

The Path of Light: Volume II © 2006 by James Kelleher

All rights reserved under International and Pan-American Copyright Conventions

This book is sold under the condition that it shall not be circulated, traded, resold, reproduced or transmitted in any form or by any means, electronic or mechanical, including photocopying, recording, or by any information storage and retrieval system, without the publisher's prior written consent, except by a reviewer who may use brief quotations in articles and reviews.

Published by Ahimsa Press

Printed in the United States by Thomson-Shore, Inc.

Book design by JTC Imagineering
Editors: Debra Infante and David Goldstein Ph.D.
Astrological Chart Designer: Marga Laube
Illustrations: Susanta Sarangi

James Kelleher's website is www.jameskelleher.com. All questions related to this book should be emailed to james@jameskelleher.com.

First Edition

Library of Congress Control Number: 2006920731
ISBN-10: 0-9774480-1-0
ISBN-13: 978-0-9774480-1-2

To M. K. Gandhi,
for taking me in,
treating me like a son,
and passing on the light.

Acknowledgements

The *Path of Light* has only been made possible by virtue of the generous efforts and blessings of the following people, to whom I am deeply grateful:

Debra Infante, for her consistent editing, researching, formatting, and modifying the text, as well as helping to create the index and glossary.

David Goldstein Ph.D., for editing and reviewing the text, as well as giving advice regarding key modifications and additions to the manuscript.

Sat Siri Khalsa, for her helpful insights after reviewing the final manuscript.

Hank Friedman, for reviewing the final text and checking chart calculations.

Marga Laube, for assistance with the book design, research assistance, creative layout of the horoscopes, and for reading and critiquing the text.

Dr. K. S. Charak, for his insights regarding key technical points.

Rajiv Tomar, for his assistance during my many trips to India, as well as coordination in obtaining the artwork for this book.

Dr. David Frawley, for his suggestions pertaining to ancient Vedic history and the nakshatras, and for his support and encouragement.

Terri Schwaderer, (my wife) for frequent advice related to grammar and design, as well as her constant encouragement, understanding, and support.

Betty Durso, for her unique ability to simplify, clarify and cut to the core of things, and thereby come up with the book's title, *Path of Light*, in a single insightful moment.

Swami Sivanandamurthy, for his encouragement and blessings during the writing of this book.

Contents

PREFACE: INTRODUCTION TO CHART ANALYSIS   11
CHAPTER ONE: INTERPRETING THE DOMAINS OF LIFE   16
CHAPTER TWO: YOGAS   25
CHAPTER THREE: DIVISIONAL CHARTS (VARGAS)   44
   Author's Journal: A Meeting with the Prince of Navamsha   54
CHAPTER FOUR: THE DREKKANAS   56
   Author's Journal: The Story of Yavanacharya   96
CHAPTER FIVE: DASHAS   98
   Author's Journal: "Look Ma, No Planets!"   110
CHAPTER SIX: TRANSITS   112
   Author's Journal: Beginner's Luck and The Power of Transits   123
CHAPTER SEVEN: THE PSYCHOLOGICAL PROFILE   127
   Author's Journal: Siddhi Ma, Grand Ma   141
CHAPTER EIGHT: HEALTH   145
   Author's Journal: Astrology On the Fly   166
CHAPTER NINE: CAREER   169
   Author's Journal: The Copper Plate Man   205
CHAPTER TEN: MONEY   210
   Author's Journal: Teet Maharaja, Yogi of the Himalaya   228
CHAPTER ELEVEN: RELATIONSHIPS AND MARRIAGE   234
   Author's Journal: Close Encounters of the Hiker Kind   273
CHAPTER TWELVE: CHILDREN   281
   Author's Journal: Varahamihira, Pig Astrologer   298
CHAPTER THIRTEEN: PARENTS   300
   Author's Journal: Two Bananas   309
CHAPTER FOURTEEN: BROTHERS AND SISTERS   311
   Author's Journal: The Nose Knows   320

CHAPTER FIFTEEN: HOUSE AND RESIDENCE   321
  Author's Journal: Baja Air   328
CHAPTER SIXTEEN: VEHICLES   333
  Author's Journal: Don't Try This At Home   353
CHAPTER SEVENTEEN: PETS   358
  Author's Journal: Misadventures in Feline Astrology   379
CHAPTER EIGHTEEN: EDUCATION   383
  Author's Journal: Bombay Beedi Baba   408
CHAPTER NINETEEN: SPIRITUALITY AND JYOTISH   412
  Author's Journal: Love Pats from Shiva   436
CHAPTER TWENTY: LIFE ACCORDING TO MARK   445
  Author's Journal: Astrologer, Predict for Thyself   492

GLOSSARY   497

BIBLIOGRAPHY   505

INDEX   509

THE AUTHOR   519

Preface:

Introduction to Chart Analysis

Chart interpretation is a complex art, which requires the astrologer to comprehend and integrate thousands of diverse factors. It is a daunting task even for the seasoned astrologer, not to mention the beginning or intermediate student. Like the waves on a vast ocean, the infinite features of the person's life are reflected in symbol through unique combinations of planets, aspects, yogas, signs, houses, nakshatras, and numerous divisional charts. The idea that any human being could master such an immense subject boggles the imagination.

The Astrologer's Attitude

As with any undertaking, the attitude with which one approaches chart interpretation is very important. It is helpful to understand from the outset that astrology is not magic. It is not a parlor trick, and those who try to use it to dazzle friends and impress people ultimately fail to derive anything profound from the horoscope. The astrologer who becomes full of himself invariably becomes motivated to impress his client with his ability to predict, and forgets that his purpose is to help the client understand his life. Astrology is not an end in itself, but a tool that has been provided to shed light on the client's experiences and lead him to higher awareness.

During the last twenty-five years, I have traveled to India many times, and have had the opportunity to meet some of India's greatest astrologers. Notable among these astrological luminaries was the late Dr. B.V.

Raman, from Bangalore. I met Dr. Raman on several occasions and had the opportunity to discuss astrology with him. He was a reserved man with a piercing intellect and a wry sense of humor. On our first meeting he asked me, "So you are an astrologer?" Something about the way in which he asked this question made me hesitate. I have never felt comfortable making such a claim, especially in the company of an astrologer of Dr. Raman's stature. I answered, "I can only say that I am a student of Vedic astrology." Dr. Raman seemed to like this response and told me that he felt the same way himself. "No one can rightly claim that he is truly an astrologer," he said. "We are all only students!"

Context is Everything

Good chart analysis begins with simple awareness and common sense. The astrologer must pay attention to the person in front of him. The client's gender, age, cultural background, appearance, and many other obvious factors must all be part of the reading. For example, a horoscope may indicate that the fifth house (children) will be activated in a positive way during a particular planetary period. If the astrologer predicts the birth of a child, however, without taking into account that the client is a 75 year-old widow, his prediction will obviously fail. A great deal of astrological assessment takes place before the astrologer even looks at the chart.

Once the student of a great jyotishi was sitting with his teacher in his consultation room. A man entered the room and asked the astrologer to read his horoscope. The teacher quickly calculated the man's chart, studied it for a moment, and began his reading. He made several accurate observations about the man's past, including an odd detail. "You have come here today, after dining on saffron rice," he said. The man was amazed by the astrologer's accuracy, and went away very happy with the reading. After the reading the student was very upset with his teacher and began to sulk. The teacher asked him what was wrong and the student replied, "I have been your student for ten years now. I have served you faithfully and worked hard to learn everything you have taught me. In return for my effort and faithful service, it has been your duty to teach me everything you know. But you have hidden this secret technique from me. You have never taught me how to tell if a man has eaten saffron rice before coming to the reading!" The teacher said, "You are right. This is a great secret and you deserve to know the method." The student looked eagerly at the teacher, "Well then, how did you do it?" he asked. The teacher said, "The man had some saffron rice grains stuck on his shirt. It looked fresh!"

The Static Chart

The horoscope has multiple dimensions. On one level it is static. It reveals the basic nature of the person. This nature never changes. A zebra remains a zebra throughout its life, regardless of his experiences. The astrologer's first job is to clearly understand the personality and overall strength of the individual. When he understands the person's unique personality patterns, he will be able to decide what choices the person will make and how he will react to particular planetary periods. Similarly, each house and planet in the horoscope has certain inherent potentials, which characterize the person's experience in the specific domains of life. The assessment of the strength or weakness of the houses and planets in the chart gives the astrologer an understanding of his innate potential. Throughout his life, the person always retains his unique personality, and he realizes only the potentials of the karmas that are reflected in his chart.

The Dynamic Chart

The chart also has a dynamic quality. Life is always changing and the chart reveals these infinite fluctuations of karma for the individual. The main tools used for this level of analysis are dashas and transits. Even though the person never changes his inherent nature, he does change within his nature. For example, a person with a Cancer Ascendant will usually seek security in some form. During the beginning phase of his life he could look to his mother to provide security. Later he may go through a long phase of life focusing on his friends as a source of security. At yet another stage in life, he might focus on his family or job for the same purpose. What remains the same is the person's typically Cancerian response to the changing phases of life. The dynamic portion of the chart is reflected by the position of the dasha rulers and transiting planets in the chart. Shifts in priorities, values, orientation, as well as events and trends in life are all reflected in the dasha and transit scheme. In this respect, the chart reflects the fructifications of karma as the soul evolves.

Prediction

The ability to predict results from a combination of the factors given above. Having deeply understood the person's nature, and taking into account the contextual factors such as the person's gender, age and cultural background, the astrologer assesses the planetary periods and transits in order to make a prediction about events in the future. The best predictions take all of these elements into consideration.

On a purely mechanical level, predictions can be easy if the astrologer has first accurately analyzed the chart's static condition. A planetary period will produce results that are in line with the planet's static potential in the chart. If the astrologer clearly understands the planet's disposition in the chart, then he can easily predict the outcome of the planet's period.

Philosophy of Prediction

As the student of Jyotish gains experience with chart analysis, he invariably becomes more confident with his predictions. Astrology is a fascinating subject, and the prospect of making an accurate prediction can be a seductive reward for a bright astrologer. At some point, however, each astrologer has to ask himself about his motivation in making predictions. Is his motivation simply to be a great astrologer and to make an accurate prediction, or is it to help the client? Is the client always helped by hearing a prediction, no matter how negative?

In this regard, astrologers are greatly divided. Some feel that the job of the astrologer is to simply reveal what he sees in the chart. Others subscribe to a philosophy that includes the occasional omission of a negative feature of the chart when it can clearly cause useless fear in the person's mind. While it is not my purpose to try to resolve this debate, there is one point that is important to consider. No astrologer knows for sure what is going to happen. Although experience in making predictions produces more confidence, it can also breed arrogance. Astrologers commonly blurt out negative predictions in such confident-sounding proclamations that it seems the event will definitely happen. The client goes away in fear, feeling that the negative event is bound to take place. What the astrologer failed to tell the person was that even though he might have seen this event happen in similar cases, he still does not know for sure if it will happen in this particular case. For this reason, great care should be taken when making negative predictions. Predictions should always be carefully worded to avoid creating unnecessary fear. The astrologer should own up to his own incapacity to reveal absolute truth and qualify his statements accordingly.

The Approach of This Book

This book is intended to be a guide to the interpretation of the Vedic horoscope. Whereas *Path of Light, Volume I* elaborated on the fundamental symbols and myths of Jyotish, this volume describes the practical process of analyzing and describing the horoscope in detail. Each astrologer at some stage needs to organize the way in which he approaches chart interpretation. Some astrologers use a house-by-house approach, describing the twelve houses of the horoscope one by one, as a way of organizing the information. Others use a planet-by-planet method in order to present the reading to the client. I have chosen to organize this book as I organize readings, theme-by-theme. Astrology is a very complex subject, and sometimes this becomes overwhelming to clients who really don't care about the countless analytical factors such as houses or planets. People come to astrologers in order to know about real life issues. They want to know more about their psychological makeup, strengths and weaknesses. They also want to know about their careers, finances, relationships, health and other aspects of life. Organizing the reading theme-by-theme is one way in which the astrologer can make the reading more understandable and meaningful for the client.

In presenting this book, it is my sincere desire that it will help aspiring students of Jyotish grasp the fundamentals of the subject. I also hope that my method of organizing and presenting this material will somehow make Vedic astrology more relevant for modern life. Most importantly, I hope that through reading both volumes of this book the student will gain an appreciation of the deep and mystical tradition out of which this astrology originates, and begin to revere it as the great *vidya* (spiritual science) that it is.

—James Kelleher
January 3, 2005

Chapter One

Interpreting the Domains of Life

The interpretation of any domain of life, such as the person's career or health, requires the ability to both analyze and synthesize the various factors within the horoscope. Because the horoscope is a veritable ocean of complex and diverse factors, chart interpretation can be a daunting task, to say the least. With this in mind, it is helpful to start by developing a clear and well-organized strategy for interpretation. The following points are intended to help the student approach the chart in a methodical way that clarifies the priorities of interpretation.

Preliminary Concepts of Interpretation
(Combining Houses, Planets and Signs)

Planets Placed in Houses

When a planet is placed in a house it contributes its energy to that house, and the significations of both the planet and the house should be reflected in the interpretation. If Venus (love and affection) is placed in the fifth house (children), the person might have affectionate and loving children. Mercury (intellect) in the same location might produce intelligent children. In both cases, a signification of the planet was combined with a signification of the house. The concept is to reflect on both the significations of the planet and the house, and to simply combine both values in an intelligent and intuitive statement.

Interpreting the Domains of Life

Planets Placed in Signs

When a planet is placed in a sign, it mixes its energy with that of the sign. The interpretation should reflect this mixture. A person with Mercury in Libra, for example, communicates in a diplomatic way. Mercury in Sagittarius, on the other hand, may indicate that the person communicates in a manner that is direct and sometimes blunt. The sign adds an important element to the texture of the interpretation.

Rulers of Houses in Other Houses (Linking Houses Through Their Rulers)

When a planet is located in a house other than its own, it carries the influence of the house of ownership to the house of placement. The interpretation should reflect the significations of both the house of rulership and the house of placement. For example, if Venus rules the third house and is placed in the tenth house, then the career might be connected with communications. In this case, the tenth house (career) has been linked to the third house (communications). The concept is to think about the significations of each house, and then create an intelligent statement that connects related values of both houses. In another example, if the ruler of the fourth house (property) is placed in the second house (money), the person might earn money through real estate. But since the fourth house also indicates the mother, the person could receive money through the mother as well. Both statements are reasonable interpretations of this combination. The art of horoscope interpretation lies in learning how to intelligently combine the significations of houses, signs, and planets into a reasonable statement. In order to become proficient at this, you first need to know the significations of each planet, house, and sign. Once you are clear on what each of these fundamentals represent, it's just a matter of thinking about their combinations and making intelligent (and intuitive) interpretations. The results of house rulers placed in the twelve houses were described in detail in *Path of Light, Volume I*.

Five-Point Domain Interpretations

The domains of life are the various areas of life in which we express and fulfill our desires. Career, health, relationships, finances, and spirituality are a few of the more prominent domains of life. Each of these domains of life is reflected in the horoscope through multiple astrological factors. In order to simplify and prioritize an effective method for interpreting the domains of life, the following five points will be emphasized: the house; the karaka; yogas; divisional charts; nakshatra and drekkana symbolism.

1. House

Each domain of life has a primary house that signifies its domain. For example, the seventh house is the house of marriage and relationships, so it is the main house that is analyzed when assessing the marriage or partnership issues in the chart. There are also other houses in the chart which signify factors that are related to marriage. For example, the eighth house is the house of joint finances and also of sexual energy, so it can be an important house to include for a more complete understanding of marriage.

Essentially, a house will thrive and produce positive results if it is strong. The house will be strong under the following three conditions:

- The house is occupied by beneficial planets
- The house ruler is positively disposed
- The house is aspected by benefical planets or hemmed in by natural benefics

A house will be weak under the following three conditions

- The house is occupied by malefic planets
- The house ruler is negatively disposed
- The house is aspected by malefic planets or hemmed in by natural malefics

These elements of house analysis were covered in the chapter on houses in *Path of Light Volume I*.

2. House Karaka (Significator) Strong or Weak

Each house has a ruler and also a significator. The house ruler is the planet that owns the sign in the house. The house significator, on the other hand, is the planet which signifies or represents the subject matter of that house. Because houses symbolize many aspects of life, they can have more than one significator. When the significator of a particular aspect of life within the domain of a house is strong, then that aspect of life is likely to manifest in a positive way. If the significator is weak, then the things it signifies will manifest with difficulty or not at all. Of course, the method of determining the strength or weakness of a house significator is the same one used for any planet, and was discussed in detail in the chapter on planets in *Path of Light, Volume I*. The following is a list of house karakas (significators).

Table of House Karakas

House	Subject	Planet
First House	Health	Sun
Second House	Wealth, Family	Jupiter
Third House	Siblings, Courage	Mars
Fourth House	Mother	Moon
	Vehicles	Venus
	Education	Mercury
	Land	Mars
Fifth House	Children	Jupiter
Sixth House	Chronic Disease	Saturn
	Acute Disease	Mars
Seventh House	Marriage	Venus
Eighth House	Longevity, Death	Saturn
Ninth House	Teacher, Wealth	Jupiter
	Father	Sun
Tenth House	Trade & Commerce	Mercury
	Employment	Saturn
	Professions	Jupiter
	Government	Sun
Eleventh House	Gains	Jupiter
Twelfth House	Losses	Saturn
	Meditation, Moksha, Liberation	Ketu

House Karaka Aspecting Its Own House

If a house karaka aspects its own house, then the significations of the house related to that planet thrive. For example, if Venus, the karaka for vehicles, is placed in the tenth house, then its aspect on the fourth house will make it more likely that the person will own nice vehicles. An important point to note here is that the aspect of the karaka does not necessarily improve other significations of the house, only those which are under the karaka's domain. Mars, for example, is the house karaka for the third house because it rules brothers and courage. If Mars is placed in the ninth house, it will aspect the third house and will produce siblings who do well in life. The third house, on the other hand, is also the house of communications. If Mars is placed in the ninth house, its aspect on the third house may produce an argumentative nature, thus producing problems in communications. Its affect on brothers and courage, however, would be beneficial.

House Karaka Occupying Its Own House

If a house karaka is placed in its own house, it strengthens some of the house significations under the domain of the karaka, however there are some exceptions. The following chart describes some of these challenges.

Interpreting the Domains of Life

Table of House Karaka Occupying Own House

Planet and House Placement	Domain of Difficulty	Comments
Sun in the ninth house	Father	May produce problems for the father, or in the relationship with the father.
Moon in the fourth house	Mother	It gives problems for the mother or in the relationship with the mother.
Mars in the third house	Younger Sibling	Mars in the third can create argumentative communications generally, including the communications with the brother. It can also give accidents, injuries or surgeries to the brother.
Jupiter in the eleventh house	Older Sibling	May produce problems for the older sibling or in the relationship with the older sibling.
Jupiter in the fifth house	Children	The standard interpretation is that this position gives problems with children. In practice, it seems to give one good child or at least a small family, which in the eyes of traditional Hindu culture is a problem.
Venus in the seventh house	Spouse	One of the partners may be more loving, passionate, affectionate, or simply more available than the other and feels that he or she does not receive enough affection.

Houses and Karakas, a Dual Approach

In order to assess any particular domain of life in the chart, it is of primary importance to know two things, the disposition of the house and the disposition of the karaka for that particular domain of life. In a chart with a Virgo lagna, for example, the fifth house (children) is the sign of Capricorn and Saturn rules the fifth house. Jupiter, however, is the significator for children in every horoscope regardless of the lagna, so Jupiter is the karaka for the fifth house. In order for a house signification to thrive, both the house (via its ruler, occupants, aspects, etc.), and the house significator should be strong. This means that in assessing any domain of life, the astrologer has two main tasks. First, he assesses the strength of the house, and then he assesses the strength of the karaka. If both are strong, the fruits of that domain of life will manifest. If both are weak, then difficulties in that area of life will result.

3. Yogas

Yogas are combinations. There are literally thousands of yogas that are described in astrological texts, which produce special effects in different domains of life. In order to thoroughly understand a domain of life, the yogas that are related to the domain should be identified and described. For example, if Venus is placed in its own sign in the seventh house, this forms a Mahapurusha Yoga called Malavya Yoga. This yoga makes the person artistic. To ignore this yoga when assessing the tenth house and the career could be a major interpretive mistake. The subject of yogas is covered later in this book.

4. Divisional Charts

Each domain of life has a primary divisional chart as well as secondary divisional charts that can be used to elaborate on the details of the domain. For example, the Dashamsha chart is the chart for career. After analyzing the tenth house and the karaka for career (the Sun), the astrologer can look at the Dashamsha chart for additional detail. This becomes particularly helpful when the astrologer is analyzing a planet's dasha and bhukti results for a particular domain of life. The subject of divisional charts is discussed in detail later in this book.

5. Nakshatra and Drekkana Symbolism

Once the astrologer has considered the impact of the houses, the karakas, the yogas, and the divisional charts that are related to a particular area of life, he can use the nakshatra and drekkana symbolism to describe the domain in more detail. The symbols of the nakshatras and drekkanas occupied by the ruler of the primary house, as well as planets placed in the primary house can sometimes provide more detail. For example, if the ruler of the tenth house is placed in the second drekkana of Virgo, which is symbolized by a man holding a pen doing his profits and losses, then the person's career could be related to accounting, bookkeeping or business in general. In another example, the placement of domain-specific planets such as the karaka or house ruler in the nakshatra of Shatabhisha, which has the basic shakti of healing, could give the person an inclination to pursue a healing profession. It could also signify that the person will go through career issues that may be related to one of the myths about Varuna, the deity of Shatabhisha. The subject of nakshatras was covered in detail in *Path of Light Volume I*. The subject of drekkanas will be covered later in this volume.

Sorting Out the Complexities in Chart Analysis

Astrology is essentially an art of putting things together, interpreting the various combinations between planets, signs, and houses. Consider Jupiter placed in the sign of Leo, in the eleventh house. Immediately we are confronted by the task of synthesizing three different sets of values: Jupiter, Leo, and the eleventh house. In fact, we actually need to synthesize more than three sets of values, if you take into consideration the houses of Jupiter's rulership, its aspects, its nakshatra placement, and various other planetary connections. It's easy to see why many people become discouraged with astrology in the beginning. There are so many factors to interpret that even the best astrologers feel overwhelmed at some time.

Having a complex task, however, doesn't mean the solution has to be complex. As a matter of fact, the solution is so simple that most people miss it completely. The basic concept when looking at a planet placed in a house and a sign, realizing that there are numerous factors to consider, is to simply analyze each factor one by one. Take them apart, one factor at a time, and one combination at a time. In the example given above, Jupiter is involved in many relationships. Start the interpretation with the relationship that is most obvious. Jupiter is a benefic and it is placed in the eleventh house. The eleventh house has many significations, such as achievements, income, friends, older brothers and sisters. So just pick one of them. It doesn't matter which one. Choose the first one that comes to your mind, or the one you are interested in at the moment, such as income, for example. Simply say something positive and Jupiterian (Jupiter is the planet of expansion) about income. Example: "This placement might improve the person's income." If Jupiter happens to be a temporal malefic, as in the case of a Libra Ascendant, then make two separate statements about Jupiter in the eleventh house. Example: 1. "Jupiter might improve the person's income." 2. "The person might have to struggle for it." If you want to focus on the signification of friendship, instead of income, then do exactly the same thing with two separate statements, one positive, and one negative. Example: 1. "The person might have successful, knowledgeable or prosperous friends." 2. "The friends might struggle for prosperity or knowledge." The point is that you don't have to synthesize several relationships into one all-inclusive statement. Life is complex, like a large ball made of many strings tied together. The chart reveals these complexities in great clarity. In order to unravel them, sometimes the best approach is to simply remove one string at a time.

The Rule of Converging Influence (Synthesis)

Once you have patiently analyzed the many factors influencing a planet or a house one by one, it will occur to you that many of the individual factors point in a similar direction. At this point, you can make use of a great astrological principle, which I call "the rule of converging influence." Simply put, this rule states that when several factors point in the same direction, they will reveal a condition or prediction that can be stated confidently, and which will be felt by the person in a way that is hard to miss. Although the great sage, Parashara, never mentioned this rule in these exact words, the rule does express one of the great maxims of Vedic astrology.

Every Combination Comes Out

Most astrologers get bogged down in an attempt to make global statements about the chart in order to synthesize many factors at once. As a result, they frequently skip or at least rush through the process of laying out all the individual combinations in the chart. This not only makes it more difficult to eventually make the desired global statement, but also overlooks an important principle. That principle is the following: Everything comes out in some way in the horoscope. Even though a combination may not be supported by ten other combinations, each saying the same thing, it doesn't mean that the combination won't manifest. It will definitely manifest in some way. Sometimes it may not manifest in an obvious way, but it will manifest either in the outer world or on a psychological level.

Chapter Two

Yogas

The word yoga means "union," "link," or "combination." In Jyotish, a yoga is a specific combination, described in the classical texts, that renders specific results. Some are very simple, involving only one planet placed in a certain sign or house. Others are extremely complex, involving several planets as well as divisional charts. The classical texts list thousands of yogas, making it impossible to discuss yogas in great depth in an introductory book. It is possible, however, to discuss some of the common yogas in a way that will make them easy to understand and to use.

Combining of Planetary Influences

Yoga means "union" or "combination." This can occur in different ways. For the purpose of defining the following yogas, the term "combination," unless otherwise stated, will refer to the following five types of relationships:

1. Two planets in the same sign.
2. Two planets mutually aspecting each other.
3. Two planets, each placed in the sign owned by the other.
4. Two planets, each placed in the nakshatra of the other.
5. Planet one in planet two's sign. Planet two aspecting planet one.

Raja Yogas

Raja Yogas are combinations that lift a person up in life, giving status and success in the profession. The most common form of a Raja Yoga occurs when two or more planets, ruling angles (houses 1,4,7,10) and trines (houses 1,5,9), combine in some way.

The most powerful version of this yoga is to have a planet that owns an angle, and a planet that owns a trine, placed in an angle in the chart. Mars and Jupiter, for example, placed in the tenth house, for a Leo lagna will give success in the profession. Planets placed in the angles of the chart tend to be expressed in prominent ways.

If the planets owning angles and trines are placed in a trinal house, this is also a very fortunate combination, leading to luck and success. The fifth and the ninth houses are houses of luck and prosperity. Any planets placed in these houses naturally thrive and fructify easily. The first house is both a trine and an angle, so any Raja Yoga falling in this house becomes particularly strong.

If Raja Yoga planets combine in houses other than angles or trines, they may produce limited results, or even negative results, if other afflictions are present. The rulers of angles and trines placed in the twelfth house (losses), for example, might produce losses or uncertainties in a person's professional dealings. This Raja Yoga position may not signify a total failure, however. Because the twelfth house is also the house of distant places, the person might experience career opportunities through travel in distant places, or even foreign countries. Similarly, in the third house (a minor dusthana), Raja Yoga planets could produce opportunities through the sibling. Instead of giving the global and obvious elevation produced by placement in angles or trines, Raja Yoga planets placed in houses other than angles and trines may produce elevation or successes via some of the specific significations of the house of placement.

It is important to note that in order for Raja Yogas to produce the best results, the lagna should be strong.

Dhana Yogas

Dhana Yogas are combinations that produce wealth or financial increase. One of the most frequent ways in which these yogas occur, is when the rulers of money houses (houses 2,5,9,and 11) combine. The second and the eleventh houses are the main houses of income. The ninth and the fifth are houses of wealth, and are connected with Lakshmi, the goddess of wealth. So any combination of these four planets by conjunction, mutual aspect, exchange of signs, etc., will produce a yoga for financial improvement. If the ruler of the ascendant combines with one of the rulers of the four money houses, this also produces a

Dhana Yoga. If these combinations occur in the money houses (houses 2,5,9,and 11) then the yoga will be quite powerful. If they occur in the angles of the horoscope (houses 1,4,7,and 10), they will also produce strong results. Placement in the dusthanas (houses 6, 8,12, and to some extent 3) will produce limited results or losses, similar to Raja Yoga planets in dusthanas. Similarly, Dhana Yogas occurring in dusthanas can give positive results that come from sources related to the dusthana house's significations. For example, a Dhana Yoga in the sixth house might produce income through a health profession. Similarly, a Dhana Yoga in the eighth house might produce income through inheritance.

It is also important to note that in order for Dhana Yogas to produce the greatest financial gains, the lagna should be strong.

Arishta Yogas

Arishta Yogas are combinations that contribute to ill health. There are three sets of planets, which become important factors in these combinations. First, the rulers of dusthanas (houses 6,8, and 12) are planets that are involved in various struggles and problems in life. Second, maraka planets (rulers of houses 2 and 7) are planets that can create death, provided the person has reached the appropriate phase of life. Otherwise, these planets simply produce ill health. Third, the ruler of the Ascendant is the planet of the physical body, so its connection to any of the planets from the first two groups of planets can produce health problems.

The most common way in which Arishta Yogas occur in the chart is when the rulers of the dusthanas combine in some way in the chart. If these planets combine with the lagna lord, they create a link to the physical body, which makes it more likely that a physical problem will occur. If the ruler of a maraka house is also involved in the combination, this may amplify the possibility of physical problems. See the chapter on health for more information on how to utilize these combinations in the horoscope.

It is important to note that in order for Arishta Yogas to produce full-blown results, the lagna should be weak. A strong lagna will give good general vitality and constitutional strength, making it difficult for disease to manifest. Jupiter in the first house also makes it difficult for major problems to manifest. Similarly, benefics placed in angles of the horoscope protect the person from health problems to a great extent.

Parivartana Yoga

Parivartana Yoga occurs when two planets exchange signs. For example, in the chart of a Libra Ascendant, if Saturn (fifth lord) is placed in the first house in Libra, and Venus (first lord) is placed in the fifth house in Aquarius, this creates a Parivartana Yoga. The planets involved in the combination become strengthened, as if they are placed in their own signs. There is also a strong bonding between the two houses involved in the Parivartana Yoga. In the previous example, the first house is a trine and also an angle, and the fifth house is a trine. The combination of these two planets, Saturn and Venus, naturally produces a Raja Yoga. The Parivartana Yoga reinforces the bond between the houses making a powerful Raja Yoga.

The particular houses and signs in which the Parivartana Yoga takes place will make a big difference in the results produced. In the example, Saturn is the Yogakaraka for the Libra Ascendant and Venus is the lagna lord. The yoga occurs between the first house and fifth house. It occurs in signs that are friendly to each of the planets. These conditions are obviously positive. If on the other hand, Jupiter (sixth lord) exchanges houses with Saturn (fourth lord), such that Saturn is placed in the sixth house (Pisces) and Jupiter is placed in the fourth house (Capricorn, where it is debilitated), quite different results will manifest. This combination links the fourth house to the sixth house (a dusthana). In spite of the fact that the Parivartana Yoga will strengthen each of the planets to some extent, the strong bond between the sixth and fourth houses will produce adverse results. The fourth house will undergo problems, struggles, and obstructions. The person could have problems with land or houses. The mother might have health problems.

Lunar Yogas

Gaja Kesari Yoga

Gaja Kesari Yoga is formed when Jupiter is placed in an angle (houses 1, 4, 7, and 10) from the Moon. This combination is actually a Raja Yoga, which promotes success and well-being in a general way. The classical texts assign an array of beneficial results to Gaja Kesari Yoga, including fame, good looks, health and wealth. These results are confined, however, to a Gaja Kesari Yoga in which the Moon and Jupiter are angular, unafflicted and strong.

Jupiter and the Moon frequently fall in an angular position to each other in the horoscope. Most of the time, however, they are not placed in the angles of the chart. Although these placements might not give the horoscope-owner wealth and fame, the yoga will frequently still give predictable results of some kind. Sometimes the results are not positive, but this is a reliable yoga, which can help the astrologer make clear predictions.

One of the easiest ways to apply this combination is to simply think of it as the "fame" yoga. When it is present in the chart, the person becomes famous on some level. Of course there are various levels of fame, ranging from "world famous," to simple popularity within one's own social or career circle. The placement of the yoga, as well as many other factors such as the strength of the lagna, the tenth house, etc., all contribute to the relative magnitude of popularity.

People who have Gaja Kesari Yoga in their charts usually have promotional ability or the ability to present themselves (or their subject of interest) in a positive light. They become good at packaging and presenting things, much like an enthusiastic teacher presents knowledge to a class. As a result, this yoga is seen in the charts of people in advertising, sales, and marketing. An example of this was seen in the charts of the employees of a New York advertising agency, where I was asked to do consultations for every employee. Out of the seventeen employees for the agency, all seventeen had Gaja Kesari Yoga in their charts. None of these people were famous themselves. But all of them were in the business of making other people famous. This yoga is a combination that makes a person able to package and present things in such a way that it becomes attractive to others. The manner in which the person presents his subject matter, either verbally, artistically, or professionally, reflects back on the person, making him popular in some way. As a result, this is frequently seen in the charts of people who work in client-professional occupations where reputation is important and "word of mouth" is a key factor in reputation building.

If malefics aspect one of the planets in the Gaja Kesari Yoga, or if one of the planets is placed in a dusthana, afflicted or weak, then the person will gain some good reputation, but he will also experience periods where the reputation suffers. This effect is more pronounced when the Moon is the afflicted planet, and it is particularly strong when the afflicting planet is Saturn.

Shakata Yoga

This combination occurs when Jupiter is in the sixth, eighth, or twelfth house from the Moon, but Jupiter should not be placed in an angle of the chart. The classical texts say that this yoga gives fluctuating fortunes, struggles, changes and setbacks. In actual practice this is a common yoga, seen in the charts of people who tend to make changes in their lives more frequently. In ancient times, making changes was often the cause of financial ruin and great difficulty. In modern times, however, our relationship to change is much different and the results of this yoga are usually more benign.

Jupiter rules over future plans and goals, knowledge, prosperity, as well as the person's spiritual path. With Jupiter placed in the sixth, eighth, or twelfth house from the Moon, the person achieves these things by first making changes or by letting go of the present conditions. A person with Shakata Yoga, for example, might quit a job in order to go to school in preparation for a new career. Frequently the change has an optimistic (Jupiterian) quality about it. The person looks forward to some new knowledge, new career, new opportunity, or new condition in the life. In order to move in the new direction, he lets go of the present condition. Eventually the ground that is lost by making the change is recovered in the new field. For example, the person could give up a steady income in order to go to school for the purpose of entering a new profession. After some time, he attains a good income again in the new profession.

If Jupiter is also placed in a dusthana from the lagna, or is afflicted by malefics, the results of this yoga can be more in line with the classical description. In extreme cases, the person can experience huge losses during the periods of Jupiter or the Moon, or when Jupiter or the Moon go through negative transits. Even in this case, however, the person eventually recovers from his losses.

Adhi Yoga

This yoga occurs when Jupiter, Mercury and Venus are placed in the sixth, seventh, and eighth houses from the Moon in any order or combination. The most powerful form of this occurs when all three of these houses are occupied by one of these planets. It doesn't matter which planet is in which house, but it is important that these planets not be afflicted or debilitated. The yoga also takes place if two of the planets are in one of these houses, and one of the planets is in another, leaving one of the three houses vacant. An example of this is found when Jupiter and Mercury are in the seventh house and Venus is in the eighth house from the Moon. It even occurs when all three planets are in only one of the houses. When Adhi yoga occurs from the Moon it is called Chandradhi Yoga. It can also occur from the lagna, in which case it is called Lagnadhi Yoga.

The classical texts give a long list of wonderful character traits, including being successful and having a good reputation, which are conferred on a person who possesses Adhi Yoga. In practice, it does seem to make the person intelligent, virtuous, healthy, and wealthy. In particular, it gives good administrative ability and is particularly good for running businesses that thrive and prosper.

Kemadruma Yoga

This combination occurs when the Moon has no planets in the sign previous to its placement or the sign after its placement. There are several conditions that cancel this yoga. Two of the most common are: 1. If there are any planets in a kendra to the lagna or the Moon, the yoga is canceled. 2. If the Moon is conjunct or aspected by a benefic planet, the yoga is also canceled.

This yoga is said to cause various kinds of miseries, such as poverty, ill health and lack of mental peace. In fact, this combination does make it more difficult to feel happy and fulfilled in life. The Moon is the mind, and especially symbolizes the ability to feel happy and secure in life. Without the support of other planets, the person feels alone, prone to depression, and unable to find ways to fulfill his needs. This yoga, however, should not be taken in isolation as indicating a miserable life. It is seen in the charts of some very successful people. In these cases, though, it still gives the person a sense of being alone or unsupported.

Sunapha, Anapha, and Durudhara Yogas

These yogas occur when the Moon has planets (other than the Sun) placed in the second house (Sunapha Yoga), the twelfth house (Anapha Yoga), and in both the second and the twelfth houses (Durudhara Yoga) from itself.

These combinations are all generally positive, giving various good results like wealth, status, and health. The main concept to understand is that it is better to have planets surrounding the Moon than to have both signs on either side of the Moon vacant.

The Pancha Mahapurusha Yogas

The Pancha Mahapurusha Yogas are five combinations that are very common and very useful in delineating the chart. Pancha means "five." Maha means "great." Purusha is a man or being. So the name refers to five great beings or five great men. Mahapurusha Yogas are five combinations that produce five great personality types, along with life conditions which correspond to their natures.

These yogas occur when any one of the planets, Mars, Mercury, Jupiter, Venus or Saturn, is placed in an angle from the Lagna or from the Moon, and is either in its own sign or exalted. Thus, these yogas occur when one of these planets is extremely strong in the chart.

The five Mahapurusha Yogas are as follows:

Ruchaka Yoga

Ruchaka Yoga occurs when Mars is in its own sign or exalted sign and placed in a kendra from the lagna or the Moon. It is said to make the person good-looking, bold, courageous, famous, adventurous, the leader of an army, or of a gang of thieves. He may have a life span of seventy years.

This yoga produces an individual who expresses the positive qualities of Mars in a very strong dose. These qualities permeate the life and make it likely that the person will even make his living in some martial way. It is common in the charts of military people, police, and athletes. It is also seen frequently in the charts of business people who are independent or self-employed.

Bhadra Yoga

Bhadra Yoga occurs when Mercury is placed in an angle from the lagna or the Moon and is in its own sign or exalted sign. The classical texts say that it makes the person strong, healthy, handsome, learned, sweet-smelling, intelligent and virtuous. The yoga also confers wealth, marriage, and children, and gives a life span of eighty years.

This combination produces the qualities of Mercury in a strong dose. The person will have a bright intellect and be skilled in language arts such as speaking, writing, and reading. If Mercury is afflicted by natural malefics, then the person may not be effective as a communicator, but may still be good at processing information. In any case, this yoga gives the ability to give and receive information on some level, and this quality will dominate the life. It is seen in the charts of writers, teachers, business people, and others for whom the process of communication dominates the life.

Hamsa Yoga

Hamsa Yoga occurs when Jupiter is placed in a kendra from the lagna or the Moon, and is also placed in its own sign or exalted sign. The classical texts say that the person will be attractive, have beautiful skin, a sweet voice, love water sports, and have a very strong sex drive. He is also intelligent and becomes very knowledgeable. He receives a beautiful spouse, comforts, prosperity, and dies in a forest at the age of one hundred years.

Hamsa Yoga obviously bestows the qualities of Jupiter in great measure. Jupiter is the planet of prosperity, knowledge, truth, the teacher, the spiritual path, and dharma. Consequently, this combination gives the person a strong sense of inner knowing. The person feels like a teacher or an expert and strives to gain the academic knowledge that will allow him to fulfill his role of advising others. People who have this yoga in their charts often become teachers, professionals, consultants, advisors, or even spiritual leaders. They gravitate towards prosperity and comfort in life.

Malavya Yoga

This yoga occurs when Venus is placed in a kendra from the lagna or the Moon and is also in its own sign or exalted sign. It is said to produce beauty, grace, education, wealth, comforts, scriptural knowledge, and an inclination toward infidelity in marriage. It is supposed to make the person an artist and he will live to the age of seventy.

In practice, Malavya Yoga elevates the energy of Venus so that it dominates the chart. Venus is the planet of emotion, so Malavya Yoga makes the person loving, kind and even compassionate. It is found frequently in the charts of healers. Venus' relational quality also makes this combination common in the charts of people who use charm and social skills in their work. Because Venus is also the planet of creativity and the arts, this yoga is frequently seen in the charts of artists and other creative types. Malavya Yoga also makes it more likely that the person will get married, or at least have romantic encounters.

Shasha Yoga

Shasha Yoga is produced when Saturn is placed in a kendra from the lagna or the Moon and is also in its own sign or sign of exaltation. The classical texts say that Shasha Yoga makes the person cruel, brave, a leader, efficient, and critical of others. He is supposed to be very sexual and has a tendency to be attracted to the sexual partners of other people.

He has devoted servants, and lives to the age of seventy.

This yoga is produced by a dominant Saturn. Consequently, all of Saturn's qualities will be expressed in a prominent way. The person will have a strong sense of responsibility, good organizational skills and management ability. He will tend to be patient, persevering, conservative, and reserved. "Devoted servants" may manifest as the person having employees who are efficient and responsible. The person also has a strong sense of commitment, and willingly accepts and follows through with responsibilities. As a result, he naturally gravitates to positions of leadership that require hard work and management skills.

Notes on Mahapurusha Yogas

In practice, Mahapurusha Yogas are very common. When one or more of these placements occur in the chart, the planet causing the yoga becomes dominant in the horoscope, and can be treated with a similar emphasis as the Sun and the Moon. Both the qualities of the sign and the nakshatra placement of the Mahapurusha planet will become dominant personality traits. The person's career will also usually be related to the planet's significations.

Having a Mahapurusha Yoga planet in the chart is not always completely positive, however. A strong planet dominating the chart can sometimes express its strength "to a fault." When Shasha Yoga is present in the chart, for example, the person might have a strong sense of responsibility that causes him to over work or to take on too many responsibilities. Hamsa Yoga can give a person a strong sense of "knowing." He might feel that he already knows things and has a strong need to teach others, whether they want to be taught or not. He might also possess a strong sense of what is right and wrong, causing him to sometimes appear to be self-righteous or judgmental. Bhadra Yoga can sometimes bring out mercurial values to a fault. The person often becomes so mental and clever that he makes other people uncomfortable. His cleverness and facility with language can also occasionally make him manipulative. Malavya Yoga can sometimes cause the person to become excessively sensual, excessively romantic or excessively self-indulgent. Finally, Ruchaka Yoga sometimes makes the person ambitious or aggressive to a fault. In some cases this produces a tendency to be feisty, argumentative or prone to anger.

Neecha Bhanga Raja Yoga

This is a combination that cancels or reverses the debilitation of a planet.

It occurs under the following conditions:

1. The ruler of the sign in which the debilitated planet is placed is in a kendra from the lagna or the Moon.
2. The ruler of the sign where the debilitated planet would be exalted is placed in a kendra from the lagna or the Moon.
3. The ruler of the sign in which the debilitated planet is placed either conjuncts or aspects the debilitated planet.
4. The ruler of the sign in which the debilitated planet would be exalted either conjuncts or aspects the debilitated planet.
5. The debilitated planet is in a Parivartana Yoga (exchanging houses) with the planet that owns the sign it is in.
6. The debilitated planet is conjunct an exalted planet.
7. The debilitated planet is retrograde.
8. The debilitated planet is exalted in the Navamsha chart.

Neecha Bhanga Raja Yoga is a Raja Yoga and is supposed to produce good results. In fact, this is a very misunderstood yoga, which many (if not most) astrologers misinterpret. It is common for jyotishis to make statements such as "Neecha bhanga doesn't work. Planets that are debilitated still give negative results, regardless of cancellation!" This opinion is based on a misunderstanding of neecha bhanga. The assumption is that since this is a Raja Yoga, it is supposed to yield fame, a rise to prominence, or at least clearly positive results during the period of the planet. Although there are some rare examples of this kind of Neecha Bhanga Raja Yoga, in the majority of cases the cancellation of the debilitation occurs in a much more subtle way.

The first thing to understand about this yoga is that it will initially produce some kind of negative condition or problem during the debilitated planet's period. This does not mean, however, that nothing good comes from the experience. In fact, the most salient feature of Neecha Bhanga Raja Yoga is that it produces improvement after initial difficulties.

Einstein's Neecha Bhanga Mercury

The classic example of Neecha Bhanga Raja Yoga occurs in the chart of Albert Einstein (see chart in the chapter on dashas) who had a Gemini lagna, with a debilitated Mercury in the tenth house conjunct an exalted Venus. Venus in this case cancels the debilitation of Mercury under condition number six listed earlier.

It is quite interesting that in the chart of Albert Einstein, the world's foremost genius, Mercury, the planet of the intellect, is debilitated. This is not a condition that the beginning student of astrology would expect to see in Einstein's chart. Yet, in the context of Mercury's neecha bhanga condition, this placement perfectly describes Einstein's intellect.

First, Mercury is debilitated in the sign of Pisces. This means that Einstein would have some problems with the linear style of processing information, which characterizes a strong Mercury. In fact, he did have problems processing information, including a tendency towards dyslexia, as well as a tendency to daydream. As a result, he had problems with his early education in the rigid and structured German schools.

It was actually during a Mercury sub-period, that Einstein even failed a critical exam, preventing him from attending engineering school, demonstrating clearly that his Mercury was definitely debilitated. Without being able to see beyond the immediate experience of failure, it would be natural to think of this event as simply a problem. Jumping to this conclusion, however, completely fails to take into consideration the global impact of that event, which can only be seen when one takes Einstein's entire life into consideration. It was actually because of failing the engineering exam that Einstein decided to study physics, a subject to which he was eminently suited.

Square Peg in a Round Hole

This brings us to an important point about neecha bhanga planets. These planets often symbolize problems that stem from trying to utilize a planet's energy in a way in which the sign of debilitation does not support. In Einstein's case, he had been constantly trying to force his mind to cope with the rigid structures of conventional academics. Actually, he was not suited to do this effectively, so it is no surprise that he had problems. As soon as he switched to physics, a field that could accommodate the global, fluid, and abstract thinking symbolized by the sign of Pisces, he began to thrive.

Blessing in Disguise

It was at exactly this point in Einstein's life, that the positive results of his neecha bhanga Mercury started to be expressed. He began to succeed in his profession, and even gained the royal status promised by the Raja Yoga. In fact, if he had not failed that engineering exam, he would never have written his *Theory of Relativity*, nor would he have attained international fame. In other words, the failure of the engineering exam was actually a "blessing in disguise," which is the trademark of Neecha Bhanga Raja Yoga.

Different Magnitudes

On the other hand, not every neecha bhanga planet produces such powerful results. Einstein's Mercury and the cancellation planet, Venus, were also in a conjunction in the tenth house, producing a powerful Raja Yoga in his chart. The strong disposition of these two planets made the cancellation of debilitation particularly beneficial. In many cases, however, the neecha bhanga effect only produces a problem that results in an opportunity. In some cases, there is no failure, but simply a problematic condition the person fixes or improves. The magnitude of the positive after-effect of this combination completely depends on the disposition of the planets involved in the yoga. If the planet that cancels the debilitation is afflicted or weak, then the improvement may be minimal or even completely denied.

Problem Solving Ability

It is also true that not every neecha bhanga planet produces problems that result in suffering. In fact, these planets often produce a powerful ability to solve problems related to the debilitated planet and to the house in which it is placed. It is common to see a debilitated planet such as Mars, the planet of surgery, placed in the second house (the mouth) in the chart of a dentist. In this case, the neecha bhanga effect gives the dentist the experience of problems related to the mouth (the teeth of his patients), which he solves, making the dental problems of other people a source of benefit. Another example of this is Jupiter placed in the fourth house in Capricorn. If the conditions of neecha bhanga are met, then this position often gives the person the ability to solve structural problems related to homes. It is a common position in the charts of contractors, or simply in the charts of people who remodel their homes. Similarly, Venus, neecha bhanga in the eighth house, sometimes makes the person a psychologist or marriage counselor. Venus' position in Virgo causes the person to first experience difficulty in his own marriage, and then enter into a deep analytical search for understanding of the dynamics of relationships. This inevitably results in the ability to share this understanding and analytical insight with other people who are having marital problems, an ability that is important in counseling professions. Ultimately, the person benefits from his own marital problems and the marital problems of others.

Some Other Common Yogas

Vasumat Yoga

Conditions: Benefics (Jupiter, Venus, Mercury) occupy the upachaya houses (3, 6, 10, 11) from the Moon or lagna.

Results: Produces wealth and a life of comfortable retirement at home.

Amala Yoga

Conditions: A benefic planet placed in the tenth house from the Moon or lagna.

Results: Charitable; likable; famous; enjoys pleasures; revered by those in authority.

Kartari Yoga

Conditions: When there is a planet in both the twelfth house and the second house from the lagna (two types).

1. Papa Kartari: Formed by malefics hemming in the lagna.
2. Shubha Kartari: Formed by benefics hemming in the lagna.

Results: Papa Kartari Yoga is an affliction to the lagna, causing a general increase of negative values, such as disease, questionable character traits, and financial problems. Shubha Kartari Yoga enhances the strength of the lagna, causing a general increase of positive values such as health, wealth, and virtuous behavior.

Note: Although this yoga is defined here in terms of the lagna, it is commonly used with reference to any house that is hemmed in by malefics or by benefics. The concept is that the significations of any house that is hemmed in by benefics will thrive, while the significations of any house that is hemmed in by malefics will suffer.

Parvata Yoga

Conditions (two types):

1. Benefics occupy the kendras and the sixth and eighth houses are vacant or occupied by benefics only.

2. Lagna lord and the twelfth house lord are placed in mutual kendras and are aspected by a benefic.

Results: Leader of a town; well-educated; lustful; famous; lucky; wealthy; public speaking ability; generous.

Kaahala Yoga

Conditions (two types):

1. Fourth house lord and the ninth house lord in mutual kendras, while the lagna lord is strong.
2. Fourth house lord exalted or in its own house, conjunct or aspected by the tenth house lord.

Results: Makes the person assertive, aggressive, and courageous; the leader of an army or the ruler of a village.

Chaamara Yoga

Conditions: (two types)

1. The lagna lord is exalted and occupies a kendra and it is also aspected by Jupiter.
2. Two benefics in conjunction in the lagna, the seventh house, the ninth house, or the tenth house.

Results: Makes the person like a king; articulate; wise; well-educated; knowledgeable about spiritual philosophy; lives until age seventy-one.

Shankha Yoga

Conditions: (two types)

1. The lords of the fifth and sixth houses in mutual kendras, while the lagna lord is strong.
2. The lagna lord and the tenth house lord occupy a movable sign, while the ninth house lord is in a position of strength.

Results: This makes the person virtuous and well-versed in spiritual subjects. It also produces ownership of land; prosperity; has a good spouse and family; and longevity up to the age of eighty-one.

Lakshmi Yoga

Conditions: Lagna lord is very strong and the ninth lord is placed in a kendra, either in his own house, moolatrikona, or exaltation.

Results: The person is beautiful, virtuous, wealthy, famous, well-educated; has a beautiful spouse and a large family.

Maha Bhagya Yoga

Conditions: For a male, the birth must occur in the daytime, and the lagna, Sun and Moon must be in an odd sign (signs 1, 3, 5, 7, 9, 11).
For a female, the birth must occur at night and the lagna, Sun and Moon must be in an even sign (signs 2, 4, 6, 8, 10, 12).

Results: Makes the person attractive, famous, of good character, a landowner, and a leader. It accentuates the best side of male assertive qualities for a man. Women who have this yoga will have beneficial feminine qualities such as grace, charm, and good character. The yoga also bestows wealth and children.

Chandra Mangala Yoga

Conditions: Mars in a conjunction with the Moon.

Results: This yoga promotes wealth. The methods of gaining wealth, however, are sometimes earthy, bawdy, rough or crude.

Maala Yoga

Conditions: The seven planets each occupy one house in a wreath-like pattern. The first planet can be placed in any house as long as the rest are placed in consecutive houses from that house forward. This means there will be twelve kinds of Maala Yogas, based on the different beginning houses.

Results: Maala Yoga enhances the values of the house of origin. If, for example, the first planet is in the fourth house, then the person will possess nice homes or might even be a leader of his town. If the yoga starts from the seventh house, then the person will have an attractive spouse and good results through marriage. However, starting from the dusthana houses (6,8, or 12), the yoga produces struggles, upheavals, and expenditures, according to the significations of the particular dusthana house.

Saraswati Yoga

Conditions: Mercury, Jupiter, and Venus placed in kendras, trikonas or the second house. Jupiter must also be strong and in its own sign, a friendly sign or exaltation sign.

Results: This produces a well-educated scholar who may have knowledge in various subjects such as language, math, or religion.

Author's Journal:

What's in a Palm?

If you ever go to India and have the opportunity to get an astrology reading from a village astrologer, it is likely that he will first look carefully at your palm before considering your horoscope. Palmistry is an closely related to the Vedic system of astrology. A glance at the palm often tells the astrologer a great deal about your basic karmic patterns and periods of life.

My astrology teacher, M.K. Gandhi, was a great palmist. He encouraged me to study palmistry while I was in London, and gave me pointers on its application. At first, I was quite hesitant to use it. Astrology seemed much more objective and even sort of scientific. Given an accurate birth date, time and place, I felt that astrology was unsurpassed in its ability to give accurate detail about the past, present, and future. So I didn't use the palm when I began to do astrology professionally.

Noticing my reluctant attitude towards palmistry, one day Gandhiji announced, "There is a psychic fair at the Charing Cross Hotel every Sunday. Go there and read palms each week."

A psychic fair? My mind balked, Palms? The whole idea of sitting at a booth at a new age fair reading palms seemed to reduce the noble science of Jyotish to a game of Trivial Pursuit. I knew the look in my teacher's eyes, however, and he was dead serious. Then he added. "You may not use a horoscope. Only read palms."

The Charing Cross Hotel was located in central London, just a short ride on the tube from Gandhiji's office in the west end. My first Sunday of reading palms was a complete disaster, total humiliation. Although I knew the basics, I was completely unprepared to give a palm reading without using a horoscope. Needless to say, for the next several weeks, I made use of every spare moment to improve my palmistry. I desperately re-read my palmistry books hoping to avoid weekly humiliation at the psychic fair. I had been working as Gandhi's assistant for a couple of years by this time, and besides preparing horoscopes and taking palm prints for his clients, I was now being allowed to take a few clients of my own. I began looking at each client's palm very carefully, comparing the features of the palm to psychological patterns and life events. Needless to say, my palmistry rapidly improved.

As I gained more confidence with palmistry, I began to use it more freely in my readings. One day, when Gandhiji was in Los Angeles and I was 'holding down the fort' in London, a man called who insisted on having a reading. The only problem was that he did not know his birth date. My first impulse was to refuse to give him an appointment. No birth date meant no horoscope. Working 'without a net' at a psychic fair where I charged five pounds for a reading was one thing. Giving a palmisty reading without a chart in London's busiest astrology office where the fee was a whopping sixty pounds was an entirely different story. The man was adamant that he wanted a reading, however, so I agreed.

When the man arrived I was a little nervous. I was wondering what I would do if I looked at his palm and didn't find what I needed to fill in the gap left by the absent horoscope. As I examined his palms, I immediately noticed the prominence of his Mercury finger (little finger), accompanied by a powerful Sun line (a line rising towards the ring finger which sometimes shows reputation and success). The Sun line was originating from his Mercury line (a line rising toward the little finger). I said, "You have made your reputation in the field of communications."

The man looked surprised and blurted out, "How famous am I?"

I paused for a moment, holding back an impulse to laugh. This man was obviously enthralled with his own brilliance. "I have no idea how famous you are," I said, "I can only tell you that whatever your level of fame, you have received it due to your ability to communicate."

"You are quite right!" the man said in his haughty British accent, "I am the *Voice of America to Pakistan*."

"Some people are legends in their own times," I thought, "this guy is a legend in his own mind!"

Over the years I have continued to use palmistry along with astrology and have always found it to be a valuable support to the interpretation of the horoscope. Whenever a person comes into my office personally, I always begin the reading by looking at his palm. Occasionally, I find something in the palm that was not evident in the horoscope. Not every client is a "legend in his own time," but the unique legend of each person's life is definitely etched in the palm. All a good jyotishi has to do is see it.

Chapter Three

Divisional Charts (Vargas)

One distinguishing feature of the Vedic horoscope is the use of divisional charts called *vargas*. Vargas are special charts designed to reveal details about specific domains of life. Instead of only using the rashi chart, most jyotishis use a minimum of two charts. The Navamsha chart is the most important varga and it is routinely calculated with every Vedic horoscope. It is used both for general evaluation of the life, as well as marriage and relationships. In addition to the Navamsha chart, Vedic astrologers commonly use a combination of several divisional charts to delineate each domain of life more specifically.

Hora Chart

The Hora chart is used for financial matters. Its calculation is based on a division of each sign into two parts of fifteen degrees each. There are various methods for calculating this chart. The author recommends the method called *parivritti dwaya*, which allots the twelve signs to the twelve sequential horas from Aries to Virgo. This is again repeated for the twelve sequential horas from Libra to Pisces.

Drekkana Chart

The Drekkana chart is based on a division of each sign into three equal parts of ten degrees each. It is primarily used to reveal details about siblings. It is also used in medical astrology for insights into health problems.

Divisional Charts (Vargas)

Chaturtamsha Chart

This chart is based on a division of the sign into four equal parts. It is used for information about the residence, as well as general happiness and well-being.

Panchamsha Chart

The Panchamsha chart is based on a division of the sign into five parts of six degrees each. It is used to obtain information about the person's spiritual practices and rituals.

Shashtamsha Chart

This chart is based on a division of the sign into six parts of five degrees each. It is used for information about the person's health.

Saptamsha Chart

The Saptamsha is the chart for children. It is based on a division of the sign into seven equal parts.

Ashtamsha Chart

This chart is derived by dividing the sign into eight parts. It can reveal upheavals, changes, accidents, surgeries, and can even provide details regarding the person's death.

Navamsha Chart

The Navamsha chart is based on dividing each sign into nine equal parts. It sheds light on the life in general, but is specifically used for marriage. It is also a useful chart for all types of relationships.

Dashamsha Chart

This is the career chart. It is based on a sign-division of ten equal parts of three degrees each. It shows the area of karma (action). It can be used to see further details about the career, hobbies, projects, and other ambitious pursuits. It also helps to predict the level and times of professional ups and downs.

Ekadashamsha Chart

The Ekadashamsha chart is based on a division of the sign into eleven equal parts. It can reveal financial matters, as well as the fructification of other desires. It ultimately shows how we manifest what we desire, as well as the likely periods of success or failure in this regard. It is also used to predict cures in the case of health problems.

Dwadashamsha Chart

The Dwadashamsha chart is based on a division of the sign into twelve parts. This is the chart that reveals details concerning parents.

Shodashamsha Chart

This chart is based on a division of each sign into sixteen parts. It can be used effectively for getting details about the person's vehicles.

Vimshamsha Chart

The Vimshamsha chart is used for the area of spiritual development. It can also be used to reveal details related to the Ishta Devata and the blessings that come from worshipping a deity.

Siddhamsha Chart

This chart is based on a sign-division of twenty-four parts. It is used for education.

Trimshamsha Chart

This chart is used for revealing difficulties in life. It can also be used to get insights about the person's character. There are different methods of calculating this chart. Even though the name suggests a division of the signs into thirty parts of one degree each, the standard method actually divides the sign into five unequal parts.

How to Use the Vargas

Vargas are used as a support to the rashi chart. They are not meant to be interpreted in isolation. When an event is shown in the rashi chart and is also indicated in the appropriate varga, then the astrologer can usually predict the event with confidence. Some of the principles of varga interpretation given below are based on the work of H.R. Sheshadri Iyer. The rest are based on the author's own experience and application.

There are two main ways to use vargas. First, they can be used in the general evaluation of the horoscope. If the astrologer is evaluating the career, for example, in addition to analyzing the tenth house of the chart, he might also examine the Dashamsha chart. This can provide further support and detail to the assessment of career. Second, the vargas can also be used as a useful tool to predict the exact outcomes of planetary periods. For example, by analyzing the particular planet's placement in a series of vargas, the astrologer might be able to determine that during the planet's period, the person will change his residence, get a raise in his employment, meet a new girlfriend, have dental surgery, and purchase a large vehicle.

Using the Vargas for General Evaluation

The basic principles of chart evaluation also apply to vargas. The analysis of each divisional chart begins with the evaluation of the first house. If the varga's lagna is strong, then it contributes support to the domain of life represented by the varga. If it is weak, then it detracts from the varga's domain. The first house also gains strength when planets occupy or aspect it. The more planets that influence the lagna of a divisional chart, the more likely it is that the varga will give prominent results.

Once the first house of the varga has been evaluated, the next step is to examine the varga's primary house or houses. The primary house or houses for each varga will be those which signify the domain represented by the varga. For example, the Dashamsha chart (tenth division) is the chart for the career. In any horoscope, the house of career is the tenth house. In the Dashamsha chart, therefore, the tenth house is the primary house. If the primary house in one of the divisional charts is strong by virtue of the placement of its ruler and other basic elements of house evaluation, then it makes it more likely that the person will experience positive results in the domain of life represented by the varga.

The varga placement of the Ascendant ruler from the rashi chart is also an important indicator of the general strength or weakness of the varga's domain. If it is debilitated, afflicted or placed in a dusthana in the varga, then the domain of the varga will suffer. Similarly, the placement and disposition of the varga's lagna lord in the rashi chart also indicates strength or weakness of the varga's domain.

The varga placement of the ruler of the primary house from the rashi chart is also important. For example, if the tenth lord from the rashi chart is exalted, well placed, and aspected by Jupiter in the Dashamsha chart, then the Dashamsha chart's domain (career) will thrive.

If the lagna of a divisional chart is vargottama (the same sign as that of the rashi), it increases the possibility of positive results in that domain of life.

Finally, the varga placement of the karaka or natural significator for the varga's domain of life is very important. For example, if Venus, the karaka for marriage, is placed in the fourth house (where it attains dig bala) in the Navamsha chart, then it contributes to overall happiness in marriage. The exception to this rule is when the karaka for the varga is in the varga's Ascendant, then it can produce negative results for the person, or the relationship with the person signified by the karaka. For example, if Jupiter (children) is in the Ascendant of the Saptamsha chart (children), it may give a small family, difficulty having children, problems in the life of a child, or some kind of problem in the relationship with a child.

Using the Vargas for Prediction

One of the most effective ways to use the vargas is in prediction. By considering the placement and disposition of a planetary period ruler in the various vargas, the astrologer can accurately predict the various nuances of the planet's period. The elements of varga evaluation are basically the same as in the general analysis of the rashi chart, except for some subtle differences that apply to specific vargas. The following twenty-five points will help in this regard.

25 Points for Varga Prediction

1. Sign strength: When a period ruler is placed in its own sign or exalted in the varga, then the planet's period will promote good results in the varga's domain of life. Similarly, if the planet is weak or debilitated in the varga, the period will produce difficulties in the varga's domain.

2. Vargottama planets: When a planet is vargottama (in the same sign in the rashi as in one of the divisional charts) then the planet will function like an exalted planet, producing mainly positive and prominent results in the varga's domain of life during the planet's period.

3. House placement: Generally, the placement of the period ruler in

angles or trines in the varga produces good results in the varga's domain during the planet's period. Trines are better than angles, and the planet should be free of affliction. Similarly, placement in dusthana houses (6,8,or 12) in a varga will produce negative results. An exception to this rule is the Vimshamsha and Panchamsha charts (used for spirituality). In these charts, the twelfth house is one of the primary houses of spirituality, so planets placed here will promote spiritual experiences. In most of the other charts, however, placement in the dusthanas suggests negative results.

4. Placement in the lagna: If the planetary period ruler is placed in the lagna of a varga, then it will give prominent results in the varga's domain during the planet's period. Prominent does not convey whether the results will be positive or negative, however, so the planet's disposition by sign, aspect, and other factors of strength or weakness must be assessed.

5. Placement in the primary house: If a planetary period ruler (major or sub-period) is placed in a primary house of the varga, then its period will produce prominent events in the domain of life signified by the varga. This result will also take place (but to a lesser extent) when the planet is in the primary house counted from the Sun or Moon. Again, whether the events are positive or negative will be determined by the sign placement, aspects, and other influences on the planet. For example, if Saturn is in Capricorn (its own sign) in the tenth house (the primary house) in the Dashamsha chart (career), then periods of Saturn will generally produce both prominent and positive career results.

6. Placement in the primary house relative to the dasha ruler: If the sub-period ruler is placed in a primary house in a varga relative to the major period ruler, then prominent results will take place as per the previous rule. For example, in the major period of Venus and the sub-period of Jupiter, if Jupiter is placed in the fourth house (home) from Venus in the Chaturtamsha chart (residence), then the person might purchase a new home or change his residence to a bigger house.

7. The ruler of the Ascendant or the primary house in the divisional chart will give prominent results related to the varga's domain of life during its period. Whether the results are positive or negative depends on the disposition of the planet. For example, if the lagna

lord for the Dashamsha chart is placed in the eighth house and is afflicted, it may produce a change or loss of career. But if it is placed in the fifth house in a friendly sign, it may produce a promotion or raise.

8. Placement with or aspect by natural benefics/malefics: When a period ruler is associated with a natural benefic planet in a divisional chart, either by conjunction or aspect, it will usually produce good results for the domain of life signified by the divisional chart. Negative results will take place in the case of aspect or association with natural malefics.

9. If the period ruler aspects the primary house in a divisional chart (either from the Ascendant, the Sun or the Moon) then its period can produce significant results for the domain of life represented by the divisional chart.

10. If two natural benefics hem in the lagna of the divisional chart, then prominent positive results will take place in the domain of life represented by the chart during the period (major and sub-period) of either or both of the two planets. Prominent negative results will take place if the two planets are natural malefics. The most powerful type of hemming-in occurs when the two planets are 2/12 (in the second and twelfth signs) from the lagna (or the primary house). Other types of hemming-in that may produce similar results occur when the two flanking planets are placed in flank in 3/11, 4/10, 5/9, and 6/8 from the lagna.

11. The karaka (natural significator) for a particular domain placed in the Ascendant of the varga for that area of life can produce negative results for that domain during the planet's period. For example, Venus (significator of the spouse) in the first house of the Navamsha chart can produce some challenges in the marriage, or for the spouse during the period of Venus.

12. If a planet is well-placed in the rashi chart (for a particular domain of life) but badly placed in the divisional chart (for that domain of life), then the planet will not give good results for that domain of life. It may give moderately negative results or partly good and partly bad results. The results may also be positive at the beginning and turn negative near the end of the planet's period. For example, if Saturn is placed in its own sign in the tenth house (career) of

Divisional Charts (Vargas)

the rashi chart (indicating good results in the career), and yet it is placed in the twelfth house, debilitated and aspected by malefics in the Dashamsha chart, then it may give good results in the career during the beginning of the period, but create problems near the end.

13. If a planet is badly placed (for a particular domain of life) in the rashi chart, but well-placed in the divisional chart (for that same domain), then the planet may produce negative results at the beginning of its period and better results near the end of the period. It may also simply give mixed results or moderately positive results.

14. If a planet is well-placed (for a particular domain of life) in both the rashi and the varga for that domain of life, then it will give first-rate, positive results. If it is badly placed in both charts, then it will give prominently negative results.

15. If a planet is badly placed in the rashi chart, but not related to a particular domain of life, yet well-placed in the varga for that domain of life, it will usually give good results in that domain of life during its period. For example, if Jupiter is in Capricorn in the sixth house in the rashi chart, yet it is placed in the fourth house (the residence) in Cancer (exalted) in the Chaturtamsha chart (the chart for residence), then the person will probably have expansive positive results pertaining to his home. The negative results related to the debilitation of Jupiter in this case may manifest in some other domain of life.

16. If a planet is well-placed in the rashi chart, but not related to a particular domain of life and yet it is prominent and badly disposed in the varga for that domain of life, then it will give negative results in that domain of life during the planet's period. For example, if Jupiter is in Cancer in the ninth house in the rashi, but in the Dashamsha chart (career) it is placed in the tenth house (career) debilitated and afflicted, then the person will have difficulties in his career during the major or sub-periods of Jupiter. The exalted placement of Jupiter in the rashi will manifest in other areas of life.

17. If a planet is neecha bhanga (cancellation of debilitation) in a varga, then its period may produce initial problems relative to the varga's domain, and better results later in the period. Alternatively, the planet's period may produce a change relative to the varga's domain.

It may also produce a problem which becomes the source of opportunity either during or after the period of the planet. For example, if Jupiter is neecha bhanga in the Chaturtamsha chart, during the period of Jupiter the person could remodel his house. Notice that in this case, the problems produced by the debilitation are simply due to the discontent with the existing home that must precede a remodel. A neecha bhanga planet often gives the ability to solve a problem. This does not mean that the person needs to suffer.

18. If a planet has dig bala (directional strength) in a divisional chart, it will give good results during its period in the domain of life represented by the divisional chart.

19. If a planet is placed at 0 degrees, 29 degrees, is combust, or defeated in a planetary war in the rashi chart, but in the divisional chart is well-placed, then it will not be able to produce much positive effect.

20. A prominently placed yogi in a divisional chart will produce good results during its period in the domain represented by the divisional chart. A similarly placed avayogi will give either mixed or negative results.

21. The eighth house is the house of upheaval, change, and metamorphosis. The third house is the eighth house from the eighth house, so it gives similar, yet less intense results. A planet placed in the eighth or the third house (but especially the eighth) will produce change, termination, or even death to the domain represented by the varga. For example, a planet placed in the eighth house of the Chaturtamsha chart frequently produces a change of residence or a remodel of the person's house.

22. The second house is a neutral house in the varga charts, except in the case of the Hora or Ekadashamsha charts (money charts), where it becomes a primary house.

23. In addition to being a chart for money, the Ekadashamsha chart is also a chart for accomplishing goals and manifesting desires in life. If a planet is in a good sign and well aspected in this chart, then the domain of life that is represented by the house in which it is located (counted from the Ascendant of the varga) as well as the domain of life ruled by that planet in the rashi chart will fructify in a good

way. If the planet is badly placed by sign, aspect, and association, then it will block these results.

24. A planet placed in the eighth house (or the first house) of the Ashtamsha chart will produce upheavals and changes in the domains of life represented by its natural significations and its rulership in the rashi chart.

25. Yogas occurring in a varga chart bear fruit in the domain represented by the varga. For example, if Venus and Saturn combine in the tenth house in Libra in the Navamsha chart (the chart for the spouse) it creates a Raja Yoga (a combination which produces rise in profession). This combination will produce a rise in the profession of the spouse. It will occur in a moderate form during the major period or sub-period of one of the planets. It will produce dramatic results during the major period of one of the planets and the sub-period of the other.

Degrees in a Varga

It is also possible to calculate a divisional chart so that it shows the degrees of each planet. Although this is an unconventional technique, it is theoretically sound and produces dependable and powerful results. Most Vedic astrology software programs provide an option for calculating vargas with degrees. The varga nakshatra placement of the lagna lord from the rashi chart, the karaka, and the varga lagna lord will add detail to the general evaluation of the varga. The varga nakshatra placement of period rulers can reveal detailed understanding of specific results manifesting during their periods. The use of nakshatra placements in various vargas will be demonstrated in examples given later in this book.

Author's Journal:

A Meeting with the Prince of Navamsha

Once on a trip to Bombay, I met Mr. C.S. Patel. Mr. Patel, an octogenarian, was one of the few remaining patriarchs who dominated Indian astrology in the mid 1900's. His book Ashtakavarga was a classic and one of the first Vedic astrology books I had read when I originally began studying astrology in Bombay. He was considered the leading authority on the subject of ashtakavarga in India. My purpose on this trip to Bombay was to meet him and to invite him to be the keynote speaker at the International Symposium on Vedic Astrology.

I had arranged to meet Mr. Patel one morning at his flat. He had given me typical Indian directions, noting a particular bank building and cinema that were near his place. The rest of the directions were confusing, but I was accustomed to finding my way in Bombay and figured that I would simply follow his directions until they failed and then ask someone on the street for directions.

As we neared Mr. Patel's neighborhood, I began to wonder. The streets were mobbed, typical of this section of Bombay, and the street names were very confusing. To make things worse, my taxi driver seemed lost and could not find the streets given in Mr. Patel's directions. After about 10 minutes of fruitless searching, I told the driver to pull over so that I could ask directions. I saw an old man, dressed in a white dhoti and Gandhi-cap standing on the corner. I got out, walked up to him and asked, "Can you tell me—"

"Mr. Kelleher, come with me!" the man interrupted. "I am C.S. Patel."

Now this may seem like a minor coincidence, but to me at that moment, on the streets of Bombay, among at least a couple of hundred thousand people, to happen upon the object of my search in this way was nothing less than a minor miracle.

    Mr. Patel led me down a series of lanes and quickly found his apartment building. I couldn't help but admire the energy he exuded. He was 80, but I could hardly keep up with him as he trotted up the four flights of stairs to his flat.

    After introducing his wife and offering me the mandatory cup of chai, we settled down in his study. We sat on cushions on the floor as we discussed various aspects of astrology. Throughout the discussion, Mr. Patel exuded complete enthusiasm and interest in astrology. 'I sure hope I am as passionate about astrology at the age of 80 as he is,' I thought. I wondered if his mental exuberance and boundless physical energy was a blessing resulting from devoting his life to the "Jyotish goddess."

    Mr. Patel then took out his latest book, Navamsha in Astrology, signed it and gave me a copy. He explained that the various uses of navamsha had been a special area of research for him. He began to talk about using the Navamsha chart and his research of navamsha in the Nadi literature. He then shared with me the following technique, which I have used frequently since that time. He said, "If you progress the navamsha of the ascendant, Sun or Moon, by a year of life for each navamsha, then you will find the times of very important life events!" He also shared with me the method of using transits in the Navamsha chart, as well as many other esoteric techniques.

    Here is Mr. Patel's progressed navamsha technique. It is a simple matter of taking the navamsha in which the Ascendant is placed as the first year of life. Age zero is shown by exact point of the Ascendant. The first birthday is represented by the longitude of the Ascendant plus 3 degrees 20 minutes. In other words, one navamsha equals one year of life. When the progressed navamsha reaches the navamsha occupied by a natal planet, then an event which corresponds with that planet will occur.

Chapter Four

The Drekkanas

Just as the zodiac is divided into twelve signs and twenty-seven nakshatras, it can also be divided into thirty-six drekkanas. A drekkana is a one-third division of a sign. From 0-10 degrees of each sign is called the first drekkana, from 10-20 degrees is the second drekkana, and from 20-30 degrees is the third drekkana.

The drekkanas are described in detail in the last chapter of the *Brihat Jataka* by Sage Varahamihira. Similar to the imagery of the tarot, the drekkanas are vivid images, rich with symbolism, which provide a fertile ground from which the intuitive astrologer can sometimes make stunning observations.

Aries

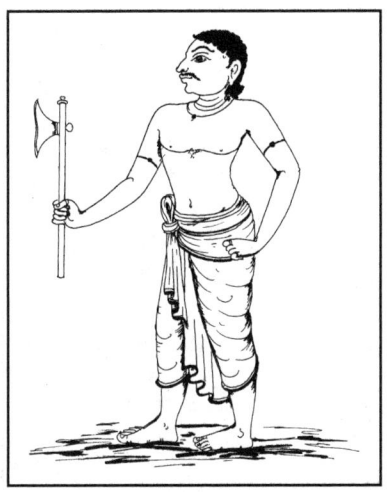

The first drekkana of Aries is a dark man with a white waistband. He has fiery red eyes and is holding an axe in the air, as if to protect.

→ This was Charlie

Notes on Symbolism:

1. Man with dark complexion: This can be used for determining physical appearance. Dark colors are signified by Saturn and can suggest delays, obstacles, pressures, or patience, perseverance, and the ability to actualize.
2. White waistband: A belt or sash. A belt maintains or holds together; white suggests purity.
3. Red eyes: Strain, stress, or anger. Red eyes are also associated with the after-effect of intoxication.
4. An axe (weapon drekkana): Assertive, combative, sometimes violent. → Charlie had a wall full of weapons. In some cases the person will actually own a weapon. An axe is also called a "parasu" and is related to Parasurama, the sixth incarnation of Vishnu, who re-established order and vanquished the arrogant warrior kings, after the revolt of the kshatriyas. In the *Mahabharata*, Parasurama became angry when Rama broke Shiva's bow, so he met him in the forest and challenged him to string another famous bow to prove his prowess. Rama did so. As a result, Parasurama knew that the purpose of his incarnation was complete, and asked Rama to carry on as the new incarnation of Vishnu. Then he retreated to an ashram to do penance. In another story, he also taught Karna the use of weapons.
5. "As if to protect": Protecting those who need refuge; gives protective tendencies. → Absolutely

The second drekkana of Aries is a one-legged woman wearing red clothes. She has the face of a horse. She looks like a water jar and is thirsty. She is always thinking about ornaments and food.

Notes on Symbolism:

1. One-legged woman: A symbol of independence; self-sufficiency; one-sided; unbalanced; insufficient support; lameness or physical disability.
2. Red clothes: Passionate; flashy dresser; possibly preferring red; assertive; bold.
3. Horse face (animal drekkana): Love of animals; instinctive; has animal-like or more physical, sexual instincts; likes cars; long face; capable of swift movement.
4. Looks like a water jar: Shapely; full of emotion; fulfillment; soothing; refreshing. This is also sometimes interpreted as pot-bellied.
5. Thirsty and thinking about food: Strong desires; never satisfied.
6. Thinking about ornaments: Beautiful dresser; egocentric; self-indulgent; likes gemstones.

The third drekkana of Aries depicts an angry and violent man with tan skin. He is lifting up a stick and is wearing red clothes. He is skilled as an artist and wants to work. He does not keep his resolutions.

Notes on Symbolism:

1. Violent man: Could be tactless; aggressive; assertive; businesslike; impersonal or cruel.
2. Tan skin: Hardened by the elements or by life; tough; thick-skinned; insensitive.
3. Stick (weapon drekkana): Tends to be angry; vindictive; aggressive; competitive; and in some cases might be violent or could actually own a weapon.
4. Red clothes: Passionate; assertive; angry; aggressive; possessing the qualities of Mars.
5. Artist: Artistic or creative ability, or highly skilled at his work.
6. Wants to work: Works hard; loves his work; seeking work.
7. Angry: Competitive; aggressive; bad temper; vindictive.
8. Doesn't keep resolutions: Unreliable; weak resolve; may not keep his word; lack of ethics or principles.

TAURUS

The first drekkana of Taurus is a woman with curly hair that has been cut. Her clothes are partially burnt. She is fond of food and ornaments. She looks like a water jar, and she is thirsty.

Notes on Symbolism:

1. Curly hair that has been cut: Well-groomed; attractive; sensual; nice hair; curly hair.
2. Burnt clothes: Tends to wear damaged clothes; could actually burn clothes; damaged reputation; reputation hurt due to misdirected passions.
3. Likes food: Good cook; eats healthy food; likes to go out to dinner; overeats; has a hard time dieting.
4. Likes ornaments: Self-indulgent; likes to dress up; vain; egocentric; joyful and self-affirming; decorative tendencies.
5. Looks like a water jar: Full emotions; refreshing; soothing. Sometimes this is interpreted as potbellied; may tend to gain weight.
6. Thirsty: Never satisfied; strong desires; chronically dissatisfied.

The Drekkanas

The second drekkana of Taurus depicts a farmer. He knows about cows, land, grain, carts, and plowing. He knows how to do house work. He is also interested in painting, music, dance and the arts in general. He has shoulders like the hump of an ox, which elevate his neck. He has a bull's face. He is hungry and wearing dirty clothes.

Notes on Symbolism:

1. Farming: Able to make things grow; good with plants. Planets falling in this drekkana will tend to thrive.
2. Cows: The symbol of sustenance; nourishment; an auspicious omen; likes animals.
3. Land: Real estate; the earth; grounded; security; stability.
4. Grain: Sustenance; a symbol of wealth.
5. Plowing: Preparation; groundwork.
6. Painting: Artistic; visual.
7. Music: Creative; hearing.
8. Dance: Creativity; physical.
9. Hunched shoulders: Poor posture; tired through hard work.
10. Bull's face: Strong will; powerful; potent; might love animals; instinctive; has more physical, sexual instincts.
11. Hungry: Not satisfied; ambitious; likes food.
12. Dirty clothes: Dresses casually; poor; works hard; affected negatively by surroundings.
13. Housework: Maintenance; tends to create security; handyman; carpenter.

Path of Light – The Domains of Life

The third drekkana of Taurus is a man with an elephant's body, brown skin, yellowish white teeth and legs like a sharabha. He wants to capture the famous animals of the forest.

Notes on Symbolism:

1. Elephant's body (animal drekkana): Kapha constitution; tendency to be overweight; an auspicious symbol of overcoming obstacles, related to Lord Ganesh; slow moving; powerful; might love animals; instinctive; has more physical sexual instincts.
2. Brown skin: Dark complexion.
3. Yellowish white teeth: Yellow is the color of Jupiter (an expansive quality similar to other symbols of this drekkana).
4. Legs like a sharabha: A sharabha is a large, mythological animal with eight powerful legs and eyes all over its forehead. In the *Shiva Purana*, Lord Rudra takes the form of Sharabha and defeats Lord Narasimha. A symbol of tremendous power, dominance, possibly overconfidence. Eight legs might indicate transformation, change, or upheaval.
5. Wants to have the famous animals of the forest: A tendency to like being near rich, famous, or successful people; a personal desire to become rich, famous or powerful; the ability to overcome powerful people or to overcome extreme odds; a desire to have pets, especially those with pedigrees.

Gemini

The first drekkana of Gemini is a beautiful woman who loves needle-

work and has adorned her body with ornaments. She has already reached puberty (menses) and is lustful; she does not have any children. She is depicted with her hands raised.

Notes on Symbolism:

1. Beautiful woman: Beautiful; special; sensitive; feminine; attractive.
2. Skilled at needlework: Needlecraft; needles used in one's occupation; weaving, literally and as a metaphor for the ability to do intricate work which threads many complex elements together.
3. Ornaments: Enjoys personal adornment; calls attention to self; self-centered; celebrating life.
4. Reached puberty: Mature; creative; fluctuating moods; potentially fruitful; creative.
5. Lustful: Sexual passion; passion for life.
6. No children: If afflicted, may not have children; or creative urges sometimes not fulfilled; on the other hand this may suggest the stage of development, just before bearing children, when a woman becomes capable of bearing children but has not yet conceived; fertility.
7. Hands raised: Reaches out to life, protesting, willful.

Dena is going into this drekkana next year
This was Megan herself
She was in her Rahu dasa when she got him

The second drekkana of Gemini is a hero dressed in armor. He has a bow in his hands, ready to fight. His face is similar to Garuda (bird-like). He loves his children (sons), sports, wealth and jewelry. He lives in a garden.

Notes on Symbolism:

1. Hero: Noble; courageous; virtuous; brave; a winner.
2. Dressed in armor: Protective; creates protective boundaries, defensive, thinks ahead.
3. Bow in hand (weapon drekkana): Aggression; ambition; and in some cases violence; may own a weapon. May own or collect tools or sharp instruments.
4. Face like Garuda (bird drekkana): Suggesting movement, especially by air; love of birds; good speaker or writer; love of flight (airplanes); adaptable; quick; powerful; courageous; musical; passionate.
(Note: Garuda is the half-bird/half-man, that Vishnu rides when he is awake. Garuda is related to speech and music. He is lustful, courageous and can take any shape he chooses.)
5. Loves children: Related to children.
6. Loves sports: Related to sports, games, play; celebration; joyful.
7. Loves wealth: Promotes prosperity.
8. Loves jewelry: Likes gems; lucky; wealthy.
9. Lives in a garden: Landscaped environments; natural environments; gardening; plants.

The Drekkanas

The third drekkana of Gemini depicts a well-dressed man, wearing ornaments, who has many gems. He is armed with arrows, a bow and a coat of armor. He excels in various aspects of the fine arts such as painting, music, drumming, dancing and poetry. He is like Varuna, the lord of the oceans.

Notes on Symbolism:

1. Well-dressed man: Attractive; presented well.
2. Gems: Prosperity, wealth.
3. Ornaments: Self-possessed; celebrates; puts the best foot forward.
4. Bow and arrows (weapon drekkana): Assertive; competitive; ambitious; penetrating; sometimes angry, occasionally violent. (See the nakshatra of Punarvasu that has a similar symbol.)
5. Coat of armor: Protective; creates boundaries.
6. Painting, drumming, dancing, poetry: Possesses various creative talents.
7. Like Varuna: Just; righteous; healing ability; paternal; pontifical; related to water; related to the heavens. (Note: Varuna is a paternal figure in Vedic mythology who is similar to God, the Father, in the Christian tradition. He rules the invisible world. He rules magical powers. He also rules the oceans, and is the dispenser of healing and medicines. He rules over the Nagas (serpent gods) and the Asuras (anti-gods). He also lays down the laws for mankind.)

Cancer

The first drekkana of Cancer represents a man with an elephant's body, a horse's neck, and legs like a sharabha. He lives in a forest near the sandalwood trees and carries leaves, fruits, and roots.

Notes on Symbolism:

1. Elephant body (animal drekkana): Kapha constitution; tends to gain weight; moves slowly; powerful; overcomes all obstacles (Like Ganesh, the elephant god), likes animals; physical, sexual desire; instinctive.
2. Horse neck: Long or thick neck; likes swift vehicles.
3. Legs like a sharabha: A sharabha is a large, mythological animal with eight powerful legs and eyes all over its forehead. In the *Shiva Purana*, Lord Rudra takes the form of Sharabha and defeats Lord Narasimha. A symbol of tremendous power; dominance; possibly overconfident. Eight legs may refer to transformation and change.
4. Lives in the forest near sandalwood trees: Beautiful home; prefers to live in seclusion; may actually live in the forest or near trees; home may be in a fragrant environment; a soothing effect.
5. Carries leaves, fruits and roots: Related to medicines and herbs; healing ability; problem solving ability; natural remedies; uses everything and doesn't waste anything.

The Drekkanas

The second drekkana of Cancer is a harsh young woman whose head is adorned (by her well-wishers) with lotus flowers. She has a snake and is leaning against a branch of a palasa tree, crying.

Notes on Symbolism:

1. Leans on a tree branch in the forest: Prefers solitude; likes to be in nature; lives in a natural environment or actually in a forest.
2. Serpents (serpent drekkena): Bound by circumstances; confined; venomous if attacked; deceptive; manipulative; seductive; hypnotic; sexual; noble; detached; rises above passions. (See the description of the Nagas under Ashlesha nakshatra in *Volume I*.)
3. Crying: Emotional, sad or depressed; tears of joy.
4. Head adorned with lotus flowers: Good reputation; celebrated by followers; famous; highly respected.

The third drekkana of Cancer is a man with a flat face, wearing jewelry, who has a snake coiled around him. He is on a boat, crossing the ocean, searching for his wife's jewels.

Notes on Symbolism:

1. Flat face: Even disposition; possibly flat or lifeless persona.
2. Serpent coiled around him (serpent drekkena): Bound by circumstances; confined; venomous if attacked; deceptive; manipulative; seductive or open to being seduced; hypnotic; sexual; may use sex to gain power; noble; detached; rises above passions. (See the description of the Nagas under Ashlesha nakshatra in *Volume I*.)
3. Adorned with gems: Wealthy; prosperous; likes or wears gems.
4. On a boat crossing the ocean: Foreign or distant travel; likes the ocean or the water; goes to great lengths to accomplish goals.
5. Searching for his wife's jewels: Subservient to spouse or partner; goes to great lengths to please others; refers to lost objects.

LEO

The first drekkana of Leo is a jackal and a vulture on a salmali tree. There is also a dog and a man wearing dirty clothes. The man is crying and leaving his parents.

Notes on Symbolism:

1. Jackal: Sneaky; cunning; lack of scruples.
2. Vulture (bird drekkana): Travels, especially by air; owns or flies planes; may have a bird for a pet; lives on the misfortune of others (as in a doctor, or some other type of consultant who benefits from the suffering of others); could benefit by the death of others as by inheritance; could prey on the weak if afflicted.
3. Dog (animal drekkana): Likes animals; animal-like sexual inclinations; a loyal friend.
4. Man with dirty clothes: Leaving parents; alienated from parents; may leave parents and live in a distant place; loss of parents.
5. Crying: Emotional.
6. Salmali tree: A mythical tree that grows in hell and is associated with torture. Yama, the god of death is said to live near the salmali tree. The thorns on this tree capture the dead. May focus on death and dying; thinks about endings and life's impermanence; may help those who are dying.

Path of Light – The Domains of Life

The second drekkana of Leo is a man with a horse's body and a bent nose, who looks as fierce as a lion. He wears a garland of white flowers on his head. He has a bow in his hand and is wearing the skin of a dark deer and a woolen blanket.

Notes on Symbolism:

1. Man with horse's body (animal drekkana): Likes animals, especially horses; physical, sexual inclinations; likes cars; moves swiftly; powerful; physically beautiful.
2. Bent nose: Prominent and distinctive character; possible unreliable instincts or questionable character.
3. Garland of white flowers on his head: Proud; famous; highly respected; self-expressive; high self-esteem.
4. Wool blanket: Dresses well; affluent; comfortable; protected.
5. Deerskin: Protected; supported; insulated.
6. Fierce as a lion: Bold; aggressive; intimidates competitors; has leadership ability; likes cats.
7. Bow (weapon drekkana): Assertive; combative; sometimes violent; occasionally possesses weapons.

The Drekkanas

The third drekkana of Leo is a man with a bear's face and who acts like a monkey. He has a long beard and curly hair. He is holding a stick in one hand and is carrying fish, fruit, and meat in the other hand.

Notes on Symbolism:

1. Bear's face (animal drekkana): Likes animals; physical, sexual inclinations; large or powerful; intimidating.
2. Acts like a monkey: Rash or foolish behavior; clever; like Hanuman (the monkey god), serves God, loyal; brave; powerful; warrior.
3. Long beard: Wise; bearded.
4. Curly hair: Curly hair.
5. Holding a stick (weapon drekkana): Assertive; competitive; ambitious; sometimes angry or occasionally violent quality.
6. Carrying fish, fruit, and meat: Provides sustenance for others through aggressive or ambitious nature, non-vegetarian.

Virgo

The first drekkana of Virgo is a virgin girl who is wearing dirty clothes although she desires nice clothes and money. She is carrying a pot of flowers and is going to her teacher's home.

Notes on Symbolism:

1. Virgin girl: Purity; innocence; potentially procreative and therefore creative potential.
2. Wearing dirty clothes: Wears old or dirty clothing; reputation tainted; first impression weak; poor; simple life; gives the impression of humility.
3. Likes clothes and money: Feels a lack of affluence; purchases nice clothing that tends to get ruined due to carelessness; in spite of giving the impression of simplicity, has strong desires for wealth, affluence and status; becomes wealthy.
4. Carrying a pot of flowers: Gives generously to others; honors and respects others.
5. Going to the home of her teacher: Gains knowledge; good education; has good teachers; becomes a good teacher; honors those who have knowledge or expertise.

The Drekkanas

The second drekkana of Virgo depicts a dark man, with hair all over his body, and a piece of cloth around his head. He has a bow in one hand and a pen in the other. He is counting profits and expenditure.

Notes on Symbolism:

1. Man with dark complexion: Dark complexion; exposed to sunlight/the outdoors; black person; possessing the qualities of Saturn.
2. Pen in his hand: Writing ability; mentally bright; may utilize other pen-like objects such as paint brushes.
3. Cloth around his head: Headband; wears hats.
4. Bow in hand (weapon drekkana): Assertive, competitive; ambitious; sometimes angry; occasionally violent.
5. Hairy body: Hairy body.
6. Counting profits and expenses: Business acumen; accounting; desire for money; worries about money; saving money; protecting wealth.

The third drekkana of Virgo is a tall woman with a fair complexion. She is dressed in white silk, and is carrying a pot and a spoon. She is going to a temple with an attitude of self-control, purity and religious sanctity.

Notes on Symbolism:

1. Tall woman: A tall person; a person of high spiritual or professional stature; a leader.
2. Yellow complexion: Liver problems; digestive problems; jaundice; Jupitarian.
3. Dressed in white silk: Purity; modesty; humility; prefers anonymity, clean, meticulous.
4. Carrying a pot and a spoon: Religious; related to ritual sacrifice.
5. Going to the temple with great sanctity: Loves sacred spaces; religiously or spiritually inclined; natural faith in the divine; seeks solitude.

LIBRA

The first drekkana of Libra depicts a man who is sitting in a shop on the roadway. He is skilled in using small balances to weigh and measure things. He has gold and diamonds in his hands to be weighed. He is thinking about their prices and the profits he can make with them.

Notes on Symbolism:

1. A man sitting in his shop on the roadway: Business owner; business acumen.
2. Skilled at using small balances to weigh and measure: Good accounting skills; mathematical; precise.
3. Thinking about the profits from gold and diamonds in his hands: Mercenary; buying and selling; wealth and prosperity in general; financial worries if afflicted.

Path of Light – The Domains of Life

The second drekkana of Libra is a man with a vulture's face who has a pot in his hand, which is ready to fall. He is hungry and thirsty and is thinking about his wife and his children.

Notes on Symbolism:

1. Man with a vulture's face (bird drekkana): Movement; travel, especially by air; could own or fly planes; might own or enjoy birds; lives on the misfortune of others (as in a doctor, or some other type of consultant who benefits from the suffering of others); could benefit by the death of others (as by inheritance). In the *Ramayana*, the Vulture King is Jatayu, who fights Ravana, the demon king, in an attempt to save Sita. He represents dharma, honor, bravery, and the willingness to put one's self in harm's way for the welfare of others.
2. Pot which is ready to fall: A sense of impending calamity or failure; a feeling that at any moment all of his efforts could be undone; worried about debts and expenses.
3. Hungry and thirsty: Strong desires; passionate; never satisfied.
4. Thinking about his wife and family: Domestic responsibilities; worry about spouse or child; strong desire for spouse and children.

The third drekkana of Libra is a man who is adorned with gems and wearing armor. He looks and acts like a monkey and scares all the other animals in the forest. He has fruit and meat in one hand and a golden quiver in the other.

Notes on Symbolism:

1. Man adorned with gems: Prosperous; successful; auspicious.
2. Wearing armor: Protective; sets firm boundaries.
3. Scares animals in the forest: Dominant; intimidating; overpowering; competitive.
4. Looks and acts like a monkey (animal drekkana): Reckless, foolish, rash; brave, courageous, bold, noble, loyal; devoted (like Hanuman); likes animals; animal-like sexual inclinations.
5. Fruit and meat: Non-vegetarian; well-nourished.
6. Golden quiver: Conserves energy; saves money; potential for aggressive action; stores belongings with great care; an auspicious symbol.

Scorpio

The first drekkana of Scorpio depicts a beautiful, naked woman without jewelry. She has serpents coiled around her feet. She is displaced from her native land and has reached a shore after a voyage across a great ocean.

Notes on Symbolism:

1. Naked woman: New beginnings; dislikes wearing clothing; vulnerability; honest; open.
2. No jewelry: Lack of pretense; dislikes ornamentation or jewelry; financial stress; simplicity.
3. Serpents wrapped around her feet (serpent drekkana): Bound by circumstances; confined; venomous if attacked; deceptive; manipulative; seductive; open to being seduced; hypnotic; sexual; noble; mystical; psychological; detached; rises above passions. (See the description of the Nagas under Ashlesha nakshatra in *Volume I*.)
4. Crosses a great ocean: Goes to great lengths to accomplish goals; long distance travel.
5. Displaced from native land: Immigration, travels to distant places or foreign countries; lives in a distant place from the place of birth; separation from home and family; feels like she doesn't belong.

THE DREKKANAS

The second drekkana of Scorpio represents a woman whose body looks like a tortoise or a water pot. She is interested in making a comfortable situation for herself. For the sake of her husband, she has a serpent coiled around her body.

Notes on Symbolism:

1. Body like a tortoise or a pot: The tortoise can be a symbol of the Kurma Avatar of Vishnu. In order to recover some valuable things which had been lost in the great deluge, Vishnu, at the time of the churning of the ocean of milk, took the shape of a tortoise and went to the bottom of the ocean to support the mountain. As a result, Lakshmi, the goddess of wealth, Soma, the Celestial Nymphs, and many others appeared. The Indian continent is also said to rest on the back of Kurma. Recovery of lost things; restoring of well being; prosperity; provides a firm foundation; stability; security; regeneration.
2. Interest in a comfortable situation: Creates material comfort and affluence.
3. Serpent coiled around her body for the sake of her husband (serpent drekkana): Subservient to spouse; restrained by marital or family circumstances; inability to get in touch with her own desires or needs; puts other's happiness before her own; bound by circumstances; confined; venomous if attacked; deceptive; manipulative; seductive; hypnotic; sexual; noble; mystical; psychological; detached; rises above passions. (See the description of the Nagas under Ashlesha nakshatra in *Volume I*.)

Path of Light – The Domains of Life

The third drekkana of Scorpio is a lion with a wide and flat face. He resembles a tortoise. He scares jackals, dogs, deer, and boars. He protects a mountainous area, which is covered with sandalwood trees.

Notes on Symbolism:

1. Lion with wide and flat face (animal drekkana): Likes animals, (especially cats); animal-like sexual inclinations; dominant; leadership abilities; royal or regal. The lion may also be related to Narasimha Avatar (The Man-Lion Avatar of Vishnu). He incarnated in order to protect a pure devotee, whose asura father wanted to kill him. He symbolizes righteous anger and wrath, protection, and unapproachable power. He is the warrior incarnate.
2. Resembles a tortoise: The tortoise can be a symbol of the Kurma Avatar of Vishnu. In order to recover some valuable things which had be lost in the great deluge, Vishnu, at the time of the churning of the ocean of milk, took the shape of a tortoise and went to the bottom of the ocean to support the mountain. Recovery of lost things; restoring well-being; prosperity; provides a firm foundation; stability; security; regeneration.
3. Scares dogs, jackals, deer, boars: Dominant; competitive.
4. Protects mountainous area covered with sandalwood trees: Protective; loves nature; environmentalist.

Sagittarius

The first drekkana of Sagittarius is a man with a human face and a horse's body. He carries a long bow, which is stretched tight in his hand. He lives in a hermitage, and protects the ascetics and articles used for the ritual sacrifice.

Notes on Symbolism:

1. Man with human face and horse's body (animal drekkana): Likes animals, especially horses; may also symbolize vehicles.
2. Lives in hermitage: Lives in a secluded spot; seeks solitude; reclusive; spiritually inclined; meditative; frequents retreat centers or ashrams.
3. Bow in hand (weapon drekkana): Assertive; competitive; ambitious; sometimes angry, possibly violent.
4. Protects the ascetics and sacrificial articles: Protective of teachers; respectful of elders; respects and protects religion or tradition; holds certain things sacred, deep within.

Path of Light – The Domains of Life

The second drekkana of Sagittarius is a beautiful woman whose color is like gold or the champaka flower. She is sitting in Bhadrasana and is picking up gems from the ocean.

Notes on Symbolism:

1. Beautiful woman: Beauty; pleasant experiences.
2. Color like gold or the champaka flower: Good complexion; likes flowers; radiant; famous; successful; noble.
3. Bhadrasana: A yoga posture meaning the throne pose; practice of yoga; spiritual practice; flexibility; yielding.
4. Picking up gems from the ocean: Easily prosperous; wealthy; likes gems; likes the water; gains deep inner wisdom.

THE DREKKANAS

The third drekkana of Sagittarius is a man with a long beard. His skin is golden and looks like the champaka flower. He is wearing white silk and a deerskin. He has a staff in his hand and is seated in the Varasana posture.

Notes on Symbolism:

1. Man with a long beard: Wise; bearded.
2. Golden skin: Radiant; famous; successful; noble; good complexion.
3. Wears white silk and deerskin: Well-dressed; affluent; pure of heart; a spiritual teacher or guru.
4. Staff in hand (weapon drekkana): Authority; assertive; competitive; ambitious; sometimes angry, occasionally violent.
5. Varasana posture: Means "a majestic seat"; inclined to occupy a position of authority; practices yoga; good posture; good health and vitality; respected.

Capricorn

The first drekkana of Capricorn is a man who has hair all over his body. He has teeth that look like a shark's. He has a pig's body and a cruel face. He has chains, nets and yokes.

Notes on Symbolism:

1. Hairy man: Hairy; virile; masculine; coarse.
2. Teeth like a shark's: Sharp teeth; lethal bite; predatory; avaricious; aggressive; cold; litigious; lawyer.
3. Pig's body: Overweight; large.
4. Cruel face: Cruel; hard-hearted.
5. Chains, nets, yokes: Binds; restrains; confines; related to jails or prisons, hunting or trapping.

THE DREKKANAS

The second drekkana of Capricorn depicts a dark woman who is wearing a lot of jewelry. She has wide eyes that resemble lotus petals and is wearing iron earrings. She is searching for many things.

Notes on Symbolism:

1. Dark woman: Saturnine; disciplined; focused; good concentration; obstacles; pressures; limitations; works hard; responsible.
2. Wearing jewelry: Wealth; prosperity; ornamentation; self-possessed; self-expressive; wears gems.
3. Wide eyes like lotus petals: Open; innocent; pure-hearted; fascinated; enlightened; wise; observant.
4. Iron earrings: Listens with discrimination; wears earrings; powerful verbal skills; works in a listening or speaking occupation; involved with technology.
5. Searching for things: Restless; always searching; curious.

Path of Light – The Domains of Life

The third drekkana of Capricorn is a man who is carrying a gem-studded water pot on his shoulder. His body is like a kinnara. He has a woolen blanket, a bow, arrows and a quiver.

Notes on Symbolism:

1. Gem-studded water pot: Wealth; prosperity; abundance; fulfillment; an auspicious symbol.
2. Body like a kinnara: A kinnara is a being with the head of a horse and the body of a human being. Kinnara means "what man." Kinnaras were noted for their ability to dance and sing.
3. Woolen blanket: Secure; well dressed; protected.
4. Bow, arrows and quiver (weapon drekkana): Assertive; competitive; ambitious; sometimes angry; prepared; able to protect self and others.

Aquarius

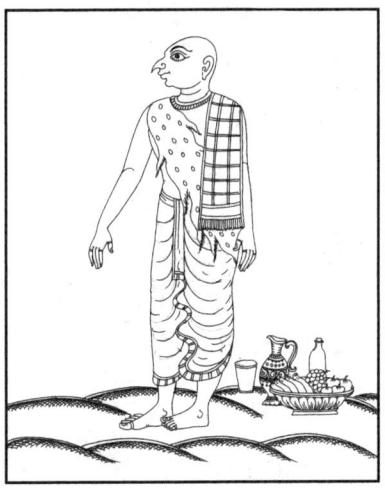

The first drekkana of Aquarius is a man with a vulture's face. He is dressed in silk clothes, and is also wearing a deerskin and a wool blanket. He is anxious about getting oils, wine, water and food.

Notes on Symbolism:

1. Vulture's face (bird drekkana): Travels, especially by air; owns or flies planes; may have a bird for a pet; lives on the misfortune of others (as in a doctor, or some other type of consultant who benefits from the suffering of others); could benefit by the death of others (as by inheritance); could prey on the weak if afflicted.
2. Anxious about getting oils, wine, water and food: Hungry; strong desires; sense of lack; poverty; obsession with food; eating disorders; insecurity about basic material survival; mental anguish or imbalance due to focusing on outer values. This can also suggest mental instability resulting from the intake of oils, wine, water or food.
3. Wearing deerskin: Insulated; protected; supported.
4. Woolen blanket; Protected against the elements; secure.
5. Silk clothes: Refined; well dressed; affluent; insulated; isolated.

The second drekkana of Aquarius is a woman who is wearing dirty clothes and who is living in the forest. She is sitting in a burnt cart, which is carrying cotton trees. She has pots on her head and she is collecting iron.

Notes on Symbolism:

1. Wearing dirty clothes: Poor; born under impoverished conditions; dresses casually or in old clothes; unconcerned with appearance or persona; struggles; miserable.
2. Lives in the forest: Lives in nature; likes wooded areas; lives alone; isolated; alienated; lonely.
3. Sitting in a burnt cart: An old truck; a broken down or damaged vehicle; an occupation which provides a meager living or which has passed its prime; something related to technology.
4. Carrying cotton trees: Wood; cloth; basic materials.
5. Pots on her head: Self-reliant; independent; succeeds through her own wits.
6. Collecting iron: Hard work; constant pressure; saturnine; hardened; tough; collects or keeps things; involved with technology.

The third drekkana of Aquarius is a dark man who has hair in his ears. He is wearing a crown. As he wanders from place to place, he carries pots containing iron, skins, gum, fruits, bark, oil and leaves.

Notes on Symbolism:

1. Dark man: Saturnine; hard working; responsible; persevering; patient or oppressed; obstructed.
2. Hair in ears: Doesn't listen; stubborn.
3. Wearing a crown: Proud; successful; leader.
4. Wandering: Wandering; distracted.
5. Carrying pots full of iron, skins, gum, fruits, bark, oil and leaves: A variety of useful substances; materials used for healing; materials used for repair work.

Pisces

The first drekkana of Pisces is a man wearing ornaments. He is on a ship crossing the ocean, searching for gems for his wife. He is holding pearls, other gems, a conch shell, and sacrificial objects in his hands.

Notes on Symbolism:

1. Man wearing ornaments: Affluent; successful; self-possessed; strong persona; concerned about the opinions of others; celebrates life.
2. Crossing an ocean: Related to travel, water, or the ocean; related to emotion or deep feelings; empathic; related to higher consciousness.
3. Searching for gems for wife: Subservient to wife or spouse; works to make a prosperous life for the sake of the spouse; benefits through partnership; tries hard to please others.
4. Holding pearls, other gems: Prosperous; successful; auspicious; blessed; possesses peace of mind; happy; wise.
5. Conch shell: Auspicious; successful; celebrated; famous; recognized.
6. Sacrificial objects: Spiritual; alchemical; ritualistic; self-sacrificing; overcomes obstacles through spiritual means.

The Drekkanas

The second drekkana of Pisces is a woman whose face is as bright and beautiful as the champaka flower. She is searching for the coastline on a ship that is sailing across the ocean. The ship has many banners on it. She is surrounded by her servants and her family, and is holding a long staff.

Notes on Symbolism:

1. Woman with a face as bright and beautiful as the champaka flower: Bright face; great beauty; sensitive; sweet disposition.
2. Searching for the coastline: Goal oriented; setting high goals; restless; living in the future; searching for enlightenment.
3. Sailing across an ocean: Related to travel; related to oceans or water; related to emotion; related to higher consciousness, covers a great deal of territory; possesses a great deal of experience.
4. Many banners on the ship: Bound to succeed; celebrated; accomplished; high status; authority.
5. Surrounded by servants and family: Supported by many people; has employees or servants; good family connections; has a position of respect and authority.
6. Holding a long staff: Authority; support; wisdom.

Path of Light – The Domains of Life

The third drekkana of Pisces is a naked man with a serpent coiled around him. He is in a pit in the forest and he is crying because he is scared of thieves and fire.

Notes on Symbolism:

1. Naked man: Defenseless; vulnerable; natural; prefers nudity; free; innocent.
2. Serpent coiled around his body (serpent drekkana): Bound by circumstances; confined; venomous if attacked; deceptive; manipulative; seductive; hypnotic; sexual; noble; mystical; psychological; detached; rises above passions. (See the description of the Nagas under Ashlesha nakshatra in *Volume I*.)
3. In a pit in the forest: Lives alone; isolated; lonely; alienated; digs himself into deeper and deeper problems; feels helpless; monastic; reclusive.
4. Crying: Emotional (tears of joy or sorrow).
5. Fear of thieves and fire: Worries about many things; fearful; gloomy; negative thinking; fear of failure; expects calamities.

THE DREKKANAS

How to Use the Drekkanas

Drekkanas can be used in different ways. One of the most obvious is to simply blend the symbolism of the drekkana image with the natural and temporal significations of the planet that is placed in the drekkana. If, for example, the ruler of the tenth house (career) is placed in the second drekkana of Virgo (a man with a pen, doing his profits and losses) then the person might do accounting, business, or may simply have writing ability. Some of the drekkana images and are easy to understand. Other images are more difficult to incorporate in the chart. Sometimes the entire image can be used. At other times it is enough to make note of the type of drekkana or its quality in general.

Types of Drekkanas

Drekkanas fall into various categories depending on the type of symbol they contain. There are various types of symbols contained within the drekkana, but there are four common symbol types that astrologers utilize frequently.

1. Sarpa Drekkanas: Sarpa means "serpent." Sarpa drekkanas are drekkanas in which serpents appear as part of the image. Serpents are the inhabitants of the underworld, which is the realm of the unconscious, so sarpa drekkanas have a complex and psychological quality. Serpents are also a symbol of the kundalini, so these drekkanas can also symbolize spiritual power. On the negative side, serpents symbolize underhanded or deceitful tendencies. They can be associated with confinement or even imprisonment. They also have the power to mesmerize, hypnotize, and manipulate. They inflict poison, which can sometimes manifest as backbiting or jealousy. For more about serpents, see Ashlesha nakshatra in *Volume I*. The qualities of serpents described under Ashlesha will apply to the sarpa drekkanas in general.

2. Ayudha Drekkanas: Ayudha means "weapon." Ayudha drekkanas contain weapons as part of the image. These drekkanas are sometimes associated with violence. In a study of over one hundred violent crimes, for example, this author found a very high incidence of ayudha drekkanas occupied by focal planets. This does not mean that having a focal planet in an ayudha drekkana will make a person an axe murderer, however. In fact, in the majority of cases, having a focal planet in ayudha drekkanas simply gives the person martial

tendencies. Ayudha drekkanas make the person more assertive and aggressive, which can produce ambitious or competitive qualities that assist the person professionally. In the chart of an emotional person, a focal planet in an ayudha drekkana will make the person more likely to express anger. If other factors in the chart suggest a lack of balance and restraint, then the addition of a key planet in an ayudha drekkana may make the person violent. How these drekkanas are utilized greatly depends on the overall tone of the horoscope, and also which planet is placed in the ayudha drekkana. The ruler of the tenth house (career), placed in an ayudha drekkana might make the person interested in careers that are related to weapons, such as law enforcement or military. The ruler of the fifth house (sports), placed in an ayudha drekkana might make the person enjoy combative sports such as soccer, football, martial arts, or fencing. If a dasha, bhukti or antara ruler is placed in an ayudha drekkana, then during that period the person could become competitive, assertive, aggressive, angry or even violent, depending on the nature of the person. If the period planet is afflicted by malefics in an ayudha drekkana, then he might be defeated by competitors or enemies during the period.

3. Chatushpad Drekkanas: Chatushpad drekkanas contain pictures of animals. These drekkanas can be interpreted in different ways. One obvious way is simply to give the person more contact with animals during his lifetime. If other factors in the chart suggest love of animals, then focal planets or the ruler of the sixth house (pets) placed in a chatushpad drekkana will allow the astrologer to confidently predict that the person will have pets. In matters of sexuality, chatushpad drekkanas suggest a more basic, physically-oriented sexual inclination.

4. Kagha Drekkanas: Kagha drekkanas contain images of birds. If the chart suggests love of animals in general, then the ruler of the sixth house placed here signifies that the person keeps a bird as a pet. In the majority of cases, however, kagha drekkanas can be used as drekkanas to symbolize travel, especially by air. In a study of over forty pilots, the author found that kagha drekkanas were usually occupied by focal planets, such as the lagna lord, the Sun, the Moon, or the ruler of the fourth house (vehicles). Kagha drekkanas will also enhance yogas for travel. For example, if a person has the ruler of the third house (short journeys) placed in the ninth house (long journeys), then this creates a combination for long distance travel.

If, in addition, this planet falls in a kagha drekkana, then it will be more likely that the person will travel frequently by air. However, if the same planet is afflicted in a kagha drekkana, then there might be problems, delays, obstacles, or even danger related to air travel.

Other Symbols

There are a variety of other symbols contained within the drekkanas. The astrologer can utilize the part of the symbolism that relates to the area of life being analyzed. The ruler of the second house (money) placed in a drekkana containing gemstones, for example, augments the financial potential of the chart. If the same planet is afflicted, then expenditure might result.

Author's Journal:

The Story of Yavanacharya

The drekkana descriptions appear in the last chapter of the Brihat Jataka *by Varahamihira, one of the most respected ancient authors of Jyotish literature. It is interesting to note that he credits the Yavanas for these descriptions. The Yavanas are generally believed to have been the inhabitants of the Greek island of Ionia. As a result of travel and trade between India and Greece, a cultural exchange took place, including the sharing of certain astrological techniques. Varshaphal, a popular method of calculating the annual horoscope, as well as the Tajika method of prashna are examples of such techniques. Tales of how this interchange took place have been passed down as part of a great oral tradition, which exists in India even to this day. Astrologers tell these stories to family members, students, and other astrologers, recounting events overlooked by more formal accounts of history.*

The following story of how Yavana astrological techniques became popular in India was told to me by Gayatri Devi Vasudev. Mrs. Vasudev is the daughter of the late Dr. B.V. Raman, who was one of the greatest Vedic astrologers of the last century. She is the editor of the Astrological Magazine, *and a great astrologer in her own right.*

"You know, most astrologers in olden times were Brahmins. Once there was a Brahmin who was the king's court astrologer. A son was born to the king, so the astrologer was asked to make his horoscope. The astrologer studied the horoscope and predicted that the king's son would live a long life and would become a powerful emperor. Unfortunately, the prince died as a young child.

"The king became very angry at the astrologer. (In those days, it was not uncommon for royal astrologers to lose their heads for missing such important predictions.) Instead of killing the astrologer, however, the king told him to leave. The astrologer traveled far and wide throughout India, and finally went outside of India, to the land of the Yavanas, which was probably the island of Ionia in Greece. He lived with the Yavanas for some time and used his astrological skills. Since he was actually a very good astrologer, his fame spread. The local king was so impressed with the astrologer's skills that he gave him his daughter, the princess, to marry.

"As time passed, various astrologers of that region heard about the Indian astrologer who had married the king's daughter and they began to come to visit him. They discussed astrology and exchanged skills. Up to this time, the astrologer did not utilize any method for calculating annual horoscopes. From one of the Yavana astrologers, he learned the method called Varshaphal. After learning this technique, he cast the Varshaphal for the year in which the Indian prince had died. He looked at the chart and immediately saw the death of the child clearly represented in the annual chart.

"Happy to know the reason for his failed prediction, the astrologer returned to India. He was received back into the kingdom where he taught the technique of Varshaphal to others, and was given the name Yavanacharya."

Chapter Five

Dashas

So far in this book we have dealt primarily with the static condition of the chart. We have shown how the various planetary positions reveal the basic wiring and potentials of the person's life. Life, on the other hand, is a constantly changing experience. In fact, the very nature of life is change. Everything is always transforming. If a horoscope has a planet placed in a particular house that promises success in the career, the success comes only at a particular period in life, not all at once at the time of birth. So Jyotish also deals with the art of predicting when the various events and trends shown in the horoscope will manifest.

Jyotish has many techniques that are used for prediction. At the basis of all of them is the following basic principle. You can only predict what is promised in the natal chart. This means that the correct analysis of the natal chart must always precede prediction. Once you are clear on what is promised in the chart, then prediction becomes a simple process of knowing how to tell when the various events of life are scheduled.

Vimshottari Dasha

The main technique for prediction in Jyotish is called the *dasha*. A dasha is a period. The most popular dasha system used in India is Vimshottari Dasha, which is a planetary period system. This is the period system that we will use in this book. There are many other good planetary period systems, however, and most of them can be used effectively for prediction. Some of them use planets and some use signs in order to predict the ups and downs of life. Learning to use the various dashas is a natural part of learning Jyotish. In this book, however, we will try to keep things as simple as possible and just stick with Vimshottari Dasha, which is the one that most Vedic astrologers use as their primary predictive tool.

Vimshottari Dasha is a planetary period cycle, which takes 120 years to complete. The full span of human life is considered to be 120 years. Each of the planets and the nodes, Rahu and Ketu, are given a major period within the 120-year Vimshottari cycle. Since this system is based on the nakshatras, the order of the periods follows the order of the nakshatras in the zodiac. The first planetary period in each horoscope is different, based on the position of the Moon. The period ruler for the first dasha will always be the planet that rules the nakshatra in which the Moon is placed. The following periods follow a set sequence, which matches the order of the nakshatras in the zodiac.

The order of the dashas is as follows: Ketu, Venus, Sun, Moon, Mars, Rahu, Jupiter, Saturn, and Mercury. If, for example, the natal Moon falls in a nakshatra ruled by the Sun, then the dasha sequence will start with the Sun and will be followed by Moon, Mars, Rahu, Jupiter, Saturn, Mercury, Ketu, and Venus.

The number of years allotted to each dasha is as follows: Ketu (7 years), Venus (20 years), Sun (6 years), Moon (10 years), Mars (7 years), Rahu (18 years), Jupiter (16 years), Saturn (19 years), and Mercury (17 years). If the natal Moon has traveled partway through a nakshatra, then the first dasha will have less than the nakshatra ruler's full number of years. The number of years allotted to the first dasha will be proportional to the remainder of the nakshatra to be traversed. If the natal Moon, for example, is exactly two-thirds of the way through the nakshatra of Krittika, this means that it has one-third of the nakshatra left before it exits Krittika and enters Rohini. Since Krittika is ruled by the Sun, the full cycle would be six years. Because the Moon has only one-third of the nakshatra left, the number of years allotted to the Sun dasha would be one-third of six years, which is two years. So in this example, the dasha sequence would begin with two years of the Sun dasha and be followed by ten years of the Moon dasha, seven years of the Mars dasha, and so on.

Dashas are also sub-divided. The main period is called the Maha Dasha. The Maha Dasha is divided into nine parts. These parts are called *bhuktis*. Each bhukti is ruled by one of the nine planets. The number of years and months allotted to each bhukti ruler is calculated in the following way. If you want to find out how many years and months will be allotted to the Venus bhukti within the Mars Maha Dasha, then look at the Venus Maha Dasha, which is a twenty year period, and determine what fraction of the total 120 years of the Vimshottari Dasha that twenty years represents. So 20/120 equals one-sixth of the total length of the Vimshottari Dasha. The Venus bhukti will be one-sixth of the seven years of the Mars Maha Dasha or fourteen months. Similarly, the Venus bhukti in each of the other Maha Dashas will be one-sixth of the total period of the dasha.

Today, dasha calculation is done by computers. It is important, nevertheless, to understand the method of calculating dashas. The preceding explanation gives the basic idea. In practice, however, most people use computers to calculate planetary periods.

Dasha Interpretation

The dasha of a planet is the period during which the planet expresses itself in its fullest capacity. In this respect, all of the planets in the chart are like singers in a chorus, who are all contributing their voices to the music. At some point, however, one singer has the opportunity to sing a solo. When a planet's period operates, the planet gives its result in a more pronounced way. If the planet's period is not operating, it still gives its influence, but in a more generalized way.

The main concept of dasha interpretation is that during the dasha of a planet, the planet gives what it promises in the natal chart. If you really understand the planet in the natal chart, then prediction will be easy. This task is not as easy as it seems, however, and there are many nuances to dasha interpretation. Here are some general rules.

Rules of Dasha Interpretation

1. The dasha lord gives results according to its nature. This is the most basic rule of dasha interpretation and is frequently overlooked by budding jyotishis who get caught up in all the mechanical intricacies of prediction. According to this rule, the planet will not behave counter to its nature. Saturn, for example, is a planet of responsibilities and pressures. It is not the planet of passion, love and romance. A strong and well-placed Saturn will tend to give better results in areas of work and responsibility. If it does give relationship or marriage, it will do so in a characteristically saturnine way.
2. The dasha lord gives results according to its house ownership. If the dasha ruler owns the fourth house, for example, then during its period events related to the fourth house are expected. The type of event is modified by the specific disposition of the dasha lord.

Sun 10°4 Cap - very weak period for me
Mars is at 29°17 Aquarius - could be equally weak

Dashas

3. The dasha lord gives results according to the house in which it is placed. If it is placed in the eighth house, for example, then eighth house results are expected. Since the eighth house signifies change, the person might go through many upheavals and transitions during that period. Dasha lords are most favorable in kendras (houses 1,4,7&10)and konas (houses 1,5&9). They produce more difficult results when placed in dusthanas (houses 6,8 &12).

4. Combining rules 2. and 3., the dasha lord gives results based on the connection between the house it rules and the house in which it is placed. If the dasha lord rules the fourth house (residence), for example, and is placed in the eighth house (change), then during its period you might expect a change of residence. (See the chapter on houses in *Volume I*, which contains a section devoted to house rulers placed in different houses for clues about how to combine the results of two houses). Generally speaking, planets that rule dusthanas produce problems in the houses they occupy during their periods. Planets which own kendras and konas produce good results in the houses they occupy during their periods.

5. The dasha lord will give results according to the natural significations of the sign in which it is placed. A planet in Libra, for example, is more likely to produce relationship events because of the natural significations related to the sign of Libra.

6. Planets placed in their own signs or exalted tend to give the positive side of the house they occupy and of their own natural significations. Planets that are debilitated tend to give the negative side of the house they occupy and of their natural signfications.

7. The dasha lord will give results according to the nakshatra in which it is placed. Here the symbol, name, shakti and mythology of the nakshatra must be considered. A planet in Purva Phalguni, which is symbolized by the conjugal bed, could produce a romantic involvement. If the planet is a malefic, though, it sometimes reverses or gives the negative side of the nakshatra. Saturn in Purva Phalguni might produce marital or relationship difficulties during its period. Similarly, if the planet is a benefic, it will produce the positive side of the nakshatra's energy during its period.

8. The dasha lord will give results according to the drekkana in which it is placed. This rule uses the symbols of the thirty-six drekkanas. For example, the second drekkana of Virgo is symbolized by a man holding a pen, calculating his profits and losses. During the period of a planet placed here, the person might do some sort of business which requires accounting, or he may simply become interested in writing.

9. The dasha lord will become more positive if it is conjunct or aspected by natural benefics. Jupiter, Venus, Mercury and the waxing Moon are the natural benefics. Benefic planets in the same sign as the dasha lord or casting an aspect on the dasha lord will create some benefit.
10. The dasha lord will become more negative if it is conjunct or aspected by natural malefics. Saturn, Mars, Sun, Rahu and Ketu are the natural malefics. If they are in the same sign as the dasha lord or if they cast an aspect on the dasha lord, then the period will contain some corresponding problems.
11. The dasha lord will become more positive when it is conjunct or aspected by temporal benefics. (See the "Table of Temporal Benefics and Malefics" in *Path of Light, Volume I*.)
12. The dasha lord will become more negative when it is conjunct or aspected by temporal malefics.
13. The dasha lord will produce results in houses it aspects. For example, Mars always aspects the fourth, seventh and eighth houses from its placement. So a person might have surgery during Mars dasha if it is placed in the third house, since Mars casts an aspect on the sixth house (health problems), which is four houses away from the third house.
14. The dasha lord will activate the planet that owns the nakshatra in which it is placed. For example, Jupiter is placed in Cancer in the first house, in the nakshatra of Pushya. Pushya is ruled by Saturn, and Saturn is placed in the sixth house, conjunct Rahu and Mars. During its period, Jupiter might produce an accident or illness, as well as create some results that are in line with its exalted, first-house placement.
15. The dasha lord will activate the planet that is placed in one of the other two nakshatras owned by its nakshatra lord. For example, if Saturn is in Ashwini in the horoscope and Venus is in Mula, then they are both placed in nakshatras ruled by Ketu. During Saturn's period, it will give both the results of its own placement as well as the results of Venus' placement in Mula.
16. A planet that is hemmed in by benefics will give positive results related to all of its significations, while a planet that is hemmed in by malefics will give negative results during its period. "Hemmed in" refers to Kartari Yoga. There are two types: Papa Kartari Yoga, which is hemming in by malefics, and Shubha Kartari Yoga, which is hemming in by benefics.
17. The dasha lord will give the results of any yoga in which it is involved. If the Moon and Jupiter are involved in Gaja Kesari Yoga,

which is a yoga that increases reputation, then during the period of the Moon or Jupiter the reputation will rise. The effects of the yoga will be more evident when the sub-period of the second planet is also operating, such as Moon major period / Jupiter sub-period, or vice versa.

18. During the period of a planet that is strong in the rashi chart but weak in the Navamsha chart, there will be positive results in the first part of the period and more negative results later in the period. If the planet is much stronger in the Navamsha and weak in the rashi, then its period will begin with difficulties and improve over time.
19. Rahu and Ketu give results according to house placement, sign placement, nakshatra placement, drekkana placement, and aspects as given in the preceding rules, except when it comes to rulership. Since Rahu and Ketu have no rulership, they are interpreted differently. To determine if Rahu or Ketu will function as a temporal benefic or malefic, interpret the results of the planet with which they are conjunct. In the absence of a conjuncting planet, interpret the results of the planet that disposits Rahu or Ketu.
20. The evaluation of the house rulerships and placement of the dasha lord may also be done from the natal Moon and natal Sun.
21. The dasha lord's disposition, as well as any yoga involvement in the various divisional charts, will reveal the type of results it will confer in the specific domain ruled by a specific divisional chart. For example, if the Moon and Jupiter are involved in a Dhana Yoga (a combination for wealth) in the Dwadashamsha chart (chart for parents), then during the period of a planet involved in that yoga, the person could receive money from a parent, or the parents themselves might experience a financial increase.

Sub-Period Interpretation

Sub-period (bhukti) rulers are interpreted exactly like major period rulers, except that they are secondary to the Maha Dasha ruler. During the major period of a planet, that planet dominates the horoscope. The sub-period ruler is subservient to the major period ruler. In this respect, a major period is like a country and the sub-period is like a state within the country. Whatever laws and rules govern the state are subservient to the laws of the country. A prosperous state within a poor country will never be as prosperous as a prosperous state within a prosperous country. In some cases a prosperous state within a poor country might be less prosperous than a poor state within a poor country. Similarly, a good major period will uplift all of its sub-periods to some extent, and a difficult major period will bring difficulty into even the best of its sub-periods.

The following rules for the interpretation of sub-periods are offered in addition to the general guidelines given for major periods:

1. The major period ruler sets the theme, while the sub-period modifies it. The sub-period ruler can't produce what is not within the repertoire of the major period ruler. For example, during Saturn's major period the overall theme is work and responsibility. Moreover, suppose Venus is well-placed and situated in the chart denoting a possible marriage. If during Saturn's major period, Saturn also has the capacity to produce marriage, then the Venus sub-period might produce marriage. However, the husband and wife may still continue to focus most of their energy on their mutual careers, while their relationship becomes something they schedule into their spare time. If Saturn is badly placed for relationships, however, then the Venus sub-period may give only a frustrated desire to find a partner. *Interesting, because of the Venus bhukti, Saturn Sub-Bhukti*

2. The major period ruler becomes an important focal point during the duration of its period and should be treated as the first house when interpreting sub-periods. In other words, if Jupiter is the major period ruler and it is placed in the fourth house in Cancer, then the sign of Cancer should be treated as the first house during Jupiter's period. The sub-period rulers should be interpreted relative to the major period ruler's position. In this example, if Mercury is placed in the ninth house in Sagittarius, then it will be in the sixth house from Jupiter, and should be treated as if it is in the sixth house as well as the ninth house. It is important to note that this technique does not exclude the normal assessment of Mercury in the ninth house from the Ascendant. It simply gives another angle from which to analyze Mercury's effects. In this example, it will produce something positive because it is in the ninth house from the Ascendant, and something more challenging because it is in the sixth house (a dusthana) from Jupiter. Analyzing the sub-period planet relative to the major period ruler's position also means that all of the previous rules about house rulership can be applied. Sub-period planets placed in kendras and konas from the major period ruler also promote good, while those placed in dusthanas promote difficulties.

3. During the major period of a malefic planet and the sub-period of another malefic planet, problems are more likely. In this context, the word "malefic" is defined as a natural malefic planet. Consider for example, an individual with a Libra Ascendant, who is experiencing the major period of Saturn and the sub-period of Mars. Also, in this chart, Mars is involved with Saturn in a Raja Yoga. In addition to having some career improvement, there will also be some difficulties during the period that are simply the result of having two natural malefics operating at the same time. Since the major period ruler in this case is a temporal benefic, and because of the Raja Yoga, the person might experience positive results in the career. Mars and Saturn are both harsh planets, so he might neglect his wife and have some minor marital problems. In this case the marital problems could be minor, due to the fact that the major period ruler has set a tone of general success in the chart. In a chart where the major or sub-period ruler is both a temporal malefic as well as a natural malefic, the problems could be more severe.
4. During the major period of a benefic, the sub-period of another benefic will promote positive effects. Again, "benefic" in this case means a natural benefic planet. Following rule 3., above, the concept is that two natural benefics are bound to give at least some positive results during their mutual major period/sub-period, even if one of them is a temporal malefic. If one or both of them are also temporal benefics, the period will be particularly positive.

Dashas: One Rule at a Time

The chart of Albert Einstein will serve to illustrate some of the preceding rules of dasha interpretation. First the rule will be stated, and then applied to the particular event.

Albert Einstein
March 14, 1879; 11:30 AM; Ulm, Germany

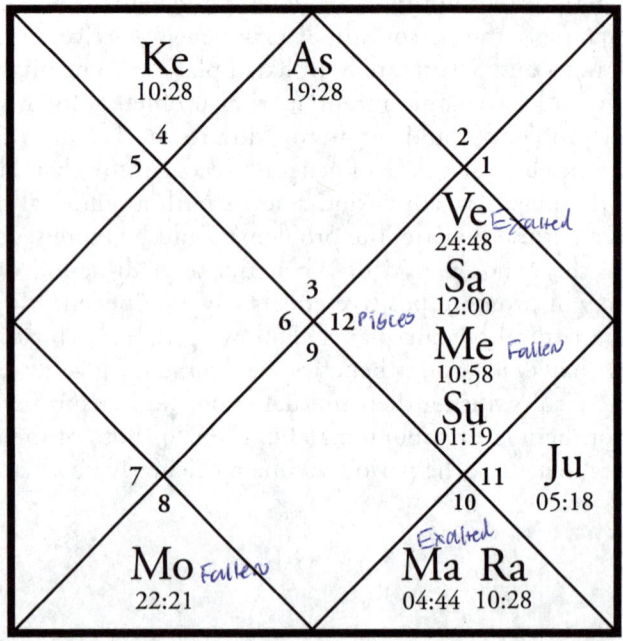

1. The period ruler gives results according to its nature. Einstein was born in his Mercury period and Mercury is the debilitated ruler of the first house. Mercury's period operated from birth to age nine. One of the prominent features of his life at that time was the problem he had with reading, and school in general. Mercury is the planet of processing information. Its debilitation shows that he had difficulty processing information, which manifested as dyslexia and daydreaming.

2. The period ruler gives results according to the house in which it is placed. In 1894, during his Ketu major period, the family business failed. Ketu (signifying losses) is placed in the second house, which

is the house of both the family and sustenance. The second house is related to food, the money necessary to put food on the table, and the family events surrounding the obtaining of food.

3. The period ruler's results are modified by the aspects of other planets. Ketu is a malefic by nature and signifies disappointment, uncertainty and losses. It is also aspected by Mars, which is not only a natural malefic but also a temporal malefic. By itself, Ketu suggests uncertainties with money. The Mars aspect significantly increases the probability that money problems for his family would manifest.

4. The period ruler gives results according to the house it owns. Saturn is the ruler of the sub-period during which the family business failed. Saturn is the ruler of the eighth house and the ninth house. The eighth house is the house of upsets, upheavals and changes. The failure of the family business produced big changes in his life. The ninth house is a kona or trinal house, signifying good results. The failure in the family business also produced much good in his life.

5. The period ruler gives the results of the natural significations of the sign in which it is placed. Ketu is in Cancer. Cancer signifies the residence or home. During the Maha Dasha of Ketu, he had changes of residence. The sub-period in which change of residence took place is seen in the following point.

6. The period ruler gives the combined results of the house in which it is placed (or aspects) and the house it owns. Saturn is the ruler of the eighth house and is placed in the tenth house. From the tenth house it throws an aspect on the fourth house. Einstein had a change (eighth house signification) of residence (fourth house signification) during Saturn's bhukti.

7. A debilitated planet gives the negative side of its natural significations during its period. Mercury is debilitated in the tenth house. During its major period, Mercury caused problems in school. During Ketu Maha Dasha, the Mercury bhukti caused Einstein to fail a crucial exam, which resulted in him not pursuing engineering but switching to physics.

8. During its period, the dasha or bhukti ruler gives the results of

any yogas in which it participates. Mercury is involved in Neecha Bhanga Raja Yoga in Einstein's horoscope. Although Mercury is debilitated, Venus is exalted and with Mercury in the tenth house, which cancels the debilitation. The effect of this yoga is to first produce a problem, and then create some improvement. This is a subtle and often misunderstood yoga. On first glance it seems that during Einstein's Mercury period, he did poorly in school. During his Ketu Maha Dasha, in his Mercury sub-period, he also failed an important entrance examination for engineering school. However, it was precisely this failure that directed him towards the study of physics, and consequently led to a highly successful career. Notice also that his career began in the field of physics at the beginning of the Venus major period when, in 1896, he began studying to become a physics teacher. Venus is the planet that cancels the debility of Mercury, thus reversing the problems experienced in Mercury's period. During the Venus period his career thrived. Venus is participating in two Raja Yogas with both Saturn and Mercury in the tenth house. Raja Yogas occur when rulers of angles and trines combine. They are most powerful when those planets combine in an angle of the horoscope. During the sub-period of Saturn (1908-1911), Einstein became recognized as the leading physicist in German-speaking Europe. In 1914, at the end of his Mercury period, he was given the most prestigious and well-paid position for a physicist in all of Europe, full professor at the Keiser-Wilhelm Gesellschaft in Berlin.

9. The period planet gives the results of the nakshatra in which it is placed. Ketu is placed in Pushya, located in the middle of the sign of Cancer. Pushya is ruled by Brihaspati, the teacher of all the gods in Hindu mythology. Ketu is a natural malefic and the significator of disappointment. During his Ketu major period Einstein was disappointed and bored by his teachers.

10. A planet that is aspected or conjunct Saturn gives its results later in its period or after some delays. Einstein gained fame and recognition in his Venus period, but not until the second half. Similarly, in his Mercury sub-period, he gained his major recognition in the last part of Mercury's bhukti. Both Venus and Mercury are conjunct Saturn.

11. The period ruler gives the results of the drekkana in which it is placed. Einstein published his *Theory of Relativity* and several other research papers in 1905 during his Venus/Rahu period. Rahu

is placed in the second drekkana of Capricorn. This drekkana is symbolized by a woman, wearing iron earrings, who is "searching out" various kinds of objects. This image can be interpreted as getting people to listen to his scientific theories (iron ear ornaments), through reading his research papers ("searching" various kinds of objects).

12. In the absence of a conjuncting planet, Rahu or Ketu gives the results of its dispositor. Ketu is placed in Cancer in the second house. This period was a difficult period for Einstein, signified by problems in school as well as changes of residence. The Moon owns the sign of Cancer making it the dispositor of Ketu. It is debilitated in the sixth house. This placement reflects both the struggles as well as the dynamic changes that took place during the period.

Author's Journal:

"Look Ma, No Planets!"

India is a vast ocean of divination techniques. Most of the astrology practiced in India has been passed down in an oral tradition and is not contained in books. For this reason I always make a point to visit local astrologers, especially the village astrologers, whenever I travel in India. Once I visited a good astrologer in a remote village in north India. I sat in his consultation room along with eight to ten other people as he answered questions. Village astrology is a group event. The concept of privacy is relatively unknown. Everyone hears the questions, no matter how personal, of everyone else. On this occasion, I noticed that for some questions, the astrologer would ask the client to take a piece of chalk and place it on a blank horoscope. The person would place the chalk on one of the astrological houses. Then the astrologer would give a quick "yes" or "no" answer based on the placement of the chalk.

When I asked him what he was doing, the astrologer explained his simple technique. He said, "If the person places the chalk on the sixth, eighth, or twelfth houses then the answer is "no." If he places the chalk on any other house, then the answer is "yes." In Jyotish, the sixth, eighth, and twelfth houses are dusthana houses, producing obstructions and disappointments.

There are a few exceptions to this rule and the technique can be refined easily by knowing what each of the houses represent. The eighth house, for example, represents upheaval and change. If the question is, "will I change my residence," then placing the chalk on the eighth house might signify a change and therefore the answer might be "yes." Similarly, the twelfth house is the house of distant places. In a question about traveling to a foreign country, putting the chalk (or any other marker) on the twelfth house might signify a "yes" answer.

A more sophisticated version of this is elaborated in the great classic, Prasna Marga. *The questioner is asked to place a coin on a blank chart. The resulting astrological sign is taken as "arudha lagna" or the ascendant for the question. Using this designated ascendant for the question, the astrologer simply fills in the planetary influences for the day and gives the reading.*

In south India they use cowry shells to choose the arudha lagna. I have visited many village astrologers who place a pile of small shells on the table and ask the client to tell them their question. Then the astrologer rubs his hand over the shells in a circular motion several times and finally grabs a handful of shells. Next he culls out groups of twelve shells until there is a remainder of twelve or less. The remainder signifies one of the twelve signs starting from Aries. This sign is taken as the arudha lagna for the question. The rest of the planets are then drawn in the chart and the astrologer offers his prediction.

Chapter Six

Transits

The natal chart is a map of the positions of the planets at the time of birth. The positions of the planets in the birth chart always stay the same throughout life. In the sky, however, the planets are constantly moving, transiting from sign to sign around the zodiac. As a transiting planet moves through a particular sign in the sky, it has the capacity to influence that sign in the natal chart as well. In a Leo Ascendant chart, for example, Jupiter's transit through the sign of Leo will influence the person's first house and thereby impact everything that the first house represents.

Classical Method

In India, various methods of transit are utilized. Many astrologers adopt the classical method of interpreting the transits of planets relative to the Moon sign, incorporating the use of an intricate system, which plots obstructions (called *vedha*) by other transiting planets. This lunar transit method plays an important part of the education of any aspiring jyotishi. Due to the complexity of this method, however, we will focus on simpler methods of transit in this book.

Transits From the Ascendant, the Sun, and the Moon

When a transiting planet moves across the sign occupying a particular house in the chart, it will impact that house and everything it signifies. The question is, however, should you plot the houses from the

Ascendant, the Sun or the Moon? As mentioned earlier, many classical astrologers primarily interpreted the transits according to the Moon's position. If a planet transits the second house from the Moon, the prediction would describe the planet's effect on finances, family matters, and other significations of the second house. Other astrologers claim that transits work best when they are plotted from the Ascendant. Still others use the Sun as the focal point and plot the houses of transiting planets from that point of view. In practice, all of the above points of reference seem to work and are valid as potential focal points when analyzing transits. In fact there are many other lagnas that can be used as well. For simplicity, in this book we will plot transits relative to the Ascendant.

How to Interpret Transits - A Simple Method for the Novice or Non-Astrologer

The first step to interpret transits is to determine which house a particular planet is transiting in your chart. This can be done in a couple of ways. The simplest and least expensive method is to purchase an ephemeris, which is a reference book that lists the motions of planets. Make sure that the ephemeris is a sidereal one, such as *The Betz Ephemeris 1940 - 2040*. Next, select a planet and find the sign it is transiting by running your finger down the column to find the day the planet entered the sign and the day it will leave the sign. This will give you the length of time of the planet's transit in that sign. Finally, determine which house in your natal chart corresponds to that sign. This will give you the house where the transit occurs.

Once you know the period of the planet's transit through a particular house, refer to the chapter on planets, in *Path of Light, Volume I*. Find the interpretation given for the placement of that planet in the various houses and read the interpretation for the house currently being transited. The results of the transiting planet will be roughly equivalent to those of natal placements, but must be modified according to common sense. If the person is 90 years old, for example, then a benefic planet transiting the fifth house will not give children.

After reading the general effect of the planet in the house, determine what houses the transiting planet rules in the natal chart. (See the "Table of House Rulers for Each Rising Sign" given in the chapter on houses in *Path of Light, Volume I*.) Then go to the chapter on houses and read the interpretation given for the appropriate ruler of a house placed in another house. For example, if the transiting planet is Jupiter and the lagna is Virgo, then Jupiter will rule the fourth and the seventh houses.

If Jupiter is transiting the tenth house in Gemini, then read the results given for the ruler of the fourth house placed in the tenth house and also for the ruler of the seventh house placed in the tenth house. This interpretation, along with the general interpretation of Jupiter placed in the tenth house (see the planets chapter) will give you a good idea about the effect of the transit.

Basic Rules of Transits For the Serious Student of Jyotish

The rules that apply to transits are essentially the same as those which apply to the natal chart. For predictions to be accurate, the astrologer needs to take many factors into consideration. The following points may be used as guidelines for interpreting transits. They are based on classical principles of chart analysis, and are also verified by the author's experience with modern horoscopes.

1. The transits of natural benefics generally produce good results to the houses they transit.
2. The transits of natural malefics generally produce challenges or difficulties to the houses they transit.
3. The temporal status of the transiting planet should be taken into consideration in order to modify or fine-tune points 1. and 2. above. Therefore, natural benefics that are temporal malefics will also produce some negative results (along with positive results) during their transit. Similarly, natural malefics that are temporal benefics will also produce some positive results (along with challenging results) during their transits.
4. The significations of the house ruled by the transiting planet in the natal chart should be integrated with the significations of the house in which it is transiting. For example, if the ruler of the ninth house (long-distance travel) transits the twelfth house (distant places) then the period of its transit may produce travel to distant places. This rule is an extension of a basic rule of natal chart interpretation, which states when the ruler of one house is placed in another house, then the significations of both houses are combined. This rule works in a similar manner in both natal chart interpretation and transit interpretation. (For a key to interpreting the rulers of various houses transiting in other houses, see the sections on house-lord placements in the chapter on houses in *Volume I*.)
5. When natural benefics (especially Jupiter) transit through signs occupied by the Sun, Moon, or by natural benefics, they tend to produce positive results. These results will take place in a general

way during the entire period of the planet's transit, but will give more specific results at the time of conjunction (when the transiting planet is within one degree of the natal planet).

6. When natural malefics (especially Saturn, Rahu and Ketu) transit through signs occupied by other planets (especially other malefics) then challenging results are likely. This becomes more likely when the transit takes place in a dusthana (sixth, eighth, or twelfth house). Negative results are also more likely when the transited house contains several planets. Negative or challenging results are likely during the entire period of the planet's transit of the house. However, more pronounced results occur at the time of conjunction (when the transiting planet is within one degree of a natal planet).

7. When a transiting planet conjuncts a natal planet, it will influence both the natural significations of the natal planet as well as the significations of the houses it rules.

8. The natal disposition of the transiting planet will have a powerful effect on its capacity to produce positive or negative results. Planets which are afflicted, placed in dusthanas, weak, or otherwise badly situated in the natal chart tend to produce more negative results during their transits. Planets that are strong and well-placed tend to give more beneficial results during their transits.

9. The sign and house placement of a transiting planet will also play an important role in its ability to produce positive or negative results. If a transiting planet is weak and badly placed during its transit, then it will produce problems both for its natural significations and for the significations of the houses it rules. If a planet transits a house in which it is strong and well-placed, then it will produce good results for the things it naturally signifies as well as the things signified by the houses it rules.

10. The transits of the dasha, bhukti and antara rulers become more important during their periods. If, for example, the bhukti ruler is transiting its sign of debilitation, is in the eighth house and afflicted by Saturn, then during the transit the person will experience difficulties. Similarly, transiting conjunctions of other planets with the dasha, bhukti and antara rulers have great significance. For example, if the antara ruler is Mercury and transiting Jupiter conjuncts natal Mercury, then the time surrounding the conjunction will produce a significant event that blends the significations of both planets.

11. Transit predictions are greatly affected by dasha/bhukti results. If the dasha and bhukti do not support an event, then the transit effect will either be unproductive or limited. If, however, the dasha,

bhukti and transit all suggest a particular event, then the prediction can be made with confidence.
12. A transit can only give what is promised by the natal chart. If the chart has combinations that deny children, then a positive transiting influence on the fifth house (children) will not produce children.

The Transit of Jupiter

Jupiter is the king of the benefic planets and generally bestows positive results. As a natural benefic, its transit is usually expansive and supportive in some way. The degree of benefit derived from a Jupiter transit, however, is dramatically affected by Jupiter's disposition in the natal chart. If Jupiter is a temporal benefic in the natal chart, then its transit will be particularly positive. If, on the other hand, Jupiter is a temporal malefic, as in the case of a Libra lagna, then the Jupiter's transit will be partially positive (because it is still a natural benefic) and partially negative (because it is a temporal malefic). Similarly, if Jupiter is strong and well-placed in the natal chart, then its transit will be beneficial. If it is weak and afflicted in the natal chart, then it will not be able to produce very positive results and may even confer negative results.

The Transit of Saturn

Saturn is a natural malefic. It is a contractive planet that pressurizes and crystallizes. As a result, its transit usually challenges a person in some way. Saturn's transit does not have to be associated with suffering, however. In fact, if Saturn is a temporal benefic, as in the case of a Libra lagna, then Saturn's transit can sometimes be a very productive and successful period. If Saturn is a temporal malefic, however, then its transit can be more problematic. Similarly, if Saturn is weak and afflicted in the natal chart it will tend to produce more negative results. If it is strong and well-placed in the natal chart, then it will tend to give more positive results. Depending on Saturn's disposition in the natal chart, its transit will range from mild pressures and responsibilities to outright difficulties and suffering.

Influence by Occupation and by Aspect

When Jupiter or Saturn transit through a house in a natal chart, they influence the chart in two ways. First, they influence the affairs of the house they occupy during the transit. Second, they influence the houses they aspect during their transit. In the case of Jupiter, this means that it will produce an influence on four houses during its transit (the house it transits, as well as the fifth, seventh and ninth houses from its transiting position). In the case of Saturn, besides the house of transit, it will also influence the third, seventh and tenth houses counted inclusively from the house it transits.

The Tandem Method of Jupiter and Saturn

Taking into consideration the fact that both Jupiter and Saturn influence four houses each at any given time, it is clear that they will also occasionally both influence the same house at the same time, either by occupation or by aspect. This is considered to be a condition that manifests events of the house, usually in a positive way and is a popular predictive technique used in some parts of India.

Jupiter Gives the Hope and Saturn Makes It Happen!

The concept behind this technique is that Jupiter is a planet which expands and promotes. It gives the hope of some positive events in the future. But Jupiter is not responsible for the actualization of these hopes and aspirations. Actualization is the domain of Saturn. In order for anything to come into concrete form, Saturn's permission is necessary. It is the planet of boundaries, form and structure. In this respect, when acting together during a transit, Jupiter brings about the plan, the optimistic attitude, and the feeling of possibility. Saturn takes that plan and puts it into concrete form, working step-by-step towards the realization of the plan. Hence, when both Jupiter and Saturn influence the same house during their transit, that house produces its results in a positive way. Jupiter gives the hope and Saturn makes it happen.

Transit Influences on Natal Planets

Extending the tandem transit principle, any planets in the natal chart that occupy houses influenced by transiting Jupiter or Saturn will also be affected during the transit. This affect will be felt in two ways: first, via the planet's significations and second, via the planet's rulership. If, Saturn, for example, aspects Venus during a Saturn transit, then during that 2 ½ year Saturn transit the person might experience pressures, delays or obstacles in the areas that Venus signifies, such as marriage or relationship. Saturn's influence will also affect any houses that Venus rules in the natal chart.

Applying the Jupiter/Saturn Tandem Technique

Although the tandem transits of Jupiter and Saturn can be used separately, they are most effective when integrated with the use of dasha and bhukti predictions. Once a prediction has been made using the dasha system, and if the mutual transits of Jupiter and Saturn concur, the prediction can be made with great confidence. Let's say, for example, that the dasha and the bhukti seem to indicate marriage. If the seventh house receives a transit influence from both Jupiter and Saturn during the predicted bhukti, then the marriage is more likely to take place. In this example, it is not necessary that both Jupiter and Saturn influence the seventh house itself. Even if one planet aspects or occupies the seventh house and the other aspects the ruler of the seventh house, then the house receives the tandem influence of both planets and good results are likely.

Zeroing-In on the Prediction Time

Saturn's transit through a sign takes approximately 2 ½ years; Jupiter's transit through a sign lasts a little more than a year. Using the tandem technique, Jupiter and Saturn will mutually influence a single house for approximately one year, during which events related to that house may become more likely. Within that one-year period the transits of the faster moving planets can be used to narrow the prediction time. The Sun, Mercury, Venus and Mars each have relatively short transit periods. If one of these transiting planets becomes more significant due to being the lagna lord, the karaka for the predicted event, the ruler of the predicted event's house, or a period ruler, then the transit of that planet can be used to narrow the prediction to a period which corresponds to the length of the planet's transit.

Lets say, for example, that Saturn and Jupiter both aspect the fourth house and the prediction is that during the particular year the person might purchase a vehicle. Let's also say that the person has a Gemini Lagna. Mercury rules the fourth house, so the transit of Mercury will be important. Since Venus is the significator of vehicles, Venus' transit might also be important. There are several ways in which these transits might trigger the event:

If the transit planet aspects the significator house *(in this case, the fourth house for vehicles)*
If the transit planet transits the significator house
If the transit planet transits the lagna
If the transit planet aspects the lagna

If the transit planet aspects or conjuncts the lagna lord
If the transit planet aspects or conjuncts the significator house lord

Pin-Pointing the Prediction

Extending the above principle, the Moon moves through a sign about every 2 ½ days. As a result, transits of the Moon can be used in a similar fashion in order to derive the 2-day period of an event. This method, although theoretically sound, is actually quite complicated to apply since during a one month period, the Moon will traverse all of the points listed above, making it difficult to choose the right one.

Significant Conjunctions

One reliable technique is to watch for significant conjunctions of transiting planets with natal planets during the prediction window. For example, if the Jupiter-Saturn window has been set and the window of prediction has been narrowed using the transit of Venus, then look to see if any significant conjunctions take place during that period. A significant conjunction involves either the significator or the significator house. In the above example where the prediction is about a vehicle, the significant planets are Venus (the karaka), the ruler of the fourth house (house of vehicles), and also the ruler of the fourth house from the Moon, the ruler of the fourth house from the Sun, and the ruler of the fourth house from Venus (Venus is used as a lagna position here as it is the karaka for vehicles). Continuing with this example, if any of these planets happen to be involved in a significant conjunction, then the period of a few days surrounding the exact conjunction may produce the predicted event.

Transits of Trinal Nakshatras

Another technique, which sometimes works for narrowing the time of prediction, is to look for the coincidence of focal planets such as the Sun, Moon, karaka, or lagna lord transiting the nakshatra that is located 120 degrees on either side of the nakshatra occupied by the significator planet. This nakshatra is ruled by the same planet as the nakshatra occupied by the significator planet. Transits here can trigger the event. A one or two-day period surrounding the exact 120 degree relationship between the transiting planet and the significator planet may be a likely time for the event to occur.

Chart 1: Anne Morrow Lindbergh
June 22, 1906; 11:15 AM; Englewood, NJ

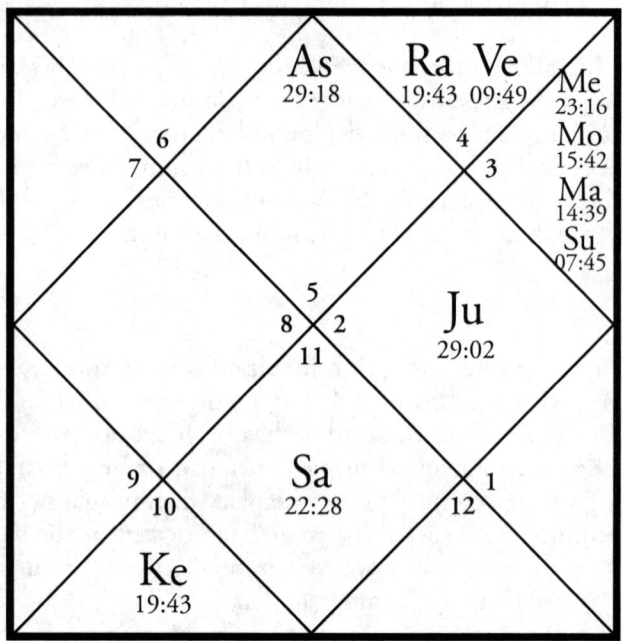

Anne Morrow Lindbergh was the wife of Charles Lindbergh, the famous aviator. She gave birth to a son, Charles Lindbergh III on June 22, 1930. She had just entered the major period of Saturn at the time. The following planets point to the event (birth of a child), illustrating some of the basic principles of transit prediction.

1. The Period Ruler: Saturn is both the major and sub-period ruler. At the time of the birth of her son, Saturn was transiting Sagittarius, her fifth house (children).

2. The House Ruler: At the time of the event, Jupiter, the ruler of the fifth house, was transiting the eleventh house of Gemini. From Gemini, Jupiter casts an aspect back to Sagittarius (the fifth house).

3. The Tandem Transits of Jupiter and Saturn: As a result of points 1. and 2., both Jupiter and Saturn were influencing the fifth house at the same time.

4. The Ruler of the Ascendant: The Sun, the ruler of the Ascendant, was also in Gemini, aspecting the fifth house.

5. The Moon: The Moon was transiting the ninth house, which is a trinal sign to the fifth house. The ninth house is actually the fifth house from the fifth house, and is an alternate house of children.

Notes on the ominous nature of the birth: It is well known that the child, Charles Lindberg III, was kidnapped on March 1, 1932, and was murdered. Some indications of this event are suggested in the planetary configurations.

1. Saturn is placed in Purva Bhadrapada nakshatra, a constellation symbolized by a funeral cot, and is the major period ruler at the time of the event.

2. Transiting Saturn was in direct opposition to Ann Morrow Lindbergh's natal Moon. This is an aspect that blocks or suppresses the qualities of the Moon. The Moon represents both the maternal qualities and also the feelings of peace and happiness. Ann's Moon is placed in Ardra, a constellation symbolized by a teardrop. The impact of this combination was to create sadness, loss, and tears.

3. The Moon at the time of the birth of Charles was in the sign of Aries, in the constellation of Bharani, which is ruled by Yama, the god of death. The basic shakti of this nakshatra is "the power to carry things away." The child was literally carried away from his crib.

4. In the child's natal chart, the dark waning Moon fell in the eighth house (death), along with Mars (violence), and Rahu (sudden and unexpected events). This caused a powerful and clear-cut Balarishta Yoga, which is a classical yoga for early death.

Chart 2: Charles Lindbergh III
June 22, 1930; 13:10 PM; Englewood, NJ

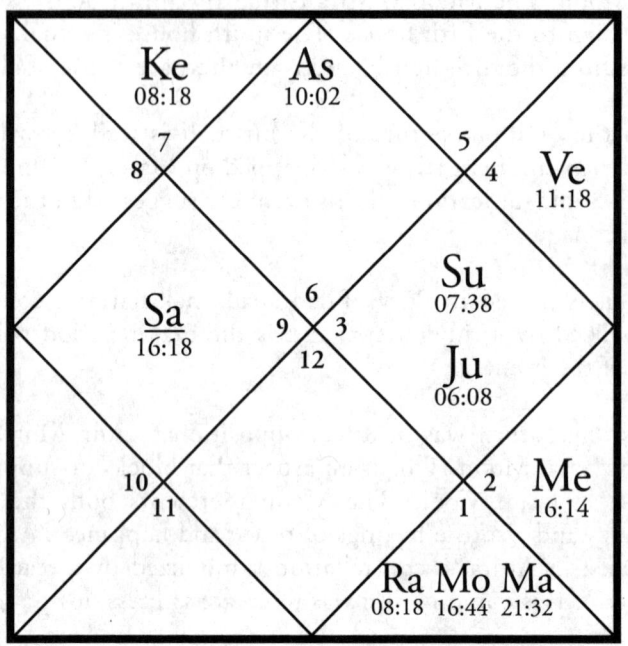

Author's Journal:
Beginner's Luck and The Power of Transits

I will never forget my first experience doing an astrology reading for a real client in Mr. Gandhi's office. I had been working for Gandhiji in London for about two years, preparing horoscopes, driving him around, and doing miscellaneous errands. Every six months, my entry permit for the UK would expire, so Gandhiji sent me out of the country for a couple of weeks. Then I could return and get a new entry permit. On this occasion, I had gone to Taormina, a beautiful resort town in Sicily. Gandhiji had arranged for me to stay with a lady who worked for Mr. Bevacqua, one of his regular clients. Mr. Bevacqua owned a London travel agency and ran tours to Italy. One of his tour guides, Jan, had reluctantly agreed to put me up in her apartment in Taormina for two weeks, as a favor to her boss.

When I arrived in Taormina, Jan met me at the airport. She was an attractive 25 year old English girl, about 5' 7" tall, with sandy brown hair. Although she was polite, I could immediately tell that Jan was not thrilled that she would have to share her flat with an American stranger.

Jan's apartment was a simple, one bedroom flat. She showed me how the sofa folded out into an extra bed as I stowed my astrology books and bag in the corner. "I hope you don't mind," Jan said, "But my boyfriend is coming from Rome to spend the weekend. I only have this one extra bed, so you two will have to share it."

"No problem," I said, choking back a mild case of homophobic discomfort. 'Beggars can't be choosers,' I thought. I realized now that Jan had gone beyond the call of duty and had agreed to take me in, even though she had planned a romantic weekend with her new Italian beau. 'No wonder she seemed a little standoffish at the airport,' I thought.

Jan's attitude towards me seemed to soften when she found out that I was into astrology. She asked me to do her chart.

"I am only a student of astrology, and not a real astrologer," I said.

That didn't seem to matter to Jan, who was an avid reader of newspaper astrology columns. I read her chart and she thoroughly enjoyed it. "I have a couple of friends," Jan said, obviously realizing that she could get some mileage for her generosity and hospitality, "Would you mind doing their charts?"

"No problem," I said.

Jan turned out to be more of a socialite than I expected. Her "couple of friends" quickly turned into twenty five, as the word spread about the American astrologer who was doing free readings at Jan's flat. Jan seemed to enjoy playing hostess as her house-jyotishi did readings for all her friends and I loved having a chance to do so many readings. Although I had been studying astrology and working for Gandhiji for a couple of years, I scrupulously avoided commenting on the charts of any of his clients who would inevitably ask me questions. I had limited my reading of horoscopes strictly to friends and family, and always prefaced my readings by claiming a beginning student's ignorance of the subject. I felt that 'real' astrology was something that took years of study and a level of awareness much greater than mine. "Mr. Gandhi is a real astrologer," I would say, "I'm just a student. If you want to get the real story, then get a reading from him."

But here in Taormina, there was an endless supply of people who were eager to have their charts done, and I was eager to have new subjects for my astrological study. So I spent the entire vacation calculating chart after chart by hand and giving readings to all of Jan's Italian friends, including her new boyfriend, who turned out to be quite a nice guy.

When I returned to London, Gandhiji met me at Heathrow Airport. On the way back to his office, he announced. "I will be leaving for Los Angeles tomorrow. If anybody calls and is desperate to have a reading, you can do the reading for them."

I couldn't believe what I was hearing. "Are you serious?" I asked, feeling completely unprepared for the task. Doing readings in Gandhiji's office for his clients was much more intimidating than doing them for free in Jan's apartment.

"Don't worry," Gandhiji said, "Just look where Jupiter is transiting and predict that something good will happen in that area of life. Look at the house where Saturn is transiting and ask if some difficulty has been taking place in that area of life. No problem."

"Alright," I agreed stiffly, secretly wondering what I was getting myself into. Gandhiji's simplified transit advice was not comforting. Making predictions using transits can be tricky. Gandhiji possessed powerful intuition that allowed him to accurately predict the results of a transit without much analysis. I didn't have that kind of confidence.

My fears abated, however, when it occurred to me that it was highly unlikely that I would actually be needed to do a reading in Gandhiji's absence. Gandhiji was like a whirlwind. When he was in London, the phone rang off the hook. Clients would call the office constantly to book appointments. He saw clients from 9 am to 10 pm, Monday through Sunday. When he would leave, however, the phone always went dead. This was a strange phenomenon, but two years as his assistant told me that I could bank on the fact that the phone would not ring much when he left. Very few people called when Gandhiji was away, and those who called would most certainly be willing to wait for him to return. 'Nobody's that desperate,' I thought. 'I'm off the hook.'

The following evening, I drove Gandhiji to the airport. When I returned to the office, the phone was ringing as I unlocked the door. 'So much for the phone theory,' I thought as I unlocked the door and ran to the phone. "M. K. Gandhi's office," I said.

"Would it be possible to see Mr. Gandhi tonight?" an emotional female voice asked.

"I'm sorry, Mr. Gandhi has just left for Los Angeles. He will be back in three weeks," I said. There was no way I was going to let this lady know that an alternative existed. "Would you like to make an appointment for when he returns?" I asked.

The lady began to sob, "I can't wait that long, I need to see someone tonight. Is there no other astrologer there? I am thinking about committing suicide!"

I couldn't believe what I was hearing. "Uh, do you think you could just postpone that for about three weeks?" I asked. "Mr. Gandhi will be back then. I'm just a student. I could see you but he's the best person to talk to."

"No, I need to talk to someone tonight!" The lady continued crying.

"Alright, alright, calm down. You can come at 8 pm." I hung up.

"I can't believe this!" I muttered out loud as I grabbed a chart form and the ephemeris. "My first formal astrology reading, and she's going to commit suicide!"

The lady arrived at 8. She was beautiful, slender, blond, elegantly dressed, and had an air of sophistication about her. I studied her face as she sat down. Her eyes were red, obviously from crying. She was obviously depressed. I stared at her chart for a couple of minutes, finding it hard to begin for some reason. I became very uncomfortable, completely unable to find anything to say. Then I remembered Gandhiji's simplistic advice about the transits of Saturn and Jupiter. I noticed Saturn's transit position in her chart. 'What the heck!' I thought.

"Saturn has been passing through your seventh house since August of 1980," I said. "Since then, you have been experiencing problems with your marriage or your relationships."

The woman looked stunned. "That's right," she said. "I got married in August of 1980 and we have been fighting constantly since that time."

'Not bad,' I thought, regaining my confidence. "Saturn will leave your seventh house in two weeks, on October 7, 1982." I said. "You can look for relief after that time."

The woman's face brightened. In fact she was so happy that she couldn't contain herself. She thanked me repeatedly as she told me the story of her impulsive decision to marry a man she had known for only two weeks. She praised me for the accurate reading of the chart, making me feel embarrassed. What I had done was so simple, that it was not worthy of anything but a good laugh. Gandhiji, on the other hand, seemed to be able to intuit the whole situation. Never before had he allowed anyone to do a reading in his office for one of his clients. Yet he had given me instructions to do this reading and even told me exactly what to say. The lady left feeling relieved and hopeful about her future. I could only feel wonder and awe at the power of astrology to lift a person's hopes and dispel depression.

After the lady left, I began to think about the prediction I had made. I was feeling a new kind of pressure now. 'What if this prediction doesn't come true,' I thought. I was worried that if the prediction did not happen, the lady might become depressed again.

Two weeks later, however, she called the office again. "I just wanted you to know," she said, "that I kicked my husband out of the house three days ago. Last week I met a new man and have fallen in love with him. I just wanted to thank you again."

When Gandhiji returned from Los Angeles, I picked him up at the airport. "It seems you have become a successful astrologer and have made an accurate prediction," he said as I lifted his bags from the baggage carousel. I looked back at him, surprised that he somehow knew what had happened. His eyes twinkled, and I recognized the familiar look on his face that told me he was teasing me.

"Well," I said, "I did make one accurate prediction, but it was beginner's luck."

Chapter 7

The Psychological Profile

In the West, the reading of the Vedic horoscope often begins with a psychological profile. The patterns of the chart reveal the various aspects of the personality and provide an important point of departure for using Jyotish as a path for spiritual growth. These psychological patterns also help the jyotishi make predictions. Unless he understands the fundamental motivations, interests, drives, attachments, fears and obsessions of the client, the astrologer can't make consistently accurate predictions.

The First House

As a point of departure for describing the personality, the first house is of primary importance. This house shows the whole life in seed form. As a result, the psychological traits ascribed to the sign and the nakshatra occupied by the Ascendant will become important aspects of the personality. Similarly, the psychological traits of the sign and the nakshatra occupied by the ruler of the Ascendant will further describe the person's nature. Finally, the planets placed in the first house will reflect noticeable aspects of the personality.

The Sun and the Moon

The Sun and the Moon are also important ingredients in assessing the psychological wiring. The sign and nakshatra qualities of each of these two luminaries add an important element to the overall picture. The house placement is also influential. In the case of the Sun, the house placement shows an area of personal identification and self-expression. This is an area in which the person seeks to express himself. For example, the Sun in the fourth house may indicate that the person identifies with his house or car. He may be proud of these things, seek them out, and see them as an extension of himself. The Moon indicates a domain in which the person seeks security and support. The person's deepest needs in life may revolve around the house location of the Moon. The Moon in the second house, for example, reveals a deep need for financial security and material comfort.

When the Sun or the Moon combines with other planets, either through conjunction or by receiving the aspect of a planet, then the personality takes on that planet's quality. If Saturn (fear and limitation) aspects the Sun (self-esteem), then the person becomes self-conscious, hesitant, and reserved. Jupiter's aspect on the Sun or the Moon, conversely, will produce optimism and confidence. In this way, each of the planets contributes its qualities to the personality when it influences the Sun or the Moon.

Psychological Domains of the Nine Planets

The sign and house placements of each of the nine planets, as well as their combination with each other will reveal additional psychological factors. Each planet represents a different domain of the psyche. In order to understand the planet's style of functioning, its sign and house placement are important considerations. For the house placement, see the chapter on houses. For the sign placements, again refer to the chapter on houses in *Path of Light, Volume I*, but read the results according to the planet's house/sign correspondence. For example, for the results of Mars in the sign of Taurus (the second sign of the zodiac), read Mars in the second house. For Mars in Gemini, read Mars in the third house, and so forth.

The primary psychological domains of the different planets, as well as the influence of other planets on them, are given below. When considering the psychological domain of a planet, the planet's association with other planets will greatly affect its style of expression. For example, if Venus is in Leo, then the person is usually demonstrative with affection and warmth. But if Venus is associated with Saturn, the style of emotional expression will be much more reserved, due to Saturn's tendency towards inhibition and fear.

There are several ways in which a planet can be associated with another planet. For the purposes of analyzing the psychological domains of the nine planets, though, we will only consider three primary relationships.

1. The significator planet is conjunct another planet
2. The significator planet is aspected by another planet
3. The significator planet is in the sign owned by another planet

In the case of Rahu and Ketu, we will only consider the conjunction. The following is a list of primary psychological domains of each of the nine planets, as well as the influence of other planets.

Sun

The Sun is the planet of the self. It shows the person's style of achieving recognition or attention. Its placement in the chart shows an area of life in which the person self-actualizes. The person will identify with this area of life and draw a good deal of his self-esteem from his ability to actualize the domain's fruits. When he is successful in this endeavor, he will be proud of himself and his self-esteem will be high. When he fails, his self-esteem may diminish. Ultimately this area of life will lead him beyond the personal ego, to the transcendent self.

Planetary Influences on the Sun

The Sun gives the following results when it is in a conjunction, aspected by, or in the sign of the following planets:

Moon: When the Sun is influenced by the Moon, the person will be nurturing, sensitive, moody, and attached to his mother.
Mars: The person is bold, assertive, physical, impulsive and fiery. He may be competitive and could enjoy physical activity or sports. On the negative side, he could also be angry, aggressive or argumentative.
Mercury: He will be verbal, mental, analytical, and communicative.
Venus: He will be charming, creative, artistic, sensual, and attracted to others who are physically beautiful.
Jupiter: Jupiter's influence gives the person a great deal of confidence, optimism, and enthusiasm.
Saturn: Saturn tempers the Sun's energy and makes the person self-conscious, hesitant, reserved and may lower self-esteem. On the positive side, the person could also be a hard worker, responsible, persevering and dependable.

Rahu: When Rahu is in conjunction with the Sun, the person projects his personality with extra energy. It can cause compulsiveness, a strong desire for recognition, or it simply makes the person obsessed with his career and other ambitious pursuits.

Ketu: Ketu's influence on the Sun creates a person who avoids recognition, and may also cause him to feel invisible or unappreciated. It makes the person intuitive and can sometimes produce spiritual inclinations. It can also manifest as an inferiority complex or low self-esteem.

Moon

The Moon is the planet of the deepest feeling and needs. It reflects the mind in its primal, emotional condition. The placement of the Moon shows an area in life that we depend on for security and support. The Moon's disposition also shows the person's ability to give and receive nurturance and support. As a result, it can reveal the person's attitudes toward his mother.

Planetary Influences on the Moon

Sun: This influence follows two patterns: First, when the Moon is in conjunction with the Sun, this means the Moon has very little light and is either a new Moon or close to a new Moon. The waning conjunction produces a good deal of introspection and spiritual energy. The person may have a tendency to be distracted and may leave his body at times. On the negative side, it can produce insecurity and a good deal of internal discontent, including a sense of not being supported. The waxing version of the conjunction is similar, but it makes the person more optimistic, active and outgoing. Second, when the Moon is in opposition to the Sun, then the Moon will be full or close to full, which is very beneficial, creating a great deal of light in the mind. The person will be fortunate, intelligent, optimistic, confident, and successful.

Mars: When Mars influences the Moon, then the person will be assertive, ambitious, passionate, possessed of an earthy physical magnetism, independent, impatient, argumentative and easily aroused to anger.

Mercury: Mercury's influence causes the mind to work very quickly and constantly. The person will be very busy, talkative, intelligent, articulate, humorous, and clever.

Jupiter:	The influence of Jupiter on the Moon creates popularity and the ability to present things in a positive package. The person will be upbeat, optimistic, fortunate, happy, gregarious, and will have the gift of gab. (Also see Gaja Kesari and Shakata Yogas in the chapter on yogas.)
Venus:	If Venus influences the Moon, then the person will be loving, kind, charming, gentle, self-indulgent, creative, sexual and sensual.
Saturn:	Saturn's influence on the Moon causes the person to put his own personal needs second and his responsibilities first. This is more intense in the case of the conjunction or a seventh house aspect. He will be a very hard worker and will be very productive. He will be very responsible, and may believe in living simply. The person may also feel like he does not receive much support from others. In negative cases, Saturn's influence can sometimes be associated with a sense of discouragement, coldness, alienation, or even depression.
Rahu:	Rahu's conjunction with the Moon creates mental unrest. The person will have strong desires and may have compulsive tendencies. The mind will be constantly active, and the attention may wander frequently. On the positive side, this aspect can create intuitive tendencies. The person will be independent and restless. He may be interested in unique or alternative subjects and may have an aptitude for astrology. In negative cases, however, Rahu causes fear, obsession, or even addictions. This is more likely if the Moon is also aspected by other natural malefics.
Ketu:	Ketu's conjunction with the Moon will cause the person to become very introspective, producing a desire for privacy, retreat and anonymity. The person will be very intuitive and could pursue a spiritual path. On the negative side, this conjunction can cause the person to be chronically dissatisfied. He may feel that he never receives enough support and could suffer from bouts of depression. He could have a strong sense of inferiority, and a tendency to avoid recognition. He may also be fearful, uncertain, or insecure. The negative traits will be more likely when the Moon is weak and afflicted by other natural malefics.

Mars

Mars is the planet of desire, ambition, will and anger. The strength and prominence of Mars in the chart will indicate the strength or weakness of the person's will. The level of the person's ambition is also revealed by the disposition of Mars. The house and sign placements of Mars will reveal an area of life in which the person naturally expresses his ambitious energy. The placement of Mars will also show how the person handles his anger.

Planetary Influences on Mars

Sun: When the Sun is with Mars, the person will be fiery, confident, hot tempered, and may possess leadership qualities. He will express his anger with flare and drama. He will have a strong will and good, ambitious energy.

Moon: When the Moon influences Mars, the person may be feisty, or emotionally reactive. In the case of the conjunction, he may be interested in pursuing activities around the home or may work out of his home. He will have a good deal of ambitious energy and will be very independent. He may have an earthy, confident, physical presence.

Mercury: When Mercury influences Mars, the person will express a great deal of energy through speech. He will possess a sharp, logical mind and may be argumentative.

Jupiter: When Jupiter influences Mars, the person becomes confident. He will have abundant ambitious energy, strong will, and will expect to succeed. He will have exuberant physical energy and enjoy physical activity.

Venus: If Venus influences Mars, the person will be passionate. He will have a high level of emotional vitality and will immerse himself completely in his various ambitious endeavors. He will be enthusiastic, sensual, sexual, and attractive.

Saturn: Saturn's influence on Mars creates delays, obstacles, and pressures to ambitious pursuits. The person may feel that progress comes in starts and stops. This may cause chronic frustration, sometimes leading to pent up anger, which the person tries to suppress. The conjunction often produces a very strong desire to succeed, sometimes at any cost. In any case, the aspect makes the person work hard. This is also an aspect that gives mechanical or technical aptitude.

Rahu: Rahu's conjunction with Mars gives the person a sense of urgency about ambitious pursuits. This may make the person compulsive or obsessed with work. He may have leadership qualities and enjoy breaking new ground in his various ambitious undertakings. He will be independent and feisty. When the person expresses anger, it may arise unexpectedly in explosive bursts. This conjunction also gives the person technical, mechanical or scientific abilities.

Ketu: Ketu's conjunction with Mars gives the person a desire to pursue activities that make him feel inspired. He may enjoy physical pursuits that produce a meditative state, such as yoga, tai chi, running, or walking. On the negative side, sometimes the person is chronically dissatisfied with ambitious activities. Sometimes this leads to a lack of inspiration and a sense of having no clear direction in life. This combination also produces technical, mechanical or scientific inclinations.

MERCURY

Mercury shows how the person's intellect works. It also shows his style of communication. The placement of Mercury can reveal a special area of interest where the person seeks information and enjoys communicating with others.

Planetary Influences on Mercury

Sun: When the Sun influences Mercury, the person will be very bright. He may feel intellectually superior to others. His communications style will be expressive and confident.

Moon: When the Moon influences Mercury the person communicates in a caring and nurturing way. He will be sensitive and his ability to reason could be influenced by his moods. This could affect his objectivity at times. In the case of the conjunction or opposition, the mind will work overtime, producing a great deal of mental activity.

Mars: If Mars influences Mercury, the person will possess a critical and analytical intellect. He will be logical and may have mathematical ability. His communication style may be argumentative, assertive, and feisty.

Jupiter: Jupiter's influence on Mercury makes the person very bright. He may be philosophical and will enjoy learning. He will have a natural ability to communicate. He will be filled with creative ideas and his communication style will be upbeat and positive. He will enjoy travel and will probably like to read.

Venus: If Venus influences Mercury then the person will be charming. He will communicate in a warm, engaging manner and will have a good sense of humor. He may possess a refined sense of aesthetics and could be interested in art, music or other creative ventures.

Saturn: Saturn's influence on Mercury produces a sense of mental pressure and responsibility. The person may worry. He might feel blocked or frustrated in the area of communications. This is especially true in the case of Saturn's seventh house aspect on Mercury, which causes the person to feel that other people are unreceptive or resistant to his ideas. On the positive side, the influence of Saturn may also make the person patient, persevering, and organized in the way he communicates. He could also possess an ability to organize and process information in an efficient manner. The conjunction sometimes gives the person the ability to concentrate. Saturn's influence also promotes psychological and philosophical thinking.

Rahu: Rahu in conjunction with Mercury can cause the person to be fascinated with various kinds of information. The mind may be very active and somewhat compulsive. Sometimes this takes the form of compulsive talking. In other cases, the person seeks information compulsively. He could be interested in progressive subjects and may spend a good deal of time on the computer or internet. He could be interested in astrology and other esoteric subjects. He may be open-minded and a very independent thinker.

Ketu: When Ketu is in a conjunction with Mercury, the person is intuitive. He may be evasive and might conceal his true thoughts and opinions. He could feel that his ideas are overlooked, unappreciated or that other people do not listen to what he has to say. He may feel that his experiences communicating with others frequently fall short of his expectations. He might be interested in subjects such as art, music, gardening, healing and spirituality. If Ketu is afflicted, the person could suffer from fears and delusions. He could also make many mistakes in conveying information, either verbally or in written form. In some cases this can cause the person to tell lies.

The Psychological Profile

Jupiter

Jupiter is the planet of truth and abundance. Its disposition in the chart shows the person's belief style, as well as their psychological orientation to money. Jupiter also shows how the person views and interacts with teachers and children.

Planetary Influences on Jupiter

Sun: When the Sun influences Jupiter the person will have a natural sense of abundance. He will be self-confident and will possess a natural familiarity with knowledge. As a result, other people will naturally trust his judgment and advice. He might be proud of his children, teachers or religion. He will be optimistic, intelligent, and will expect to succeed.

Moon: When the Moon influences Jupiter, the person will be upbeat, gregarious and knowledgeable. He could have public relations skills and will be popular. He will receive a good education and will have good teachers. He will have a natural confidence with knowledge and will gain a good reputation. He will be fortunate, and will be comfortable and secure in his attitudes about money. He will also possess instinctive faith in the basic principles of truth and virtue.

Mars: If Mars influences the Jupiter, the person will actively pursue his education and will put a good deal of energy into gaining knowledge. He will also pursue his financial goals with abundant energy. He may argue with his teachers, or become critical of them. He may enjoy arguing about religion or politics, and may have strong opinions and beliefs. He will be quite willing to spend his energy working hard to earn money, but he could also be equally willing to spend his money.

Mercury: When Mercury influences Jupiter, the person will be very interested in gaining knowledge. He may be an avid reader and a good student. He will enjoy philosophical discussions. He will also possess a good facility with language. He could have a natural ability to grasp spiritual and philosophical concepts. He will enjoy communicating with his children and also his teachers. He will probably enjoy travel.

Venus: If Venus influences Jupiter, the person will enjoy comfort and affluence. He will feel as if he should be wealthy. If he is not wealthy, then he may tend to associate with wealthy people. He may also enjoy travel, preferring luxury accommodations.

This placement can sometimes make the person self-indulgent, and in some cases creates a tendency to spend money.

Saturn: If Saturn influences Jupiter, the person could experience many ups and downs in life. He may possess the ability to prepare well in order to advance his future plans. He may also have conservative financial attitudes, or may be doubtful or hesitant in his use of financial resources. Sometimes this creates an inner sense of financial lack. The person could also doubt his own knowledge. In some cases, this gives a constant desire to gain more knowledge. For others, it can reflect a resistance to gaining knowledge that stems from fear and self-doubt. The person might also be attracted to structured and organized religions or philosophies.

Rahu: If Rahu is conjunct Jupiter, it produces unconventional beliefs and philosophies. The person will be independent, and will be interested in alternative subjects. This combination is also called Guru Chandala Yoga, which they say "makes the person a heretic," an outcast who adopts unconventional attitudes. In some cases the person's beliefs will be very intense, and he will reject the religion or belief system of his family. This combination is more likely to produce negative experiences related to religion and beliefs when it is also aspected by Mars or Saturn.

Ketu: If Ketu is in a conjunction with Jupiter, the person could possess a natural intuition and faith in the divine. This is a combination that causes the person to intuit what is true and real. The person will easily transcend beliefs and experience the truth first hand. If he meditates, he could attain higher states of consciousness. He will idealize his teachers and his spiritual path. In the financial realm, this combination sometimes brings selflessness or idealism. It can also give the person an intuitive approach towards money. If the combination is afflicted by Saturn or Mars, however, then the person could experience financial losses and expenditure.

Venus

Venus is the planet of love, affection, marriage, pleasure, and enjoyment. Its placement shows the person's capacity to receive love and affection, as well as his emotional style. Venus also signifies higher aspects of emotion, including impersonal or unconditional love. Venus is the indicator of art, music and all forms of creativity, so it shows how the person experiences creativity in its various forms. (Also see Venus in the chapter on relationships and marriage.)

Planetary Influences on Venus

Sun: If the Sun influences Venus, the person will be charming and will express his emotions with warmth and charisma. He will be attracted to people who are physically beautiful and charming. He will also have a strong sense of aesthetics and may possess creative talent in some area. Females with this combination may be demonstrative with the feminine side of their personality, and may enjoy dressing in a way that calls attention to their beauty.

Moon: The Moon's influence on Venus makes the person loving and warm. He will be charming, nurturing and sympathetic. He will be very sensual and sexual. He could be very attached to his mother.

Mars: If Mars influences Venus, the person will be passionate. He will believe in romance, and will possess a strong dose of physical sexuality. Being a person of powerful emotional vitality, he will express his enthusiasm by projecting himself wholeheartedly into his various endeavors. In negative cases, this combination can cause sexual problems. For example, if Saturn also influences the combination, it sometimes frustrates the desire for passion. Rahu and Ketu's influence sometimes creates unconventional or compulsive sexual impulses.

Mercury: If Mercury influences Venus, the person is charming and finds it easy to communicate love and affection to others. Communications also become an important element in relationships. This may also give the person an interest in artistic and creative pursuits.

Jupiter: If Jupiter influences Venus, the person may seek out relationships and friendships among people who are prosperous or knowledgeable. He will seek comfort and affluence. He will enjoy traveling for pleasure. He may also become self-indulgent.

Saturn: The influence of Saturn on Venus causes emotional reserve. The person may be capable of emotional commitment, but also feels emotionally frustrated. Ultimately his experience of emotional lack stems from deep-rooted emotional fear. He may be good at being charming in business situations, but is usually afraid to express the most vulnerable side of his feelings. He is afraid to truly reveal himself emotionally, so he wears an emotional suit of armor. (This influence has been covered at length in the chapter on love and relationships.)

Rahu: When Rahu is conjunct Venus, the person will be open to all kinds of people from all walks of life. He will be attracted to foreigners and may have friends who are unconventional. He may also be prone to sexual or relationship addictions. (This aspect was covered at length in the chapter on relationships and marriage.)

Ketu: When Ketu is conjunct Venus, the person idealizes love. This can mean that he yearns to find his soul mate, yet is chronically dissatisfied with his real-life partner. As a result, this can cause the person to hesitate to fully commit himself in relationships or marriage. This combination can also cause the person to spiritualize his relationship in a good way, choosing a partner with whom he shares an inspirational interest or spiritual path.

Saturn

Saturn is the planet of commitment and responsibility. Its disposition in the chart shows the person's capacity to follow through on commitments, to work hard, and to meet his responsibilities.

Planetary Influences on Saturn

Sun: If the Sun influences Saturn, the person may be reserved, patient, persevering and hardworking. He will possess a strong sense of responsibility. He could also feel blocked and frustrated. He may be attracted to work that involves organizing or managing.

Moon: If the Moon influences Saturn, the person may take on many domestic responsibilities. He will put his own needs second, and those of his home and family first. At work he will also put the needs of others above his own. He will work hard and may forget to take care of his own needs. There may be a tendency towards depression. He may also have problems expressing his emotions.

Mars: If Mars influences Saturn, the person will express a good deal of ambition in his work, yet he might also feel frustrated. This influence makes the person very hard working, but also

	causes him to experience progress in starts and stops. He might also have mechanical ability.
Mercury:	If Mercury influences Saturn, the person may take on many mental responsibilities. He might spend a good deal of time processing or organizing information. If Saturn conjuncts Mercury, he may have good ability to concentrate and possess a good memory, or just the opposite if other afflictions to Mercury exist. He could also worry excessively.
Jupiter:	If Jupiter influences Saturn, the person will gain a good deal of support in the process of carrying out his responsibilities. He will find it easy to be organized and have an ability to prepare well.
Venus:	If Venus influences Saturn, the person will make friends easily in the work environment. He will be social and charming in work situations. He will enjoy his work and will have a reserved, somewhat formal demeanor. He will have a natural understanding of the commitment and hard work that is necessary to form lasting relationships. Particularly in the case of the conjunction, he might equate responsibility and service with love, desiring a spouse who is practical and hardworking. He could also substitute responsibility for expressing love, masking his fear of true intimacy with the willingness to work hard for the sake of increasing the material condition of his marriage or family.
Rahu:	If Rahu conjuncts Saturn, the person will have a sense of urgency about work. This could simply cause him to be a hard worker or a workaholic. Rahu gives the desire for revolutionary change and freedom. Saturn constrains Rahu's revolutionary energy, so the person feels frustrated. Compulsive work is often an outlet for venting this feeling.
Ketu:	If Ketu is in a conjunction with Saturn, the person may be a perfectionist. He will idealize work and responsibility. Ironically, he will also be chronically dissatisfied with his work and will sometimes yearn to give it up.

Rahu

Rahu is a planet of attachment and obsession. Its placement by house, sign, nakshatra and conjunction, reveals an area of life in which the person is fascinated or possibly obsessed in a positive way. On the negative side it can show areas of fear, addiction or compulsion. The conjunctions of other planets with Rahu were covered previously.

Ketu

Ketu is a planet of detachment and spirituality. Its placement in the chart shows an area of life in which the person feels a deep need for a spiritual experience. The person will feel a need to experience an exalted and ideal experience in the areas of life represented by the house, sign, and nakshatra in which Ketu is placed. Conjunctions of other planets with Ketu also produce this effect in the domain of the conjuncting planet. On the negative side, Ketu tends to cause the person to hold a very high standard in these same domains of life, so its placement can also show areas of chronic dissatisfaction and disappointment. If it is associated with multiple negative influences, it can produce fear, violence, and other negative mental conditions.

Author's Journal:

Siddhi Ma, Grand Ma

"Have you heard of Siddhi Ma?" my host, Captain Singh, asked.

My wife and I were staying at the summer home of the Maharaja of Balrampur in Nainital, a beautiful mountain town in the heart of the Himalayas. Captain Singh, who manages the Maharaja's estate, knows that I am always on the lookout to meet saints and yogis during my travels in India. On this occasion, we were taking a small group of westerners on a three-week pilgrimage. The opportunity to meet a lady saint was appealing. "No, who is she?" I said.

"She was once a very wealthy lady who was a close disciple of Neem Karoli Baba. She renounced the world many years ago, lived a life of total renunciation, meditation and devotion to God, and became enlightened. She has an ashram nearby and she is there right now. Would you like to meet her?" he asked.

Captain Singh, of course, knew that our reply would be "yes." He had already given instructions to get two cars ready. So, along with seven people from my group, Terri and I got into one of the cars and enjoyed the mountain scenery on the half-hour ride to Siddhi Ma's ashram.

Siddhi Ma's ashram is located on a small river that flows through a heavily wooded mountain ravine just outside Nainital. We crossed the river on a footbridge and left our shoes at the gate to the ashram. As we walked barefoot through the gateway, ashram workers were busy scrubbing the concrete with brushes and water. A daily affair at Siddhi Ma's ashram, the effect of constant cleaning gave the place a sense of spotless purity, which was augmented by the pristine natural setting. Captain Singh sent word to

Siddhi Ma in order to arrange a meeting. I stood next to one of the brightly painted temples in the ashram complex waiting, as the others milled in and out of the various smaller temples.

"Are you English?" the voice came from behind me.

I turned to meet a girl in her early twenties, along with her husband. She seemed to be curious about our group so I explained that I was an astrologer from the United States and that I frequently bring people to India on pilgrimage-style trips.

When she heard I was an astrologer, the girl became excited. She said, "I hope you don't mind me asking this, but would you be able to answer a question for me?"

I agreed, and the three of us found a spot to sit down, while I calculated her chart on a small pocket PC that I carry while traveling.

"My question is about my career," she said.

"Your chart shows that you would be good in a creative field. Art, music, or photography might be good options," I said.

A look of relief crossed her face. "I am very much interested in photography," the girl said. "I want to do it professionally, but I have been having doubts." She had a Gemini Ascendant, with Venus exalted in the tenth house, creating a beautiful Malavya Yoga. "Do you think I could succeed in this field?" she asked.

I told her to be confident and follow her interest.

The impact of my words seemed to lift a heavy burden from her mind. She thanked me profusely, which felt a little embarrassing, considering that no great astrological feat had been accomplished. The chart was simple and clear-cut. Any beginning jyotishi could have interpreted it easily. I was struck by the impact of this great science. I also wondered if, like many pilgrims who seek the darshan of saints in remote regions of the Himalayas, this girl might have carried this question in search of clarity and resolution. I wondered if in this mountain hermitage, in the presence of its spiritual matriarch, I had unwittingly become a messenger to deliver the insight which the girl sought.

I put away my little computer and watched the girl and her husband walk away.

"Siddhi Ma will see us now," Captain Singh said as he walked towards me.

We entered Siddhi Ma's room in single file. She was sitting on a grass mat on the floor and we all gathered around her, sitting cross-legged, filling up her little room. My wife, Terri, sat next to me and beside her was Randy Barron, one of the members of our group. Siddhi Ma appeared to be around eighty years old. She was dressed in the typical white sari worn by female Indian renunciates and nuns, giving her a Mother Theresa-like appearance. Her sparkling eyes combed through the group, seeming to check into each soul personally. She immediately started asking questions of the group, simple things like, "Where are you from? What kind of food do you eat? Where are you going on your journey?" etc.

Very quickly the group became animated. Faces began to beam as Siddhi Ma's easy compassionate energy lifted the hearts of each member of the group. I felt myself moved by the simplicity of her life and the deep love that she obviously embodied. 'What great luck,' I thought. The opportunity to have darshan (the uplifting, radiant spiritual energy) from such a great soul is rare. In the presence of an enlightened being, words are not necessary. I felt my consciousness shift into the familiar experience of bliss that I have often felt in the presence of saints.

After a few minutes of sitting with Siddhi Ma, I felt Terri's hand searching for mine. I took her hand and looked at her. I could see that her eyes were welling up with tears and that she was holding back her need to cry. I held her hand for the remainder of our meeting with Siddhi Ma. Finally, we said goodbye, each of us touching the feet of the lady saint, as a gesture of respect to a great teacher.

Outside, in the courtyard, Terri and I found a place to sit. "Are you alright?" I asked.

In a tone saturated with emotion she said, "When I looked at Siddhi Ma, I saw my grandmother!"

With this emotional declaration, the floodgates opened and Terri began to sob. I held her as she cried and thought about the deep sense of loss which Terri had felt upon losing her maternal grandmother several years earlier and the even deeper sadness she had felt when, earlier that same year, her mother had died. Her heart had been melted by waves of unconditional love and compassion radiating from Siddhi Ma who had sensed her sadness and appeared to her in the form of her grandmother.

Seeing that Terri was crying, Randy Barron came over to check in. "Are you alright Terri?" he asked.

Terri continued to sob, so I answered for her, "She just had a very powerful experience with Siddhi Ma."

"Me too," Randy said. "I actually saw my grandmother!"

Terri stopped crying and looked up. "Your grandmother?" she asked.

"Yes," Randy said, "I was looking at Siddhi Ma's face, but only saw the face of my grandmother. I felt a great sense of love and compassion coming from her. It was quite remarkable."

"I saw my grandmother too," Terri said.

"You're kidding!" Randy exclaimed.

We waited silently for the others while we tried to absorb the minor miracle that had just occurred. I couldn't help but think of the mysterious *ways in which the divine spark finds its way into the hearts of the sincere seeker. This is why people come to ashrams and seek out enlightened teachers, I reminded myself. The darshan of a saint is truly a rare blessing.*

Chapter Eight

Health

As in the delineation of any area of life, the starting point for analyzing the health is the Ascendant. The Ascendant represents the body, so its strength or weakness shows a person's constitutional strength or weakness. This point is very important. If a chart has a very strong Ascendant, then the owner of the chart will usually maintain good health, regardless of difficult planetary periods or transits. If the Ascendant is weak, then health problems are more likely and more easily triggered by difficult dashas.

Each rising sign has its own predispositions toward disease. If the Ascendant is weak, then the area of the body ruled by the sign rising may be predisposed to illness. The following list shows the parts of the body that are ruled by the various rising signs.

Signs and Parts of the Body

Aries: head
Taurus: face
Gemini: shoulders, neck, upper chest
Cancer: heart
Leo: stomach
Virgo: waist, bowels
Libra: lower abdomen
Scorpio: sexual organs
Sagittarius: thighs
Capricorn: knees

Aquarius: legs
Pisces: feet

Houses and the Body

Similarly, each house of the horoscope represents particular organs. If the house is weak and afflicted, then it is more likely that those organs will be weak or manifest disease. Again, the following list will show the organs related to each house of the horoscope. Note that the organs related to the signs are roughly the same as those related to the parallel houses. In other words, Aries represents the head and is the first sign of the zodiac. The first house of the horoscope is the head as well. Similarly, Taurus and the second house represent similar organs and diseases.

First House: the body in general, constitutional strength, general vitality, head, appearance, brain, hair, longevity
Second House: mouth, teeth, face, right eye, nails, cheeks, nose, chin
Third House: right ear, right hand, shoulder, upper arms, collarbone, throat, nervous system
Fourth House: chest, lungs, diaphragm, breasts (Some authorities say this house also represents the heart.)
Fifth House: heart, stomach, liver, gall bladder, pancreas, spleen, half of the duodenum, pregnancy, foregut, small intestine.
Sixth House: diseases and ill health in general, midgut, small intestine, mesentery, appendix, upper part of the large intestine, kidneys, waist, injury, operation, accidents.
Seventh House: ovaries, testes, prostate, rectum, kidneys, groin, semen, sexual diseases, sex drive, urinary system, last part of the large intestine (hindgut).
Eighth House: genitals, incurable or chronic diseases, longevity, depression, poisoning, escaping death, bites, anus.
Ninth House: hips, thighs
Tenth House: knees, spine
Eleventh House: legs, left ear, left hand, also a general house of disease (being the sixth house from the sixth house)
Twelfth House: feet, left eye, sleep disorders, mental disorders, institutions such as hospitals and asylums

Planets and the Body

Each planet also signifies certain body parts and diseases. These significations are given below.

Sun: general health, vitality, digestive fire, heart, bones, back, right eye, baldness, burns
Moon: body fluids, stomach, breasts, blood (white blood cells), mental problems, stomach, left eye, lymph, face
Mars: muscles, blood (red blood cells), head, bone marrow, bile, energy level, endometrium, accidents, injuries, surgery, burns, poisoning, pain, fever
Mercury: skin, navel, neck, lungs, nervous system, speech, ears, throat, nose, thyroid
Jupiter: liver, gallbladder, part of the pancreas, spleen, circulation, right ear, feet, fat
Venus: face, eyes, semen, sexual organs, urinary system, kidneys, part of the pancreas, appendix, tear glands
Saturn: longevity, bones, left ear, calves, knees, teeth, chronic problems, tiredness, depression, the lymphatic system, problems due to exposure to the elements, cancer
Rahu: fears, boils, ulcers, incurable ailments, poisons, bites, foot disease, chronic diseases, heart palpitations, cancer, skin diseases, accidents, hiccups, fainting
Ketu: problems due to misdiagnosis or wrong medicine, fevers, infections, parasites, deafness, surgery, poison, fears, phobias, hard-to-diagnose ailments

Nakshatras and the Body

Each nakshatra signifies a particular part of the body as well. If a nakshatra is occupied by a natural malefic, it is possible that its corresponding body part could produce problems. If the nakshatra is occupied by two natural malefics, then it becomes more likely that the body part will be a source of problems. If three natural malefic planets occupy a nakshatra, however, then the organ or body part becomes a first-rate candidate for disease, weakness or injury.

If a nakshatra is occupied by only a single natural malefic, it may only indicate a tendency for the nakshatra's body part to produce problems. If the planet and house which represent the same body part are weak and afflicted, then the affliction to the nakshatra becomes a confirming element which adds confidence to the prediction.

Table of Nakshatras and Parts of the Body

Nakshatra	Body Part
1. Ashwini	knees
2. Bharani	head
3. Krittika	waist
4. Rohini	both legs
5. Mrigashira	both eyes
6. Ardra	hair
7. Punarvasu	fingers
8 Pushya	mouth
9. Ashlesha	fingernails
10. Magha	nose
11. Purva Phalguni	right testicle or ovary
12. Uttara Phalguni	left testicle or ovary
13. Hasta	both hands
14. Chitra	forehead
15. Swati	teeth
16. Vishakha	both arms
17. Anuradha	heart
18. Jyeshtha	tongue
19. Mula	both feet
20. Purva Ashadha	right thigh
21. Uttara Ashadha	left thigh
22. Shravana	two ears
23. Dhanishtha	back
24. Shatabhisha	both sides of the chin
25. Purva Bhadrapada	right ankle
26. Uttara Bhadrapada	left ankle
27. Revati	armpits

Ayurveda and Vedic Astrology

Ayurveda, the traditional healing system of India, describes three bodily humors that must be in balance for good health to be maintained. These three humors are Vata (wind), Pitta (bile) and Kapha (phlegm). Individuals have their own unique balance of Vata, Pitta, and Kapha. This ideal state of equilibrium, which is also reflected in the horoscope, is the individual's constitutional type that is usually expressed in terms of the predominant and secondary humor. Thus, someone with a predominance of Vata and a secondary Pitta constitution would be called Vata-Pitta. Over time, the person either stays near their state of doshic balance or, more commonly, drifts away from it. A Pitta-Kapha person, for example, might develop a predominance of Kapha due to living a sedentary lifestyle combined with improper diet.

Theoretically, both the constitutional type and the directions of imbalance can be seen in the Vedic chart. Because of the complexity of Ayurveda, the chart is best used only as a support to the Ayurvedic diagnosis. Determining the constitutional type through pulse reading and other means is an art form that takes an Ayurvedic physician years to master. Although the horoscope gives many important clues, which can support the process of diagnosis, it should never be used as the sole means of diagnosis.

Planetary Relationships to the Three Doshas

Sun: Pitta
Moon: Kapha and Vata
Mars: Pitta
Mercury: Vata, Pitta and Kapha
Jupiter: Kapha
Venus: Vata and Kapha
Saturn: Vata
Rahu: Vata
Ketu: Pitta

As mentioned earlier, the Ayurvedic system of healing is both deep and complex, requiring years of training. It is also true that there is very little written about the application of Vedic astrology to Ayurveda. Those wishing to use Vedic astrology to gain insights into health from the Ayurvedic point of view should first study Ayurveda, and then apply the fundamentals of Vedic astrology. By learning both systems thoroughly, the natural relationships between them emerge.

In general, however, certain clues to the person's ayurvedic type can be seen by analyzing the disposition of the Ascendant, the ruler of the Ascendant, the Sun and the Moon. These focal points generally suggest the constitutional type. If the majority of these focal points fall in kapha signs or nakshatras, or if they are conjunct or aspected by kapha planets, then the person will tend to be a predominantly kapha type. Imbalances are usually shown through the disposition of the sixth house and the ruler of the sixth house. The eighth house and its ruler also give insights into the nature of imbalances. For example, if the vata planets Saturn and Rahu are placed in the sixth house, the person might be a compulsive worker. He might lead a hectic and pressured lifestyle, which can produce a vata imbalance.

The Organ-Based Approach to Medical Astrology

One of the simplest ways to study health in the horoscope is with an organ-based approach. This method is fairly straight forward, and is focused on determining whether a limb or organ of the body is strong or weak. It is very important to note, however, that everybody, even an Olympic athlete, has a weak link physically. Finding a potential for disease or weakness in the Vedic chart does not mean that the person will definitely experience the problem. In fact, locating a potential problem in the chart can sometimes be very effective preventive medicine, allowing the person to take direct measures to strengthen that part of the body before a problem takes place.

1. Determining the Constitutional Strength

The first house is the house of the constitutional strength and general vitality. A strong first house gives a strong body that is generally resilient to disease. Similarly, if the Sun is strong, energy and vitality abound. The Moon can also be an important focal planet to consider here. The first step in assessing health or disease patterns is to assess the relative strength of the constitution. A person with a very strong constitution and high vitality level will probably not experience the disease patterns indicated in other parts of the chart until he is very old. A weak constitution and low vitality, however, makes the person susceptible to experiencing problems with the challenged organs or parts of the body more easily.

2. Determining the Organ or Part of the Body That is Susceptible to Disease

Various clues to potential problems with organs or parts of the body are expressed in the chart. These clues are revealed by the planets, houses, nakshatras, signs, and drekanas (1/3 division of the sign). In this book we will only deal with planets and houses. For a more in-depth study of medical astrology, the serious student can refer to *Essentials of Medical Astrology* by Dr. K.S. Charak.

Afflicted Planets and Houses

If a planet or a house is weak or afflicted, then the organ it signifies may have a tendency to be weak. The relative weakness or strength of planets and houses was covered *Path of Light, Volume I*. Planets or houses that receive multiple negative influences by natural malefics can be very susceptible to problems. For instance, the Sun (the heart), placed in Libra (its weakest sign) in the sixth house (the house of disease), conjunct Rahu and Saturn, and aspected by Mars, raises the concern about the heart dramatically. This placement also may bring problems related to the sixth house (intestines, kidneys, and health in general). Simply having one of these indications alone is usually not usually enough to give a big problem. When three or more negative factors influence a planet or a house, the astrologer can usually safely conclude that the relevant organ or body part will have problems. Whether the problem will come at age seven or at age ninety-seven, however, is a matter related to the strength of the first house and the planetary periods that operate during the person's life.

Predicting the Time of Illness and Recovery

The time of illness can be predicted in the major periods and sub-periods of planets that are in the following conditions in the Rashi chart or the Shashtamsha chart.

Periods That Promote Disease, Illness or Injury

1. The period of a weak, debilitated or afflicted lagna lord.
2. The period of a weak, debilitated or afflicted planet placed in dusthanas (the sixth, eighth or twelfth houses).
3. The period of a weak, debilitated or afflicted planet placed in the eleventh house (sixth from the sixth house).
4. The period of a planet that is badly afflicted in other parts of the chart, not mentioned above, can sometimes give problems related to the part of the body ruled by the house, the sign and the nakshatra of occupation.

5. The periods of dusthana rulers do not usually favor recovery in most cases. An exception to this concept occurs when the sixth lord is placed in its own sign in the sixth house, which sometimes produces recovery.
6. Theoretically, the periods of natural malefics placed in the sixth house are supposed to produce good health. In practice, they frequently produce health problems. This is particularly true when the natural malefic is with another planet or aspects another planet. If it is conjunct or aspected by another natural malefic, then the period becomes very likely to produce health problems.

Periods That Promote Recovery From Disease, Illness or Injury

1. The period of a strong and well-placed lagna lord.
2. The period of Jupiter placed in the first house.
3. The period of Jupiter aspecting the first or the sixth house.
4. The period of a planet that is aspected by Jupiter.
5. The period of a well-placed temporal benefic in the Rashi chart.
6. The period of a planet placed in a Shubha Kartari Yoga for the Ascendant. (flanking of the Ascendant by natural benefics).
7. The period of a strong and well-placed ruler of the sixth house, especially if it is aspected by Jupiter or associated with a natural benefic.
8. The period of a strong and well-placed ruler of the eleventh house (sixth from the sixth house) especially if it is aspected by Jupiter or a natural benefic.
9. The period of a strong, unafflicted natural malefic in the sixth house gives good recuperative power, but may also initially give problems.

Using the Shashtamsha Chart for Predictions About Health

The divisional chart for health matters is the Shashtamsha chart. The positive or negative health results of a major period or sub-period planet will be powerfully influenced by its position in the Shashtamsha chart, based on the conditions given above. Additionally, natural benefics that are placed in angles and trines of the Shashtamsha chart, and which are free of aspects from natural malefics, tend to promote good health and recovery. This varga is particularly sensitive to the influence of natural malefics. Planets which are afflicted by natural malefics in the Shashtamsha chart suggest health problems. Multiple influence of natural malefics are particularly aggravating. Natural malefic planets that aspect other planets in Shashtamsha chart can also produce problems.

The periods of planets which are involved in multiple afflictions due to conjunctions with or aspects by natural malefic planets will produce negative results for health. If the period planet is also badly disposed in the rashi chart, then the period will quite likely produce a problem. If a planet is strong and well-placed for health matters in the rashi chart, but badly afflicted in the Shashtamsha chart, then the period may still produce minor health problems. Similarly, a planet that is badly disposed in the Rashi chart, but well disposed in the Shashtamsha chart may only confer minor health problems. For more noticeable and serious conditions, the planet should be in a negative condition in both charts.

Great care should be taken in predicting illness and disease. Before making any predictions the astrologer should check strength of the constitution in general. If the person's chart suggests a strong constitution, due to a powerful and well-placed lagna lord or the presence of Jupiter in the lagna, then the person may not experience any major problems, even though the period suggests ill health. Similarly, if the person's chart suggests a weak constitution because of multiple afflictions to the Ascendant, the lagna lord, and the Sun, then the person could have health problems even during the period of a well-placed planet. During the periods of badly placed planets, the owner of such a chart will be very likely to experience more pronounced health problems. The art of predicting periods of ill health and recovery must be based on a clear understanding of the strength of the person's overall constitution.

The Shashtamsha chart can also be used to discover other details regarding the person's health, besides the time of illness and recovery. For example, the second house of the Shashtamsha chart relates to the money spent in dealing with health matters. If a planet is afflicted in the second house, its period could simply create general expenditure on health matters rather than health problems. Similarly, a planet placed in the eleventh house, could produce health activities done in groups.

An afflicted planet in the Shastamsha chart may produce a problem related to the body part signified by the house, but not in every case. The planet's natural signification, as well as its various placements in the Rashi and Shashtamsha will all give clues to the affected body part.

Below are interpretations of typical results of the periods of planets placed in the twelve houses of the Shashtamsha chart. These are modern applications based on classical principles. These results should not be taken in isolation, and should always be supported by the planet's position in the Rashi chart.

Planets Placed in the Twelve Houses of the Shashtamsha Chart

First House (the body in general): A planet placed in the first house of the Shashtamsha chart will give prominent results related to health. If the planet is weak and afflicted by malefics, then ill health will result. If it is strong and free of influence from natural malefics, then good health or recovery will take place. For example, the period of Venus, placed in Libra (its own sign) in the first house of the Shashtamsha chart, will usually produce improvement in the health or at least maintain a previous condition of good health.

Second House (teeth, diet, face, mouth, money): A planet that is placed in the second house of the Shashtamsha chart may give results related to the preceding significations which will be positive or negative depending on the planet's positive or negative disposition in the chart. For example, Mars (surgery) placed in the second house is a typical placement for dental surgery or cosmetic surgery to the face. If this house is afflicted, the afflicting planet's period can also produce expenditures related to health. On the other hand, if the period planet is placed in the second house and is involved in a Dhana Yoga, its period can produce gains related to health. For example, if a person has the ruler of the eleventh house placed in the second house, this produces a Dhana Yoga (see the chapter on yogas). This could signify an insurance payment due to an injury. In the case of a health professional, it could simply symbolize a raise in salary or income.

Third House (communications, information, the hands, arms, neck, ears): If a planet is placed in the third house of the Shashtamsha chart, it can give positive or negative effects for the above significations, based on its positive or negative disposition. Keep in mind that the third house is a minor dusthana house (the eighth house from the eighth house), so afflicted planets placed here can give general difficulties and should be watched carefully. A positive and strong planet in the third house may allow the person to gain information that will be beneficial for health, either through books, the internet, classes, or conversation.

Fourth House (chest, stomach, breast, lungs): Unless it is afflicted, a period planet placed in the fourth house of the Shashtamsha chart will generally give good results for health during its period. An exception to this would be a strong, unafflicted natural malefic, that is aspecting another planet. For example, an unafflicted Saturn in the fourth house may cause some problems during its period due to its aspect on the sixth house, especially if any planets occupy the sixth house. Of course, planets placed in the fourth house that are afflicted by natural malefics generally produce health problems.

Fifth House (heart, stomach, liver, gall bladder, spleen, duodenum, intestines, pregnancy): If a period planet is placed in the fifth house, it generally gives good results for health, provided it is strong and free of aspects from natural malefics. If it is afflicted here, however, it can cause general health problems, which could be connected to the organs of the body given above. This is also the house of education, so sometimes a period planet placed here can indicate attending classes related to health. For, example, during the period of Mars (muscles of the body) placed in the fifth house of the Shashtamsha chart, the person could take an exercise class. If Mars is afflicted here, the person could pull a muscle during the exercise class.

Sixth House (diseases and ill health in general, large intestine, kidneys, waist, the primary house for the Shashtamsha chart): Planets placed in the sixth house of the Shashtamsha chart frequently produce health problems during their periods, especially if they are also afflicted by natural malefics. The health problems often pertain to the planet's natural significations. If the planet placed in the sixth house is exalted or in its own sign and also free of the influence of natural malefics, it can indicate improvement for health. This is particularly true if Jupiter also aspects the sixth house planet. For example, if Saturn is the sub-period planet and is placed in Aquarius in the sixth house of the Shashtamsha chart, the person could begin a strict discipline involving an exercise class (Aquarius rules groups of people) during the period of Saturn.

Seventh House (ovaries, testes, prostate, anus, groin, semen, sexual diseases, sex drive, urinary tract, bones): If a period planet is placed in the seventh house unafflicted, then its period is generally positive for health. If the period planet is weak and afflicted by natural malefics, then it can produce problems. The seventh house of the Shashtamsha chart also includes health-oriented relationships, involving doctors and other people who are consulted. A planet placed here can sometimes give positive or negative events in one's relationships with healthcare workers. This house is also connected to contracts and legal issues that pertain to health.

Eighth House (genitals, incurable or chronic diseases, longevity, depression, poisoning, escaping death, bites): The eighth house is another primary house in this chart. The period of a planet placed in the eighth house of the Shashtamsha chart will tend to give health problems. This tendency will be aggravated substantially if the planet is influenced by natural malefics. A positive and well-placed planet in this house can suggest therapeutic activities that improve health. Massage therapy, psychotherapy, yoga, and other transformational practices are examples of positive eighth house activities.

Ninth House (hips, thighs): The period of a planet placed in the ninth house of the Shashtamsha chart will generally give good results, unless it is afflicted by malefic planets. This is also the house of advisors, so it can be associated with finding a good doctor or receiving a good result from the advice of doctors. If afflicted, it could show that the advice of the doctor might be flawed in some way. The ninth house is also a travel house, so a positive planet placed here can indicate positive results through travel. For example, a conjunction of Jupiter and Venus here could produce a long-distance trip to a luxurious health spa during a Jupiter or Venus period.

Tenth House (knees, spine): If a planet is placed in the tenth house of the Shashtamsha chart, its period will give generally positive results, unless it is weak or afflicted by natural malefics. This is also the house of career, so powerful planets located here can sometimes indicate good results for the career of a healthcare professional.

Eleventh House (legs, left ear, left hand, also a general house of disease): The eleventh house in any divisional chart shows the potential of actualizing the desired outcome of the varga's domain. The desired outcome of health is often good health or recovery from disease. A strong planet placed here can suggest recovery from disease or general improvement for health, especially if it receives the aspect of Jupiter or Venus. If the planet is debilitated or afflicted by malefics, it could produce health problems. Since the eleventh house is the sixth house from the sixth house, it is also a primary house for the Shashtamsha chart. The placement of a weak and afflicted planet in the eleventh house gives a strong inclination to produce health problems during its period. This is also the house of groups of people. As a result, planets placed here sometimes produce involvement in team sports, exercise classes, or other group events related to health during their periods.

Twelfth House (feet, left eye, sleep disorders, mental disorders, institutions such as hospitals and asylums): Planets placed in the twelfth house in the Shashtamsha chart are inclined to produce difficulties for health during their periods. This is particularly the case if the planet is afflicted by natural malefics. An unafflicted benefic planet in the twelfth house can actually improve the person's health due to its aspect on the sixth house. Malefic planets placed here, even if unafflicted, tend to aggravate health due to their aspect on the sixth house. The twelfth house is also the house of distant places and retreats. Similar to planets placed in the ninth house, positive placements here sometimes suggest travel related to health. This effect is magnified if the period planet also participates in a yoga for travel. (For more on yogas for travel see the chapter on yogas.)

Chart 1: This is the chart of a woman who dislocated her left shoulder in Rahu/Venus period. The houses of the shoulders are the third house (right shoulder) and the eleventh house (left shoulder).

Rashi chart: Ketu is placed in the eleventh house and Rahu aspects the eleventh house. The eleventh house also receives the aspect of Saturn. The ruler of the eleventh house is Venus, which is placed in the twelfth house (a dusthana). Notice that Venus (the sub-period ruler) is in the eighth house from Rahu (the major period ruler), which is a difficult placement for the sub-period planet. Venus is also the ruler of the sixth house (health problems, accidents, etc.). Venus' placement in the twelfth house (distant places) indicated the accident took place while she was traveling. She was swimming at the time (Venus is in a water sign).

Shashtamsha chart: Rahu is placed in the second house and is afflicted by Mars. Relative to the Sun and Moon, Mars is placed in the eleventh house (left shoulder). Venus is placed in the tenth house and is also afflicted by Mars. Relative to the Sun and the Moon, Venus also rules the eleventh house (left shoulder). The aspect of Mars in the Shashtamsha chart is particularly important in cases of injury or surgery. In this case, Mars rules the first house and the eighth house (accidents), making its influence more significant.

Chart 1: Dislocated Shoulder
December 30, 1948; 6:33 AM; San Antonio, TX

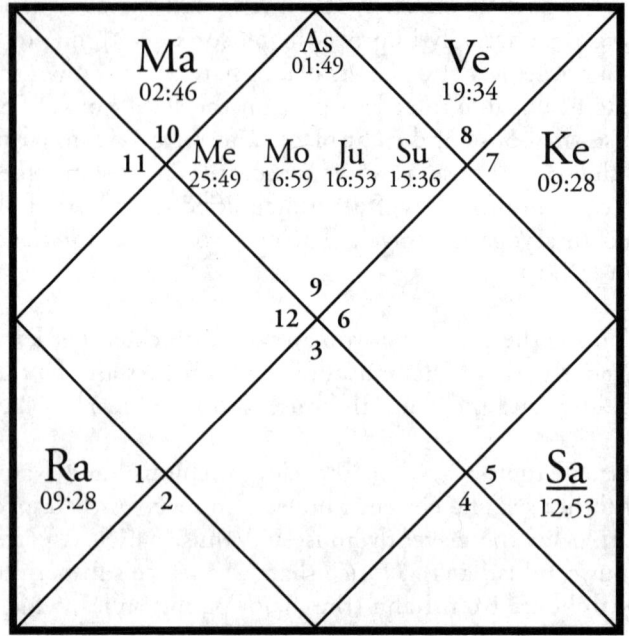

(D6) Shashtamsha

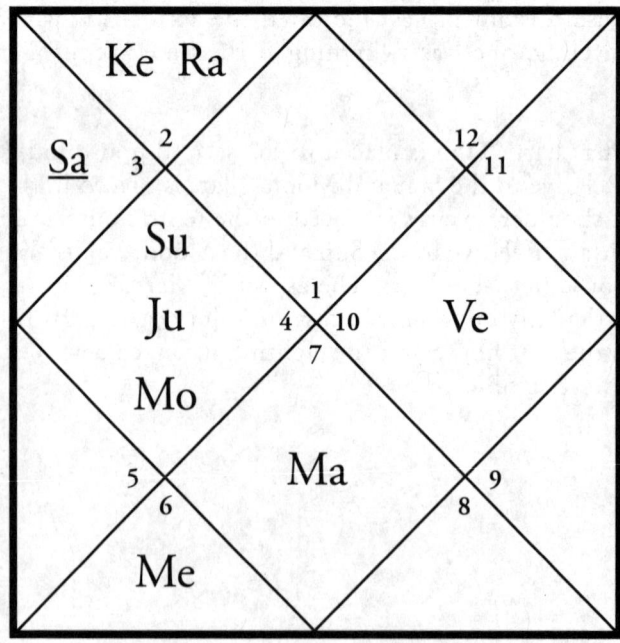

Chart 2: Ram Dass
April 6, 1931; 10:40 AM; Boston, MA

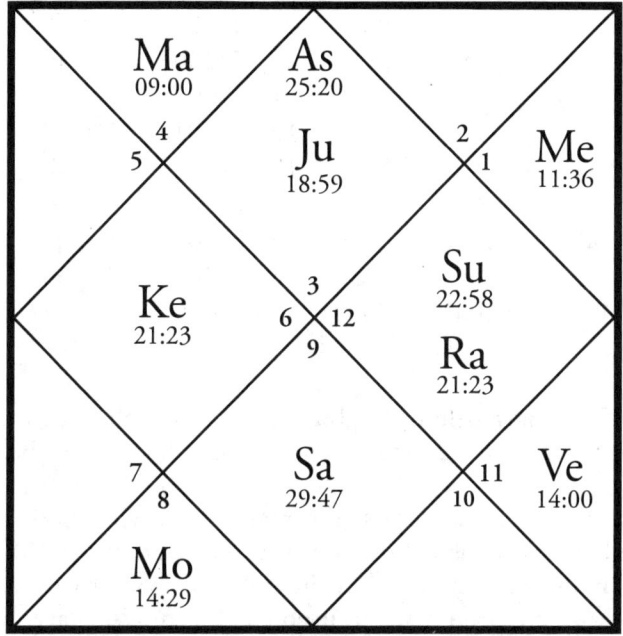

(D6) Shashtamsha

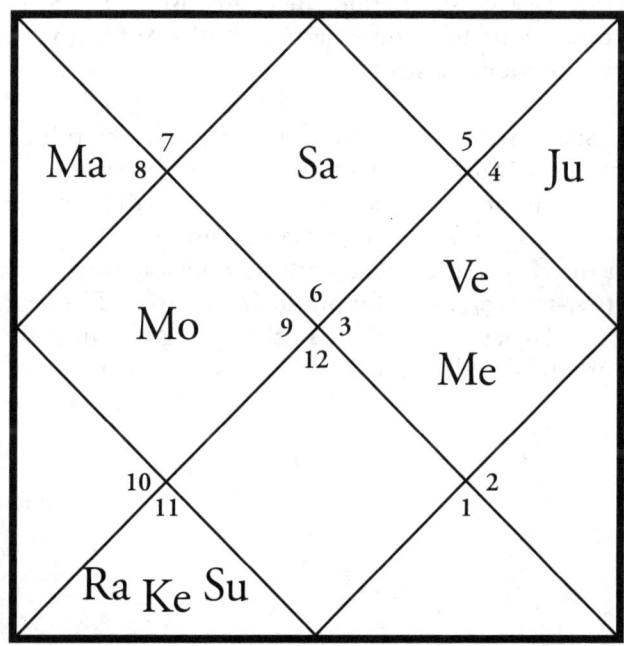

Dashas

05/15/1994	Ma	Ma	01/26/2004	Ra	Ju
10/11/1994	Ma	Ra	06/21/2006	Ra	Sa
10/30/1995	Ma	Ju	04/27/2009	Ra	Me
10/05/1996	Ma	Sa	11/14/2011	Ra	Ke
11/14/1997	Ma	Me	12/02/2012	Ra	Ve
11/11/1998	Ma	Ke	12/02/2015	Ra	Su
04/09/1999	Ma	Ve	10/26/2016	Ra	Mo
06/08/2000	Ma	Su	04/27/2018	Ra	Ma
10/14/2000	Ma	Mo	05/16/2019	Ju	Ju
05/15/2001	Ra	Ra			

Chart 2: This chart belongs to Ram Dass, the well-known American spiritual teacher, who suffered a stroke in his Mars/Saturn period.

Rashi chart: Notice that Mars, the planet signifying both the blood vessels and the head, is debilitated in the second house. Mars is also the ruler of the sixth house (health problems). Saturn is the ruler of the eighth house (chronic health problems). From its placement in the seventh house it aspects the first house (head). Mars (the major period ruler) and Saturn (the sub-period ruler) are also in a 6/8 relationship with each other. Due to a combination of all these factors, the Mars/Saturn period produced a stroke.

Shashtamsha chart: Mars is placed in Scorpio in the third house and receives an aspect from Saturn. Mars is also the powerful ruler of the third house (a minor dusthana). It aspects Rahu/Ketu and the Sun in the sixth house. Saturn is placed in the first house and aspects Mars. Its position in the first house, along with its rulership of the sixth house, makes it a first-rate candidate for producing a stroke. The fact that both period rulers (Mars and Saturn) are so clearly negative in both the Rashi and the Shashtamsha charts, makes their results easy to predict.

Chart 3: Breast Cancer
August 1, 1947; 7:18 PM; San Francisco, CA

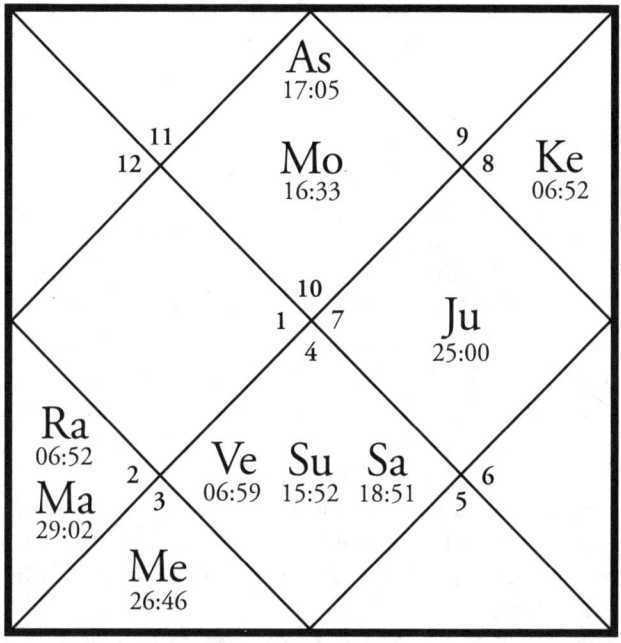

(D6) Shashtamsha

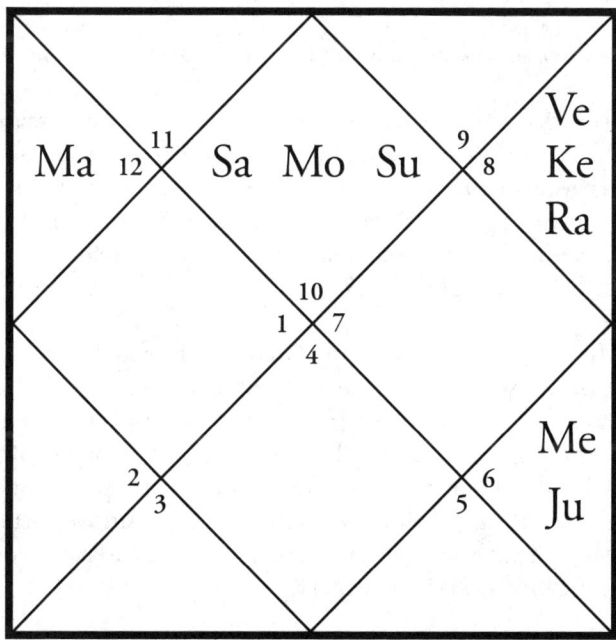

Chart 3: This is the chart of a woman who has struggled with breast cancer. The disease was first diagnosed in December of 1999. A lumpectomy was performed in January of 2000. General factors in the horoscope that indicate breast cancer are as follows:

Rashi Chart:
1. The Moon is the karaka for the breasts. It is placed in the Ascendant (the body) and is aspected by Saturn (karaka for disease). The Moon is also aspected by the Sun, which is the ruler of the eighth house (surgeries and chronic illness).
2. The Sun, eighth lord (chronic diseases) and karaka for health and vitality, is placed in the constellation of Pushya (symbolized by the udder of a cow), and is in a close conjunction with Saturn.
3. The ruler of the fourth house (the breasts) is placed in a conjunction with Rahu, which is placed in Krittika nakshatra (symbolized by a blade), suggesting surgery to the breasts. Both Rahu and Saturn are important influences in cases of cancer.
4. Saturn is also the ruler of the second house (things which are taken through the mouth) and is placed in Ashlesha. Ashlesha's shakti is "the power of poison," suggesting treatment through chemotherapy, which is toxic to the body.

Shashtamsha Chart: In the Shashtamsha chart, the Moon is in the first house along with Saturn and the Sun (eighth lord).

(At the time of onset and surgery she was in the period of Saturn/Ketu.)

Saturn Dasha: Saturn is a natural malefic (karaka for disease) and is placed in the seventh house (a maraka house), conjunct the Sun (eighth lord). Saturn is also the lagna lord, so it represents the physical body. Afflictions to the lagna lord can produce health problems during the lagna lord's period. This is particularly true if the malefic planet also rules the sixth or the eighth house.

Ketu Bhukti: The bhuktis of natural malefics in the dasha of a natural malefic are prone to expressing negative results in various domains of life. In this case, Ketu is placed in Scorpio. Scorpio is the eighth sign (related to the eighth house). Planets placed in Scorpio often given challenging results during their periods. Ketu is also placed in the eleventh house (sixth house from the sixth), which is an important house connected with health matters. Ketu also receives an aspect of Mars, a natural malefic and karaka of surgery.

Shashtamsha Chart: Saturn (lagna lord) is placed in the lagna with the eighth lord (Sun), creating a disease-prone major period. The Moon is also with Saturn and the Sun, indicating a disease process involving the breasts. Ketu is in the eleventh house indicating a disease-prone sub-period.

Transits: At the time of diagnosis, transiting Mars and Ketu (bhukti ruler) were passing through Capricorn (the lagna) in close conjunction to the natal Moon (karaka for the breasts). The conjunction or aspects of other transiting planets to the transiting dasha or bhukti ruler radically affects the planet's period results.

In this case, the transit of two powerful malefics in conjunction with the Moon, reflected serious health problems connected with the breasts. Debilitated transiting Saturn (dasha ruler) was passing through the fourth house (the breasts). From the fourth house, Saturn cast its aspect on transiting Ketu and the natal Moon. The influence of three natural malefics on the karaka for the breasts produced an obvious result.

(In May of 2002, she was diagnosed with cancer in the right breast. The period was Saturn/Venus.)

Saturn Dasha: Saturn's dasha was discussed earlier.

Venus Bhukti: Venus, the ruler of the fourth house (breasts) from Saturn (dasha ruler), is placed in the seventh house in Pushya nakshatra. Pushya is symbolized by the udder of a cow, a symbol of the breasts. Venus is in a conjunction with Saturn (a natural malefic).

Shashtamsha Chart: Venus is in Scorpio (the eighth sign, frequently problematic) placed in the eleventh house, (the sixth from the sixth) which is related to health matters. It is in a conjunction with Rahu and Ketu.

Transits: At the time of diagnosis, Saturn (dasha ruler) and Venus (bhukti ruler) were passing through the sign of Taurus. They were in a conjunction with transiting Rahu, Mars, and Mercury. Together, this five-planet transiting conjunction passed over natal Mars and Rahu. Two principles are utilized here. First, when the transiting dasha or bhukti ruler conjuncts transiting natural malefics, negative results often occur during the period. Also when the dasha or bhukti ruler transit over natural malefics in the natal chart, negative results often occur during the planet's period.

(Surgery took place in October of 2002. Although the dasha and the bhukti were the same, the transits were different at the time of surgery.)

Transits: Venus (bhukti ruler) was transiting through Libra in the tenth house. At first glance, this transit seems positive. A closer look reveals that Venus is flanked on both sides by transiting malefics. Transiting Sun and retrograde Mars were on one side and Ketu was on the other. This produced a transiting Papa Kartari Yoga, which negatively affected Venus' bhukti results. This was complicated by the fact that transiting Venus was also in retrograde motion at the time.

(She had a third surgery for breast cancer on Sept 18, 2003. The period was Saturn/Sun.)

Saturn Dasha: Saturn's major period has already been discussed.

Sun Bhukti: The Sun (sub-period ruler) is the ruler of the eighth house (chronic diseases, death) placed in the seventh house, a maraka (death) house. Planets placed in maraka houses (second and seventh houses) frequently produce illness during their periods. The Sun is also in a conjunction with Saturn (period ruler and lagna ruler) which is a natural significator for illness. For a Capricorn Ascendant, Saturn rules the physical body. The combination of the eighth lord (chronic disease) and the lagna lord (the body) is a clear indication of health problems.

Shashtamsha Chart: The Sun is also the ruler of the eighth house in the Shashtamsha chart. It is placed in the first house, where it is in a conjuction with Saturn. When the major and sub-period rulers conjunct in a divisional chart, they suggest prominent events related to the divisional chart's domain. If such a conjunction is placed in the first house of a divisional chart, then the events will be even more noticeable. The fact that this was a surgery, a negative health event, is related to the fact that both Saturn and the Sun are natural malefics, in addition to their relationship as rulers of the first and eighth houses respectively.

Transit: At the time of the surgery, Saturn (period ruler) was transiting Gemini in the sixth house (disease). The transiting Moon (karaka for the breasts) was in a conjunction with Saturn. The Sun (sub-period ruler) was passing through Virgo in Purva Phalguni nakshatra (symbolized by a healing cot). The transiting received the eighth house aspect from transiting Mars, which was retrograding through Shatabhisha nakshatra (a nakshatra related to illness and healing). The conjunction or aspect of transiting malefics to the transiting period ruler significantly modifies the events produced in its period.

Author's Journal:

Astrology On the Fly

In India, Jyotish takes on many forms. Astrologers have learned to adapt it to each situation according to need. In fact, good jyotishis often do not need to refer to ephemerides or computers to calculate charts. Instead, they simply do the chart in their head, on the go.

The day I met J.N. Sharma, the great prashna astrologer, illustrates this kind of astrology nicely. Although my own astrological practice generally revolves around birth chart interpretation, prashna (question astrology) has always been a supportive tool. Frequently a question chart can give a very detailed picture of coming events, so I use them liberally in my practice. I had heard about J.N. Sharma from a friend, who told me that he was one of Delhi's best prashna experts, and I was looking forward to meeting him. On this occasion, my friend set up a meeting, which was supposed to take place at a New Delhi restaurant over lunch. Unfortunately, during the morning before our meeting I began to feel nauseated. I decided to keep the appointment, however, thinking that the feeling would pass.

   On the way to the restaurant, I began to feel very uncomfortable. My body ached, and the nausea increased. I opened the window of the car to get some air, only to be suffocated by the thick and toxic New Delhi smog. The very thought of food made me cringe. As our car pulled up to the restaurant, my friend pointed out Mr. Sharma, who was waiting for us outside. My whole body ached as I got out of the car. My friend introduced Mr. Sharma to me, and as I shook his hand, I could see the puzzled look on his face. "Are you alright?" he asked.

   Not surprised that I looked as bad as I felt, I said, "Yes, I'm OK. I just need to sit down for a second."

Dizzy, I started to squat down to get my balance when, all of a sudden, in one gigantic, uncontrollable convulsion, I regurgitated my breakfast and part of the previous night's dinner right next to Mr. Sharma's feet!

Some people bring a great astrologer flowers. Others bring him fruit. My only consolation was that I did not actually hit his feet, but aimed my offering skillfully so as to simply adorn the space in front of his feet.

Concerned, Mr. Sharma repeated "Are you alright?"

"Yes, Yes," I said, "I'm OK. Let's just go into the restaurant."

Inside the restaurant, I quickly realized that I was actually very sick. While my friend and Mr. Sharma ordered dinner, I laid down on the bench of the booth at which we were seated. I can't remember what we talked about, but I remember that I managed to eke out some sort of pleasant conversation, while assuring them both that I was really OK. Then a thought occurred to me, why not put an astrological question to Mr. Sharma. So I asked, "Mr. Sharma, can you do a prashna right now, and tell me when I will recover?"

Mr Sharma thought for a moment and then said, "At this time, Virgo lagna is rising, Mercury is in the eighth house. It is in a purn ithasala yoga with Jupiter. You will recover quickly, in one or two days!"

'Incredible,' I thought. I said, "The way I feel, a one or two month recovery would be more in line. If I recover in one or two days it will have to be due to a miracle!"

As it turned out, a miracle is exactly what took place. The next day I dragged myself out of bed and I went to see Hans Baba, a great yogi who was staying outside New Delhi. As I approached his manch (a hut on stilts) I could see him sitting on his porch, completely naked, in spite of the cold morning air. Hans Baba took one look at me and asked, "You are not feeling well?"

"No," I said, "It's my stomach."

He pointed for me to stand under his porch. He then put his leg over the side and placed his foot on my head. He said, "You will begin to feel warm now." Then he began to chant loudly, while he channeled healing energy into my stomach. Immediately I began to feel warm. It was a nippy January morning and I was wearing a down parka, which I quickly shed. I continued to feel warmer and warmer and eventually began to sweat. Finally, I took off my outer shirt and stood there in my tee shirt. I had always heard that great yogis are able to control their body temperature and to withstand cold temperatures. Now I was experiencing the energy, by which this phenomenon is possible, first hand. I immediately began to feel better. After about twenty minutes, the nausea was completely gone and I felt great.

Mr. Sharma's prediction had been exactly correct. When I returned to the United States, I began focusing on prashna again. For the next year I worked with Mr. Sharma once a week for an hour over the phone, learning some of his unique predictive techniques. I used the real question charts from my clients for our weekly discussions. The result was that my use of prashna greatly improved. When I think about our meeting and the disgusting omen which accompanied it, I can only say that the science of nimitta (omenology) is not always an easy one to interpret. In retrospect, I guess the act of regurgitation might have symbolized a release of ignorance. In any case, it is the mark of a great teacher that no matter what the student brings as an offering, he reciprocates with knowledge.

Chapter Nine

Career

One of the most important facets of chart interpretation is the delineation of the career, which is usually signified by the tenth house. To say that the tenth house is only about career, is to vastly limit its signification. Actually, the tenth house is the house of karma, which means "action." In this respect it signifies not only the actions that a person performs in his career, but also actions related to his avocation and hobbies. This, along with the fact that in today's world there are literally thousands of different types of professions, makes the task of exactly pinpointing a person's profession a challenging one, to say the least.

For this reason, instead of trying to tell the person an exact profession for which he is suited, the judicious astrologer may be well advised to give his client a description of the qualities which play into the person's action-wiring. If a person is creative, has specific ability to design things, and is technically inclined as well, there might be several possible professions for which he is suited. By simply describing the characteristics of the career and then suggesting some example jobs which combine some or most of those characteristics, the astrologer puts the client on the right track without boxing him in with a narrow job definition.

Of course the best fit in defining the career occurs when most or all of the characteristics in the chart describe a single profession. In reality, however, few people are lucky enough to have a single job that combines all of their talents and abilities. When this does happen, the person usually feels blessed by a very positive and profound connection to his work. When the chosen profession fits some, but not all of the person's talents and abilities, he will usually feel that the job lacks a certain quality, which he can sometimes fulfill by exercising some of those abilities in pursuits outside of the profession. The popular notion that every person must have a job that matches every one of his talents and abilities may be unrealistic. In this respect, if the astrologer reinforces the idea that the goal of life, as far as the career is concerned, is to find the job-equivalent of a "soul mate," then he may be unwittingly setting the person up for chronic dissatisfaction in the area of career.

These are only a few of the obstacles that litter the path to accurate assessment of the career. Bearing in mind the complexity of this task, here are a few important points of departure for judging the career.

Five Points of Departure for Judging Career

1. The Ascendant
2. Dominant career planets
3. The ruler of the tenth house
4. Planets aspecting the tenth house
5. The Sun

1. The Ascendant

Finding the career in the horoscope starts with the Ascendant, which is the hub of the chart. In fact, no matter what area of life is being considered, one should always keep the particular tendencies of the Ascendant in mind. In the case of the career, however, this is particularly true. For example, if the chart has a Leo Ascendant, the person is attracted to jobs with authority. Leos need to be in charge. They also tend to have high expectations and are not usually satisfied with low positions. So even if the rest of the chart seems to indicate working as an employee for a company, a Leo-type will not be quite satisfied with mere service without some measure of authority. If the Leo person has to work for someone else, he might be happier if he at least has some position of authority within the company. Better yet, self-employment in a service-oriented field might give him a sense of fulfillment concerning the need to rule. In sum, it's important to remember the tendencies of the rising sign when determining the career patterns for specific careers. It is also important to consider the qualities of the Sun and Moon signs.

The following is a simple list of basic career tendencies of the signs. This is to be used in conjunction with the more thorough descriptions of the signs given in *Path of Light, Volume I*.

Aries: police or military, technical, scientific, competitive, athletics, fitness, industry, exploration, entrepreneur

Taurus: finance, banking, beauty, musical, artistic, throat-related, public relations, buying and selling, food business, stockbroker

Gemini: communications, language, sales, education, writing, music, art, math, accounting, business, more than one career at a time

Cancer: science, water-related, agriculture, real estate, hospitality, restaurants, hotels, healing professions that require a nurturing quality, housekeeping, architecture, archeology, nursing

Leo: authority, power, leadership, politics, drama, art, music, medicine, investment, entertainment, athletics

Virgo: all healing modalities, service, analysts, secretaries, language, accountants, business, teaching, mathematicians, engineering, computer science

Libra: art, music, drama, diplomacy, politics, legal, public relations, business, consulting

Scorpio: business, psychology, science, investigation, astrology, philosophy, medicine, insurance, financial planning, mortgage broker, accounting, banking, hospice, mortuary, all kinds of therapists

Sagittarius: professionals (teachers, doctors, lawyers), philosophers, outdoor work, horses, finance, athletes, veterinarians

Capricorn: executives, business, science, technology, managers, politics, organizational work, administration

Aquarius: humanitarian, social work, chemistry, dentistry, technology, astrology, metaphysics, electricians, engineering

Pisces: healers, psychics, charity, music, art, photography, film, travel

2. Dominant Career Planets

Certain planets, by virtue of their placement in the chart, gain the ability to greatly influence the career. There are three main ways in which this occurs: First, if a planet is placed in the tenth house, it becomes a primary contributor to the profession. Second, planets placed in the first house also play an important role in the career. Finally, if a person has a Mahapurusha Yoga in the chart (see the chapter on yogas), then the planet involved in the Mahapurusha Yoga will become a first-class determinant of profession.

Planets Placed in the Tenth or First Houses

Sun: leadership, government, self-expression, authority, creativity
Moon: public relations, advertising, connections to females
Mars: business, competitive careers, athletics, physical occupations, martial occupations, technical work, surgeon
Mercury: communications, writing, teaching, analytical professions, accounting
Jupiter: credentialed professions, teaching, doctors, lawyers, advisors
Venus: creativity, artists, musicians, designers
Saturn: management, service
Rahu: technical, cutting-edge or progressive fields, alternative and unconventional occupations
Ketu: healing, artists, spiritual occupations

Mahapurusha Yogas

The Mahapurusha Yogas are combinations that occur when either Mars, Mercury, Jupiter, Venus or Saturn is exalted or is placed in its own sign, in an angle from the Ascendant or the Moon. This yoga is fairly common, and as a result, the beginning astrologer frequently underestimates it. The function of a Mahapurusha planet is to bring its qualities to the foreground and dominate the horoscope. Like the Sun or the Moon, the Mahapurusha planet becomes a major focal point in the chart. Its sign and nakshatra placement also gain great prominence. For this reason, when a Mahapurusha Yoga is present, the Mahapurusha planet has a great deal of influence over the career.

In general, Mahapurusha planets reflect natural strength according to the signification of the Mahapurusha planet. If Ruchaka Yoga is present, then the person will reflect the qualities of Mars in a strong way. Although the classical texts say that this combination produces a military leader, this is only meant as a guideline. In fact, this yoga amplifies all the qualities of Mars. For example, Mars rules the muscles of the body, so the person might be athletic. Since Mars rules ambitious energy and independence, the person may be self-employed. There are many ways in which Mahapurusha planets can express themselves, as described in the following examples.

It is also important to pay attention to the particular sign and nakshatra in which the Mahapurusha planet is placed. Mars in Aries in Ashwini in the tenth house, for example, could produce a person who is a self-employed gardener. This occurs because the Ashwini Kumars, the deities that rule Ashwini, were the gardeners of the gods in the Hindu mythology. The same Mars in Aries, in Bharani, in the tenth house, however, could indicate a career in law enforcement. The constellation of Bharani is connected to Yama, the god of death, who judges the souls at the end of life. By blending the qualities of the planet with those of the sign and nakshatra of its placement, the astrologer will find important clues to the person's profession.

In general the five Mahapurusha planets produce the following possibilities for career.

Ruchaka Yoga: (Mars) athletes, business, mathematics, science, mechanical occupations, technical jobs, leadership, physical jobs, military or martial occupations.

Bhadra Yoga: (Mercury) mental pursuits, analysts, writers, teachers, information processors, business, sales.

Hamsa Yoga: (Jupiter) doctors, lawyers, teachers, consultants, experts and other credentialed or certified professionals.

Malavaya Yoga: (Venus) artists, musicians, healers, and professions that require relational skills.

Shasha Yoga: (Saturn) managers, organizers, people who have employees, and those who are required to take on a great deal of responsibility.

3. The Ruler of the Tenth House

One of the most important elements in determining the profession is the house and sign placement of the ruler of the tenth house. When the ruler of the tenth house is placed in another house, then that house is linked to the profession. If it is placed in the sixth house (health), for example, the career might relate to medicine or healing. The same type of work might also be indicated if the tenth lord is placed in Virgo, which is the sixth sign of the zodiac. Remember, the twelve zodiac signs correspond in sequence to the twelve houses of the chart. So the sixth sign, Virgo, is interpreted in similar fashion to the sixth house.

If the ruler of the tenth house is in its own house, then the sign it occupies becomes the determining factor. The navamsha placement of the ruler of the tenth is also an extremely important factor. Other important factors are the sign of the Ascendant in the Dashamsha chart, as well as the planets placed in the first house. The planets placed in the tenth house of that chart are also important. Finally, the Dashamsha chart placement of the ruler of the tenth house from the Rashi chart plays an important role.

Results of the Tenth Lord Placed in the Twelve Houses

The results of the tenth lord placed in the twelve houses as well as the results of other house rulers placed in or aspecting the twelfth house was discussed in *Path of light, Volume I*, in the chapter on houses.

4. Planets Aspecting the Tenth House

As with planets placed in the tenth house, planets aspecting the tenth house can have a strong influence on the profession. First, the aspecting planet projects the qualities of its nature on the career. This influence will be similar to that of planets placed in the tenth house. (see Planets Placed in the Tenth or First houses on p. 172) Secondarily, the aspecting planet also conveys the influence of the house it rules to the tenth house, causing the profession to take on the qualities of that house. For example, if the ruler of the third house aspects the tenth house, the person may work in a communication-related profession.

5. The Sun

The Sun is the primary karaka for career. Its placement in the chart is an important element in judging the career. If the Sun is strong and well-placed, then the person will project himself into his career with confidence. If the Sun is weak or afflicted, then the person may experience difficulty in realizing his career potential. The following list contains interpretations of the Sun, placed in the twelve houses or signs of the chart.

First House or Aries

Career is linked to the self.
Self-employment; self-directed; likes to work alone; leadership; wants

to be first or best in his field; becomes famous; could be a pioneer in his field.

Second House or Taurus

Career is linked to money, food, speech, possessions, family.
Business; buying and selling; work in finance; public speaking; teaching; cooking; restaurants; family business.

Third House or Gemini

Career is linked to communications, information, hands, various creative expressions, short journeys, siblings.
Professions that involve lots of communicating; work for companies which specialize in communication; information processing work; technology; writing; teaching; crafts; music; delivery or errand services; accounting; working with the hands; working with brothers or sisters.

Fourth House or Cancer

Career is linked to home, mother, family, vehicles, real estate, education, institutions or foundations.
Office in the home; having a shop or an office; work in real estate; nursing (nurturing, related to the mother); teaching; work connected to vehicles such as car sales; fishermen; cab drivers; working for or founding institutions; working with family members, especially the mother; homemakers.

Fifth House or Leo

Career is linked to children, speculation, entertainment, writing, publishing, the arts.
Teachers; professional mothers and fathers; entertainers; writers; publishers; artists; musicians; actors; stockbrokers; financial planners.

Sixth House or Virgo

The career is linked to service, health, analysis, accounting, criticism, pets or animal care.
All health-related professions; lawyers; judges; prison workers; employment by others rather than self-employment; if self-employed then work

involves providing a service to others, meticulous attention to detail.

Seventh House or Libra

The career is linked to partnership, law, diplomacy, banks, clients, contracts, business, spouse.
Working in partnership with others; political careers; banking; consulting or other client-based professions; business; lawyers; judges; contractors; working with the spouse.

Eighth House or Scorpio

The career is linked to upheavals and changes, the subconscious, the kundalini, other people's money, insurance, death, transformation, the occult.
Psychologists and therapists of all kinds; yoga teachers; bankers; brokers; financial planners; insurance agents; morticians; hospice workers; astrologers; researchers; diagnosticians; work that involves constant change and constant challenge; changes of career.

Ninth House or Sagittarius

The career is linked to dharma, father, travel, cosmic law, universities, knowledge, philosophy, religion.
Teachers; priests; university professors; professionals who have advanced degrees or expertise; doctors; lawyers; judges; philosophers; professions which give a sense of purpose; work connected to the father; airlines; work-related long-distant travel.

Tenth House or Capricorn

The career is linked to fame, reputation, status, respect, and productivity.
The profession will give reputation, honor, respect and status, but the particular profession will be connected to the sign in the tenth house.

Eleventh House or Aquarius

The career is linked to friends, groups, community, society, humanity, achievement, money, increase.
Social work; humanitarian work; community service; teaching and other group work; working with friends or making friends at work;

working in teams; achievement through the job; success; financial gains through the profession.

Twelfth House or Pisces

The career is linked to loss, interruption, retreats, meditation, introspection, foreign countries, uncertainty.
Interruptions in the career; jobs involving tasks which are constantly interrupted as part of their natural course; hospital or prison work; psychology; meditation instructor; working in seclusion; intuitive work; working in foreign countries or distant places; travel through the work; disappointments in the career; loss of job; difficulty finding a direction.

Dealing with Complexities

Finding someone's career in his or her chart is a complex and sometimes difficult nut to crack. The chart may show talents, abilities and predispositions, but it does not always show a distinct career or job. Part of the problem lies in the ever-changing nature of the culture. Today in the west, people are working at jobs that were unknown even ten years ago, not to mention in the days of the ancient rishis. The art of giving pertinent advice regarding the profession requires not only a high degree of astrological proficiency, but also a broad range of knowledge about different types of contemporary professions available in a particular cultural setting. In other words, it is not enough to look at a horoscope and simply give pat definitions of astrological combinations for certain types of careers. Rather, the person's real life situation must be thoroughly considered.

Along the same lines, not everyone has a single career to which they are best suited. People are much too complex to fit into one compartment or box. Most individuals are a combination of various talents, abilities and predispositions. A particular chart may show mathematical ability, an ability to cook, athletic ability, an ability to work with the hands, a knack for public relations, an ability to play a stringed instrument, a great memory, mechanical ability, a nurturing and caring nature, and a passion for technology. Finding a single job that can utilize all these talents, or even most of them, is not an easy task.

Career Patterns

One solution to this dilemma is to approach the process of career analysis with the intention of simply revealing the different career patterns instead of choosing a profession for the client. It is also important to remember that career, from the astrological point of view, means the action that fills your day. This might indicate vocation, but it also might include avocations, hobbies or other activities. In any case, when you simply spell out the tendencies in the chart, certain patterns naturally emerge. With a little knowledge of the components of contemporary professions, possible career choices will be apparent. In the previous example, where the person showed musical ability, a passion for computers and sales ability, a natural choice might be a sales career in the popular music industry. Taking the interest in technology, mechanical ability and ability to work with the hands into consideration, the same person might do well in a business related to high tech repair or hardware development.

Some Typical Career Patterns

Each career requires certain talents and abilities. Individuals who possess the qualities required of a particular job, naturally do well in that job. No single astrological pattern will show the career in the chart. Instead, the art of finding the career in the chart actually consists of identifying a series of patterns which, taken together, might be useful in a particular occupation. First, try to understand which psychological traits are necessary for particular careers. The next step is to identify various astrological combinations that will produce those qualities. It is useful to remember, however, that there are many ways to produce the same or similar qualities astrologically.

Here are some examples of qualities necessary for some of the more common professions and some possible astrological combinations that might produce those qualities. The qualities for these professions are not exhaustive. By the same token, the combinations listed are by no means the only ways to produce these attributes. They are only meant as examples. In actual practice, there are many different sets of qualities that could be useful in any profession, and there are unlimited ways to produce a given characteristic astrologically. What is important is not to memorize the particular combination, but rather to understand the basic reasoning behind the combination.

Healing Profession

Compassion: focal points (Sun, Moon, Ascendant or first house ruler) in Pisces or the twelfth house; Venus in Pisces or conjunct Ketu; Venus in an angle from the Moon or the Ascendant, especially if it is in own sign or exalted (Malavaya Yoga).

Technical and scientific aptitude: a strong fifth house with some connection to malefics (technical or scientific planets); Mercury or the Moon strong and connected with natural malefic planets.

The tendency to become an expert or a professional: focal points (Sun, Moon, Ascendant, or first house ruler) associated with Sagittarius, Jupiter or the ninth house; Jupiter in the tenth house from the Ascendant, Sun or Moon.

The ability to give support or nurture another person: focal planets in the fourth house or Cancer.

Healing ability: Ketu in the first or the tenth house; Moon, Ascendant, or other focal planets in Ashwini, Uttara Phalguni, Chitra, Mula or Shatabhisha nakshatras; focal planets in the sixth house (health) or eighth house (therapies) or in Virgo or Scorpio.

Ability to work with and benefit through patients: focal points in Libra or the seventh house; strong seventh house; strong eighth house (money coming through clients or patients).

The type of healer will be signified by planets which are located in key positions in the chart. For example, If a planet is placed in the sixth house, the Ascendant, or is in conjunction with the sixth lord, the ascendant lord, the Sun or the Moon, the person will pursue a healing style in line with the planets significations. Ketu in one of these placements usually gives an inclination to alternative medicine. Jupiter is related to more conventional healing modalities. Mars prominent suggests surgery or possibly acupuncture. Rahu suggests technological fields such as radiology, and also signifies dentistry and chiropractic. Mercury may produce a career in psychology or psychiatry, especially if it is aspected by Saturn.

Teacher

Expert or professional: Jupiter, Sagittarius or the ninth house prominent; Jupiter in the tenth house from the Sun, Moon or Ascendant.

Speaking ability: strong second house (speech and education), Mercury strong.

Persuasiveness and communications ability: third house strong; Mercury strong; focal points in Gemini or the third house; Jupiter in the first, fourth, seventh, or tenth house from the Moon (Gaja Kesari Yoga); Jupiter aspecting Mercury.

The ability to read the psychology of the student: Moon, Mercury or the Ascendant associated with Ketu; focal planets in the twelfth house; Ketu in the third house; focal planets in the eighth house.

Nurturing ability: focal points in Cancer or the fourth house.

Ability to work with and have good experiences with children (if a primary school teacher, for example): focal planets in the fifth house or in Leo; fifth lord from the Ascendant or Moon in the tenth house or visa versa; focal planets conjunct Jupiter; benefics in the fifth house from the Moon, Sun or Ascendant.

Organizational or management ability: Saturn strong and in an angle, especially if it is in its own sign or exalted (Shasha Yoga); Saturn beneficially aspecting focal planets; focal planets in Capricorn, the tenth house, Virgo or the sixth house.

A connection to groups of people: Aquarius or the eleventh house prominent; the ruler of the tenth house in the eleventh house or Aquarius; Jupiter conjunct the Moon.

Connection to institutions; fourth house or Cancer prominent.

Engineers and Other Technical Professions

Technical ability: fifth house and tenth house strong and linked to malefics (technical planets); focal planets strong and similarly associated with malefics; focal points in logical and/or technical signs (Aries, Gemini, Virgo, Scorpio, Sagittarius, Capricorn, Aquarius); conjunctions or mutual aspects of malefics that are prominently placed.

Note: Saturn - Mars combinations bring mechanical ability. Rahu represents computers, electronics and other new technologies. Ketu represents very refined technologies and alternative technologies.

Expert or professional: Jupiter, Sagittarius or the ninth house prominent; Jupiter in the tenth house from the Sun, Moon or Ascendant.

Ability to work for a company: (in the case of employed technical professionals) focal planets in the sixth house, Saturn strong and in the upachaya houses (third, sixth, tenth or eleventh houses); tenth lord from the Ascendant, Sun or Moon in the sixth house (employment by others).

Ability to work with clients (in the case of a consultant): seventh house or Libra prominent; eighth house strong and influenced by benefics (money coming through clients or contracts); tenth lord in the seventh house or the seventh lord in the tenth house.

Self-employment: (in the case of an owner of a technical business) focal planets in the first house or Aries; tenth lord in the first house or visa versa; all or most of the planets above the horizon (between the seventh and the first houses); Sun in Aries or Leo.

Ability to write and publish (in the case of a software designer or technical writer): focal planets in the fifth house; the tenth lord (which should also be a technical planet or be associated with technical planets) in the fifth house or fifth lord in the tenth house; strong fifth house from the Ascendant, Moon and Sun.

Lawyers

Expert or professional: Jupiter, Sagittarius or the ninth house prominent; Jupiter in the tenth house from the Sun, Moon or Ascendant.

Ability to work with clients and legal matters: seventh house or Libra prominent; eighth house strong and influenced by benefics; tenth lord in the seventh house or seventh lord in the tenth house.

Argumentative ability and competitive nature: focal planets or the Ascendant associated with a strong Mars; malefics in the sixth house (ability to defeat enemies); Mars or other malefics in the third, sixth, seventh, tenth or eleventh houses; Jupiter and Mars in mutual aspect (opposite each other); Mars aspecting or conjunct Mercury.

Analytical ability: focal points in Virgo, sixth house, or associated with a strong Mercury.

Persuasiveness and communications ability: third house strong; Mercury strong; focal points in Gemini or the third house; Jupiter in the first, fourth, seventh, or tenth house from the Moon (Gaja Kesari Yoga); Jupiter with or aspecting Mercury.

Capacity for work within structure and organizational ability: Saturn strong and in an angle, especially if it is in its own sign or exalted (Shasha Yoga); Saturn beneficially aspecting focal planets; focal planets in Capricorn, the tenth house, Virgo or the sixth house.

As with engineers, lawyers can be self-employed or they can work for a law firm. They can also practice different kinds of law. The particular type of law will depend upon other factors. Environmental law, for example, is related to the fourth house. International law is related to the ninth and the twelfth houses.

Business

Organizational or management ability: Saturn strong and in an angle, especially if it is in its own sign or exalted (Shasha Yoga); Saturn beneficially aspecting focal planets; focal planets in Capricorn, the tenth house, Virgo or the sixth house.

Ability to profit through buying and selling: focal planets in the second house or in Taurus; tenth lord in the second house or Taurus in either the Rashi or Navamsha charts.

Salesmanship: the Moon (working with public) powerful and in an angle from the Ascendant; Jupiter in an angle from the Moon (Gaja Kesari Yoga); Mercury associated with Ketu; Ketu in the third house.

Communications ability: Mercury powerful and angular; the third house strong and occupied by benefics; Mercury aspected by Jupiter or associated with benefics; Mercury conjunct Mars (gives energy in communications); Venus conjunct Mars (passion) and placed in the second house (speech) or third house (communications).

Competitiveness, drive: Mars in the second house (money), third house (errands and tasks), sixth house (competition and work), seventh house (tenth from the tenth), tenth house (career), or in the sign of Capricorn. (Note: Any career needs ambition. Owning and succeeding at a business, however, takes a high degree of drive and enterprise, as well as an intrinsic faith in one's own ability to prevail in the world of work.)

The ability to understand a particular type of product varies, depending on the product. For example, an understanding of food is produced by primary connections to Taurus, the second house or Venus. An understanding of automobile parts would be produced by technical combinations (explained previously), as well as a powerful fourth house (vehicles). Each area of business will have its own nature and must be analyzed in a similar way.

Artists, Musicians, Actors, Writers

Creative ability: Venus strong and in angles or trines from the Ascendant or the Moon (if Venus is also in its own or exalted sign and in an angle, this creates Malavaya Yoga, which makes creative energy a central theme for the chart); Mercury similarly placed creates Bhadra Yoga, which makes the person a writer; Other combinations for general creativity include: Venus conjunct the Sun, Moon or Mercury; Moon in the nakshatras of Rohini, Purva Phalguni, or Dhanishtha; focal planets in Libra, Leo, Gemini or Taurus.

Ability to put creative ideas into form: Saturn conjunct or aspecting Venus; Venus in Capricorn or Aquarius; Venus in the tenth house.

Ability to gain reputation through the arts (making a living at art depends entirely on reputation): Gaja Kesari Yoga (Jupiter in the first, fourth, seventh, or tenth house from the Moon); Raja Yogas (rulers of angles and trines combined) involving the tenth and the fifth houses; tenth house powerful; eleventh house powerful; Ascendant powerful.

Imagination: Venus, Mercury or the Moon conjunct Ketu or Rahu, or placed in Aquarius, Pisces or the twelfth house.

Charm, charisma, ability to win friends and influence people: Venus on the Ascendant; Leo Ascendant with Rahu; Venus conjunct the Sun or Mercury; Venus in the third house; Malavaya Yoga; Venus conjunct Mars (passion) and placed in the first house (persona); Mercury in Gemini (wit, cleverness with language); Mercury in the first house. There are literally hundreds of ways to create a charming personality astrologically. Most of them boil down to channeling emotional-sensual energy (Venus) or mental-communicative energy (Mercury) through the personality.

Career Themes

After thoroughly elaborating all the career combinations, it is common for two or three discrete patterns to emerge. The same chart may reveal sets of talents that would be good for a career in psychology or as a restaurant owner. In such cases, it is important to remember that the chart shows the different themes of action. These themes are analogous to the different muscle groups in the body. Like different muscle groups, all of these talents and traits need to be exercised. If a person decided to only exercise his biceps and not the triceps, his arms would quickly get out of balance. Similarly, if a person works at a highly technical career sixty hours per week, but finds no time to use his musical talent, an important part of himself begins to wither.

Predicting Ups and Downs in Career

The major or sub-period of a planet will produce positive or negative results for the career, depending on the planet's placement in the Rashi chart and in the Dashamsha chart. The guidelines for judging the positive or negative results of planetary periods were given in the chapter on dashas. In addition to those guidelines, the following points will help in judging the dasha's effect on the career.

Noticeable Results: Not every planetary period will produce pronounced career events. When assessing the career results of a major or sub-period, it is helpful to first decide if the period ruler qualifies as a prominent planet for the career. The planet's overall disposition will determine whether the planetary period's influence on the career is positive or negative. Period rulers become prominent career planets and tend to give noticeable career results under the following conditions:

1. A period planet is placed in the tenth house in the Rashi or the Dashamsha chart.
2. A period planet rules the tenth house in the Rashi or Dashamsha chart.
3. A period planet aspects the tenth house in the Rashi or Dashamsha chart.
4. A period planet rules the first house in the Dashamsha chart.
5. A period planet is placed in the first house of the Dashamsha chart.
6. A period planet aspects the first house of the Dashamsha chart.

7. A period planet is in the above conditions relative to the Sun or Moon.
8. A sub-period planet which is in one of the above situations relative to the major period planet.

Positive Results: A planet will give positive results for career, under the following conditions:

1. It is one of the above mentioned prominent career planets and is strong and well-placed in the Rashi or Dashamsha chart, preferably in both.
2. It is a prominent career planet, placed in a Raja Yoga in either the Rashi or Dashamsha chart.

Negative Results: A planet will give negative results for the career under the following conditions:

1. It is one of the above mentioned prominent career planets and is debilitated, afflicted, or poorly placed in the Rashi or Dashamsha chart, preferably in both.

Note: For career, the influence or aspect of strong and well-placed natural malefics may actually give good results under many conditions. Natural malefics such as Mars (ambition and drive), Saturn (hard work and responsibility) and Rahu (compulsive desire) have the potential to promote the career domain. As a result, the astrologer should proceed carefully when judging the effects of an afflicted period ruler on the domain of career.

The Dashamsha Chart

The divisional chart for the career is the Dashamsha chart. The placement of a major or sub-period planet in this varga will give important clues to the specific career results produced during the period. As mentioned above, the most noticeable career results usually take place when the planet has become a prominent career planet. On the other hand, in cases where the planet does not qualify as a prominent planet for career, its placement in the Dashamsha chart can still give the astrologer a good idea about the types of career events the planet is likely to produce during its period.

The following results show the general effect of the major or sub-period rulers when they are placed in the twelve houses of the Dashamsha chart. These interpretations are modern applications based on classical principles and have been found to give consistent results in the author's own practice. The specific results will vary depending on the positive or negative disposition of the dasha, bhukti or antara ruler in the Dashamsha chart. The period ruler's placement in the Dashamsha chart should not be used in isolation. It should be used in conjunction with the planet's placement in the Rashi chart. These interpretations are general guidelines and do not take the Dashamsha house rulership of the planet into consideration. To further modify and refine the interpretation, the reader should refer to the results given in the section on houses in *Path of Light, Volume I*. For example, if the ruler of the fourth house in the Rashi chart is placed in the eighth house, this normally suggests change of residence, as per the house interpretations given in *Volume I*. However, if a period ruler is the ruler of the fourth house in the Dashamsha chart, and is placed in the eighth house of that chart, then a change of the workplace or office could take place during the planet's period. The prediction, however, should be modified according to the age and practical circumstances of the client.

Planets Placed in the Twelve Houses of the Dashamsha Chart

First House: If a period planet is placed in the first house of the Dashamsha chart, it will produce prominent career results. The positive or negative quality of the results will depend on the positive or negative disposition of the planet. For example, an exalted Saturn here might produce a successful period as a manager during a Saturn major period or sub-period.

Second House: If a period planet is placed in the second house of the Dashamsha chart, its period will produce financial events related to the profession. If the planet is involved in a Dhana Yoga (yoga for money), the person may experience financial increase through work, especially if it is also aspected by Jupiter. If the planet is involved in a negative placement, the result may be the opposite. For example, a debilitated and afflicted Mars placed here might suggest financial losses, cut in pay, or business expenditure during a period of Mars.

Third House : If a planet is placed in the third house of the Dashamsha chart, its period can produce a good deal of communications-oriented activities. It can also suggest many short journeys or errands connected to work. These activities will be positive or negative depending on the disposition of the planet. For example, a debilitated and afflicted planet placed here might indicate difficulties in communications in the work place during the planet's period. On the other hand, the third house is also a minor dusthana house (eighth house from the eighth) and should be watched carefully for career changes as well (see the results for the eighth house that follows).

Fourth House: If a planet is placed in the fourth house of the Dashamsha chart, it becomes a somewhat prominent planet due to its aspect on the tenth house. This is also the house of the workplace, so planets placed here produce results pertaining to the office, shop, studio or even the work cubicle. For example, the ruler of the eighth house placed here will give a change of office or workplace. A strong Venus placed here may motivate the person to paint or decorate his office.

Fifth House: A period planet placed in the fifth house of the Dashamsha chart will generally give good results for career, unless it is weak and afflicted. This is also the house of education, so the periods of planets placed here often cause the person to pursue work-related education. This is also a house of creativity and children, so these activities also can become more important during the planet's period.

Sixth House: Planets place in the sixth house tend to produce struggle and hard work during their periods. In the Dashamsha chart, this could simply mean that the person is working hard during the period, which is not necessarily negative. The sixth house is the house of employment, however, so it gains the status of being a primary house in this chart. A strong and well-placed planet in this house could produce an improvement in the conditions of employment such as a raise, promotion, or bonus. For a business owner, the same condition could cause him to hire employees or simply manifest good results from employees. Of course these effects will be the opposite in the case of weak and afflicted planets.

Seventh House: Planets in the seventh house of the Dashamsha chart always aspect the Ascendant, so they become capable of producing prominent career results. A period planet placed here will tend to produce career events that are related to other people, such as partnerships, collaborations, legal matters and client-related events. The positive or negative quality of these events will depend on the positive or negative disposition of the period planet.

Eighth House: Planets in the eighth house of the Dashamsha chart tend to produce change of direction in the career. The most dramatic version of this is a complete change of career, which would be more likely if such a major change was also reflected in the Rashi chart. On a more subtle level, however, this placement commonly produces a change of job in the same field, or simply a new direction or new project within the same job. The positive or negative quality of the change will depend on the positive or negative disposition of the period planet. This placement can also produce therapeutic activities in the case of health professionals.

Ninth House: If a planet is placed in the ninth house of the Dashamsha chart, its period will usually produce good results for the career in general, unless the planet is weak and afflicted. This is a house of higher education, so period planets here sometimes produce educational efforts. It is also a house of long distance travel, so the planet's period can sometimes include work-related travel. In fact, because the Dashamsha chart includes the entire field of action, even pleasure travel can be indicated here.

Tenth House: If a planet is place in the tenth house of the Dashamsha chart, it will give prominent results for the career during its period. This is the primary house for the Dashamsha chart. For example, an exalted Mars placed here might indicate an increase in authority in the work. A debilitated planet, on the other hand, could indicate a layoff or some other career problem. If the debilitated planet is neecha bhanga (canceled debilitation), then the problem could be overcome or become a blessing in disguise later on.

Eleventh House: If a planet is placed in the eleventh house, it can produce financial gains and successes during its period, unless it is weak and afflicted. Financial gains are more likely if the planet is also involved in a Dhana Yoga (yoga for money, see yoga chapter). For example, if the ruler of the fifth house is placed in the eleventh house, it could produce a raise or increased profits through business. This effect will be strongly amplified if Jupiter also influences the eleventh house. The eleventh is also the house of attainment, so a planet placed here can allow the person to finish important projects during its period. The eleventh house is the house of groups, so it sometimes signifies activities related to teams, groups or the community.

Twelfth House: If a planet is placed in the twelfth house of the Dashamsha chart, its period can sometimes seem to be a time of unclear direction in the career. This is also the house of distant places, so period planets placed here commonly produce work-related travel as well. The positive or negative quality of these events will depend on the positive or negative disposition of the planet.

Chart 1: Albert Schweitzer
January 14, 1875; 11:50 PM; Kayserberg, Germany

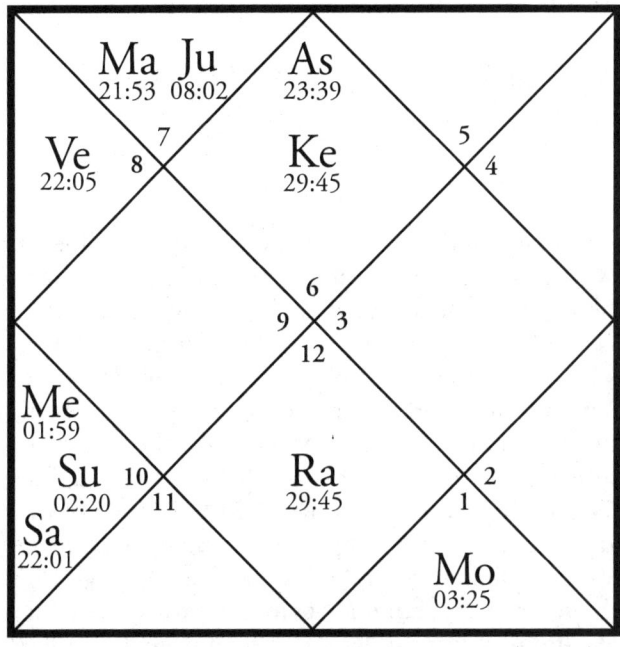

(D10) Dashamsha

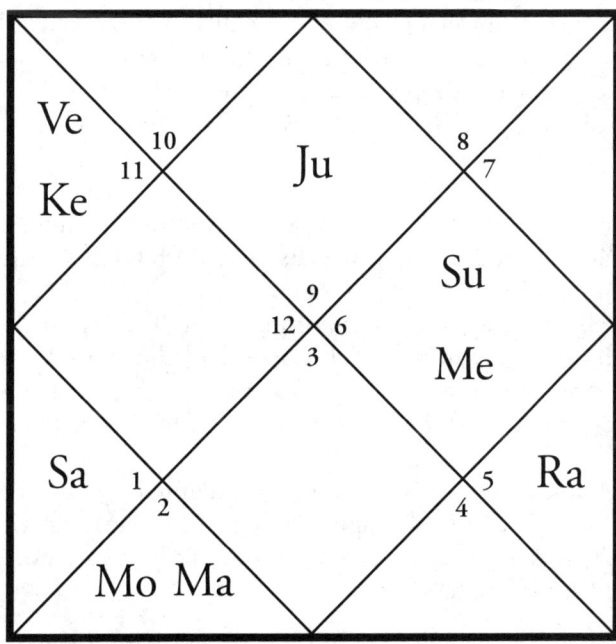

Dashas

01/14/1875	Ke	03/30/1916	Ma
03/29/1880	Ve	03/301923	Ra
03/30/1900	Su	03/30/1941	Jp
03/30/1906	Mo	03/30/1957	Sa

Career of Albert Schweitzer

One of the most famous doctors in the last century was Albert Schweitzer. Schweitzer was known for his great contributions as a humanitarian and healer in the heart of Africa. He was also known as a great theological writer. Before either of these careers surfaced in his life, however, Schweitzer was a world-class concert organist. He seemed to have boundless energy and enthusiasm, working an average of eighteen hours daily.

He was once interviewed by a news reporter who asked him to reveal the secret of his great capacity for work. Schweitzer said, "It's simple, I never work at anything past the point when I get tired of it." His habit was to tend to patients for a couple of hours, write in his journal, do paperwork, take a walk, dig a ditch, and above all, play his organ every day. Even though he was a famous doctor with a serious clinic in Africa, he never gave up his music. In fact, he brought his organ to the middle of the African jungle so that he could continue to nurture his musical side. In this way, Schweitzer exercised his different talents and abilities and achieved a kind of planetary balance. The result was limitless energy, enthusiasm and a deep sense of purpose.

These three occupations are reflected in Schweitzer's chart in the following ways.

Organist: Hasta nakshatra (the hands) rising; Venus in the third house (the house of music); three planets in the fifth house (creativity).

Writer: All of the above combinations generally support creative activities. In addition, Schweitzer had the second drekkana of Virgo rising, which is symbolized by a man with a pen. Mercury (writing) is also placed in the fifth house (creativity).

Healer: Ashwini nakshtra (healing) is occupied by the Moon. The Moon is also in the eighth house (therapeutic activities). Virgo (healing) is the lagna. Hasta nakshatra supports healing through the hands.

In addition to these general career patterns, Schweitzer had a Raja Yoga produced by Mercury (ruler of the tenth house) and Saturn (ruler of the fifth house) conjunct in the fifth house. This contributed to his rise in professional success. His fine reputation and fame were augmented by Gaja Kesari Yoga.

Schweitzer also traveled extensively for his work, first as a concert organist and later as a doctor in Africa. This is reflected by Mercury, ruler of the tenth house (career) conjunct with the Sun, ruler of the twelfth house (distant places).

Timing

Most of Schweitzer's childhood and youth took place during the major period of Venus. Venus' placement in the third house in both the Rashi and the Dashamsha charts, is one of the combinations responsible for his musical ability. During that period he became a great organist, focusing on the works of Bach. He also became a noted academic expert on Bach during that time.

At the end of Schweitzer's Sun period he decided to study medicine so that he could become a missionary. The Sun is the ruler of the twelfth house (charity). It was during Sun dasha/Ketu bhukti that Schweitzer entered medical school. Ketu rules the constellation of Ashwini and is a planet of healing. Notice that in the Dashamsha chart, Ketu (an important significator of healing) is placed in the third house (information) and in the sixth house from the Sun (healing). He was at the end of the Sun period and about to enter the Moon period. The Moon is placed in Ashwini in the eighth house (therapeutic activities). In the Dashamsha chart, the exalted Moon is placed in the sixth house (healing). This is the most important placement in the chart with respect to healing ability. At the end of a major period, a person often feels an inclination to move in the new direction shown by the next major period. Schweitzer's desire to study medicine is a good example of this. He spent the next seven years (most of the Moon period) studying medicine. He became a physician during the last part of the Moon period. The Moon, like Saturn, often gives its results at the end of its period. Schweitzer realized his dream of becoming a doctor in Moon dasha/Ketu bhukti, near the end of the Moon period.

After becoming a physician, the First World War broke out in Europe. Schweitzer spent a few years in an internment camp and later experienced ill health for a few years. It wasn't until 1924 that he moved to Africa and began the work for which he became famous. Rahu's eighteen-year period began in 1923. It is common that at the beginning of a new dasha, major changes take place in a person's life. Rahu rules foreign countries and exotic places. It is placed in the seventh house, the house of relationships, which includes the doctor-patient relationship. Rahu is also placed in the constellation of Revati, which is associated with travel and also caretaking of other people.

Schweitzer worked in his clinic in Africa for the remainder of his life. From the onset of his Jupiter period, however, his reputation as a humanitarian began to spread. Notice that Jupiter is placed in the first house of the Dashamsha chart, creating a Hamsa Mahapurusha Yoga. In December 1953, Schweitzer received the 1952 Nobel Peace Prize. This took place during Jupiter dasha/Moon bhukti. The Moon and Jupiter form Gaja Kesari Yoga in Schweitzer's Rashi chart. Gaja Kesari Yoga is a combination for reputation and fame. Although his reputation grew throughout the Jupiter period, it culminated in Jupiter dasha/Moon bhukti. Again, the Moon frequently gives its results late in its period. The Moon's sub-period extended from September 1952 to January 1954. The award was announced in late 1952, but awarded in December of 1953.

Chart 2: Galileo Galilei
February 15, 1564; 3:31 PM; Pisa, Italy

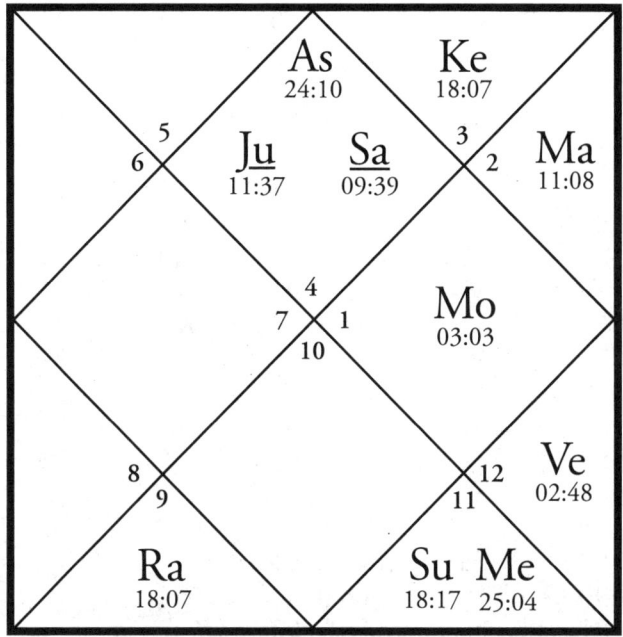

(D10) Dashamsha

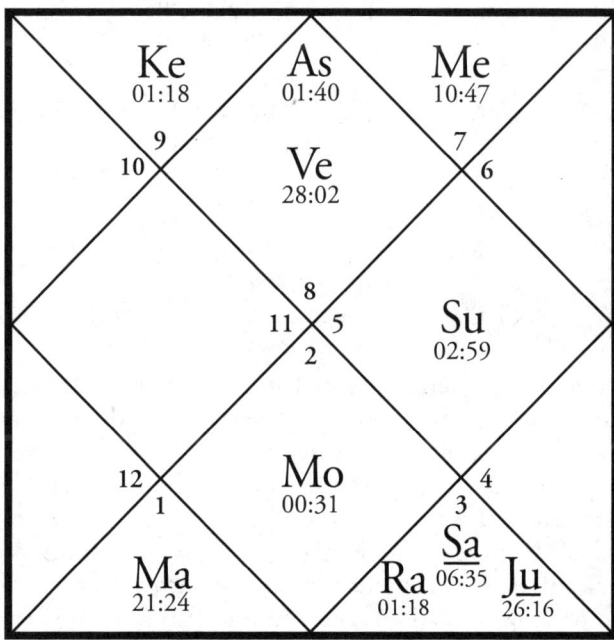

Path of Light – The Domains of Life

Dashas

Date			Date		
06/12/1564	Ke	Mo	05/20/1601	Mo	Me
01/11/1565	Ke	Ma	10/19/1602	Mo	Ke
06/09/1565	Ke	Ra	05/20/1603	Mo	Ve
06/28/1566	Ke	Jp	01/18/1605	Mo	Su
06/03/1567	Ke	Sa	07/20/1605	Ma	Ma
07/12/1568	Ke	Me	12/16/1605	Ma	Ra
07/09/1569	Ve	Ve	01/03/1607	Ma	Jp
11/08/1572	Ve	Su	12/10/1607	Ma	Sa
11/08/1573	Ve	Mo	01/18/1609	Ma	Me
07/10/1575	Ve	Ma	01/15/1610	Ma	Ke
09/08/1576	Ve	Ra	06/13/1610	Ma	Ve
09/09/1579	Ve	Jp	08/14/1611	Ma	Su
05/10/1582	Ve	Sa	12/19/1611	Ma	Mo
07/20/1585	Ve	Me	07/19/1612	Ra	Ra
05/19/1588	Ve	Ke	04/02/1615	Ra	Jp
07/20/1589	Su	Su	08/25/1617	Ra	Sa
11/06/1589	Su	Mo	07/01/1620	Ra	Me
05/08/1590	Su	Ma	01/19/1623	Ra	Ke
09/13/1590	Su	Ra	02/06/1624	Ra	Ve
08/07/1591	Su	Jp	02/06/1627	Ra	Su
05/26/1592	Su	Sa	01/01/1628	Ra	Mo
05/08/1593	Su	Me	07/02/1629	Ra	Ma
03/14/1594	Su	Ke	07/20/1630	Jp	Jp
07/20/1594	Su	Ve	09/06/1632	Jp	Sa
07/20/1595	Mo	Mo	03/21/1635	Jp	Me
05/20/1596	Mo	Ma	06/26/1637	Jp	Ke
12/19/1596	Mo	Ra	06/01/1638	Jp	Ve
06/19/1598	Mo	Jp	01/30/1641	Jp	Su
10/19/1599	Mo	Sa	11/19/1641	Jp	Mo

Career of Galileo Galilei

Galileo is famous for being one of the fathers of modern astronomy. He is credited with many important astronomical observations, including several that confirmed a heliocentric model of the solar system. Through the use of one of the first telescopes, he also discovered four satellites around Jupiter.

Galileo was actually a mathematician. As a boy, he studied in a monastery and wanted to become a monk. His father wanted him to become a doctor, however, so he removed him from the monastery. From

1581- 1585 Galileo attended the University of Pisa where he began to study medicine. During that time he developed an interest in mathematics and natural philosophy. He left school after four years without a degree, and began to pursue mathematics independently, studying with a private tutor.

Rashi Chart: Galileo's chart is interesting in several ways. His lagna is Cancer, which is occupied by exalted, digbala Jupiter, forming Hamsa Yoga. This yoga is seen in the charts of people who gain knowledge or expertise in a subject and is common in the charts of professionals, scholars, and teachers. Jupiter is also placed in Pushya nakshatra, which is ruled by Brihaspati, the teacher of all the gods, furthering the predisposition to gain great knowledge in life. Saturn's conjunction with Jupiter gave him a thirst for knowledge, and gave him a willingness to work hard at gaining knowledge.

His high intelligence level and academic prowess are also reflected by Venus being exalted in the ninth house (education). Venus, the planet of pleasure and self-indulgence, is frequently overlooked as a planet of knowledge. In mythology, Venus was Shukra, the guru of the demons. He was a highly advanced yogi who had an abundance of knowledge that matched Brihaspati (Jupiter), who was the teacher of the gods. Galileo's great academic abilities are clearly indicated through the exaltation of both Venus and Jupiter (teacher-planets), and Venus' placement in the ninth house (higher education).

The Moon (lagna lord) is placed in the tenth house (career). This produced a strong orientation towards career. The Moon (the mind) is in Ashwini nakshatra, a nakshatra connected with medicine and science. The Sun (the father) is placed in Shatabhisha, which is also an important nakshatra of healing. It is noteworthy that Galileo began the study of medicine at the insistence of his father.

The reason for his resistance to becoming a doctor may be found in several ways. First, the Sun (the father) is placed in the eighth house (rebellion) indicating a need to reject his father and to control his own life. Next, the ruler of the ninth house (father) is in a conjunction with Saturn (resistance), indicating a natural resistance to the advice of his father. Furthermore, Mercury (the intellect) is placed in the eighth house (science) creating a deeply investigative intellect, and the mind of a scientific researcher.

Interest in mathematics is associated with Mars. The fifth house is the house of the intellect. It shows intellectual activities, so it reveals the subjects that one studies in school. When Mars (mathematics) is placed in or aspects the fifth house the person may study math.

Surya Lagna: From the Sun sign, Mars (mathematics) rules the tenth house (career). It is placed in the fourth house (educational institutions and foundations). Galileo taught at universities and was on the boards of several institutions. The fourth house is also the home. Under house arrest later in his life, he was forced to work out of his home.

Chandra Lagna: This pattern is repeated from the Moon sign, where the ruler of the tenth house (career) is Saturn (management and administration). Saturn is placed in the fourth house from the Moon (home, educational institutions, foundations) and is in a conjunction with an exalted Jupiter. Jupiter's exaltation, its role as a mahapurusha planet, and its placement in Pushya nakshatra have already been discussed as a three-fold inclination towards teaching. Saturn's conjunction with Jupiter simply modifies this inclination to include management and administration. This is expressed by Galileo's role as Chairman of the Mathematics Department at the University of Pisa.

Events

In 1588 (Venus dasha/Mercury bhukti) Galileo got a job as a teacher of mathematics at the University of Pisa. This was his first big teaching job. Up to this point he was doing private tutoring in his home town of Florence.

Venus Dasha: Venus' connection to knowledge and to teaching has been discussed earlier. Its placement in the house of higher education gave Galileo a great love of knowledge and teaching.

Mercury Bhukti: Mercury (education), the ruler of the fourth house (educational institutions, home) is placed in the twelfth house (distant places) from Venus (dasha ruler). This is the reason that he moved out of the area to teach in a distant place. Mercury is also placed in the third drekkana of Aquarius, symbolized by a man wearing a crown (a leader, teacher), with hair on his ears (the organ of learning). He is moving from place to place carrying a pot filled with iron, gum, skin, fruits, bark, oil and leaves (changing his residence due to his work).

Dashamsha Chart: Venus is placed in the first house of the Dashamsha chart. Planets placed in the first house of a divisional chart give prominent events (often new beginnings) in the domain of life indicated by the divisional chart. In this case he began an illustrious career as a teacher. Venus is placed in Scorpio, a sign related to math and science. Mercury (karaka for the intellect and education) is placed in the twelfth house where it receives the aspect of Mars from Aries. As ruler of the eighth house, placed in the twelfth house, Mercury is involved in Vipareeta Raja Yoga, a combination which lifts a person up after pushing through problems. In this case, Mercury's placement in the twelfth house is related to the tremendous upheaval, change, and uncertainty related to the change of residence (to a distant place) that was necessary to take the job. The mutual aspect of Mars (Dashamsha lagna lord) and Mercury connected the job to mathematics.

Transit: Jupiter was transiting Cancer in 1588, casting its aspect on Venus. It was passing through the fifth house (education) from Venus (dasha ruler) and in a conjunction with natal Jupiter. When a planet transits over its own natal position, it usually reflects a new beginning with respect to the planet's significations.

In December of 1592 (Sun dasha/Saturn bhukti) Galileo obtained the Chair in Mathematics at the University of Padua. This was a six-year contract which included a substantial raise in salary.

Sun Dasha: The Sun (authority and karaka for career) is placed in the eighth house (change) in the Rashi chart showing a change in the career.

Saturn Bhukti: Saturn is placed in the first house of the Rashi chart in a conjunction with exalted Jupiter. This placement has been discussed earlier. Saturn represents management, authority figures, and administrative activities. Jupiter represents teaching. The combination produced the chairmanship of the math department. It is noteworthy that this event took place in Sun/Saturn. Normally, this period is predisposed towards a fall from power or status, especially when Saturn and the Sun are in a 6/8 relationship with each other as they are here. In this case, however, Saturn is in conjunction with an exalted Jupiter which is placed in the first house. Jupiter in the first house makes the person a leader. When Saturn is conjunct or aspected by Jupiter, its period usually produces the fruits and full manifestation of whatever Jupiter promises. Jupiter's period gives a hope or aspiration, but Saturn makes it happen.

Dashamsha Chart: The Sun is placed in the tenth house (career) in its own sign. When a planet is placed in the tenth house (the primary house) of the Dashamsha chart, its period produces prominent results in the person's career. The placement of the Sun in its own sign shows that the event was positive. Since both the Sun and Leo are related to leadership, he received a leadership position in his work. Saturn (bhukti ruler) is placed in the eighth house (change) of the Dashamsha chart, producing a change in his career. Since Saturn also rules the Dashamsha fourth house (place of work), its placement in the eighth house also changed his place of work.

Using degrees in the Dashamsha chart, the Sun is placed in Magha, a nakshatra symbolized by a throne room. Galileo obtained the "chair" in mathematics! The Dashamsha drekkana position of the Sun is also relevant. The Sun is placed in the first drekkana of Leo in the Dashamsha chart, which is symbolized by a man who is leaving his home and family behind. The Sun is not only the karaka for the career, but also the ruler of the Dashamsha tenth house, placed in the tenth house. Its placement in the first drekkana of Leo gives a general tendency to change the residence for the purpose of the job. During the period of the Sun this tendency fructified. The new job required Galileo to change his residence to Padua.

Transit: In December of 1592, Jupiter was in a conjunction with Venus. These two teacher-planets (Brihaspati and Shukra) were transiting the sixth house (employment) from the Ascendant, and the eleventh house (gains) from the Sun. From this position, Jupiter also cast its fifth house aspect on the Moon (lagna lord) which is placed in the tenth house (career).

Saturn (bhukti lord) was transiting Cancer, triggering the natal Jupiter-Saturn conjunction. Saturn was also aspecting the Moon in the tenth house (career). When a house receives the combined transiting aspect of both Jupiter and Saturn, positive events fructify in that house.

In 1599 (Moon dasha/Jupiter bhukti) Galileo got a new contract that raised his salary and was retroactive to December of 1598.

Moon Dasha: The Moon is placed in the tenth house (career). This is an obvious period which emphasizes prominent career results.

Jupiter Bhukti: Jupiter and the Moon are involved in Gaja Kesari Yoga, a combination which gives recognition, reputation, and prosperity. Jupiter is also in Hamsa Yoga, which raised his professional status during its sub-period. Jupiter is placed in the fourth house (education) from the Moon.

Dashamsha Chart: Jupiter is placed in the second house (money) from the Moon (dasha ruler). Using degrees in the Dashamsha chart, Jupiter is placed in Punarvasu, a nakshatra with the shakti of creating prosperity. It is conjoined with Saturn, ruler of the ninth house (wealth) from the Moon. This creates a Dhana Yoga relative to the Moon. Since the conjoining planet is Saturn, the effects were delayed until the second half of the period. It is interesting to note that the raise was retroactive, so that the salary increase covered most of the Jupiter sub-period.

Transit: Jupiter was transiting Cancer over his natal Jupiter, again triggering a new cycle of teaching activity. This is the same transit which triggered his first real important job in 1588. Cancer is also the fourth house (education) from the Moon.

In the fall of 1609 (Mars dasha/Mercury bhukti) there was a tremendous boost in Galileo's career. He began a series of telescope observations which, over the next three months, became the foundations for an important book, Sidereus Nuncius.

Mars Dasha: Mars is the tenth lord (career) and the yogakaraka (ruler of an angle and trinal house) for a Cancer Ascendant. It is placed in the eleventh house (achievement), which makes the period likely to produce success.

Mercury Bhukti: Mercury is placed in the eighth house (scientific research) and in the tenth house (career) from Mars, indicating career success, through scientific discoveries.

Dashamsha Chart: Mars is the ruler of the Dashamsha lagna, placed in its own sign, Aries, and mutually aspecting the sub-period ruler. Planets which are in mutual aspect in a divisional chart tend to bring prominent events related to the domain of the divisional chart. As mentioned previously, Mercury is involved in Vipareeta Raja Yoga in the Dashamsha chart, contributing to the rise in Galileo's career. The mutual aspect of Mars and Mercury also brought mathematical and scientific tendencies. Using degrees in the Dashamsha chart, Mercury is placed in Swati, a nakshatra whose desire is to "roam freely throughout the universe," making the Mercury bhukti a natural time for observations through a telescope.

Transit: Mars was transiting Virgo in the third house (investigation, information, communication). From this position it aspects the tenth house (Aries, its own sign).

In March of 1610 (Mars dasha/Ketu bhukti) Sidereus Nuncius *was published. This book instantly made Galileo a European celebrity, and earned him a position as the "Mathematician and Philosopher" to the Grand Duke of Tuscany. He was also given a position as the sixth member of the prestigious Accademia dei Lincei.*

Mars Dasha: Mars is placed in the eleventh house (impact on the masses). It is also placed in the constellation of Rohini. In mythology, Rohini was the favorite wife of the Moon. In the story, all of the Moon's wives were desperate to get the Moon's attention because he was so dazzled by Rohini's beauty and creativity. During this period, Galileo became the center of attention in high circles of society and royal courts. Rohini is a creative nakshatra. Mars' (technical and scientific matters) placement in this nakshatra enabled him to write a book on a scientific subject.

Ketu Bhukti: Ketu is similar to Mars in astrology, yet it has a higher, more refined and abstract quality. Mars represents technical matters, but Ketu represents esoteric, cutting-edge technologies. Ketu signifies the etheric plane as well as the vertical direction and things above one's head. In this respect, the fact that Galileo's book dealt with heavenly bodies and esoteric principles of astronomy and mathematics is clearly reflected in Ketu's natural significations. Ketu is placed in Gemini (written and oral communications) in the third house (communications) from the Moon.

Dashamsha Chart: Mars' disposition in the Dashamsha chart was discussed in the previous section. Ketu is placed in the ninth house (a trinal house) from Mars, indicating positive results during the period. Ketu gives the results of its dispositor, Jupiter. Relative to Mars, Jupiter is the ruler of the ninth house (knowledge, publishing, teaching) placed in the third house (writing, communicating), a combination for writing and publishing. Since the ninth and third houses are both travel houses, the same combination also suggested long-distance travel, as well as long-distance communications. Jupiter is placed in the eighth house (research) of the Dashamsha and is involved in Guru Chandala Yoga, a combination that produced unconventional and revolutionary ideas.

Using degrees in the Dashamsha chart, Jupiter (Ketu's dispositor) is placed in Punarvasu nakshatra. The deity of Punarvasu is Aditi, the mother of all the gods. In Sanskrit, Aditi means "primordial vastness," referring to the unbounded space that had to be present first before all of the gods could manifest. Her name is literally related to outer space, the heavenly firmament. Galileo's groundbreaking book, *Sidereus Nuncius*, was a treatise describing many of his astronomical observations.

The use of degrees in divisional charts can also be extended to drekkana positions. In this case, Ketu is placed in the second house (education) in the Dashamsha chart and is in the first drekkana of Sagittarius. This drekkana is symbolized by a man with a bow who lives in a hermitage and protects the ascetics and the articles used for the rituals. This may also be used to symbolically describe Galileo's rise to the position of Mathematician and Philosopher to the Grand Duke as well as his position in the Accademia dei Lincei. Used symbolically, the halls of science are like a hermitage and these prestigious positions gave Galileo a protective role in insuring that the sacred science rituals would reveal the truth.

Transit: Mars (dasha ruler) was still transiting Virgo as was discussed previously during the Mercury bhukti. Ketu (bhukti ruler) was transiting Capricorn where it was in a conjunction with transiting Saturn. Together these two planets were transiting the tenth house (career) from the Moon. Ketu gives the results of the planet that it conjuncts. In this case it gave the results of a powerful Saturn, the tenth ruler of the tenth house from the Moon. Jupiter was transiting Gemini across natal Ketu, clearly producing positive transit support for the bhukti ruler.

In December of 1610 (Mars dasha/Venus bhukti) Galileo made observations of Venus and demonstrated that Venus goes through phases, confirming the Copernican theory that Venus transits around the Sun.

Mars Dasha: Discussed in earlier examples.

Venus Bhukti: First, the obvious relationship of Venus (bhukti ruler) to Galileo's ground-breaking observations of the planet Venus is startling. Venus is Mars' dispositor, and is exalted in the eleventh house (society, the masses, successes, achievements) from Mars. During this period he enjoyed great acclaim and acceptance among high society, royal courts, and in Rome.

Dashamsha Chart: Mars' position in the Dashamsha chart has already been discussed. Venus is placed in the first house of the Dashamsha chart, suggesting new projects in the career connected with Venus.

Transits: In December of 1610, Mars (dasha lord) was transiting the tenth house (career) in its own sign, Aries. It was conjunct the Moon (lagna lord). Venus (bhukti lord) was transiting Capricorn in the tenth house (career) from the Moon. From this position, Venus also aspects the Ascendant. Jupiter was transiting Cancer. This transit was discussed in previous examples, and it is the third time that Jupiter's return to Cancer triggered prominent career events.

In December of 1614 (Rahu dasha/Rahu bhukti) a Dominican friar, Niccolo Lorini, began preaching against Galileo in Padua. This began a series of attacks which Galileo had to defend throughout the Rahu period. In 1615 (still Rahu/Rahu) Lorini filed a written complaint against Galileo.

Rahu Dasha: The onset of a new planetary period initiated a new phase in Galileo's life. Previous to this period, Galileo enjoyed the full benefit of positive planetary cycles. He began his career in the Venus major period. Venus is exalted in the ninth house. The following period was that of the Sun, which is the karaka for career and is placed in its own sign in the Dashamsha chart. During the Moon's period, he enjoyed benefits derived from the Moon's status as lagna lord, nicely placed in the tenth house. Mars, the yogakaraka, gave him his biggest boost, conferring fame and prosperity. Rahu, on the other hand, is the first badly placed planet in the dasha sequence. It is placed in the sixth house (enemies, struggle, and diseases) and is aspected by Mars. In this case, Mars' status as a natural malefic trumps its status as yogakaraka. Although it still helped him to progress in his career, Mars' warrior qualities aggravated Rahu's (the serpent) tendency towards backbiting and fighting. During the entire Mahadasha, Galileo had to continually watch his back and fend off his enemies. Rahu is placed in Purva Ashadha, a nakshatra symbolized by a winnowing basket (which separates wheat from the chaff). This nakshatra is associated with judgment, indicating that he was judged by his enemies (sixth house placement of Rahu).

Dashamsha Chart: Rahu is placed in the eighth house, a dusthana house related to power struggles and conflicts. It is also in a conjunction with Saturn, reinforcing the negative placement and bringing censure. Rahu's conjunction with Jupiter is particularly interesting. The conjunction of Rahu and Jupiter is called Guru Chandala Yoga, which is said to make the person "a heretic or outcast." In this case Galileo was literally branded as a heretic by the fanatical monk. Using degrees in the Dashamsha chart, Rahu is placed in Mrigashira nakshatra. One of the characteristics of this nakshatra is intense inquisitiveness along with a tendency to initially disbelieve what is said until proof is presented. It is interesting that this challenge by the monk ultimately led to Galileo being subjected to the Inquisition.

Transits: In December of 1614, Rahu was transiting Pisces in a close conjunction with transiting Saturn. Together these two planets transited the ninth house (the church, priests) moving across natal Venus. Venus in mythology was Shukra, the guru or priest to the demons. Rahu was a demon, who cursed the Sun and the Moon, so Rahu is associated with curses. Saturn is also associated with curses in mythology. The affliction of such a powerful Venus by transiting Rahu and Saturn, in the ninth house (religion), clearly reflects a "curse" on Galileo by a high member of the clergy. A curse is nothing more than ill will directed towards another person. In this case, the Dominican friar followed through on his ill will by continuing to discredit Galileo. Transiting debilitated Mars (tenth lord) was also retrograde in Cancer (lagna) during this period.

In January of 1621 (Rahu dasha/Mercury bhukti) Galileo was elected Consul of the Academia Florintino.

Rahu Dasha: Rahu's (dasha ruler) capacity to also give some positive results during its period comes via the aspect of Mars (yogakaraka).

Mercury Bhutki: Mercury's (bhukti ruler) role has been discussed earlier. Mercury's sub-periods have consistently produced positive career results. Relative to Rahu, Mercury rules the tenth house, giving it the potential to continue its positive results during the Rahu dasha.

Dashamsha Chart: In the Dashamsha chart, Mercury is placed in the fifth house (a trinal house) from Rahu showing positive career results.

Transits: In January of 1621, Rahu was in Scorpio, transiting the fifth house (academics, education, and a trinal house) in a conjunction with transiting Venus. Venus' role in producing high achievements and academic glory has been discussed previously. In the previous example, Rahu and Saturn, two malefics, afflicted natal Venus. In this case, Rahu simply benefits by the conjunction of a single transiting benefic planet. This transit also took place in the tenth house (career) from the Sun.

In April of 1633 (Jupiter dasha/Saturn bhukti) Galileo was formally threatened with torture and was interrogated by the Inquisition. He was put under house arrest. A plea bargain was struck, and he pled guilty to a lesser charge. He was given a sentence of imprisonment by house arrest.

Jupiter Dasha/Saturn Bhukti: The conjunction of Jupiter and Saturn has been discussed earlier. In the previous examples, periods of Saturn gave good results, allowing the positive and hopeful results of Jupiter to fructify. This is because Jupiter is good for Saturn. Saturn, on the other hand, is bad for Jupiter, holding it back and constraining Jupiter's capacity to give positive results. Since this was the dasha of Jupiter, Saturn's bhukti acted to negate Jupiter's expansive energy, so the effects were primarily negative. Saturn is also the ruler of the eighth house, giving it the potential to create significant upheavals and changes during the period.

It is also important to note that Jupiter is involved in Gaja Kesari Yoga, a combination which can give a person reputation and fame. In this case, due to the influence of Saturn, it gave ill fame. This is what happens when Gaja Kesari Yoga is associated with Saturn. The person's fame fluctuates, sometimes giving negative reputation during sub-periods of Saturn.

Dashamsha Chart: The conjunction of Saturn and Jupiter is repeated in the Dashamsha chart. When a conjunction of planets takes place in a divisional chart, it produces prominent results in the domain of that chart. The positive or negative quality of the events can be described by the positive or negative disposition of the planets involved in the conjunction. In this case, Jupiter and Saturn are placed in the eighth house (a dusthana) with Rahu, a natural malefic, symbolizing extremely negative events related to the career. Using degrees in the Dashamsha chart, the placement of Saturn (sub-period ruler) in Mrigashira (searching, challenging) explains the Inquisition. It is noteworthy that the initial challenges to Galileo came during the Rahu bhukti, but fructified with the threat of torture and house arrest by the Inquisition during the Saturn bhukti. Rahu and Saturn are both in Mrigashira, reflecting a negative investigation into Galileo's work.

Transits: Jupiter was transiting Taurus and the eleventh house (the group, society, successes) but was in opposition to transiting Saturn which was in Scorpio. This transiting opposition further emphasized the resistance of his community and the fall in his career. It is noteworthy that Rahu (the serpent, curses) was again transiting the ninth house (priests, clergy) moving across natal Venus. Again Rahu was with another malefic planet, Mars, indicating the aggressive actions against Galileo by the clergy. This is the same Rahu transit that took place in 1614 at the time that he was denounced by Niccolo Norini. This time, Rahu finished the job.

On January 8, 1642 (Jupiter dasha/Moon bhukti) Galileo died.

Longevity is a complex subject, and it is not the purpose of this chapter to discuss the role of Jupiter and the Moon in producing death. It is interesting however, that Jupiter and the Moon are involved in Gaja Kesari Yoga, a combination which confers high reputation and fame. They are angular in the chart, indicating prominent results. The fact that Galileo died during this period clearly shows that his reputation and fame continued after his death. Even the circumstances around the death itself (dying under house arrest), became a highly recognized historical event.

The Author's Journal:
The Copper Plate Man

Once I was sitting with Swami Sivanandamurthy in his living room. I was telling him about the Brighu reading that I had received from the Karoi Pundit.

Swamiji said, "Yes, India is a land of so many divination techniques. Everything is here." He paused for a moment and then said, "And then there is the copper plate reader."

"Copper plate reader?" I asked, with a smile on my face and my curiosity peaked.

"Yes," Swamiji said. "I have a disciple, the Vice President of India, who went to see this man in Orissa who reads copper plates. The plates are blank. Then when you ask your question your answer appears on one of the blank plates in Sanskrit."

"Your're joking," I said. This was too much of a stretch for my Western mind to believe. But the man who was telling me this was Swami Sivanandamurthy. I asked him to continue.

He said, "Yes, the Vice President went to see the copper plate man back when he was the governor of Andhra Pradesh. The copper plate man predicted that he would become the Vice President suddenly and unexpectedly. That is just how it happened. The Vice President wasn't even a contender for the position. A sudden turn of events at the last minute gave him the appointment."

"Interesting," I said. "I would like to go see this copper plate man. How do I find him?"

Swamiji told me that the Vice President was the one who knew the whereabouts of the copper plate man and he assured me that he would ask him next time he came to visit.

A few years and a couple of visits to Swamiji's ashram went by. I was sitting with Swamiji one afternoon when the phone rang. Swamiji answered it, had a brief conversation with the caller and hung up. "You are going to get your wish," he announced. "The Vice President's secretary will be coming to visit tomorrow. He will tell you how to find the copper plate man."

Swamiji introduced me to the Vice President's secretary, Mr Tiwari, as "James Kelleher, a great astrologer from the USA." I found this comment both comical and embarrassing considering that it is actually Swami Sivanandamurthy who was the only one in the room who could rightly be called "a great astrologer." His deep astrological knowledge and profound intuition had been demonstrated to me on many occasions. A little embarrassed, I greeted Mr. Tiwari and then asked him about the copper plate reader. Mr Tiwari told me that the copper plate man lived outside of Bhubaneshwara, and that his entire family had consulted this man. He graciously offered to call his brother, the former Minister of Tourism of the state of Orissa, and arrange for him to take me to get a reading. I accepted.

Later, when Swamiji was out of the room, Mr. Tiwari asked me to look at his chart and make some predictions. I declined. I told him that as long as I was at Swamiji's ashram, I didn't feel comfortable doing readings for people. I felt that Swamiji was the real authority and the one to ask. I offered to do a reading for him back in Delhi, however, at a later time.

Mr. Tiwari took me up on my offer and when I returned to Delhi, he invited me to dinner. It is common in India that astrologers "sing for their supper." Rather than showing respect through paying a fee, as is customary in the United States, Indians frequently give the astrologer fruits, flowers, or other offerings like hospitality and a meal. For this reason, I have never charged a fee in India. Mr. Tiwari's driver picked me up at eight p.m. and drove me to his residence near the government section of Delhi. The car pulled up through an iron gate and around a circular driveway in front of a huge, white, lighted mansion. The Vice President's mansion had beautiful gardens and a low-keyed stately appearance. Mr. Tiwari's home was next door. I did his chart, answered his questions, and then we had a fabulous dinner, prepared by Mrs. Tiwari.

"Can you tell me more about the copper plate man?" I asked.

"Yes," he said. "He comes from a 500 year-old line of pundits who are devotees of Swami Achyutananda, a saint who lived several hundred years ago. The story is that the first pundit had a dream in which he was instructed to go to a certain place and find a stack of copper plates. When he awoke from the dream, he followed the instructions and actually found a stack of blank copper plates. The dream also instructed him on how to use the plates to give readings. Apparently the pundit took one disciple of his own and passed the copper plates to him at the time of his death. This tradition has been carried down for the past 500 years. When you go for a reading, the pundit asks you to think of your question. Then the answer appears on one of the plates in an ancient dialect of Sanskrit. He reads you the answer. All this is supposed to occur courtesy of the spiritual blessings of Swami Achyutananda."

I was fascinated by Mr. Tiwari's description of the copper plate man and asked him if he could give me directions to find him.

"Of course," Mr. Tiwari said. He immediately picked up the phone and placed a call to his brother in Bhubaneshwara, a large city in Orissa. His brother, the former Minister of Tourism for the state of Orissa, agreed to take me to meet the copper plate man.

I couldn't believe the devastation, as I looked out the window of the car on my way to see the copper plate man. Only six weeks had passed since the state of Orissa had been hit by a devastating tropical storm. Tens of thousands of lives had been lost as the 150 mph winds flattened forests of coconut trees and eradicated entire villages. The pundit's village is located two hours from Bhubaneshwara, Orissa's largest city. The village was one of the hardest hit by the tropical storm. I was wondering if the pundit had survived. Mr. Tiwari had arranged for me to meet his brother, who in turn arranged to have his son take me to see the pundit.

The pundit's village looked like a war zone. Most of the grass huts and other mud houses were gone. The road was now clear, but rubble and snapped trees lined either side. We made our way off the main road and through a maze of small dirt roads, asking people for directions as we went. Everywhere people were busy cleaning up and rebuilding their roofless, three-walled, broken homes. As we slowly moved down the narrow dirt road to the pundit's house, I was not optimistic. Although there was a chance that he had survived, it was likely that he would be occupied with the reconstruction of his home. "We have arrived," the driver said, as we pulled up to the only undamaged house in the whole neighborhood.

'Incredible,' I thought. 'Whoever Swami Achyutananda is, he sure takes care of his disciples!'

When we arrived, the pundit was just returning from the river where he was taking his bath. He was bare-chested, and wore an ankle-length, white, cotton cloth wrapped around his waist. He told us to meet him later at the Mangala Temple and that he would give me a reading.

The area where the pundit does the readings is pure rural India. He sits in a little hut next to the Mangala Temple. People come from all over and wait in line, sometimes all day, in order to see him. I was already a vegetarian, but I was told that on the day of the reading, the questioner must not eat meat, fish, or eggs. Also, being a westerner, I was asked to change my clothes and put on a dhoti, the traditional white cloth of a Hindu, before entering the hut. Seeing my lack of appropriate attire, a local villager offered to lend me his extra dhoti, which was drying on a bush. As he helped me tie it properly, I couldn't help but notice that he seemed mesmerized by me. Finally, he asked, "European?"

"No, American," I said.

"I have never seen an American," the man said. At that moment, I became aware that as far as this man was concerned, I might as well be from outer space. I was in a part of rural India that had not changed much in the past 500 years.

As I entered the hut, the pundit bowed to me and we both sat down cross-legged on the floor. He showed me the stack of copper plates, which looked like thin copper rulers in a stack, like a deck of cards. He asked me to think of my questions. I had previously thought of four questions. Since I did not have any burning questions at that time, I had struggled a bit to come up with my questions. I decided to ask three very ordinary questions. I also decided to ask a question for my wife. I decided that she might like finding out how a particular investment might do. I had no particular emotional charge on any of these questions. There was one question, however, that I did not want to ask. It was about my wife's health. She had been getting dizzy spells that year and I was a little worried. She had not yet consulted a physician about it and I didn't want to ask the pundit, on the off chance that he might make a dramatic negative prediction.

The pundit showed me the copper plates and encouraged me to look at them closely, using a magnifying glass. Seeing that I was satisfied that they were indeed blank, the pundit began, "Think of your question and separate the copper plates using this piece of chalk," he said in the local language.

The interpreter translated and I thought of my questions, trying to block the one about my wife's health out of my mind. I knew that the idea was that the answer would appear on the copper plates somehow. What I didn't know, however, is that the questions would also appear on the plate. I took the piece of chalk and separated the stack of plates, selecting a single plate. The pundit showed me the plate, which miraculously now had finely etched Sanskrit script on it. He began to read, "You have four questions. One is about your business, one is about your health, one is an academic question and the fourth question is about your wife. But about the wife there are two questions, one is about her business and the other is about her health!"

I was flabbergasted. Not only had the pundit zeroed in on my exact questions, but he had included the one question that I had an emotional charge on, the one question that I did not want to ask. He then went on to give very brief, but accurate answers to the other questions. When he got to the one about my wife's health, however, he went into great detail, describing the symptoms exactly and even referring to an ayurvedic text which he had written on palm leaves, sitting next to him on the table. The copper plate suggested ayurvedic herbs and even gave recommended doses.

I never got to try out the herbs, because my wife's health actually improved on its own a few months later. The copper plate reading had its effect, however. It reminded me that India is a mysterious place, and allowed me to enter into a time warp, and experience a slice of what getting a reading in ancient India might have been like hundreds of years ago. Later, over dinner at his home, Mr. Tiwari's brother also told me of the many astounding predictions made for him in the past by the copper plate reader. "Yes, yes," he said in almost the same words as Swami Sivanandamurthy, "India has so many divination methods. Everything can be found here!"

Chapter Ten

Money

"One wishing for prosperity should not dwell in a place devoid of a good astrologer. For he is the Eye, and no sin will creep in where he stays."— Brihat Samhita, Chapter 2

As with other areas of life, the horoscope reflects the karmas related to money and material prosperity. On one level it shows the likely areas in which a person might make or lose money. It also shows psychological patterns that either contribute to or hinder the sense of prosperity. One person becomes wealthy, yet always feels he is poor. Another person may have limited means, yet always feels that he has more than enough. In some cases, a sense of limitation in the financial area of life might even inhibit a person from making an attempt to improve his or her financial condition. The chart can also show the relative level of financial success the person is likely to achieve, as well as the probable times of gain or loss. In this way, the chart has the potential to become both a means to understand and enhance one's financial potential, and also as a method for promoting equanimity in the face of one of life's greatest attachments.

Indicators of Money

Jupiter, the Karaka for Money

Any study of finances in the chart begins with Jupiter's disposition. A strong Jupiter immediately gives the person an edge with money. A weak Jupiter makes prosperity more difficult. Jupiter is also a key planet for showing the person's psychological programming around money and prosperity, as well as the likely area in which "fortune" or prosperity can be located.

Money Houses

The houses of money are the second, eleventh, ninth and fifth. The second house is the house of money as a source of sustenance. The eleventh house is the house of gains and the multiplier house. It is also the second from the tenth house (career) so it shows money through one's career. The ninth house is the house of overall wealth and general abundance. The fifth house is a house of past good karma, general luck, and is associated with wealth through investments in the stock market and other areas which involve some degree of risk. The fifth house is also the ninth house from the ninth house so it is another house of general wealth.

Rulers of Money Houses

The rulers of the money houses (second, eleventh, ninth, and fifth) are planets that indicate financial gain. Their position and connections in the chart give clues to sources of wealth and periods of financial improvement.

Yoga Point

The yoga point in a horoscope is a generally beneficial point that can be used effectively for predicting positive events, including financial gain. It is calculated by adding the longitude of the Moon to that of the Sun, and then adding the resulting sum to 93 degrees 20 minutes. The resulting point in the horoscope is called the yoga point, which is a prosperity point in the chart.

Yogi and Duplicate Yogi

The yoga point will fall in a particular nakshatra and sign. The planetary ruler of the nakshatra is called the yogi and the ruler of the sign is called the duplicate yogi. These are both planets that promote prosperity.

Avayogi

The avayoga point is determined by adding 186 degrees degrees 40 minutes to the yoga point. The avayogi is the nakshatra ruler of the constellation occupied by the avayoga point and is a planet that promotes expenditure, financial losses or poverty.

How To Use the Yogi, DuplicateYogi, and Avayogi

Although it has other uses, in financial astrology the yogi is a planet of prosperity. If it is well-placed in angles or trines, or if it is associated with other money planets, then it will produce wealth. If, on the other hand, it is badly placed in dusthana houses, is weak or afflicted, then it can produce the opposite result. The idea is that the yogi should be strong and supported to give good results. The duplicate yogi can be treated as another yogi, so it is interpreted in the same way.

Similarly, the yoga point and the nakshatra in which it falls becomes a point of prosperity within the chart. Planets that fall in this nakshatra tend to prosper. For example, having Jupiter, the natural significator of prosperity, placed in the yoga point nakshatra will significantly augment Jupiter's tendency to give wealth.

The avayogi is a planet of financial problems. If it is strong, well placed and supported, then it promotes financial hardship. If it is weak and afflicted then it promotes financial gains.

The Source of Wealth

The placements of Jupiter, the rulers of the money houses, the yogi, duplicate yogi and yogi point indicate potential sources of wealth in the chart. If two or more of these indicators combine in a particular house, then that house becomes more inclined to produce wealth though the areas it signifies. The following is an interpretation of the sources of prosperity when Jupiter and/or other money indicators are placed in the twelve houses.

First House: This gives general prosperity. The person may benefit from positions of authority, or by the use of the personality. He may have independent means and be self-reliant regarding money.

Second House: The person can gain through speaking, teaching, buying and selling, food, financial markets, or other second house indications. Money planets here also produce a yoga for financial gains which tend to manifest in the periods or sub-periods of the money planets.

Third House: There may be benefits through short journeys, errand-like activities, communications, or siblings. Jupiter's placement here seems to be quite a good placement for money, due to the aspect of Jupiter on the eleventh house (gains) and the ninth house (abundance). Since the third house is an upachaya house, the person tends to improve his prosperity level gradually over time.

Fourth House: The person may gain through property, houses, real estate, family, education, foundations, or the spouse's profession. Money indicators here also cause the person to relate to money as an important element of security in life.

Fifth House: This produces gains through writing, publishing, creativity, children, teaching, sports, or the stock market. This is a good position for prosperity, indicating powerful "positive karma" coming from past lives, which promotes wealth in this life. Money planets here produce a yoga for financial gains that may fructify in the dashas or bhuktis of the money planets.

Sixth House: The person may gain through healing work, service to others, or through a job in the employment of others. This is a house of struggle; it suggests that hard work may be necessary in order to achieve prosperity. It is also an upachaya house, suggesting the possibility of improvement in the prosperity level as time goes on.

Seventh House: The person may gain through the spouse, partnership, clients, legal matters, contracts, or other people in general. Here, and in the eighth house as well, Jupiter and other money indicators bring money from outside sources. In other words, the person tends to develop profitable relationships.

Eighth House: The person may gain through all of the things listed in the seventh house. He might also benefit through therapies, astrology, occult, the spouse's income, insurance, and inheritance.

Ninth House: This produces gains through the father, travel, higher education, teachers, religion, or some other dharmic activities. This also gives the person a generous and expansive spirit and a natural sense of abundance. It is a good placement for overall prosperity and wealth. Money planets placed here produce a yoga for financial gains that produces its results in the periods or sub-periods of those planets.

Tenth House: The person might gain through the career. This is a good placement for financial gains through the profession. There might also be gains connected with the government.

Eleventh House: The person might gain through friends, networking, marketing, group activities, social causes, humanitarian work or other activities that impact the masses. This is an excellent placement for overall wealth. The eleventh house is a house that multiplies and amplifies what it influences. Jupiter placed here tends to make it easy to achieve desired goals and magnifies the prosperity level.

Twelfth House: The person might gain through long-distance travel, distant places, foreign countries, institutions, charities, or retreats. This is a more difficult placement for achieving prosperity because the twelfth house is a house of expenditure, loss, and uncertainty. Jupiter and other money planets placed here frequently cause expenditure, and often make the person feel that their financial future is uncertain. Nevertheless, many people with money planets here do thrive through the things related to the twelfth house.

The Source of Wealth - A Key to Investing

When a chart has two or more key money planets combining in a particular house, then the person will tend to prosper according to the significations of that house. This works on the same principle listed previously, denoting Jupiter placed in various houses. If the ruler of the second house and the ruler of the ninth house combine in the fourth house, for example, the person could profit through real estate (a fourth house signification). Taken together, the rulers of the second, eleventh, ninth and fifth, along with the planets Jupiter and Venus, give very practical information that can be used to find intelligent sources for investment. A few applications of this principle are given below.

Some Typical Investment Styles

Real Estate: A strong fourth house and money combinations located in or aspecting the fourth house. The eighth house is important here, because getting loans from banks is also important in real estate.

Stock Market: A strong fifth house and money combinations influencing the fifth house. If the eighth house is particularly strong as well, then one might benefit by taking the advice of a broker. If the eleventh and the eighth houses are strong, then mutual funds might be particularly beneficial.

Bonds: The eighth house strong and influenced by money planets.

International or Overseas Investments: The fifth house strong and well-aspected, and the twelfth house strong and influenced by money combinations.

Collectibles: The second house and the indicator for the particular type of collectible must be strong and influenced by money combinations. For example, if the person is collecting art, then Venus must be strong. If he is collecting firearms, then Mars must be strong.

In all of the above cases, it is important to remember that no single house is capable of giving prosperity. Prosperity is usually the outcome of several complementary influences. The first house, for example, must be strong enough to give the physical health, vitality, personality and ego strength with which to pursue and claim the potentials for wealth suggested in the other areas of the chart. Similarly, the Moon as the indicator of the mind, must be in a good situation. For first-rate prosperity, the Ascendant, the Moon and Jupiter must be strong, and there must be some powerful yogas or combinations for money as well.

Positive Combinations for Money

When the money planets listed previously combine with each other, the lagna lord, or with Jupiter, the financial results are usually favorable in a more pronounced way. This is more pronounced when the combinations fall in angles (houses 1, 4, 7, and 10), trines (houses 1, 5, and 9), or in the second or eleventh houses. Similarly, the rulers of the second, eleventh, ninth, and fifth placed in each other's houses promote prosperity.

Combinations for Loss of Money

Combinations or links between the money planets (or the houses they rule) and the twelfth house (loss) or its lord, usually show expenditure. Similar combinations between money planets and the sixth house or its lord may indicate debts, struggles or disagreements with money. Money planets connected to the eighth house suggest upheavals and changes with money. It is important to note, however, that each of these combinations has a positive potential as well. A money planet in the twelfth house, for example, can bring money from distant places or foreign countries. In the sixth house, the same planet might bring income through service, employment, or a health profession. In the eighth house, inheritance, insurance, clients, contracts or other eighth house matters become possible sources of financial benefit. Whether these combinations produce gains or losses is determined by the relative strength and nature of the planets involved. However, aspects by malefics render these combinations more likely to produce financial problems.

Jupiter and Venus

Money planets (the yogi, duplicate yogi, and the rulers of the second, eleventh, ninth, and fifth houses) conjunct or aspected by Jupiter or Venus usually promote prosperity. On the other hand, if a money planet is connected with Saturn, Mars, Rahu, or Ketu, it may signify expenses and other financial problems, especially if two or more of these malefics influence the money planet. Malefics frequently promote ambition, however, so in some cases they can actually promote material gains. Saturn in the second house or conjunct the second lord, for example, may promote a hard-working attitude towards money, which may give slow and steady gains. Much depends on whether the malefic planet is a temporal benefic or malefic (see "Table of Temporal Benefics and Malefics" given in *Path of Light, Volume I*). By the same token, even multiple influences on money planets or houses by natural malefics can sometimes signify financial gains. If the person makes his money through technology, for example, it is common to see multiple malefic influences on a money planet or house. This is because the natural malefics, Mars, Saturn, Rahu and Ketu, are also technical planets. When they combine in the chart, they frequently bring a technical connection.

Psychological Patterns Regarding Money

Before making predictions of financial gain or loss, the astrologer must first assess the overall psychological makeup of the client's horoscope. This process begins with an overall analysis of the lagna, the Sun, Moon, the lagna lord, Jupiter, the yogi and the rulers of the second and eleventh houses. The disposition of these focal points, as well as the characteristics of the signs and nakshatras of their placement should be considered carefully before making predictions. In addition to this, planets placed in the second house will give important keys to the person's psychology of finance. Similarly, the house placement and planetary combinations of the second lord will also reveal financial attitudes.
In addition to these general indications the following combinations may provide clues to the person's psychology related to money.

The Sun in the second house or conjunct its lord: The person will identify with money and prosperity. This means that if the financial situation is good, the person will be proud of his prosperity, resulting in high self-esteem. If the financial situation is difficult, it will contribute to low self-esteem. Normally, this drives the person to invest a great deal of time and energy in becoming prosperous, and is a generally good placement for acquiring wealth. Having one's self-esteem tied to financial success, however, presents an obvious philosophical dilemma. The slightest hiccup in the person's financial condition can radically undermine his self-image. On the highest level, the Sun located here shows that the pursuit of money can be a tremendous vehicle for helping the person transcend his limited ego-identification with wealth in the process of finding unbounded awareness and ultimate freedom. Constantly asking the question, "Who am I?" when feeling proud or humble financially, can be a good technique for facilitating this process.

The Moon in the second house or conjunct its lord: The person will seek money as a means to security. He may also have changeable attitudes towards money. If financial matters go well, the person will feel happy and secure. If finances falter, he will feel insecure and worried. The tendency to be attached to money and the comforts it provides can give the person powerful, unconscious drives towards creating prosperity and wealth. The same attachment can also bring mental anguish when affluence and comfort is not available. This position offers fertile ground for examining the roots of security and happiness. Whether rich or poor, the person with the Moon in this position is challenged to discover real security within.

Mars aspecting or conjunct Jupiter, money houses, or their lords: The person may have a strong desire to have money, but may also have a strong desire to spend it. Mars sometimes brings expenses. The person may also get into disagreements or arguments about money. On the positive side, the ambition and energy of Mars can contribute to significant financial gains in many cases. A key to working with these influences is to learn to emphasize the ambitious side of Mars while moderating the desire to spend.

Jupiter strong and unobstructed: This shows a natural sense of abundance. The person usually does not worry about money, feeling that abundance is part of his birthright. This attitude helps him gravitate toward prosperity. The sense of financial security will be greater if Jupiter falls in one of the money houses or in the angles. It is also more pronounced if Jupiter conjuncts or aspects the Moon, the Sun, or the ruler of the Ascendant.

Jupiter weak or afflicted: This suggests a sense of lack, inhibition, worry, or other negative mental states regarding money. The person tends to be conservative in regard to financial decisions and may be thrifty.

Venus conjunct or aspecting Jupiter, money houses, or their lords: Venus is a natural benefic so it usually enhances the sense of prosperity and gives the person the ability to create affluence and comfort. The person sometimes tends to purchase only the finest quality items and derives great pleasure from the things money can buy. Sometimes, however, this leads to self-indulgent expenditure on expensive things. The person sometimes has an inner feeling he should be prosperous, so even if he isn't wealthy himself, he will be attracted toward other people who are prosperous.

Saturn aspecting or conjunct Jupiter, money houses, or their lords: The person feels a need to work hard for money and may have many delays, blocks, responsibilities, or pressures regarding finances. The financial situation might have big ups and downs periodically. The person may have the tendency to worry about money, even if he or she earns well. On the positive side, this same influence of Saturn teaches patience and perseverance, which can be a key to overcoming the frustrations sometimes associated with these combinations. It also favors a long-term, step-by-step approach to gaining wealth.

Rahu conjunct Jupiter, money houses or their lords: The person might be compulsive or even fearful about money. Sometimes this just gives him an overwhelming drive to earn well. He might like to gamble or take financial risks, and may lose money as a result. He might have unconventional attitudes towards money or earn through unconventional means. In some cases, there can be an unrealistic sense that some unexpected event, such as winning the lottery, might bring big gains. The person also tends to get overextended financially. On the positive side, this aspect gives the person innovative and unconventional ways of making money. He sometimes uses technology in the process of making an income. Frequently these combinations give a positive expectancy that "anything can happen" with money, and sometimes the person actually experiences unexpected gains.

Ketu conjunct Jupiter, money houses or their lords: This sometimes causes a constant sense of fear, uneasiness or uncertainty regarding finances. The person might also feel that it is hard to hold on to money. On the other hand, this combination is also seen in the charts of many wealthy individuals who use the intuition of Ketu to enhance their ability to make investments. If other aspects in the chart agree, then the "easy come, easy go" attitude which is sometimes produced by these combinations, helps the entrepreneur or speculator retain his peace of mind in the midst of dynamic ups and downs with money. These combinations can also produce an attitude of selflessness, charity and detachment with money. The person feels that money is not the main point of his life and develops a "day at a time" approach to making money. In this way, money becomes a vehicle for growth of awareness and spiritual development.

Indu Lagna

Indu Lagna is an important lagna that is used specifically for determining profits and losses. It is calculated in the following way:

Each of the planets is said to have a certain number of rays (Sun-30, Moon-16, Mars-6, Mercury-8, Jupiter-10, Venus-12, Saturn-1). To calculate Indu Lagna, take the number associated with the planet which rules the ninth house from the Ascendant and add it to the number of the planet which rules the ninth from the Moon. Divide the sum by 12. Take the remainder only and count that many signs from the Moon sign. The resulting sign is called Indu Lagna.

How To Use Indu Lagna

Indu Lagna is a focal point for financial matters. When the Indu Lagna falls in the second, eleventh, ninth or fifth houses, it is generally favorable for finances. Similarly, the first, fourth, seventh and tenth houses are good placements. When the Indu Lagna is placed in dusthanas (third, sixth, eighth, and twelfth houses), it can produce problems corresponding to the significations of that dusthana house. Money planets, the yogi or duplicate yogi placed in or aspecting the Indu Lagna promote general prosperity. The avayogi's influence here, on the other hand, promotes financial problems. A positive financial result is also realized when financial planets form Dhana Yogas using the Indu Lagna as the first house.

How To Determine the General Prosperity Level of a Horoscope

First find the Indu Lagna and notice where it is placed. Angles, trines, the second and the eleventh houses are preferable, but sometimes the eighth house can be a good house for money through inheritance or business. See if any planets are associated with Indu Lagna. For prosperity, it helps when a combination of money producing planets influence this lagna. The rulers of the second, eleventh, ninth, and fifth houses, as well as the yogi and duplicate yogi all support prosperity. The avayogi, and the rulers of the sixth, eighth, and twelfth houses are usually adverse for money.

Next, check the general disposition of the yogi and duplicate yogi. It is good if the yogi and duplicate yogi are both strong, and best if they are both strong and combine with each other by conjunction or mutual aspect. But if either the yogi or the duplicate yogi is strong and supported and the avayogi is weak or afflicted, then this still promotes wealth generally.

Of course, the natural significator for wealth is Jupiter. A weak and afflicted Jupiter suggests financial problems, while a strong Jupiter suggests general abundance.

Look for Dhana Yogas in the chart. These are combinations of financial increase and are produced when the rulers of the first, second, eleventh, ninth, and fifth houses combine in a sign or mutually aspect each other. Other positive money combinations are also produced when the ruler of one money house occupies another money house; for example, the ruler of the eleventh house, placed in the second house. If any of these placements combine with the yoga point, the yogi, duplicate yogi or Indu Lagna, then they are amplified.

Finally, check the Ascendant of the chart. It goes without saying that a strong Ascendant is usually important for the realization of financial gains. If the Ascendant happens to fall on the yoga point or in the yoga point's nakshatra, this promotes wealth. If the Ascendant is in a conjunction with the yogi, then it tends to produce steady wealth in life. The duplicate yogi conjunct the Ascendant also promotes wealth, while the avayogi brings a tendency to have financial problems.

Chart 1: George Harrison
February 24, 1943; 11:42 PM; Liverpool, England

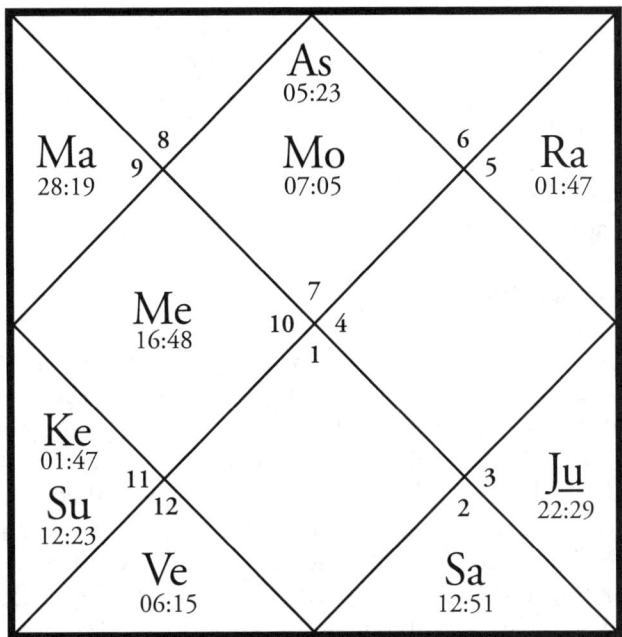

Assessing the General Level of Wealth

George Harrison's chart shows his high level wealth in the following ways. First, the Indu Lagna falls in the fourth house in the sign of Capricorn. Mercury (the yogi and ruler of the ninth house) is placed in the Indu Lagna. Jupiter, the significator of wealth is placed in the ninth house. The Sun, the ruler of the eleventh house, is placed in the fifth house and is aspected by Jupiter from the ninth house, as well as Saturn (yogakaraka and fifth house lord). These are powerful indications of wealth.

Timing

George Harrison's rise to fame took place in his Jupiter period that began in July of 1960. By 1962 the Beatles were on their way to international fame and fortune. Jupiter gave him great wealth for the following reasons. First, Jupiter is the natural significator of wealth. It is placed in the ninth house, the house of wealth and abundance, and is located in the constellation of Punarvasu. The basic shakti of Punarvasu is "the power to create prosperity." Jupiter is also in mutual aspect with the second house lord, Mars, and also aspects the Sun, the eleventh house lord, which is placed in the fifth house.

On the negative side, Jupiter is a temporal malefic for a Libra lagna. This chart clearly exemplifies how a planet can play two roles at the same time. On one hand, Jupiter's temporal status caused Harrison to have arguments and disagreements with his fellow Beatles, causing the ultimate break-up of the band before the Jupiter period ended. However, even as a temporal malefic, Jupiter was still capable of giving him prosperity according to its favorable placement in the chart.

Divisional Charts for Money

There are two divisional charts which are particularly useful for finances. The first is the Hora chart, which is a division of the sign by two. There are different methods to calculate this chart. The method used in this book is called *parivritti dwaya*, popularized by Iyer. In addition to the Hora chart, the Ekadashamsha chart, sometimes called the Labhamsha chart, is also quite useful for money. This chart is based on dividing each of the signs into 11 equal parts. In this book will we will use a standard or continuous method of calculation, instead of Iyer's method which leaves out the sign of Taurus.

Both the Hora and the Ekadashamsha charts are interpreted in the same manner. The important houses in these charts are the "money houses" (houses 2, 11, 9, and 5). The concept of Dhana Yogas (combinations which link the money houses) has been described earlier. When Dhana Yogas or other money combinations occur in either of the two divisional charts for money, they enhance the overall financial potential of the chart. The following guidelines will help in using the Hora and Ekadashamsha charts.

General Assessment of Wealth Using Divisional Charts

1. The placement of the ruler of the Ascendant from the Rashi chart in divisional charts for money is important. Placement in the money houses (houses 2, 11, 9, and 5) is best. Placement in houses 1, 4, 7, and 10 is good. Other indications of strength such as exaltation, own sign, and dig bala also contribute to overall prosperity. Placement of the lagna lord from the Rashi chart in a dusthana in the Hora or Ekadashamsha chart is detrimental to wealth. This is particularly true if the planet is also subject to other negative influences such as debilitation or aspects by malefics.

2. The placement of the lagna lord from either of the two divisional charts is an important factor. As in the previous point, this planet should be strong and supported in its own chart in order to enhance finances.
3. The placement (according to point 1.) of the money planets (from the Rashi chart) in the Hora or Ekadashamsha charts also contributes to the overall money situation.
4. The placement of the karaka for wealth (Jupiter) in the Hora and Ekadashamsha charts is also an important factor in the overall assessment of wealth.
5. The placement of the yogi (from the Rashi chart) in the Hora and Ekadashamsha chart is similarly important.

Period Rulers in the Hora and Ekadashamsha Charts

1. During the period of a planet that is strong and well-placed in the Hora or the Ekadashamsha charts, there will be good results for the person's finances. If the planet is weak, afflicted, and placed in dusthanas, there will be problems with money.
2. During the periods of planets involved in Dhana Yogas in the Hora or Ekadashamsha charts, there will be financial increase or improvement.
3. During the periods of planets that are involved in Neechabhanga Yoga (see the chapter on yogas) there will be initial problems with money which may lead to improvement later in the planet's period.
4. In the Hora or Ekadashamsha charts, the aspect or association of the period ruler with Jupiter or the yogi (from the Rashi chart) will greatly enhance the financial results during that planet's period.

Path of Light – The Domains of Life

Chart 2: From Riches to Rags
January 13, 1940; 5:52 PM; Minneapolis, MN

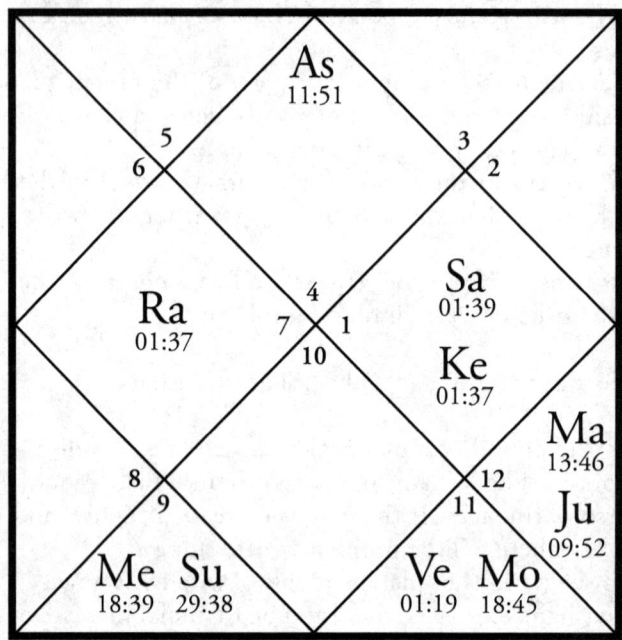

(D2) Hora

(D11) Ekadashamsha

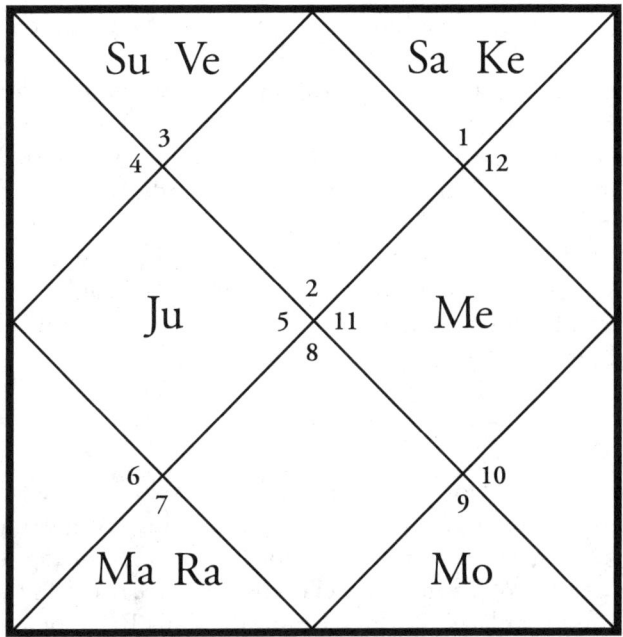

Assessing the General Level of Wealth

This is the chart of a man who built a successful business, sold it for millions of dollars, and then lost it all.

Rashi Chart: Indu Lagna falls in the sign of Scorpio in the fifth house. The fifth house is a favorable house, but Scorpio is a sign of upheaval and change. The Indu Lagna is also aspected by Jupiter, the yogi, which is placed in its own sign in the ninth house from the Ascendant (the house of wealth and prosperity), and is placed in the fifth house from the Indu Lagna. Jupiter is also conjunct Mars, the fifth lord and the yogakaraka for Cancer lagna. This produces a powerful Dhana Yoga. The lagna lord, Moon, and the eleventh house lord, Venus, are in a conjunction in the eighth house, which is both an important house of business and a house of fluctuations, upheavals and changes. The lagna lord is also conjunct the yoga point which falls at 21 degrees of Aquarius, again showing the probability of gains.

Divisional Charts: The lagna lord (Moon) from the Rashi chart is placed in a the fourth house (dig bala) in the Hora chart. In the Ekadashamsha chart the Moon is placed in the eighth house, showing upheavals and changes. It receives a beneficial aspect from Jupiter, however, which also contributes to wealth from outside sources. Jupiter is both the karaka for wealth and the yogi in this chart. It is well-placed in both divisional charts. In addition, the powerful Mars/Jupiter conjunction from the Rashi chart, is repeated in the Hora chart, where Mars becomes the ruler of the second house (a money house), placed in the fifth (another money house).

Summary: The position and strength of Jupiter, the yogi, as well as Jupiter's aspect on the Indu Lagna are strong indicators of a high level of wealth and prosperity. This is supported by the conjunction of the lagna lord with the yoga point, as well as the positions of key planets in the divisional charts. Yet the fact that the yoga point falls in the eighth house and the Indu Lagna falls in the eighth sign (Scorpio) shows fluctuations of fortune.

Timing

During Mercury's major period he built and sold a business, making him a multi-millionaire. Mercury is in Sagittarius, a sign ruled by Jupiter. This allows Mercury to trigger Jupiter's results during its period. Mercury is also involved in Vipareeta Raja Yoga because it is the ruler of the twelfth house, placed in the sixth house. This Raja Yoga made him successful in his career.

Divisional Charts: Although Mercury is placed in the twelfth house of the Hora chart, it is exalted. Relative to the Moon, it functions like a powerful ninth lord, contributing to wealth. The twelfth house placement, in this case, simply created natural uncertainties which arise in the process of building a business. In the Ekadashamsha chart, however, Mercury is powerfully placed in the tenth house, where it receives the aspect of Jupiter. These placements greatly enhance Mercury's financial potential.

During the Ketu period he lost everything and became homeless. There are two main conditions that contributed to this result. First, Ketu is a natural malefic and the significator of loss. Second, an important rule of interpretation for Ketu is that Ketu gives the results of the planet with which it is conjunct. In this case, Ketu is in a conjunction with Saturn. Saturn is the duplicate yogi. Normally the duplicate yogi would increase wealth. In this case, however, Saturn is debilitated and conjunct Ketu causing financial loss. He remained homeless until the end of the Ketu period. At the beginning of the Venus period he got a job and found a place to live.

Divisional charts: The conjunction of Ketu and Saturn in Aries is repeated in the Hora chart. This clearly shows that this combination was slated not only to produce career problems, due to the tenth house placement in the Rashi chart, but also to produce financial disaster. In this case the placement also shows the area in which the disaster occurred. Relative to the Moon, the conjunction is placed in the fourth house (real estate). His financial ruin was triggered by the purchase of a huge piece of real estate that drove him to bankruptcy. In the Ekadashamsha chart, the same Ketu/Saturn conjunction in Aries is placed in the twelfth house (losses), making the event hard to miss for even the novice jyotishi.

Author's Journal:

Teet Maharaja, Yogi of the Himalaya

Teet Maharaja
April 15, 1892; 11:55am; Calcutta, India

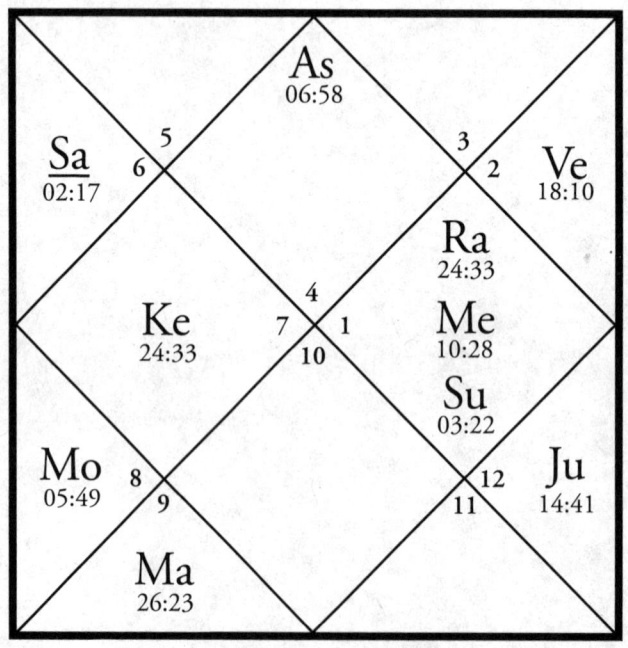

"Stop the car here!"
   Rajiv pulled the car off the road at the turnout.
   "Look at that!" I said.
   We both got out of the car and crossed the narrow mountain road to get a clearer view. In the distance we could see the six Himalayan peaks of the

Nanda Devi Range. Nanda Devi East, Nanda Devi Main, Panch Chuli, Trishul, Nanda Khat, and Nanda Khot rose high above the clouds at 24,000 feet. An accomplished climber, outdoorsman and longtime friend, Rajiv had climbed to the summit of two of these giants in 1991. His experience as a mountaineer, as well as his knowledge of many of the back roads and byways in the Himalayas, made him the perfect traveling companion for this excursion. We were traveling on a remote mountain road at six thousand feet, on our way to Jageshwar, a sacred pilgrimage site in the Himalayas. Jageshwar is one of the twelve Jyotirlingams, which are special places of worship for Lord Shiva. It is believed that the divine energy of Shiva, in the form of a lingam (phallic symbol) of light manifests on a subtle etheric level here. Rajiv had been suggesting that I visit Jageshwar for years. Standing there, taking in the majestic Himalayan ramparts, I was beginning to understand why Rajiv had been so impressed by the place.

Jageshwar itself is tiny. It consists of a handful of tea stalls and simple shops for basic provisions. It is a forested mountain village, which contains 124 ancient temples. Nestled next to a river and tall evergreen trees, the ancient temple complex dominates the village. The dark stone temples rise up amongst the forested backdrop to blend the awesome power of Shiva with the pristine beauty of Mother Nature in a perfect union of Shiva and Shakti.

After getting a room at the Government Rest House, Rajiv and I explored the temples. We were particularly interested in visiting the Mahamrityunjaya Temple, which is devoted to Shiva in his manifestation as "The Great Victor Over Death." This is the only such temple in all of India, and is reputed to be the site of many miraculous healings. We arranged to have a Mahamrityunjaya yagya performed the following day for one of my clients and spent a half-hour meditating inside the temple.

"Would you like to go see Teet Maharaja?" Rajiv asked as we walked out of the Mahamrityunjaya Temple.

"Of course," I said. I had met Teet Maharaja once before at the home of the King of Balrampur. He is the guru to the King and had come to visit once when I was staying at the King's summer palace. Born in 1892, at the age of four, his mother gave him to a gurukulam, a spiritual school run by a guru. At ten years of age he formally became a monk, renouncing all possessions and vowing to take only food that was offered to him in a prescribed manner. Taking the name, Swami Prakashanada, he began to study yoga, meditation, various aspects of Indian philosophy and Jyotish under the guidance of his guru. He lived for many years at high altitudes in the mountains, where he constantly practiced meditation, fasting and prayer. After spending the greater part of his youth in the Himalayas, he

finally came down to the foothills near Nainital where he spent many years meditating in a cave in the Teet Forest. In 1927, the British Government gave him the Teet Forest as well as the title, His Holiness, Maharaj of Teet. Over the years he came to be known as Teet Maharaja.

Maharaji's ashram is located about two kilometers from the Nainital temple complex. It is a simple place, with a single temple and a series of whitewashed adobe rooms to accommodate guests and students. As Rajiv and I walked up the path to the ashram, we could hear the exuberant voice of Maharaji in the distance. He seemed to be calling out instructions to one of the workers at the ashram. We entered the ashram grounds and could see him sitting in front of the temple, his golden robe and silver hair illuminated by the late afternoon sun. He sat cross-legged on a bed that had been placed outside a small temple. Seeing us, he shouted, "Welcome, welcome, you have come! Sit, Sit!"

We sat down on lawn chairs beside him. My first observation was that in mid November, at eight thousand feet in the Himalayas, I was freezing! I was wearing long underwear, a wool sweater, a fleece jacket and a gortex shell. Maharaji, on the other hand, sat there comfortably wearing nothing more than a thin flannel robe. 'Not bad for 110 years old!' I thought.

The remainder of the afternoon was spent in easy conversation with Maharaji. His eyes danced and his voice had a joyful tone, as he told us about his life and discussed an array of topics ranging from travel to Jyotish. When the conversation eventually gravitated to astrology I asked him, "Are you also an astrologer?"

"Oh yes, yes, I had to study all the spiritual sciences as a young man. I have also taught astrology to my students for many years."

My curiosity was now aroused, so I asked, "Would you be willing to look at my chart?"

"Oh yes, yes, no problem. Tell me your birthdate, time and place," he said.

I gave Maharaji the required information and he got out an antique, tattered almanac. Over the past century in India, the most common, quick method for astrologers to calculate a horoscope has been to use an almanac-ephemeris that includes hundreds of pre-calculated horoscopes, tables of rising signs and other quick reference tools. Maharaji flipped through the worn pages of his ancient book and quickly came up with my chart. He made some brief observations that were very accurate. After he was done, I asked him if I could look at his horoscope. He gave me his birth data and I calculated his chart on my pocket PC.

We spent the remainder of our two days in Jageshwar with Maharaji. Dur-

ing the whole time he was animated and full of life. At one point, I made a passing comment that in spite of my warm jacket I still felt cold and asked him how he managed to stay warm in his thin flannel robe. He immediately sprang to his feet and quickly walked halfway across the courtyard. "Sit!" he said in a commanding tone.

I sat cross-legged on the ground and watched him. He sat down on a straight-backed chair and put his legs in full lotus in one graceful motion. "Now breathe!" he shouted.

He started to demonstrate the breathing exercise he wanted me to do. "Hmmff, hmmff, hmmff, hmmff," he breathed vigorously expelling the air from his diaphragm in a pranayama technique which I knew to be called "the bellows."

I copied his breathing, "Hmmff, hmmff, hmmff."

"Do it properly!" he roared. With his eyes sparkling and an enthusiastic smile on his face, he continued to direct my breathing in this way for the next fifteen minutes.

"I once was stranded for three weeks in the mountains above Jyotir Math in the middle of winter," Maharaji explained, after we finished the pranayama. "There was a terrible storm, leaving me snowbound in my cave. No one could reach me to bring me food. I had to fast for three weeks in sub-zero weather, so I did six hours of this pranayama technique each day. I had no problem staying warm."

'Indeed,' I thought, 'Maharaji is truly a man who has mastered the various practices of yoga.' Through his years of austerity and rigorous spiritual practice, he has elevated his consciousness, and has extended his life span to an extraordinary length. At 110 years old, his appearance is that of a healthy man in his early seventies. I marveled at his vitality and radiant energy. 'What a great example of a yogi!' I thought. 'I better get with the pranayama!'

I got up off the ground and moved back to my chair. As I sat down, a man with his wife and son approached Maharaji. "Maharaji, my son is psychologically disturbed and needs your help," the man said.

Maharaji looked annoyed. "Not now. Go away," Maharaji said softly.

Disappointed, the man and his family moved across the courtyard to the other side of the ashram compound where they lingered for a while. Rajiv and I sat with Maharaji and continued our discussion. We asked Maharaji about his life as a Himalayan yogi and listened with great interest as he told us about walking the length and breadth of India on foot. "Because I am a yogi, I have lots of time," Mahariaji said with a grin. "I like to walk."

"Maharaji, Maharaji, we have to go now. You must help my son. He is crazy and needs to be healed!" The man and his family had returned for a second attempt at getting Maharaji's help. He was now pleading for Maharaji's intervention.

"Alright then!" Maharaji said with irritation, "Sit." The boy sat beside Maharaji on a folding chair. Maharaji looked at him for a few seconds and then said, "You had a fight!"

The man and his wife looked at each other nervously. Maharaji had obviously struck a nerve. After an awkward moment of silence, the woman spoke up, "No, no, Maharaji. It was actually the other man who stabbed my son and put him in the hospital."

"Don't tell me what happened! I know what happened!" Maharaji said in a commanding tone. "Lift your shirt," he said to the boy. Maharaji examined the wounds on the boy's torso. The boy pulled his shirt back on and Maharaji announced, "Alright, I have healed him, now go!"

As they were going, the boy's father squatted near Maharaji and offered him a large sum of money. Rajiv leaned over and whispered in my ear, "He is trying to bribe Maharaji! Maharaji has already healed the boy. The way he has offered this money is obviously a bribe of some sort!" Maharaji refused the money and ordered the man to leave.

After the family had left, Maharaji turned his attention once again to Rajiv and me. He told us what had just transpired. "This man and his wife conspired to murder one of their relatives," he said. "They got their son to commit the murder. In the process, the relative put up a struggle and the boy was injured. After the murder, the boy was arrested. His father bribed a local judge to let the boy off and also to see that the property of the dead relative was transferred into his name. The boy was being bothered by the ghost of the dead relative, so he seemed to be crazy." Maharaji added, "They commit a sin by killing their relative, then they want me to commit a sin by taking a bribe!"

Evening came and Maharaji went inside. Before he left, he made sure that Rajiv and I received dinner, some rice, dhal and chapattis. We ate and went back to Jageshwar, where we rested at the Government Rest House for a couple of hours. We planned to leave the next morning, so about 9:00 pm, we returned to the ashram to say goodbye. The forest was completely dark as we walked up the path to the ashram, flashlights in hand. A faint light could be seen in the hut of Maharaji's cook and another in Maharaji's hut. We arrived at Maharaji's door and Rajiv knocked as he simultaneously called Maharaji's name.

"Yes, yes, come in, welcome, sit down," Maharaji's voice had its usual joyous, musical tone. We entered the room and found Maharaji sitting cross-legged on the floor. In the middle of the concrete floor was a small fire, framed in by adobe bricks, which smoked up the entire room and vented through the open window. Maharaji sat there next to the fire, wrapped in a wool blanket. He was a picture perfect Himalayan yogi, sitting in his hut in the mountains, except for one detail. On the floor, in front of Maharaji was a Dell laptop computer. I almost laughed out loud at the contrast and innocence of this East meets West scene.

"What are you doing Maharaji?" I said with a comical grin on my face. As I got closer I could see that he was playing solitaire on the computer.

"Yes, yes, sit, sit, you are welcome. I received this gift from one of my students from America. I am playing this game. You know, I am a yogi from the Himalayas. I have lots of time."

The next day, Rajiv and I returned to Nainital. As we wound down the mountain road we stopped again at the vista point to take pictures of the Himalayas. It was a nippy, clear morning and Nanda Devi and the other peaks stood high against the mountainous horizon. We stood there in silence for a few minutes, taking in the awesome sight of these Himalayan giants. I thought about Maharaji, as a young yogi, surviving for three weeks in his snowed-in cave by doing constant pranayama. I said a silent prayer, a salutation to these highest of all mountains, which have produced yogis and saints for thousands of years. "Shall we go?" Rajiv asked as he started to move towards the car, "We have about a six-hour drive back to Nainital."

"Don't worry, don't worry," I said in my best imitation of Maharaji's Indian accent, "We are yogis from the Himalayas, we have lots of time!"

Chapter Eleven

Relationships and Marriage

The desire to give and receive love in partnership with another person is one of the most fundamental human urges. The horoscope can be used to attain insight into the many facets of a person's relationship experience. First, it shows the fundamental patterns of the individual's relationship psychology. It can also reveal many details about the type of partner one might attract. It is not uncommon for a competent Vedic astrologer to describe the psychology, profession, and even the financial prospects of the husband, simply by looking at the chart of the wife. The chart can also give clues concerning places one might find romance or even marriage. And of course, Vedic astrology has some great techniques for predicting the time of marriage and relationships.

The Lagna (Rising Sign)

Each rising sign has its own idiosyncrasies and tendencies in romance. Someone with Gemini rising, for example, may be talkative, playful, sexual and somewhat fickle. A Scorpio lagna, on the other hand, might be passionate, fall deeply in and out of love at the drop of a hat, keep many things secret, and be jealous and possessive. Knowing the basic tendencies of the lagna, as well as the Sun and Moon signs, is the first step in understanding the relationships in the horoscope. These tendencies are described in *Path of Light, Volume I*, in the chapter about the astrological signs.

Venus, the Planet of Love and Sexuality

Venus represents affection, love, pleasure and sex, so it is naturally the main indicator of marriage and relationship. The placement of Venus and its general disposition in the chart will give insights into the individual's emotional nature, his ability to give and receive love, and his ability to attract a loving and fulfilling relationship. If Venus is well-placed and strong, then the person will have an easy time giving and receiving affection and warmth. He will easily attract a loving and beautiful partner and will feel fulfilled in marriage or relationship. If, on the other hand, Venus is weak and poorly placed in the chart, the person will have problems attracting and/or maintaining a loving relationship. Of course, Venus is not the only factor to consider in this regard. Actually, it is one of several factors. It is an important factor, however, and should not be overlooked. In order to learn how to determine if Venus is weak or strong, see the section on strength and weakness of planets earlier in *Path of Light, Volume I*.

Venus in the Twelve Signs

Venus operates differently in each sign. The following is a brief description of the particular style of emotional expression when Venus is placed in each of the astrological signs. In the chart of a female, the characteristics below will be displayed in her own personality. In male charts, the qualities listed may reflect his own emotional nature, but to some extent, may also be seen as qualities in the female he chooses as a partner.

Aries: The Aries Venus is passionate, assertive, aggressive, competitive in love, impulsive, adventuresome, self-centered, and enthusiastic. A woman with this placement might be assertive emotionally or sexually. She may be willing to ask the man out on a date, for example. She may also be the one who initiates sexual relations. Men with this placement may be naturally drawn to this kind of passionate, assertive woman.

Taurus: With Venus in Taurus, the person displays lasting affection. She is constant, loyal and loves deeply. She is very sensual and her sense of touch is especially sensitive. She places a good deal of importance on the affluence or material comfort produced by the relationship. In a man's chart this often brings a beautiful wife, or sometimes a wife with a beautiful voice. In a woman's chart it suggests a desire to find material comfort and prosperity through marriage.

Gemini: For the Venus in Gemini person, communications are an important element of relationships. She likes change, variety, and gets tired of emotional or sexual routines easily. She is very sexual, sensual, and playful, but can also be somewhat fickle. Humor and charm are valued as important elements of the romantic exchange. Men with Venus in Gemini may attract beautiful, cheerful, talkative, charming, or intelligent partners. Women with Venus here seek husbands or boyfriends with whom they can communicate. In both cases, if Saturn aspects Venus here, it brings much sexual passion and sensuality.

Cancer: With Venus in Cancer, the person is sensitive. As a result, her feelings can be easily hurt. She seeks relationship and marriage in order to provide both emotional and financial security. She may also look to relationships for emotional support. She can also give support and nurturing to others. Being sentimental, moods can sometimes fluctuate and be unpredictable. Men with this placement may look to their wives for maternal nurturing. Women with Venus in Cancer may seek partners who can provide them with security, home and family.

Leo: People with Venus in Leo are passionate, very sexual, and somewhat dramatic emotionally. They are outgoing, loyal, and like to be the center of attention in their relationships. They are very warm-hearted, proud of their partners, but can also be possessive or jealous. The typical Leo-Venus person needs lots of attention and praise, and can sometimes be self-centered or selfish. A man with Venus in this position usually looks for a physically attractive, sometimes vain woman, who might have a dramatic, somewhat flashy style. In a woman's chart this placement causes a tendency for her to focus on her beauty, clothes, and personality style. It may make her a bit of a princess or prima donna as well.

Virgo: Venus is debilitated in Virgo, unless the debilitation is canceled (see the section on neecha bhanga for the conditions of cancellation of debility in this volume). People who have Venus placed in Virgo tend to channel their emotions through the intellect. They analyze and evaluate their emotions. They strive to understand rather than feel their emotions. As a result they sometimes have difficulty accessing their real feelings. They can be critical of their partners, and may seek partners who are intellectually stimulating, critical, or analytical. Men with this placement often attract intellectual, mental, or pragmatic women as partners. Women with Venus in Virgo may express much of their femininity in a mental or verbal way. In both cases this can be a very sexual and passionate placement, especially if Saturn also aspects Venus.

If Venus is in the condition known as neecha bhanga (debilitation canceled) then the person might have initial difficulties with emotional fulfillment due to having an excessively mental emotional style. This usually ends up working to his advantage. This is a good placement for a marriage and family counselor, who benefits by the ability to analyze and understand emotional relationships. By the same token, the neecha bhanga Venus can give an ability to understand emotions and relationships even if the person doesn't become a psychologist.

Libra: When Venus is in Libra, the person is loving, warm, sensitive, charming, stylish, and partnership-oriented. She will be good at harmonizing and love companionship. This placement of Venus usually makes the person considerate, empathetic, and flexible. Naturally diplomatic and fair, the person seeks a relationship for the aesthetic style and refinement it contributes to life. Libras dislike gross behavior, seeking mental stimulation as well as sensuality. Both men and women with this position of Venus usually seek beautiful partners with refined manners and style. They do not like arguments or anything that disrupts the harmony of the relationship.

Scorpio: The person with Venus in Scorpio will be passionate, sensual, jealous, secretive, and sometimes calculating. He will take romantic involvements very seriously and usually go through many ups and downs in romance. He will usually have a good deal of sexual power and charisma. He can fall in love intensely and easily. The typical Scorpio person can also be controlling or manipulative. Women who have Venus in Scorpio may use their charm, femininity and sexuality to influence or even manipulate their partners. They may also seek a wealthy partner. Men with this placement may tend to attract dominant, manipulative or controlling wives or girlfriends.

Venus in Scorpio has a deeply spiritual side, however. Scorpio is the sign of both passion and metamorphosis. Here, Venus gives the capacity for a deep and passionate emotional connection. Relationships may go through difficulties, but they also have great potential for regeneration. In its best light, the Scorpio Venus causes a person to look at his relationship as a vehicle for deep inner transformation and self-knowledge.

Sagittarius: When Venus is in Sagittarius, the person expresses emotions frankly and honestly. He will seek a spiritual or purposeful approach to marriage and relationship. He will be socially outgoing and warm.

He will have conventional moral and sexual attitudes. He will also seek a spouse or partner within his/her own religious or social group. Men with this placement may seek a prosperous, well-educated or physically tall wife. Women with Venus here may seek marriage as a way of giving purpose and meaning to life.

Capricorn: The person with Venus in Capricorn will be emotionally reserved, repressed, or inhibited. He makes a stable and steady partner because he tends to be emotionally patient. He can sometimes be harsh or unfeeling. He dislikes emotional outbursts and is drawn to hard-working or successful partners. He is dignified, proud, and uses relationship as a means to achieve status. He tends to marry late. The Capricorn-Venus person is also emotionally responsible, and works hard at relationship. He can sometimes lapse into stagnant emotional and sexual routines. He desires commitment, and understands that relationships require compromise. Men who have this position often seek women who are career-oriented. Women with Venus in Capricorn sometimes marry for position or money rather than romantic love. If Venus is placed in the twelfth house, or is idealized in other ways (such as conjunct Ketu), then this placement may give the person the capacity to blend the responsible and committed qualities of Saturn with unconditional love and devotion. In any case, this position of Venus makes the person passionate as a result of a deep need for affection and warmth, which underlies the emotional reserve reflected by the placement.

Aquarius: When Venus is in Aquarius, the person will be emotionally independent, warm, but somewhat impersonal. She will be spontaneous, seeking intellectual stimulation through emotional relationships. She might also have unconventional relationships. She needs her lover to also be a friend. She will be open to all sorts of people, and sometimes she can have unconventional sexual attitudes, liking excitement and stimulation emotionally and sexually. She dislikes being controlled or manipulated and seeks emotional freedom. Men with this placement sometimes seek brilliant or creative women. Women with Venus in Aquarius can be impulsive free spirits, who sometimes feel confined in marriage or committed relationships. Sometimes the person with Venus in Aquarius holds tenaciously to an inner ideal of perfect love, which they continue to seek throughout life. This can lead them into chronic dissatisfaction with their real-world partners, who never seem to measure up to their ideal standards. On the other hand, it sometimes leads them to a realization of universal, impersonal love which gives them emotional stability and fulfillment.

Pisces: In Pisces, Venus is exalted. This causes the person to have a romantic nature. Being selfless and idealistic, she will marry for love. She is highly emotional, inspirational, and falls deeply in love. She is also subject to romantic illusion, sometimes seeing what she wants to see in a partner, rather than what is actually there. The Pisces-Venus person is compassionate, sympathetic, and sensitive. Men who have this placement seek beautiful, sensitive women who are romantics, artists, or compassionate healers. Women with Venus here are usually in love with being in love, seeking the deepest and most profound kind of romantic partnership.

Venus with Other Planets

Venus can also combine with other planets in various ways. Understanding these combinations can give important insights into emotional patterns that often make or break a relationship. The following is a description of some of the more common Venus combinations.

Venus Conjunct the Sun: When Venus is with the Sun it tends to magnify the creative, loving and affectionate side of Venus in the personality. The partner may be charming, creative or physically beautiful. As long as these planets do not fall within four degrees of each other, the relationship or marriage may be affectionate, with occasional arguments.

Venus Combust: If Venus is placed within four degrees of the Sun, its rays are blotted out by the Sun's brilliance. This condition is called combustion. Venus combust is supposed to render the planet weak. In actual practice, the planet's qualities will be strong in the personality of the person. Venus combust, for example, will produce a personality that is charming, fun loving and creative. It frequently produces a beautiful, creative, or charming spouse as well. These are not signs of weakness. The problem with the combustion of Venus seems to be in the person's ability to enjoy the pleasures provided by Venus. For example, he might, have a beautiful wife, but also work so hard at his job that it overshadows the enjoyment of the marriage. In combination with other negative factors in the chart, however, a combust Venus can also deny marriage. The key to understanding the effect of Venus' combustion on marriage is to remember that by itself it is usually not bad for all aspects of marriage, only the sense of ultimate fulfillment and pleasure in the marriage.

Moon Conjunct Venus: When the Moon is with Venus the person's nature is very loving and affectionate. This combination gives a sensual and passionate nature. This is especially true for women, and it is also seen when Venus falls in the fourth, seventh or tenth houses from the Moon. The partner or spouse may have a youthful appearance and have qualities like the sign of Cancer, such as sensitivity and the ability to nurture. There may be a close personal intimacy with the partner as well. On the other hand, Venus and the Moon together is sometimes associated with fickleness, emotional neediness, or other lunar problems on the part of the person or the spouse.

Mars Conjunct Venus: When Mars and Venus are in the same sign they are conjunct by Vedic standards. This usually signifies passion, with an emphasis on the physical aspect of sexuality. Usually this means that the person is inclined to become involved romantically due to initial physical attraction. They do not always make wise decisions in romance as a result. Since sexual passion and romantic magic are such an emphasis, relationships often only last as long as the sexual interest lasts. If the partner becomes disinterested in sex, the person with the conjunction feels very frustrated. For this reason, this combination is not usually associated with long-lasting relationships, and it becomes important for people with this combination to find partners who can match their level and style of sexual interest.

There are many exceptions to this, however. Passion can be channeled in different directions. In many cases, the passion released by this conjunction is not channeled into sexuality, but into some other area of life, usually associated with the house in which the conjunction is placed. In the third house, for example, it may give a passion for music. In the second house, it may bring a passionate way of speaking or a great love of food. In the first house, it may give a passion (or great love) for one's self. In most cases, however, it does indicate intense sexual drives. A similar result takes place when Mars and Venus mutually aspect each other, as well as when Venus and Mars exchange signs (Parivartana Yoga).

Those who have the Mars-Venus conjunction in their charts have a "passionate wiring." They are usually not very well suited to be celibate monks or nuns. Recognizing the need for a healthy sexual relationship is part of tuning in to this combination. Taking care to choose a partner who can share the sexual aspect of life with a similar intensity is one of their keys to relational harmony. It can also be helpful if they choose a partner who shares their passion for the matters signified by the house in which the placement is located. For example, if Mars and Venus are conjunct in the twelfth house, the person might enjoy having a partner who loves to travel or who is spiritually inclined. It is equally necessary for those with this conjunction to practice being aware of the role that strong desires play in their romantic perceptions. Mars-Venus people don't always think with their heads when it comes to romance. Their deep need to experience passion sometimes takes on an urgency that may cause them to shelve their better judgment or even to disregard the feelings of their partners.

Mercury Conjunct Venus: When Mercury is conjunct Venus, it makes the person charming. It also gives them a good ability to convey affection and warmth verbally. It causes the person to place a good deal of emphasis on communications in relationship. They like sharing and communicating with their partners. Sometimes their partners will have a mercurial nature, with Mercury, Virgo, or Gemini prominent in the their horoscope.

Jupiter Conjunct or Aspecting Venus: When Jupiter and Venus combine, there is usually support, prosperity, affluence and comfort associated with relationship. In general, Jupiter helps to promote the financial aspects of relationship and marriage. It expands the opportunities for relationships to occur and also provides solutions to problems that come up within existing relationships. This conjunction, especially, may indicate marriage to a wealthy person or prosperity that comes after marriage. These effects, as with all planetary combinations, are greatly modified by the particular sign and placement of the planets. If Jupiter is a functional malefic, it can also create struggles and problems in marriage. In such cases, however, Jupiter does not lose its natural benefic qualities completely, and continues to give opportunities and support through the relationship.

Venus Conjunct or Aspected by Saturn: These are combinations of emotional inhibition. Saturn restricts Venus' natural capacity to give and receive love. Those with Saturn influencing Venus, especially in the case of the conjunction, feel hesitant to express their deepest and most intimate emotions. They are sometimes emotionally reserved and rather undemonstrative with affection. They can still be socially gregarious, however, and are usually very passionate on the sexual level. Perhaps this comes from a deep need for love and affection brought on by the combination. Saturn-Venus people usually have an easier time with the physical aspect of sex than with opening the heart and expressing love. It is equally difficult for them to believe that they are truly loved by others. In the case of the conjunction, there is usually a tendency to form long-lasting relationships or marriages. Sometimes these relationships stagnate, becoming routine and tedious. This conjunction frequently causes a person to stay in a marriage or relationship past the point when it is serving them. Those with Saturn influencing Venus usually feel that they are not really worthy of being loved. As a result they sometimes feel that if they let go of a marriage or relationship they will not find another. Sometimes they can trace this feeling to early childhood experiences in the home. In some cases there may have been an absent, harsh, or demanding parent, usually the father.

It is important to remember, however, that the emotional inhibitions, doubts and fears produced by Saturn-Venus combinations are not really produced by early childhood experiences. Childhood is simply the first place where the emotional pattern is experienced. These emotional patterns are actually the result of karmic impressions incurred in previous births. For this reason, delving into the experiences and traumas of childhood and trying to heal parental relationships is only a small part of working with Saturn-Venus problems. Clearly understanding the nature of Saturn and playing by its rules seems to allow the person to transform his emotional experience.

Saturn, on its positive side, represents strength, structure, responsibility, patience, and perseverance. If Saturn is afflicting any planet, then it is issuing a challenge to take personal responsibility for strengthening the significations of that planet. In the case of a Saturn-Venus combination, we are challenged to make personal efforts to open up the heart. Instead of waiting for the magic moments when we spontaneously feel warmth and affection for others, Saturn demands that we practice and consciously exercise expressing love. Instead of blaming our lack of emotional fulfillment on bad luck, an unaffectionate spouse or a harsh parent, we are challenged to realize that love is something we can create within ourselves.

Hence, it becomes necessary to practice opening the heart, much the same as a musician practices an instrument. This is a good analogy because this same combination is seen in the charts of musicians and artists as well. Once the musician learns all of the techniques, scales, arpeggios and other fundamentals, only then can music flow spontaneously. Saturn is structure and discipline; Venus is art and love. With a little effort, Saturn's influence gives us the capacity to actualize any Venus value (art or love), bringing it out of the realm of inspiration and into the real world. Most people want the experience of opening the heart, to be spontaneous. In fact, it is a popular notion that love and affection are artificial if one has to make an effort to express these feelings. With the Saturn-Venus combination, however, deliberate effort is always necessary.

At first the Saturn-Venus person feels very awkward as he confronts his fear in his attempt to break through his emotional ice. He plans in advance to give a hug to a friend, compliment or praise his wife, or to tell his mother that he really loves her. His regular attempts to give love and affection seem stiff and formal at first, causing much discomfort. With repetition, however, the discomfort, awkwardness and lack of spontaneity eventually subside and the real emotional strength of this combination begins to emerge. Instead of having to wait for the emotional mood to strike in order to express affection, the Saturn-Venus person learns to simply "turn on" affection and warmth at will. Instead of waiting for people in his environment to push his emotional buttons in just the right way, he becomes emotionally self-sufficient, able to love anyone, anytime. Like an accomplished musician who has thoroughly practiced the fundamentals of his instrument, he starts to transcend the mechanical emotional techniques and begins to make real heart-music.

Rahu Conjunct Venus: Rahu is a planet of change and innovation. Combined with Venus it tends to stimulate Venus' sensual side and increases the need for excitement. This combination can bring a sense of urgency or even compulsiveness in relationships or marriage. It stimulates the creative and impulsive sides of Venus and adds an impulsive quality to relationships. These tendencies have obvious problematic implications for long-term committed relationships. One way to work with this energy is to consciously create plenty of variety and change in the various aspects of the relationship.

This combination can also simply indicate anguish. Sometimes a person feels that he does not deserve the kind of treatment or the kind of suffering that he experiences in relationship. Rahu often gives a feeling that events and experiences in relationships are happening from the outside, undeserved and uncontrollable. It frequently gives the person the feeling of not having a choice, which is usually a mirage, rooted in a deep attachment to the relationship. If the person lets go of his sense of urgency about the relationship, the possibility of creating a better situation in the relationship will usually emerge.

One idiosyncrasy of this combination is marriage or partnership to a person from a different background, possibly from a foreign country. Sometimes the spouse has a dark complexion. Rahu likes separateness. A difference in backgrounds brings a type of natural distance between a couple which can offset some of Rahu's more difficult qualities.

Rahu is a planet of independence. Conjunct Venus or placed in the seventh house, it suggests a tendency for relationship to bring the person toward independence. This might mean divorce in the case of an afflicted Rahu. In many cases it gives rather benign periods of separation from the partner. The person's partner, for example, might travel for a living. In any case, it is important to recognize that Rahu's association with either Venus or the seventh house indicates a need for distance in relationship. Since Rahu is also a rather compulsive planet, it is also common for people with this combination to feel a sense of urgency about being in a relationship. Sometimes the compulsive or excessive desire to have a good relationship is the very thing that causes separation. This makes it more difficult to find a balanced approach to creating "healthy distance" in the relationship.

Nevertheless, many people with these combinations have satisfying and happy relationships. Usually, they use distance as a way to recharge their emotional batteries. Sometimes they choose partners who are very different or unconventional. Sometimes the partner travels or the couple takes separate vacations. Other times, they simply make their marriage different or unconventional in some way. The basic idea is that in order to survive, the Rahu marriage should allow the person plenty of individual freedom.

Ketu Conjunct Venus: Ketu is the planet of moksha, liberation and detachment. It is a highly spiritualized influence. Conjunct Venus or in the seventh house, it suggests a spiritual approach to relationships. The person is often disappointed with the material expectations of the relationship. The person learns to let go of expectations and conditions as a result. In its best form, this combination indicates a spiritually-oriented partnership, usually having some unconventional quality. Those with Ketu conjunct Venus usually have a very idealized inner picture of the perfect partner. This picture is nearly impossible to fulfill. Whether they know it or not, they are looking for moksha or spiritual liberation, through marriage or relationship. Of course, the partner who tries to fill this need, unless he or she is a true saint, will probably fall short of the expectation.

This combination is seen in the charts of people who have trouble with commitment in relationship. It makes the relationship difficult to pin down and secure. This is usually because Ketu sometimes brings an inner sense of being let down by loved ones. The person doubts the dependability of love. Sometimes there is an early family experience in which a parent or other family member has fallen short of the person's expectations. This pattern actually goes back much further than childhood, however, and is rooted in past lives.

Along with the tendency to doubt love, this combination brings high expectations of love. This is an obvious contradiction in terms, but it is exactly the reason that those with Venus conjunct Ketu find it difficult to find total fulfillment in love. They are looking for the highest spiritual experience through relationship, yet relationships always fall short of delivering what they seek. Like a monk who renounces the world and goes off to a cave to meditate, the Ketu-Venus person eventually realizes that what he seeks is impossible to find in the material world. He gives up, lets go, and renounces the attachment to romance.

At this point, those who have this conjunction in their natal charts are faced with choosing one of two options. Either they renounce relationships altogether, or they simply renounce the expectations and conditions of the romanticized approach to relationships. If they choose to go the second route, then the task is to create a spiritualized, unattached, selfless and unconditionally loving relationship.

Taking this route, many Ketu-Venus people have succeeded in creating very happy relationships. These are people who learned to let go of their impossible expectations, doubts, and fears in relationships. They take the relationship or marriage a day at a time. Sometimes they opt to not get married, but to simply live with their partner. They feel no need to spend all of their time with their partner, enjoying solitude as much as they enjoy partnership.

Among those who have this combination and manage to succeed in their relationships, are many meditators. Ketu is the planet of meditation, the ultimate detachment. Influencing Venus or the seventh house, it creates an intimate link between relationship and meditation. This means that if Ketu has produced disappointment and depression due to a romantic loss, meditation is the medicine to heal the emotional wound. In a way, we can say that Ketu produces its emotional disappointments in order to motivate us to meditate. Looking at this idea in another way, those who have this combination and who also meditate are more likely to tune-in to their relationships in a way that Ketu supports. Ketu-Venus people are well advised to practice regular meditation in order to enhance the positive side of the relationship experience.

Regular meditation, a detached attitude, and frequent periods of solitude, can actually be good strategies for Ketu-Venus people wishing to preserve their relationships. The key seems to be to let go of expectations and even to release the idea that the partner will be there tomorrow. The willingness to let go seems to work in favor of preserving the relationship, rather than losing it. If you let go of what Ketu touches, it usually has no need to take it away from you. If you hold on to the thing Ketu touches, it takes it away or makes it a source of disappointment.

Other Important Placements of Venus

Venus in the Seventh House: Venus is the planet of love. The seventh house is the house of relationship. Simple logic would suggest that Venus would give great results with this placement. In reality, however, this does not manifest. In Vedic astrology the karaka (natural significator) of a house does not do well in its own house. A natural significator of a house is the planet that naturally rules the same domain as the house. The karaka is different than the ruler of a house, which is the planet ruling the sign in that house. Venus is said to give some problems for relationships in the seventh house.

In practice, Venus in the seventh seems to give a deep desire for sensuality, passion and romance in relationship. This Venus placement indicates a very loving and affectionate spouse, and in many cases it is actually the spouse, rather than the individual, who is in search of passion and romance. But there is usually a lack of balance between the partners in the area of affection, with one partner feeling that the relationship is lacking in affection and passion.

Venus in the First House of the Navamsha Chart: This is roughly equivalent to Venus in the seventh house. In some schools of thought, the natural significator is not good in the first house of the divisional chart related to its signification. The Navamsha chart is a chart for marriage. Venus is the planet of marriage. The results may be similar to that of Venus placed in the seventh house.

Malavaya Yoga: Malavaya Yoga occurs when Venus is placed in the first, fourth, seventh, or tenth houses from the Ascendant or the Moon, and is also placed in its own sign or exaltation sign. This gives a strong dose of romantic and emotional vitality, as well as sexual energy. It can be a very good placement for relationship. This placement usually brings sensuality and romanticism, however, which sometimes leads to disappointment. In any case, if it is not afflicted by malefics, it gives warmth and increases the potential for a successful and fulfilling marriage or relationship experience.

On the positive side, Venus in the seventh house can be a good placement for the cultivation of compassion, unconditional love, and devotion. Many who have this placement in their horoscopes actually have very positive relationships or marriages simply by emphasizing the higher aspects of love.

Venus Retrograde: Most classical literature suggests that when a planet is retrograde (apparently moving backward in the zodiac), it is stronger than when in direct motion. A strong planet may not always give good results, however, and a retrograde Venus usually has some challenges to offer. While it might create generous doses of emotional, creative, sensual and sexual energy, retrograde Venus is sometimes associated with relationship problems. It frequently makes the experience of love and affection a complex and deeply psychological experience. Sometimes it makes the person emotionally compulsive. Retrograde Venus may also produce unconventional relationships. The success of the person's relationship may also hinge on how much psychological homework he or she has done in this area. In fact, the key to successful relationships with Venus retrograde in the chart seems to be reflection. The relationship, in this case, becomes a tool for unraveling deeply complex emotional patterns. From this vantage point, Venus retrograde can also offer the potential for significant emotional growth and fulfilling relationships.

The Seventh House

The seventh house represents relationships in general. The disposition of this house reveals how the person views and experiences relationships of all kinds. The seventh house is the house of "other people," as it is exactly opposite the Ascendant, the house of the personal ego. It represents one's relational environment and relational style, partnership and one-to-one interaction. It reflects our ability to cooperate, adjust, bargain, and negotiate. It shows how easy or difficult we find the process of achieving harmony with another person.

On the romantic level, the seventh house is the house of marriage. It shows our experience in romantic partnerships. For this reason, the disposition of this house is extremely important in the overall assessment of marriage and relationship.

Planets in the Seventh House

If a planet is placed in the seventh house, it will powerfully influence the person's marriage or relationship experience. The spouse or the relationship partner will possess the qualities associated with that particular planet. The results for each planet placed in the seventh house are given in *Path of Light, Volume I* in the chapter on houses.

The Ruler of the Seventh House

The placement of the ruler of the seventh house is an important factor in understanding relationship tendencies. Its placement can also offer insights helpful in describing and understanding the spouse.

Ruler of the Seventh House Exalted or in its Own Sign: The seventh house is the first house for the partner. When the ruler of the seventh is exalted or in its own sign, then the partner will be strong in some way. This might mean he or she will have strong health, a strong personality, high intelligence, or self confidence. A strong seventh lord also enhances the possibility for marriage or a committed relationship to take place.

Ruler of the Seventh House Debilitated: If the ruler of the seventh house is debilitated, it may indicate weakness of some kind in the partner or spouse. Usually the particular area of weakness is related to the nature of the planet. If Mars rules the seventh house, for example, its debilitation may signify that the partner is defensive, insecure, or emotional. Saturn, the planet of responsibility, may suggest that the partner has problems with responsibility or commitment in some way. Similarly, other debilitated planets can produce problems in the partner that are characteristic of the planet's nature. A debilitated seventh lord also makes marital harmony more difficult to achieve and may suggest difficulty in getting into a relationship or marriage.

Ruler of the Seventh House Neecha Bhanga (debilitation canceled): If the ruler of the seventh house is neecha bhanga, then the above condition may be overcome or it may be a blessing in disguise. For example, a debilitated Saturn as ruler of the seventh house, may cause the partner to have a love-hate relationship with work and responsibility. He might have an attitude of resistance toward responsibility that causes him to avoid working if possible. While this may seem to be a problem, the neecha bhanga condition suggests that this could be a hidden blessing. The desire to avoid routines or responsibilities might spur the partner to seek freelance work or self-employment, enabling him to become more successful. Einstein had the ruler of his Ascendant, Mercury (the planet of the intellect) in Pisces (the sign of dreams and intuition) neecha bhanga. This made him a dreamer and he did poorly in his early education. Yet this was the key to his genius as well. Similarly, a neecha bhanga seventh lord may indicate qualities in the spouse that are only a problem from a conventional point of view, but which could turn out to be a source of hidden strength.

Sometimes this condition also suggests that the spouse goes through initial problems in life that are overcome later. The same could be said for the relationship in general terms. When someone has a neecha bhanga seventh lord, he might initially go through difficulties in marriage, which he later works out. Another possibility is a difficult first marriage that ends in a divorce, but which leads to new and important insights about relationships, bringing a much better relationship later.

The Ruler of the Seventh House Placed in the Twelve Houses

The house placement of the ruler of the seventh house is also an important factor for understanding marriage. These results were given in *Path of Light, Volume I*, in the chapter on houses.

Using the Navamsha Chart for Support

The Navamsha chart is the chart for marriage. It can be used to confirm what is seen in the natal chart. It can also be used to further elaborate on details about the partner's career, health, finances, and other aspects of the partner's life. The Navamsha can be used in different ways. One simple and effective method is to take the Ascendant of the Navamsha as the Ascendant of the partner. Taken in this way, the tenth house becomes the partner's career house, the second house becomes the house of the partner's finances, and so forth.

The Placement of the Lagna Lord in the Navamsha: The placement of the Rashi lagna lord in the Navamsha chart is important. If it is weak and afflicted, then the person's experience of relationship will be problematic. If it is strong and aspected by benefics, then it contributes to a positive experience in relationship.

The Placement of the Navamsha Lagna Lord: The placement of the Navamsha lagna lord in the Navamsha chart as well as its placement in the Rashi chart is also important. The strength or weakness of these two placements must be considered in the overall assessment of the chart.

Planets Placed in the First House of the Navamsha Chart: When a planet is placed in the first house of the Navamsha chart, it behaves like a planet placed in the seventh house of the Rashi chart. The effect of the nine planets placed in the seventh house in the Rashi chart was discussed in *Path of Light, Volume I*.

Yogas in the Navamsha Chart

As with other divisional charts, yogas can be effectively used in the Navamsha chart. The effects of common yogas found here will be applied to the partner or to the partnership. The results of yogas occurring in the Navamsha chart will take place during the major and sub-periods of the planets involved in the combinations. The following are combinations that commonly occur in the Navamsha chart and can be used effectively for accurate predictions.

Travel Associated with Relationship: The travel houses are the twelfth (distant places), the ninth (long-distance travel) and the third (short-distance travel). The following combinations linking these houses produce travel: lord of the twelfth in the ninth; lord of the ninth in the twelfth; lord of the twelfth in the third; lord of the third in the twelfth; lord of the ninth in the third; lord of the third in the ninth. Also, the rulers of the twelfth, ninth and third houses in a conjunction or mutual aspect cause travel. If Jupiter is involved, it amplifies the effect. If Ketu is involved, then the travel will be to a foreign country. If one of the above combinations occurs in the Navamsha chart, then a travel event for the spouse or partner may take place during the periods of the yoga-producing planets. This could mean that the person goes on a trip with his spouse or significant other. It could also mean that the person's partner or spouse travels on his or her own during the period.

Financial Gains for the Partner or Partnership: Dhana Yogas bring financial improvement. When they occur in the Navamsha chart, then they improve the financial condition of either the partner individually or the partnership. See the chapter on yogas and also the chapter on money for more about Dhana Yogas.

Career Success for the Partner: Raja Yogas suggest career success. If a Raja Yoga exists in the Navamsha chart, then the partner may have a rise in his career during the period of the planets involved in the yoga. For more on Raja Yogas, see the chapter on yogas in this volume.

The tenth house in the Navamsha chart is the house of the partner's career. If the period planet is placed in the tenth house or if it rules the tenth house, then prominent results for the partner's career may result. The positive or negative quality of the results will be determined by the positive or negative disposition of the period planet.

Health Predictions for the Partner: If the ruler of the seventh house from the Rashi chart, or the rulers of the first house or the seventh house from the Navamsha chart are placed in either the sixth house (partner's health relative to the Navamsha lagna) or the twelfth house (the sixth house from the seventh house) in the Navamsha chart, then the health of the partner may be described by those planets. If the planet is weak and afflicted by natural malefics, then ill health or other physical problems may occur. If it is strong and aspected by benefics, the partner's health could improve in some way.

Residence Events for the Spouse or Partnership: If the period planet is placed in the fourth house or rules the fourth house in the Navamsha chart, then it tends to produce events related to the residence for the spouse or the partnership. Here are some common combinations:

1. Change or remodel of residence: lord of the eighth in the fourth house; lord of the fourth in the eighth house.
2. Purchase of residence for the couple: lord of the fourth in the eleventh or second house or vice versa.
3. The couple moves out of the area (to a distant place, which doesn't necessarily mean a foreign country): lord of the fourth in the twelfth or the ninth house or vice versa.

If one of these residence combinations involves Mars and Saturn, combining their energies by either conjunction or mutual aspect, then the couple could build a house or do some kind of mechanical work on the house. If the combination is produced by a powerful Venus, then the couple will beautify the existing home or purchase a luxury home.

Other Domains of Life: The preceding examples are given not as strict rules, but rather as guidelines in using the Navamsha chart. Extending the basic principles, events in various domains of life for the partner can be predicted by simply noting the houses that the period planet rules or occupies in the Navamsha chart. The positive or negative quality of the event always depends on the positive or negative disposition of the period ruler.

Gathering Support for Predictions Made with the Navamsha Chart

Ideally, it is best to have several indications from various angles before making a prediction. The first place to look for support is the Rashi chart, which is the most important of all the charts. There are, however, other charts which can be used for supporting predictions about the spouse. For example, if the period ruler is afflicted in the sixth house of the Navamsha chart, it suggests the possibility of ill health for the spouse. If the same planet either rules or is placed in the twelfth house of the Shashtamsha chart (health) and is afflicted, then the prediction can be made more confidently. Notice that the Shashtamsha chart is a chart for the person's own health. We are able to use it to predict the health of the spouse as well because the twelfth house is the sixth house (health) from the seventh (spouse). In the Shashtamsha chart as well as the Rashi chart the twelfth house indicates the health of the spouse.

Similarly, the other divisional charts can be used to predict events for the spouse by interpreting the varga, using the seventh house as the lagna. Here are a few other examples to illustrate which houses to consult in various divisional charts for specific events in the life of the partner or spouse.

The partner's career: the fourth house (tenth from the seventh house) in both the Rashi chart and the Dashamsha chart.

The partner's finances: the eighth house (second from the seventh) and the fifth house (eleventh from the seventh) in the Hora chart, Ekadashamsha chart and the Rashi chart.

The partner's car: the tenth house (fourth from the seventh) in the Shodashamsha chart and the Rashi chart.

Applying this method to the other vargas, the number of possibilities for additional predictions is greatly increased.

Exploring Details of the Spouse or Partner's Life

Finding details about the partner or spouse in the chart is actually not difficult. It simply requires a clear understanding of the fundamentals of chart interpretation. The basic premise is to use the seventh house as the first house for the partner and then interpret all of the other houses relative to that point. The eighth house, for example, is the second house from the seventh so it is the partner's money house. The ninth house is the partner's third house, and so forth. Examination of the partner's career occurs from the fourth house from the Ascendant. The fourth house is the tenth house (career) from the seventh house (partner). This makes it the partner's career house. The analysis is exactly the same as was discussed in the chapter on career, except that everything is analyzed using the seventh house as the Ascendant.

Chart 1: Woman with Acupuncturist Husband
October 28, 1955; 4:13 AM; Honolulu, HI

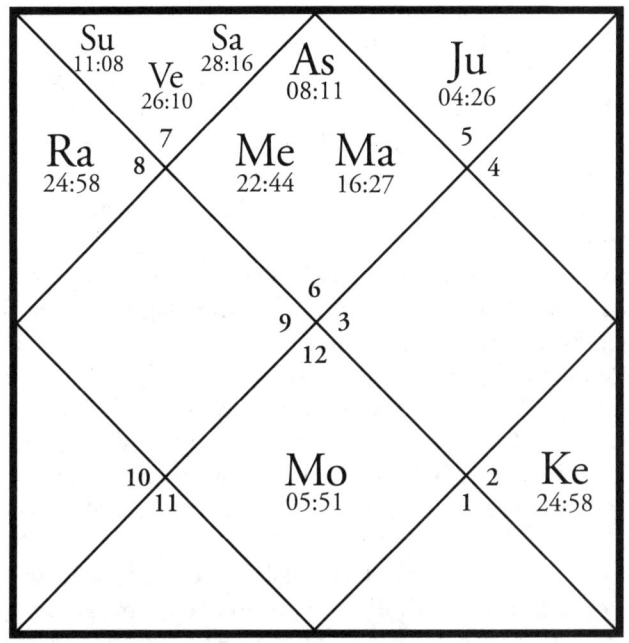

(D9) Navamsha

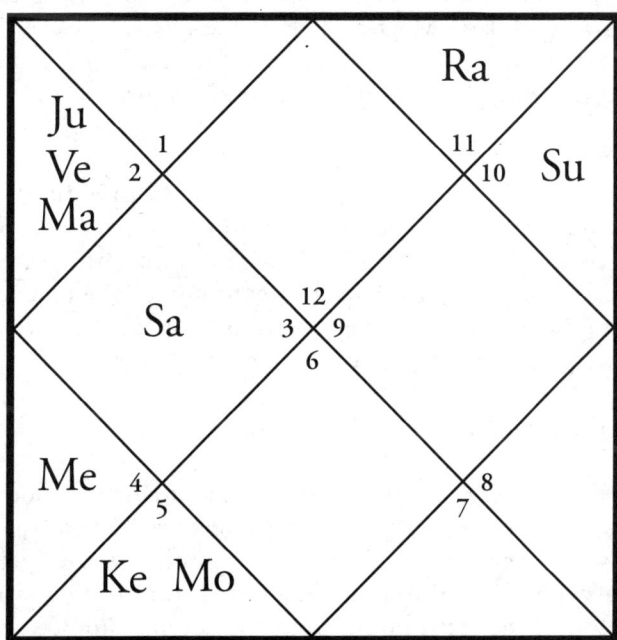

Chart 1 is the chart of a woman whose husband is an acupuncturist. Her chart reflects many details about her husband.

First, the general personality of her husband is suggested by the sign (Pisces) and planet (Moon) occupying the seventh house. This combination suggests an idealistic, intuitive, and spiritually-oriented partner.

Using the seventh house (Pisces) as the lagna for the husband, the chart has an Adhi Yoga (Jupiter, Mercury and Venus in the sixth, seventh, and eighth houses). This suggests that the husband is successful, knowledgeable, prosperous, virtuous and has administrative ability. All these things are true about her husband.

The sign in the seventh house is Pisces, one of the signs of compassion and selflessness. It is an important healing sign.

The tenth house from the seventh house gives a clue about the husband's profession. This house is occupied by the sign of Sagittarius (the sign of professionals and knowledgeable experts). Sagittarius is ruled by Jupiter, which becomes the husband's tenth lord. Jupiter is placed in the sign of Leo, which becomes the husband's sixth house (health) because it is six houses away from the seventh house. So he is in a healing profession.

Jupiter is in Leo, the sign of authority and leadership. It is also in Magha, a constellation symbolized by a throne room, and her husband was the president of his state acupuncture association.

Magha's planetary ruler is Ketu. Ketu is related to healing, and is also the planet of Buddhism. Magha's deity is the Pitris, who are the ancestors, signifying things that come from ancient traditions. All of of these symbols suggest acupuncture and oriental medicine.

Using the Navamsha chart to further describe the native's husband's career, the Navamsha lagna is Pisces (idealism and inspiration). The first house and the tenth house are ruled by Jupiter. Jupiter is in Taurus in the third house (communications) with the ninth lord (higher education). This links his work to themes of communication and education. He was a teacher of meditation earlier in his life. He was on the board of directors for an acupuncture college as well.

Extending the Principle

In the same way, other aspects describing the life of the spouse can be clearly seen by looking at the pertinent houses relative to the seventh. You can also use the Navamsha chart in a similar way to get support and further detail. For information about the health of the partner, for example, look at the sixth house from the seventh house (the twelfth from the natal Ascendant). Then look at the Navamsha sixth house for support. For information about the spouse's first younger brother or sister, look at the third house from the seventh house (ninth from the Ascendant) as well as the Navamsha's third house. To find out about the health of the first younger brother of the spouse's mother (the maternal uncle), look at the sixth house from the seventh as the house of the maternal uncle, and then the sixth house from that house (the natal fifth house), as the house of his health. This last example is purposely a little complicated and removed from the partner's immediate life. The point, however, is that there is really no limit to what can be seen using this method. It is one of the great keys to deriving detail from the Vedic chart. This is how a good astrologer can give accurate information and predictions to questions like, "Can you tell me about the health of my uncle?"

Of course, this approach has only been applied to the house of marriage or relationship. But it can easily be applied to other relationships as well. For information about the spouse, the seventh house is used as the Ascendant. For information about the younger brother, use the third house as the Ascendant. From here, the tenth house from the third house is the brother's career. The sixth house from the third is the brother's health and so on. Once you know which house signifies a particular relative, boss, friend, client, or competitor, the same fundamentals can be applied using that house as the first house.

Second Marriage and Beyond

According to the ancient jyotishi-sage Kalidasa, the second house is the house of the second spouse. The reasoning behind this is that the second house is the eighth house (death) from the seventh house (first spouse). So the second house signifies the death or the end of the first marriage. This logic can still apply in modern times because the eighth house (from the seventh) can also be used to signify the symbolic, as well as the literal death (and rebirth) of a marriage. Using Kalidasa's approach, each subsequent marriage is eight houses from the previous one. The seventh house is the first marriage. The second house is the second marriage. The ninth house is the third marriage and so on.

Although some astrologers use Kalidasa's method effectively, there is another school of thought that uses the ninth house as the house of the second spouse. This is because the ninth house is the third house (sister) from the seventh house (wife). In ancient times, it was a common practice to marry the sister of the wife if the first wife died. In modern times, remarriage to the sibling of one's spouse is not a common practice. Nevertheless, the ninth house is still used effectively by many modern Vedic astrologers (including the author) as the house of the second spouse. Using this approach, each subsequent marriage is located in third house from the one before it. In other words, the first marriage is the seventh house, the second marriage is the ninth house, the third marriage is the eleventh house, and so forth.

It is up to the serious student of Vedic astrology to test these methods and decide which works best to locate the sequential marriages in the chart. Once decided upon, details about the various spouses are derived using the same techniques mentioned previously.

Harmony or Disharmony in Marriage

There are many astrological factors that contribute to marital harmony or disharmony. Here are a few important points to consider.

Marital Harmony

1. Venus is the karaka or significator of marriage. If it is strong and well-placed then harmony in marriage is likely.
2. If the seventh house and its ruler are strong, aspected by benefics, and free from the influence of malefics, then marriage will be harmonious.
3. The ruler of the first house represents the individual. The ruler of the seventh house represents the spouse. If these two planets are in a sympathetic relationship, then there will be marital harmony.

Friendship, mutual respect and general harmony occur between the husband and wife when the rulers of the first house and the seventh house (or the house of a subsequent marriage) are:
A. Placed in the signs of planets that are friendly to each other (see "Table of Planetary Friendship" in *Volume I*)
B. Placed in a 3/11 or 5/9 relationship from each other

Marital Disharmony

1. A weak and afflicted Venus makes marital harmony more difficult.
2. Disharmony and disagreement may result if the seventh house or its lord is weak or influenced by malefics.
3. Disharmony and disagreement may take place when the rulers of the first house and seventh house are placed in a 6/8 relationship from each other.

4. When the rulers of the first and the seventh houses are placed in a 2/12 relationship from each other, then one of the partners, (the one whose planet is placed in the twelfth from the other), becomes a source of disappointment or uncertainty to the other partner.

Will Marriage Take Place?

The house of marriage is essentially a house of partnership. This means that it can include more than just traditional marriage. It can include alternative marriage-like relationships, where two people commit to each other in an emotional-sexual bonding. Determining astrologically whether the partners will choose a traditional marriage or an unconventional one is a matter of understanding the planetary influences on Venus and the seventh house. Determining whether a relationship of either kind will actually take place, on the other hand, is a matter of understanding the intrinsic strength of the seventh house and Venus. If the seventh house and Venus are strong, then relationship will usually take place. If they are weak, then the prospects for marriage become more difficult. In this case, however, a marriage might still take place, but it will be much more challenging.

Another factor, which radically affects marital prospects, is the lagna. If the first house is weak, the person might be too shy, self-conscious, unfriendly, unattractive, or physically ill, to take advantage of his potential for partnership. On the other hand, if the first house is strong, then the intelligence, charm, physical beauty and good health of the individual may offset a difficult seventh house, raising the prospects for marriage and diminishing marital problems to a great extent.

When Will Marriage Take Place?

Once it has been determined that marriage is possible, the task of predicting the time of marriage is accomplished by the use of dashas and transits. The most likely periods for marriage are as follows.

Dashas That Produce Marriage

1. During the period of a well-placed Venus
2. During the period of the seventh lord or a planet placed in the seventh house
3. During the period of the second lord or a planet placed in the second house
4. During the period of the eleventh lord or a planet placed in the

eleventh house
5. During the period of the yogakaraka
6. During the periods of the lords of houses 1, 2, 7, or 11 in the Navamsha   *Mars rules Aries, the 7th Ruler in Navamsha*
7. During the period of a planet that is well-placed in the Navamsha chart
8. During the period of the planet that is placed in or which owns the seventh house from the Moon or Venus
9. During the period of a planet that rules the nakshatra of any of the above planets

Transits That Produce Marriage

1. The combined aspects of Jupiter and Saturn

Once the dasha and bhukti have been selected, then the timing of marriage is narrowed by the use of transits. For this purpose, the combined aspects of Saturn and Jupiter are sometimes very useful. As mentioned earlier, Jupiter aspects houses 5, 7, and 9 from its placement. Hence, including its house of transit, Jupiter influences four houses at all times. Similarly, Saturn influences its house of transit and also casts aspects on houses 3, 7 and 10 from its transit placement. According to this method, when Saturn and Jupiter both aspect the seventh house, or the seventh lord, this becomes a likely time for partnership or marriage. If in addition to aspecting the seventh house and/or the seventh lord, Saturn and Jupiter also aspect the first house and/or the first lord, then the transit will be particularly powerful for producing partnership.

2. The transit of the dasha or bhukti lord

If the planet that rules the dasha or bhukti transits or aspects the seventh house, this can be a likely time for partnership or marriage.

3. Transits of the seventh lord and lagna lord

If the seventh lord transits the lagna or transits the sign occupied by the lagna lord, this becomes a likely time for partnership or marriage. By the same token, if the lagna lord transits the seventh house, or the sign occupied by the seventh lord, marriage is likely.

Hopefully, marriage will occur!! Rahu Transiting the Sun (Lagna Ruler) at the same time around that Rahu matures (age 41). My Rahu is right on my Descendent.

Chart 2: John F. Kennedy
May 29, 1917; 3:00 PM; Brookline, MA

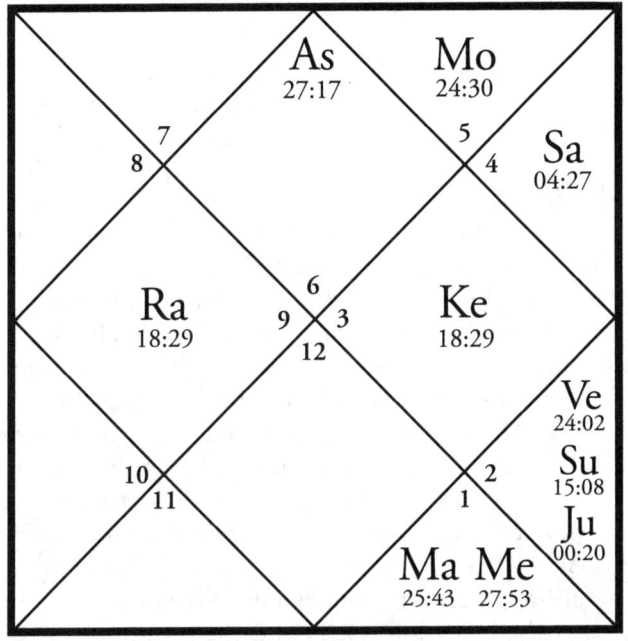

(D9) Navamsha

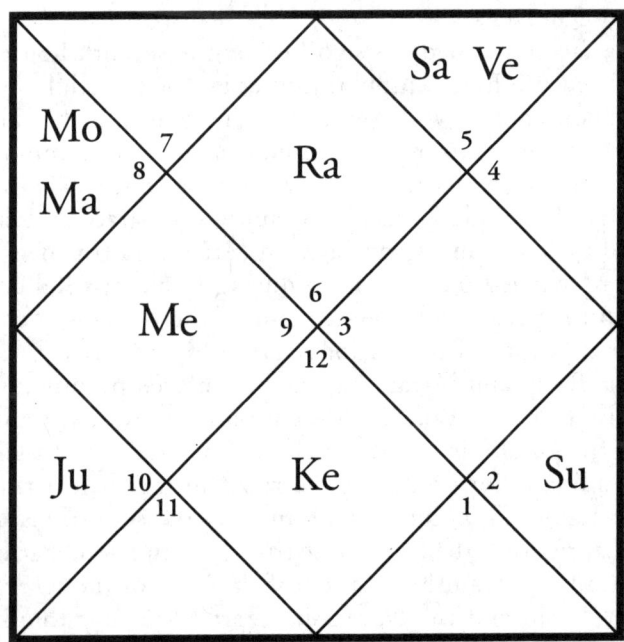

Dashas

08/28/1943	Ra	Ra	03/17/1955	Ra	Ve
05/11/1946	Ra	Jp	03/17/1958	Ra	Su
10/03/1948	Ra	Sa	02/09/1959	Ra	Mo
08/10/1951	Ra	Me	08/10/1960	Ra	Ma
02/27/1954	Ra	Ke	08/28/1961	Ju	Ju

Let's consider marriage in the chart of John F. Kennedy. First, Kennedy was known to be a passionate person who had many extramarital affairs. This is reflected in several ways in his chart. His Venus is placed in Mrigashira (see the myth of Brahma chasing his daughter in the nakshatra chapter in *Path of Light, Volume I*). He also has his Moon in Purva Phalguni nakshatra, which has "the power of procreativity" as its shakti. The ruler of the Ascendant, Mercury, is placed in Krittika, along with Mars. All of these nakshatras have a tendency toward a high libido and infidelity. This is compounded by the fact that his Mars and his Venus are in a 2/12 relationship, which is usually associated with a tendency to compartmentalize emotional and physical aspects of sexuality. As a result, he found it hard to experience both physical and emotional happiness with one woman. It is further compounded by the fact that the lagna lord (self) and the seventh lord (spouse) are in a 2/12 relationship, which makes it difficult to experience marital harmony in general.

His wife, Jackie Kennedy, is signified by the seventh house and the ruler of the seventh house, Jupiter. Jupiter is in the ninth house (abundance) in a conjunction with Venus, which, in turn, is the ruler of the ninth house, placed in its own sign. This is a powerful combination for prosperity, suggesting marriage to a wealthy person. Jackie came from a wealthy family. Similarly, Jackie's beauty, style, grace and charm are all signified by Venus in its own sign, in Mrigashira (the deer's head).

They were married on 9/12/1953 during Kennedy's Rahu/Mercury period. Rahu is placed in the Ascendant of the Navamsha chart indicating that it is a focal period for relationships. Mercury, lagna lord for both the Rashi and Navamsha charts, is placed prominently in the fourth house of the Navamsha. Mercury also rules the seventh house (marriage) from Rahu in the Rashi chart. Both Rahu and Mercury are primary candidates for producing marriage during their periods.

Transits: Rahu (dasha lord) was transiting the sign of Capricorn at the time. Capricorn is the fifth house (romance and good karma). Capricorn is also the Navamsha location of the ruler of the seventh house of both the Rashi and the Navamsha charts. Mercury (bhukti ruler) was transiting Virgo, which is the Ascendant of the Navamsha chart. Jupiter (seventh lord) was transiting Gemini, in the seventh house from Rahu (period ruler) in the Rashi chart.

Path of Light – The Domains of Life

Chart 3: Jacqueline Kennedy Onassis
July 28, 1929; 2:30 PM; Southampton, NY

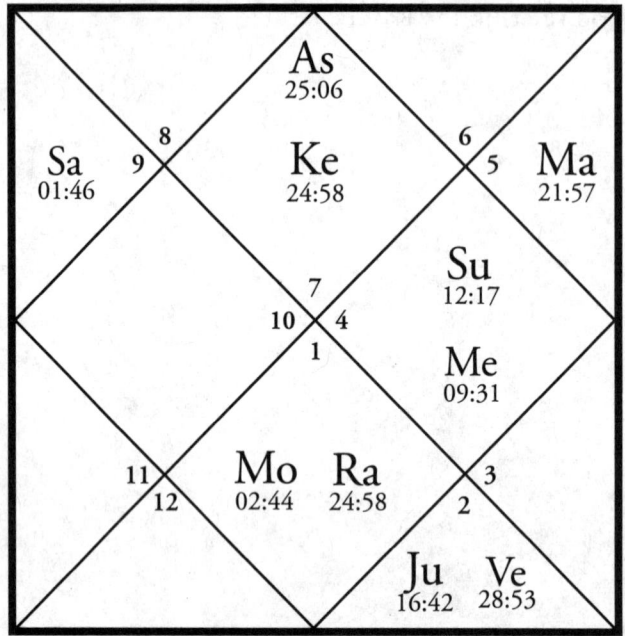

(D9) Navamsha

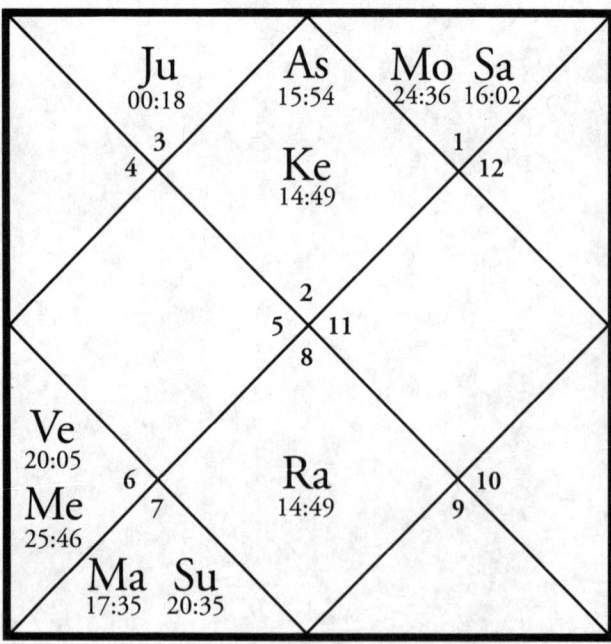

Dashas

04/21/1945	Ve	Jp	12/20/1968	Mo	Ve
12/21/1947	Ve	Sa	08/21/1970	Mo	Su
02/20/1951	Ve	Me	02/20/1971	Ma	Ma
12/21/1953	Ve	Ke	07/19/1971	Ma	Ra
02/20/1955	Su	Su	08/06/1972	Ma	Jp
06/09/1955	Su	Mo	07/12/1973	Ma	Sa
12/09/1955	Su	Ma	08/21/1974	Ma	Me
04/15/1956	Su	Ra	08/18/1975	Ma	Ke
03/09/1957	Su	Ju	01/15/1976	Ma	Ve
12/27/1957	Su	Sa	03/16/1977	Ma	Su
12/09/1958	Su	Me	07/22/1977	Ma	Mo
10/15/1959	Su	Ke	02/20/1978	Ra	Ra
02/20/1960	Su	Ve	11/02/1980	Ra	Jp
02/19/1961	Mo	Mo	03/28/1983	Ra	Sa
12/21/1961	Mo	Ma	02/01/1986	Ra	Me
07/22/1962	Mo	Ra	08/21/1988	Ra	Ke
01/21/1964	Mo	Jp	09/08/1989	Ra	Ve
05/22/1965	Mo	Sa	09/08/1992	Ra	Su
12/21/1966	Mo	Me	08/03/1993	Ra	Mo
05/21/1968	Mo	Ke			

Jacqueline Kennedy Onassis: A Relationship Chronology

Jacqueline Kennedy Onassis' chart provides a graphic example of how a person's destiny with their various relationships is etched in the horoscope.

First, she has a Libra Ascendant. The lagna is placed in Vishakha nakshatra, which is ruled by Indragni, a deity comprised of two gods in one body. This gave her the desire for an intense and close relationship. Another name for this nakshatra is Radha, which makes the myths about Radha and Krishna, the divine lovers, relevant. Although this lagna gave the hope of a divine union, Ketu's close conjunction with the Ascendant shows her deep disappointment with her marriage. Placed in the seventh house from the Moon, Ketu also reflects the many secretive, romantic affairs of her husband.

The seventh house in Jackie's chart is occupied by the Moon and Rahu which shows that her mind was obsessed and disturbed by the marital situation.

The ruler of the seventh house is Mars, which is placed in the eleventh house, promoting the success of her husband. Relative to the seventh house, Mars is placed in the fifth house, showing that her husband had a strong libido. It is also placed in Purva Phalguni, a nakshatra symbolized by the conjugal bed, reiterating this quality. Being the ruler of the seventh house, Mars in Purva Phalguni describes her husband's financial condition in an interesting way. Purva Phalguni is ruled by Bhaga, the god of wealth. As described in *Path of Light, Volume I*, the name Bhaga, in Sanskrit, means the "inherited share," which describes a right of passage prevalent in the ancient tribes of India, where a young person, having attained adulthood, was given his share of the tribal wealth. As if following a script written in Jackie's horosocope, when John F. Kennedy turned twenty-one years of age, his father, Joseph Kennedy, gave him a million dollars.

Of course, it is also important to mention Jackie's powerful Venus, karaka for marriage. This gives her the emotional vitality and ability to attract a partner. Venus is also in a conjunction with Jupiter, the karaka for husband in a woman's horoscope. Venus is placed in the eighth house (partner's money), showing that she married a wealthy man. The eighth house is also the house of death, however, which foreshadows the assassination of her husband. Venus is placed in Mrigashira nakshatra, which has the *prinana shakti*, or the power to fulfill one's desires. The shadow side of Mrigashira, reflected in the seduction myth of Brahma chasing his daughter across the heavens, is also relevant as it symbolizes the philandering nature of her husband. (See *Path of Light, Volume I* for more about the various nakshatra myths).

On September 12, 1953, Jacqueline married John F. Kennedy (Venus dasha/Mercury bhukti).

Venus Dasha: Venus is a natural period for marriage. It is the karaka of marriage, and in this case it is placed in its own sign in the Rashi chart, giving it the power to easily express its significations. Venus' nakshatra and house placement were discussed previously.

Mercury Bhukti: Mercury is a benefic period. Ruling the ninth house (dharma), it is placed in the tenth house (career, and also the house of the President), suggesting that the marriage would lead to career success for her husband and also for herself, in her role as First Lady.

Navamsha Chart: In the Navamsha chart, Venus and Mercury are placed in a conjunction in the fifth house. When two planets are in conjunction in a divisional chart, their mutual major/sub-periods can produce prominent events for the domain of that chart. In this case the conjunction of these two planets forms a powerful Neecha Bhanga Raja Yoga, which literally lifted her husband (and herself) up to the status of royalty.

Using Degrees in the Navamsha Chart: Mercury, the sub-period ruler, is placed in Virgo at 25 degrees in Chitra nakshatra in the Navamsha chart. Chitra produces a charming and charismatic nature, which clearly describes her husband. What is more startling is that her husband's (John F. Kennedy) Ascendant was 27 degrees of Virgo, in Chitra nakshatra.

Combined Transit of Jupiter and Saturn: Jupiter (karaka of the husband) was at 1 degree of Gemini aspecting Libra which is the seventh house (marriage) from the Moon. Jupiter had also recently (three weeks earlier) passed over Venus, the major period ruler and karaka of marriage. Saturn (yogakaraka) was transiting Libra, her lagna, which is also the seventh house from the Moon, thus producing the dual influence of both Jupiter and Saturn on the seventh house from the Moon.

John F. Kennedy's Chronic Health Problems

John F. Kennedy had chronic health problems including colitis, malaria, Addison's disease and chronic back pain. From the beginning of their marriage, he took multiple medications for variety of symptoms. It is noteworthy that in the Navamsha chart, the three major period rulers covering the time-span of the marriage are all challenged. Venus is debilitated. The Sun is debilitated and afflicted by malefics, and the Moon is also severely afflicted in the twelfth house. The affliction of these planets in the Navamsha chart clearly show the health problems of her husband, not to mention the problems in their relationship due to his womanizing.

On October 21, 1954, John F. Kennedy had back surgery (during Jackie's Venus dasha/Ketu bhukti).

Venus Dasha: Venus (marriage) is placed in the eighth house (surgery) in the Rashi chart.

Ketu Bhukti: Ketu is placed in the seventh house (spouse) from the Moon and in the sixth house (health problems) from Venus (dasha lord) in the Rashi chart.

Navamsha Chart: In the Navamsha chart, Venus is debilitated, reflecting the general predisposition towards health problems for the husband during the twenty year period of Venus. Ketu is placed in the Navamsha lagna, where it is afflicted by Mars (surgery) from the sixth house (health problems). This placement clearly shows that during this period the husband could have health problems related to surgery.

It is also interesting that this surgery failed, which is one of the significations of Ketu, a planet which signifies disappointments. This sub-period triggered a significant worsening of John F. Kennedy's condition. During the Sun period which followed, he was in chronic pain, and had further unsuccessful surgeries. He had to take a long list of drugs, including cortisone, testosterone, amphetamines, and methadone just to get through each day. This shift is reflected in the condition of the two major period rulers, Venus and the Sun.

Navamsha chart: Although Venus is debilitated, it is with exalted Mercury in the fifth house. The Sun, on the other hand, is debilitated, placed in the sixth house, conjunct Mars, and aspected by Saturn. Jupiter's aspect on the Sun may show some minor relief due to the advice and medications received by doctors, but this is greatly outweighed by the multiple negative influences on the Sun. Seen through the prism of Jackie's Navamsha chart, the failed surgery in the Venus/Ketu period simply set the stage for the onset of a new and more difficult period for her husband's health.

Transits: Saturn, along with the Sun and Mercury, was transiting Libra in a conjunction with Jackie's natal Ketu (sub-period ruler). The conjunction of natural malefics with the natal dasha or bhukti ruler produces problems during the dasha or bhukti period. Mars was in Capricorn, powerfully aspecting the seventh house (husband), as well as the natal Moon, Sun, and Mercury. The aspect of transiting Mars on the natal Mercury and Sun is particularly significant. Taking the seventh house as the lagna for the husband, Mercury rules the sixth house, so it shows the type of health problems experienced by the husband. The Sun is the karaka for the spine, so this combination shows that her husband had back problems. The combined aspects of both Mars (surgery) and Saturn (illness) on the seventh house, the natal Moon, Mercury and the Sun, acted in concert with the dasha/bhukti influences to produce the surgery. An important transit principle to remember here is the following: *Just as the combined influences of transiting Jupiter and Saturn usually act to fulfill the significations of the houses they mutually influence, the combined influences of two or more transiting natural malefics generally act to undermine the significations of the houses or planets they mutually influence.*

On November 25, 1960, Jackie gave birth to a son, John F. Kennedy Jr. (during Sun dasha/Venus bhukti).

Although this chapter primarily deals with marriage, the birth of Jackie's son is given here as an example of an important event during the marriage. It also illustrates the use of the Navamsha chart as a chart that can show other types of relationships besides marriage.

Sun Dasha: The Sun is the ruler of the fifth house (children) from the Moon placed in the constellation of Pushya in the Rashi chart. Pushya is symbolized by the udder of a cow and is related to motherhood.

Venus Bhukti: Venus is in a conjunction with Jupiter, karaka of children in the Rashi chart and is also placed in the eleventh house (fulfillment of desires) from the Sun. It is also placed in the constellation of Mrigashira, which has the shakti of fulfilling desires. Venus also aspects the fifth house (children) from the Sun.

Navamsha Chart: Venus is Navamsha lagna lord, placed in the fifth house with the ruler of the fifth house. This placement in the Navamsha chart clearly points to a marital event related to children.

Combined Transit of Jupiter and Saturn: Jupiter and Saturn were transiting Sagittarius in Jacqueline's third house along with the sub-period and lagna lord, Venus. They were in conjunction with Jackie's Saturn, the ruler of the fifth house (children). It is also important to note that the third house is the eleventh house (attainment of desires) from the fifth house (children). The combined influences of Jupiter and Saturn in the third house promoted the fruition of the desire for a child. In Jackie's chart, Sagittarius is also the ninth house from the Moon. The ninth house is the fifth house from the fifth house and is an important house for children.

In January of 1961 Jackie's husband, John F. Kennedy, was elected President of the United States (during her Sun dasha/Venus bhukti).

Sun Dasha: The Sun is the karaka for leadership and is placed in the tenth house (career) in Jacqueline's chart. In the chart of a married woman who does not have a prominent career of her own, the career of her husband can be reflected in her tenth house. The Sun in the tenth house suggests career success. Of course this event triggered a new career for Jacqueline as well, as First Lady.

Venus Bhukti: Venus is in its own sign and in a conjunction with Jupiter. It is also placed in the eleventh house (fulfillment of desires) from the Sun in the constellation of Mrigashira. This allowed the period to produce fulfillment of desires.

Navamsha Chart: Venus (bhukti ruler) is placed in the fifth house of the Navamsha chart. The fifth house is the house of the king. Venus is the ruler of the Navamsha lagna and is placed in a conjunction with the ruler of the fifth house. This produces a Raja Yoga in the Navamsha chart. Raja means "king," and Raja Yogas usually bring a rise in status in the career. In this case it literally made Kennedy a type of king.

The Sun is seriously afflicted in the sixth house (enemies) in the Navamsha chart. The period in which a person begins an undertaking can reveal the outcome of that undertaking. In this case, his election during Jacqueline's Sun period produced many enemies which ultimately contributed to his assassination.

Combined Influence of Jupiter and Saturn: Jupiter and Saturn were transiting Sagittarius at the time of the inauguration. Taking the seventh house as the lagna for the husband, Sagittarius is the ninth house. From this lagna, Jupiter rules the ninth house (and is transiting its own sign) and Saturn rules the tenth house. Their conjunction in the ninth house constitutes a transiting Raja Yoga, which lifts the husband up in his career. It is noteworthy that the Sun (dasha ruler) was transiting Capricorn, the tenth house (the husband's career) from the seventh house. Venus (bhukti ruler) was transiting Aquarius in the eleventh house (success) from the seventh house.

From January to June of 1962 John F. Kennedy became involved in an affair with the actress Marilyn Monroe (during Moon dasha/Mars bhukti).

Moon Dasha: Jackie entered the Moon period in 1961. The Moon is seriously disturbed in her chart. First the Moon (the mind) is placed in the seventh house (marriage) in a conjunction with Rahu. The Moon-Rahu conjunction creates fear, obsessions, and compulsions. The Moon is also placed in Ashwini nakshatra. Ashwini is ruled by the Ashwini Kumaras, the twin healers of the gods. Once the Ashwini twins tried to tempt a beautiful young princess away from her old, blind husband by telling her that she would be better off with one of them because they were young and virile and handsome. Although the Ashwini twins did not succeed in seducing the princess, this story shows how Ashwini nakshatra can bring an inclination to be attracted to the young and the glamorous. Ashwini types are sometimes challenged to learn to see their partners with their hearts rather than their eyes. Although this is Jacqueline's Moon, it is placed in the seventh house of her chart, which is the house of her husband, suggesting that the "attraction to glamour" theme might be played out by her husband. Rahu's association with the Moon here produces compulsion and addiction, which is the reason that John F. Kennedy's version of the Ashwini myth is filled with infidelities.

Mars Bhukti: Mars is the ruler of the seventh house in the Rashi chart, so it represents the spouse. It is placed in the eleventh house, which is the fifth house (romance and sexuality) from the seventh house. Mars in the fifth house produces a strong libido. It is also placed in the nakshatra of Purva Phalguni, which is symbolized by the conjugal bed and has the shakti of procreativity. This placement is largely responsible for Jacqueline's choice of a man with powerful sexual urges. The onset of the Mars sub-period simply expressed this tendency in her husband in a more powerful way.

Navamsha Chart: Mars is the badly afflicted ruler of the seventh house (spouse) in the Navamsha chart, placed in the sixth house (separation, disputes, struggles, divorce), indicating difficulties in marriage during this period.

Note: It was also during the Mars sub-period that the Bay of Pigs event took place, which was a huge embarrassment for Kennedy. The Mars placement in the sixth house of the Navamsha chart shows disputes, warfare, enemies and problems in general for Jackie's husband.

The Cuban Missile Crisis took place in October, 1962, during her Moon dasha/Rahu bhukti. Jackie's husband John F. Kennedy was assassinated on November 22, 1963.

Moon Dasha: The Moon is placed in the seventh house in a conjunction with Rahu showing problems connected with the husband during the period of the Moon.

Rahu Bhukti: Rahu is placed the seventh house in Bharani, a constellation connected with death. It is in a conjunction with the Moon, which makes the mutual periods of the Moon and Rahu produce the death of Jacqueline's husband.

Navamsha Chart: In the Navamsha chart the Moon is placed in the twelfth house (losses) in a conjunction with Saturn. This placement demonstrates the informative use of degrees in the Navamsha chart with startling clarity. Both the Moon and Saturn are in Bharani nakshatra, ruled by Yama, the god of death. The Moon is also afflicted by Mars and the Sun from the sixth house. This combination produces a powerful yoga called Balarishta Yoga, which is normally used in assessing longevity. Balarishta Yoga, if found in the Rashi chart, produces death in childhood, usually before twelve years of age. In the Navamsha chart, however, Balarishta Yoga can produce the death of the spouse. In this case, the death of the spouse took place relatively early in their marriage, after only ten years. Cases like this make it very clear that yogas can effectively be used in divisional charts.

Transits: Rahu (bhukti ruler) was transiting Gemini in Ardra nakshatra, which is symbolized by a teardrop. This brings the potential for experiences related to tears. Relative to the Moon (dasha lord) and to the seventh house (husband), Rahu was also transiting the third house. The third house is the eighth house from the eighth house, so it is one of the houses connected with death. Rahu is also aspected by transiting Mars (enemies/violence) from Scorpio, its own sign. Mars was also at twenty six degrees of Scorpio, putting it within two degrees of an exact opposition with Jacqueline's lagna lord Venus, showing that Jackie was also present at the time of the assassination. Mars was transiting the sixth house from transiting Rahu (enemies) and the eighth house from the natal Moon (death). Mars was also transiting Jyeshtha nakshatra, a constellation related to vanquishing enemies in warfare. This combination produced the attack by a powerful enemy and the slaying of John F. Kennedy. It is also interesting that the Moon (dasha ruler) was in an exact conjunction with transiting Saturn at the time of the assassination. Once again it becomes clear that no single factor produced this event, but rather a combination of many powerful factors. The combined influences of transiting Rahu and Mars only triggered the underlying inclination produced by the disposition of the dasha and bhukti rulers.

Jacqueline married Aristotle Onassis in October of 1968 during her Moon dasha/Ketu bhukti.

Moon Dasha: The many afflictions to Jacqueline's Moon that have previously been discussed led to a great deal of sadness during the period of the Moon. The Moon is placed in the seventh house, however, so it continued to also bring the need to connect with a partner. The

Moon is also placed in the constellation of Ashwini. Once again the Ashwini myth about the beautiful princess who married the old blind hermit became relevant. This time the myth was played out verbatim. Aristotle Onassis, the Greek shipping magnate, was much older than Jackie. News of the engagement made the whole world curious, as were the Ashwini Kumaras when they asked the young princess, "Beautiful young princess, what are you doing with this old blind hermit?"

Ketu Bhukti: Ketu signifies foreign things, so if a person finds a romantic partner during this period, the person will be Ketu-like, which may include unconventionality, being different, spiritually-oriented or foreign. Ketu is placed in Vishakha nakshatra, a nakshatra ruled by Indragni, two gods in one body. This suggests the desire for a partner. As discussed earlier, the ancient name for Vishakha is Radha, the name of the consort of Krishna, which also suggests the tendency to partner. It is also noteworthy that Ketu is a planet of detachment, uncertainty, and losses, so marriages that begin in Ketu periods sometimes do not last.

Transits: Transiting Jupiter and Ketu were passing through Virgo in Jackie's twelfth house. When the bhukti ruler (Ketu in Jackie's chart) is joined by a transiting natural benefic, then the period brings positive results. In this case, the transiting benefic was Jupiter, the karaka of the husband. Jupiter's conjunction with Ketu in the twelfth house in a woman's horoscope can produce marriage to a foreigner. This placement would at least produce foreign travel, which also took place for Jackie during the Ketu period. Transiting Jupiter also aspected natal Jupiter (husband) and Venus (marriage), and had very recently moved into Virgo from Leo, where it aspected the seventh house of Jackie's chart. Saturn had also been transiting Aries (Jackie's seventh house) only a few weeks earlier and had just retrograded into Pisces. Once again the dual influence of Saturn and Jupiter on the seventh house played an important role in promoting the marriage.

Aristotle Onassis died in March of 1975 (during her Mars dasha).

Mars Dasha: Mars is the ruler of the seventh house, so it represents the partner. It is placed in Purva Phalguni nakshatra which is ruled by Venus. Venus is the ruler of the eighth house placed in the eighth house. This gave it the potential to create upheaval, change, and death during its period. Purva Phalguni is also a nakshatra ruled by Bhaga, the god of prosperity. In Sanskrit, Bhaga means "the inherited share." This placement, combined with the nakshatra dispositor's placement in its own sign in the eighth house with Jupiter, produced a powerful combination for inheriting wealth. After the death of Onassis, Jackie inherited a fortune.

Transits: Transiting Mars, ruler of the eighth from the Moon and the eighth from the seventh house was in Capricorn. From this position it cast a powerful aspect onto Mercury, the bhukti ruler, as well as to the Moon and Rahu in the seventh house. Transiting Saturn was passing through the ninth house, casting its third house aspect on natal Mars (dasha ruler and the ruler of the seventh house). Transiting Ketu (losses) was in the eighth house (death) conjoining both natal Jupiter (husband) and Venus (marriage). In this case, the dasha ruler, bhukti ruler and both karakas for marriage were afflicted by transiting malefics, clearly pointing to a negative event related to Jackie's husband, Aristotle Onassis.

Author's Journal:

Close Encounters of the Hiker Kind

Have you ever wondered about what motivates people to hike for miles into the wilderness, give up creature comforts, sleep in a tent, put up with mosquitoes, and brave unpredictable weather? I have. In fact, I wonder about this frequently! Usually, however, this kind of inner questioning comes to me just before I put on my backpack, and set out, once again, for some remote place in the mountains.

On one particularly nippy October morning, I had an unusually strong dose of this kind of thinking. Along with four other hiking friends, Diane, Jeff, Mark and Betty, I had spent the previous night at a motel near Yosemite National Park. We got up early that morning and drove the spectacular mountain route across Tyoga Pass to Bridgeport, California, a picturesque cowboy town, on the eastern edge of the Sierras. We stopped briefly at the Bridgeport Ranger Station to get a wilderness permit, and then continued to the trailhead. After rearranging several items in my pack and tightening all the straps, I heaved the pack carefully onto my knee and then to my back. I cinched down the waistband and shoulder straps, and turned toward the bright faces of my four friends who had also donned their packs and were ready to go.

In the next eight days we would cover more than fifty miles together, crossing the Sierra Mountain range on foot, through some of the most spectacular and rugged wilderness on earth. My forty-five pound pack suddenly felt heavy as I thought about the steep switchbacks and high ridges we would have to navigate.

"Too late to turn back now!" I nervously joked to the others. Immediately

the armchair psychologist within me kicked in, eloquently expressing the perennial question. 'Why in the hell am I doing this!' I groaned to myself.

The beginning of a hike, especially a long backpacking trip, almost always creates a nervous sense of self doubt. I mostly wonder if I can handle the physical exertion and high altitudes. Hiking with weight on your back isn't easy, especially above eight thousand feet. But over the years I have learned a few tricks that help me get in shape for mountain treks. I usually increase my exercise routine, especially hiking up hills, for a couple of months prior to a long trip. I also load up my backpack and hike around in the hills near my home in Los Gatos.

On this morning, as we started up the trail, I soon adjusted to the weight of the pack and found an easy pace. I could tell that my conditioning program had worked, and quickly felt my doubts begin to fade. After a mile of dense forest hiking in the chilly mountain air, we suddenly broke into a vast, sunny, alpine meadow which lay at the feet of the towering peaks of the Sierras. I managed to put some distance between me and my hiking companions and soon found myself completely alone, in the middle of a three-mile long meadow filled with wild flowers and alpine grasses. I walked silently along the trail, looking ahead at the awesome granite peaks that lay in my path. I drew in a deep breath and as I let it out, I could feel the stress and fast pace of the so called "civilized world" leave me. As if remembering some forgotten secret, I thought, 'This is why I come here!'

At this point you might be wondering what my camping trip story has to do with astrology. To be perfectly honest, in some ways it has absolutely nothing to do with astrology and may not really belong in an astrology text. On the other hand, I have always thought that backpacking is the perfect metaphor for life. Not to use a cliché, but learning to be a "happy camper" is what life is all about as far as I am concerned. The horoscope shows "the path" an individual soul will tread in life. Sometimes the path is easy and sometimes difficult, but the whole point of astrology is to help a person meet the ups and downs of life with awareness and a happy attitude. Backpacking is the art of carrying your own baggage over undulating terrain, and simultaneously enjoying the scenery along the way. Learning to backpack simply makes a person better at living life!

Although there is no formal backpacking remedial measure in the Vedic astrology repertoire, it is a time honored technique in India. For thousands of years, yogis have walked deep into the Himalayas, carrying only a few simple things, living for years in the deep silence of caves or forests.

On one trip to the Himalayas, I met a great yogi who was more than 110 years old who had made continuous treks throughout his lifetime, through the Himalayan wilderness, through all kinds of weather, clad in nothing but a loin cloth. Even the common householder in India instinctively understands the value of taking long journeys, and annually goes on pilgrimages, frequently on foot, to visit remote shrines or temples. From ancient times, people from all parts of the world have been drawn to the mountains as a place which strips away excess, reveals the self, and forces one to rely on spirit alone.

 As I reached the edge of that big alpine meadow, I couldn't help but feel a kinship with all the yogis, adventurers, mountain climbers and naturalists from the past. A sense of exhilaration filled me as I started up a long set of switchbacks towards our first campsite, an alpine lake at 8,000 feet. Along the way, I took a break, and waited for the others. We hiked the rest of the way together and made camp by dusk.

During the next three days we established our hiking routine, covering about eight miles a day and reaching camp by about 3 p.m. The October weather was typical for this part of the Sierras, warm, sunny and bug free. We hiked in tee shirts and shorts. The trail along the way was one breathtaking vista after another, one waterfall after another, and each day was a day walking through a new mountain paradise.

 On the fourth day, about twenty-five miles into the hike, we took a layover day next to a lake. We each found spots to do laundry and to bathe along a creek that drained down from the lake. It was about 80 degrees that morning as I walked barefoot, hopping from stone to stone, for about a half a mile down the creek. Finally, I found a secluded pool, deep enough to sit in up to my neck, but shallow enough to be warmed by the afternoon sun. 'There is only one thing that beats hiking through the mountains,' I thought, 'and that's skinny dipping in a mountain stream!' I dropped my shorts, took off my shirt and entered nirvana.

Later that afternoon, one of my hiking companions, Diane, sat down with me in camp to talk astrology. I usually bring the charts of people I hike with along on these trips. Diane had never had an astrology reading, so I was initiating her into the language of the stars. I talked for half an hour or so about her personality, career, etc. and then I said, "Now let's talk about relationships."

 At that moment something caught my eye on the other side of the lake. There, lumbering along the meadow by the edge of the forest were two black bears, coming in our direction. "Look!" I said to Diane, pointing excitedly towards the bears. We both got up and watched the bears for a few minutes as they stopped and foraged by the lake and then continued towards us.

 "Quick, let's hang the food," Diane said, and we scrambled to get our food bags.

Now anybody who has ever backpacked in or around Yosemite National Park knows that you have to have a good strategy for protecting your food from bears, especially when you are three days from the nearest road. Yosemite bears are smart, especially when it comes to getting a backpacker's food bag. The time-honored method for dealing with this has been to hang your food bags from a tall tree. While this method works, it only works if you have a very tall tree, a very long rope, and a little luck. With Yosemite bears, you need a lot of luck. These bears have been known to send their cubs up a tree and out onto a limb over which a backpacker's food bags are hung. The cub breaks the limb and tumbles to the ground along with the bag, rope and branches. Then the mother and cub scramble off, bag in mouth, for a tasty afternoon snack.

On a previous trip, while camping at Rancheria Falls with my friend George, we made the mistake of hanging our food over a branch directly above our tent. It was a rainy night, so even though we knew this was a bad idea, we didn't feel like getting soaked while looking for the perfect branch. In the middle of the night I suddenly woke up to the sound of branches snapping in the tree above. I could hear a bear, probably a cub, in the tree above us trying to get our food. "George!" I whispered as I shook him. George emerged begrudgingly from a deep sleep. "George!" I said with an urgent tone, "there's a bear above the tent in the tree."

"What do you think we should do?" George asked in groggy tone.

"Well, if we stay here, the bear could fall right on top of the tent," I said. "On the other hand, if we run, we have to go out into the rain in our underwear. And if it is a bear cub that is up there, then the mother will not be far off. If we get in between the mother and her cub accidentally, then we're toast!"

Crack! Snap! A small branch fell on our tent. I was seeing visions of that bear cub hurling through the air towards our tent. "Let's get out of here!" I said.

We grabbed our flashlights and darted out through the tent vestibule into the cold, rainy night, probing in every direction with our flashlights to see if the mother could be sighted. Not seeing her, we turned the flashlights towards the tree just in time to see the cub scrambling down from the tree to make his escape. Luckily, the only thing we lost was our dignity.

With this and several other bear encounters etched in my mind, I quickly grabbed the food bags as Diane arranged the rope. Together we counterbalanced thirty pounds of food ten feet in the air, and then returned to the edge of the meadow to look for the bears.

"They're gone!" Diane said. We scanned the entire meadow around the lake and by the edge of the forest.

"Better keep our eyes peeled," I said. "They might be headed in our direction. Bears can smell food miles away."

We sat down on a log near the food bags, looking out at the lake. I returned to the astrology reading. "Omens have always been an important part of Vedic astrology," I said. "We saw two bears at the exact moment that I changed the subject of your reading to the area of relationships. You will undoubtedly attract a relationship in the near future."

Just then, Mark and Betty walked into the campsite after a day-hike to a nearby lake. "Did you see the bears?" I asked.

"Where?" Mark asked.

Diane told them about the bears and we all speculated about the odds of outwitting the bears with our strung-up food bags. In Yosemite Valley, a mere twenty miles away, backpackers are not allowed to hang their food anymore. Instead, they are required to carry bear canisters, bulky, heavy, bullet-proof metal containers that bears can't penetrate. The park rangers tell stories of bag-savvy bears performing miracles in order to get hanging food bags. In the past, campsites within the park were equipped with bear wires, pre-strung wires set high between two trees, over which backpackers could throw a line and string up food. The bears, however, simply send up their cubs who, apparently having trained with Ringling Brothers Circus, do a high-wire act that includes shinnying out on the wire and twanging the bag line until it breaks.

Although technically not inside the Yosemite Valley, we were inside the Yosemite National Forest. Everyone, except Diane, had encountered bears many times on other trips, with no mishaps. On those trips, however, we were always within a day's hike from civilization. This time we were three days out, and in country where the bears make an art of outwitting hapless campers.

Mark changed the subject, "It sure is nice to hike this far into the wilderness. We haven't seen even one hiker since day one."

It was true. We were completely alone, camped on the Pacific Crest Trail, in a spectacular spot, surrounded by huge evergreens, a lake, a stream, eagles, bears, and deer.

"This is one of the great benefits of doing such a remote hike," Mark said.

At that moment, I saw something on the side of the meadow. Something was moving by the edge of the forest. Thinking it might be the two bears, I got up and took a few steps forward. Coming out of the forest, I could see a single hiker making a quick pace into the meadow. "It's a hiker!" I said.

Mark got up to take a look. "He's hiking fast," Mark said.

We watched as he deftly crossed the drainage stream over a fallen log. He was tall, bearded, and as he got close, we could see that he was wearing nylon hiking pants, with zippers up the side. He had the zippers completely open for ventilation. He wore a bandana around his neck and was carrying what appeared to be an eighty-pound pack.

"Hello there!" I shouted as the hiker neared the camp.

"Hi!" he said as he approached. "Didn't expect to see anybody this far out," he said. His eyes immediately found our bear bags. "Think that's gonna work?" he asked.

"Hope so, or else we're gonna have a long, hungry walk home," I said.

"Where are you coming from?" Mark asked.

"Canada," the hiker said.

Mark and I exchanged a surprised glance. "Where you headed?" I asked.

"Mexico," he said calmly.

"That's a long walk," I laughed. I was thinking, 'This is better than meeting a bear!'

The Pacific Crest Trail runs a course along the rim of the Cascade and Sierra Range all the way from British Columbia, Canada, down to Mexico. Every year, a few brave souls hike the entire route, in a period of about five to six months. Hiking the Pacific Crest is the Boston Marathon of back-packing. More than 1500 miles of some of the roughest, most spectacular terrain on earth.

"When did you start?" Mark asked.

"May," the hiker said, "I had to plan out the food very carefully. I take enough for a week in my pack, and pack the rest in a large box. I send the box to a mountain town somewhere down the trail, hike down to it and restock my provisions each week. Then I send it to the next drop."

"How many miles do you cover in a day?" I asked.

"I average about thirty miles a day," he explained.

"Thirty!" I gasped. I had been feeling pretty good about my measly eight miles a day, but also pretty tired at the end of each hike. This guy was doing thirty miles a day!

The hiker continued to explain that he gets up at the crack of dawn, breaks camp in fifteen minutes and hits the trail immediately. He hikes until the sun goes down, only stopping to refill his water bottle and eat. He had started in late May and intended to complete his trip by November. It was crucial that he clear the northern California section of the mountains by early October in order to avoid the snow.

We continued to talk, but the hiker seemed restless. His tall, gaunt, wiry body seemed to have a mind of its own. He sort of paced while he talked, as if he couldn't contain his boundless energy.

"How do you deal with bears?" I asked. The hiker got a serious look on his face as his clear, determined eyes met mine.

"Well, that's my only worry," he said. " I've read a lot about these Yosemite bears. Everywhere else I hang my food. Here, I am not eating any cooked food. I am camping away from developed campsites and keeping the food bag inside my tent. I also say my prayers before I go to sleep!"

"You're brave," I said. "Sleeping with your food bag seems like a good way to have a bear for a bunk mate!"

The hiker explained that this was the preferred method of Pacific Crest Trail hikers when they pass through the Yosemite area. Apparently they are more concerned about protecting their food than they are about protecting their bodies from bear claws.

"I think I'll just hang my food," I said.

"Well, nice talking to you. I've gotta get going. There's still about an hour of daylight left," the hiker said.

We wished him good luck as he power-hiked down the trail. "He hikes like the energizer bunny," Betty chimed in.

"No kidding," Mark said.

I couldn't help but think what a great adventure and challenge he had set for himself. "Cranking out thirty miles a day would be a little too intense for my blood," I said.

"Me too" Diane said.

Yet the thought of hiking from Canada to Mexico through the mountains was totally captivating. Even a weekend in the wilderness changes a person, makes them more self-sufficient, happier, less complicated, and more flexible. "I can't imagine what six months of backpacking would do to your head," I said.

Mark agreed.

Our trek through the mountains continued on the following days to produce consistent magic. Our pace was easy and the terrain forgiving. We had already crossed the three huge ridges which separated us from the western side of the Sierras and we were now on a downhill course. My body felt strong, having fully adjusted to the daily hiking and extra weight. My mind was calm and expansive. There comes a point in every backpacking trip when boundaries dissolve, the ceaseless chatter of the mind falls away, and a hiker feels at one with the natural settings around him. I had reached that point on the first day and was now feeling completely free.

My hiking friends and I have an unspoken understanding that each of us hikes at our own pace. There is absolutely no pressure or expectation to hike fast or slow. Each person finds his own balance. During the last three days of the trip, I took full advantage of this, sometimes hiking far behind the group, and other times well out in front. This gave me the opportunity to hike completely alone, experiencing the feeling of total self-sufficiency and intimate solitude. Near the end of the hike, I started down the last section of trail called "the wall," a long series of switchbacks so-named *because they traverse a nearly vertical face of about a thousand feet. At the first switchback, a spectacular view of Hetch Hetchy Reservoir and Dam came into site far below. I would soon be crossing that dam and the trip would be over. I thought about the hiker we had met a few days before and wondered where he might be camping that night. I thought about how good it felt to be completely self-sustained in the middle of such a spectacular environment. 'Who needs the Himalayas,' I thought as I walked down the rocky trail. 'A person can live like a yogi even in California!'*

Chapter Twelve

Children

As with any of the other areas of life, the accurate assessment concerning children through the chart depends on the disposition of two main factors. The first factor is Jupiter, the karaka for children. Jupiter shows the person's general capacity to have children as well as his experience during the process of having and raising children. A strong, well-placed and unafflicted Jupiter makes it likely that the person will not only have children, but will find the experience of being a parent enjoyable and rewarding. A weak, poorly placed and afflicted Jupiter, on the other hand, will indicate that the person will experience difficulties either in having children, or during the process of raising children. The second factor is the fifth house, which is the general house of children. The disposition of the fifth house, via its ruler, planets placed in the fifth house, and aspects on the fifth house, is the most important factor in determining if the person will have children. If the fifth house is strong and influenced by benefics, then children are likely. If it is weak and afflicted by malefics, then having children may either be denied or involve difficulties.

The Ruler of the Fifth House

Positive Placements

Placed in the fifth house: If the ruler of the fifth house is placed in the fifth house, it greatly strengthens the house and makes it very likely that the person will have children.

Aspecting the fifth house: If the ruler of the fifth house is aspecting the fifth house, then it fortifies the house and makes it likely that the person will have children.

Placed in angles or trines: If the ruler of the fifth house is placed in houses 1, 4, 7, or 10 (angles) or houses 1, 5, or 9 (trines), then it strengthens the house and contributes to the likelihood of having children.

Negative Placements

Placed in a dusthana: If the ruler of the fifth house is placed in houses 6, 8, or 12 (dusthanas), then it weakens the house and makes it likely that difficulties will be experienced regarding children. The simple placement of the ruler of the fifth house in a dusthana, without affliction, does not usually deny children, but only brings mild difficulties in raising them. (For more on the house placement of the ruler of the fifth house, see the section on the fifth house in the chapter on houses in *Path of Light, Volume I.*)

Association with other planets: If the fifth house is associated with natural malefics then it produces problems regarding children. This association can take place in the following ways: natural malefics placed in the fifth house; natural malefics aspecting the fifth house; natural malefics placed in the same sign as (or aspecting) the ruler of the fifth house. If two or more malefics influence the fifth house then the resulting problems may become more serious.

Denial of Children: Complete denial of children is not produced by one single factor in the horoscope and should not be predicted unless a combination of negative factors exists. For example, if the fifth house is weak and afflicted, yet Jupiter is strong, then the person may still be able to have children, but could experience problems related to children. Even in cases where there are afflictions to both Jupiter and the fifth house, children may still be possible. Denial of children usually results when there are severe afflictions to both Jupiter and the fifth house, via its ruler, occupants, and other negative factors listed above.

Delay of Children

Delay rather than denial of children: Saturn is the planet of delays. The association of Saturn with Jupiter or the fifth house can cause delay in having children. This association can take place in the following ways.

1. Jupiter or the ruler of the fifth house placed in a conjunction with or aspected by Saturn.
2. Saturn placed in or aspecting the fifth house.
3. Jupiter or the ruler of the fifth house placed in a sign ruled by Saturn.

If the disposition of Jupiter and the fifth house are relatively positive, yet Saturn is associated with Jupiter or the fifth house, then delay is likely. Saturn comes to maturity at the age of thirty-six, and often delays the time of having children to mid-thirties in general. Saturn's influence usually makes the person very cautious and deliberate about having children, due to having a strong sense of the responsibilities involved in being a parent. The person hesitates to have children early in life. There is usually a desire for all the necessary factors to be in place before having a child such as financial security, marriage, and career stability. In many cases the person does have a choice, but consciously delays having a child to the point when the biological capacity for childbearing begins to diminish. Around the mid-thirties, the couple may realize that if they are going to have a child, then they must push through their doubts and hesitation and make deliberate efforts to conceive a child.

Adoption and Other Alternatives

Adoption of children is shown in the horoscope by combinations that promote unconventional action in the area of children. One of the most common placements for adoption is Rahu or Ketu in the fifth house. Merely having Rahu or Ketu in the fifth house, however, does not ensure that the person will definitely adopt children. Rahu or Ketu's presence can have many different meanings depending on other combinations in the chart. In any case, Rahu or Ketu's placement in the fifth house will usually manifest as an unconventional approach to children. Some of the other unique options that occur when Rahu or Ketu are placed in the fifth house are: modern technical means of having children, such as artificial insemination; the use of surrogate mothers; and alternative methods for promoting fertility, such as Ayurveda and Traditional Chinese Medicine. It is also possible that the person could have a child naturally, but use an alternative philosophy in raising or educating the child.

Rahu's combination with Jupiter is called Guru Chandala Yoga, and it is said to cause the person to become a heretic. *Chandala* means outcast, so this aspect causes the person to have unconventional beliefs. This definition especially applies to children, because Jupiter is the significator of children and Rahu represents unconventional things.

The constellation of Shatabhisha, which is ruled by Rahu, is also associated with adoption. This constellation is related to a myth about a king who purchased a son (symbolic of adoption). (See Shatabhisha nakshatra in *Path of Light, Volume I*) The other two constellations ruled by Rahu, Ardra and Swati, can also be associated with adoption. Similarly, Krittika nakshatra is sometimes associated with adoption. In the story of Agni, (given in *Path of Light, Volume I*), he seduced the six wives of six rishis. These six ladies collectively nurtured one single offspring that resulted from the intercourse. As a result, Krittika nakshatra is sometimes associated with having more than one mother, surrogate mothers, or adoption. If the Ascendant, the Moon, the ruler of the fifth house, or Jupiter fall in any of the above nakshatras, then the possibilities of unconventional experiences with children become higher.

Complications with Giving Birth

Multiple afflictions by natural malefics to the fifth house can show miscarriage, abortion, surgical procedures, premature birth, or other complications. This tendency is more pronounced when one of the malefics is either Mars or Ketu. When both Mars and Ketu influence the fifth house, then this tendency is amplified.

Chart 1: Woman with History of Miscarriages
December, 25, 1961; 12:43 AM; San Francisco, CA

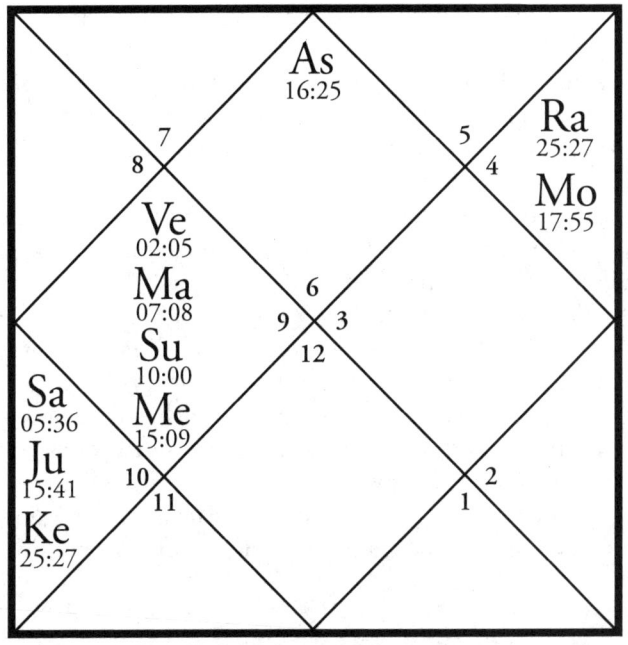

(D7) Saptamsha

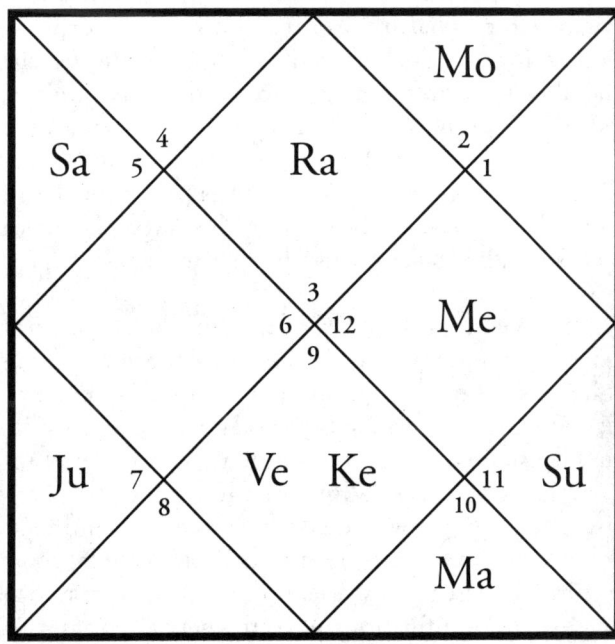

Chart 1 is of a woman who had a child early in life, and then had several miscarriages. Saturn, the ruler of the fifth house is in its own sign, which gives the ability to have children. Jupiter, the significator of children is neecha bhanga (see Neecha Bhanga Yoga in the chapter on yogas), causing problems regarding children that are possible to overcome. Ketu's placement with debilitated Jupiter suggests miscarriages. This is further suggested by the Moon (motherhood) which is conjunct Rahu and aspected by Mars.

Jupiter is also in a conjunction with Ketu, which gives the inclination to adopt alternative and unconventional philosophies. The placement of this combination in the fifth house suggests that unconventional events will take place in the domain of children.

Author's note: This woman came to me to ask if she would be able to have another child. Although she was age forty-one and had experienced several miscarriages in the past, I told her that having a child might still be possible if she tried alternative measures. I referred her to my wife, who is a well-known acupuncturist specializing in fertility. After a regime of herbs and acupuncture treatments for eight months, the woman gave birth. The baby was one month premature, but was healthy.

Dasha and bhukti: Ketu represents herbal medicine and alternative healing. It also is responsible for the unexpected complications producing the premature birth. Saturn, as fifth lord in Capricorn, suggests the possibility of having a child late in life. Jupiter, being neecha bhanga, indicates the ability to overcome previous problems. Jupiter conjunct Ketu suggests the possibility of benefiting from an alternative approach. The period of giving birth was Venus-Ketu. Venus is in Mula, a nakshatra whose basic desire is for progeny. Ketu is placed in the fifth house with Jupiter and Saturn. Ketu gives the results of the planets with which it is conjunct, so it allows her to give birth after delays.

Saptamsha chart: Venus is the ruler of the fifth house, making it a primary period for having children. Venus aspects the first house, which also re-emphasizes prominent events related to children. Ketu is conjunct Venus. When major and sub-period rulers conjunct in the Saptamsha chart, it usually produces prominent events related to children. Yet, Ketu is a planet of losses. Why didn't it produce the loss of a child through miscarriage, which would also have been a prominent event? In fact, throughout the Venus major period, Ketu's general role had been to promote miscarriages. In this case, however, the woman began to use some of the positive significations of Ketu (herbs, natural healing, and meditation) to remove Ketu's negative significations (loss through miscarriage). The saying, "Use a thorn to remove a thorn," aptly describes the way in which a little knowledge about the positive and negative traits of a planet can sometimes turn a negative condition into a positive one.

First Child, Second Child, Third Child

The fifth house is the house of children in general, but it is specifically the house of the first child. The second child is the younger sibling of the first child, so it is represented by the seventh house, which is the third house (younger sibling) from the fifth house. Similarly, the ninth house is the house of the third child; the eleventh house is the house of the fourth child; and so on.

How To Describe the Children

The fifth house is the house of the first child, so the sign in the fifth house can be used as the Ascendant for the first child. The characteristics of this sign will describe the personality of the first child. The sign and house placement (using the fifth house as the temporary lagna) of the ruler of the fifth house will also describe the first child. For example, if the sign in the fifth house is Aries, and Mars is exalted in the sign of Capricorn, then the first child will be assertive and independent, like the sign of Aries. He will also be very confident and ambitious because the ruler of the fifth house is exalted and placed in the tenth house (counted from the fifth house). This placement would make the first child successful in his career and it would also create a Ruchaka Yoga (see the yoga chapter) relative to the fifth house. Similarly, the signs in the seventh, ninth, and eleventh houses, as well as the rulers of those houses, will help describe the qualities of the second, third and fourth children, respectively.

 This technique can be extended to include a description of the career prospects, marriage, education and any other aspect of life of the various children. In order to describe the career of the first child, simply turn the chart around so that the fifth house is the lagna, and interpret the chart from that point of view. Counting from the new lagna, locate the tenth house and its ruler and describe the career according to the principles given in the chapter on career. The process is the same for describing the marriage prospects of one of the children. For example, to describe the spouse of the third child, first locate the house of the third child (the ninth house). Next, make this house the temporary lagna. It might help at first to simply turn the chart around or even redraw the chart so that the sign in the ninth house actually appears in the lagna position. Next, locate the seventh house from the new lagna. The sign in this house as well as the placement of its ruler will describe the spouse of the third child.

Harmony or Disharmony with Children

In order to tell if the person will get along with his various children, first locate the house of that particular child and describe the child's nature. If the nature seems gentle and sociable, then this contributes to harmony. If the nature is independent and rambunctious, this contributes to conflicts. The same logic must be applied to the owner of the horoscope. If his personality is loving and kind, nurturing, consistent, and full of other qualities necessary for good parenting, then this will contribute to harmony. If not, then problems will result.

The next step is to look at the relationship between the ruler of the first house (the person) and the ruler of the house signifying the specific child. If these house rulers are in a 3/11 or a 5/9 relationship, then there will be a friendly and harmonious relationship between the person and that child. (A 3/11 relationship means that counting inclusively from one of the pair of planets, the other is three houses away. Counting from the other planet, the first planet is eleven houses away, and so forth.) If the relationship is 6/8, then disharmony will result. If the relationship is 1/7, then the personality styles of parent and child will be opposite and could create conflict, especially if one or both of the planets is a malefic. If the relationship is 2/12, then the person and the child will not connect, and may feel that they do not quite understand each other. If the relationship is 4/10, then there may be occasional tension, especially if malefic influences are involved. If these two planets are placed in the same sign, then the level of harmony depends on the nature of the two planets. If the planets are friends, then harmony will result; if they are enemies, then disharmony between parent and child will occur. In any case, whether these two planets are friendly or unfriendly will be a contributing factor to the overall harmony of the relationship.

How Many Children?

Predicting the number of children can be done in a number of ways. If the fifth house is occupied or aspected by any planets, the number of children may correspond to the number of planets that influence the house. If any of the planets that influence the house are weak, combust, or at zero degrees, then they should not be counted. The ruler of the fifth house may also indicate the number of children. If it is placed with other planets, then the number of planets involved in the combination, including the ruler of the fifth house, may indicate the number of children. Similarly, these methods can be applied to the fifth house from the Moon and the fifth house from Jupiter.

Timing Children

The following periods are likely times for having children:

1. The period of the ruler of the fifth or the ninth house (the fifth house from the fifth) *Coming up soon*
2. The period of a planet occupying the fifth (or ninth) house
3. The period of a planet aspecting the fifth (or ninth) house
4. The above three dispositions can also be counted from the Moon or Jupiter
5. The period of Jupiter (karaka for children)
6. The period of a well-placed Moon (karaka for motherhood)

If moon is poorly placed - damages motherhood

The Saptamsha Chart

The Saptamsha chart is the divisional chart for children. This chart is very useful in determining the time of having children, as well as indicating events in the children's lives. As with other divisional charts, a planet placed in the lagna of the Saptamsha chart becomes a strong candidate for prominent events related to children, and therefore a candidate for producing children during its period. Whether the events are positive or negative depends on the positive or negative placement of the planet by sign and aspect. See the chapter on divisional charts for more clarification on this point.

Since children are a fifth house matter, the fifth house becomes the primary house in the Saptamsha chart. Planets placed in the fifth house of this varga will also produce prominent results related to children during their periods. The period of the ruler of the fifth house will also produce prominent results. Again, the positive or negative quality of those results will depend on the planet's disposition by sign, association, and aspect. The ninth house should also be considered here. It is the fifth house from the fifth house, so it becomes another primary house in the Saptamsha chart.

As in the list for timing children given above, other candidates in the Saptamsha chart include a strong Jupiter; a well-placed and strong Moon; planets that are placed in or aspect the fifth or ninth house; and planets connected to the fifth house from the Moon or Jupiter by rulership, placement or aspect.

In addition to timing birth, the Saptamsha chart can also be used to describe the events in the lives of children during the various planetary periods. For example, if a planet is placed in the tenth house of the Saptamsha chart, then the person's child might experience events related to the career that are in-line with the planet's nature and disposition in the chart. This can become confusing if the person has more than one child, so the method given under the previous section "How to Describe the Children" will be useful in sorting out the various elements in the lives of each of the children. For example, the career of the first child can be seen from the second house (the tenth house from the fifth house). The career of the second child will be seen from the fourth house (the tenth house from the seventh house), and so on. If the person only has one child, however, then the best method is to use the lagna of the Saptamsha chart as the lagna of the child and interpret the chart in a regular manner.

The following results show the general effect of the major or sub-period rulers when they are placed in the twelve houses of the Saptamsha chart. These interpretations are modern applications based on classical principles and have been found to give consistent results in the author's own practice. The specific results will vary depending on the positive or negative disposition of the dasha, bhukti or antara ruler in the Saptamsha chart. The period ruler's placement in the Saptamsha chart should not be used in isolation. It should be used in conjunction with the planet's placement in the natal chart. These interpretations are general guidelines and do not take the Saptamsha house rulership of the planet into consideration. To further modify and refine the interpretation, the reader should refer to the results given in the section on houses in *Path of Light, Volume I*. For example, if the ruler of the fourth house in the Rashi chart is placed in the eighth house, this normally suggests change of residence, as per the house interpretations given in *Volume I*. If, on the other hand, a period ruler is the ruler of the fourth house in the Saptamsha chart, and is placed in the eighth house of that chart, then the change of residence could take place for a child during that planet's period. The prediction, however, should be modified according to the age of the child. For a small child living at home, this could mean that the child's bedroom or his classroom could change. For an older child living away from home, it could indicate a change of residence or a remodel to the home.

Period Rulers in the Twelve Houses of the Saptamsha Chart

First House: If the period planet is placed in the first house of the Saptamsha chart, the period will produce prominent events related to children. This placement can produce positive or negative events related to the education or travel of the first child, the spouse or partner of the second child, and the education or creative involvements of the third child. In the absence of weakness or affliction, this placement generally suggests positive results.

Second House: If the dasha, bhukti or antara ruler is placed in the second house, then its period will produce results related to money, food, or speech for children. For infants and small children, this period could reflect events connected with learning to speak. It could also represent events related to diet. This house can also indicate the money that the parent spends on the child, as well as the child's own earnings in the case of older children. For the first child this placement produces events connected to the career (or education in the case of younger children). For the second child, this period could produce generalized change. In the case of the third child, the focus may be on health. The positive or negative quality of the events depends on the positive or negative disposition of the period planet in the Saptamsha chart.

Third House: If a period planet is placed in the third house of the Saptamsha chart, the children will experience communication and information-oriented experiences during the planet's period. This placement is typical for education-oriented experiences. It is also a placement that brings the children's communications with the parent into the spotlight. For the first child it represents experiences related to friends and groups. For the second, it can produce events related to education. For the third, it reflects one-to-one relationships, including marriage in the case of older children. The positive or negative quality of the events depends on the positive or negative disposition of the planet in the Saptamsha chart.

Fourth House: If the ruler of a planetary period is placed in the fourth house of the Saptamsha chart, it will produce events related to the home, room, or school of children in general. The person may travel to visit his grown child's home, or the child could come to visit him in his home. This placement may create uncertainties or travel for the first child. It can indicate career-related results for the second child, and may reflect general challenges and changes in the life of the third child. The positive or negative quality of the events will depend on the positive or negative disposition of the period planet in the Saptamsha chart.

Fifth House: The fifth house is a primary house for the Saptamsha chart. If the dasha, bhukti, or antara ruler is placed in the fifth house of the Saptamsha chart, the person will experience prominent results related to children during the planet's period. For example, a strong planet placed here can sometimes produced the birth of a child. In the absence of a negative disposition of the planet, this placement generally produces positive results. This is also a house of education for children in general. This placement can produce events related to friends and groups for the second child, and travel or education for the third child. If the person has grown children, this placement can sometimes produce grandchildren or may reflect having more contact with grandchildren.

Sixth House: If the ruler of a period is placed in the sixth house of the Saptamsha chart, the period may produce struggles, arguments or health issues related to children. If the planet is strong or associated with natural benefics, then it can improve health and suggests successful efforts connected with children. In the absence of a positive disposition, however, this placement tends to be negative. This placement can also produce events related to money, speech or food for the first child. In the case of the second child it may produce a period of general uncertainties, self-doubts, travel, or spiritual development. It shows the career (or education in the case of a small child) of the third child.

Seventh House: When the ruler of a planetary period is placed in the seventh house, the person may experience prominent events related to the second child. This is the house of partnership and marriage, so this placement can also produce relationships or marriage for one of the children. Similarly, the period may reflect events for the spouse of a child. The positive or negative quality of the events will depend on the positive or negative disposition of the planet in the Saptamsha chart.

Eighth House: Placed in the eighth house of the Saptamsha chart, a period ruler will produce change related to children during its period. The nature of the change may be related to the Saptamsha houses ruled by the period planet. If the planet rules the tenth house, for example, there could be a change of career. If it rules the seventh house then a child's relationship may go through an intense period of metamorphosis or change. A period ruler in the eighth house also can reflect events related to the house (or room) of the first child, and the money, speech or food of the second child.

Ninth House: If the period ruler is placed in the ninth house of the Saptamsha chart, the person could have prominent results related to children during the period. Being the fifth house from the fifth, this placement can also produce results related to grandchildren. For the first child, this placement may produce results related to education. For the second child, it can represent communications-oriented events. If the person has three children, then prominent events related to the third child may be emphasized. In the absence of negative factors, this placement tends to produce positive events.

Tenth House: If the ruler of a major period or sub-period is placed in the tenth house, then the career, or education or hobby in the case of younger children, may be brought into focus. For example, a strong planet placed here could suggest that a child has an improvement in his career. This placement may reflect the condition of the health of the first child. It produces results related to the house or room of the second child. It can focus on the money, speech or diet of the third child. The positive or negative quality of the events depends on the positive or negative disposition of the planet in the Saptamsha chart.

Eleventh House: If a period planet is placed in the eleventh house, it can produce successes or achievement related to children. This could be a period of having a child, for example. It could also suggest that a child achieves some desired goal or brings something to conclusion. This placement may also reflect events related to friendships and groups for children. For the first child, this period can produce one-to-one relationship events. For the second child, the events may be related to education, creativity or romance. For the third child, it can suggest communications-oriented events. The quality of the events will depend on the positive or negative disposition of the planet.

Twelfth House: In the absence of mitigating beneficial influences, a period ruler placed in the twelfth house can produce uncertainties or disappointments related to children. This is the house of distant places, however, so this is a typical placement for travel-related events connected with children. For example, the period can cause the person to take a trip with a child, or travel to visit a child in a distant place. For the first child, the period suggests general changes and lack of stability. For the second child, the period may bring events related to health or employment into focus. For the third child, events related to the house or the room may be emphasized. The positive or negative nature of the events depends on the strength, weakness and general disposition of the planet.

The Combined Transits of Jupiter and Saturn

Ideally, the birth of a child will be reflected by several astrological factors simultaneously. First, the major period planet should indicate the potential for childbirth. Next, the sub-period planet should indicate a child. Once the appropriate dasha and bhukti have been located, then the transits of Jupiter and Saturn in combination become a helpful tool. If both Jupiter and Saturn influence the fifth house by transiting through the house, aspecting the house, or by aspecting the house ruler, then the period becomes ripe for producing a child. If the dasha and bhukti are promising and only Jupiter influences the fifth house, this may also produce a child. This technique is normally applied to the fifth house, because it is the house of children in general, but it can also be applied to the seventh house, in the case of predicting the second child, and the ninth house in the case of a third child.

Of course a little common sense goes a long way in predicting children. The astrologer needs to take the person's age and circumstances into consideration. If the client is a forty-two year old female who is desperate to have children, she may have difficulty simply due to her age, regardless of positive astrological indications. It is helpful to remember that from about the age of thirty-six, females begin to slowly lose fertility. The odds of pregnancy in the late thirties and the early forties are much less than the years previous to age thirty-six. Similarly, it can be helpful to ask the person if they are planning to have children before making predictions. Modern methods of birth control and family planning can override astrological indications in making predictions about having children.

Chart 2: Charles Lindbergh
February 4, 1902; 1:30 AM; Detroit, MI

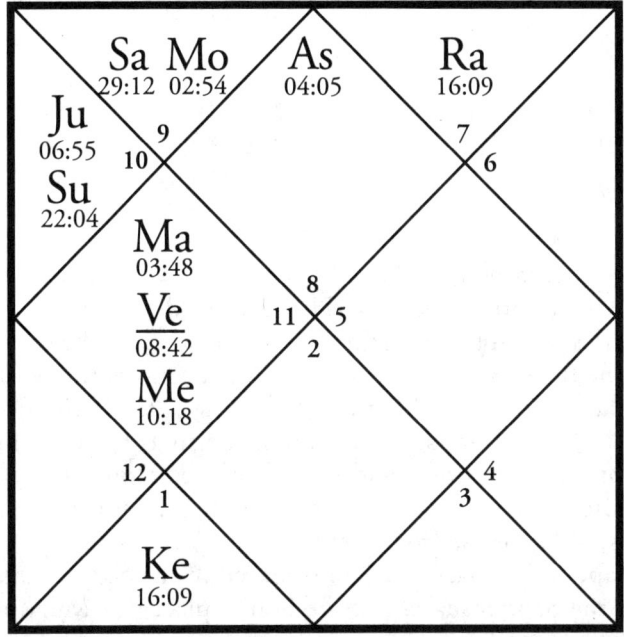

(D7) Saptamsha

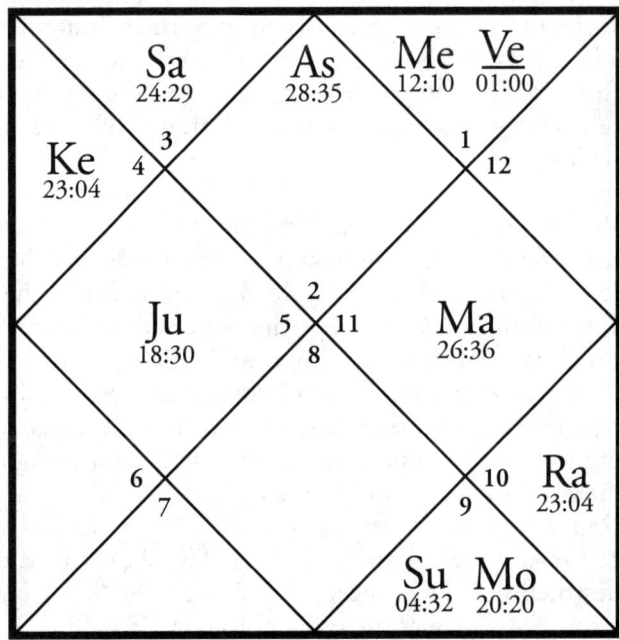

Dashas:

04/22/1927	Su	Su	12/15/1931	Su	Ke
08/10/1927	Su	Mo	04/21/1932	Su	Ve
02/08/1928	Su	Ma	04/22/1933	Mo	Mo
06/15/1928	Su	Ra	02/20/1934	Mo	Ma
05/10/1929	Su	Jp	09/21/1934	Mo	Ra
02/26/1930	Su	Sa	03/22/1936	Mo	Jp
02/08/1931	Su	Me			

Charles Lindbergh was the famed aviator who was the first person to cross the Atlantic in an airplane. His first child was born on June 22, 1930. Charles was in the major period of the Sun and the sub-period of Saturn at the time. Notice that the Sun is in a conjunction with Jupiter, which is the karaka for children and also the ruler of the fifth house. Saturn is in the sign of Sagittarius (even the signs ruled by Jupiter are prone to produce children) and placed in the second house (family). Saturn is also in conjunction with the Moon, which is the ruler of the ninth house (fifth house from the fifth).

In the Saptamsha chart, the Sun is placed in the eighth house. Using degrees in the Saptamsha chart, the Sun is placed in Mula nakshatra. Mula's desire is "to find the root of all progeny." The Sun is also aspected by Jupiter, the karaka for children. Saturn is the yogakaraka, and the ruler of the ninth house, which is an important house of children. It is placed in the second house (family) and in the constellation of Punarvasu, which is associated with the deity, Aditi, the mother of all the gods. These placements gave the dasha and bhukti rulers (Sun/Saturn) the tendency to produce a child.

It is important to note that Lindbergh's Rashi chart had some serious blemishes regarding children. First, Jupiter (fifth lord and karaka for children) is debilitated, conjunct a malefic (Sun), and hemmed-in by the malefics Saturn and Mars. In the Saptamsha chart, the Moon is placed in the eighth house conjunct the Sun, and aspected by Saturn and by Jupiter, the eighth lord. This combination is called Balarishta Yoga, which is used to predict death of children. Occurring in the Saptamsha chart, this combination suggests the early death of a child. It is interesting to note that Lindbergh's son, Charles Lindbergh III, also had a potent Balarishta Yoga in his Rashi chart.

As mentioned previously, using degrees in the Saptamsha chart, the Sun is placed in the constellation of Mula. The shakti of Mula is "the power of destruction." The aspect of Saturn on the Sun triggered the destructive force of this placement. The fact that the birth took place during such a negative dasha and bhukti combination (Sun/Saturn) does not bode well for the longevity of the child.

On March 1, 1932, during his Sun dasha and Mercury bhukti, the Lindbergh child was kidnapped and murdered. Mercury is placed in Shatabhisha nakshatra in the Rashi chart. Here it is in the company of Mars, the twelfth lord, Venus, and also receives the aspect of Saturn. The Shatabhisha story about the king who was asked by Varuna to sacrifice his son was played out in a literal but highly negative form. (See *Path of Light, Volume I* for stories related to Shatabhisha).

In the Saptamsha chart, Mercury is conjunct Venus (ruler of the sixth house) and placed in the twelfth house (losses). It receives the aspect of Jupiter (eighth lord). These influences suggest losses related to children.

It is also noteworthy that Lindbergh has Kala Sarpa Yoga (all planets hemmed in between Ketu and Rahu) in his chart. As the leading planet in this yoga, Ketu's placement in Bharani nakshatra in the sixth house becomes even more influential.

Author's Journal:

Varahamihira, Pig Astrologer

(As told to me by Mrs. Gayatri Devi Vasudev)

Once there was a man named Aditya Dasa who was a Sun worshiper. He had a son, who he named Mihira, which is one of the names of the Sun.

Being an astrologer himself, Aditya Dasa taught Jyotish to Mihira. When he became proficient in astrology, Mihira became the court astrologer of King Vikram Aditya, a very well-known king during a golden period in Indian history.

King Vikram Aditya had a son, and Mihira was asked to read his horoscope. After casting the horoscope, Mihira told the king, "This boy will be killed by a varaha, a boar!" Mihira also gave a specific date on which this unfortunate event would take place.

The king was so shocked and upset that he said, "My son will never be killed by a pig. I will make sure of it! If your prediction comes true, I will give you my kingdom. If it does not come true, you will be banished from the kingdom forever."

In order to ensure that the prince would not be killed by a pig, the king built a huge multi-story palace-fortress and confined the prince to the top floor. The prince lived safely in the palace, as everyone waited for the predicted date of death to arrive. As the date approached, everyone in the palace was placed on special alert, and all pigs were removed from the areas surrounding the palace. The king did everything possible to make sure that the prediction would fail.

When the fateful day arrived, the prince was playing in a courtyard at the top of the fortress, when a flagpole fell, killing him instantly. The *guards rushed to the boy's side, only to find that his head had been struck by a brass ornament which had been on the top of the flagpole. The ornament was that of a boar.*

After this incident, Mihira was given the title of Varaha (boar) Mihira. He later became the most illustrious astrologer of his time.

Chapter Thirteen

Parents

In addition to the information already given on this subject in the chapter on houses (see the fourth house for the mother and the ninth house for the father), the method (given in the chapter on children) of turning the chart around so that either the fourth house (mother) or the ninth house (father) becomes the lagna, can be used in order to obtain more details about the parents. Counting from the new lagna, subsequent houses become the parent's second house, third house, and so on. Similarly, the Moon's sign can be used for the lagna for the mother, while the Sun's sign can be used as the lagna for the father. If the person asks the question, "How will my father's health go in the next year?" The astrologer can answer by examining the condition of the sixth house (health) from the Sun (karaka for father), and the sixth house from the ninth house (father), which is the second house from the Ascendant. The same technique can also be applied to the Dwadashamsha chart.

Using the Dwadashamsha Chart

The Dwadashamsha chart is the key divisional chart used to give predictions about the mother and father. All of the general rules of varga interpretation given in the chapter on divisional charts can be applied to this chart. In addition to those guidelines, here are some additional points that may be helpful.

The primary houses for the mother are the fourth house and the house occupied by the Moon. The primary houses for the father are the ninth house and the house occupied by the Sun. Period planets placed in these houses give prominent results for the particular parent during their periods. Remember, however, that the ninth house is the sixth house from the fourth house, so it can also be used as the house of the mother's health. For example, a weak and afflicted planet placed in the ninth house, may create problems for the father generally, or for the mother's health specifically, during its period. Deciphering the difference between these alternatives is usually a matter of considering the significance of the period planet in the Rashi chart and other vargas.

The karaka for the mother is the Moon. Moon periods tend to produce events connected with the mother. In a major period of the Moon, a sub-period of a natural malefic planet can sometimes produce negative events related to the mother that are characteristic of the planet's natural qualities. Sub-periods of natural benefics will tend to produce positive results for the mother. For example, a Moon/Ketu period may produces losses or disappointment related to the mother. Similarly, the Sun is the karaka for the father, and its period will behave in a similar way for the father.

Yogas and the Dwadashamsha Chart

As with other divisional charts, yogas can be used in the Dwadashamsha chart. If a yoga appears in the Dwadashamsha chart, the effect of the yoga will apply specifically to the parents.

Dhana Yogas: Dhana Yogas (combinations for financial increase) in the Dwadashamsha chart will produce financial increase related to parents. This might mean that the person's mother, father or both parents experience a financial gain during the period of the planet. Alternatively, the period could produce a financial gain for the owner of the horoscope, but the gain might come through the person's parents. The exact manifestation of each yoga is a matter of carefully scrutinizing the period ruler's involvement in the Rashi and divisional charts. In this example, the planet's position in the Hora and Ekadashamsha charts (financial vargas) might give important clues. If the period planet falls in the ninth or fourth houses in either of these divisional charts, it could reinforce the connection between the parents and money during the planet's period. Final verification, however, should be derived from the Rashi chart. For example, if the ruler of the seventh house in the Rashi (the eleventh house from the ninth) is placed in the tenth house in the Rashi chart (the second house from the ninth), then it produces a Dhana Yoga for the father. In this case, the astrologer might predict that the financial gain will take place for the father specifically.

Gaja Kesari Yoga: Gaja Kesari Yoga is produced when the Moon and Jupiter are placed in houses 1, 4, 7, or 10, relative to each other. This yoga was covered in the chapter on yogas. It is a yoga that has a wide variety of applications. When applied to career, this yoga produces connections to the public such as advertising, marketing, sales, promotion, presentations and growth of reputation. When applied to family matters, however, it creates group events related to the family, such as family reunions or get-togethers. It can also be applied to social contacts and public events of the parents. If it is connected to the tenth house in the Dwadashamsha chart, then it can indicate typical career-oriented events for one of the parents' careers. If this yoga is present in the Dwadashamsha chart, it will manifest during the periods of Jupiter and/or the Moon. It will also manifest during the periods of planets placed in the same signs as Jupiter or the Moon in the Dwadashamsha chart.

Neecha Bhanga Yoga: Neecha Bhanga Yoga was covered in the chapter on yogas. It was described as producing initial problems followed by some improvements. Alternatively, this yoga can produce a problem that later becomes a blessing in disguise. A Neecha Bhanga Yoga found in the Dwadashamsha chart will produce results related to the parents. The specific area of the parent's life that will be affected will depend on the nature of the planet, as well as its house placement in the Dwadashamsha chart. For example, a neecha bhanga Mars, placed in the sixth house of the Dwadashamsha chart, might suggest a successful surgery (overcoming a problem) during a major period or sub-period of Mars. Placed in the fourth house (home environment), the same neecha bhanga Mars could suggest a landscaping project (Mars is the karaka of land) around the home for both parents.

Raja Yogas: Raja Yogas found in the Dwadashamsha chart promote the career, status and success of the parents. If the parents are retired then the yogas simply suggest successful accomplishment of projects and other involvements by the parents.

Yogas for Travel: As mentioned in the chapter on yogas, the houses of travel are the ninth, twelfth, and third. Combinations of these houses, via the placement or combinations of their rulers, produce travel in their periods. When these combinations occur in the Dwadashamsha chart, then it sometimes produces travel related to parents. For example, if the ruler of the ninth house is placed in the twelfth house in the Dwadashamsha chart, then the person's parents might travel during the major or sub-period of the planet involved in the yoga. This could also mean that the owner of the horoscope travels to visit his parents (or vice versa) during the period.

Planetary Period Rulers Placed in the Twelve Houses of the Dwadashamsha Chart

First House: If the dasha, bhukti or antara ruler is placed in the first house of the Dwadashamsha chart, the person may experience prominent events pertaining to parents. This could mean that he has more prominent contact and interaction with his parents during the period, or that the parents have more noticeable events occur in their own lives. The planet and sign in the first house may indicate the nature of the events. The positive or negative quality of the events will depend on the positive or negative disposition of the planet.

Second House: If a strong and well-supported period planet is place in the second house of the Dwadashamsha chart, the parents may experience financial gains or may purchase desirable items during the planet's period. This placement sometimes suggests that the person will have financial gifts or support from the parents. If the period planet is afflicted or weak, then the parents could have expenses or financial problems during the period. This could also mean that the person could give money to his parents or experience some financial problems due to his parents. This placement may suggest health problems for the father.

Third House: If a strong and beneficially disposed planet is placed in the third house of the Dwadashamsha chart, the person will experience positive communications with his parents during its period. This could also indicate that the parents will experience many positive short trips, or become involved in information-gathering activities, such as taking a class. If the planet is afflicted and weak, then the person might experience disagreements or other communications problems with his parents. This could also mean that the parents experience communications problems of their own with other people.

Fourth House: If a strong and well-aspected planet is placed in the fourth house of the Dwadashamsha chart, the person may experience positive events related to the mother during the planet's period. This can also mean the person visits the home of his parents or that the parents come to visit him in his home. If the planet is weak and afflicted, then the person may experience negative interactions with the mother. This may also be an unsettled period for the father.

Fifth House: If a strong and supported planet is placed in the fifth house of the Dwadashamsha chart, the person will generally experience positive events related to parents during the period. This may simply indicate a period of good health, prosperity and general happiness for the parents. This placement can also suggest educational support by the parents. If the planet is weak or afflicted, the parents may have general stresses in their lives. There could also be some emotional strain or negative events connected with education that is somehow related to the person's parents.

Sixth House: Unless it is well-supported and strong, a planet which is placed in the sixth house of the Dwadashamsha chart normally suggests problems related to parents during its period. If it is associated with natural malefics, then this placement may suggest health problems for one of the parents. This need not be a dramatic illness, and could even reflect simple and common ailments. If the planet is strong and supported, then it can suggest good results for one of the parents through employment. It may also produce an improvement in health for one of the parents.

Seventh House: A strong and positive planet placed in the seventh house of the Dwadashamsha chart can produce positive events shared by both parents during the planet's period. This placement can indicate a time during which the parents' relationship is harmonious, or even show the re-marriage of a single parent. It can also produce a period of harmony between the person and his parents. If the planet is weak or afflicted, then the period can produce disharmony, either for the parents or between the person and his parents. This placement can also be associated with difficulties through legal matters, contracts, or consultants for the parents.

Eighth House: If a well-supported and strong planet is placed in the eighth house of the Dwadashamsha chart, the person may experience financial gains through the parents. This placement can also cause the parents to obtain unearned income through loans, gifts, insurance or other outside sources. It can be associated with a period of change that is an intense, but productive period in the life of a parent. If the planet is weak or afflicted, then the period will involve change that will be more difficult. If other factors agree, then this period can sometimes be associated with the death of a parent. In most cases, however, such dire consequences are not the result, and the parent simply experiences health problems, changes, expenses or other challenges.

Ninth House: A strong and positive planet placed in the ninth house of the Dwadashamsha chart can produce positive events related to the person's father during its period. This placement is also good for the health of the mother, and may suggest healing or involvement in activities that improve the health. It can also be associated with positive, long-distance travel experiences related to the parents. If the planet is weak or influenced by malefics, then the mother or father may experience health problems or other concerns.

Tenth House: If the planet placed in the tenth house of the Dwadashamsha chart is strong and supported, then one of the person's parents could experience success and progress in the career during the planet's period. This placement can also suggest positive projects that the person does for his parents or with his parents. If the planet is weak and afflicted, then the period may produce general problems related to parents, especially in the domain of action, projects, and career.

Eleventh House: The placement of a positive and supported planet in the eleventh house of the Dwadashamsha chart generally suggests good results related to parents. The person could attend a group event such as a party or family reunion that a parent also attends. This can also be a period in which a parent becomes more involved with friends, groups or organizations. The period can also produce financial gains, finishing of projects, or attainment of desires on the part of the parents. If the planet is afflicted or weak, then the parents or person's experience of the things listed above might contain negative elements.

Twelfth House: A strong and supported planet placed in the twelfth house of the Dwadashamsha chart sometimes suggests positive experiences connected with distant places, either for the parents or for the person in his relationship with the parents. For example, the person could travel to a distant place to visit a parent, or a parent could travel during this period. If the planet is weak or afflicted, then the parents could experience a period of uncertainty, losses, or expenses. This could also cause the person to experience a period of uncertainty or disappointment regarding his parents.

Prince William
June 21, 1982; 9:03 PM; London, England

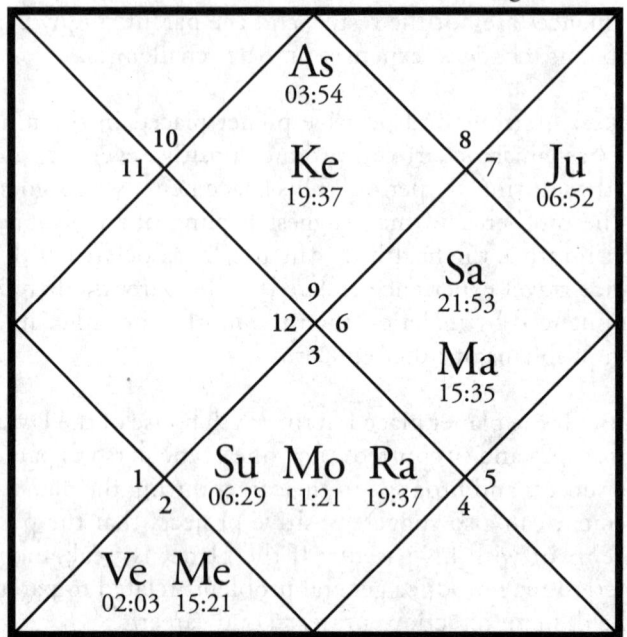

(D12) Dwadashamsha

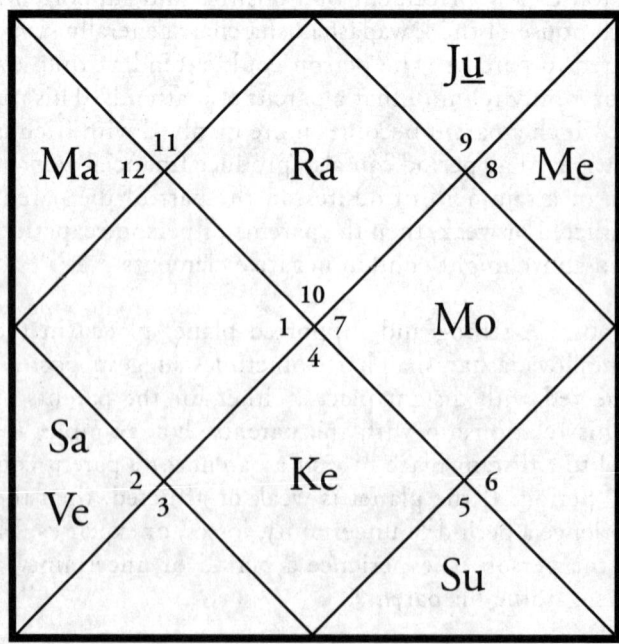

Dashas

02/03/1993	Ra	Ma	09/04/2004	Jp	Su
02/21/1994	Jp	Jp	06/23/2005	Jp	Mo
04/11/1996	Jp	Sa	10/23/2006	Jp	Ma
10/23/1998	Jp	Me	09/29/2007	Jp	Ra
01/28/2001	Jp	Ke	02/22/2010	Sa	Sa
01/04/2002	Jp	Ve			

Prince William is the son of Prince Charles and Princess Diana of Great Britain. His mother, Diana, died in a foreign country on August 31, 1997, during William's major period of Jupiter and sub-period of Saturn. Notice that in William's Rashi chart, the Moon is in the seventh house in a conjunction with the Sun and Rahu. It is also aspected by Saturn, and these conditions produce the initial potential for loss of the mother.

The following points reflect this event in the Jupiter dasha, Saturn bhukti.

Rashi Chart

1. Jupiter is placed in the eleventh house, which is the eighth house (death) from the fourth house (mother).
2. Saturn (sub-period ruler) is the ruler of the fourth house (mother) from Jupiter (the major period ruler), and is placed in the twelfth house (losses) from Jupiter.
3. Saturn is in a conjunction with Mars. Together, both malefics aspect the fourth house (mother) from the Ascendant.
4. Saturn and Mars are both fourth from the Moon (mother) and Saturn is the sub-period ruler. From the Moon, Saturn rules the eighth house (accidents) and Mars rules the sixth house (also accidents).

Dwadashamsha Chart

1. Jupiter is the ruler of the twelfth house (losses and distant places), and is placed in the twelfth house.
2. Saturn rules the lagna of the Dwadashamsha chart, showing that prominent events for one of the parents will take place during its period.
3. Saturn is placed in the sixth house (accidents and injuries) from Jupiter in the Dwadashamsha chart.

4. Saturn and Mars hem in the Dwadashamsha fourth house (a primary house in this varga), forming a Papa Kartari Yoga (hemming in by malefics). This yoga creates difficulties for fourth house matters (mother).

Transits in the Rashi Chart

It is noteworthy that Saturn (the sub-period ruler) was transiting Prince William's fourth house (mother) at the time of her death. Saturn is the planet of death.

Author's Journal:

Two Bananas

(As told to me by Mrs. Gayatri Devi Vasudev)

Once there was a Jain teacher named Narapatijaya Acharya who was very accomplished in Prashna and the use of omens. One day he was sitting at home when a worried man came to his house and said, "My sons are missing. Can you help me?"

Narapatijaya Acharya said, "Please sit and wait while I make the horoscope."

In the meantime, a woman came to the house carrying a bunch of bananas. She gave the bunch of bananas to Narapatijaya Acharya's wife. His wife plucked two bananas from the bunch and took them to the kitchen. She put one of the bananas in the frying pan to cook. The other, she put in a vessel of water to keep it from becoming black.

Narapatijaya Acharya observed all of this. Before the man could provide any details of his question, Narapatijaya Acharya said, "Your two sons are dead. One has drowned in the sea. The other has been killed and buried in the sand by robbers."

The man was very upset by this, and he immediately ran to the seashore and found his two sons' bodies. One had been washed up on the shore. The other son's mutilated body was found buried in the sand.

When asked how he made this prediction, Narapatijaya Acharya said, "At the time of the man's arrival, a woman also came to the house with a bunch of bananas. Two bananas were plucked from the stock. This represented the man's two sons. My wife put one in water, so one son drowned. She pealed the other, cut it into pieces, and put it in oil to fry. So I concluded the other son had been killed with knives and buried the sand."

Path of Light – The Domains of Life

"These omens simply indicate what is going to happen as a result of your good or bad karma in your last birth. At the time of entering (when the client enters the astrologer's office, or when the astrologer enters the client's home) if the astrologer hears the Vedas being chanted, mantras recited, sees a bull facing the house, hears cows mooing sweetly, or if he finds a gentle and fragrant breeze blowing, then he should predict good health and prosperity." —Prashna Marga

1st born ~~first~~
Child of the ~~second~~ younger
Sibling

Seventh House

Spouse of the first younger
Sibling

Ninth House

3rd house
Joesph

4th House — Sarah would have a
Sarah   teen child, but the
                  relationship with
5th House   7th   this child would be
Paul   Matthew non-existent (Fallen
                  Saturn in 1st house
                  of Drekana)

Jack
is going
to have
a many — 7th house of
new child the Drekkana

Chapter Fourteen

Brothers and Sisters

The topic of brothers and sisters was covered in the chapter on houses, (the third house), in *Path of Light, Volume I*. The third house is the house of siblings in general. The disposition of the third house and the placement of its ruler can give important clues about the siblings. (Read the results for the placement of the ruler of the third house placed in each of the twelve houses, given in that chapter, as well as the description given for the placement of the nine planets in the third house.)

When describing siblings from the horoscope, however, it is important to understand that the third house can be used in two ways. First, it is the general house of brothers and sisters. In this respect it gives a generalized view of the person's experience with his siblings. Second, the third house is also the specific house of the next younger sibling. If the person has several brothers and sisters, each will be represented by a different house.

Locating a Specific Sibling in the Horoscope

The principle used to find specific siblings in the chart is simple. The next younger sibling is the third house. The fifth house represents the person's second younger sibling. This is because the fifth house is the third house (next younger sibling) from the third house (next younger sibling). Counting from the lagna, which represents the person himself, each younger sibling, in order, will be three houses away from the previous one. Similarly, the eleventh house (counting three houses previous to the first house) is the house of the next older sibling. Three houses previous to the eleventh house, the ninth house is the house of the second older sibling (the next older sibling to the next older sibling).

Describing a Specific Sibling

In order to describe a specific sibling from the chart, first locate the house which represents that sibling. Next, describe the sign and planets occupying that house. The disposition of the ruler, especially the qualities of the nakshatra and sign it occupies, will be particularly important in the description of the sibling. If the ruler of the specific sibling's house is debilitated, then that brother or sister may be weak in some way, either physically or in terms of the personality. If, on the other hand, the ruler of a sibling house is exalted, then the sibling will be strong in terms of the planet's nature. For example, let's say that the ruler of the ninth house is Saturn. Saturn, then, signifies the second older sibling. Let's say that Saturn is placed in the sixth house in Libra. Because Saturn is exalted in Libra, the second older sibling will possess a strong sense of responsibility, patience, perseverance and management abilities, which are the qualities of a strong Saturn. Because it is placed in the sixth house (the tenth house from the ninth house), that sibling will manifest the Saturn qualities in his occupation and could become a manager. This placement will also make it likely that the second older sibling will have a strong physical constitution.

This description can be furthered by the use of the nakshatra and even the drekkana occupied by the ruler of the sibling's house. In the previous example, if Saturn is also placed in the constellation of Chitra, the sibling could possess the ability to design things and be charismatic. If it is also placed in the first drekkana of Libra, which is symbolized by a man sitting by the side of the road in a shop, then the sibling might own and manage a retail store or apply his management skills to marketing. In this way, by working with the various symbols of the sign, nakshatra and drekkana occupied by the ruler of the sibling's house, the description can become quite detailed.

Harmony or Disharmony With Siblings

In order to determine if the person experiences harmony or disharmony in his relationship with a particular sibling, two factors must be considered. First, the relative strength and nature of the house and house ruler for that sibling must be considered. For example, a client may ask, "How does my relationship with my brother, who is my next older sibling, look?" Because the next older sibling is represented by the eleventh house, the first consideration must be the disposition of the eleventh house and its ruler. If the eleventh house is afflicted by malefics, and if the ruler of the house is debilitated and afflicted, then the person will experience his older brother as weak and problematic. If the eleventh house and its ruler are strong and well-disposed, then the person will experience his elder sibling as strong, intelligent, and well-behaved. In other words, the first step in understanding the person's relationship with the sibling is the general assessment of the sibling's character. If the character of the sibling is sweet, charming and personable, then it is more likely that the person will get along with him.

On the other hand, even a strong and well-behaved sibling can be problematic at times. To further understand the level of sympathy between the person and his sibling, examine the relationship between the ruler of the first house (the person) and the ruler of the house of the specific sibling. This method is borrowed from the Tajika system and was described in the chapters on children and relationships. In the previous example, if the lagna is Leo, then the Sun rules the first house (the person), and Mercury rules the eleventh house (the next older sibling). Let's say that Mercury is placed in the third house in Libra and the Sun is placed in fifth house in Sagittarius. The fact that they are in a 3/11 relationship, (the Sun is three houses from Mercury and Mercury is eleven houses from the Sun), produces a positive and harmonious relationship between the person and his older brother. See the chapter on children for further elaboration on this technique. As a reminder, planets placed in 3/11 and 5/9 relationships are harmonious. Planets in 6/8, 2/12, 1/7, and 4/10 relationships are inharmonious. The harmony level between planets in conjunction depends on the friendship relationship (See the "Table of Planetary Friendship" in *Path of Light, Volume I*) between the two planets.

The Drekkana Chart

The Drekkana chart is the divisional chart for siblings. The techniques given above can also be applied to this chart, as can the technique of turning the chart around and using the house of the specific sibling as a temporary lagna (see the chapter on children for more details on this technique). For example, if you want to know about the first child of the person's third older sibling, first locate the house of the third older sibling (the seventh house). Now make the seventh house the temporary lagna. Counting from this point, locate the fifth house from it. The fifth house from the seventh house is the eleventh house. This house becomes the house of the first child of the sibling.

As with other vargas, any yogas appearing in this chart can be interpreted in terms of the person's siblings. Dasha planets will also give results for brothers and sisters, according to their placement in the Drekkana chart.

Below are typical results given by planets placed in the twelve houses of the Drekkana chart. As with the other divisional charts, these results should be modified according to the planet's house rulership in the Drekkana chart, as well as its positive or negative disposition according to sign placement, aspect, and other defining factors. For interpretations of the various house placements and house rulerships, the reader can refer to the chapter on houses in *Path of Light, Volume I*. These results should be modified to reflect events in the lives of siblings.

Planets Placed in the Twelve Houses of the Drekkana Chart

First House: A primary house; siblings in general; the children, especially the first child of the second older sibling. A dasha planet placed in the first house will signify that during the planet's period, the person will experience prominent events related to brothers or sisters in general. The positive or negative nature of the events will be associated with the positive or negative disposition of the planet.

Second House: Financial matters related to siblings in general; the residence of the first older sibling; the health of the second older sibling; the career of the second younger sibling. If a planet is placed in the second house, it can produce financial gains or losses (in the case of afflicted planets) for one of the siblings in general. It can also signify financial events for the person himself, which are related to one of his siblings. If the person has an afflicted planet in this house, and he has a second older sibling, this period could produce health problems for that sibling. If the planet is strong and positive, however, then the second older sibling's health (or employment) could improve. Similarly, the career of the second younger sibling could wax or wane according to the disposition of the planet.

Third House: A primary house for the Drekkana chart; siblings in general; the first younger sibling specifically; the children (especially the first child) of the first older sibling; the spouse or relationship of the second older sibling; gains and friendships for the second younger sibling. A planet placed in the third house of the drekkana chart usually produces prominent results connected with one of the siblings during its period. Since this is a general house of siblings, the affected sibling does not necessarily have to be the next younger sibling. The period planet placed here will also give positive or negative results to the other domains listed above, depending on its positive or negative disposition by sign, aspect, and association with other planets.

Fourth House: Home and real estate for siblings in general; the health of the first older sibling; the financial matters of the first younger sibling; the house of upheaval and change for the second older sibling. If a period planet is placed in the fourth house of the Drekkana chart, one of the person's brothers or sisters may experience home or house-related events, such as purchase of property, remodeling, or landscaping. This planet can also produce financial ups or downs for the first younger sibling, depending on the planet's positive or negative disposition in the chart. It can also indicate changes for the second older sibling.

Fifth House: Second younger sibling; children for siblings in general; education for siblings in general; the spouse or partner for the first older sibling; long-distance travel and higher education for the second older sibling. If a period planet is placed in the fifth house of the Drekkana chart, the person might have more contact with his second younger sibling during the planet's period, or that sibling might have more prominent events in his own life. This planet's period can also signify relationship events for the first older sibling, which will be positive or negative depending on the planet's disposition. Unless this planet is afflicted, the fifth house placement is generally good for the overall well being of siblings as well as the person's relationship with them. It may signify the birth of a child for one of the brothers or sisters, for example, or may simply point to more prominent events in the lives of the sibling's children.

Sixth House: Health for siblings in general; struggles and disagreement related to siblings in general; the finances of the second younger sibling; the house or home of the first younger sibling; the house of upheavals and changes for the first older sibling; the career of the second older sibling. If a planet is placed in the sixth house of the Drekkana chart, the planet's period can bring positive or negative results for the significations listed above, based on the positive or negative disposition of the planet. If the planet is afflicted here, then arguments or disagreements with one of the siblings might result. This could also be a period of general struggle and difficulty for a brother or sister. For example, it could signify a period of health problems for one of the brothers or sisters.

Seventh House: Relationships; partnerships or marriage for siblings in general; the children (especially the first child) of the first younger sibling. If a planet is placed in the seventh house of the Drekkana chart, it can produce relationship events for siblings in general. For example, if the planet is strong and positive, then its period sometimes produces positive relationship events such as marriage, birth of children or prosperity for a spouse. If it is negatively placed, then the period can suggest disharmony in marriage or other relationships.

Eighth House: Upheaval; change; death; transformation; the second younger sibling's home; the career of the first older sibling; the health of the first younger sibling; money from outside sources related to siblings. During the period of a planet placed in the eighth house, the person will have negative or positive results for the values listed above, based on the positive or negative disposition of the planet. For example, a debilitated or afflicted planet placed in the eight house could cause one of the siblings to go through a period of suffering, involving significant live changes. On the other hand, a well-placed planetary period ruler could indicate a successful period for the career of the next older sibling.

Ninth House: A favorable house for siblings in general; travel; the second older sibling; the spouse or partnerships for the first younger sibling; the children (especially the first child) of the second younger sibling. If a planet is placed in the ninth house of the Drekkana chart, then its period will usually produce favorable results for brothers and sisters in general. Its positive or negative disposition will determine whether it produces positive or negative results for various house significations listed above. For example, a badly afflicted planet placed here could indicate a separation or divorce for the first younger sibling. A positive planet, could suggest travel for one of the siblings, especially if it is the ruler of the third or the twelfth house.

Tenth House: The career of siblings in general; upheavals and changes for the first younger sibling; the financial affairs of the second oldest sibling; the health of the second younger sibling. If a planet is placed in the tenth house, its period will produce either positive or negative events for the things listed above, depending on the planet's positive or negative disposition. For example, a positive and strong planet in the tenth house could indicate career advancement for one of the brothers or sisters.

Eleventh House: The next older sibling; the spouse of the second younger sibling; friendships and gains for siblings in general. If a planet is placed in the eleventh house, the period will produce prominent results if the person has an older sibling. This could mean that the person has more interaction or contact with the older brother or sister. The positive or negative quality of the relationship will depend on the positive or negative disposition of the planet. If the person doesn't have an older sibling, then a period planet placed in the eleventh house might indicate events related to desired goals, achievements, or financial gains for siblings in general.

Twelfth House: Distant places; losses; uncertainty; the next older sibling's finances; the house or residence of the second older sibling; the career of the first younger sibling; the house of upheavals and changes for the second younger sibling. If a period planet is placed in the twelfth house of the Drekkana chart it will give positive or negative events related to the significations given above, depending on the positive or negative disposition of the planet. For example, it may produce a period of uncertainty in the life of one of the siblings or in the person's relationship with a sibling. It could also signify a period when a sibling travels to a distant place, or is living in a distant place.

Sister Purchases A House
July 22, 1949; 6:25 PM; San Jose, CA

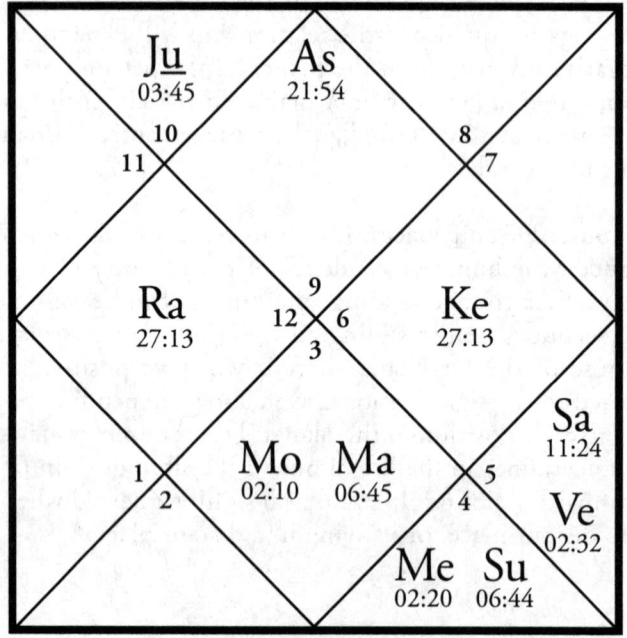

(D3) Drekkana

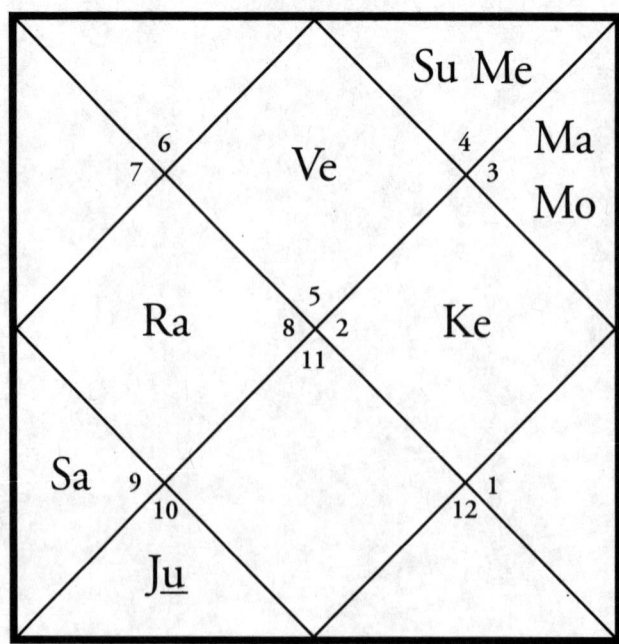

In the example chart the person's sister purchased a house during the period of Saturn/Jupiter. This event is reflected in the chart in the following ways.

Rashi Chart

1. Saturn is ruler of the third house (next younger sibling). It is placed in Magha nakshatra, which is symbolized by a throne room and is a very typical nakshatra for real estate events.
2. Saturn is in a conjunction with Venus, ruler of the sixth house, which is the house of property for the next younger sibling (the sixth is the fourth house from the third house). Venus is also placed in Magha.
3. Saturn also aspects the sixth house (fourth from the third), the house of property for the sibling.
4. Jupiter, the sub-period ruler, aspects the sixth house, which is the fourth house (real estate) from the third house.

Drekkana Chart

1. Saturn is the ruler of the sixth house, which is the fourth house (property) from the third house (next younger sibling).
2. Jupiter is placed in the sixth house.
3. From Saturn, the major period ruler, Jupiter rules the fourth house. Jupiter is placed in the sixth house (sibling's property).
4. Saturn and Jupiter are in a Parivartana Yoga (exchanging signs), thereby strengthening their bond.

Jupiter is Neecha Bhanga

Jupiter is neecha bhanga (canceled debilitation – see the definition in the chapter on yogas) in both the Rashi and the Navamsha charts. This caused her younger sister to initially have a problem getting the money to buy the house. (Notice that Jupiter is in the second house (money) from Saturn in the Drekkana chart.) When a yoga is repeated in both the Rashi chart and the divisional chart, it usually means that the yoga will manifest in a pronounced way in the area of life represented by the divisional chart. Later in the period she was successful getting financing. She also purchased a house that needed repairs, and even started some of those repairs during the sub-period of Jupiter.

Author's Journal:
The Nose Knows

You don't have to be an astrologer to use *nimitta* (omens) to predict the outcome of questions. All you have to do is look around you whenever you have any serious question. If you are sharp, you will pick up all sorts of clues from your everyday environment. Your body also gives clues. In fact, there is a whole system of prediction based on which nostril is more clear at the time of the question. This is called *swara*. Here's how it works. On Sunday, Tuesday and Saturday, if, at the time of asking a yes-no question, the right nostril is more clear, then the answer is "yes." If the left is the clearer one, then "no." On Monday, Wednesday, Thursday and Friday it is reversed, left is "yes," right is "no." This may sound like mumbo jumbo, but then, I suppose astrology sounds like mumbo jumbo to many people. This system is based on esoteric principles related to the *ida* and the *pingala*, two types of subtle energy that run up the spine in different channels on different days of the week. Anyway, it is a fantastic system, and it works. It may take some time to perfect this technique, because part of the art of *swara* has to do with how to ask the question. Even so, you'll have fun trying, and you might even find that it is a convenient way to make difficult decisions. So the next time you are standing in your kitchen and your six-year old comes up to you and asks, "Mommy, can I have some candy?" Just press your fingers against your nostrils, check your breath on both sides, and say, "Sorry dear, wrong nostril!"

Chapter Fifteen

House and Residence

The fourth house is the house of residence. This area has been covered in *Path of Light, Volume I*, in the house chapter, under the fourth house section. The placements of the ruler of the fourth house, given in that chapter, as well as the planets placed in the fourth house, show the person's general experience with homes, property, and real estate.

The fourth house also represents the mother, happiness, and vehicles. It is sometimes difficult to sort out these significations by only looking at the fourth house in the Rashi chart. For this reason, each of these areas has a different divisional chart. For the mother, the divisional chart is the Dwadashamsha chart. For vehicles, the recommended varga is the Shodashamsha chart. For homes, it is the Chaturtamsha chart. Each of these areas also has a special karaka. For the mother the karaka is the Moon. For vehicles, the karaka is Venus. For real estate, it is Mars. Distinguishing real estate from other fourth house significations is a process of considering not only the fourth house, but also the karaka (Mars) and the divisional chart (the Chaturtamsha chart).

Mars and Venus, the Karakas for Real Estate

Mars is the most common karaka for land and houses. This may be because in ancient times, houses were simple structures which mainly provided protection from the elements. In modern times, however, houses are frequently viewed as symbols of luxury and comfort. This is perhaps the reason that the great classic, *Phala Deepika*, lists Venus as the karaka for houses. The disposition of Mars and Venus in both the Rashi and the Chaturtamsha charts will show the person's potential for acquiring real estate. A strong and well-placed Mars or Venus in both charts will make it easier to acquire homes and land. When analyzing the chart for ownership of land specifically, Mars is the karaka. When considering the chart's potential for houses, both Mars and Venus are the karakas.

Primary Houses of the Chaturtamsha Chart

In the Chaturtamsha chart, the primary houses are the first house and the fourth house. The seventh house is also important because it is the fourth house from the fourth house. Planets placed here also aspect the Ascendant. The tenth house is also important as planets in the tenth house aspect the fourth house. All of these placements can be counted from the Moon as well.

The Eleventh House

The eleventh house is the house of acquisitions. The ruler of this house as well as planets placed in the eleventh house of the Chaturtamsha chart become important for purchasing or acquiring homes. The eleventh house is also a house of finishing things. If the person has begun a house project previously, then he could finish the project during the period of a planet in the eleventh house.

Change of Residence

The eighth house is the house of change. Planets placed in the eighth house suggest change of residence or changes within the residence during their periods. If the ruler of the eighth house is placed in or aspects the fourth or the first house, the person could change his residence as well. This could mean that the person completely changes his place of residence. It could also mean that he simply remodels or paints his house.

There are also other houses that sometimes become involved in a change of residence. The third house is the eighth house from the eighth, so planets placed in the third house also can occasionally produce a change of residence. The twelfth house is the house of distant places, so planets placed in the twelfth house can sometimes produce a change of residence to a distant place (out of the person's area). Planets placed in the ninth house (long-distance travel) can have a similar effect.

Contemporary Significations of the Twelve Houses in the Chaturtamsha Chart

The following significations are modern applications of classical principles applied to the twelve houses in the Chaturtamsha chart.

First House: The home in general; the front of the house; the entrance to the house; the ground floor. A planet place here will give prominent results related to the home during its period. The disposition of the planet determines whether the results are positive or negative. This house also reflects the general appearance of the home.

Second House: Financial matters related to the house; documents related to the house; the kitchen; pantry; places where money and other valuables are kept. Planets placed here may produce expenditure related to homes. If the planet in the second house also rules the first or the fourth house, then the person could purchase a home or make a significant purchase related to the home during the period. If the planet is weak and afflicted, then there could be more negative expenses related to the home.

Third House: Errands; communication and information related to the house; the windows; the driveway; the road outside the home; the path or walkway leading to the house. Planets placed in the third house produce a good deal of information-gathering and errand-like activity related to homes during their periods. This is also a house of selling a home, because it is the twelfth (letting go) from the fourth. It is connected to the windows in the house. It also rules information-appliances such as telephones and computers in the home.

Fourth House: The home in general; the foundation of the house; the floor; the basement; domestic harmony within the home; the bedroom of the first child (twelfth house from the fifth house). Planets placed here will give prominent results related to the home during their period. The placement of the ruler of the fourth house will also be important. (See the chapter on houses for the placement of the ruler of the fourth house in the other houses.)

Fifth House: Fortune; good luck; creativity; education; first child; the recreation room; the shrine to one's deity; puja area; the second-floor bathroom (eighth house from the tenth house); the study; library or bookshelves. Planets placed here will produce generally positive results pertaining to the home. The person could decorate or design a home during a period of a planet placed in or ruling the fifth house.

Sixth House: Illness; maintenance; service; work; rentals; the shop or work room; the bedroom of the second child. In the Chaturtamsha chart the sixth house represents the medicine cabinet, as well as places where general home repairs are done. It also represents the place where pets are kept, such as the doghouse or stable. Planets placed here can sometimes produce problems, repairs, or other difficulties related to the home during their periods. If the planet is strong and positive, then the person might do general maintenance of the house during the planet's period. The sixth house also represents rental homes. A period ruler in this house can sometimes show activities in dealing with tenants or rental properties.

Seventh House: Partnership pertaining to the house; legal matters pertaining to the house; the back part of the house; the bathroom for the master bedroom (eighth house from the twelfth house); the third floor (in a three story house). Planets placed in, or ruling, the seventh house in the Chaturtamsha chart can sometimes produce events related to roommates or house partnerships. These planets may indicate the outcomes of legal issues related to the house during their periods. The seventh house can also show events related to the garage (fourth house from the fourth house).

Eighth House: Change; the bathroom; plumbing; the bedroom of the third child. Planets placed in the eighth house produce either change of residence or change within the residence during their periods. Remodels, painting, landscaping, or other renovations fall within this domain.

Ninth House: Long-distance travel; father; the place of study or worship; the road or walkway leading to or near the back of the house; the windows in the back of the house; the main second-floor bedroom. Planets placed in the ninth house produce generally positive results for the home during their period. They can also suggest change of residence to distant places. Any real estate events that are related to the father also become possibilities during the period of planets placed here.

Tenth House: The office; the roof; the second floor in the case of a multi-story house. Since a planet placed in the tenth house will aspect the fourth house, it becomes an important planet reflecting prominent results for property. During its period, a tenth house planet will promote noticeable events related to the home. The tenth house is a house of career, so it is related to home projects. It is also the house of the office, so planets placed here sometimes produce events related to one's office or place of work.

Eleventh House: Acquisitions; gains; neighbors; the living room; the community. A strong and beneficial planet placed here can motivate the person to obtain a house during its period. This house also rules the culmination of projects and obtaining of desires, so the periods of planets in the eleventh house frequently enable the person to finish home projects. This house also rules over neighbors and the neighborhood and will reflect the general harmony of the person's experience with neighbors.

Twelfth House: Distant places; uncertainty; expenses; the master bedroom; retreats; meditation room. Planets placed in the twelfth house sometimes show a change of residence to a distant place. Sometimes the person simply travels during the planet's period and is away from home as a result. Afflicted planets in this house can suggest expenditure and uncertainty related to the home in general.

Woman Purchasing a House
August 14, 1952; 4:14 AM; San Jose, CA

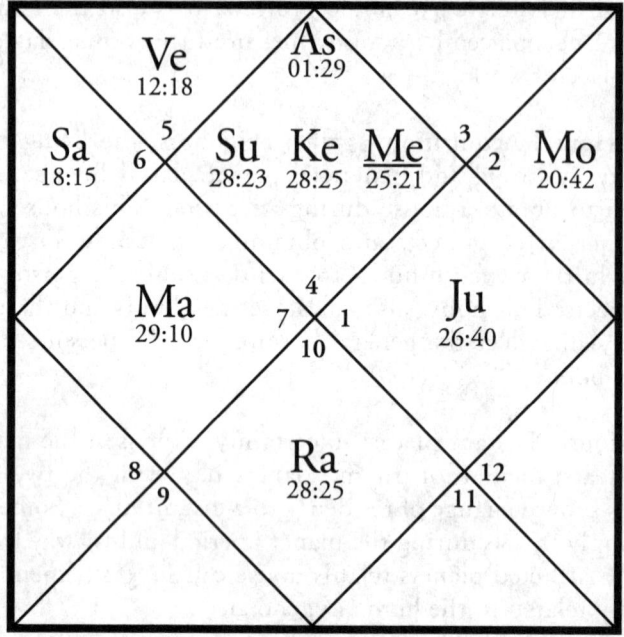

(D4) Chaturtamsha

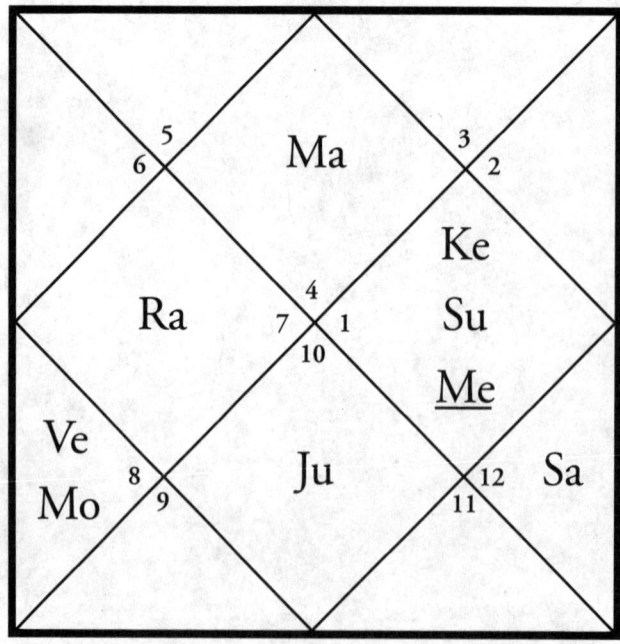

In this example chart, the woman purchased a house in 2002, in the major period of Saturn and the sub-period of Venus. The astrological features producing this event are as follows:

General Ability to Purchase a Home

1. Mars, the karaka for houses, is placed in the fourth house (homes) and aspected by Jupiter. Its placement in the twenty ninth degree of Libra made it difficult to purchase a house, but the aspect of Jupiter alleviated this difficulty.
2. The fourth house is relatively strong. Although its ruler, Venus, is involved in Papa Kartari Yoga, it is also aspected by Jupiter. Jupiter also aspects the fourth house.
3. Venus (karaka for houses), the ruler of the fourth house, is in Magha nakshatra, which is symbolized by a throne room and frequently associated with homes.

The Rashi Chart

1. Venus (karaka for houses), the sub-period ruler, is the ruler of the fourth house (the home) in the Rashi and Chaturtamsha charts. It is placed in the constellation of Magha in the second house (buying and selling), giving the tendency to purchase a home during its period.
2. The Papa Kartari Yoga created difficulties in getting financing, which were offset by the aspect of Jupiter. She got financing after initial difficulties.
3. Venus is also placed in the fourth house from the Moon.

The Chaturtamsha Chart

1. Venus, sub-period ruler and ruler of the fourth house in both charts, is placed in the fifth house, which is positive because it is a trinal house. It is in a conjunction with the lagna lord, making it a very powerful indicator of acquiring property.
2. Saturn, the major period ruler, is also placed in a trinal house in the Chaturtamsha chart.
3. Notice that relative to the lagna of the Chaturtamsha chart, Venus is five signs ahead and Saturn is five signs behind. In other words, both planets are flanking the lagna at an equal distance from either side of the lagna. This condition was discussed in the chapter on divisional charts as producing significant events during the major period and sub-period of the two flanking planets.

Author's Journal:

Baja Air

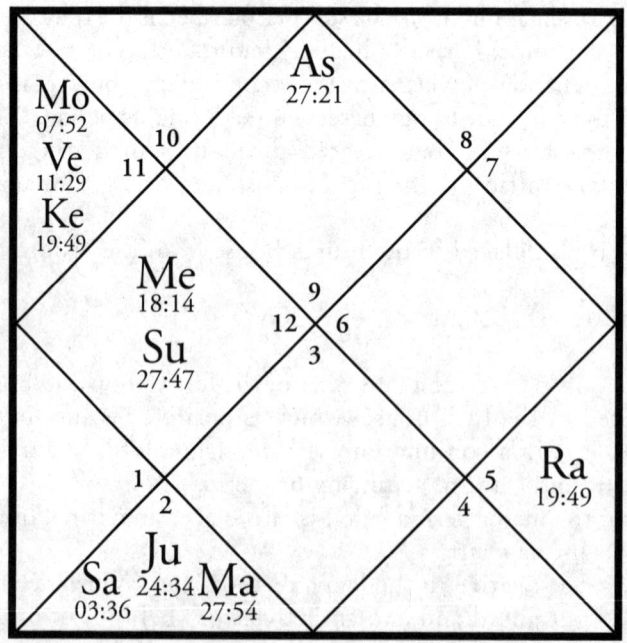

Chary Fernandez
April 11, 1942; 2:00 AM; Tijuana, Mexico

The plane buffeted as I banked to the left to follow the coastline. I was flying south at 2,000 feet, along the coast of the Sea of Cortez on the Baja Peninsula. My two friends, Mark and George, had put their lives in my hands, innocently trusting that, as a novice pilot with only 300 flying hours in my log book, I would land them safely in Mulege, Baja, Mexico.

We had departed from a dark and chilly San Jose, California at 5 a.m. and had a smooth ride through southern California. In San Felipe, Mexico, we managed to clear Mexican customs without any problem. We were a couple of hundred miles down the Baja Peninsula, when we hit moderate turbulence and my four-seat Cessna Cardinal became a bucking bronco. "There's no turning back now!" I joked. "Are you okay George?"

George, who had confessed his fear of flying before we took off, was on his first long trip in a small plane. A long-time backpacking buddy, he and I had previously taken one short flight to Lake Tahoe in calm air for a weekend backpacking trip. This trip, however, was 1,000 miles over terrain that offered no place to land in case of an emergency.

"Our only choices for landing now are the rocks or the ocean!" I yelled.

George groaned and laughed at the same time. "Now you tell me!" he said as he cinched up his seatbelt.

I gave the controls to Mark, who was sitting in the co-pilot's seat. "Think you can keep the plane straight and level while I check the map?" I said.

"No problema," Mark said. Mark had taken the controls on numerous occasions and I was confident that he was up to the task of keeping us from crashing. The turbulence we were experiencing was not serious, just a little exciting. I got out my map and studied it.

"I've got an idea," I said, "Why don't we land in Punta San Francisquito?"

"Where's that?" George's voice chimed in on my headset.

"It's a dirt strip, right next to the beach, about 150 miles from nowhere. You have to use a 4-wheel drive to get there on land, over very bad dirt roads. But it is a favorite hangout for pilots on their way down the Baja Coast. They have about ten palapas (open air grass huts) and a white sandy beach. They say the food there is supposed to be pretty good."

"I'm game," Mark said.

"Sounds great!" George agreed.

"According to the map, we should be coming up on it in about 15 minutes," I said. I took the controls back from Mark, gave him the map, and started a slow descent.

"It should be just beyond the next point over there," Mark said.

I ran through my prelanding checklist, silently repeating the words to myself, "Carb heat, cowl flaps, gas, under carriage, mix, prop, seatbelts." We flew over the rugged outcropping of rocks which Mark had just pointed out, as the grass huts of Punta San Francisquito came into view. Below us, way out here in the middle of nowhere, was the shimmering greenish blue water of the Sea of Cortez, a mile-long, white sandy beach, and a handful of grass huts.

"Bet it's a long drive to the nearest Safeway!" Mark said.

I took the plane out over the water, banked left and made my radio call. "San Francisquito traffic, Cardinal 13733, left base, landing, San Francisquito."

As we came in for a landing, from two hundred feet, we could see three people sitting on the beach next to a palapa, watching us, obviously curious about their new visitors. I landed on the dirt and taxied over to a tie down near the beach. "Not bad for my first time landing on dirt!" I said.

"Ugh," George groaned. "Now you tell me!"

As we got out of the plane, we were met by Hernardo, one of the owners of the palapa business at Punta San Francisquito. He took us to our palapa and explained that it would cost us $20 a day per person, including food. Our palapa, which had three bunks with clean linen, was right on the beach. Nothing but white sand, the sun and the Sea of Cortez. "Maybe we should just forget the rest of the trip and stay here!" Mark suggested.

Around 7 p.m., Hernardo called us for dinner. We walked over to the cooking hut where we met Chary, the cook and caretaker of Punta San Francisquito. Chary cooked a Mexican vegetarian meal for us and we learned first hand why San Francisquito has a reputation for the best food in Baja. Chary seemed to be mid-50ish, friendly, and very contented with life. I was intrigued by her way of life here in the middle of Baja, so when Chary walked by my hut the next day as I was sitting, reading and lounging, I started up a conversation with her. In the process I got her birthdate and asked her how she had come to live in such a remote place.

Whenever I travel, I make it a point to get the birthdate, time and place of people I meet along the way. I like to hear their stories and often reflect on the events of their lives in the light of their horoscope. In the course of traveling, it is common for me to meet people who have led unique, exciting, successful, or simply interesting lives. What is less common, however, is to meet someone who has led an interesting life, and also found peace along the way. Such a person is Chary.

"I was born in Tijuana," Chary said. "I grew up there and when I was a teenager my family moved to San Diego. I got married, had kids, and worked for many years in the office of a trucking company. My life wasn't really going very well though. Life in San Diego was too fast and pressured. Work was stressful. My marriage was not good. My husband and I were not getting along and I was getting pretty fed up with him. As it turned out, my boss was also the owner of this place, San Francisquito. The place had been run down and wasn't being used. He suggested to me that I could come down here, fix it up, and if I liked it, I could run the place and be the cook. I didn't know how I would like living so far away from everything, but I decided to give it a try. My son took me down here in his pickup. It was a very long drive over very bad, dusty roads. I remember that it was about 110 degrees and we had driven for about 12 hours. Just before we arrived here, we got totally lost and started driving around in circles in the desert. We were getting pretty desperate and knew that we had to find our way soon because our gas was almost gone. Then I saw someone walking in the distance. I called to him and he came and told us that he was a fisherman and that he lived and fished at Punta San Francisquito. He showed us the road, and we realized that we had spent more than an hour lost in the desert, yet we were actually less than a mile away from our San Francisquito. When we arrived, I took one look the water and the beach and said, 'I'm home, I don't need anything else.' I have been here ever since. I have a small house at the end of the beach. My life is simple and relaxed. I have been much happier ever since I came here."

It was interesting to consider Chary's experiences in the light of her horoscope. She has a Sagittarius ascendant with Mercury placed in the fourth house in Pisces, indicating that she would live and work near the water. Her chart is a striking example of how karma expresses itself on a very clear schedule. During the period of Saturn, from 1974 to 1993, she was involved in work, stress and pressure while living in San Diego. All of these things were clearly signified by Saturn and were quite evident in her chart. Then, in August of 1993, Saturn's period ended and Mercury's seventeen year period began. Chary made her move to San Francisquito in September of 1993. The karmic pattern that promised a life living and working by the sea manifested exactly on schedule, at the beginning of the period of Mercury.

It is also interesting to look at the chain of events that leads a person to such a life-altering change. Previous to 1993 Chary had been struggling, straining and constantly putting burdens on herself. She was living a high-pressure life in San Diego, under the illusion that somehow she was limited and that she had to accept limitation, hard work and pressure in her life. She was getting more and more frustrated and had reached her breaking point. Finally, in 1993, she simply got fed up and gave up on her old, complicated way of life. Unconsciously, she adopted what Mahatma Gandhi called "simple living, high thinking." Which means that by simplifying life and letting go of the many possessions and complications which cause worry and strain, the mind naturally goes to a more peaceful state. According to various Eastern philosophies, simple living is one of the major keys to being happy in life. Without realizing it, Chary had stumbled across one of the great keys to happiness. Out of frustration and despair, at her lowest point in her life, she picked up that key and used it. Miraculously, it opened a door to a happy, contented way of life and delivered her from suffering.

We spent the remainder of our trip sitting in the sun, reading and napping in Punta San Francisquito. After we took off from San Francisquito for our return to the US, I made one last circling pass, rocking our wings as we said goodbye to Chary and the simple life. Halfway back to the border, we encountered moderate turbulence again. This time, it was strong enough to make me a little nervous. As the plane bounced around, jarring and shaking us up and down, I tightened my seat belt and held the yoke tightly.

"Is this normal?" George asked nervously from the back seat.

"Just a little moderate turbulence," I said. "Nothing to worry about." What I didn't tell George was that even though the turbulence was not technically "severe" I was feeling just a shade beyond my comfort zone. I had been in wind such as this before, but never for such a long time and not over terrain this harsh and remote. If we went down here it would be either in the Sea of Cortez or on the jagged rocks of the Baja Coast, so there was nothing to do but push on to the US border. After two hours of turbulence, my knuckles were white as I clenched the yoke. Every muscle in my body was tense as I pushed through and reacted to every buffet and bounce, trying to keep the plane level. At one point the small ladder, which I keep in the baggage compartment to check my fuel, flew up and cracked the back window of the plane. I cursed myself for not packing it more carefully, and while George applied some duct tape to the window and tried to stow the ladder, I continued to plough through the turbulent air. In the early afternoon, we finally crossed the US border, landing in a stiff wind at Calexico International Airport.

As I taxied to the US customs ramp I could feel the muscles in my body begin to relax. "Home safe and sound," I said, trying to put George at ease about the bumpy ride. To myself I was thinking of Chary and her trip to San Francisquito. 'I better check my chart,' I thought. 'Maybe I just came out of a little Saturn period!' I took a deep breath, thanked God for bringing us home safely, and made a silent promise that I would live a simpler life!

Chapter Sixteen

Vehicles

In assessing any domain of life through the horoscope, it is always important for the astrologer to take the cultural context of the person who owns the horoscope under consideration. In the case of vehicles, this is particularly important. For example, if the person lives on the west coast of the United States, and has a strong fourth house and a strong Venus in his chart, this will usually allow the person to own a good vehicle. If the person lives in India, however, he may not own a car, in spite of good astrological indications, simply because owning cars in India is financially difficult for the average person. Even if the person lives in an American city where most people take mass transit, such as New York, good astrological combinations for cars may fail to produce a vehicle. For this reason, taking the cultural context into consideration at the time of assessing vehicles is mandatory if accurate predictions are to be made.

Astrological Factors for Purchasing Vehicles

In addition to cultural factors, certain astrological factors will also affect this decision. The fourth house is the house of vehicles. If the house and its ruler are strong and influenced by benefic planets, it becomes likely that the person will own vehicles. The disposition of Venus is also important in this regard. A strong and well-placed Venus can cause the person to own good cars and other vehicles. Finally, the Shodashamsha chart, which is the divisional chart for vehicles, gives more specific information about the vehicle. A strong Venus in this chart supports the total prospect of purchasing vehicles. If the Shodashamsha lagna and its ruler are strong and well-placed, it makes owing a good vehicle more likely. The disposition in the Shodashamsha chart of the Rashi chart lagna lord and fourth house ruler are also important.

Astrological vs. Cultural Factors

Both cultural and astrological factors must be taken together. In India, where relatively few people own cars, more powerful astrological factors are necessary in order to own a vehicle. Even when a person in India has a powerful chart for owning a car, he may own a motor scooter or even a bicycle instead of a car. By contrast, on the west coast of the United States, most people own cars. In this context, even negative astrological factors can produce purchase of vehicles. Ultimately, the key to determining the potential to purchase a car is simply experience. After seeing hundreds of horoscopes from a particular region, the astrologer begins to understand what kinds of astrological factors are necessary for the purchase of cars and other vehicles.

Predicting the Time of Purchase of a Car

If the chart and the culture give the potential to purchase a vehicle, then prediction should be made using the dasha and bhukti rulers. The following periods are likely for obtaining a vehicle.

In the Rashi Chart

1. Period ruler placed in or aspecting the fourth house from the Ascendant, Sun, or Moon
2. Period of a well-placed fourth lord
3. Period of Venus, especially if it is placed in or aspecting the fourth house from the Ascendant, Moon, or Sun

In the Shodashamsha Chart

1. Period of the Shodashamsha chart lagna lord or of a planet placed in the lagna
2. Period of the Rashi chart lagna lord placed in houses 1, 4, 7, or 10 of the Shodashamsha chart
3. Period of the Rashi chart fourth lord placed in houses 1, 4, 7, or 10 of the Shodashamsha chart
4. Period of the Shodashamsha chart fourth lord or a planet placed in

the fourth house
5. Period of a strong and positive planet placed in houses 1, 4, 7, or 10 of the Shodashamsha chart
6. Period of Venus placed in houses 1, 4, 7, or 10 of the Shodashamsha chart

Major and Sub-Period Combinations

1. Sub-period ruler is strong and beneficial and placed in the fourth house from the major period ruler in the Rashi
2. Sub-period ruler is beneficially placed in houses 1, 4, 7, or 10 from the major period ruler in the Shodashamsha chart
3. Sub-period planet and the major period planet hem in the first house or the fourth house of the Shodashamsha chart (See the chapter on divisional charts for various types of hemming-in.)

Determining the Type of Vehicle

In order to determine the type of vehicle the person will obtain during a planetary period, the astrologer should first of all consider that the person will tend to purchase vehicles that are in line with his general character, based on his Ascendant and other factors in the chart. If the person is conservative and frugal, then it is unlikely that he will purchase a sports car. The sign and planets in the fourth house of the Rashi chart, as well as the lagna and fourth house of the Shodashamsha chart, are key factors in determining the general style of vehicle the person prefers.

After considering the general style suggested in the chart, the sub-period ruler at the time of purchase could give more specific information regarding the style of vehicle.

Types of Vehicles Signified by the Nine Planets

Sun: sports cars; flashy cars; convertibles; cars that make a personal ego-statement; red cars; limousines
Moon: family cars; white cars; small cars
Mars: red cars; fast cars; powerful cars; jeeps and off-road vehicles; motorcycles
Mercury: green cars; small cars; economy cars
Jupiter: big cars; sports utility vehicles; expensive cars; yellow cars
Venus: luxury cars; stylish cars; white cars; expensive, well-designed cars

Saturn: practical cars; trucks; work cars; black or blue cars; conservative and well-built cars; used cars
Rahu: dark cars; multicolored cars; foreign cars; covered cars
Ketu: Asian cars; foreign cars; covered cars

Significations of the Twelve Houses of the Shodashamsha Chart

The following significations for the Shodashamsha chart are modern applications based on classical principles. These significations are given for American cars and other cars in which the driver's seat is the left front seat. For British cars and other cars with a right-side front driver's seat, the order and significations of the houses should be reversed.

First House: the car in general; the front part of the car; front bumper; the front seat passenger and his seat.

Second House: the fuel; carburetor; left headlight; horn; financial matters related to the car; the driver's license; the vehicle's registration; the left front windshield.

Third House: the left front window; left front door; left front fender; telephone; radio; GPS; the road; communications connected with the car.

Fourth House: the rear passenger and seat which is diagonal to the driver's seat; gas tank; the under-part of the car; the garage.

Fifth House: left rear fender, window, and door; engine compression; the CD player and other non-radio entertainment systems; the owner's manual; events related to children in the car.

Sixth House: mechanical problems; left rear headlight; repairs; maintenance; accidents; injuries; work-related driving; health-related driving.

Seventh House: the rear part of the car; rear bumper; the rear passenger and seat which is diagonal to the front passenger's seat; contracts and contractors (mechanics) related to the car; leases; legal matters related to the car; parking places around town.

Eighth House: accidents; the engine; right rear headlight; restoration; the odometer; breakdowns and other general problems; car insurance and insurance settlements; exhaust system; muffler.

Ninth House: right rear door; right rear window and fender; long-distance trips in the car; advice and advisors (also mechanics) related to the car.

Tenth House: the driver and the driver's seat; police and law enforcement related to the car.

Eleventh House: right front window, fender and door; obtaining a car

Twelfth House: tires; hubcaps; car expenses; distant places visited in the car; uncertainties related to the car; general car problems; the right front windshield; the right headlight

Planetary Period Rulers Placed in the Twelve Houses of the Shodashamsha Chart

The twelve houses of the Shodashamsha chart shed light on the details of the person's experience regarding cars or other vehicles. The following significations for the Shodashamsha chart are modern applications of fundamental principles in Jyotish.

First House: The first house of the Shodashamsha chart represents the car in general. Planets placed in the first house can produce prominent events related to vehicles. A strong and positive planet in the first house can produce the purchase of a car during its period. A weak or afflicted planet suggests problems related to vehicles.

Second House: If a strong and well-disposed period planet is placed in the second house of the Shodashamsha chart, the person could receive money from the sale of a car, or even earn money by using a car. If the planet is afflicted or weak, this can cause extra expenses related to the car due to repairs, fuel, or operating costs.

Third House: If a strong and supported period planet is placed in the third house of the Shodashamsha chart, the person will take positive or enjoyable short trips in his car during the planet's period. If the planet is weak and afflicted in the third house, there could be car problems that occur while traveling on the road. The person may also experience negative communications related to the car.

Fourth House: This is also a prominent house in the Shodashamsha chart that represents the car in general. If a dasha, bhukti, or antara planet is placed here, its period can produce prominent results related to vehicles. The positive or negative nature of the results will depend on the positive or negative disposition of the planet. A planet placed in its own sign or exalted in the fourth house, for example, could cause the person to purchase a vehicle during its period.

Fifth House: If a period planet is strong and supported in the fifth house of the Shodashamsha chart, it can produce general enjoyment and positive experiences related to driving. The person could benefit by using his vehicle for attending classes or for transporting children. An afflicted planet in this house may give only minor problems related to the car, but it could also produce car problems that occur while driving to a class or while transporting children.

Sixth House: If a period planet is placed in the sixth house of the Shodashamsha chart, it may produce car problems, repairs, or expenses during its period. If the planet is weak and afflicted, then it can produce accidents, fender benders, or pronounced expenditure related to the car. If it is strong and influenced by benefics, the person could derive benefit through using the car to drive to work or to perform various services.

Seventh House: If a dasha, bhukti, or antara ruler is placed in the seventh house of the Shodashamsha chart, the person may experience prominent events associated with cars during the period. A strong and positive planet placed here can cause the partner to purchase a car. This placement can also cause the person to lease or purchase a car. A neecha bhanga planet here may give the person a desire to clean up his garage. A weak or afflicted planet in the seventh house can indicate difficult interactions with mechanics or legal problems related to the car. It can also produce disharmony or disagreement with others, which is related to the vehicle.

Eighth House: If a period planet is placed in the eighth house, there can be changes related to the vehicle. If it is weak or afflicted here, the planet's period can produce accidents, repairs, or expenses. If the planet is strong and influenced by benefics, it can suggest improvements and solutions to mechanical problems.

Ninth House: If the ruler of a period or sub-period is placed in the ninth house of the Shodashamsha chart, it usually gives good results related to vehicles, unless it is afflicted or weak. If the planet is strong and associated with benefics, then it can produce a long and enjoyable trip in the vehicle (or in commercial vehicles). This placement can also cause the person to use the car (or public transportation) to go to school. If the planet is weak and afflicted, then it can produce minor expenditures or stresses related to the vehicle. This can also reflect unreliable advice from mechanics.

Tenth House: If a period ruler is placed in the tenth house of the Shodashamsha chart, the person could use his vehicle for work. A positive and strong planet placed here can sometimes cause the person or his partner to purchase a car. If the planet is weak and afflicted, it can indicate general problems related to the car. If the person is mechanically inclined, malefic influences can cause the person to do repairs or other mechanical work on the vehicle during the planet's period.

Eleventh House: If a dasha, bhukti, or antara ruler is placed in the eleventh house of the Shodashamsha chart, the person may experience trips in the vehicle that include friends or groups during the period. A strong and supported planet here can produce the purchase of a vehicle, while a weak and afflicted planet will produce obstructions to the purchase of a car. A planet placed here influenced by natural malefics can also produce repairs or expenses related to the car.

Twelfth House: If a period ruler is placed in the twelfth house of the Shodashamsha chart, the person could experience expenditure and uncertainty regarding his vehicle during the planet's period. A strong and supported planet placed here can indicate that the person will travel in his vehicle (or a commercial vehicle) to a distant place.

Chart 1: John F Kennedy, Jr.
Nov 25, 1960; 00:22 AM; Washington, DC

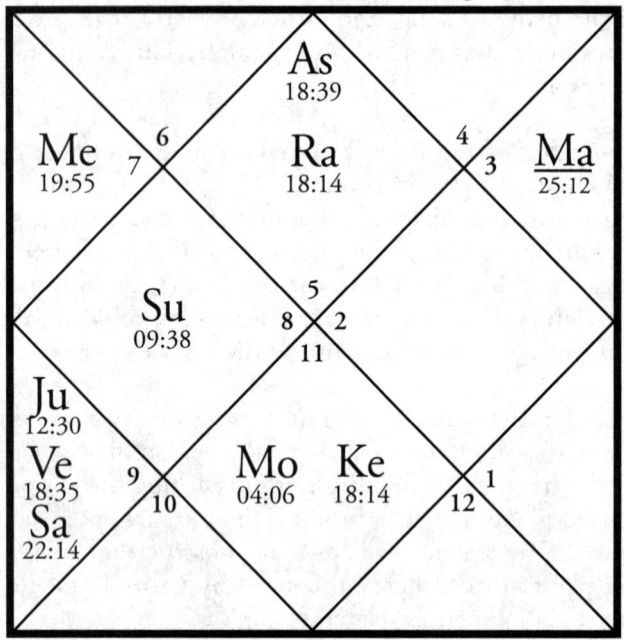

(D16) Shodashamsha

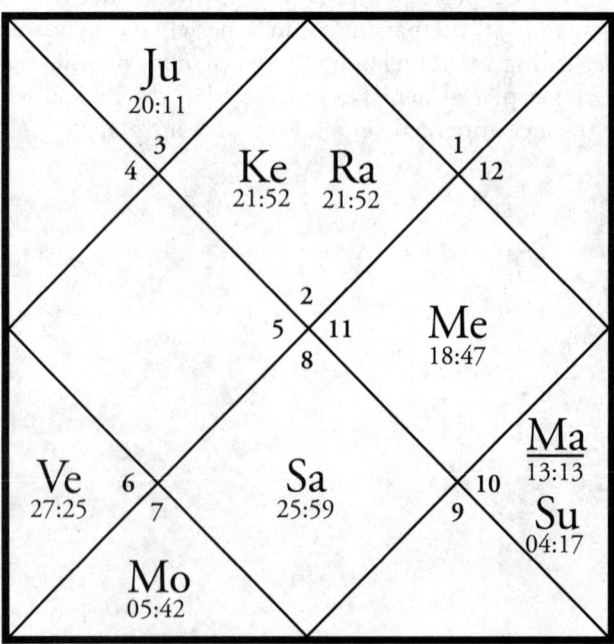

Dashas

03/30/1996	Sa	Sa
04/03/1999	Sa	Me

John F. Kennedy, Jr. was the son of American President John F. Kennedy. He had a strong interest in various kinds of vehicles, which is reflected in the following ways.

First, the Sun (Ascendant lord) is placed in the fourth house (vehicles). This indicates that he identified with his vehicle, seeing it as a mark of status and an important expression of his self image. The Moon is placed in the fourth house from the Sun, reiterating a strong attachment to the areas represented by this house (vehicles, homes etc.).

Description of the vehicle: The planets in the fourth house (from the Ascendant, Sun, or Moon) can give an indication of the type of vehicle a person tends to purchase. In this case, the Sun in the fourth house suggests a vehicle that is showy or flashy. Shortly before his death, Kennedy purchased a restored 1965 GTO. The Moon is placed in the fourth house from the Sun in a bird drekkana. Bird drekkanas are commonly associated with aircraft. He was an airplane enthusiast who owned not only a Piper Saratoga, but also a two-seated powered parachute.

In August of 1996, Kennedy purchased a refurbished 1965 GTO. A muscle car known for its power and flashy style.

Saturn dasha/Saturn bhukti: Saturn's period began in 1996. Saturn is the ruler of the fourth house from the Sun. It is placed in the second house (buying and selling) from the Sun and is in a conjunction with Jupiter and Venus (karaka for vehicles and ruler of the fourth house from the Moon). Kennedy had a natural predisposition towards owning flashy cars. Saturn's contribution was to make this vehicle a used car. The two planes purchased by him during this period were also used. Saturn rules things that are used or old.

Shodashamsha chart: Saturn is placed in the seventh house, where it has dig bala, in the Shodashamsha chart. Planets placed in dig bala in a divisional chart produce powerful results in the divisional chart's domain. Saturn also rules the fourth house from the Moon and is placed in the constellation of Jyeshtha in the Shodashamsha chart. This nakshatra is ruled by Indra, the king of the gods and is associated with great power.

The power of the GTO is an important part of its cult-image.

Transits: At the time of the purchase, Jupiter was transiting Sagittarius, in a conjunction with natal Saturn and Venus. As previously discussed, Saturn rules the fourth house (vehicles) from the Sun, and Venus is the karaka for vehicles. Transiting Saturn was in Pisces, casting its aspect on natal Jupiter, Venus, and Saturn in Sagittarius. When both Saturn and Jupiter influence the same house, that house, as well as the occupants of that house become strengthened and often produce fruits. In this case, the Jupiter-Saturn transiting influence affected the ruler of the fourth from the Sun (Saturn) and the karaka for vehicles (Venus), thereby stimulating the urge to purchase a vehicle. Transiting Venus (vehicles) was passing through Gemini in the eleventh house (acquisition of desires). It was aspecting natal Saturn, Jupiter, and Venus. It was also in a conjunction with natal Mars, ruler of the fourth house (vehicles) from the lagna.

On October 12, 1996, Kennedy took his first flying lesson. He had always been interested in flying. As editor of the magazine, George, *his office was in the same building as a popular aviation magazine. He asked the magazine's editor if there was any type of flying that did not require a great deal of training. The editor told him to look into powered parachute flying. Kennedy followed up on this advice and took his first flying lesson in a powered parachute.*

Transits: The dasha and bhukti are the same for this event and have already been discussed. Although the transits of Saturn and Jupiter are the same for this event and generally indicate significant events related to vehicles, the transits of the faster moving planets are interesting to note. Venus, the karaka for vehicles, was transiting the first house. When a planet transits the first house, it frequently triggers events related to that planet's significations.

On the day of his first lesson, the Moon and the Sun were in a conjunction in Virgo. This was amavasya, the last waning lunar day, when the Moon was completely dark. This day is sacred to the Pitris, the spirits who have left the body and gone to the spiritual realm. Starting important undertakings that are intended to grow and thrive on this lunar day invariably leads to failure or disappointment. This was not a good day for Kennedy to begin his first flying lesson. In this case, it led him to eventually leave his body and enter the spiritual realm due to a later plane crash.

The Sun (lagna lord) was transiting the second house (purchases) along with Mercury, the Moon, and Rahu (strong desires). Taken together, these factors produced a strong or obsessive desire to make a purchase. He also purchased his first powered parachute on that day.

In April of 1998, Kennedy received his private pilot's license and in May of 1998 he purchased his first airplane, a Cessna 182.

Saturn dasha/Saturn bhukti: This period has been discussed earlier. Saturn's powerful position in the Shodashamsha chart (seventh house in dig bala) simply shows a predisposition towards acquiring vehicles.

Transits: Saturn (period ruler and ruler of the fourth house from the Sun) was transiting Aries in the ninth house (long-distance travels). It was passing through Ashwini nakshatra. In mythology the Ashwini Kumars rode through the sky in golden chariots. This nakshatra is particularly related to fast vehicles, so Saturn's transit in Ashwini became a particularly important time for events related to travel.

At the time of purchasing the plane, the Sun (ruler of the first house, the self) and Mars (ruler of the fourth house, vehicles) were transiting Taurus, casting their aspects on the natal fourth house.

In April of 1999 Kennedy purchased a Piper Saratoga, a six-seat, single engine plane. He died in a crash in this plane on July 18, 1999.

Saturn dasha: Saturn has already been discussed as to its propensity for causing purchase of vehicles. While it may not be possible for most astrologers to predict that he purchased four vehicles during the sub-period of Saturn, it is clear that the purchase of vehicles is a strong inclination. The fact that he had a fatal airplane crash during this period is based on the following factors:

First, Saturn is the ruler of the sixth house (a dusthana related to accidents and injuries) and the seventh house (a maraka house related to death) in the Rashi chart. Saturn is also placed in a conjunction with Jupiter, which rules the eighth house (accidents). Jupiter is placed in Mula nakshatra, which has the power of destruction as its shakti. This makes Jupiter's influence as eighth lord particularly destructive. This destructive quality is amplified by the aspect of Mars on Jupiter and Saturn. Together, Jupiter and Saturn surround Venus (karaka for vehicles) producing a clear combination for vehicular accidents.

Shodashamsha chart: Saturn is placed in the seventh house (a maraka or death-producing house). It is also placed in Scorpio, which is the eighth sign, producing similar results as the eighth house. Saturn is also aspected by Rahu (karaka for accidents) in the Shodashamsha chart.

Saturn is placed in Jyeshtha nakshatra in the Shodashamsha chart. This nakshatra is ruled by Indra, the king of the gods. Indra's vehicle was a great white elephant named Airavata. Airavata had two tusks. It is interesting that Kennedy purchased a large white airplane. The propeller of the airplane consists of two blades (symbolized by the tusks). In mythology, Airavata was decapitated by Shiva, who used his head to replace the head of Ganesha. This part of the story can be seen symbolically as the destruction of Kennedy's vehicle. Although the use of degrees in divisional charts is not a conventional technique, the use of nakshatra and drekkana symbolism in these charts can frequently produce useful and sometimes startling details.

Mercury bhukti: Mercury bhukti began in April of 1999, exactly at the time of his purchase of the Piper Saratoga. Mercury is placed in the third house (accidents, being the eighth house from the eighth) in the sign of Libra (an air sign). Mercury is also placed in the second drekkana of Libra which is a pakshi (bird) drekkana. Pakshi drekkanas often figure prominently in the charts of pilots. Saturn and Mercury hem-in the fourth house. When two planets hem-in a house, then that house can be activated during the mutual dasha and bhukti of the two planets. Mercury is also in Swati nakshatra. Swati is ruled by Vayu, the god of the wind, and is symbolized by a young sprout swaying in the wind. This nakshatra suggests tenuous beginnings. The drekkana symbolism also suggests uncertainty. The drekkana is symbolized by a man who is holding a pot that is about to fall. These symbols clearly show the fact that Kennedy had purchased a more complex airplane and was feeling uncertain about his ability to fly it. The Piper Saratoga is a six-seat aircraft which is more powerful and more difficult to fly than the Cessna 182 Skylane which was Kennedy's first plane. Analysis of the crash by the National Transportation Safety Board confirms that he was flying above his skill level when the crash took place.

Shodashamsha chart: Mercury is placed in the fourth house (vehicles) from Saturn (dasha lord), clearly reinforcing the potential for prominent events related to the vehicle to take place during its period. Although it is not aspected by natural malefics, it is aspected by Jupiter. Jupiter is the ruler of the eighth house (accidents) in both the Rashi and Shodashamsha charts. Mercury is also placed in Shatabhisha nakshatra. Shatabhisha is ruled by Varuna, the god of the ocean. Kennedy crashed in the ocean. Shatabhisha is also related to addictions and the need to let go of obsessions (see *Path of Light, Volume I*) under Shatabhisha nakshatra) as depicted in the story of the king who was asked by Varuna to sacrifice his son. The clear culprit in Kennedy's crash was his strong attachment to arrive at his destination. His inability to cancel his trip in spite of clear signs of foul weather and darkness led to his demise. When a planet is in Shatabhisha, there can be a need to let go of urgency and obsession. In this case, in the Shodashamsha chart it is related to vehicles. Mercury in Shatabhisha in the tenth house (the pilot) produced a strong sense of urgency related to piloting his plane. He pressed on, in spite of deteriorating conditions, when he should have turned back.

Transit: Saturn (period ruler) was transiting Ashwini nakshatra. This nakshatra is associated with vehicles as previously mentioned. Saturn was also debilitated (in Aries). Since Saturn is the ruler of the fourth house from the Sun in the Rashi as well as the fourth house from the Moon in the Shodashamsha chart, this transit indicated the potential of damage for the vehicle. Aries is also the sixth house (damage) from the fourth house (vehicles), suggesting problems or accidents for the vehicle.

At the time of the crash, Mercury (bhukti ruler) was retrograding through Cancer. It was in a close conjunction with transiting Rahu (accidents) and was hemmed in by Rahu and the Sun (lagna lord) forming a transiting Papa Kartari Yoga. Cancer is the twelfth house (distant places) in Kennedy's chart. Cancer is also the eighth house (accidents) from natal Saturn (dasha ruler) and Venus (karaka for vehicles). This transit clearly reflected the potential of problems during the flight.

The symbolism of the Rahu-Sun influence on transiting Mercury is also worth noting. In mythology, Rahu had an urgent desire to attend a banquet in order to steal the nectar of the gods. This resulted in having his head cut off (See *Path of Light, Volume I*). He became the sworn enemy of the Sun at that time. As a result, he now gobbles up the Sun when he is close to him in the sky. This was the mythological explanation for eclipses. It is interesting to note that Kennedy was on his way to a wedding banquet at the time of the crash. Darkness was setting in, causing impaired visibility. Again, his inability to let go of the desire to attend the banquet resulted in his demise.

Chart 2: More Cars and Airplanes (Anonymous)

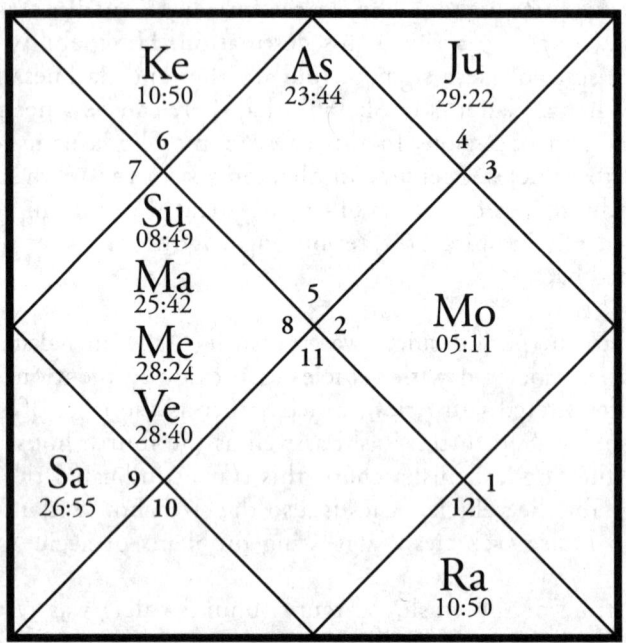

(D16) Shodashamsha

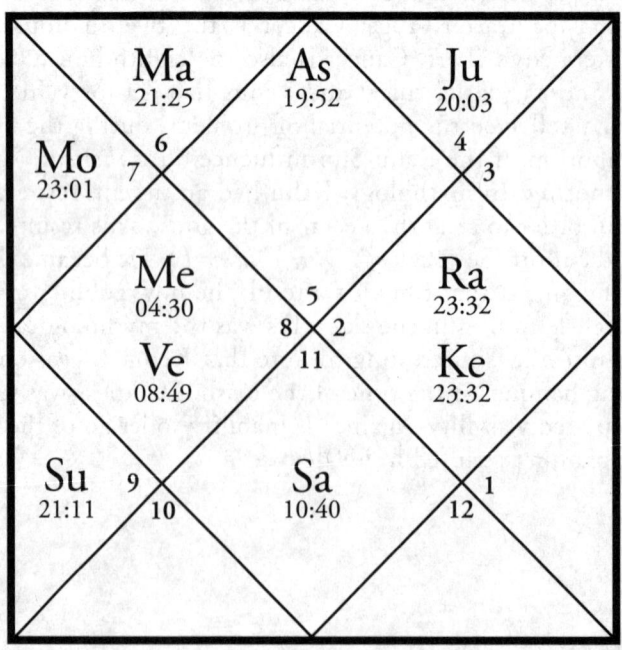

Vehicles

Dashas

01/24/1951	Ra	Ra	09/24/1973	Jp	Me
10/06/1953	Ra	Jp	12/31/1975	Jp	Ke
02/29/1956	Ra	Sa	12/06/1976	Jp	Ve
01/05/1959	Ra	Me	08/07/1979	Jp	Su
07/25/1961	Ra	Ke	05/25/1980	Jp	Mo
08/12/1962	Ra	Ve	09/24/1981	Jp	Ma
08/12/1965	Ra	Su	08/31/1982	Jp	Ra
07/07/1966	Ra	Mo	01/23/1985	Sa	Sa
01/06/1968	Ra	Ma	01/27/1988	Sa	Me
01/23/1969	Jp	Jp	10/06/1990	Sa	Ke
03/13/1971	Jp	Sa	11/15/1991	Sa	Ve

Nov 25, 1931; 00:30 AM; Vienna, Austria

"On February 15, 1951, I was driving a '51 Plymouth for a car dealer near Brinkley, Arkansas. I tried to pass a truck on a slushy road and lost control, plunging down a 20-foot embankment. I landed on the roof. The highway patrol officer was German, and used to be a military policeman in Berlin. We had a nice chat, speaking in German. I drove the car back to Memphis with the crushed roof, and dated the car dealer's daughter that very evening. He was not impressed."

Rahu dasha/ Rahu bhukti: Rahu is a karaka for accidents. It is placed in the eighth house (accidents) in the Rashi chart.

Shodashamsha chart: Rahu is placed in the eighth house (accidents) from the Moon, suggesting an accident in a vehicle. Rahu is in the tenth house (roof) of the Shodashamsha chart. The damage was to the roof of the car. Using degrees in the Shodashamsha chart, Rahu was placed in the constellation of Mrigashira, which signifies roads. Mrigashira is also associated with the story of misguided passion, as when Brahma chases his daughter and gets his head cut off by Shiva. In this case, after returning the car, he took out the owner's daughter on a date, to the chagrin of the owner.

Transits: Transiting Rahu (period ruler) was in an exact conjunction with transiting Mars (ruler of the natal fourth house, vehicles). Transiting Jupiter (ruler of the eighth house, accidents), transiting Venus (karaka for vehicles), and transiting Sun (lagna lord) were in Aquarius, which is the fourth house (vehicles) from the Sun.

"About October of 1957 I bought my first car, a 1951 Plymouth 2-door. I bought the car 'as is'. It had a bad cylinder and the head gasket belched greasy oil smoke like a diesel with a bad injection pump."

Rahu dasha: Rahu has already been discussed.

Saturn bhukti: Saturn is the ruler of the fourth house (vehicles) from the Sun. It is placed in the second house (purchases) from the Sun. Saturn symbolizes old or used cars.

Shodashamsha chart: Saturn is placed in Aquarius (moolatrikona) in the seventh house (dig bala) in the Shodashamsha chart showing a strong tendency to purchase a vehicle during the period. Saturn is also placed in the constellation of Shatabhisha, which is a constellation related to hard to diagnose or hard to treat health problems. In the Shodashamsha chart, this reflects mechanical problems for the car.

Transits: Saturn (bhukti ruler) was transiting the fourth house (vehicles) in a close conjunction with transiting Venus (karaka for vehicles). Transiting Jupiter and Mars (ruler of the fourth house), were in a close conjunction in the second house (purchases) in Virgo.

"In June of 1959 I drove the Plymouth to Memphis to visit friends after my graduation from MIT. The car broke down before the return trip. My friend loaned me the money to buy a white, compact, a sweet-smelling 1960 Nash Rambler station wagon."

Rahu dasha/Mercury bhukti

Mercury bhukti: Mercury is placed in the fourth house (vehicles) in Scorpio (change) in the Rashi chart. It receives the aspect of Jupiter, which is placed in the twelfth house (distant places). These influences account for the long trip and the change of vehicle.

Shodashamsha chart: Mercury is also placed in the fourth house (vehicles) and is vargottama (in the same sign as in the Rashi chart) in the Shodashamsha chart. The placement of Mercury in the fourth house in the Rashi chart gave a clue that a fourth house event may take place. But it is still unclear whether that event will be related to vehicles, homes, the mother, or the education. The placement of Mercury in the fourth house of the Shodashamsha chart, however, clearly shows that a significant vehicle event will take place.

The involvement of friends in the purchase of the new car is also clearly indicated. Mercury rules the eleventh house (friends) and is placed in the fourth (vehicles) in the Shodashamsha chart. It is also placed in Anuradha nakshatra (in the Shodashamsha chart), which is ruled by Mitra, the god of friendship (see *Path of Light, Volume I*). It receives the aspect of Jupiter, ruler of the eighth house (loans) in both the Rashi and the Shodashamsha charts.

Transits: Rahu (period ruler) was transiting Virgo in the second house (money). Here it was aspected by transiting Saturn, indicating expenses. Transiting Mercury (bhukti ruler) was passing through the eleventh house (friends) and was also receiving the aspect of transiting Saturn (delays, obstacles). The eleventh house is also the house of acquiring desires, as well as being the eighth house (change) from the fourth house (vehicles).

"In September of 1967 I was living in Munich, Germany, working as the supervisor for a flight mechanics group. We worked on Tornado Fighter Bombers. I bought a beautiful 1966 Volvo."

Rahu dasha/Moon bhukti

Moon bhukti: The Moon is exalted in the tenth house, where it aspects the fourth house (vehicles). The Moon is placed in Krittika nakshatra, which is related to mechanical precision. The exalted status of the Moon in Krittika led to the purchase of a car known for its high mechanical quality. The Moon is also aspected by Mars (ruler of the fourth house) Venus (karaka for vehicles) and the Sun (lagna lord). The Moon is also placed in the third house (change) from Rahu (period ruler).

Shodashamsha chart: The Moon is in Libra (style and beauty). Both Libra and Taurus (the Rashi placement of the Moon) are signs of beauty and style, producing a desire for a vehicle which was aesthetically pleasing. The Moon is also placed in the third house (change) in the Shodashamsha chart, repeating the pattern in the Rashi chart. The third house is the eighth house (change) from the eighth house, indicating the potential for a change related to the vehicle.

Note: Saturn is placed in its own sign in the seventh house in the Shodashamsha chart. This creates Shasha Mahapurusha Yoga, which gives management ability and according to the classical texts, gives the person "good servants." This suggests the managing of other workers. When present in the Shodashamsha chart, this yoga can make the person a manager or supervisor in work related to vehicles. In this case, he was a supervisor of flight mechanics.

Transit: Although it is not known where the Moon (sub-period ruler) was transiting at the time of this event, the Sun (lagna ruler), Venus (karaka for vehicles) and Jupiter were passing transiting Leo (lagna). Mars (ruler of the fourth-vehicles) was transiting the fourth house in its own sign (Scorpio). The Venus-Jupiter-Sun transit led to a self-indulgent expenditure related to vehicles, while the Mars transit produced the fruits of the fourth house. When the ruler of a house transits its own house it frequently expresses the significations of that house.

"On March 3, 1986 I bought a new 1986 Nissan pickup."

Saturn dasha/ Saturn bhukti: Saturn's role has been discussed earlier. It is the ruler of the fourth house from the Sun and is also well placed (dig bala) in the Shodashamsha chart.

Transits: Transiting Saturn (dasha ruler), Mars (ruler of the fourth house) and the Moon were in the fourth house in Scorpio. As in the previous example, Mars, the ruler of the fourth house, was transiting the fourth house. The Moon acted to trigger the combination. Jupiter, the Sun (lagna lord) and Venus (karaka for vehicles) were in a conjunction in Aquarius in the seventh house. Notice the similarity of these transits to the previous example where the same three planets were transiting the Ascendant. Aquarius is also the fourth house (vehicles) from the Sun and Venus. Aquarius is also the sign in which Saturn (dasha ruler) is placed in the Shodashamsha chart.

"On March 18, 1991, I bought a Nissan Sentra."

Saturn dasha/Ketu bhukti

Ketu bhukti: Ketu is placed in the second house (purchases) where it aspects the fourth house (vehicles) from Saturn (dasha ruler).

Shodashamsha chart: Ketu is placed in the fourth house (vehicles) from Saturn (dasha ruler). Its dispositor (Venus, the karaka for vehicles) is placed in the fourth house (vehicles, and dig bala for Venus). This produces a powerful tendency to acquire a vehicle during this period.

Transits: Ketu was transiting Cancer (the fourth zodiacal sign, related to vehicles) and was in conjunction with exalted, transiting Jupiter). Ketu also represents asian things, so he bought an asian car. Transiting Mars (ruler of the fourth house, vehicles) was in Taurus, casting its aspect on the fourth house. Transiting Jupiter was also casting its aspect on the fourth house, promoting the event. The transiting Moon was in the fourth house triggering the purchase.

"On December 29, 1984, I was flying a Lockheed L-100-30 to Cafunfo, Angola during the war. I was on the downwind leg of an approach for landing when my plane was mistaken for a Cuban mercenary transport, causing the Unita ground forces to open fire on my plane. Shortly before turning to the base leg of the pattern, a crew member reported hearing clicking sounds coming from the plane. As we turned to the final approach, another crew member reported smoke coming from the circuit breaker panels. By the time we landed, the fire had filled the cabin with smoke. My exit route was blocked by flames, so I had no choice but to exit via the left window. It was a twelve-foot drop to the ground. I injured my foot as I hit the ground and limped painfully away from the plane. The Unita forces continued to fire on us, and I could hear the bullets zipping by me. I managed to get the attention of the army commander, and when he realized that we were not Cubans, the shooting stopped. They loaded us on land rovers and drove us into the forest. We were later returned to our home base."

Jupiter dasha/Rahu bhukti

Jupiter dasha: Jupiter is the ruler of the eighth house (accidents) and it is exalted in the twelfth house (distant places). It is placed in Ashlesha nakshatra, which is related to serpents. Ashlesha is also connected with warfare through its desire, which is to overcome enemies (*See Path of Light, Volume I* for the desires of each nakshatra). Jupiter is also placed at 29 degrees of Cancer (gandanta), which frequently produces problems.

Rahu bhukti: Rahu is the karaka for accidents. It is placed in the eighth house (accidents) in Pisces, where it receives the aspect of Jupiter, the ruler of the eighth house (accidents). When a planet is placed in the eighth house and is aspected by the eighth lord, its period becomes particularly problematic. Jupiter is placed in Uttara Badrapada, which is symbolized by a funeral cot, showing the threat to life. Uttara Badrapada and its neighbor, Purva Bhadrapada, are both associated with fire, because the funeral cot is burned in the cremation ceremony. They are called "the scorching pair." This is the reason the accident involved fire.

Pisces represents the feet, so his feet were injured as he jumped from the burning plane.

Shodashamsha chart: Jupiter (dasha ruler) is again the ruler of the eighth house exalted in Ashlesha (using degrees in the Shodashamsha chart) in the twelfth house. Rahu is placed in the tenth house, which represents the sky above. The tenth house in the chart for vehicles is an important house for air travel. Rahu is also placed in the eighth house (accidents) from the Moon. It is also in the sixth house (accidents and injuries) from the Sun (lagna lord). These influences clearly reinforce the patterns found in the Rashi chart, showing that the accidents and injuries suggested in the Rashi chart would occur due to an accident in a vehicle.

Rahu is also placed in the constellation of Mrigashira (in the Shodashamsha chart). Mrigashira is related to the myth of Brahma chasing his daughter through the sky and then having his head snipped off. (*See Path of Light, Volume I* for the myths and symbols of Mrigashira). In this case, the plane was shot down while crossing the sky.

Transits: Saturn, Ketu, and Mercury were in a conjunction in Scorpio in the fourth house (vehicles). Rahu (sub-period ruler) was transiting the tenth house (the sky) in Krittika nakshatra (ruled by Agni, god of fire) where it received the aspects of transiting Saturn, Ketu and Mercury.

More importantly, Rahu was receiving the aspect of transiting Mars (war), from the seventh house (also related to war). Furthermore, transiting Venus (karaka for vehicles), was at zero degrees of Aquarius and was in a conjunction with transiting Mars, ruler of the fourth house (vehicles). From this position both the natural karaka for vehicles (Venus) and the ruler of the house of vehicles (Mars) were aspecting the lagna of the Shodashamsha chart, indicating a prominent event related to vehicles. Mars aspect on Rahu indicated that the event would involve violence.

Jupiter (dasha ruler) was transiting Sagittarius (a sign symbolized by a weapon) in conjunction with transiting Sun (fire). Jupiter was also in a conjunction with natal Saturn. When the major period ruler transits the sign where a malefic is placed in the natal chart, then the period can produce difficulties.

Last, but not least, the Moon was transiting the eighth house and was in an exact conjunction with natal Rahu at the time of the incident. Although it is not always possible to time an event to the exact day, it is interesting to note the important role played by the Moon in triggering the exact time of an event.

Author's Journal:
Don't Try This At Home

"*You will need a permit if you are going trekking,*" the agent said.

I was sitting in the Yak and Yetti Travel Agency, a little hole-in-the-wall on a crowded lane in Katmandu, inquiring about a two-week trek into the Annapurna Sanctuary.

The agent sat at his desk, smoking a cigarette and drinking a cup of chai, as he described my itinerary. "*First you will make a two-week loop near Annapurna,*" *he said.* "*You will stay at tea houses. We will provide a porter. After your trip you can go river rafting for a few days if you like.*"

"*River rafting? Uh . . . is it safe?*" *I asked. I had a friend in California who led river rafting trips. He had been trying to get me to go on one of his trips for the past few years. I had almost gone with him the previous year, but had to cancel at the last minute.*

"*Yes, completely safe, no problem!*" *The agent said.*

A red flag went up in my mind. "*Are you absolutely sure?*" *I countered,* "*I know that there are different levels of white water, I have a friend who runs river trips and he told me that the levels go from one to six. Level six is unrunable. Level five is only for experts and is very dangerous. Level four is big water and also not recommended for novices, so I don't want anything above level three.*"

"*Yes, yes,*" *the agent said,* "*It's level two, level three, nothing bigger than that. You can easily do it!*"

The next morning I got up early and went to the trekking permit office. Before I left, I grabbed a book and put it in my daypack. Saturn was transiting the seventh house from my Moon and during that year, it made its complete degree-wise opposition to the Moon three times. On the day of going for the permit, the opposition was exact.

I had planned this trip to Nepal, partly as a strategy for overcoming the influence of Saturn. Earlier in the year, during the first exact opposition of Saturn to the Moon, I had been in Seattle doing astrology readings. I was asked to do an interview on an evening news program on KIRO TV, hosted by Steve Raeble, an ex-Seattle Sea Hawk quarterback-turned TV anchorman. On the way to the interview, I got stuck in a big traffic jam and arrived at the studio late. Somehow the interview still worked out, in spite of my late arrival. After that interview, nearly 200 people called for readings. I let myself get so swamped with readings that I nearly burnt out. This Nepal trip was a reaction to overwork, and a strategy for dealing with Saturn's second opposition to the Moon. "Last time I got stuck in a traffic jam," I muttered as I picked up the book, "I better bring something to read this time."

As I neared the trekking office I looked at my watch. It was 8:00 am and the line was already halfway round the block. I found a place in line and sat on the ground. The wait in line took eight hours. So I passed the time reading and talking to the other trekkers. Although many of the trekkers were annoyed and impatient, I had expected the long wait. I was secretly proud of retaining my peace of mind and staying relaxed. I was the only person in line who had thought to bring a book. 'Outsmarting Saturn just takes a little planning,' I thought.

Trekking through the Annapurna Sanctuary was a lifetime experience. Each day my porter and I hiked for several hours along some of the most spectacular and exotic mountain trails on the planet, arriving at our tea-house accommodations exhausted and hungry in the early afternoon. At the high point of the route, we crossed a 14,000 foot pass next to Annapurna itself, stopping for a short while to take in the ancient mountain's mystical presence as it rose above the clouds to catch the morning rays of the sun.

My smug attitude about "outwitting Saturn" was quickly leaving me though. Even though I was not stuck on a freeway or overworking to the point of exhaustion, I was still working hard in another way. The trekking was hard, sometimes grueling. The Nepalese seem to be totally unaware of the art of making switchbacks in their trails. Instead, they make stairs out of stones which simply go straight up the mountains. Compared to the Himalayas, the California Sierras (where I usually hike), are like tiny foothills. The Himalayas are gargantuan and totally intimidating. As I stumbled into my tea-house bed each night, I couldn't help but think that I had traded one sort of saturnine exhaustion for another. At 14,000 feet, the temperature was bitterly cold, about 15 degrees Fahrenheit, a fringe benefit of Saturn, the great significator of cold. I am really not complaining, because I thoroughly enjoyed hiking in Nepal. I am simply acknowledging Saturn's power to influence planets in a person's horoscope. In some cases, there is nothing you can do. If other cases, however, you may be able to chose the way in which you experience Saturn's influence, as I did. You can make new plans, work your attitude, and see the glass as "half full." All of these things will definitely help, but there is really no way to outwit Saturn.

This point came into focus, in the form of learning a lesson, during the river rafting portion of the trip. Now you might ask, "What were you thinking, to go on your first river rafting trip in Nepal's Himalayas, during a powerful Saturn influence?"

I know it sounds foolhardy (maybe it was) but I don't believe in practicing fear-based astrology, so I usually do what I want to do, regardless of what the planets are suggesting. In this case, I decided to proceed with caution, in spite of Saturn, and in spite of the little voice in my head that kept telling me that the travel agent may not have been telling me the complete story about the river. "Don't worry," his voice kept repeating over and over, "only level two or three, no problem!"

Our rafting party was small, only two boats, and a total of ten people from various nationalities. From Katmandu, we took a three-hour bus ride along a narrow road, which wound its way through incredibly steep mountains, frequently traversing narrow ledges next to thousand foot drops to the Trisuli River below.

We arrived at our departure point and the guides set up the boats. The crew in my boat consisted of a Japanese mountain climber, three Italians, and myself. Our river guide, Ravi, began by showing us how to maneuver the boat. River rafting requires team work. It is essential that every member of the crew work together and follow the guide's commands. In order to turn the boat to the left, for example, all the paddlers on the right side of the boat must paddle forward, while those of the left paddle backward. "Left back" was the command that signaled this maneuver, while "right back" signaled a right turn. Ravi shouted these commands as we practiced turns on our first stretch of the Trisuli, which seemed totally calm and tranquil. 'The guide wasn't kidding,' I thought to myself, 'This isn't even white water.' I was secretly disappointed that the Trisuli River was so tame. Although I didn't want to do anything dangerous, paddling all day on a calm river seemed like it might get a little boring.

Apparently the Italians shared my observation, because they started joking about the river and disobeying the commands of the guide. They were irreverent and unconcerned, making fun of Ravi's military style, as we floated down the river. As our raft turned a bend in the river, Ravi raised his voice and shouted, "Now you people, see ahead one rapid. This rapid's name is 'Roller Coaster.' Now you do what I say or you die!"

We all looked ahead to get a look at "Roller Coaster." It was huge!

As we entered the white water, Ravi began to shout commands. "Forward!" Both sides paddled forward. A huge wave pounded the side of the raft turning it to the right. "Left back!" he yelled as he dug in his rudder-oar to straighten the raft. The front of the raft rose as it climbed a giant wave. As it came over the crest of the wave the Italians shouted, "Aaaaahhhh." On the other side of the crest, the raft began to enter a deep hole. "Roller Coaster" was living up to its name. The raft disappeared into the hole and buckled as the front smashed against the bottom of a giant wave, turning the raft to its side. Two of the Italians were knocked to the floor of the raft. The raft rode up the other side of the wave sideways and was hit by another wave from the left side of the boat. The left side of the raft rose up, and from my place, sitting on the right tube, it became clear we were about to flip.

I hit the water backwards, head first, looking up at a perpendicular raft, filled with flailing arms, and life jackets. After five seconds submerged in the roiling bowels of the Trisuli River, I surfaced and looked around for the raft. Miraculously it had not flipped, but had righted itself. One of the Italians had also fallen out of the raft and was floating twenty yards downstream from me. We had cleared the main part of the rapids and were now floating through a fast, but deeper part of the river. I swam to my paddle, which was floating ten feet away, and slowly made my way to the raft. The others pulled me on board.

This was the first of several sets of big rapids which we encountered that day, and the first of two times I fell out of the raft during the trip. Later that day, we made camp on a sandy beach. In the evening, around the campfire, I asked Ravi, "What level was that rapid where I fell out?"

"Level five," he said in a matter-of-fact way.

"Level five?" I said, "They told me that this was level three!"

"No, this river has some level three rapids but it also has three sets of level five," Ravi said.

"Isn't that sort of dangerous for beginners?" I asked.

Ravi was silent.

"Have you ever had any injuries on these trips?"

"Not in this part of the river," Ravi said, "but just below here there is a slightly bigger rapid and during a trip last year the raft flipped and one of the clients in my raft died!"

"Thanks for telling me," I groaned.

I managed to make it safely through the next two days of rafting, and learned quickly how to paddle in big water. Even the Italians changed their attitude towards Ravi, and started working as a team in the raft.

The rafting experience during my Saturn-Moon opposition was amazing, and I don't regret it in any way. But I wonder at the wisdom of choosing to go on a white water rafting trip during such a challenging aspect. Since that time I have rafted several class five rivers in California with my friend, but none of them have had white water as big as the Trisuli River. It's one thing to live an active life and do the things you want to do in spite of astrological aspects. It's quite another to tempt fate. As an astrologer, I sometimes encourage clients to be cautious during difficult aspects. Other times, I advise them to be courageous, and not to hesitate to make plans when challenging aspects occur. In this case, however, I think the advice I have for those who read this story is, "Don't try this at home!"

Chapter Seventeen

Pets

In ancient times, animals were an integral part of daily life. Accordingly, the authors of the great classical works on Jyotish included significations for animals in their texts. During each period of history and in each culture, the role of animals has changed. In modern western countries, keeping animals as pets has become quite common. This is especially true in the United States and Canada, where many people look at their pet dog or cat literally as a member of their family. The deep attachment that many people feel for their pets cannot be ignored, so the analysis of pets in the horoscope should be included in the study of modern Jyotish.

Significations of Signs, Drekkanas, and Nakshatras

Signs

The signs of the zodiac are categorized as quadruped (four-footed animals), biped (human), multi-footed (crabs, centipedes, etc.), or footless (fish).

Aries: quadruped
Taurus: quadruped
Gemini: biped
Cancer: multi-footed
Leo: quadruped
Virgo: biped

Libra: biped
Scorpio: multi-footed
Sagittarius: (first half of sign) biped, (second half of sign) quadruped
Capricorn: (first half of sign) quadruped, (second half of sign) footless
Aquarius: biped
Pisces: footless

Drekkanas

Many of the 36 drekkanas contain animal symbolism. These drekkanas are categorized as animal, bird, or serpent drekkanas.

Animal Drekkanas

Aries (second drekkana): woman with a horse's face
Taurus (second drekkana): man with shoulders of an ox and the face of a bull
Taurus (third drekkana): man with an elephant's body, legs of a sharabha, captures the famous animals of the forest
Cancer (first drekkana): man with an elephant's body, horse's neck, legs of a sharabha, lives in the forest
Leo (first drekkana): depicts a jackal and a dog
Leo (second drekkana): man with a horse's body, fierce as a lion, has a deerskin
Leo (third drekkana): man with a bear's face, acts like a monkey, carrying fish
Libra (third drekkana): man who acts like a monkey and scares the other animals of the forest
Scorpio (third drekkana): a lion that resembles a tortoise, and scares jackals, dogs, deer, and boars
Sagittarius (first drekkana): man with a horse's body
Capricorn (first drekkana): man with a pig's body and teeth like a shark
Capricorn (third drekkana): man with the body of a kinnara

Bird Drekkanas

Gemini (second drekkana): man with a face like Garuda
Leo (first drekkana): depicts a vulture
Libra (second drekkana): man with a vulture's face
Aquarius (first drekkana): man with a vulture's face

Serpent Drekkanas

Cancer (second drekkana): woman with a snake
Cancer (third drekkana): man with a snake wrapped around him
Scorpio (first drekkana): naked woman with snakes coiled around her
Scorpio (second drekkana): woman with a serpent coiled around her
Pisces (third drekkana): a man with a snake coiled around him

Nakshatras

Listed below are the nakshatras that also contain symbols, shaktis, or desires related to animals, birds, or serpents.

Ashwini: symbolized by a horse's head, the meaning is "owning horses"
Mrigashira: symbol is the head of a deer
Ardra: desire is "to gain lordship over the animals"
Pushya: symbol is the udder of a cow
Ashlesha: symbol is a coiled serpent, deities are the Nagas (deified serpents)
Uttara Phalguni: desire is "to become lord of the animals"
Chitra: deity is Vishvakarma who incarnated as a monkey
Swati: deity is Vayu, the god of the wind (related to birds)
Uttara Ashadha: symbol is the tusk of an elephant
Purva Bhadrapada: one-footed goat
Uttara Bhadrapada: deity is a sea serpent
Revati: desire is "to become lord of the animals," basis above is "cows," basis below is "calves," deity is Pushan, the caretaker of the animals

Animal Table for Signs, Drekkanas, and Nakshatras

Signs	Type	First Drekkana	Second Drekkana	Third Drekkana
Aries	Animal		Animal	
Nakshatras in Aries		Ashwini (horse)		
Taurus	Animal		Animal	Animal
Nakshatras in Taurus				Mrigashira (deer)

Signs	Type	First Drekkana	Second Drekkana	Third Drekkana
Gemini	Human		Bird	
Nakshatras in Gemini		Mrigashira (deer)	Ardra (lord of animals)	
Cancer	Crab	Animal	Serpent	Serpent
Nakshatras in Cancer			Pushya (udder of a cow)	Ashlesha (serpents)
Leo	Animal	Animal/Bird	Animal	Animal
Nakshatras in Leo				Uttara Phalguni (lord of animals)
Virgo	Human			
Nakshatras in Virgo		Uttara Phalguni (lord of animals)		Chitra (Vishvakarma, incarnated as a monkey)
Libra	Human		Bird	Animal
Nakshatras in Libra		Chitra (Vishvakarma, incarnated as a monkey)	Swati (Vayu, related to birds)	
Scorpio	Scorpion	Serpent	Serpent	Animal
Nakshatras in Scorpio				
Sagittarius	Animal (second half of sign)	Animal		
Nakshatras in Sagittarius				Uttara Ashadha (elephant tusk)

Signs	Type	First Drekkana	Second Drekkana	Third Drekkana
Capricorn	Animal (first half of sign)	Animal		Animal
Nakshatras in Capricorn		Uttara Ashadha (elephant tusk)		Dhanishtha
Aquarius	Human	Bird		
Nakshatras in Aquarius				Purva Bhadrapada (one-footed goat)
Pisces	Fish			Serpent
Nakshatras in Pisces		Purva Bhadrapada (one-footed goat)	Uttara Bhadrapada (sea serpent)	Revati (Pushan, the caretaker of the animals; desire to be lord of the animals)

Planetary Significations for Animals

Sun: dogs, cats, cattle, lions, quadrupeds in general
Moon: fish, amphibians, horses, horned animals, cows, water animals, small animals, deer
Mars: dogs, quadrupeds in general, wild animals, aggressive animals, predatory animals, vultures, eagles, roosters, pigeons, elephants, goats, poisonous insects, tigers, lions, serpents
Mercury: cats, birds
Jupiter: horses, elephants, large animals, whales, dolphins
Venus: horses, elephants, birds, (beautiful animals or birds)
Saturn: work animals, homeless animals, serpents, goats, dogs, donkeys, camels, horses, oxen, crows
Rahu: serpent, reptiles, insects, creatures that sleep too much, poisonous creatures
Ketu: vulture, deer, insects, serpents, animals that conceal themselves

Common Domestic Animals in the West

In the West, the most common types of pets are dogs, cats, birds, horses, and fish. The classical texts list several planets that can be used to signify each of these animals, which can lead to some confusion. It is important to understand that a planet symbolizes a certain style of energy, and can be used flexibly to signify different animals in different contexts. The following explanations can help to clarify this point.

Dogs: Mars is the primary significator of most domesticated dogs. Dogs tend to be assertive and martial, protecting their territory. They bark at anyone who comes to their home. Dog-pets of this type are related to Mars. Some dogs are not aggressive, but are primarily attention seekers, full of enthusiasm and a strong desire for appreciation and affection. This kind of dog is related to the Sun. The first drekkana of Leo and the third drekkana of Scorpio are also related to dogs. Homeless dogs that are dirty and malnourished are signified by Saturn.

Cats: Mercury is the primary significator of cats. Cats are quick and agile, always landing on their feet. The Sun, however, rules the sign of Leo, which is related to cats as well. In this respect the first drekkana of Leo represents dogs, whereas the second drekkana of Leo represent cats. So the Sun can represent both cats and dogs.

Fish: The Moon is the best significator for fish. In the West, small fish are kept in fish tanks. The Moon also represents small animals. If the person keeps exotic fish or tropical fish, then Rahu or Ketu may also combine with the Moon. The water signs of Cancer, Scorpio, and Pisces, as well as the constellation of Shatabhisha, are also important for designating water animals.

Horses: Jupiter (large animals) is the best significator for most horse-pets in the West. In western countries horses are more of a pet and typically used for occasional riding on weekends or for pleasure. Saturn represents work and service. Saturn can be used to signify a horse as long as the horse is doing heavy and continuous work, such as a pack horse, or a horse that is use to pull a plough or cart. If the horse is viewed by its owner as a constant source of transportation, then Venus (karaka for vehicles) can be the significator.

Birds: Various birds are signified by different planets. The following list of significators given in *Phala Deepika* can serve as a point of departure.

Sun: goose
Moon: crane, partridge
Mars: rooster, vulture, eagle
Jupiter: swan, pigeon
Venus: parrot, peacock
Mercury: parrot
Saturn: crow, cuckoo bird
Rahu and Ketu: owls

How To Tell If the Person Will Be a Pet Lover

There are several astrological factors that contribute to a love of animals. First, the position of the Ascendant, or focal planets such as the lagna lord, the Sun, or the Moon in key signs, nakshatras or drekkanas that are connected with animals can produce a love of animals. The placement of focal planets in the sixth house or in conjunction with the sixth house ruler can also produce the love of animals. Venus' position is also important because it is the planet of love and affection. If Venus is placed in any of the positions mentioned above, then love of animals is also likely.

Venus conjunct or aspected by Saturn in combination with other factors, often contributes to a love of animals. This conjunction shows that the person may have a deep need for love and affection, finding it hard to access unconditional love in the human realm. As a means of addressing this need, the person sometimes turns to animals, learning early in life that having a pet allows them to give unconditional love without the risk of disappointment.

Fear of Animals or Problems from Animals

If a focal planet such as the Sun, Moon, or Ascendant lord is heavily afflicted and placed in a nakshatra or drekkana related to animals, then fear of animals or problems related to animals may result. Similarly, if the sixth or eleventh house is afflicted by natural malefics, or if the rulers of either of these houses are weak or afflicted, then negative experiences related to animals can result. Rahu or Ketu in combination with any of the above placements can increase the tendency to fear them.

The Shashtamsha Chart

The Shashtamsha chart (D-6) can be effectively used for determining details regarding animals. The following interpretations can be used as a guideline for interpreting dasha or bhukti results of planets placed in the twelve houses of the Shashtamsha chart. This should be further refined by taking the planet's house rulership into consideration. The positive or negative quality of the events will of course depend on the positive or negative disposition of the period planet.

It goes without saying that before making predictions regarding pets, it should first be determined if the person is a pet lover and, in fact, has pets. The period planet should also have some connection to signs, houses, drekkanas, or nakshatras related to animals in the Rashi chart. By calculating the Shashtamsha chart to include the degrees, the same connections can be determined for that chart.

First House: When a period planet is placed in the first house of the Shashtamsha chart, there may be prominent events related to animals during the planet's period.

Second House: This placement may produce events related to the pet's diet or to expenditures that are related to the pet. In some cases it could reflect buying, selling or income related to animals.

Third House: If a period ruler is placed in the third house of the Shashtamsha chart, the person may become involved in short distant journeys or errands related to their pet. This placement may also reflect the nature of communications related to the pet or with the pet.

Fourth House: This placement pertains to the home of the pet. For a dog, this may reflect the doghouse. For a bird, it may represent the birdcage. For animals that live in the person's home without any special house, cage, or room, this placement produces results related to the pet's experience in the home.

Fifth House: The fifth house placement of a period ruler produces generally positive results related to pets. It is a good placement for playfulness and games. If the pet is not neutered, then this placement can sometimes represent mating and other events connected with offspring.

Sixth House: When a period planet is placed in the sixth house of the Shashtamsha chart, the person may experience prominent experiences connected with pets. Afflictions to this house can reflect health issues for the pet. A strong and benefic planet here may simply indicate positive and important events connected with pets in general.

Seventh House: A period planet placed in the seventh house can produce relational experiences for the pet. If the person has more than one pet, it can show relative harmony or disharmony in the interaction between the pets. Positive planets in this house can indicate mating for pets that are not neutered. This might also indicate obtaining an additional pet or a companion for the current pet. Negative planets and natural malefics here can show fights with other animals or aggressiveness toward humans during the period.

Eighth House: If a period ruler is place in the eighth house, there may be changes related to the pet during its period. If it is seriously afflicted by natural malefics, then the pet could experience health problems, accidents, injuries or in extreme cases, death. He might also run away or get lost.

Ninth House: This placement produces generally positive results connected to pets. In some cases it can be related to travel with the pet.

Tenth House: A period planet placed in the tenth house of the Shashtamsha chart suggests practical activities, projects, or work connected with the animal. Unless seriously afflicted, it may simply symbolize a period during which the pet is generally active.

Eleventh House: Like the sixth house (pets), the eleventh house (sixth house from the sixth house) is an important house for pets. Benefic or strong planets placed here generally reflect prominent positive events connected to the pet. Malefics and afflicted planets here may produce health problems, or a temperament problem for the pet. This house, as well as the tenth house, may be important for awards or achievements through various types of animal competitions or shows.

Twelfth House: This placement can produce uncertainties connected with pets. It may suggest that the pet is in a distant place, leaves home, or gets lost. This can also indicate that the person travels with the pet. Malefics placed here can sometimes affect health adversely.

Ekadashamsha, The Chart for the Pet's Health

The Ekadashamsha chart (D-11) is also related to pets and animals in general. This chart is related to the eleventh house, which is the sixth house (pets) from the sixth house (pets). The eleventh house is also the sixth house (health) from the sixth house (pets), so the Ekadashamsha chart becomes the health chart for the person's pets. Planets that are afflicted, debilitated, or generally ill disposed in this chart may reflect physical discomfort or health problems for pets. Planets that are strong, well placed and associated with natural benefics bring good health or recovery from disease.

Other Divisional Charts

Pets can also be reflected in other divisional charts.

Navamsha chart: Because a pet can be an important and purposeful bond, the Navamsha chart can also give clues. The sixth house of the Navamsha chart can be used for this purpose. The Navamsha placement of the ruler of the sixth house from the Rashi chart is also an important placement.

Drekkana, Saptamsha and Dwadashamsha charts: The pets of brothers or sisters can be revealed through the sixth house and sixth lord in the Drekkana chart. The pets of children or parents can similarly be seen in the Saptamsha or Dwadashamsha charts.

Animal Lover
May 27, 1946; 6:15 PM; Richmond, VA

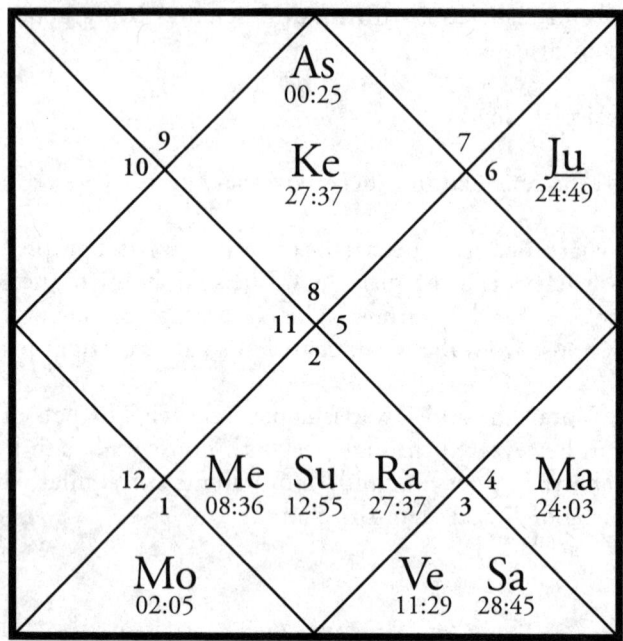

(D6) Shashtamsha

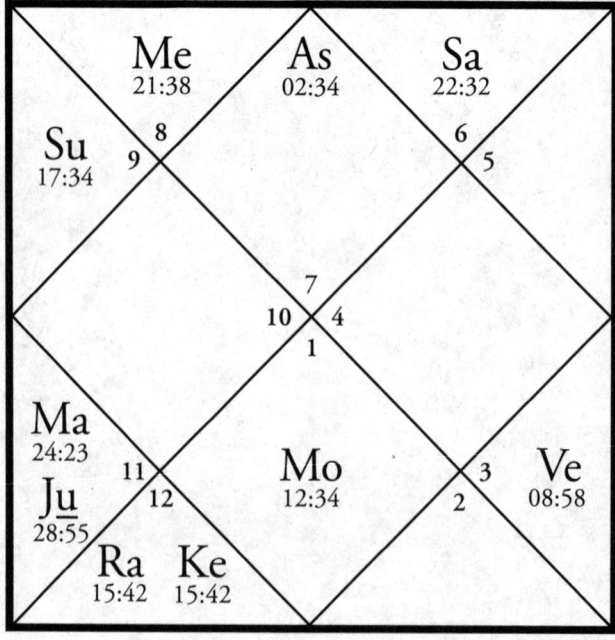

(D11) Ekadashamsha

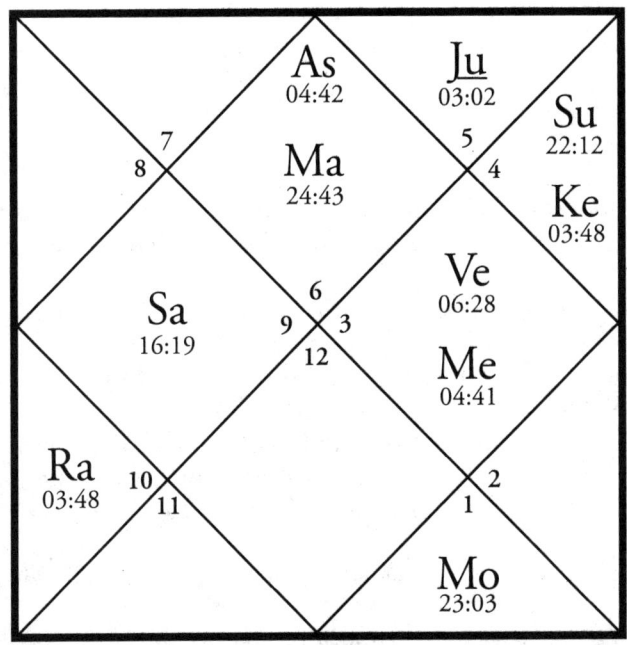

Dashas

08/21/1955	Ve	Su	03/21/1981	Mo	Jp
08/20/1956	Ve	Mo	07/21/1982	Mo	Sa
04/21/1958	Ve	Ma	02/19/1984	Mo	Me
06/21/1959	Ve	Ra	07/21/1985	Mo	Ke
06/21/1962	Ve	Jp	02/19/1986	Mo	Ve
02/19/1965	Ve	Sa	10/21/1987	Mo	Su
04/20/1968	Ve	Me	04/20/1988	Ma	Ma
02/19/1971	Ve	Ke	09/17/1988	Ma	Ra
04/20/1972	Su	Su	10/05/1989	Ma	Jp
08/08/1972	Su	Mo	09/11/1990	Ma	Sa
02/06/1973	Su	Ma	10/21/1991	Ma	Me
06/14/1973	Su	Ra	10/17/1992	Ma	Ke
05/09/1974	Su	Jp	03/15/1993	Ma	Ve
02/25/1975	Su	Sa	05/15/1994	Ma	Su
02/07/1976	Su	Me	09/20/1994	Ma	Mo
12/14/1976	Su	Ke	04/21/1995	Ra	Ra
04/21/1977	Su	Ve	01/01/1998	Ra	Jp
04/21/1978	Mo	Mo	05/27/2000	Ra	Sa
02/19/1979	Mo	Ma	04/03/2003	Ra	Me
09/20/1979	Mo	Ra	10/20/2005	Ra	Ke

This is the chart of a lady who has been a life-long animal lover. During her life she has had various animals as pets including sheep, rabbits, lizards, snakes, cats, dogs, Guinea pigs, and turtles.

Her love of animals is reflected in the following ways in the Rashi chart:

1. The Moon (a focal planet and a planet of attachment) is placed in the sixth house (pets) in Ashwini nakshatra (symbolized by a horse's head).
2. Venus (love and affection) is placed in Ardra nakshatra, which has the desire "to rule over the animals."
3. The Sun is placed in the second drekkana of Taurus (animal drekkana) in the seventh house (relationships).
4. Jupiter (a great benefic) is placed in the sixth house (pets) from the Moon. It is also placed in the eleventh house from the Ascendant, which is the sixth house from the sixth house (pets).

Different animals that she owned are signified in the following ways:

Dogs: The ruler of the sixth house is Mars (dogs). It is debilitated in the ninth house, so she has had dogs with health problems. The Moon (small animals) is placed in Aries in the sixth house (pets). Her Moon is placed in Ashwini nakshatra (ruled by the Ashwini Kumaras, who were twins). She had two small dachshunds. The Moon is also placed in the first drekkana of Aries. This drekkana is symbolized by a man holding a stick as if protecting something, and who has red eyes. The Moon in this position gives the impression of two small dogs that bark at strangers as they protect their territory. The Sun is also an indicator of dogs. It is placed in the seventh house in an animal drekkana.

Cats: The Sun is also a significator of cats. It is in a conjunction with Mercury, another significator of cats. Mercury (cats) is the ruler of the sixth house (pets) from the Moon.

Birds: Venus (significator of beautiful birds) is placed in a bird drekkana. Venus is also the ruler of the sixth house (pets) from the Sun.

Snakes: Mars is the ruler of the sixth house (pets) from the lagna. It is placed in Ashlesha nakshatra (symbolized by serpents) and is in the last drekkana of Cancer, a serpent drekkana.

Her first deep bond with an animal occurred on April 12, 1956 when she got a Siamese cat named Happy.

Dasha/Bhukti: Venus Dasha/Sun Bhukti

Venus Dasha: Venus is placed in Gemini in the constellation of Ardra. The desire of Ardra is "to gain lordship over the animals." Venus is also in a conjunction with Saturn. The Venus/Saturn conjunction reveals a deep need for affection and warmth. Those who have this aspect often feel that love and affection is difficult to experience in human relationships. They frequently look to animals as an outlet for the expression of unconditional love. The sign of Gemini is ruled by Mercury and is therefore related to cats.

Sun Bhukti: The Sun (one of the significators of cats) is placed in the middle drekkana of Taurus. This is an animal drekkana. It is also placed in the seventh house (relationships). Those who have the Sun placed in the seventh house usually identify with their relationships. The Sun is in a conjunction with Rahu (foreign and exotic things), so she got a Siamese cat.

Divisional Chart

In the Shashtamsha chart Venus (dasha ruler) is the lagna lord. It is placed in the ninth house (a favorable house), indicating that this period would be generally beneficial for having pets. The Sun (bhukti ruler) is placed in the third house where it mutually aspects Venus. This ties it to Venus and suggests the likelihood of prominent events related to pets during this period. The Sun is also the ruler of the eleventh house (obtaining desires) in this chart. This allowed her to obtain a pet during the Sun's sub-period.

Transits

At the time of receiving the pet, the Sun (sub-period ruler) was passing through Revati nakshatra. Revati is ruled by Pushan, the caretaker of the animals. Transiting Venus (dasha ruler) was at 14 degrees of Taurus in a close conjunction with the natal Sun (sub-period ruler). Relative to the natal Sun, Venus rules the sixth house (pets).

On Feb 23, 1972 Happy, the Siamese cat was lost in a snowstorm.

Dasha/Bhukti: Venus Dasha/Ketu Bhukti

Venus Dasha: Venus' relationship to animals was discussed earlier. It is noteworthy that Happy's life tracked the Venus period. Happy came to her in the beginning of the Venus cycle and was lost at the end. Venus is a period of life in which relationships often play an important role. In this person's case, her most important relationship was with her cat. In her own words, "Having a pet is like being married. It's a deep bond."

Ketu Bhukti: Ketu is a period that frequently brings losses. During the Venus major period, it sometimes produces the loss of a relationship. Ketu symbolizes things that are hidden or lost. In the natal chart, Ketu is placed the sixth house (pets) from Venus. It is in the sign of Scorpio, a sign of upheavals, changes and death.

Divisional Chart

Shashtamsha chart: Ketu (a malefic and significator of losses) is placed in the sixth house (pets). It is aspected from the twelfth house (losses) by Saturn (a potent natural malefic). As a result, this produced a negative event connected with pets during the sub-period of Ketu.

Transits

Transiting Saturn was at 6 degrees of Taurus, in a close conjunction with natal Mercury (one of the significators of cats and the ruler of the sixth house from the Moon). Ketu (bhukti ruler) was transiting in the sign of Cancer, in a loose conjunction with Mars (the debilitated ruler of the natal sixth house). Transiting Mars (a malefic that is in a weak situation in the natal chart) was passing through the sixth house (pets). Transiting Venus (dasha ruler) was passing through Revati nakshatra (related to pets in general). The transiting Moon (which is placed in the sixth house in the natal chart) was passing through the eighth house (death) and in conjunction with Venus (dasha ruler) and Saturn (a malefic) on the exact day of the loss.

On June 25, 1974, she got a miniature dachshund named Vicky.

Dasha/Bhukti: Sun Dasha/Jupiter Bhukti

Sun Dasha: The Sun has been discussed previously. It is placed in an animal drekkana and in the seventh house, producing a strong tendency to bond with animals.

Jupiter Bhukti: Jupiter is placed in the eleventh house (the sixth house from the sixth), which is also a house of pets. It is also placed in the sixth house from the Moon (pets).

Divisional Chart

Shashtamsha chart: Jupiter is the ruler of the sixth house (pets) in the Shashtamsha chart. It is placed in the fifth house (a trinal house denoting positive events) in the sign of Aquarius. Aquarius is the eleventh sign of the zodiac. Like the eleventh house, it tends to produce the actualization of desires.

Transits

At the time of getting the dachshund, the transiting Sun (period ruler) was passing thorough Ardra nakshatra, which has the desire "to rule over the animals." The Sun was in an exact conjunction with Venus, a natural benefic and the ruler of the sixth house (pets) from the Sun. Transiting Jupiter was at 24 degrees of Aquarius. From Aquarius, Jupiter was aspecting the sixth house from the Sun (pets). Aquarius is also the eleventh house (the sixth house from the sixth and therefore related to pets) from the Moon.

In August of 1977 she moved with Vicky from Virginia to Los Angeles, California.

Dasha/Bhukti: Sun Dasha/Venus Bhukti

Both the Sun's and Venus' natal positions have been discussed earlier in terms of their relationship to pets.

Divisional Chart

Shashtamsha chart: The Sun (dasha ruler) is placed in the third house, which is the eighth house from the eighth house and therefore related to changes. Venus (bhukti ruler) is the ruler of the eighth house in the Shashtamsha chart. Having both the dasha and bhukti rulers connected to the two houses of change makes a change very likely. Venus is placed in the ninth house, so the change involved long-distance travel.

Transits

Saturn, ruler of the fourth house (home) in both the Rashi and the Shashtamsha charts, was transiting through Cancer in a close conjunction with natal Mars (ruler of the sixth house). The transiting Sun (dasha ruler) was transiting Libra, in the twelfth house (distant places). Transiting Venus (bhukti ruler) was in Cancer in the ninth house (long-distance travel).

Vicky got ulcerated colitis from the winter of 1983 to the spring of 1984.

Dasha/Bhukti: Moon Dasha/Saturn Bhukti (onset of illness)/Mercury Bhukti (recovery)

Moon Dasha: The Moon is placed in the sixth house (pets), giving prominent experiences with pets.

Saturn Bhukti: Saturn (a natural malefic) is placed in the eighth house (a dusthana) in conjunction with Venus (ruler of the sixth house from the Sun). This suggests a negative experience related to pets.

Mercury Bhukti: Recovery took place during Mercury's sub-period. Mercury is a natural benefic and is aspected by Jupiter. Jupiter is placed in the sixth house from the sixth house, which is the house of the health of pets.

Divisional Charts

Shashtamsha chart: In the Shashtamsha chart, Saturn (bhukti ruler) is placed in the sixth house from the Moon (dasha ruler), where it is aspected by Mars (another natural malefic), indicating a negative experience related to pets. The sixth house rules the intestinal tract and Vicky developed ulcerative colitis, a condition involving inflammation of the intestines. The aspect of Mars indicates bleeding and ulcers. Mercury is placed in the second house. It is aspected by Saturn, which gave some delay in recovery, but this influence could not offset the aspect of Jupiter on Mercury in the Rashi chart.

Ekadashamsha chart: The Ekadashamsha chart is specifically related to the health of pets. The Moon is placed in the eighth house in this chart, receiving an aspect from Mars, the eighth lord. Sixth lord, Saturn (bhukti ruler at onset), is placed in the fourth house and is also aspected by Mars (eighth lord). Mercury (bhukti ruler during the recovery) is placed in its own sign and is conjunct Venus, indicating recovery. Mercury is the lagna lord (body) for this chart. Placed in its own sign, Mercury promotes physical health of the pet. Mercury is also aspected by Saturn, indicating that recovery took place after a delay.

Transits

Transiting Saturn (bhukti lord) was passing through Libra, which is the sixth house (pets) from the natal Sun. It was aspecting the natal Moon, which is placed in the sixth house (pets) from the lagna. Saturn was also aspecting natal Mars, debilitated ruler of the sixth house. Hence, it produced problems related to pets.

On January 20, 1990 she got a miniature dachshund named Sara.

Dasha/Bhukti: Mars Dasha/Jupiter Bhukti

Mars Dasha: Mars is the ruler of the sixth house (pets). It is debilitated, suggesting that pets acquired during this period may also have problems. Mars rules dogs as described.

Jupiter Bhukti: Jupiter (a benefic) is placed in the eleventh house (sixth house from the sixth) which is an important house of pets. Jupiter is also placed in the sixth house (pets) from the Moon. The eleventh house is also the house of acquisition and attainment of desires. A benefic placed here suggests the ability to gain one's desires. Combined with its sixth house placement relative to the Moon, Jupiter's position in the eleventh house suggests the acquisition of a pet.

In March of 1995 Sara almost died. She went into a catatonic state. The veterinarian gave her steroids and she immediately recovered.

Dasha/Bhukti: Mars Dasha/Moon Bhukti

Mars Dasha: As mentioned earlier, Mars is the debilitated sixth lord, signifying problems for the pet.

Moon Bhukti: The Moon is placed in the sixth house, which by itself does not indicate health problems for the pet. The key to the health problem is indicated in the Ekadashamsha chart, the divisional chart for the health of pets.

Ekadashamsha chart: Mars (dasha lord) is the eighth lord, placed in the first house, a placement detrimental to health. The Moon (bhukti lord) is placed in the eighth house (death), where it receives the aspect of Mars (eighth lord). Calculating the Ekadashamsha chart to include degrees reveals that the Moon is in the nakshatra of Bharani, which is ruled by the deity Yama, the lord of death. The Moon also receives an aspect from Jupiter, which overcomes the problem and brings recovery.

She got Amber, another dachshund, on October 28, 1990. Amber had constant health problems, including ear mites, diabetes, digestive problems, an inability to gain weight, pancreatitis, and kidney disease.

Dasha/Bhukti: Mars Dasha/Saturn Bhukti

Mars Dasha: Mars (a natural malefic) is the ruler of the sixth house, so it is qualified to give experiences related to pets. It is debilitated in the ninth house. The debilitated condition of Mars produced a "debilitated" pet.

Saturn Bhukti: Saturn (another natural malefic) is placed in the eighth house (a dusthana). It is also in the twelfth house (a dusthana) from Mars (dasha lord). Saturn is in a conjunction with Venus, the ruler of the sixth house (pets) from the Sun. Receiving the dog in the Mars/Saturn period in this case was foreshadowed by the inevitable health problems that plagued the dog throughout its life.

Divisional Charts

Shashtamsha chart: Mars and Saturn are in a 6/8 relationship in the Shashtamsha chart. Saturn is placed in the twelfth house (a dusthana) in this chart.

Ekadashamsha chart: The Ekadashamsha chart is the specific divisional chart for the health of pets. Mars (dasha lord) is the ruler of the eighth house (chronic disease) in the Ekadashamsha chart. It is placed in the first house (the body), which promotes disease. Saturn (bhukti lord) is the ruler of the sixth house (disease) in the Ekadashamsha chart. Mars and Saturn are both powerful natural malefics and are mutually aspecting each other in the Ekadashamsha chart, clearly indicating the animal's health problems during this period. In the Ekadashamsha chart, afflicted Mars rules the third house (ears). Saturn aspects Venus (kidneys and pancreas).

On May 27, 1955 she got a bird, a parakeet named Patrick Henry.

Dasha/Bhukti: Venus Dasha/Venus Bhukti

Venus is the ruler of the sixth house (pets) from the Sun. It is placed the second drekkana of Gemini, which is a bird drekkana. She had parakeets throughout her entire Venus period.

Her parakeet died in 1974 during the Sun's period.

During the period from 1974-1997 she had no birds. This period spanned the second half of the Sun period, all of the Moon period, and all of the Mars period. None of these planets are associated with birds in the horoscope.

She got a pair of cockatiels (birds) in 1997.

Dasha/Bhukti: Rahu Dasha/Rahu Bhukti

Rahu (exotic birds) is the nakshatra dispositor of Venus, so Venus' results will exhibit during Rahu's period. Venus' association with birds was discussed earlier.

On January 29, 1999 she got a parrot named Coco, who was a good talker.

Dasha/Bhukti: Rahu Dasha/Jupiter Bhukti

Jupiter is placed in the eleventh house (the sixth from the sixth). It is also placed in the sixth house (pets) from the Moon. Jupiter is a natural benefic, so it produced a positive event.

On February 27, 2000, Coco fell and injured his wings causing them to bleed. The owner chased Coco around the house for 40 minutes in order to capture him and take him to the veterinarian. After that incident the parrot was paranoid, and wouldn't let his owner touch him. She gave Coco away on June 6, 2003. The new owners mated him with another parrot and he was happy.

Dasha/Bhukti: Rahu Dasha/Jupiter Bhukti

The bird's injury took place during the Rahu dasha. Rahu rules paranoia. The event occurred at the end of the Jupiter bhukti. Jupiter is relatively well-placed in the chart so it would normally suggest good results. The negative results are clarified by the transits and divisional chart.

Divisional Chart

Ekadashamsha chart: The Ekadashamsha chart shows the health events of pets. Jupiter is placed in the twelfth house (losses). Jupiter is also placed in the eighth house (a dusthana) from Rahu in the Ekadashamsha chart. It is hemmed in by malefics forming Papa Kartari Yoga. Calculating the Ekadashamsha chart to include degrees, Jupiter falls in the nakshatra of Magha, which is associated with the shakti of leaving the body. Finally, in the Ekadashamsha chart, Jupiter falls in the first drekkana of Leo, a bird drekkana, represented by a man who is crying and leaving his home and family behind. Hence the event led to having to give away her bird.

Transits

Jupiter (bhukti ruler) was transiting the sixth house (pets) in a conjunction with transiting Saturn. Rahu (dasha ruler) was transiting Cancer, where it was in a conjunction with the debilitated natal Mars.

Dasha/Bhukti: Rahu Dasha/Saturn Bhukti

Saturn Bhukti: During the Saturn bhukti, she was forced to give the bird away. Saturn's negative relationship to animals has been previously discussed. It is placed in the twelfth house (losses) from Rahu in the Ekadashamsha chart. Saturn is also placed in the twelfth house (losses) in the Shashtamsha chart where it aspects Rahu (period ruler), which is placed in the sixth house.

Author's Journal:

Misadventures in Feline Astrology

In December of 1984, I had just moved to Seattle with my girlfriend, Terri (later we got married). Terri was from California. She was feeling homesick and missing her family as well as California's sunny weather. Terri was a big cat lover, so I decided to get her a cat for Christmas.

My brother had a girlfriend, Peggy, who was a veterinarian. I asked Peggy if she knew of any new cat litters where the owners were selling kittens. I told her I was looking for a really special kitten. Peggy checked around and found a litter of half Siamese/half Manx kittens. "They are only six weeks old, which is a little early to take them away from their mother, but it might be alright," Peggy said.

I called the owner and asked about the kittens. "Yes, they are extremely cute," she said. "We have five kittens left."

"I hope you don't think this is a strange question," I said, "but do you happen to know their birth date?"

"Sure," the owner said, "it was November 16th."

"Great," I said, "How about the time of birth, do you happen to know that?"

"Why do you want to know the time?" the owner asked.

"Well, I am an astrologer, and this is a present for my girlfriend," I said. "I was thinking I would like to do the cat's horoscope."

There was a pause on the other end of the line, "Uh huh. Well, let's see. It was in the afternoon. . . . Let me check with my wife." He put down the phone for a minute and then came back. "She says that it was around 3:30 in the afternoon."

"Fantastic," I said, "I'll come right over."

'What a stroke of luck,' I thought. 'He knows the birth time. I can include the kitten's horoscope as part of the Christmas present!'

Many times, owners forget the time when their pregnant mother cat delivers her litter. Cats also frequently give birth when their owners are not present. Having a birth time and being able to do the kitten's chart seemed to add a unique element to the gift, so I was highly motivated to find a kitten for Terri among this litter.

I got out my ephemeris and table of houses (no computer astrology in those days) and calculated the horoscope. I saw the Aries ascendant, with the lagna lord, Mars, placed in the tenth house. This indicated a strong constitution, and an outgoing nature. The moon was in Magha. 'Good, he'll be like a mighty lion,' I thought. Jupiter and Venus were in the ninth house, nicely placed. 'Good enough,' I thought, quickly passing over the Sun and Mercury conjunction in the eighth house, 'It's a strong chart.'

I met the owner and he showed me the litter. Four cute little balls of fur wiggled around their sleeping mother, competing for a place next to her. Off to the side, however, was a grayish white explorer who seemed to be curious about the entire room. He was the cutest of the lot, as well as being a bundle of energy and personality. "I'll take him," I said.

On Christmas eve, I gave the kitten to Terri. I first gave her the Christmas card. I had drawn the horoscope inside the card.

"A horoscope?" Terry asked with a puzzled look on her face. "Are you giving me a reading for Christmas?"

"A reading is part of the present," I said, "But this chart belongs to someone very special."

I had tied a bow around the kitten's neck and put him in a basket. He was not pleased with this arrangement and made lots of noise, so I hid him in the bedroom closet. I got the basket and Terri opened it. When she saw the kitten, she was beside herself with excitement. "A kitten," she cried, "He's darling!"

"What shall we name him?" I asked.

After some deliberation, she settled on Washake, named after a famous Native American chief from the Seattle area. Terri was very happy with her new pet.

Proud of my present-selecting capability, the next day I got the Christmas card with the kitten's horoscope drawn on it and gave Terri the astrological reading for Washake. "He will be strong and assertive," I said, "His Mars is exalted in the tenth house. He will have a good constitution and a long life. He will see himself as the king of the jungle because of his Magha Moon."

I was getting into my new role as cat astrologer, and was humorously enjoying telling Terri all the wonderful and amazing qualities possessed by her new little kitty, Washake. 'He's just a kitten,' I thought. 'It's not the same as a person's chart.' I wasn't really sure how much these personality traits would actually manifest in a cat, but it didn't matter. I was trying to make my new girlfriend feel good, and was willing to exaggerate the cat's positive traits a bit in order to do it. It was cute and funny, and Washake was very cooperative. He exemplified each of the traits I described, even at the tender age of six weeks. He roamed all over the house, poking his nose into everything, pestering both of us endlessly.

Washake
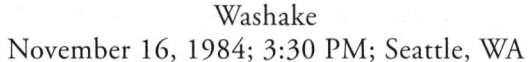

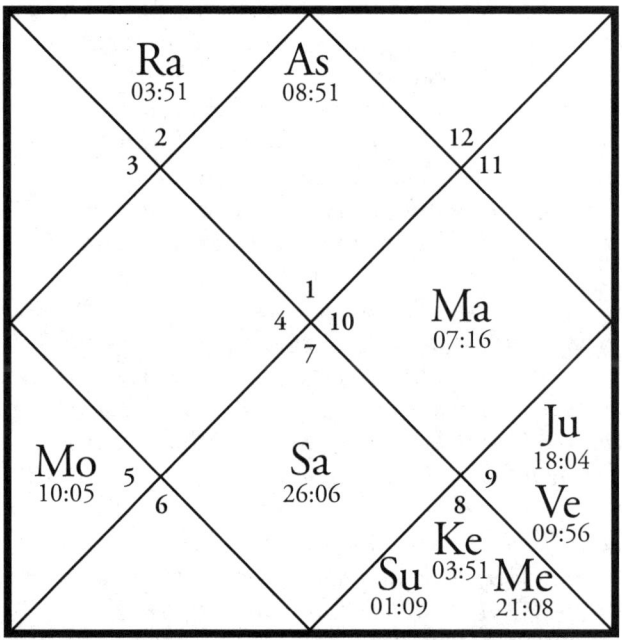

In fact, he just wouldn't stop. Like a true Leo Moon, Washake demanded total attention. He followed both of us around, climbed all over us, and in my non-cat-lover-view, made a total nuisance of himself. At night, he roamed around the bedroom, meowing loudly to be lifted up onto the bed. Two minutes after lifting him on to the bed, he would jump off the bed and roam around the room again. Five minutes later, he was meowing to be lifted up again. This went on for weeks. Although Terri was still excited with her new kitten, I began to have second thoughts.

In addition to his unbounded energy, Washake's eighth house Sun and Mercury gave him some compulsive behaviors as well. Very soon after came to live with us, we noticed that he had developed the habit of sucking on blankets or anything else he could get in his mouth. He drooled as he did this, which I found disgusting. This sometimes occurs when a cat is separated from his mother too early. This habit stayed with him for the rest of his life.

Washake grew into a giant cat, typical of the Manx half of his breeding. His lagna lord, Mars, was placed in Uttara Ashadha, which is signified by the tusk of an elephant. Like Ganesh, he was big and could overcome any obstacle. Like Muhammed Ali, his tenth house Mars formed Ruchaka Yoga. The ancient astrological texts say that this yoga makes the person a military general. When I had originally seen this yoga in the chart, I had thought it to be "cute," seeing that as a kitten, he was a fearless explorer. I failed to consider what a military-general-cat might be like as an adolescent or an adult. Washake terrorized the neighborhood. Even though he had been neutered, he fought aggressively with other cats.

This aggressive trait extended to people as well. Washake allowed people to pet him only for a few seconds before he would bite them. Even Terri, who was the only one he allowed to pet him, was not immune to his biting or scratching, and her arms frequently bore the evidence of Washake's brutality.

Washake lived to the ripe old age of seventeen. In spite of his sucking, drooling, biting, and scratching, Terri continued to lavish him with love and affection until the end. In fact, over time, I even became mildly attached to Washake. I have never been a big animal lover, but living with Terri, I have slowly come to appreciate and even love our pets.

Washake taught me some good lessons. In the future, I will never take a kitten from its mother too early. I will also never again take the chart of a pet lightly. I will insist on an accurate birth time and will screen the animal carefully. Only well-balanced, affectionate, mild-mannered, non-compulsive kitties will be allowed to enter my house. And I will never again, try to impress a girl with a cat.

Chapter Eighteen

Education

Like the other domains of life, education is reflected in various ways in the horoscope. Each planet and each house in the horoscope can potentially be related to education in some way, but some houses and planets are of primary significance.

Houses of Education

Various classics attribute education to different houses in the chart. The second house, the fourth house, and the fifth house are all mentioned in this regard. The ninth house is also a house of education. Sometimes this leads the beginning student to become confused about which house to analyze, but there really should be no confusion. As with every domain of life, education can be viewed from many points of view. As a result, several houses can offer insights about education. The following descriptions of the education houses will clarify this idea.

Second House: Many authors list the second house as a house of education, since it is the house of speech. In ancient times, most education took place on a verbal level. Knowledge was passed down in an oral tradition, so speech was the vehicle of education. In the present day, the mode of education has shifted to emphasize reading, rather than speaking, so the second house may not be quite as important as it once was for interpreting education. Teachers still stand in front of classrooms and speak to the class, however, so the second house is still a relevant house of education.

Fourth House: The fourth house represents the school the person attends. This is because the fourth house represents environments, houses, buildings, foundations and institutions. Most formal education involves spending a great deal of time in a school, which is an institution as well as an educational environment. This house can be used effectively in order to describe the type of school the person attends, and to determine when the person might change schools.

Fifth House: The fifth house is the house of the mind, and intelligence in general. This house reveals what subjects the person finds fascinating. It can reveal the major areas of study, and the subjects in which the person might excel.

Ninth House: The ninth house is the fifth house from the fifth house, so it reflects a higher octave of intelligence. Traditionally, this is the house of the guru or teacher. Since most formal education is intimately connected to teachers, this house is very important. The ninth house not only shows the person's relationships with his teachers, but also the quality and effectiveness of those teachers. It is not only a house of education in general, but it can specifically be used to reflect higher education in universities.

Third House: Although this house is rarely mentioned as a house of education by classical authors, it has become an important house in modern times. The third house is the house of information and communication, so it reflects the person's ability to process information. It shows the person's skill in completing homework, and accomplishing the various tasks of the classroom. Whereas the second house is the house of speech and the voice, the third house rules language itself. It would be a mistake to overlook this house when considering education, especially in modern times when success depends on reading ability and computer skills. The third house is also the eleventh house (achievement of goals) from the fifth house (the study of subjects), so it indicates how the person performs on tests.

Planets and Education

Mercury, the Karaka of Education

Mercury rules the intellect, so it is an important karaka of education. Reading, writing, language ability, analyzing, and critical thinking all fall within its domain. If Mercury is strong, the person will be verbal and intellectual. He will have a natural ability to accumulate knowledge, to process information, and will be good with language. Mercury rules intelligence and cleverness of the mind, so a strong Mercury is essential in order for the person to perform well academically.

Mercury's dasha or bhukti provides the general inclination to learn. It produces curiosity, the desire to read, take classes, communicate, write, and assimilate knowledge. The specific results of a Mercury period depend on the disposition of Mercury in the chart.

Mercury In the Twelve Signs

Aries: This placement favors the study of writing, logic, mathematics, science, and technology. The person will have an energetic, bright mind, and will be assertive in pursuing knowledge.

Taurus: This placement favors the study of finance, business, marketing, landscape, interior design, real estate, business, and the arts.

Gemini: Mercury in Gemini produces multiple talents and favors the study of accounting, logic, music, writing, language arts, and healing. If this placement falls in the first, fourth, seventh, or tenth house from the Ascendant or the Moon then Bhadra Yoga is formed, accentuating language ability and general intelligence.

Cancer: This placement favors the study of education, finance, healing, biology, archaeology, social work, history, culinary arts, horticulture, architecture, and public relations.

Leo: This placement favors the study of the healing arts, history, language arts, art, music, and various technologies. The person will be very bright and may distinguish himself in his education.

Virgo: This placement may promote the study of the healing arts, language arts, accounting, psychology, statistics, business, architecture, or design. The person will have a highly analytical mind and will be very bright. If this placement falls in the first, fourth, seventh, or tenth house from the Ascendant or the Moon, then Bhadra Yoga is formed, which raises the level of intelligence and language ability dramatically.

Libra: Mercury in Libra favors the study of the arts, music, literature, design, political science, social sciences, and architecture. The person will have a very refined intellect, but may be indecisive, and may occasionally become scattered.

Scorpio: This placement is good for the study of science and technology. It favors research, psychology, education, mathematics, healing arts, business, and the occult. The person will have a penetrating intellect, and the power of concentration.

Sagittarius: This placement favors the study of education, language arts, law, foreign languages, religion, philosophy, and the healing arts. It promotes a broad and liberal education, and suggests that the person will be bright. The person may become a knowledgeable expert in his field, or may obtain professional certification.

Capricorn: Mercury in Capricorn promotes the study of business, economics, real estate, mathematics, government studies, and technical subjects. The person will have an organized, structured intellect and will possess a patient persevering approach to learning. If Mercury is afflicted here, then he may worry or experience delays or obstacles to learning.

Aquarius: This placement promotes the study of science, technology, medicine, dentistry, chemistry, mathematics, and astrology. The person will be very bright, innovative, and may distinguish himself in his education. He may also consider his intellect to be superior to that of other people.

Pisces: Mercury is debilitated in Pisces. This placement may produce a highly intelligent mind, but the person could have difficulty with some aspect of communication or information processing. In some cases this can produce difficulty reading or writing. In other cases, there may be problems with attention. The person will possess a global type of intellect, causing him to absorb information more through osmosis than by learning in a linear fashion. This placement favors the study of psychology, technology, mathematics, physics, education, oceanography, veterinary medicine, and foreign languages.

Jupiter, the Karaka of Knowledge

Jupiter rules teachers and knowledge in general. Whereas Mercury rules over bits and pieces of information, Jupiter signifies broad concepts, and global understanding. Jupiter's placement and strength in the chart reveals the person's general comfort level with knowledge. A strong Jupiter makes it more likely the person will have access to good teachers and be confident with knowledge. A weak, afflicted, or debilitated

Jupiter can produce problems with teachers, difficulty getting a good education, and self-doubt regarding knowledge.

For example, a debilitated Jupiter frequently gives the person a feeling that he never knows enough to be an expert in his chosen field. In some cases, this can lead the person to over prepare before going forward with work. If Jupiter is neecha bhanga, however, self-doubt regarding knowledge may act as fuel that drives the person to learn more. In this case, no matter how much the person knows and understands, he always feels that he needs to learn more. For this reason, care should be taken in assessing Jupiter in the chart. Sometimes a debilitated Jupiter is found in the charts of highly educated people.

Similarly, an exalted Jupiter does not necessarily indicate that the person is highly educated. Jupiter exalted gives the person a natural confidence with knowledge. In some cases this produces a sense of "I already know that," which undermines the person's motivation to learn. The person may have a hard time learning because they feel like a cup that is already full. The sense of already knowing prohibits the assimilation of further knowledge.

Other Planets and Education

Moon: Although Mercury is the karaka of education, the Moon represents the mind. The Moon is associated with feelings, needs and global awareness. If the Moon is strong in the chart, then the mind will be settled and capable of steadiness and concentration. If the Moon is weak or afflicted, then the mind may be restless or disturbed, which can affect concentration.

Sun: The Sun represents self-esteem and self-expression. Although it is not directly connected with education, it does show areas where the person seeks to express himself. In this respect, the Sun's position can play a major role in the selection of a field of study.

Mars: Mars represents will-power, energy, and motivation, all of which are important for education. Although it is not an intellectual planet, a weak Mars can sometimes suggest that the person is unmotivated. A well-placed Mars can bring the motivation and ambitious energy necessary to achieve academic excellence. Placed in the fifth house, Mars produces a logical mind, mathematical ability, and a good deal of mental energy.

Venus: Venus is usually thought to be the planet of the arts and creativity.

It is frequently overlooked as a planet of education. In mythology, however, Venus was Shukra, the guru of the demons. He was a great yogi with spiritual power and knowledge that rivaled Brihaspati (Jupiter), the guru of the gods. For this reason, a prominent Venus associated with the Ascendant or houses of education can signify a high intelligence level as well as access to fine teachers.

Rahu: Rahu represents unconventional values. If Rahu is associated with the fourth house, for example, the person may go to an unconventional or alternative school. In the fifth house, it sometimes suggests an unconventional program of study. If Rahu is with the Moon or Mercury, however, it can affect concentration, making the mind restless and distracted. This effect can also take place if the Moon or Mercury is placed in Swati nakshatra, which is ruled by Rahu. Swati's shakti is "the power to scatter like the wind," which can make the mind scattered and unfocused. This will be more problematic if the Moon or Mercury is also afflicted by other natural malefics.

Ketu: Ketu represents unconventional values similar to Rahu. Both Ketu and Rahu also represent the astral plane. Ketu's association with the Moon or Mercury can disturb concentration and may cause distraction. The Moon or Mercury placed in Magha nakshatra, which is ruled by Ketu, is especially prone to producing a distracted mind. This is due to Magha's basic shakti, "the power to leave the body." This will be more problematic if the Moon is afflicted by another natural malefic.

How To Tell If the Person Receives a Good Education

Assessment of education is based on two primary factors. The first factor is the house of education, which is primarily the fifth house, but the ninth house may also be considered as well. The second factor is the karaka or significator of education, which is Mercury, along with Jupiter, which represents knowledge and the ability to learn from teachers. If these factors are intact in the chart, strong and well-disposed, then the person will receive a good education and have an easy time in his educational experience.

Divisional Charts for Education

Siddhamsha Chart

The Siddhamsha chart (D-24) is the divisional chart for education. If a dasha or bhukti lord is prominently placed in this chart, then its period will produce pronounced educational activities. If a planet is strong and associated with natural benefics in the Siddhamsha chart, then positive and pleasant educational experiences will result during its period. If the period ruler is placed in a dusthana (houses 6, 8, or 12) and is afflicted by natural malefics, then there may be failures, breaks in the education, or changes of educational direction during its period.

In addition to its utility as a tool for determining dasha and bhukti results, the Siddhamsha chart also provides additional clues about the general strength of the chart regarding the person's education. The placement of the lagna lord (from the Rashi chart) in the Siddhamsha chart is an important factor. Similarly, the placement of the fourth, fifth and ninth lords (from the Rashi chart) in the Siddhamsha chart also help to clarify educational experiences. Along with these factors, the disposition of the lagna, the fourth, the fifth and the ninth houses in the Siddhamsha chart can give important information about education which supplements the Rashi chart.

The nakshatra and drekkana placements of key planets in the Siddhamsha chart are also important. In order to determine the nakshatra placement of a planet in the Siddhamsha chart, the Siddhamsha chart has to be calculated in such a way as to include the degrees. Most Vedic astrology software programs include this calculation feature as an option.

Dashamsha Chart

Even though the Dashamsha chart is primarily related to career, it can be used for hints about educational activities. If a period planet is placed in or rules the fifth house in the Dashamsha chart, it frequently promotes activities connected to education. This is also true for the planet placed in or ruling the ninth house. The Dashamsha chart is related to action, so it reflects all kinds of ambitious pursuits, not just those related to employment. However, it is especially helpful for seeing career-related education.

Divisional Charts For the Education of Children

Saptamsha Chart for Children: Many people are more interested in the education of their children than their own education. The Saptamsha chart can be a helpful tool for this purpose. The disposition of the houses of education in the Saptamsha chart will give information about the education of the child. The fifth house in the Saptamsha chart shows the general education of children. This can be used as the primary house of education for the child if there is only one child. If the person has more than one child, however, then the fifth house becomes the house of the first child and the fifth house from the fifth house (ninth house) becomes the first child's education. The seventh house becomes the house of the second child, so the eleventh house (the fifth house from the seventh house) becomes the house of the second child's education. Similarly, the fourth house is the house of the school. The eighth house (the fourth house from the fifth house) can be used for the first child's school. The tenth house (the fourth house from the seventh house) can be used as the second child's school. This pattern can be continued for subsequent children.

Siddhamsha Chart for Children: The Siddhamsha chart can also be used in a similar way for the education of the children, using the fifth, seventh and ninth houses as the lagnas for the first, second and third child respectively. Then analyze the fifth house from each of these lagnas to describe the education of that particular child, and use the fourth house from each child's lagna as the child's school.

Determining the Major Subject of Study

The fifth house is the house of intelligence and the mind. It shows the types of subjects that are studied in school. The ninth house (fifth house from the fifth house) can also be used for this purpose. Planets which occupy or aspect these houses, as well as the disposition of the ruler of these houses, give important clues to the type of education the person receives. This will be true for the Rashi chart as well as the Siddhamsha chart.

In general, natural benefics tend to produce an interest in studying liberal arts subjects. Malefic planets promote the study of science, mathematics, and technology. The following interpretations list some of the possible areas of study for the nine planets when they are placed in or aspect the fifth (or ninth) house. These interpretations should be modified to reflect the sign in the fifth or ninth house.

Sun: drama, art, physical education, business management, medicine, history, administration, politics.

Moon: healing arts, nursing, teaching, liberal arts, architecture, real estate, biology, oceanography, culinary arts.

Mars: math, technologies, science, engineering, computer science, physical education, geology, archeology, biomedical science.

Mercury: language arts, foreign language, writing, music, accounting, education, music, psychology, business, mathematics, computer science.

Jupiter: education, law, medicine, philosophy, religion, and other subjects that lead to professional certification.

Venus: art, music, political science, finance, design, real estate, education, architecture, social sciences.

Saturn: engineering, business, technical subjects, accounting, vocational education.

Rahu: computer sciences, sciences, unconventional subjects, metaphysics, astrology, alternative medicine, foreign languages, chemistry, physics, astronomy, aeronautics.

Ketu: computer sciences, sciences, exotic or esoteric subjects, research, foreign languages, history, archeology, astronomy, music, art, healing arts, botany, herbology.

How To Describe the School

The fourth house is related to the educational institution. The disposition of this house, both in the Rashi and the Siddhamsha charts, can reveal the type of school that the person attends. The analysis of this house can also be used to answer questions put by parents regarding the best kind of school for their child. The influence of various planets on the fourth house from the lagna, and also from the Sun or Moon as the lagna in either of these charts can help to characterize the school. The following significations can be used as guidelines for the influence of the nine planets on the educational institution.

Sun: prestigious or famous schools, schools in hot or sunny climates.
Moon: public schools and liberal arts schools, schools near water.
Mars: technical schools, military schools, sports-oriented schools, trade schools.
Mercury: language schools, schools with excellent academic programs.
Jupiter: excellent schools that are conventional, parochial schools, professional certification schools, seminaries, big schools in terms of either

campus area or population.
Venus: schools with good art or music programs, schools known for their party atmosphere, real estate schools, design schools, schools with beautiful campuses.
Saturn: business or technical schools, schools with structured environments, schools in cold or restrictive environments.
Rahu: unconventional or alternative schools, foreign schools, technical schools.
Ketu: unconventional or alternative schools, foreign schools, technical schools, private schools, seminaries.

How To Tell If the University Will Be Nearby Or In a Distant Place

The fourth house in the Rashi and the Siddhamsha charts signifies the school. Any connection to the twelfth house (distant places) or the ninth house (long-distance travel) can indicate that the person attends a school in a distant place. The sign of Sagittarius is the ninth sign of the zodiac (similar to the ninth house) and the sign of Pisces is the twelfth sign of the zodiac (similar to the twelfth house). Placements of the ruler of the fourth house in either of these signs can also signify attending a school in a distant place. Typical combinations for studying in a distant place are:

1. The ruler of the ninth house placed in the fourth house
2. The ruler of the fourth house placed in the ninth house
3. The ruler of the twelfth house placed in the fourth house
4. The ruler of the fourth house place in the twelfth house
5. The ruler of the fourth house in Pisces or Sagittarius
6. The ruler of the ninth house conjunct or in mutual aspect with the ruler of the twelfth house
7. The ruler of the ninth house conjunct or in mutual aspect with the ruler of the fourth house
8. Jupiter or Ketu in the fourth house

If Rahu or Ketu are also involved in any of the above combinations, in either the Rashi or the Siddhamsha chart, then the person may go to school in a foreign country. Alternatively, they may go to a distant place in their own country, but choose to attend an unconventional school.

In the absence of the above combinations, the person may choose a school that is closer to home. If the ruler of the fourth house is placed in the fourth house from the lagna or the Moon, or if it is in a conjunction with the Moon, then the person may attend a school near his home and family.

It is also important to consider whether the chart as a whole reflects a desire to travel. If the chart contains several indications of travel in general, then this will promote studying in a distant place. If many factors in the chart show insecurity and resistance to travel, however, then the person may stay close to home.

Teachers

The disposition of Jupiter and the lord of the ninth house can describe the person's teachers. If both of these planets are strong and well-disposed, then the person will have access to good teachers. If either or both of these planets are weak, afflicted, or placed in dusthanas, then the person may have difficulty finding a teacher, or he may simply have ineffective teachers.

Relationship with Teachers

The relationship between Jupiter (teacher) and the lagna lord (self), as well as the relationship between the ninth lord (teacher) and the lagna lord (self), shows the harmony or lack of harmony between the person and his teachers.

Friendly Relationships with Teachers

1. If the two planets in one or both of the above listed pairs (lagna lord and either Jupiter or the ninth lord) are friendly to each other (see "Table of Planetary Friendship" in *Path of Light, Volume I*).
2. If the two planets in one or both of the above pairs are located in a 3/11 relationship or a 5/9 relationship from each other.
3. If the two planets in one or both of the above pairs are located in signs owned by friendly planets (see "Table of Planetary Friendship" in *Path of Light, Volume I*).

Inharmonious Relationships with Teachers

Afflictions to Jupiter or the ninth lord can show disharmony. The aspect of Mars on Jupiter sometimes causes criticism by teachers or arguments with teachers. The following relationships between the above listed pairs of planets can show disharmony with teachers.

1. If the two planets in the above listed pairs are unfriendly to each other (see "Table of Planetary Friendship" in *Volume I*).

2. If the planets in one or both of the pairs are located in a 6/8 relationship from each other.
3. If the planets in the above pairs are placed in the signs of mutual enemies (see "Table of Planetary Friendship" in *Volume I*).
4. If the planets in the above pairs are located in the seventh house from each other and at least one of them is a natural malefic.

It is important to note, that the overall personality of the individual must be taken into consideration before evaluating his relationship with teachers. For example, if the person has several combinations in his chart suggesting that he is reserved, careful in his speech, a good student, polite, humble and generally friendly, then an inharmonious relationship between the lagna lord and either Jupiter or the ninth lord will not create much of a problem. In this case the person may not care for the teacher, but will not experience major difficulty. Against the background of an extremely rebellious personality, however, combinations that produce disharmony with teachers can bring major conflicts and seriously disturb the education.

Popularity in School

Popularity and social adjustment in school is a feature that is governed primarily by the Rashi chart. If the person has several combinations in the Rashi chart that suggest positive social skills, then it is more likely that he will be liked and popular among his classmates. There are many people, however, who have friendly and charming personalities, but do not experience popularity during their school years. For this reason, the disposition of the Moon (reputation and social instincts) in the Siddhamsha chart will show the person's reputation in school. If the Moon is strong and well-placed, the person gets along with his friends at school and is well-liked. If Jupiter is in the first, fourth, seventh or tenth house from the Moon, then Gaja Kesari Yoga is formed. If this yoga occurs in the Siddhamsha chart, then the person will experience popularity at school. If the Moon is weak, placed in dusthanas, or afflicted by natural malefics, however, then the person may feel that he has limited friends or that he is not well-liked.

The eleventh house in the Siddhamsha chart is also important for social status in school. If the eleventh house is strong and occupied or aspected by benefics, then the person will enjoy friendships and social acceptance during his school years. If the eleventh house is weak or is occupied or aspected by malefics, then the person may experience difficulty in making friends at school.

Educational Achievements

Distinction in education is determined to a great extent by the general disposition of the Rashi chart. If the person has several factors in the Rashi chart that combine to produce a confident, intelligent, responsible, and ambitious personality, then it becomes much more likely that he will do well in school and distinguish himself in some way. In addition to these general factors, if Raja Yogas occur in the Siddhamsha chart, the likelihood of high achievement in education becomes greater.

The eleventh house in the Rashi chart shows the person's general ability to achieve goals, while the eleventh house in the Siddhamsha chart signifies his ability to achieve educational goals. If the eleventh house in both of these charts is strong, via its ruler, planets placed in it, and aspects upon it, then the person will achieve his educational goals easily. This also applies to finishing educational projects, completing programs, and attaining degrees.

The tenth house is the house of karma or action. This house shows the person's ability to execute projects and to perform well on various tasks. In the Siddhamsha chart, the tenth house represents actions related to education such as homework, projects, and general classroom performance. If this house is strong, then the person will work hard and will be an efficient and organized student.

If the eleventh house in the Siddhamsha chart is significantly stronger than the tenth house, then the person will achieve high marks in school with a minimum of effort. This must be supported by other indications of high intelligence in the chart. If the pattern is reversed and the tenth house is significantly stronger than the eleventh house in the Siddhamsha chart, then the person will have to work very hard to achieve good grades.

Tuition, Scholarships and Financial Aid

The houses of money and money planets (see the chapter on money) in the Rashi chart show the person's relationship to money in general, while the money houses and money planets in the Siddhamsha chart show the person's relationship to money as it pertains to education. If the disposition of the money factors in the Rashi is strong, then the person may be able to finance his education without assistance. If the rulers of money planets combine in the lagna or with the lagna lord, then the person may pay his own tuition. If money planets combine in the fourth or ninth house, or with the lords of these houses, then the parents may pay the tuition. If the money planets combine in the eighth house or with the eighth lord then the person may receive a scholarship or financial aid. Since the eighth house is the house of money coming from outside sources, however, these combinations can also indicate money from parents for tuition.

Dhana Yogas occurring in the Siddhamsha chart show financial gain related to education. Such combinations can bring loans, grants, scholarships, and parental assistance. Yogas for expenditure and poverty (see the money chapter) occurring in the Siddhamsha chart may signify difficulties in financing the education.

Timing Education Events

In general, the events suggested in all of the above sections on education will occur in the dashas and bhuktis of the planets that are described as signifying the events. In making predictions about education, particular attention should be given to the disposition of the dasha or bhukti ruler in the Siddhamsha chart. The following placements of dasha or bhukti rulers in the Siddhamsha chart are based on placements in houses. They should be further modified according to house rulership. For clues to interpreting the results of a specific house ruler placed in a specific house, see the chapter on houses in *Path of Light, Volume I*.

Dasha or Bhukti Rulers Placed In the Twelve Houses of the Siddhamsha Chart

The following interpretations describe the results of planets that are placed in the twelve houses of the Siddhamsha chart. By checking the planet's placement in both charts, various dimensions of the education experience can be described. Generally, if the planet is strong and associated with natural benefics, it will produce positive results pertaining to its house of occupation and rulership. If it is debilitated and afflicted by natural malefics, then negative results will occur.

First House: If the dasha or bhukti ruler is placed in the first house of the Siddhamsha chart, the person will experience prominent events connected with education.

Second House: Placement of a dasha or bhukti ruler in the second house of the Siddhamsha chart can indicate expenditures and other financial matters connected with education.

Third House: When the period ruler is placed in the third house of the Siddhamsha chart, it can signify the process of studying and gaining information in school. If the person is already in school, it can reveal the person's experience through study and taking tests. Because the third house is the eighth house from the eighth house (change), this placement is sometimes associated with changes of school or educational program. Because it is an upachaya house (a growing house), the placement of a period planet in the third house of the Siddhamsha chart can produce initial educational difficulties followed by improvement.

Fourth House: A period planet placed in the fourth house of the Siddhamsha chart can produce prominent events related to education, especially events connected with the school.

Fifth House: If a period planet is placed in the fifth house of the Siddhamsha chart, the period will be highly likely to produce prominent educational events. Unless it is afflicted or weak, a period planet placed here will generally give positive results.

Sixth House: If the dasha or bhukti ruler is placed in the sixth house in the Siddhamsha chart, then the period will produce struggle, obstacles, and a great deal of effort related to education. If the planet is afflicted by natural malefics, then obvious failures or criticism could result. If the person is studying medicine or healing, then this placement may not produce as many problems.

Seventh House: If the period planet is placed in the seventh house of the Siddhamsha chart, then it promotes educational events through casting its aspect on the Ascendant of the chart. It can also produce friendships, teamwork or partnerships in school.

Eighth House: If the period planet is placed in the eighth house of the Siddhamsha chart, then the person will make changes in his educational program or his school. If the planet is afflicted by malefics, then failures and other problems could occur.

Ninth House: If a dasha or bhukti ruler is placed in the ninth house of the Siddhamsha chart, it can produce prominent education events. Unless it is afflicted or weak, the period will produce positive events in the education.

Tenth House: A period planet placed in the tenth house of the Siddhamsha chart promotes professional development and other educational events that are directly related to one's career. Alternatively, it can simply represent active involvement in various school projects.

Eleventh House: If a dasha or bhukti ruler is placed in the eleventh house of the Siddhamsha chart, then the person may attain degrees or finish programs during its period. This house promotes the attainment of educational goals. It also reflects group activities and social experiences at school.

Twelfth House: If the period ruler is placed in the twelfth house of the Siddhamsha chart, then the person may experience disappointment or losses in education. If the planet is afflicted by natural malefics, then failures or low grades may result. On the other hand, because this house signifies distant places, it is a common placement for attending school in a distant or foreign location.

EDUCATION

Chart 1: Woman With a Degree in Archeology
August 14, 1952; 4:14 AM; San José, CA

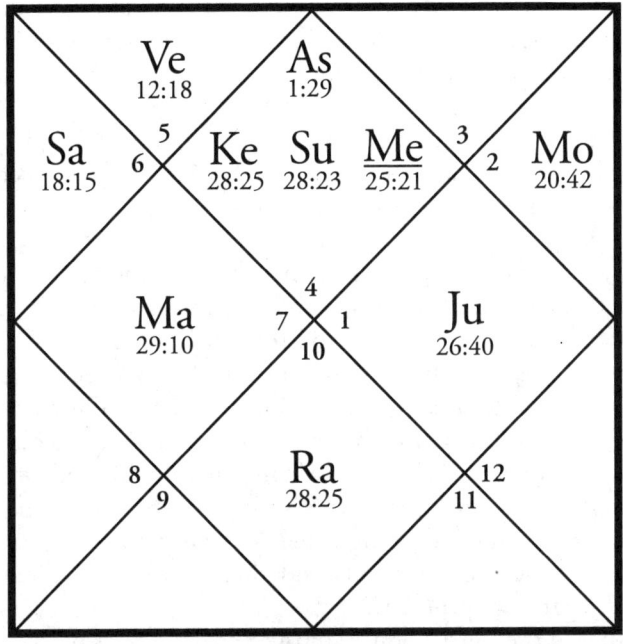

(D24) Siddhamsha

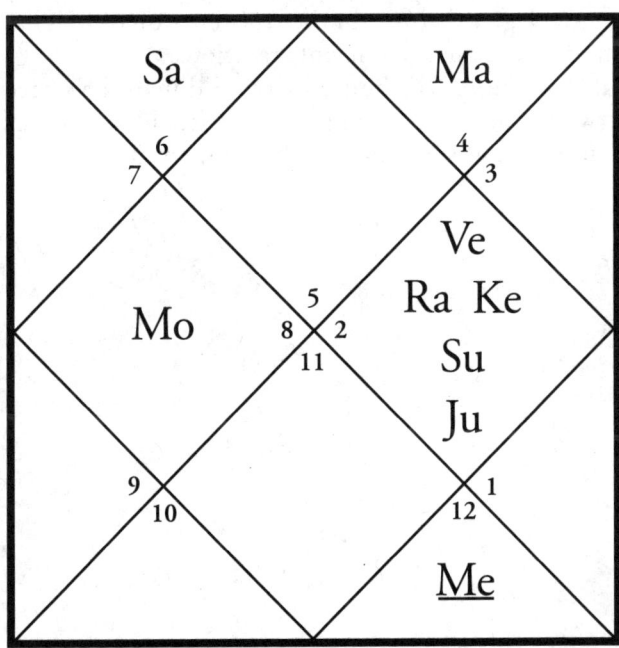

This is the chart of a woman who received her degree in archeology. The following points show the educational direction. She became an archeologist and frequently worked on archeological digs. She now occupies an administrative position with the state, overseeing the protection of important archeological sites.

1. The ruler of the fifth house (Mars, karaka of land) is placed in the fourth house (land and environments). Mars is also placed in Cancer (environment) in the twelfth house (the past) in the Siddhamsha chart.
2. Mars, ruler of the fifth house (education) in the Rashi chart is debilitated in the twelfth house (uncertainties and losses) in the Siddhamsha chart. She experienced interruptions during her education and found it especially difficult to finish her master's degree.
3. Mars and the Moon are both debilitated in the Siddhamsha chart. They exchange houses, forming a Parivartana Yoga. This is a form of Neecha Bhanga Raja Yoga, a combination that allows a person to benefit from a problem or to solve a problem. In this case, her archeological education taught her to examine the "debilitated" remains of ancient civilizations and then to excavate them, thereby benefiting from a problem.
4. The ruler of the fourth house (in the Rashi chart) is placed in Magha nakshatra. Calculating the degrees in the Siddhamsha chart, the Siddhamsha lagna also falls in the constellation of Magha. Magha is a constellation related to ancient traditions.
5. The ruler of the fourth house of the Siddhamsha chart is placed in the twelfth house, showing that she attended a school in a foreign country or distant place. She studied at Oxford University briefly.

Chart 2: Man Who Studied Architecture
November 25, 1951; 4:35 AM; Renton, WA

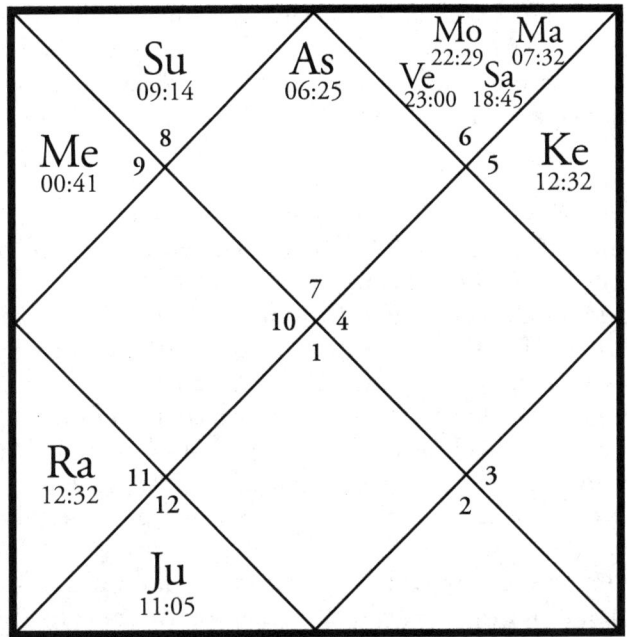

(D24) Siddhamsha

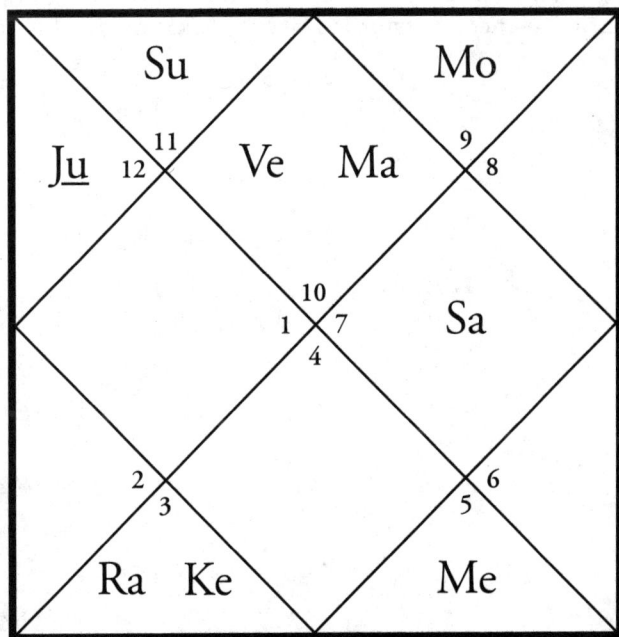

This is the chart of a man who studied architecture at the University of Washington. He did not become an architect, but made his living creating handicrafts, such as flutes. He had many recollections of being a Native American Indian in his past lives. As a result, he had a great dislike for living indoors, so while attending school, he chose to sleep on the campus lawn in a sleeping bag. The following points reflect his education.

1. Both the Ascendant and the ruler of the Ascendant in the Rashi chart are in Chitra, a constellation ruled by Vishvakarma, the celestial architect and craftsman.
2. The ruler of the fourth and fifth houses in the Rashi chart is Saturn. Calculating the Siddhamsha chart to include degrees, Saturn is placed in the tenth house of the Siddhamsha chart in Chitra, reiterating the importance of this nakshatra in defining education.
3. In the Rashi chart, Saturn rules the fourth house. It is placed in the twelfth house that normally would suggest going to school in a distant place. Although his family lived in the greater Seattle area, he slept and lived outside during his university years. The twelfth house represents things that are outside or beyond boundaries, uncertainty, distant places, wandering, and freedom. The ruler of the fourth house placed in the twelfth in this case suggested that school represented uncertainty, wandering, freedom, and going beyond boundaries. Hence, he chose to sleep outside during his education.

EDUCATION

Chart 3: An Educational Biography (Anonymous)
October 31, 1938; 9:35 AM; Lhokseumawe, Indonesia

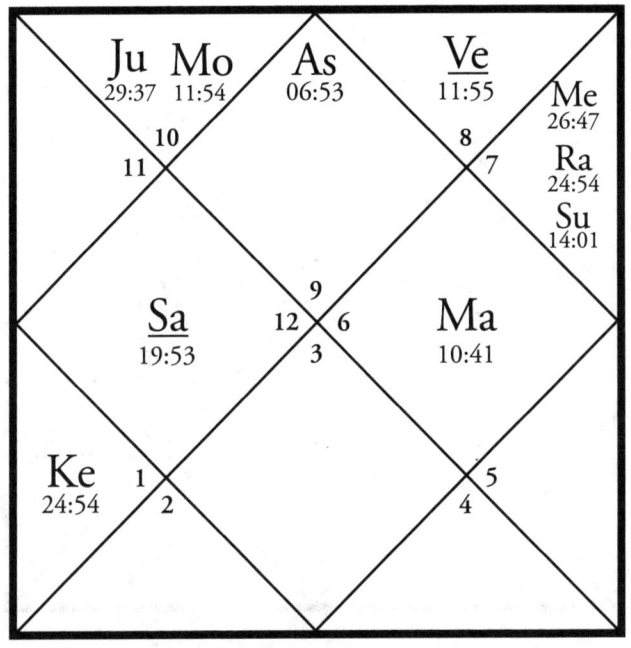

(D24) Siddhamsha

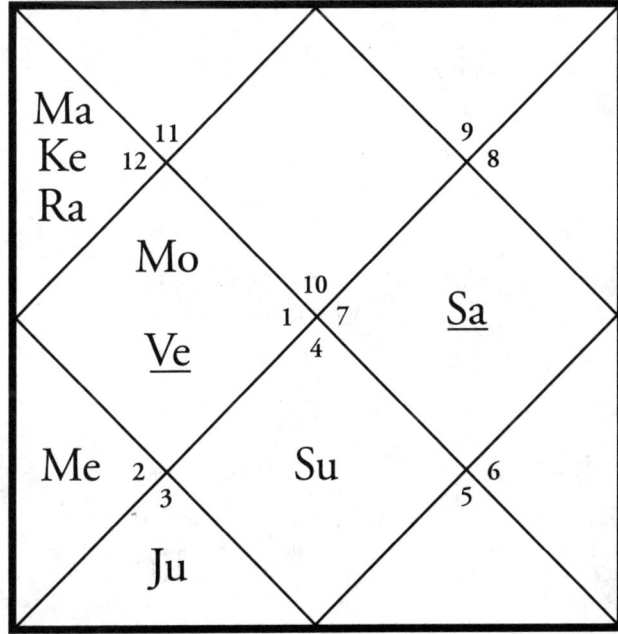

(D2) Hora

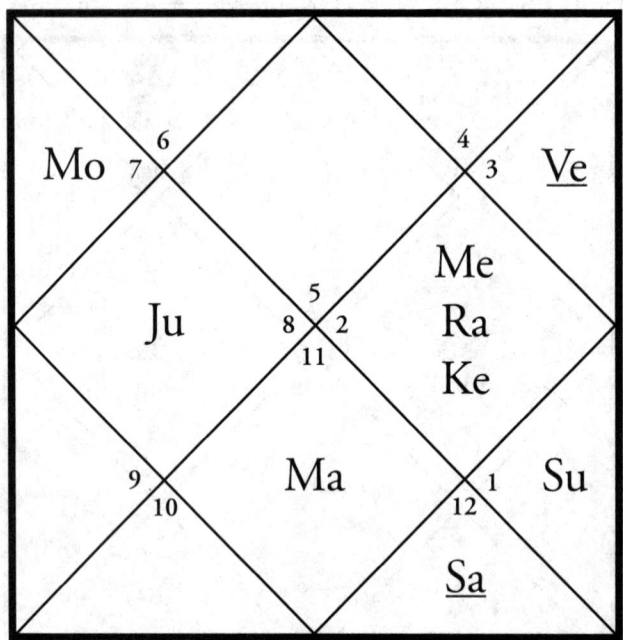

(D11) Ekadashamsha

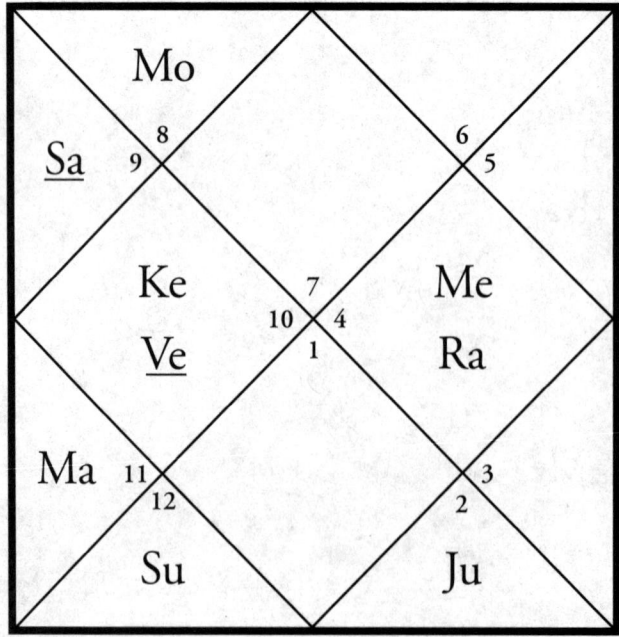

This is the chart of a Dutch man who was born in Indonesia. His father was in the military and stationed in Indonesia when he was born. In March of 1942 (Moon dasha/Saturn bhukti) the Japanese army took control of Indonesia and, along with his parents, he was put in an internment camp. His initial education took place in the camp. Life in the camp was very basic and restrictive. The living compounds consisted of rudimentary houses, surrounded by fences. Saturn is placed in the fourth house (home, education, and environment) where it restricts and frustrates environmental factors and the educational experience. It is aspected by Mars in the tenth house (government), showing the influence of the military government and the great frustration of that period. The camps were very uncomfortable and crowded. His mother and other family members beat him and made him a scapegoat. This was a very unhappy period of his life.

Education of children was prohibited by the Japanese, so it took place in secret. Groups of children would congregate in one of the houses and women would teach them orally. There were no books or written materials. His education began during Moon dasha/Mercury bhukti. Mercury (karaka of education) is placed in the eleventh house (groups and community) conjunct Rahu (which shadows or hides things), indicating his secret education. His education continued during Ketu bhukti. Ketu also covers or hides things and is placed in the fifth house, the house of education.

In August of 1945, after the atomic bomb was dropped on Hiroshima, the Japanese surrendered. He and his family were released from the internment camp. In February of 1946, he moved to Holland. This took place during Moon dasha/Venus bhukti. Venus is the ruler of the sixth house (a dusthana lord), placed in the twelfth house (prisons). This is called Vipareeta Raja Yoga, a combination that overcomes problems by destroying the significations of the twelfth house.

During the period from 1946 to 1951 he attended seven elementary schools, moving back and forth between Indonesia and Holland due to his father's work in the military. Finally in 1951 his parents sent him to Holland to live with his aunt. There he began attending a good gymnasium (Dutch elementary school). From this point onward, his place of education was stable. He did well in school and had positive feedback from his teachers.

Although this period began at the end of his Moon dasha, it essentially tracked his Mars mahadasha. The events of a new dasha are often foreshadowed during the last part of the previous dasha, which provides a transition into the new period. Mars is the ruler of the fifth house (education) and is placed in the tenth house in Hasta nakshatra. The shakti of Hasta is "the power to grasp or attain what one desires," suggesting that he would realize his aspirations regarding his education during the period. Mars is also placed in the second drekkana of Virgo, which is symbolized by a man with a pen, indicating the ability to study. Mars is aspected by Saturn, however, producing delays and obstacles. When a period planet is aspected by Saturn, it usually produces delays, obstacles, and pressures in the first part of the period. Mars is also aspected by Jupiter (teachers), which produced good teachers and a positive relationship with them.

The delaying effect in the Mars dasha is reiterated by Mars' placement in the Siddhamsha chart. Mars is placed in the third house of the Siddhamsha chart with Rahu and Ketu. The third house is the eighth house (changes) from the eighth house, indicating changes in education. The third house is also an upachaya (growing) house. Planets that fall in the third house of the Siddhamsha chart indicate difficulties in education in the beginning of their periods followed by improvement as the period progresses. This is especially true when the period planet is also conjunct a natural malefic. In this case, Mars is conjunct Rahu and Ketu, symbolizing change and uncertainty, which characterized his educational experience during the first part of the Mars dasha.

In the Siddhamsha chart, Mars is also the ruler of the fourth house (the school) placed in the third house. The third house is the twelfth house (distant places and foreign countries) from the fourth house. It is also placed in Pisces (distant places and foreign countries) and in conjunction with Rahu and Ketu (foreign countries) indicating that during this period his school changed to a foreign country.

In 1956 he began his university studies, majoring in sociology. This took place during his Rahu dasha/Rahu bhukti. New phases of life often start at the beginning of new mahadashas. Rahu gives the results of the planet with which it is conjunct, which is Mercury, the karaka of education. Rahu (revolutionary concepts) and Mercury are both placed in the eleventh house (successes, achievements, groups) in the nakshatra of Vishakha (self-empowered successes). This combination points to the study of sociology and successes in his education during the period.

In the Siddhamsha chart, Rahu is placed in the third house with Mars, the ruler of the fourth house (the school). This placement was discussed earlier. It suggested studying in a distant place and changes of school location. He moved to a city at a distance from his home to attend the university. The move created problems at first, but after some adjustment he did well in school. The campus was located in several different locations around the city, so he constantly rode a bicycle long distances between classes. The third house is the house of short distance inter-city travel. In this sense, throughout his university studies, he was constantly changing his classroom from place to place.

At the end of 1957 he changed his major slightly to focus on a different aspect of sociology. This took place during Rahu dasha/Jupiter bhukti. Jupiter (karaka of knowledge and higher education) is neecha bhanga in the Rashi chart, indicating a problem to overcome. Jupiter is placed in the fourth house (school) from Rahu (the period ruler), indicating that the remodeling effect of the neecha bhanga planet would affect education in some way.

In the Siddhamsha chart Jupiter rules the ninth house (higher education) from the Moon. It is placed in the third house (change) from the Moon. Jupiter is aspected by Mars, which rules the eighth house (change) from the Moon, indicating a change in educational direction during Jupiter's bhukti.

Also, at the end of 1957 during the Jupiter bhukti, he received a scholarship based on financial need. Jupiter (karaka for finances) is neecha bhanga in the Rashi chart in the second house (money), indicating initial problems with money, followed by a solution. The planet that canceled the debilitation of Jupiter is the Moon, the ruler of the eighth house (money from outside sources such as loans, grants, and scholarships).

In the Siddhamsha chart, Jupiter (karaka of finances) is placed in the sixth house. It aspects the ruler of the first and second houses (Saturn), as well as the second house, indicating the ability to overcome financial problems during the period.

In the Hora chart (D-2 used for finances) Jupiter is placed in the fourth house (education institution) in Scorpio (the eighth sign indicating money from outside sources).

In the Ekadashamsha chart (D-11 used for financial gains) Jupiter is placed in the eighth house (money from outside sources), again confirming the scholarship.

In May of 1965 he got his doctorate in sociology. This took place during Rahu dasha/Ketu bhukti. Ketu is placed in the fifth house (education). In the absence of any conjuncting planet, Ketu gives the results of its dispositor, which is Mars. Mars is placed in the tenth house in Hasta nakshatra. Hasta's shakti, "the power to actualize one's desires and place it in the hand," was mentioned earlier. Mars is also placed in the ninth house (higher education) from the Moon and from Jupiter, where it receives aspects from both Saturn and Jupiter. Saturn's aspect produced the initial delay due to the obvious efforts necessary to achieve a doctorate. Jupiter (the teacher and the professional) gave the beneficial and expansive influence that produced a doctoral degree.

Author's Journal:

Bombay Beedi Baba

In 1975, I met my Guru, Gandhiji. Gandhiji was a great jyotishi and also an enlightened spiritual adept. When I received my first Jyotish reading, I didn't even believe in astrology. I was curious, but skeptical. I didn't know what to expect, but I certainly was not prepared for what he told me in that reading. He said, "You will become an astrologer and travel around the world many times."

The Mark of a Great Jyotishi

Some people say it is the mark of a great jyotishi when his predictions come true. In this case, I guess my teacher wasn't going to take any chances, because he followed his prediction by offering to make me his assistant and to teach me astrology. I accepted his offer thinking that I would then go to London, which is where his office was located. Instead, Gandhiji took me to Bombay where we stayed in his flat for a week. At the end of the week he said, "I have to go to London but I will be back soon. In the meantime, you can read the astrology books in my library." He came back five months later!

Although this style of teaching seems rather unorthodox, I guess it worked in my case, because from the moment Gandhiji left, I was consumed with an intense desire to learn astrology. I spent more than twelve hours a day pouring through his books on Vedic astrology, doing chart after chart, and teaching myself the basics.

There was a German man, Herman, also staying at Gandhiji's flat. Herman spent most of his time writing a book, but he would periodically take the train into central Bombay when he had writer's block or when he got bored. One day Herman went into Bombay to meet a saint he had heard about. When he returned he told me about the saint, saying that he seemed to be a great soul. I have always been interested in meeting great yogis and asked Herman to take me to see him. Herman refused, saying that he was too busy. To make matters worse, Herman took a rather condescending tone and told me that I really couldn't go see him on my own because this saint, who they called "Beedi Baba," lived in the red light district, which was a very old and complicated section of Bombay. He told me that I would never find the saint because this area was a maze of narrow lanes and alleyways.

Of course, I had just finished reading several books on prashna, so I cast a chart for the time of hearing about the saint. There was a nice ithashala yoga between the neecha bhanga ruler of the first house (the questioner) and the ruler of the ninth house (the significator of spiritual teachers). I immediately discounted Herman's admonition and set out for Bombay on my own.

As I shuffled through the crowded narrow lanes of inner Bombay, I wondered if Herman might have been right. How could anyone find his way in this pandemonium? I had entered a world of chaos filled with utterly dilapidated three-story buildings, honking horns, cows roaming the streets aimlessly, the smell of incense, spices, urine, and samosas cooking on street vendors' carts. Bombay was a shipwreck, out of which, ironically, emanated an intangible, yet strangely magnetic energy. I found myself powerfully attracted to this ancient city, and threw away the feeble directions Herman had given me. I knew I was in the general vicinity of Beedi Baba's house. There were only around seven hundred thousand people in this area. It was obvious; I would just ask someone for directions!

As odd as this seems, this method of getting around in India usually works out pretty well. I saw a man doing laundry, ironing a shirt with an old fashioned iron. He was filling the back of the iron with hot coals from his stove. "Beedi Baba kaha hai," I asked in my rudimentary Hindi.

"That way," the man responded with a smile, enjoying the fact that I had spoken to him in his native tongue.

For about a half an hour, I wove in and out as I walked, bumping against the throngs of pedestrians who filled the busy lanes, repeating the same question periodically. I was enjoying the fact that I had completely lost myself in the belly of this ancient city, and couldn't even think of how I would find my way back. Yet many of the people I asked seemed to know Beedi Baba. I was beginning to wonder, however, if they were just trying to get rid of me by pretending to know Beedi Baba and giving me a bogus direction to *follow.* I asked again at a flower cart, "*Beedi Baba kaha hai.*"

"His house is there," the flower seller said, pointing across the street to an old building.

I jogged the remaining few yards to the teacher's door, in order to dodge a rickshaw. The door was open so I poked my head in and said, "I am looking for Beedi Baba."

A middle-aged lady dressed in a royal blue sari beckoned for me to come in and pointed to a ladder-like staircase.

I entered the dark building and started up the steep ladder towards the second floor where I could see a doorway. Halfway up the ladder the lady in the blue sari raised her voice and started chattering at me in Hindi. Confused, I turned around, not understanding what she was saying. A man said, "Your shoes, your shoes, leave them down here."

Embarrassed by forgetting to take off my shoes, I turned completely around and began my hurried descent. Unfortunately, the darkness, pitch of the ladder, and my impatience combined at that moment and my foot slipped from the ladder, causing me to half tumble, half slide down the ladder, clamoring to the floor in a painful heap.

I apologized to the lady and the man as I picked myself off the floor and painfully removed my shoes. I climbed the ladder-stairs once again, and entered the door at the top. As I entered, I found myself at the front of an attic-like room, filled with about twenty-five people. At the front of the room a very old man, with failing health, sat in silence. He looked at me for a moment as if he was deciding whether to let me in, after I had made so much racket on the stairs. After an awkward moment, he pointed to the back of the room and said, "Sit there."

I made my way to the back, edging by the sitting devotees, half of whom sat with their eyes closed. I found a place and sat cross-legged on the floor. Beedi Baba said nothing, he just sat, eyes open, gazing out the window down at the street. After several minutes he mumbled something to his translator in Hindi. "Baba is saying there is nothing other than the self, the self alone is," he repeated for the group.

Again a long silence as Baba sat gazing. My first reaction was simply that I found it interesting that this man did not speak much. He was not giving a talk. I was aware, however, that something was happening which was not on the level of speech. I could feel a powerful silence in the room, much like the feeling of being with my own teacher, Gandhiji. My agitation from falling down the stairs seemed to disappear and I felt a sense of peace. We sat there like this for the next hour until finally Beedi Baba dismissed the group. "Go now," he said.

While returning to the train station, I reflected on what had just hap-

pened. In the middle of one of the most impoverished cities in the world and in the midst of utter pandemonium I had found a pocket of profound peace and tranquility, which somehow made the chaos actually make sense. I returned to my teacher's flat on the outskirts of Bombay and continued my astrological studies.

A few years later I picked up a book, I Am That, *by a famous saint I had heard about named Nisargadatta Maharaj. This man had been a cigarette shopkeeper, who had an inner awakening. There was a picture of this man inside the book cover. It was Beedi Baba! A "beedi" in Hindi is a cigarette.*

Chapter Nineteen

Spirituality and Jyotish

The birth chart shows quite clearly how each individual perceives the world differently. As a result, it reveals the type of spiritual path a person might tread. The ancient seers who originally brought Vedic knowledge to the world knew that every person is different. They knew that we each view the world through our own special glasses. They took this into account when they devised the various spiritual practices. For mental and intellectual types, an intellectual system of yoga (spiritual practice leading to union or self-actualization) was devised. For emotional and romantic types, the recommended spiritual practice was of a devotional nature. For the physically inclined, they devised a system of exercises and postures that led the awareness to a meditative state. For those who were suited to the direct approach of inner union, various techniques of meditation were given.

The Style of Spiritual Practice

The twelfth, ninth, eighth, and fifth houses are particularly important when it comes to determining spiritual practices and activities. Here are some guidelines that can be used to determine which meditation or style of spiritual practice is suitable for an individual.

Significations of Key Houses and Signs

1. Twelfth House/Sign of Pisces: meditation; introspection; retreat; travel; Raja Yoga (the royal path of meditation)

Spirituality and Jyotish

2. Eighth House/Sign of Scorpio: kundalini; astrology; psychology; deep inner transformation; mysticism; tantra; other unconventional paths

3. Ninth House/Sign of Sagittarius: beliefs; guru; life purpose; religion; philosophy

4. Fifth House/Sign of Leo: mantras; yantras; rituals, the personal deity

Planets and Spirituality

Sun: The Sun is the soul, the inner light of consciousness.

Moon: The Moon represents the mind, especially the aspect of the mind that feels and needs. It is the receptive maternal and feminine aspect of life, and signifies the path of surrender. It is also a social planet, which sometimes produces involvement with spiritual communities or groups.

Mars: Mars represents physical approaches to spirituality. It is also the significator of the will, so it shows the person's capacity to follow through with spiritual practices.

Mercury: Mercury is the planet of the intellect. Those with a dominant Mercury frequently follow the path of Gyana Yoga, the path of the intellect. Mercury gives the ability to discern the truth through intellectual means. It also shows the person's potential for deriving benefit from spiritual literature. Mercury is the planet of the breath as well, so it signifies breathing techniques such as pranayama.

Jupiter: Called *Guru*, Jupiter is the planet of spiritual teachers, beliefs, dharma, and spirituality in general. Its disposition in the chart will dramatically affect the person's spiritual progress.

Venus: Venus is the planet of emotion. It symbolizes Bhakti Yoga, the path of devotion. It brings an approach to spirituality that emphasizes interpersonal relationships. It can also signify the use of art, music or other creative modalities as meditation. In Hindu mythology, Venus was Shukra, the guru of the asuras. He was a very great yogi, known for his great knowledge and intense spiritual practice. Venus is often underestimated as a planet of spirituality. Properly placed, it can confer great spiritual progress.

Saturn: Saturn is the planet of strength gained through hard work. Its spiritual style is to produce an inclination towards the practice of austerities, detachment, work, routines, disciplines, and Karma Yoga, the path of action and service.

Rahu: Rahu represents unconventional beliefs and practices, the astral plane, practices involving the chakras, esoteric teachings, foreign and heretical beliefs, and fanaticism.

Ketu: Ketu is the planet of moksha, or spiritual liberation. Its placement and disposition in the chart will also contribute to the person's ability to meditate and reflect. It is a primary significator of spirituality, which enables the person to experience detachment and enlightenment. Ketu signifies non-structured techniques like Vipassana, or other techniques that do not use mantras. It is also a significator of Buddhism, foreign or heretical teachings, pilgrimage, and spiritual healing.

Nakshatras and Spirituality

Ashwini: Brings intuition, healing ability, interest in psychology and introspection.

Bharani: Brings a strong sense of righteousness and purpose via its deity, Yama, the lord of dharma.

Krittika: Brings the desire for purification and sacrifice.

Rohini: Can bring devotional tendencies and the desire to unite with God.

Mrigashira: Can bring a constant, restless search for God.

Ardra: Can bring the power to make a spiritual effort and great compassion for others.

Punarvasu: Can bring unbounded awareness, via its deity, Aditi, whose name means "primordial vastness." It also brings an interest in yoga and philosophy.

Pushya: Brings access to spiritual teachers and the power to create spiritual energy. This nakshatra amplifies the spiritual power of planets placed within it.

Ashlesha: Brings interest in psychology and a desire to activate the kundalini.

Magha: Brings the power to leave the body, astral projection, intuition, sensitivity to the spiritual realm, and the desire to connect with ancient traditional spiritual paths.

Purva Phalguni: Can bring devotional tendencies and creative instincts.

Uttara Phalguni: Can bring a desire to serve others selflessly.

Hasta: Can bring the ability to get results from the practice of mantras.

Chitra: Can allow the person to accumulate merit through virtuous conduct.

Swati: Can bring tenuous beginnings with spiritual practices, but good progress over time. Swati may also make it difficult to stay one-pointed.

Vishakha: Can give an intense, fiery devotion to God and a desire for union.

Anuradha: Can produce the path of devotion.

Jyeshtha: Can give shamanistic tendencies, as well as the ability to conquer the senses.

Mula: Can give intense desire for the deepest reality, as well as the capacity to overcome fear and suffering.

Purva Ashadha: Can bring the power to discern the truth as well as an ability to transmit spiritual energy to others.

Uttara Ashadha: Can bring the ability to achieve any goal, including enlightenment.

Shravana: Can bring the ability to make spirituality a priority, and also to integrate it with other aspects of life. The person may become very knowledgeable about a vast array of spiritual knowledge.

Dhanishtha: Can bring access to the inner circles of spiritual organizations as well as spiritual status and reputation.

Shatabhisha: Brings spiritual awareness through letting go of attachments and addictions. It brings the ability to give up conventional belief systems that inhibit the perception of reality.

Purva Bhadrapada: Acts to elevate consciousness through the intense fire of spiritual passion. It brings the awareness of the transitory nature of life and a desire for moksha. This nakshatra greatly amplifies the power of spiritual planets placed within it. *[handwritten: Mars and Rahu here practically guarantees a witch or a magician]*

Uttara Bhadrapada: Similar to Purva Bhadrapada, elevates consciousness, but with less volatility. It gives the ability to activate the kundalini and amplifies the energy of spiritual planets placed within it.

Revati: Brings elevation of consciousness through caring for others and by the realization that life is temporary.

Life Purpose and the Ninth House

Being in one's dharma, or life purpose, means being in touch with the total flow of life. Astrologically this means accepting and integrating the natural indications of the whole chart, while remaining absorbed in a state of transcendent self-awareness. From this point of view, no single house takes precedence over another in showing the purpose of one's life. Eating, sleeping, doing the dishes, taking out the garbage, doing one's job—all of these become equally important parts of being in one's dharma. So each house contributes to the total picture.

Practically speaking, however, there are certain activities that tend to give us the ability to better connect with our sense of purpose. An important clue to these dharmic areas of life can be seen by examining the ninth house and its ruler. The basic idea is that any planet occupying the ninth house will take on a "purposeful" quality. This will apply to both the significations of the planet and to the houses it rules. If Mercury, the planet of the intellect, occupies the ninth house, for example, then academic learning and the development of the intellect might give one a sense of purpose. If the first house happens to be Taurus in this example, then as the ruler of the second house, Mercury might also allow the person to derive a sense of purpose from the pursuit of financial goals or through acts of generosity with money. Because Mercury, in this case, would also rule the fifth house, the raising of children might be another vehicle for the development of purposefulness. Similarly, the house placement of the planet ruling the ninth house also points to a domain in which the sense of purpose can be cultivated.

In this way, the chart points to important areas of life that can assist the overall spiritual evolution of the individual. It is also noteworthy that these areas of purposefulness are not always related to activities that are typically called "spiritual." In the above case, deriving spiritual awareness and a sense of purpose from the pursuit of money is exactly opposite of the expected stereotype of spiritual action. Money is typically regarded as "the root of all evil" by various religions. Having it connected to the spiritual path may seem totally out of line with conventional spirituality. If one reads the *Bhagavad Gita*, however, it becomes quickly apparent that the conventional ideas about what is and what is not spiritual action are not always the ideas promoted by the sages. In the *Gita*, for example, Krishna encourages Arjuna to uphold righteousness and fulfill his duty as a warrior, even to the point of killing his relatives as a means of spiritual evolution. Performed with dispassion and purpose, any dutiful action can lead to the transcendent. The various links between the ninth house and other houses and planets provides us with clues to finding unique areas in which a person naturally connects with dharma and experiences a sense of purpose that facilitates progress towards self-realization.

Extending this idea, the fifth house is also a dharma house. Even though the ninth house seems to have a more direct link to duty and purpose, the fifth is the ninth house from the ninth house, so it becomes an important factor in the consideration of duty and purpose in life. This house and its ruler can be used as secondary factors in identifying areas of dharmic emphasis in the chart.

Styles of Meditation in the Chart

Just as the ninth house and its ruler reveal clues about the sense of purpose, the twelfth house reveals the type of meditation that is suited to the individual. The twelfth house is the house of moksha, liberation from karmic bondage. Unlike the first house, which is a house of crystallized ego, the twelfth house is where the ego dissolves into the state of pure, unbounded awareness. It represents the process of introspection, reflection, and meditation. Its various connections, via the house placement of its ruler and planets placed in the twelfth house, show important elements that contribute to the person's individual meditative approach.

The following interpretations are modern applications of classical principles of Jyotish. They have been applied successfully to modern horoscopes by the author. Although these interpretations are given for the twelfth lord's placement in different houses, the interpretations work in reverse as well (when the planet ruling the pertinent house is placed in the twelfth house). If the planet happens to rule a current dasha or bhukti, then the results will manifest during that planet's period.

The Twelfth Lord Placed in the Twelve Houses

First House (the physical body, the personality): This placement favors the practice of hatha yoga, Tai Chi or Chi Kung. Sometimes this also indicates the use of the personality as a kind of meditation. Religious leaders, charismatics, and trance channels fall into this category.

Second House (the voice, food, money): The person will benefit by chanting mantras, using verbal affirmations and singing. The voice becomes a vehicle for intuition and the person's speaking style frequently takes on a "stream of consciousness" quality. If the intuition is developed, then the person's words will naturally come true. Learning to eat consciously and intuitively also becomes important. Charity and selfless sharing of resources is another approach that enhances the spiritual process. The person can benefit from the practice of *aparigraha* (limiting attachments and possessions and living simply). Mahatma Gandhi called this approach, "simple living, high thinking!"

Third House (music, the hands, short journeys, and the communications process): The person can use music or working with the hands as a meditation. This is also a combination for intuition expressed through communications processes like writing or talking. This is also a good placement for practicing what the Buddhists call "walking meditation."

Fourth House (the home): This suggests the meditative value of environmental activities such as gardening and landscaping. People with this placement also derive spiritual benefit by creating a sacred space in their home, such as a shrine or small temple. The use of Vastu (sacred architecture, the Vedic form of Feng Shui) can also be a valuable spiritual tool.

Fifth House (mantras, yantras, rituals, creativity, children): This placement allows the person to benefit through the practice of a meditation that involves the use of a mantra (or yantra). The person might also perform rituals such as pujas and homas. Meditation on the form or mantra of the ishta devata (personal deity) can also be indicated. Raising children might be an appropriate spiritual practice. The person could also use the creative process as a type of meditation.

Sixth House (work, service, health): This suggests service (seva) as a spiritual practice. It can also suggest healing work as sadhana. The challenge of dealing with personal health issues might also provide food for meditation. This placement also suggests that meditation can be an effective remedy for health problems and diseases.

Seventh House (relationships, marriage, and partnerships): Relationships become the vehicles for meditation. An extension of this idea is that the practice of meditation will help to solve problems in relationships. Similarly, relationships will drive the person inward toward the practice of meditation. The divine is externalized, so this is an excellent placement for devotion to a personal deity and the practice of Bhakti Yoga (the path of devotion).

Eighth House (kundalini and yoga): The person will benefit through meditation techniques that focus on the chakra system. It also suggests kundalini-oriented techniques such as shaktipat (energy transmission from an enlightened teacher). This placement of the twelfth lord also allows the person to derive benefit from the practice of hatha yoga.

Ninth House (guru): This placement promotes meditation on the guru, initiation by a guru, or the use of a technique suggested by a teacher. It may also indicate meditation on the family deity, performing charity, and making pilgrimages. It is a first-rate yoga for the development of spiritual awareness.

Tenth House (mantra siddhi, career): The activities of the career can produce a flowing, meditative state. Extending this, the career will tend to improve through the practice of meditation. This is also the house of mantra siddhi (power coming through the practice of a mantra), so the twelfth lord placed here can be good for enhancing mantra meditation, producing tangible outcomes such as providential help, healing and other miraculous happenings.

Eleventh House (friends, community, humanity, goals): The person might practice a meditation that extends loving kindness or compassion to all beings. He might enjoy meditating in groups. Satsang (spiritual community) may be an important part of the spiritual path. This is also a good placement for goal-oriented meditations aimed at manifesting a particular desire.

Twelfth House (ashrams, foreign countries, formlessness): If the twelfth lord is in the twelfth house and is not influenced by any other planet, then the meditation will primarily be related to the nature of the twelfth lord. Pilgrimages, retreats or time spent at ashrams will also be beneficial.

In addition to the connections between the twelfth house and other houses in the chart, it is important to consider the natural significations of planets connected with the twelfth house or its ruler. As indicated previously, each planet has its own spiritual style. This is also true when it comes to meditation. Here are the results of the nine planets when they are placed in the twelfth house or when they are connected with the twelfth lord.

Meditation Styles Indicated by Planets in the Twelfth House or Connected with the Twelfth Lord

Sun: This placement favors meditation techniques that focus on the inner light, either in visual form or through a mantra such as the Gayatri mantra. Hatha yoga is also helpful. The Sun here can also cause a person to identify with the practice of meditation, deriving a sense of self-worth from positive experiences in meditation. Meditation can be a great cure for self-doubt and self-consciousness, which usually accompanies this placement. If afflicted, it can produce spiritual egotism, where the person enjoys calling attention to his experiences in meditation. He could also have a need to believe that the meditation he practices is better and higher than that practiced by others.

Moon: The Moon in the twelfth house is good for meditations on the Goddess in her various forms as the Universal Mother. Meditations on Lord Shiva or Lord Krishna can also be indicated. The Moon also favors meditation that focuses on the element of water. Reflective techniques such as meditation on the inner abode of peace and security can also be indicated. The practice of meditation will result in a greater sense of security and happiness.

Mars: Mars in the twelfth house indicates active or physical meditations. Hatha yoga is a meditation that uses the physical muscles as the vehicle for meditation. In other traditions, Tai Chi and Chi Kung use the body in a similar way. The practice of meditation will result in better physical energy and stamina.

Mercury: Mercury's connection to the twelfth house can indicate techniques that use the breath such as pranayama. Modern versions of this have also become popular in the west, such as Rebirthing and Holotropic Breathwork. The practice of meditation might also result in better memory and improved communication skills.

Jupiter: When Jupiter is connected to the twelfth house, the person could benefit from meditating on the form of the teacher or guru. In any case, Jupiter's influence on the twelfth house suggests the importance of seeking out a good teacher for instruction in meditation. Even without the influence of Jupiter here, it is generally advisable to find a good teacher when learning meditation, but more so in the case of Jupiter's influence on the twelfth house. Jupiter's influence also favors spiritual development generally. The person usually has positive experiences in meditation. Meditation also produces a natural sense of prosperity and may even be a key to developing the person's financial potential.

Venus: Venus' connection to the twelfth house usually makes meditation enjoyable. It can suggest a meditation that has a devotional quality. It might also favor a technique that focuses on the heart chakra. Meditations on some form of the Goddess, either visually or by use of a mantra, may also be indicated. When Venus is in the twelfth house, regular meditation will lead to better relationships and is a prerequisite for happy marriage.

Saturn: If Saturn has an influence on the twelfth house, then it is very important for the person to create a regular routine of meditation. Otherwise, there will be resistance and obstruction to meditation. This placement allows the person to make real progress, but only by making efforts to adhere to the disciplines of sadhana. Hard work and service also become natural vehicles for meditation.

Rahu: When Rahu is connected with the twelfth house, the person tends to practice a meditation connected with the chakras or kundalini. Rahu also produces an interest in various alternative and revolutionary forms of meditation. In some cases, it gives an interest in astral projection. In any case, the mind will be restless during meditation, frequently going on tangents or following streams of thought. For this reason, the person might benefit from practicing a technique of meditation that does not force or push out thoughts. It is also important that the technique is not too monotonous.

Ketu: Ketu is the planet moksha or liberation. Its connection with the twelfth house is very good for spiritual development. Ketu favors "no-technique" techniques such as Vipassana. It is also said that "Ketu is a Buddhist," so other Buddhist forms of meditation are also possibilities. In any case, Ketu is a minimalist, a non-material, non-structured graha, and so minimalist techniques such as mindfulness or simply watching the breath usually suit this placement.

[handwritten margin note: This does not surprise me at all, since my Ketu on the Ascendent partakes of 12th house energy.]

Mantras and the Ishta Devata

Each person has an individual deity called the ishta devata, which is reflected in the chart. Whether or not the person is Hindu, knowing the nature of this deity can help him understand the personality of the deity, which helps remove obstacles along the spiritual path. Identifying the ishta devata allows the person to cultivate a relationship with a particular aspect of the divine that is particularly harmonized with his own nature.

Various methods for identifying this ishta devata are given in the classics. Basically, the fifth house is the house of the ishta devata and the fifth lord can sometimes be used as an indicator. Planets located in or aspecting the fifth house also give important clues to the deity's nature. Planets in the twelfth house from the Ascendant or from the atmakaraka (the planet with the highest degree in the natal chart) can also reveal the person's ishta devata. Generally, the idea is to take the most powerful and supportive of these planets as the indicator of the deity. If two or more planets are involved, they sometimes reveal a specific deity by their combination. It is also important to consider the nature of the deity that rules over the nakshatra occupied by the fifth lord.

The following list, gives the names of some deities commonly associated with the various planets. It is important to note that the deity represented by a particular planet or combination of planets may vary from culture to culture. The Moon, for example, might represent Durga, the Divine Mother, in India. In Italy, however, where Hindu gods are relatively unknown, the same Moon might indicate that Virgin Mary is the object of the person's devotion and prayers. Instead of a Hindu mantra, the person might say the Hail Mary prayer in repetition. The point is that in both cases, it is a maternal deity who is worshipped. Also, for those who are specifically interested in Hindu gods, there will still be some variation from country to country. In India, where people generally know about the various gods and goddesses of their mythology, it is more common and acceptable for a person to adopt a practice of worshipping a deity that might not be well known in the West. In recommending a deity to a typical western practitioner of yoga and meditation, however, it is important to take into consideration the person's level of interest and exposure to the Vedic tradition.

Table of Ishta Devatas

Planet	Common Use	Bengali Tantric Goddesses	South Indian Tantric Goddesses	Parashara Incarnations of Vishnu	Parashara's *Hora Shastra*, Chapter 3
Sun	Rama/Shiva	Matangi	Tripura Bhairavi	Rama	Agni (fire)
Moon	Durga, Mahadevi, Krishna, Shiva	Bhuvaneshvari	Tripura Sundari, Bhuvaneshvari	Krishna	Varuna (Water)
Mars	Kartikeya, Subramanya, Hanuman	Bagalamukhi	Bagalamukhi	Narasimha	Kartikeya
Mercury	Vishnu	Tripura Sundari (Bala)	Matangi	Buddha	Vishnu
Jupiter	Ganesha	Tara	Tara	Vamana	Indra
Venus	Lakshmi	Kamala	Kamala	Parasu Rama	Sachi Devi
Saturn	Shiva	Kali	Kali	Koorma	Brahma
Rahu	Durga	Chinnamasta	Dhuvamati	Varaha	None listed
Ketu	Rudra	Dhuvamati	Chinnamasta	Meena	None listed

In addition to the preceding table, the South Indian classic, *Prashna Marga*, gives the following correlation between planets and deities.

Ishta Devata According to *Prashna Marga*

Sun

Sun: Shiva
Sun in first drekkana of common sign: Subrahmanya
Sun in second drekkana of common sign: Ganesha

Moon

Moon: Durga
Weak Moon: Bhadrakali
Weak Moon and in a sign of Mars: Chamundi (with dark attributes)

Mars

Mars in odd signs: Subrahmanya, Bhairava
Mars in even signs: Chamundi, Bhadrakali

Mercury

Mercury in movable and common signs: the avatars of Vishnu
Mercury in the first or second drekkanas of a fixed sign: Krishna
Mercury in the third drekkana of a fixed sign: Vishnu, in general

Jupiter

Jupiter: Vishnu, in general
Jupiter signifies divinity in general, and so the deity can be taken from the nature of the sign occupied by Jupiter and by the planets associated with Jupiter.

Venus

Venus in the house of a benefic: Lakshmi
Venus in houses 3, 6, 8, or 12: Yakshi
Venus in own sign: Annapoorna
Venus in rajasic signs (signs of Mercury or Venus): Lakshmi
Venus in tamasic signs (signs of Mars or Saturn): Yakshi

Venus in odd signs with male planets: Ganesha

Saturn

Saturn: Sastha, Kiratha

Rahu

Rahu: Serpent God

Yogas That Promote Spiritual Development

As previously mentioned, the primary houses of spirituality are the twelfth, ninth, eighth, fifth and fourth houses. When these houses combine their energies via the placement of their rulers, they produce a strong tendency for spiritual evolution. These combinations can take place in the following ways.

1. Ruler of the 12th house placed in the 9th, 8th, 5th, or 4th house
2. Ruler of the 9th house placed in the 12th, 8th, 5th or 4th house
3. Ruler of the 8th house placed in the 12th, 9th, 5th, or 4th house
4. Ruler of the 5th house placed in the 12th, 9th, 8th, or 4th house
5. Ruler of the 4th house placed in the 12th, 9th, 8th, or 5th house

In addition, if the rulers of the spirituality houses combine with each other in other houses of the chart, it can also produce elevation of spiritual awareness.

The addition of the two karakas (significators) of spiritual development, Jupiter and Ketu, to any of the preceding combinations greatly enhances their spiritual power. Jupiter and Ketu in combination with each other is also a great combination for spiritual development.

Divisional Charts for Spirituality

The main divisional chart for spirituality is the Vimshamsha chart. This chart can be used for spirituality in general. It is the varga of *upasana*, which means worship or devotion. It can reflect all aspects of the person's spiritual journey, and is especially good for revealing his connection to his ishta devata. The Vimshamsha chart can also be used for predicting periods of spiritual growth, as well as periods when spiritual growth is frustrated.

The Panchamsha chart can be used specifically for determining the style of the person's spiritual practices. Just as the fifth house is the house of mantras, rituals and other techniques, the Panchamsha chart (the fifth division) shows the details regarding the various types of sadhana.

When looking at the Vimshamsha chart or the Panchamsha chart, the various house meanings should be applied to the domain of spirituality. There is a subtle but important difference, though, between these two charts. In the case of the Panchamsha chart, the house meanings pertain specifically to the spiritual practices themselves. The Vimshamsha chart, on the other hand, is related to the overall spiritual evolution, which may also include spiritual practices, but is more focused on the totality of spiritual growth. With this in mind, the house meanings, planetary placements and yogas given in this chapter can be applied to both charts.

Planetary Periods That Produce Spiritual Development

The major periods or sub-periods of planets involved in any of the yogas given earlier will produce significant spiritual development. The quality of spiritual experiences will vary based on the nature, rulership and disposition of the period lord. The ruler of the twelfth house, for example, may produce an inclination to meditate, resulting in unbounded awareness. The ruler of the eighth house, on the other hand, can produce a more intense transformation process.

The period ruler's placement in the Vimshamsha and Panchamsha charts is very important. The placement of the period ruler in the lagna, the twelfth, ninth, or fifth houses of the Vimshamsha or Panchamsha chart will produce prominent spiritual development during the planet's period, especially if it is associated with Jupiter or Ketu. If a planetary period ruler is involved in a spirituality-producing yoga in both the Rashi and the divisional charts (Vimshamsha and Panchamsha charts), then the planet's period will produce very prominent spiritual results. If the period planet does not seem to be connected to the area of spirituality in the Rashi chart, but is prominently placed in the Vimshamsha or Panchamsha charts, its period can still produce moderately good results.

The spiritual results of a period ruler can be clarified further by taking its specific house placement in the Vimshamsha and Panchamsha charts into consideration. These results will be similar to the results given previously in this chapter under the heading, "The Twelfth Lord Placed in the Twelve Houses." When interpreting these results, simply read the results for the house in which the period ruler is placed. It is important to remember that the effects of a period ruler in the two divisional charts will vary slightly. The Panchamsha chart is specifically for spiritual practices, while the Vimshamsha chart is for spirituality in general. Also, remember that the results given for the twelfth lord placed in the twelve houses pertains to the person's overall spiritual disposition, while a period planet placed in the twelve houses of a divisional chart only gives its results during its period. In this respect, it is also important to remember that the period planet can only express itself on the background of the person's nature. For example, if a person has many patterns in the natal chart that indicate sensuality and love of comfort, the mere placement of a period ruler in the second house will not necessarily produce fasting or modifications to the diet.

The major period of Ketu is one that naturally brings the person's awareness to the divine. Ketu's process, though, involves the development of a distaste for the outer world. Ketu is the planet of detachment, so during its period the person may feel like being alone. Sometimes the person becomes aloof or distant. If Ketu is badly placed in the chart, the person could feel dissatisfied, lonely, or even depressed. Discontented with outer circumstances, the person turns within to find fulfillment. Of all the nine planets, it is Ketu that gives the mind the greatest inclination to seek the divine.

Jupiter's period is also a natural period for spiritual development. This period frequently produces a desire to gain spiritual knowledge, and gives the person contact with spiritual teachers. This effect will be noticed more clearly when Jupiter is placed in one of the houses of spirituality, and especially if it joins Ketu or one of the rulers of the other houses of spiritual development.

Chart 1: Spiritual Devotee
February 1, 1969; 9:05 AM; Kumbakonam, India

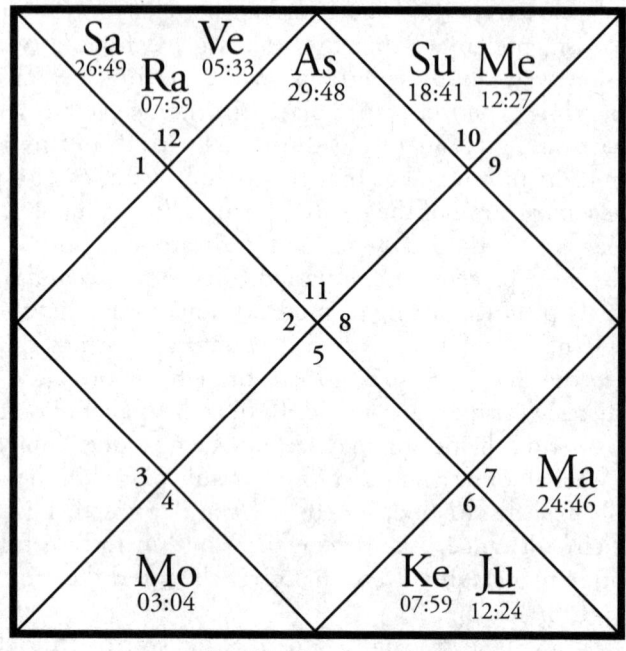

(D20) Vimshamsha

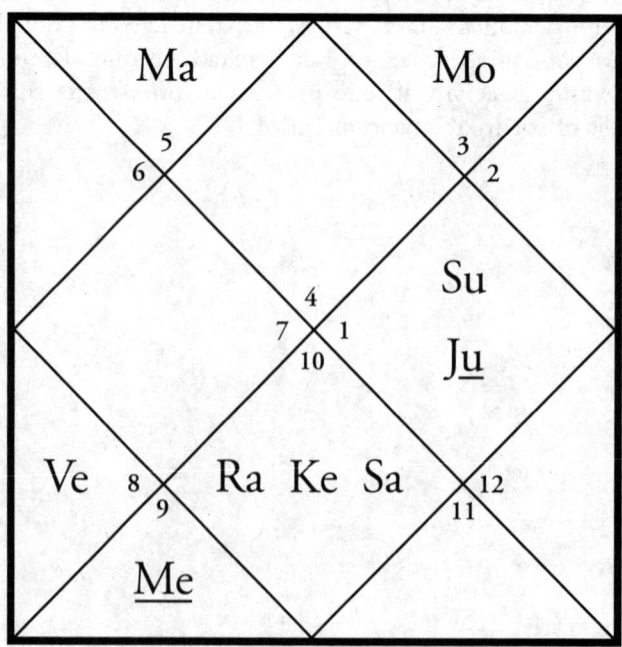

(D5) Panchamsha

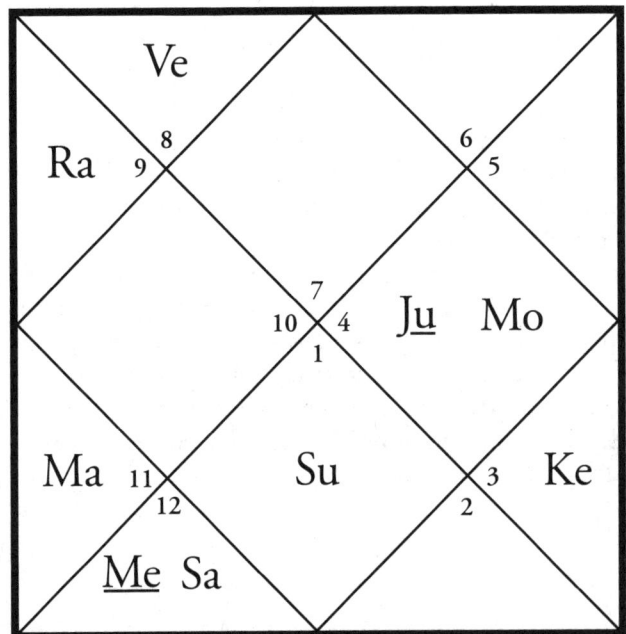

In this anonymous example chart, the ruler of the fifth house is placed in the twelfth house. This combination is good for a mantra practice. The twelfth house is also aspected by Jupiter, which rules the second house, the house of the voice. This caused a vocalized practice of the mantra. Notice that the planet that owns the fifth house is Mercury, which indicates Vishnu according to one school of thought. Mercury is also in the nakshatra of Shravana, which is ruled by Vishnu. In both the Vimshamsha and Panchamsha charts, Mercury is the ruler of the twelfth house (meditation), aspecting its own sign from the sixth house. In the case of the Panchamsha chart (spiritual practices), Mercury is conjunct Saturn, ruler of the fifth house (mantras). The person was initiated by a highly respected guru in the practice of a Vishnu mantra, and instructed to chant this mantra orally.

It is also important to note that not everyone with this combination will practice a mantra to Vishnu. Other supportive factors must be present. Notice, for example, that the ascending nakshatra in the Rashi chart is Purva Bhadrapada, a nakshatra that gives a great spiritual inclination. Jupiter is conjunct Ketu in the eighth house as well.

The dasha scheme is also a vital element. In spite of various spiritual combinations, the person will not pursue spiritual aspirations such as initiation into a mantra unless the proper period has arrived. In this case, she was initiated during the major period of Mercury and the sub-period of Rahu. Rahu is conjunct Venus (ninth lord) and is placed in Pisces (the sign of moksha). It is also placed in the second house (the voice).

Panchamsha chart: In the Panchamsha chart, Rahu is disposited by exalted Jupiter which is placed in the tenth house. This creates Hamsa Yoga which was triggered during Rahu's period. Hamsa Yoga frequently makes a person a teacher or advisor when found in a Rashi chart. It can also give access to good teachers. In the Panchamsha chart (the chart for spiritual practices), however, it can produce initiation into spiritual practices by a guru. In some cases it can also cause the person to teach meditation or other spiritual practices. Jupiter is also involved in Gaja Kesari Yoga, which can be associated with fame. Triggered by Rahu's sub-period, these combinations clearly reflected her spiritual initiation by a famous spiritual teacher.

Chart 2: Swami Sivananda
September 8, 1887; 6:16 AM; Tirunelveli, India

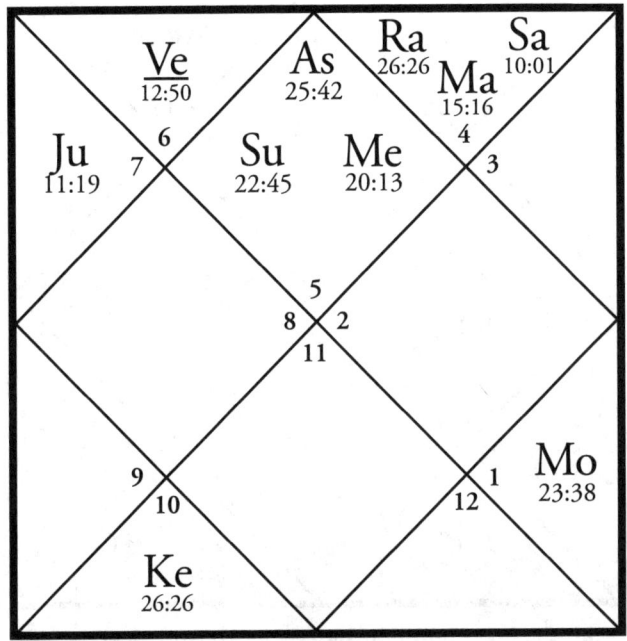

(D20) Vimshamsha

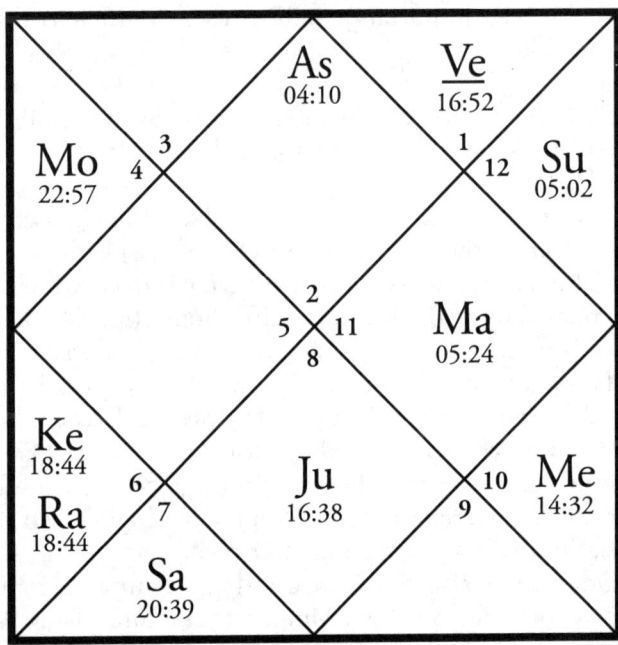

(D5) Panchamsha

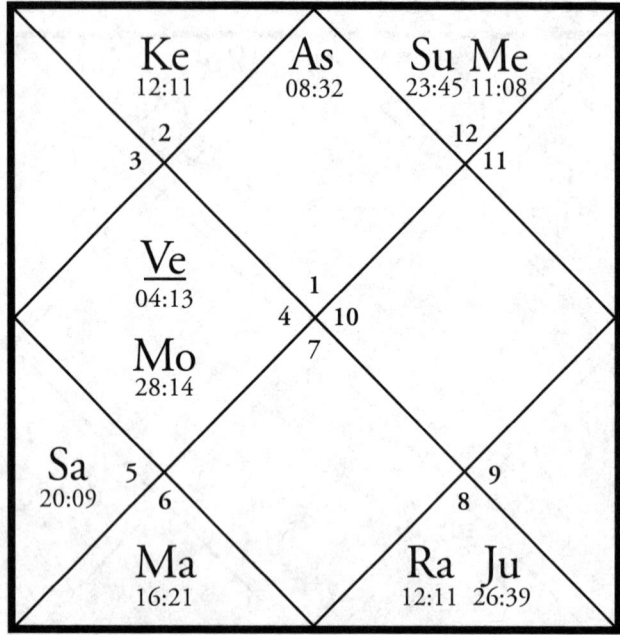

Swami Sivananda was one of India's most-well respected saints. He was a great Vedic scholar and medical doctor, as well as a great devotee of Shiva. He had several important combinations in his chart that reflected these conditions in his life.

1. Sivananda has a Leo Ascendant, occupied by the Sun. This gave him a strong sense of self and sound health. It also made him a natural leader.
2. The ruler of the ninth house (Mars) is placed in the twelfth house and the ruler of the twelfth house (Moon) is placed in the ninth house. This created a powerful Parivartana Yoga, which links the ninth house (dharma) with the twelfth house (moksha). This combination produced a strong inclination towards spirituality. Notice that Mars is neecha bhanga, indicating that he would first have a problem (Mars in Cancer gives insecurities, such as change of residence and uncertainties regarding sustenance), and that the problem would later become a blessing in disguise. As a result, he left his home and material support behind, devoting himself to a life of renunciation, relying on nothing but divine support.
3. Sivananda's chart also has a yoga called Srikanta Yoga. This yoga is formed when the Sun, the Moon and the lord of the Ascendant

are placed in an angle or a trine and in their own sign, exalted or in a friendly sign. According to the classical text, *Phala Deepika*, by Mantreswara, this yoga causes the person to "have a rudraksha rosary around his neck, have his body smeared with sacred ashes, be magnanimous, and always meditating on Shiva. He will be virtuous and tolerant to other's faiths. He will be mentally and spiritually strong and delight in the worship of Shiva." This description accurately depicts Swami Sivananda. It also demonstrates the value of studying the many yogas described in the classical texts.
4. Jupiter, the ruler of the fifth house and the general significator of spirituality, is placed in the third house and in a mutual aspect with the Moon. This combines the ruler of the twelfth house (Moon) and the ruler of the fifth house (Jupiter), to produce the practice of Japa Yoga (chanting of mantras). The fifth house rules mantras. The twelfth house is the house of meditation and introspection.

Notable Events in the Life of Swami Sivananda

During his primary school days (age 5-11 years) he was an honors student, winning awards and competitions. This occurred during the Sun's dasha. Notice that the Sun is the ruler of the first house and is placed in its own sign of Leo, in the first house. This produced leadership, excellent reputation, recognition and elevation of status.

During the Moon's period, he continued to do well in school, and achieved honors and recognition. The Moon is placed in the ninth house in Aries and involved in Gaja Kesari Yoga, a combination for fame and recognition.

During the Mars period, he left India and traveled to Singapore to become a doctor and work in a hospital. This event occurred in Mars dasha/Venus bhukti. Mars is the planet of ambition placed in the twelfth house (distant places). Mars is also placed in Pushya nakshatra, which is related to nurturing and also to working in various professions that involve credentials and certifications. Mars is also neecha bhanga (see Neecha Bhanga Yoga), indicating that he would do problem-solving work in a distant place.

Vimshamsha Chart: Mars is the ruler of the twelfth house (moksha), which is an important house in the Vimshamsha chart. Mars is placed in the tenth house (action and career) showing that during the Mars period Sivananda's spiritual development would be linked to his work.

Panchamsha Chart: Mars is the ruler of the first house of the Panchamsha chart, indicating that its period would produce prominent events related to spiritual practice. It is placed in the sixth house (service and healing) in Hasta nakshatra. Hasta is symbolized by the hands indicating hands-on healing work as the mode of spiritual practice.

Rashi Chart: Venus is placed in the second house in Hasta nakshatra (the hands) and is also neecha bhanga (problem-solving with the hands). Venus is also placed in a nakshatra (Hasta) that is ruled by the Moon. According to the great sage, Satyacharya, a planet will not only give its own results during its period, but will also give the results of the planet that rules the nakshatra in which it is placed. The Moon is the ruler of the twelfth house (distant places), placed in the ninth house (long-distance travel). This is a combination for long-distance travel. From Mars, the dasha lord, Venus rules the fourth house (home). Thus, the Venus sub-period within the Mars major period qualified to produce a change of residence to a distant place.

Vimshamsha Chart: Venus is the ruler of the Ascendant in the Vimshamsha chart. It is placed in the twelfth house, the house of moksha, which is a focal house for this chart. The twelfth house is also a house of distant places. Venus is aspected by exalted Saturn (ruler of the ninth house, the spiritual path), which is placed in the sixth house (service). These combinations support performing healing service as a spiritual path during the Venus sub-period.

Panchamsha chart: Venus is the ruler of the seventh house, which is the house of relationships in the Panchamsha chart. In this case it reflected the relationship-oriented spiritual practice. Venus is placed in the fourth house in Pushya nakshatra. Pushya is ruled by Brihaspati, the teacher of the gods, indicating a spiritual practice as an advisor (doctor). Pushya is also symbolized by the udder of a cow, indicating the giving of sustenance and nurturing to others as a spiritual practice.

The most significant recorded spiritual event in Sivananda's life occurred in 1923 when he returned to India and renounced the world. Shortly after that time he met his Guru. This was during his Rahu dasha and Mercury bhukti. Rahu is placed in the twelfth house (moksha) in a conjunction with Saturn (effort) and Mars (desire). This led him to make herculean efforts in his spiritual practice during the Rahu period. Mercury, the sub-period ruler, governs the twelfth house from Rahu. Rahu's dispositor, the Moon, is placed in the ninth house, further predisposing him to advancing spiritually.

Vimshamsha Chart: Rahu is placed in the fifth house (spiritual practices) of the Vimshamsha chart. Mercury is placed in the ninth house (the spiritual path) of the Vimshamsha chart. Mercury is placed in Shravana nakshatra which is symbolized by three footprints and is related to the story of Vamana kicking the demons out of heaven and restoring the gods to the heavens. (See *Path of Light, Volume I* for the story of Vamana.) This nakshatra is frequently associated with important changes which are related to the process of reestablishing one's highest priorities.

Panchamsha Chart: Rahu is placed in a conjunction with the ninth lord, Jupiter (dharma), in the eighth house (changes) in the Panchamsha chart. The eighth house is not only the house of general upheavals and changes in life, but is also a moksha house, reflecting the process of deep spiritual transformation and change. Mercury is placed in the twelfth house (house of moksha) in Pisces (sign of moksha) and is placed in Uttara Bhadrapada nakshatra. Uttara Bhadrapada is ruled by Ahirbudnya, the serpent of the deep, a symbol of the kundalini. These placements clearly reflect the important spiritual events during Mercury's sub-period.

Author's Journal:

Love Pats from Shiva

"*You are in the medical line?*" *the astrologer asked.*

"*Yes,*" *my friend, Ken, answered.*

We were visiting an astrologer in Uttarkashi. Tracing the Ganges to its source at Gangotri, Ken and I had started our journey into the Himalayas from Rishikesh, traveling by jeep along a narrow, winding, mountain road. After seven hours in the jeep, we had arrived in Uttarkashi, our first layover destination, where we met our mountaineer guide and porters. After making arrangements with the guide and purchasing provisions for our trek, Ken and I decided to visit a local astrologer, just to get a second opinion.

"We are going to attempt to hike from Gangotri to Kedarnath via Uden Col, an 18,000 foot pass," Ken said to the astrologer, as we sat in his little office. "What do you think? Should we go?"

The astrologer had heard about the route, which was the highest of three trekking routes, and frequently blocked by snow. The past three days had dumped heavy snow on the higher elevations and Ken and I were nearly ready to cancel the trip altogether. The jyotishi cast a question chart, scrutinized it for a minute and said, "You can go, but there will be problems if you go on the higher route. You should go on the lower route."

When picking a good time for an event, it's not always possible to get perfection. Among Vedic astrologers there is a joke about the astrologer who wanted to get married, but wanted to find the perfect astrological match. He finally found her at age 99. Then he wanted to pick a perfect day to get married. For this, he waited until he was 150 years old. On this India trip, I was steering around a Mars/Ketu conjunction which inconveniently occurred in October. Logistically, the only time to go into the Himalayas is September or October, when the weather is usually good, so I had to decide whether this conjunction warranted canceling the trip.

Although the conjunction had a certain formidable aura about it, I didn't think it would be physically harmful, so I decided to plan the trekking portion of the trip in September, so that we could at least avoid the conjunction's most intense phase. I had picked a good muhurtha (auspicious time) to begin the trip, knowing full well that, in the big picture, the astrological aspects were not very promising.

The previous two weeks had brought unseasonably late rain storms to north India. In the Himalayas, landslides had washed out many roads, and heavy snow covered the higher elevations. From my home in the United States, I kept in touch with my friend, Rajiv Tomar, who was guiding a tour group in the foothills of the Himalayas. He gave me daily weather reports, and we discussed the possibility of canceling my trip. Two days before my India flight departed, however, the rain stopped and I decided to chance it.

From Uttarkashi we continued by jeep to Gangotri, a small village at the end of the road, located at 11,000 feet, 14 miles from where the Ganges River emerges from the glacier. Although we did consider the astrologer's advice seriously, we ultimately decided that we would make our final decision based on the weather. If the weather was clear, we would attempt the high route, but with any hint of rain or snow, we would either cancel or take the lower route. In the meantime, we needed to spend a night at a higher altitude in order to allow our bodies to adjust to the lack of oxygen, and prepare for the 18,000 foot elevation which would come later in the trip. So we decided to hike 14 miles up to the glacier at Bojbasa and spend the night.

The hike to the source of the Ganges at Bojbasa was a pleasant surprise. In the early 90's I trekked in Nepal for a couple of weeks. Although the Nepal Himalayas were spectacular, the trails were like little freeways, crowded with many trekkers and covered with litter. In contrast, I was surprised to find this route along the Ganges to be a pristine, well-cut trail, relatively crowd-free.

When we arrived at the glacier, we hiked over the rocks to get as close as possible. I found a place on the rocks about 40 feet from where the Ganges rushed out from the glacial ice cave. I leaned down, washed my face in the icy water and began drinking with my hands. All of a sudden, there was a roaring, cracking sound from across the river. I looked up and saw a large chunk of the glacier fall 50 feet and splash into the river. Surrounded on three sides by the mammoth ice, I began to feel uneasy. Glaciers are always moving and changing, so sitting at the foot of a large glacier can be risky. I stood up and backed away slowly.

Ken, who was a few yards away, suggested, "Maybe we should say the Mahamrityunjaya Mantra." This is the great mantra to Lord Shiva, which is often recited by devout Hindus for protection from disease and accidents. The Ganges River is sacred to Shiva, and in mythology it is said to be Shiva's hair, so we both quietly began to chant the mantra.

I stood still, facing the icy river, watching the glacier on the other side as I recited the mantra. It was an awesome mass of brownish ice 70 feet high. Painfully aware of its capacity to move, I felt like I was standing in front of a huge frozen tsunami. Behind me was a steep embankment of broken rocks and ice. After a minute of chanting I heard rumbling behind me, followed by a whizzing next to my ear as several large rocks began to fall from the steep embankment next to the glacier. "Aihhh!" I yelled, as a small rock hit me in the head, and another larger rock hit my back. I quickly turned to face the oncoming rocks. I moved quickly to the left as a softball size rock flew towards me, missing my head by a couple of inches. I moved quickly out of the rock-fall zone and stood at a safe distance rubbing the painful bump on my head caused by the rock. "Shiva seems to have given me a slap on the head, reminding me to be respectful," I said to Ken.

We returned to Gangotri the next day and planned the trek to Kedarnath. I picked a (relatively) good muhurtha (beginning time) for our departure the next morning. The weather was clear, so we decided to attempt the hike to Kedarnath, via Uden Col, along the high route. "Even if we hit weather and have to turn back," I suggested, "we will at least get to experience some very spectacular hiking at the base of 25,000 foot peaks." Both Ken and I agreed that in spite of the astrologer's advice, we should attempt the high route. We had come half-way around the world for this trek, so we wanted to at least make an attempt.

We spent the next two days hiking up the Shiva valley, following a raging river by the same name. Since this route is only occasionally taken by mountaineers, the path was narrow, very steep, and relatively undeveloped. Ken and I frequently exchanged expressions of disbelief, as the trail traversed narrow ledges, along cliffs which often plummeted 200 feet to the icy, level six white water below. Trying to stay alert, we kept an eye on our porters and cook, who deftly navigated the treacherous terrain with their heavy loads strapped to their heads.

At 13,000 feet, the trail became less steep as we passed through a large stand of bhojpatra trees. The golden leaves and white bark, against the backdrop of the Shiva River's dancing rapids, produced a spectacular fall setting for a well-earned rest stop. I peeled some bark from a bhojpatra tree. Used for thousands of years by ancient jyotishis for writing astrological yantras, the thin whitish bark separated easily from the tree to produce an instant sheet of parchment.

On day two, the trail faded out as we climbed an extremely steep, grassy-sod face. At 15,000 feet, we reached Rudragaira, a base camp from which mountaineers make their attempts to summit the intimidating 25,000 foot giants that protrude in every direction. The sky was clear. The temperature was 60 degrees, perfect hiking weather. Between the giant peaks which surrounded us, we could see the lower, snow-laden saddle of Uden Col in the distance. This 18,000 foot pass would be the high point of our ten-day journey. It would take one more day to get to the base of Uden Col. Then it would take one grueling twelve-hour day to cross it, and to lower ourselves down the back side of the pass on ropes. From there it would take another week to cross the Katling Glacier, cross another high pass, and finally reach Kedarnath.

In the evening after dinner, I walked over to thank the cook, Dhani Ram, who was tidying up the cooking area. At 5' 6", 120 pounds, his skin was dark brown and leathery, from years of living in the mountains. He was the hardest worker in our entourage, rising each day at 4 a.m. in order to make breakfast. He happened to know his birth time, so I calculated his chart on my palm pilot.

Dhani Ram
April 13, 1956; 4 AM; 300 km west of Pokhara, Nepal

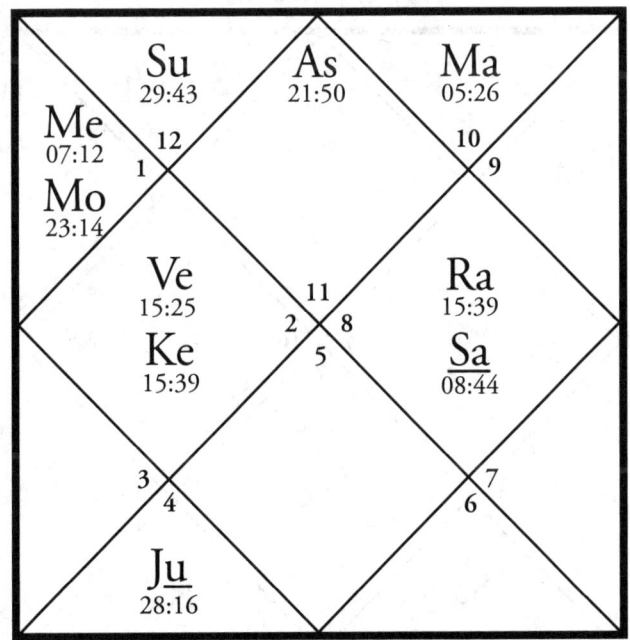

(D7) Saptamsha

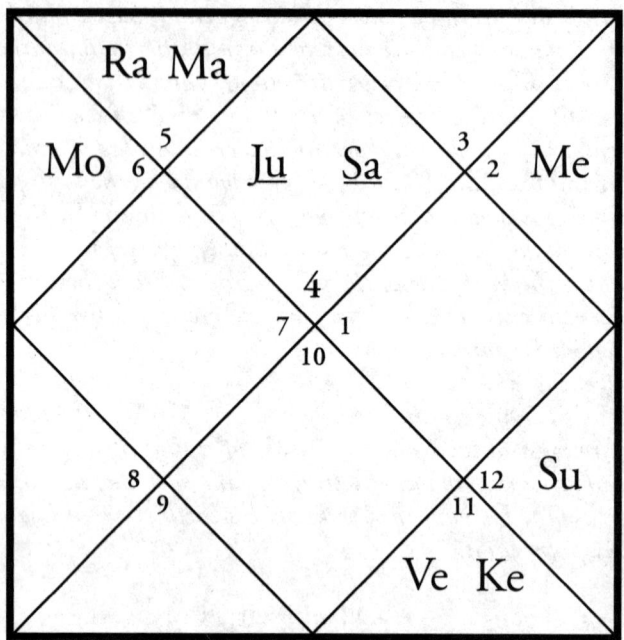

(D9) Navamsha

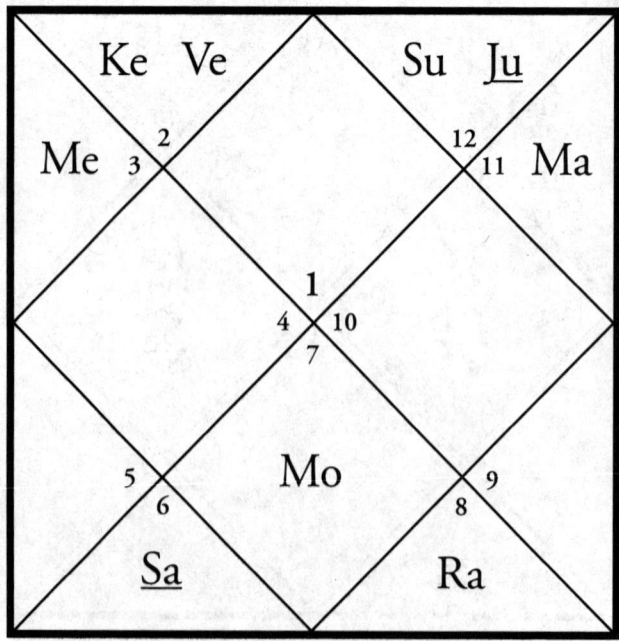

(D10) Dashamsha

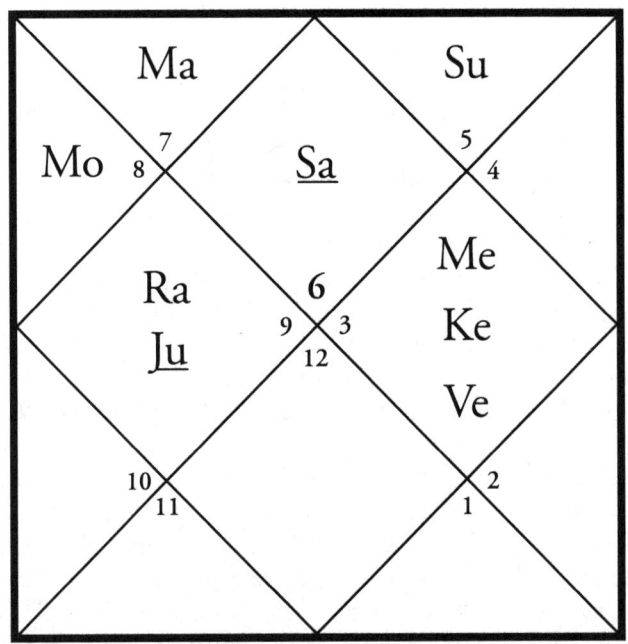

Dhani Ram was born in Nepal on April 13, 1956 at 4 a.m., in a small village, 300 km west of Pokhara. I spoke to him in Hindi. He smiled, revealing his partially broken teeth, as he answered my questions about his life. As I looked at his broken teeth and shining face, I imagined myself to be in the presence of Pushan, himself. In Dhani Ram's horoscope, his Sun is in the second house (food) in Revati nakshatra, which is ruled by Pushan, the deity who is the caretaker of travelers. Revati's shakti is the power of nourishment. In mythology, Pushan had his teeth broken by Shiva (see the story of Pushan in Path of Light, Volume I*). Dhani Ram's role as the cook for trekkers seemed a natural choice of career.*

The Aquarius lagna gives Dhani Ram his inclination towards working with groups. His lagna lord, Saturn, is placed in the tenth house in a conjunction with Rahu. This placement produced compulsive work and herculean efforts made in the career. The tenth house is the house of things that are above the head (high altitudes).

His Venus forms Malavya Yoga, a Mahapurusha Yoga, which makes the person an artist. In Taurus (food) this yoga made him a master of the culinary arts. His Mars, ruler of the tenth house (career) is placed in the twelfth house (distant places) indicating travel connected with the profession. From the Moon, Mars forms Ruchaka Yoga, which causes the person to act like a military general. Dhani Ram displayed this characteristic as he gave orders to the troops (the porters) to help him with the kitchen and dishes. Also, from the Moon, Jupiter produces Hamsa Yoga. This yoga makes a person an advisor, teacher, or professional. In this case, Jupiter placed in the fourth house (hospitality, home) made him a hospitality professional, giving him the ability to provide nourishment and support to the trekking team by providing a central environment for food.

Born in a small village 300 kilometers west of Pokhara, Nepal, Dhani Ram was married at age 23, during Moon dasha/Rahu bhukti. The Moon dasha is a typical period for marriage. Rahu is in Anuradha nakshatra (partnership). In the Navamsha chart, Rahu is disposited by Mars (which is also the Navamsha lagna lord), which is placed in the eleventh house (fulfillment of desires). The eighth house placement of Rahu in the Navamsha chart, as well as its eighth house placement from the Moon in the Rashi chart led me to suspect that his marriage may not have been totally happy.

The first of Dhani Ram's six children was a daughter, born in March of 1981 during Mars dasha/Mercury bhukti. Mars qualifies to produce children due to being ruler of the fifth house in the Saptamsha chart. Mercury is the ruler of the fifth house, and is placed in a conjunction with the Moon in the Rashi chart. In the Saptamsha chart, Mercury is in the eleventh house (fulfillment of desires) where it aspects the fifth house (children).

Dhani Ram began as a trekking cook in March of 1978, during Mars dasha/Rahu bhukti. As mentioned earlier, Mars (the planet of physical exercise) is the exalted ruler of the tenth house (career), placed in the twelfth house (distant places), suggesting strenuous travel connected with the career. Rahu is conjunct the lagna lord, Saturn, and is placed in the tenth house (career and also high places), invoking the previously mentioned compulsion to go to high places.

One of the high points (no pun intended) of his career, was when Dhani Ram climbed Kedardom, a 22,000 foot Himalayan peak, as part of a climbing expedition. This occurred in April of 1982 during Mars dasha/Ketu bhukti. Mars has already been discussed. Ketu is placed in a conjunction with yogakaraka Venus in the Rashi chart. In the Dashamsha chart, Ketu is again conjunct Venus in the tenth house (high places). Using degrees in the Dashamsha chart, Ketu is placed in the constellation of Mrigashira, which is connected with well-trodden paths. The conjunction with Venus here also creates Chaya Graha Yoga, a raja yoga that lifts a person up in career.

The sun went down early and by 9 p.m. the stars were out. Ken and I walked fifty yards from camp and found a spot in the rocks from which to view the spectacular night sky. At 15,000 feet the air is extremely thin, providing excellent views from the world's best natural observatory. "There's the Pleiades," Ken said, pointing to the northwest.

I found the seven-star formation (which looks like six stars, since one is a dual star). "Krittika nakshatra," I said, as I recalled the story of Agni, its ruler. Agni was deified fire. Once he became infatuated with the seven wives of the seven rishis, who are represented by the seven stars of the constellation. He masqueraded as their husbands and seduced each of the wives. This deception worked on six of the wives, but the seventh wife saw through his disguise and rejected him. Later, the six wives took the collective semen and nurtured it in a collective womb. Out of this, Kartikeya, the god of war was born.

By 9:30 p.m., the temperature had fallen to 28 degrees Fahrenheit, so we cut our stargazing short in favor of warm sleeping bags. The porters, cook and guide were huddled around a small fire, twenty-five yards from our tents, talking, laughing, and singing Nepalese folk songs. As I lay in my sleeping bag, I listened to their gentle voices for a few minutes, and then fell into a deep sleep.

At 4 a.m., prompted by the need to pee, I woke up and got out of my tent. It was snowing. Hoping that it would abate by morning, I returned to bed. At 7 a.m., however, there were three inches of snow on the ground. Our guide, who was an experienced mountaineer, made the decision to return. Having spent a good deal of time backpacking in the California Sierras, I have a healthy respect for mountain weather. This time I didn't need a "love pat" from Shiva to get my attention. We made a quick descent down the extremely steep trail. I'll never forget standing at the top of Rudragaira, looking over our route down a 1,000 foot face. About as steep as an expert-level ski run, the previous day's ascent had required the use of both hands and feet. Now, covered with three inches of snow, the trail had disappeared, and I wondered whether we would simply end up sliding down the mountain. I was especially concerned about the porters, each of whom carried more than sixty pounds of gear.

Although we all slipped and fell a few times on the way down, the experienced porters, most of whom were Nepalese, navigated the snowy course without any problem. We returned to Gangotri tired, hungry, cold, and with a renewed reverence and respect for the power of nature.

Our decision to take the high route had proven to be the right one, because snow had covered and blocked the low routes as well. The Uttarkashi astrologer had been correct that we would meet obstructions on the trip. He was even correct in advising us that we could still go on the trip, but he had been mistaken that the lower routes would be a better option. Such is the nature of astrological analysis. Although the chart may reveal certain *inevitable conditions, giving advice based on horoscope analysis can be a tricky business. One must always blend intuition and a practical knowledge of the real-life situation with astrological factors, in order to arrive at wise decisions. It also goes without saying, that it is important to pay attention to omens and signs. But don't wait for a slap from Lord Shiva to put you on the right track!*

Chapter Twenty

Life According To Mark

Mark
October 31, 1952; 6:30 PM; Seattle, WA

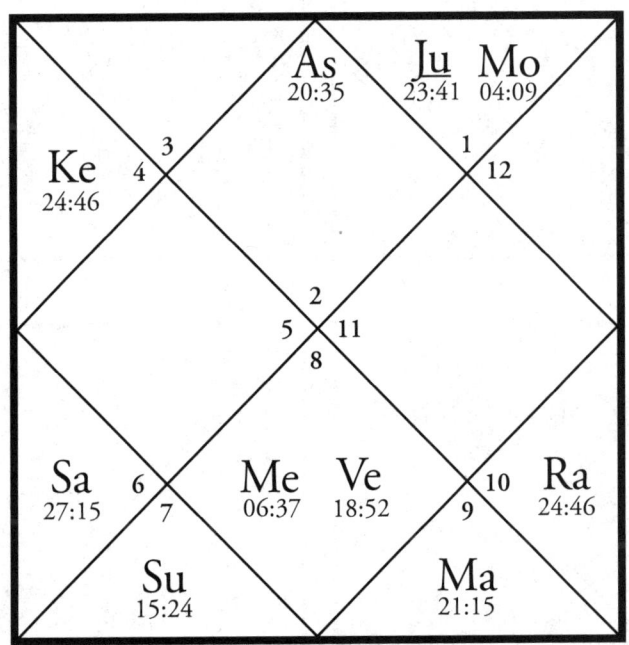

Path of Light – The Domains of Life

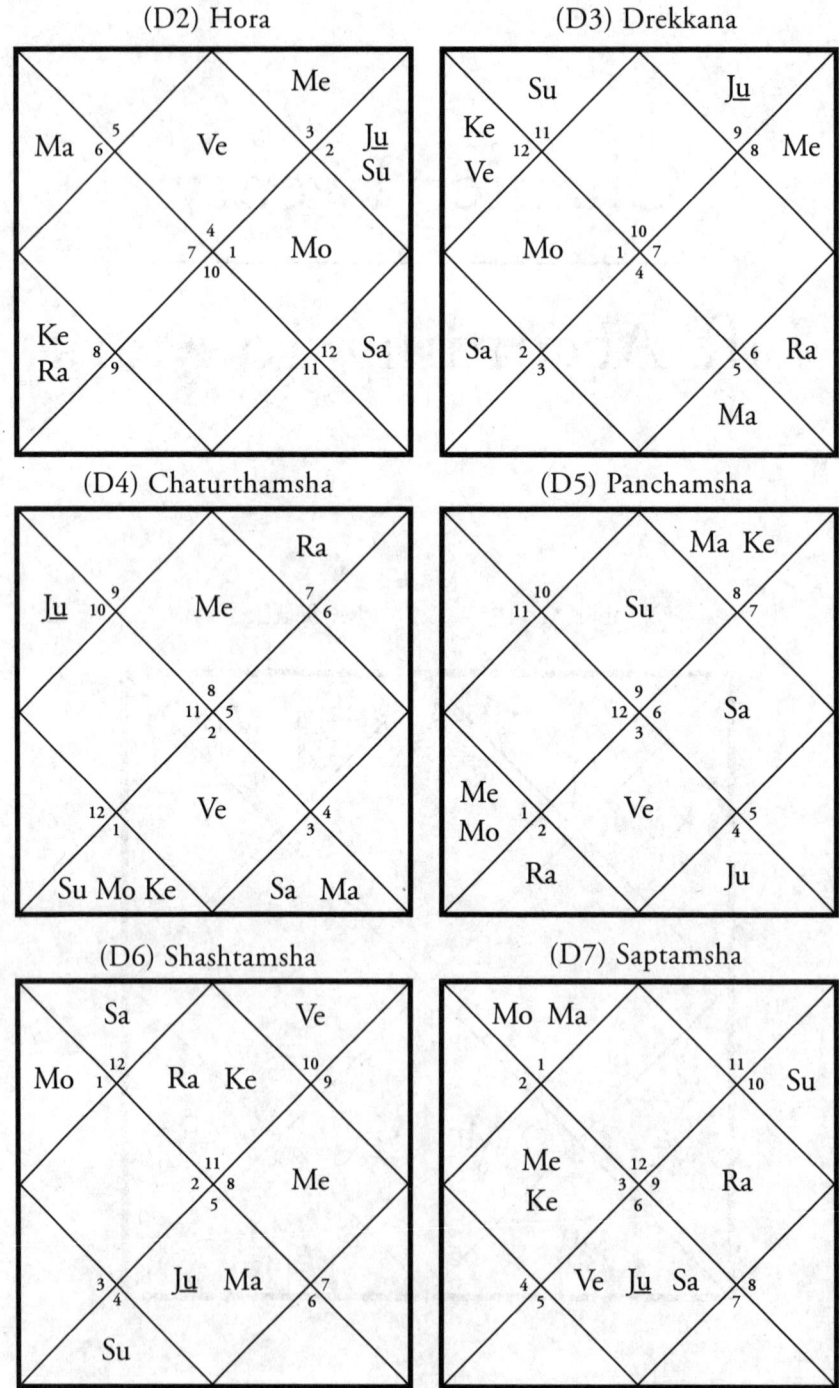

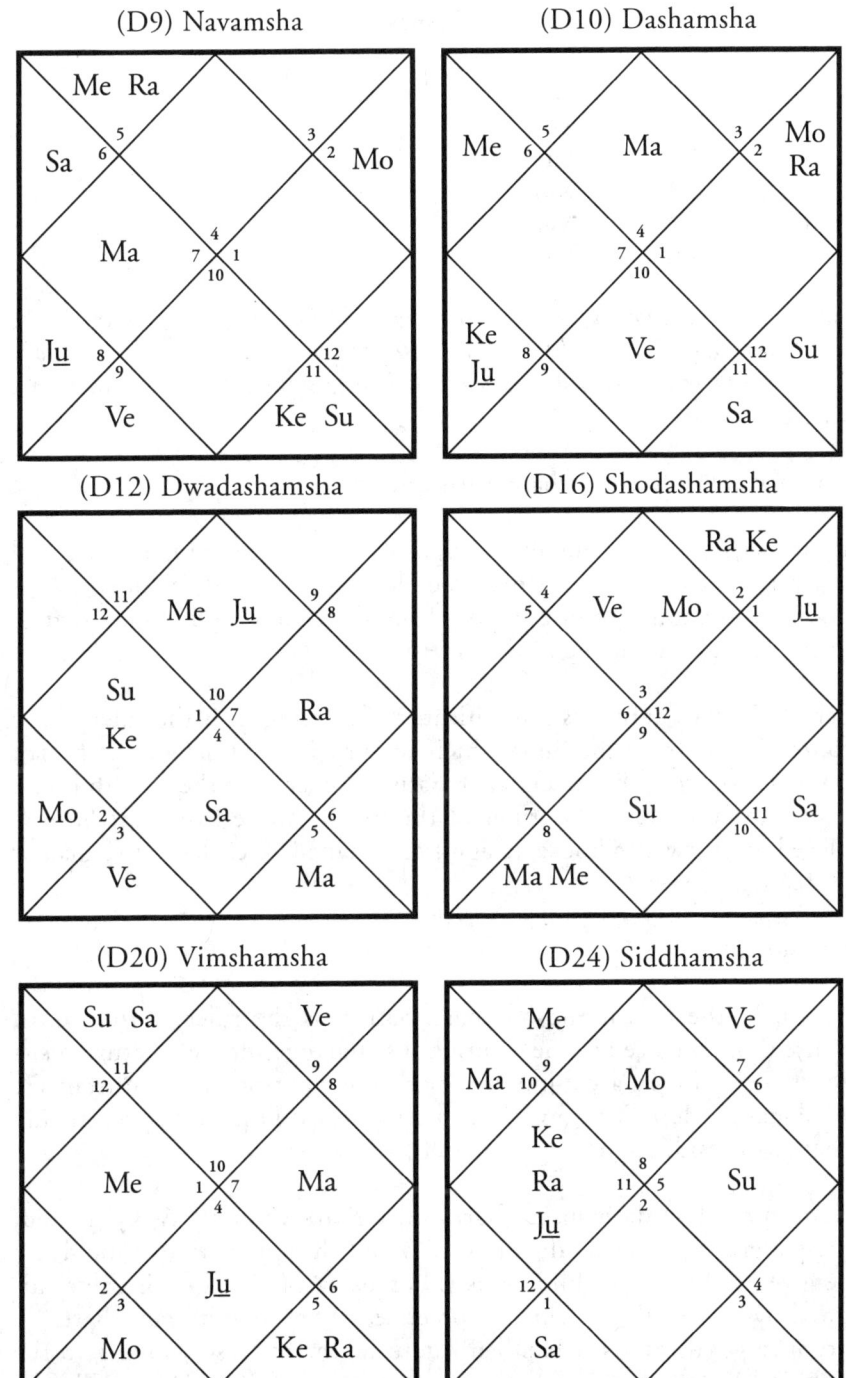

Dashas

08/25/1950	Ke
08/25/1957	Ve
08/25/1977	Su
08/25/1983	Mo
08/25/1993	Ma
08/25/2000	Ra

"My earliest memory is of changing my residence. This took place in the late summer of 1955, when I was 2 ½ years old. My family moved to a forty-acre farm in Kent, Washington. It had lots of animals, a garden, and an orchard."

Dasha/Bhukti: Ketu Dasha/Saturn Bhukti

Ketu Dasha: Ketu is one of the significators of gardening and natural environments. It is also a planet of letting go and detachment. It is placed in the fourth house (home) from the Moon, signifying a change of residence to a bucolic environment.

Saturn Bhukti: Saturn is a significator of farming. It is the ruler of the fourth house from the Sun (which in turn is the ruler of the fourth house (Leo) from the Ascendant). Saturn is placed in the twelfth house from the Sun. When the ruler of the fourth house (from the Sun) is placed in the twelfth house, it signifies a change of residence to a distant place.

Divisional Charts

Saturn in the Chaturtamsha chart: Saturn is the ruler of the fourth house (home) placed in the eighth house (change) in the Chaturtamsha chart. It is also in a conjunction with the ruler of the Chaturtamsha Ascendant, Mars. This makes it a first-rate candidate for producing change of residence during its period.

Ketu in the Dwadashamsha chart: Since Mark was only two years old, the parents were very influential. It is said that predictions should not be given for a young child. This is because a child's chart is overshadowed by that of the parents. In practice, however, children's charts do produce good results if handled carefully. In this case, looking to the Dwadashamsha chart provides an important clue. Ketu is placed in the fourth house in the Dwadashamsha chart (parents). Ketu gives the results of its dispositor, the planet owing its sign of placement, which is Mars. As the ruler of the fourth house (home) placed in the eighth house (change), Mars signifies change of residence for parents during Ketu's period.

"In September of 1958, on my first day of kindergarten, my cat was hit by a car on the road. This was a traumatic event for me. The car had squashed her head, and I found her mangled body on the road. This was when I first became aware of death, and for the next several months I asked my mother probing questions like, 'Will I die?' and 'Where do you go when you die?'"

Dasha/Bhukti: Venus Dasha/Venus Bhukti

Venus Dasha/Venus Bhukti: Venus rules love, affection and attachment. It is also the ruler of the sixth house (pets). It is placed in the seventh house (relationships) in a conjunction with Mercury, the significator of cats. Venus is also placed in the eighth house (death) from the Moon. It is flanked by a debilitated Sun and Mars, forming a Papa Kartari Yoga. Venus also receives an aspect from Saturn, which is itself placed in the sixth house (pets) from the Moon. All of these factors predispose Venus to produce a negative pet experience during its period.

Transits and Nakshatra Symbology

Transiting Saturn was at 25 degrees of Scorpio, in conjunction with natal Venus. It is important to note Saturn's position in the Rashi chart. It is placed in the sixth house (pets) from the Moon, suggesting difficult experiences related to pets. Saturn also aspects Venus in the Rashi chart. These conditions predispose Saturn to produce a significant event during its transit over Venus.

Rahu is a significator of accidents. Rahu was at 29 degrees of Virgo, having just moved into the sixth house (pets) from the Moon. Here it came into an immediate and close conjunction with Saturn. This had two effects. First, the conjunction of transiting Rahu with natal Saturn in the sixth house from the Moon signifies a negative sixth house (pets) event. Second, transiting Rahu's conjunction with natal Saturn amplifies the negative quality of Saturn's natal aspect on Venus, as well as transiting Saturn's conjunction with natal Venus.

Mars is the significator of violent events. At the time of the accident,

Mars had just moved into the sign of Taurus. From Taurus, transiting Mars cast its aspect on natal Venus, the period ruler. It also cast a very close aspect on natal Mercury (significator of cats).

Mercury is the significator of cats. At the time of the accident transiting Mercury had just entered the sign of Leo and the constellation of Magha. The shakti of Magha is "the power to leave the body," which is related to the soul departing at the time of death. In this position transiting Mercury received an exact aspect from transiting Mars (in Taurus), as well as an aspect from transiting Saturn (in Scorpio).

"In late May of 1961, when I was 8 years old, I fell off my bike and broke my front teeth. Someone had stolen the stem cover off the tires of my bike. My cousins were visiting and I wanted to impress them. My dad had a friend who had some kids who kept their bikes in an open garage near my house. So I rode up to their garage with my cousins and stole the caps off their bikes. On the way back I started riding my bike with no hands to show off to my cousins. I fell off my bike, hit my face on the cement, and broke my teeth."

Dasha/Bhukti: Venus Dasha/Sun Bhukti

Venus Dasha: Venus is the karaka for the face and mouth. It is also the ruler of the sixth house (diseases and accidents). As mentioned earlier, it is aspected by Saturn (bones and teeth) and hemmed in by Mars and the Sun (Papa Kartari Yoga). These factors qualify Venus to produce a negative health event related to the mouth or teeth.

Sun Bhukti: The Sun is placed in the sixth house (diseases and accidents) and is debilitated. Relative to Venus, it is placed in the twelfth house (a dusthana house). The Sun is also one of the planets that hems in Venus, which is the reason it triggered a negative health event in its bhukti.

Divisional Chart

Shashtamsha Chart: Venus is placed in the twelfth house, a dusthana house. The Sun, the bhukti ruler, is placed in the sixth house, a dusthana and the house of accidents. Venus and the Sun are in mutual aspect in the Shashtamsha chart.

Transits and Nakshatra Symbolism and Mythology

Saturn, significator of the teeth and bones, had just turned retrograde and was transiting at 6 degrees of Capricorn. From this position it cast a close aspect on the Sun, the sub-period planet. It is noteworthy that Saturn was in the constellation of Uttara Ashadha, which is symbolized by the tusk of an elephant, a symbol of broken teeth.

How Ganesha Broke His Tusk

Once a great sage named Ved Vyasa decided to write a great epic called the Mahabharata. *He needed someone who would write it down for him as he recited the words, so he went to Lord Ganesha and asked him if he would be the scribe. Lord Ganesha agreed. Ved Vyasa said, "I will tell you the story, but you must take it down quickly so that you don't interrupt or stop me at any time." Ganesha said, "I will do what you ask, but if you stop or hesitate, I will stop writing and your story will never be written." Ved Vyasa agreed, but added, "I agree to your condition, but you must also agree to fully comprehend the meaning of the words as you write them, and not just blindly write what I say." Ganesha agreed and they started writing the* Mahabharata. *But Lord Ganesha needed a pen in order write, so he broke a bit off his tusk and used it as a pen.*

The transit of the period ruler is always significant. Venus is the dasha ruler. At the time of the accident, Venus was transiting in the constellation of Revati, where it was in an exact opposition to natal Saturn. Revati is ruled by the deity, Pushan. In mythology, Pushan had his teeth knocked out by Rudra because he was eating a sacrificial offering. The story is given in *Path of Light, Volume I.*

Mars is the significator of violent events. Transiting Mars was debilitated and passing through the third house (short journeys—he was riding his bicycle). At the time of the accident, transiting Mars was conjuncting natal Ketu and closely aspecting the natal Sun (bhukti ruler).

"In late May of 1965, I broke my right forearm. It was the first little league game of the year. It was early in the game. I played first base. The batter hit a ground ball to Jack Anderson, the third baseman. Jack threw the ball to me at first base, but the ball went wide to my left. I had to stretch towards the runner to catch the ball and the runner collided with me, breaking my arm. When I cried, the assistant coach scolded me and goaded me into getting up and finishing the rest of the game. The next day I went to the doctor and found out that the arm was broken."

Dasha/Bhukti: Venus Dasha/Rahu Bhukti

Venus Dasha: As discussed earlier, Venus is the ruler of the sixth house (accidents). It is hemmed in by malefics and receives an aspect from Saturn, qualifying it to produce negative health events.

Rahu Bhukti: Rahu is a significator of accidents. It is placed in the third house (the right forearm) from Venus.

Divisional Chart

The Shashtamsha Chart: In the Shashtamsha chart Rahu is placed in the first house, signifying a significant health event during its bhukti. It receives the aspect of Mars, another significator of accidents. Jupiter also aspects Rahu, suggesting recovery.

Transits

Rahu was the bhukti ruler. At the time of the accident it was transiting at 20 degrees of Taurus, in an exact conjunction with the Ascendant (the physical body).

Saturn was transiting at 22 degrees of Aquarius, throwing a powerful aspect to the natal Venus, the dasha ruler and the lagna lord.

Mars was transiting at 22 degrees of Leo, placing it in exact opposition with transiting Saturn. Mars was also throwing a powerful aspect on natal Venus, the dasha ruler and the lagna lord.

The dasha ruler and lagna lord, Venus, was near 20 degrees of Taurus, where it was in an exact conjunction with transiting Rahu.

"In November 1965 I moved to Minnesota. This event was significant. Before that time I identified with being a 'good kid.' After that time, however, I started to hang out with kids who were considered to be 'hoods' and began flirting with the dark side. I started smoking, drinking, and had many sexual encounters. I learned that the bad boy persona had many payoffs, and I started identifying with the rebellious kids.

For example, shortly after moving, an incident took place in my shop class. My teacher was the classic bully shop teacher, a total jerk. On this particular day, someone had stolen something from the shop class. The teacher was mad and he was rousting one of the hoods, who he thought was the most likely thief. He had his hand on the kid's shoulder and was physically intimidating him while he accused him of the theft. The kid was denying it, and I happened to know that he didn't do it. Even though I didn't particularly like the kid, I piped up and said, 'I know who did it and it wasn't him.' The teacher demanded that I tell him the name of the thief, but I refused. He got so mad that he slapped me across the face. I became an instant celebrity in the 8th grade, and I realized that being rebellious was a good way to get attention."

Dasha/Bhukti: Venus Dasha/Rahu Bhukti

Venus Dasha: Venus indicates love, affection, sexuality and social relations in general. It is placed in the sign of Scorpio, which signifies upheavals and changes of various kinds. Scorpio is a sexually precocious sign, and is often associated with forbidden or dangerous liaisons. Venus is also placed in the constellation of Jyeshtha, a nakshatra ruled by Indra, the king of the gods. In mythology, Indra was amorous, seductive, and was fond of becoming intoxicated by drinking soma.

Rahu Bhukti: Rahu is the significator of revolution, rebellion and change. It is placed in the fourth house (residence) from the Sun (which is in turn the ruler of the fourth house from the Ascendant). Rahu represents outcasts and all sorts of unconventional attitudes. The Rahu sub-period during the dasha of Venus is a very typical time for changes of residence, and a change towards more unconventional relationships. This is also a typical period for career changes.

Divisional Chart

Chaturtamsha Chart: Rahu (bhukti ruler) is placed in the twelfth house (distant places) in the Chaturtamsha chart, signifying a change of residence to a distant place.

Transits and Nakshatra Symbolism and Mythology

At the time of the move, Rahu was at 11 degrees of Taurus, in the constellation of Rohini. Its transit of the Ascendant caused him to revolutionize his persona and project himself as a rebel.
It is noteworthy that natal Rahu is placed in the constellation of Dhanishtha. One of the Sanskrit meanings of Dhanishtha is "a dwelling place," so it is related to residence. Since Rahu represents change, this placement can be related to change of residence. The constellation

is ruled by eight deities called the Vasus. The desire of Dhanishtha is "to revolve around the summit of the gods." Its shakti is "the power to give wealth and fame." So this constellation is also associated with one's ability to achieve a reputation among the chosen or the elite. It gives a desire to be accepted by the elite or inner social circle, represented by the Vasus. Rahu, however, is an outcast, so in this case, Mark's desire was to be included among the inner circle of outcasts. For more symbolism of Dhanishtha nakshatra, see *Path of Light, Volume I*.

In fact, Rahu also has a strong mythological connection to the desire to be included in the inner circles. In the story of Rahu, he tried to be included at the banquet of the gods and ended up getting his head cut off. This story, as well as the symbolism of the constellation of Dhanishtha, is directly related to the events that resulted from the change of residence. (See *Path of Light, Volume I* for the story of Rahu.)

It is important to note that the rebellious behavior that was triggered by Rahu was only a part of a bigger pattern in the horoscope. There are several combinations in the chart that point to a deep need for acceptance and approval by others. First, the Sun in Libra shows a tendency to identify with partnerships and relationships. Next, the desire of the rising nakshatra, Rohini, is "to attract a lover and unite with her." Further, the ruler of the Ascendant, Venus, is placed in the seventh house, the house of relationships. All of these things suggest that Mark had a strong tendency to derive his self-worth from his friendships and partnerships. Another significant factor is the placement of the Moon in the constellation of Ashwini. Mythologically, the Ashwini Kumaras were barred by Indra from gaining a place among the gods. They proved themselves however, by bestowing immortality on Rishi Cyavana. (See Ashwini nakshatra in *Path of Light, Volume I*.) As a result, they were allowed to partake in the soma offering and were admitted to the assembly of the gods. Ashwini people frequently feel the need to prove themselves. This is confirmed by Mark.

"I met my first real girlfriend in June of 1967. This was an exciting time in my life. There was an abandoned cabin in the woods by a lake near my house. I took her there to drink and make out. Although I didn't have intercourse with her, I got to third base. My parents had a speedboat, so we spent the summer cruising the lake, swimming and water skiing. It was at this time that I also started hanging out with older kids."

Dasha/Bhukti: Venus Dasha/Rahu Bhukti

Venus Dasha: Venus dasha was analyzed previously with reference to sexuality. Its placement in the seventh house in Scorpio and in Jyeshtha nakshatra continued to produce precocious sexual behavior throughout its major period.

Rahu Bhukti: Rahu is the significator of revolution and change. The Rahu bhukti of Venus dasha is typically a time of sexual and social revolution. This period is notorious for infatuations. It can either create or separate relationships. Rahu is placed in the constellation of Dhanishtha, a nakshatra ruled by Mars. Mars (male sexual energy) is placed in the eighth house, the house of sexual energy and the sexual organs.

Transits and Nakshatra Symbolism and Mythology

In 1967, Rahu was transiting Aries, which was Mark's twelfth house. The twelfth house is related to sexuality because it represents the bedroom, as well as secret hideaways. In June of 1967, Rahu also entered Ashwini nakshatra. Ashwini is also a sexually assertive and precocious nakshatra. In mythology, the Ashwini Kumaras approached a princess in a hut by a lake, tried to seduce her and steal her from her husband. Ashwini is also a constellation related to various types of fast vehicles, including boats. (See Ashwini nakshatra in *Path of Light, Volume I*.)

"At the end of August in 1967, my family moved back to Kent, Washington. I didn't want to move. At first I got back together with my old friends and tried out for the football team. In September, I got injured, so I couldn't play football. After that, I started hanging out with the delinquent kids, and became attracted to the girls who had promiscuous reputations."

Dasha/Bhukti: Venus Dasha/Rahu Bhukti

The analysis of the major period and sub-period with reference to change of residence was given previously.

Transits

In August of 1967, at the time of the change of residence, Rahu was in an exact conjunction with his natal Moon. Rahu is the bhukti ruler, and is the natural significator of change. The Moon is a significator of the family, security, and the home, and is placed in the twelfth house (distant places).

"In January of 1968 I met Rhonda, my first major girlfriend. Although our

relationship was on again-off again in the beginning, we eventually stayed together for about three years. It was at this time that I met all the hoods and changed my social affiliation to that group. I became popular among my new friends and I also started taking drugs in the spring of 1968. I lost my virginity with Rhonda in June of 1968."

Dasha/Bhukti: Venus Dasha/Jupiter Bhukti

Venus Dasha: The analysis of Venus dasha with reference to sexual behavior was given previously.

Jupiter Bhukti: Jupiter is placed in the twelfth house (the bedroom). It is also placed in the constellation of Bharani, which is symbolized by the womb, suggesting the progression of sexual activity to include intercourse. The general tone of Jupiter's sub-period during the dasha of Venus is usually self-indulgence. Jupiter is also involved in Gaja Kesari Yoga, a combination that brings popularity and social acceptance.

Divisional Chart

Navamsha Chart: Jupiter, the sub-period ruler is placed in the fifth house (romance and sexuality) in the Navamsha chart. It is also placed in the seventh house (relationships and sexuality) from the Moon in the Navamsha chart. Jupiter is in the sign of Scorpio, which is a very sexual sign.

Transits and Nakshatra Symbolism and Mythology

At the time of gaining acceptance in the new social circle and beginning to take LSD, Venus, the dasha ruler lord, was transiting the constellation of Ashwini. The story of how the Ashwini Kumaras gained acceptance into the assembly of the gods again becomes relevant. It is also noteworthy that when they gained acceptance by the gods, they were allowed to partake in the soma offering. Soma is the elixir of the gods, which makes them immortal, and can be used to symbolize the use of hallucinogenics and other recreational drugs.

At the time of losing his virginity, Venus, the dasha lord, was transiting the constellation of Rohini, which has the basic desire "to attract a lover and unite with her." Mars was also in conjunction with Venus (a combination for sexual passion), but in the constellation of Mrigashira. Mrigashira is also a constellation of sexual passion and seduction. (See the myths and symbols of Rohini and Mrigashira in *Path of Light, Volume I*.)

"In the summer of 1968 my parents and my brother went away on a fishing trip. I decided to have constant parties at my house while they were away. I invited all my friends over and we had a wild time, taking drugs, having sex, and listening to Jimi Hendrix. Unfortunately, my parents came home early. I freaked out because I knew I would be in big trouble. One of my friends convinced me that the best strategy was to run away. At the time, this seemed to me to be a very cool thing to do, so we ran away together. In order to get money, we started burglarizing houses. Our strategy was to first drive up and case a house. Then we would find a way to get in, usually using a sliding glass door or open window. We were mainly looking for checks. Once we had someone's checkbook, we would go into a store and forge the checks. I used the same story each time. I would go to a grocery store and select a few items. Then I would go to the cashier and tell him that my parents were getting ready to go camping and didn't have time to come in personally. I would give him a check that was already made out for more than the total charge. I had a rather innocent looking face, so the storeowner usually believed me, and gave me cash back as change. During my two weeks of being on the run, I met some older teenagers, who were seasoned burglars and much more hardened criminals. I realized that I was headed for serious trouble. I was also getting tired of hiding out, and realized that I didn't like the life of crime, so I went home. My parents grounded me for a month."

Dasha/Bhukti: Venus Dasha/Jupiter Bhukti

Venus Dasha: Venus is in Scorpio in the Rashi chart, hemmed in by malefics. Scorpio is a sign that can easily turn to the dark side.

Jupiter Bhukti: Jupiter is retrograde in the twelfth house in the Rashi chart. The twelfth house is a house of retreats and hideaways. Jupiter is placed in the sixth house from Venus. The sixth house is the house of thieves and theft. Jupiter is also in Bharani nakshatra, a constellation ruled by Yama, the god of death. In mythology, Yama was given rulership over dharma, or cosmic law. So this nakshatra is related to the law. (See *Path of Light, Volume I* for the story of how Yama came to rule dharma.) Jupiter's retrograde condition in Bharani in the sixth house from Venus suggests actions that are contrary to the law.

Transits and Nakshatra Symbolism

At the time of running away and burglarizing the houses, Venus, the dasha ruler, was transiting the constellation of Ashlesha and in conjunction with Ketu. Ashlesha is ruled by serpents and signifies the underworld and deceptive and unethical behavior.

Saturn signifies restriction and confinement. Saturn had recently entered the twelfth house (institutions, jails) in July of 1968 and was moving toward a conjunction with his natal Moon. It stopped short of the conjunction and turned retrograde, backing out of the sign of Aries. At the time of the burglaries, Saturn had just become stationary and was about to turn retrograde. This transit was hinting at the possibility of jail, but stopped short due to the incomplete conjunction with the Moon. It gave a one-month period of being confined to home, but it also foreshadowed a more serious incarceration to come.

"In the spring of 1969 a friend of mine and I were looking for some thrills, so he talked me into burglarizing a house. We cased some houses in the Renton highlands and chose one to rob. We entered the house and looked around inside. I saw a gun hanging in its holster on a closet door. I picked it up and was shocked to see a stamp on the gun. It was the insignia of the Washington State Patrol. I had inadvertently entered the house of a policeman! I took the gun and three thousand dollars before leaving the house. A few weeks later, my friend got in trouble for another crime, and in order to get himself out of trouble, he turned me in for the burglary. I was arrested, expelled from school, and was put in the youth center. The Seattle Youth Center was a serious place for serious young criminals. The kids there were tough and very scary. Brutal fights broke out daily. I was terrified, but somehow I managed to survive for two weeks. After I was released, the judge ordered me to go to counseling during the rest of the spring. By the end of the spring the whole thing was resolved, and I had changed my attitude about crime and life in general. A couple of weeks in jail made me realize that the benefits of a life of crime were vastly outweighed by its heavy price."

Dasha/Bhukti: Venus Dasha/Jupiter Bhukti

This was discussed previously.

Transits

By the early spring of 1969, Saturn returned to the sign of Aries in Mark's twelfth house, and began to move towards the conjunction of his natal Moon once again. The conjunction took place in mid-April, at about the time he was put in the youth center. After the conjunction was complete and Saturn began separating from the Moon, he was released and entered counseling. The twelfth house is related to both incarceration and introspection. It is one of the primary houses of psychology. Saturn gave him a harsh wake-up call that caused him to become reflective about his life. This was a major turning point in his life.

"In the fall of 1969 my father gave me my first car, a brand new 1969 Ford Mustang."

Dasha/Bhukti: Venus Dasha/Jupiter Bhukti

Venus Dasha: Venus is the significator of vehicles. It is placed prominently in the Rashi chart.

Jupiter Bhukti: Jupiter aspects the fourth house (vehicles) in the Rashi chart.

Divisional Chart and Nakshatra Symbolism

Shodashamsha Chart: Venus is in the first house in the Shodashamsha chart, making it a first-rate period for owning a vehicle. Jupiter is placed in the eleventh house of the Shodashamsha chart (attainment of desires), which gave him the ability to obtain a car. Venus represents luxury cars or stylish cars. Jupiter represents expensive cars. His father bought him a new 1969 Ford Mustang.

It is interesting to note that he has his Moon in Ashwini nakshatra, a constellation symbolized by a horse's head (mustang). This nakshatra is associated with fast vehicles and fast driving, both of which apply in this case. (See *Path of Light, Volume I* for more information about the mythology and symbolism of Ashwini nakshatra.)

"From 1969 to 1971 I had several car accidents."

Divisional Chart

In the Shodashamsha chart Saturn also aspects Jupiter. Saturn rules the eighth house (accidents) in the Shodashamsha chart.

Transits

The accidents continued during the entire time that Saturn was transiting the natal twelfth house, moving over his Jupiter (bhukti ruler) and the

Moon. Saturn is the eighth lord (accidents) of the Shodashamsha chart. Saturn is also placed in the sixth house (accidents) from the Moon in the Rashi chart.

"In June of 1970, all remnants of my criminal persona left me. I began to identify with being an easy-going drug-taking hippy."

Dasha/Bhukti: Venus Dasha/Saturn Bhukti

Saturn Bhukti: Saturn bhukti began on June 25, 1970. Saturn is the yogakaraka and a planet symbolizing reserved behavior. Placed in the fifth house (emotions and recreational activities), it brought a psychological shift that produced a more moderate and responsible demeanor.

"In August of 1971 after taking some LSD, I had my first profound spiritual experience. I was at a huge party with over a hundred people. I was hallucinating, seeing flashing police lights and hearing sirens. I couldn't recognize any of the people there, even though I had grown up with most of them. I started to panic. My girlfriend Rhonda and a few friends took me to Rhonda's house in order to calm me down. I sat down in Rhonda's living room and started pondering my unsettled and unhappy life. I thought deeply about how I lied occasionally. It occurred to me that my life would be much happier if I just always told the truth. This insight about the value of simply telling the truth seemed profound at the time. I wondered if following all the other ethical rules might also make life easier. I asked Rhonda to bring me a copy of the Bible. As I read various passages related to virtuous conduct, a startling realization came to me. The purpose of virtuous conduct became crystal clear. I realized that right action was not something that a person should practice in order to please God or even to be good or holy. In fact, right action seemed to be the only kind of action that leads to a better life, a life of happiness and peace of mind. I realized that virtue had a payoff, a clear and tangible result. It seemed to be the only intelligent choice in order to produce a life of positive and pleasurable experiences. As I read, I became excited, and started sharing my new insights with my friends. The fact that I had been hallucinating and panicking earlier had not really bothered my friends. Now that I was reading to them from the Bible and preaching the value of virtuous living, my friends decided that I had definitely gone over the edge, so they gave me some thorazine to bring me down. The insight stayed with me after I came down, however, and it changed my life after that. I now saw ethical behavior as a means for a good life. Although I continued to take drugs for awhile, they really didn't work very well for me anymore."

Dasha/Bhukti: Venus Dasha/Saturn Bhukti

Venus Dasha: Venus is the ruler of the Ascendant and is in Scorpio, a sign of deep transformation and change.

Saturn Bhukti: Saturn is the yogakaraka and therefore symbolizes constructive or useful limitation. It is placed in the fifth house, a dharma (cosmic law) house. Saturn is also placed in the third drekkana of Virgo, which is symbolized by a tall woman going into a temple. Saturn is placed in the nakshatra of Chitra. The shakti of Chitra is "the power to accumulate merit." In other words, Chitra is associated with the ability to see the benefit of doing right action.

Divisional Chart

Vimshamsha Chart: Saturn is placed in the second house in Aquarius, its moolatrikona sign. This qualifies Saturn to produce spiritual progress and insights during its period. The second house is associated with speech and food. In this case, his spiritual insight was associated with food (ingesting LSD) and was also related to speech (telling the truth).

"In the fall of 1971 I began attending the University of Puget Sound, in Tacoma, Washington. Some of my friends started getting into heroin. I tried it a few times, hoping that it might deliver a more fulfilling experience through drugs, but I was disappointed. I also recognized its addictive properties and realized that it could quickly lead me into trouble. I was studying psychology in college, and in late November I read an article about the research that had been done on Transcendental Meditation. I knew right away that I wanted to learn how to meditate. I went to an introductory lecture and was told that if I wanted to start, I would have to quit using drugs first. I immediately stopped using drugs, and in January of 1972 I was initiated into meditation. During my second meditation, I had a profound experience. I had a clear vision of a bright light coming towards me. This alarmed me so I tried to get away. The light hit me, exploding inward and leaving my whole brain buzzing in a blissful state of unbounded awareness."

Dasha/Bhukti: Venus Dasha/ Saturn Bhukti

The results of this dasha/bhukti combination, with reference to drug use and spiritual experiences, were discussed previously.

Divisional Chart

Vimshamsha Chart: This was discussed earlier with reference to the Venus/Saturn period and spiritual awareness.

Transits and Nakshatra Symbology

Saturn, the bhukti ruler, began its retrograde motion in mid-September of 1971 in Taurus, which is the first house of the chart. Normally the transit of Saturn across a Taurus Ascendant leads to more responsible behavior because Saturn (responsibility) challenges the person to take responsibility for himself (the first house represents the self). When a planet becomes retrograde, however, it frequently reverses its trend and sometimes causes the person to experience a more introspective version of its lesson. At the time of attending the meditation lecture, Saturn had just moved into the constellation of Krittika. Krittika nakshatra is ruled by Agni. The shakti of Krittika is "the power to burn or purify." This is connected to the yagya, an ancient fire ritual that is part of the foundation of the Vedic tradition. It is noteworthy that before learning to meditate, his teacher performed a puja, which is a Vedic ritual related to the yagya. He was asked to first purify himself by abstaining from the use of drugs. In his meditation experience, he was hit by an explosion of light. Agni is deified fire and represents the fire of consciousness within.

"In July of 1972, still reeling from my initial meditation experience, I went to Japan in search of monasteries and Buddhist monks. I intended to study Zen, so I went to several monasteries looking for a teacher. My experiences in meditation were motivating me to travel, as part of a deeper search for enlightenment. I visited a few monasteries, but couldn't find a teacher. Instead of enlightenment, I got cholera and a bad staph infection. The staph infection resulted in a two-year case of boils which were very painful."

Dasha/Bhukti: Venus Dasha/Saturn Bhukti

Venus Dasha: Venus dasha was discussed earlier as it relates to spiritual experiences. Regarding contracting cholera and the staph infection, the following points are relevant: Venus is the ruler of the Ascendant (the body). Venus is subject to Papa Kartari Yoga, being hemmed-in by the malefic planets, Sun and Mars. Both the Sun and Mars are hot, pitta planets (boils are caused by excess heat).

Saturn Bhukti: Saturn is the ruler of the ninth house (long-distance travel, spiritual path, gurus, higher education), and is placed in the fifth house (education). Saturn is placed in the third drekkana of Virgo, which is symbolized by a tall woman, dressed in white, going into a temple, carrying a pot and a spoon with a great sense of sanctity. Hence, he traveled to monasteries. Saturn is also a natural malefic, which aspects Venus (period ruler and lagna lord), so it produced obstacles, delays, and contributed to health problems.

Divisional Chart

Shashtamsha Chart (used for health): In the Shashtamsha chart, Venus is placed in the twelfth house (a dusthana and also the house of distant places). It is aspected by the Sun. The Sun is not only a natural malefic, but it is a participant in the Papa Kartari Yoga afflicting Venus in the Rashi chart. Saturn is placed in the second house, (diet) and is in a water sign (Pisces). He got cholera by drinking contaminated water.

Transits and Nakshatra Symbology

Venus, the dasha ruler, was passing through the constellation of Magha at the time of the trip. Magha is associated with ancient traditions and ancient cultures. Its shakti is "the power to leave the body," so it is associated with the spiritual realm in general. (See Magha nakshatra in *Path of Light, Volume I*.)

Saturn had just moved into the constellation of Mrigashira, which is associated with roads and well-trodden paths. It is a constellation of restless wandering and searching. (See Mrigashira nakshatra in *Path of Light, Volume I*.) Saturn was also transiting the sign Taurus (food), where it brought health problems related to diet.

"When I returned home, I went back to my second year of college. In the fall of 1972, I had my first full-blown enlightenment experience. I was meditating in my bedroom. There was a full moon that night, and the moon could be seen against the horizon, between layers of fog that were just settling in. I put my attention on the moon, and in a totally clear experience of infinite awareness, I spontaneously realized the self within as the same essential consciousness at the basis of everything in the universe. I experienced unity consciousness for about one hour. This experience began a year of blissful meditation experiences mixed with frequent symptoms of higher consciousness. I felt like Saint Francis of Assisi, and I was sure that I was on the verge of enlightenment."

Dasha/Bhukti: Venus Dasha/Saturn Bhukti

This was discussed earlier with reference to spiritual experience.

Divisional Chart

Vimshamsha Chart: This was also discussed earlier.

Transits and Nakshatra Symbology

Saturn, the bhukti ruler had recently begun its transit through the constellation of Punarvasu. Punarvasu is ruled by the deity, Aditi, the mother of all the gods. The name Aditi in Sanskrit means "primordial vastness." She represents the unbounded awareness that had to first be present before all of the gods could manifest. The nature of his spiritual experience was unbounded awareness, and perception of the primordial self. The experience was triggered by the vision of the moon, a maternal symbol, again related to Aditi, the mother of the gods.

"In the late fall of 1972, I started the Mucusless Diet, a diet promoted by Arnold Ehret, which completely eliminates the so-called mucous-forming foods. I existed for one year on nuts, seeds, fruits, vegetables, and various kinds of juices. In addition, I started fasting regularly. My weight fell to 102 lbs. by the next summer. Although I got over the boils, I became very thin and emaciated."

Dasha/Bhukti: Venus Dasha/Saturn Bhukti

Venus Dasha: Venus rules Taurus, which is the first house (the body). Taurus signifies food. Venus is also placed in the sign of Scorpio (transformation and change through various kinds of therapies).

Saturn Bhukti: Saturn (restriction) aspects the second house (diet) causing the tendency to restrain or control the diet.

Divisional Chart

Shashtamsha Chart: In the Shashtamsha chart, Saturn (restriction and control) is placed in the second house (diet) in Pisces (a sign related to idealistic or spiritualistic practices such as fasting).

Transits

Saturn (bhukti lord) was passing through Taurus, the lagna (body). Taurus is also the second house (food) from the Moon in the Rashi chart, encouraging discipline and restriction of the diet. Ketu had just started its eighteen month transit of Gemini, the second house from the lagna. Ketu represents renunciation. Ketu's transit of the second house is typical for renouncing food through dieting or fasting.

"In October or November of 1972, I decided that I wanted to become a healer. My goal was to combine teaching meditation with a healing practice, including both chiropractic work and nutrition. I was attending Evergreen College at that time. I remember being motivated by the feeling that if I could become a healer/meditation teacher, it would be very cool. I wanted to be cool, so I decided to pursue these career goals."

Dasha/Bhukti: Venus Dasha/Saturn Bhukti

Venus Dasha: Venus is placed in the seventh house (the tenth house from the tenth house), which is a prominent career placement. The seventh house is the house of clients. Venus is in Scorpio, a sign that signifies therapies of different kinds. Venus is the ruler of the sixth house (healing).

Saturn Bhukti: Saturn is the ruler of the tenth house (career) placed in the fifth house (education, good karma, and a dharma house). Saturn's nature is to bring things into concrete manifestation through effort and organization. Its solid placement in the chart led him to clarify his career goals in a field that gave him a sense of purpose. Saturn also prompted him to make plans to pursue further education. Saturn is also placed in the third drekkana of Virgo (a tall woman, dressed in white, going into a temple), suggesting that the career could somehow be linked to a spiritual theme (meditation teacher).

Divisional Chart

Dashamsha Chart: Venus is placed in the sign of Capricorn (career) in the seventh house (a prominent placement for this chart). Saturn is the ruler of the eighth house (change of career) placed in its own sign in the eighth house. This is a clear indication of a change of career direction during the Saturn bhukti. Because Saturn is strong, the career change was positive and involved concrete plans and efforts.

Contextual Factors

Even though this event took place in the Venus dasha/Saturn bhukti, it is important to note that the decision to become a healer sprang from a bigger pattern in the chart. First, in the natal chart the Moon is placed in Ashwini, a healing nakshatra, ruled by the Ashwini Kumaras, who were the healers of the gods. The Sun is placed in the sixth house (health) and is neecha bhanga. Neecha bhanga planets were discussed in the chapter on yogas. One of the features of this yoga is the ability to solve problems in the domain represented by the house in which the yoga takes place. In this case, he expressed his problem solving ability in the area of health. Then, his Venus (ruler of the first and the sixth houses) is placed in the seventh house (clients or patients) in the sign of Scorpio (therapies). This produced a desire to interact with people one-on-one. Rahu in the tenth house from the Moon suggests an alternative career. Rahu is also a significator of alternative healing modalities. The ruler of the tenth house (career) from the Moon is Saturn, which is placed in the sixth house (health) from the Moon. Added to these factors is the overall desire to be accepted by other people, which was discussed earlier.

"In August of 1973, I attended a long meditation retreat in Humboldt, California. There I met a Greek girl from New Jersey. I was attracted to her and she seemed to like me, but I had become interested in celibacy as a means of enhancing spiritual progress, so I didn't get involved with her physically. After the retreat, she wanted to come home with me, but I didn't take her up on it. I returned home in late August."

Dasha/Bhukti: Venus Dasha/Saturn Bhukti

Venus Dasha: Venus is placed in Scorpio, a sexual sign, and in the seventh house (relationships). Venus is also in Jyeshtha nakshatra, which is related to sexual attractions. (See Jyeshtha nakshatra in *Path of Light, Volume I*.)

Saturn Bhukti: Saturn (restraint) is placed in the fifth house (romance and sexuality). It is placed in the sign of Virgo (the virgin). Saturn is also in the nakshatra of Chitra. Chitra's shakti is "the power to accumulate merit or to store up good karma." Saturn is also placed in a drekkana symbolized by a tall woman, dressed in white, going into a temple, with a sense of sanctity. Hence, he met a woman and remained celibate.

"In September of 1973, I went to Europe for nine months of TM teacher training. Teacher training lasted from September of 1973 to June of 1974. We spent several hours each day doing extended meditation, yoga and pranayama in the Swiss Alps. For the last three months, we were in constant contact with Maharishi Mahesh Yogi. He met with us every day for about an hour and gave us each personal instruction. After I got home I was totally blissed out and started teaching meditation."

Dasha/Bhukti: Venus Dasha/Mercury Bhukti

Venus Dasha: Venus dasha's predisposition towards travel and spiritual progress was discussed earlier.

Mercury Bhukti: Mercury signifies communications, study, teaching and other verbal activities. It is placed in the seventh house, in the sign of Scorpio, where it produced a desire to transform others through speech. This is a placement found in the charts of many therapists, counselors, coaches and teachers. Mercury rules the twelfth house (moksha, meditation) from the Sun. Mercury also rules the fifth house (mantras) from the Ascendant.

Divisional Charts

Vimshamsha Chart: Mercury is the ruler of the ninth house (gurus and the spiritual path) and is placed in the fourth house (an angle house, a moksha house, and therefore a prominent placement) in the Vimshamsha chart. This signified significant spiritual events during the Mercury period. The ruler of the ninth house (long-distance travel) placed in the fourth house (residence) is also a combination that sometimes creates a change of residence involving long-distance travel. Occurring in the Vimshamsha chart, this combination suggests that the change of residence was related to spirituality. Using Venus as the lagna, Mercury is the ruler of the tenth house (career) placed in the fifth house (education and teaching). Hence he moved to Switzerland to take a meditation teacher training course.

Panchamsha Chart: The Panchamsha chart can be used for spiritual practices. It is noteworthy that Mercury is the ruler of the tenth house (career) placed in the fifth house (spiritual practices and education) in this chart. This repeats a pattern that suggests a link between professional education and spiritual practices.

Contextual Factors

It is important to note that the dasha and bhukti rulers only triggered a bigger pattern of spirituality in the horoscope. First, in the Rashi chart, the Moon is placed in the twelfth house (moksha), producing a strong inclination towards reflection and meditation. It is fortified by Jupiter, the karaka of spiritual knowledge. The ruler of the twelfth house (meditation) is Mars (the muscles of the body), which is placed in the eighth house (yoga and other therapies). This combination produced an interest in Hatha Yoga. Saturn, the ruler of the ninth house (spiritual path), is placed in the fifth house (mantras and spiritual practices) in a drekkana symbolized by a woman going into a temple. Without this overall pattern suggesting an interest in spirituality, the dasha-bhukti periods would not have produced such a dramatic series of events.

"I continued teaching meditation for the next two years, with good success. I teamed up with a friend who was also a meditation teacher. I traveled from town to town throughout the Pacific Northwest, and taught hundreds of people to meditate."

Dasha/Bhukti: Venus Dasha/Mercury Bhukti

Mercury Bhukti: His teaching activity continued throughout the bhukti of Mercury, which has already been discussed in this regard.

"In September of 1976, I teamed up with a different teaching partner in order to pursue a project to start a retreat center. Unfortunately, he and I did not get along and immediately started experiencing communication problems. Our partnership lasted only three months."

Dasha/Bhukti: Venus Dasha/Ketu Bhukti

Venus Dasha: Venus is in Scorpio in the seventh house. This gives the inclination towards power struggles and other complications in partnerships.

Ketu Bhukti: Ketu (retreats, disappointments, losses) is in the third house (communications) creating problems in his communications with others. Ketu is also placed in the constellation of Ashlesha. Ashlesha's shakti is "the power of poison." A malefic placed in Ashlesha in the third house can easily produce communication problems. Ketu is also the planet of detachment and is frequently associated with separations in partnerships.

Transits

Saturn (obstructions) was transiting the third house (communications) in the sign of Cancer. It had just entered the constellation of Ashlesha, and was moving to an exact conjunction with Ketu (the sub-period ruler). This aggravated Ketu's negative effect on communications, creating a great deal of frustration.

"From October of 1976 to March of 1977 I felt like I was floating. I seemed to lack a direction and was going nowhere. My parents were concerned. In March of 1977 I started moving towards chiropractic college, getting prerequisites out of the way at the local community college."

Dasha/ Bhukti: Venus Dasha/Ketu Bhukti

Ketu Bhukti: Ketu (detachment) bhukti is frequently a period of floating. This feeling persisted throughout the entire bhukti of Ketu. The period produced moment-to-moment experiences and an inability to focus on clear-cut goals. Ketu (healing) in the third house (information) also suggested a desire to gain knowledge about healing.

Divisional Chart

Siddhamsha Chart: Ketu is placed in the fourth house (school) in the Siddhamsha chart. It is in a conjunction with Jupiter (karaka of teachers and knowledge). Its dispositor, Saturn, is placed in the ninth house (higher education) from the Sun.

Transits

Saturn continued to conjunct Ketu, producing frustration and delay. Saturn (effort and concentration) also promoted returning to school through its transit of the third house (information). It challenged him to focus and concentrate on accumulating knowledge. Rahu (a sense of urgency) entered Virgo and the fifth house (education) in March of 1977, producing a desire to go to school.

"In September of 1977 I got my pilot's license."

Dasha/Bhukti: Sun Dasha/Sun Bhukti

Sun Dasha/Sun Bhukti: The Sun is the ruler of the fourth house (vehicles). It is placed in the sign of Libra (an air sign). It is also placed in Swati nakshatra, ruled by Vayu, the god of the wind. Swati's basic desire is "to roam freely throughout the universe." The Sun is also in the second drekkana of Libra, a bird drekkana. Hence, the desire to fly in a plane manifested in the Sun's period.

Divisional Chart

Shodashamsha Chart: In the Shodashamsha chart the Sun is placed in the seventh house in Sagittarius. The seventh house is the fourth house (vehicles) from the fourth house, and is therefore a prominent house in this divisional chart. From this position, the Sun also aspects the lagna. Furthermore, the Sun receives Jupiter's aspect from the eleventh house (attainment of desires), indicating the ability to attain his license.

"I started chiropractic college in January of 1978."

Sun Mahadasha Begins

The Sun is the karaka of career. It is placed in the sixth house (healing), suggesting the interest in pursuing the healing arts. The Sun is placed in the second drekkana of Libra, which is pictured as a man with a vulture's face. Vultures are creatures that derive their sustenance from the suffering of others. Although healing is a compassionate practice, healers do profit from the suffering of others. The Sun also rules the bones and the skeleton. In mythology, the Sun was the father of the Ashwini Kumaras, who were the gods of healing.

At the beginning of a new major period, it is typical for a person to take major new directions in life. The onset of this new dasha brought a new way of thinking, followed by a significant change in his life experiences.

Divisional Chart

Siddhamsha Chart: The Sun is placed in the tenth house (career) in Leo (own sign) in the Siddhamsha chart. The fact that it is in its own sign in the tenth house suggests that the period brought prominent educational events that were directly connected to a profession.

Transits

At the time of beginning chiropractic school, Saturn was passing through Leo in the fourth house (educational institution and residence) of the Rashi chart. This created the change of residence. Jupiter was transiting the third house (information) from the Ascendant and the fourth house (educational institution and home) from the Moon. The Sun (period ruler) entered the ninth house (higher education and also the spine) in mid-January.

"In the fall of 1977, I met my future wife and we got married on March 31, 1979."

Dasha/Bhukti: Sun Dasha/Sun Bhukti and Sun Dasha/Rahu Bhukti

He met his wife in Sun/Sun and he married her in Sun/Rahu.

Sun Dasha: The Sun is placed in Libra (relationships and marriage). It is placed in the seventh (marriage) house from the Moon, where it is aspected by Jupiter and the Moon. The Sun is also placed in the second drekkana of Libra. The second drekkana of Libra is symbolized by a man with a vulture's face, who has a pot in his hand, which is ready to fall. He is hungry and thirsty and is thinking about his wife and his children. This drekkana clearly suggest that the Sun dasha would produce an interest in getting married and having children.

Rahu Bhukti: Rahu (exotic and foreign conditions) is placed in the ninth house (education and long-distance travel). He met his wife in a college class and she was a native Hawaiian.

Divisional Chart

Navamsha Chart: The Sun (dasha ruler) is placed in the eighth house and in a conjunction with Ketu. Normally this position would not produce marriage. Ketu produces uncertainties and lack of commitment. The eighth house represents upheavals and changes. In this case, the wife was from a very different (almost foreign) culture. Ketu represents foreigners and exotic people. This eighth house placement, along with Ketu's conjunction, foreshadowed future difficulties in the marriage, which did take place. Rahu (bhukti ruler) is placed in the second house (family) of the Navamsha chart. Planets placed in the second house qualify to produce marriage.

Transits

At the time of marriage, Jupiter was transiting at five degrees of Cancer, casting an aspect on natal Venus (karaka of marriage) and on the seventh house (marriage).

"I initially attended chiropractic college in Davenport, Iowa. I didn't like the school, so in July of 1978 I changed to a chiropractic school in Portland, Oregon."

Dasha/Bhukti: Sun Dasha/Mars Bhukti

Sun Dasha: The Sun is the ruler of the fourth house (the educational institution) placed in the sixth house (healing and also struggles). It is neecha bhanga (the Sun is debilitated, but the debilitation is canceled due to the position of Venus, the Sun's dispositor, placed in an angle). Neecha Bhanga Yoga frequently gives an initial problem or failure, followed by a change that brings better results. The Sun is in the second drekkana of Libra, symbolized by a man holding a pot that is about to fall (suggesting a feeling of impending failure or impending change).

Mars Bhukti: Mars is placed in the eighth house of the chart, suggesting significant upheaval and change during its period.

Divisional Charts

Chaturtamsha Chart (residence): In the Chaturtamsha chart, Mars is placed in the eighth house (change) where it reiterates the placement in the Rashi chart. This suggests that the upheavals and changes taking place in the Mars period would include a change of residence.

Siddhamsha Chart (education): In the Siddhamsha chart, Mars is placed in Capricorn in the third house. The third house is the eighth house from the eighth house. Planets placed in the third house of divisional charts sometimes indicate change. Mars is placed in the sixth house from the Sun, indicating discontent and struggle. It is aspected by neecha bhanga Saturn, which is the ruler of the fourth house placed in the sixth house. Saturn's placement in the chart produced a change of school. Its aspect on Mars shows both frustration with the school in Iowa and the change of school to Portland during the Mars bhukti.

(Note: By itself, the Siddhamsha chart only hints at the change of school.

Taken together with the Chaturtamsha chart (residence), a change of school is quite clear.)

Transits

Saturn was transiting the fourth house (the environment, residence and educational institution). Mars (bhukti ruler) and Venus (lagna lord) were also transiting Leo in the fourth house. Rahu (change) was transiting Virgo, in the fifth house (education).

"In August of 1979 my car broke down and I bought a Subaru."

Dasha/Bhukti: Sun Dasha/Jupiter Bhukti

Sun Dasha: The Sun is the ruler of the fourth house (vehicles) placed in the sixth house (problems). It is involved in a Neecha Bhanga Yoga, suggesting an initial problem that is later overcome or fixed. Hence, he bought a car after having a problem. Here again the placement of the Sun in the second drekkana of Libra is relevant. This drekkana depicts a man who is holding a pot which about to fall, and who is thinking about his wife and family. This suggests that he was worried about impending problems with the car, and felt he needed to take care of his wife by getting a different car.

Jupiter Bhukti: Jupiter is in a conjunction with the Moon, which is located in Ashwini nakshatra (vehicles). Ashwini is ruled by the twin gods, the Ashwini Kumaras, who drove golden chariots through the heavens. (*See Path of Light, Volume I*).

Divisional Chart

Shodashamsha Chart (vehicles): The Sun is aspecting the Ascendant of the Shodashamsha chart, promoting the tendency for its mahadasha to produce vehicle ownership. Jupiter is placed in the eleventh house (attainment of desires) in the Shodashamsha chart. The placement of a strong and positive planet in the eleventh house of a divisional chart causes the planet's period to produce attainment of desires that are related to that chart. In the case of the Shodashamsha chart, this produced the attainment of a vehicle. Jupiter, the Sun's dispositor, is also aspecting the Sun in the Shodashamsha chart, forming a strong bond between the dasha and bhukti rulers. Jupiter is also the ruler of the fourth house (vehicles) from the Sun, and placed in the fifth house (luck) from the Sun.

Transits

Saturn (obstructions and problems) was transiting Leo in the fourth house (vehicles). The Sun (dasha ruler) and Venus (lagna lord) were also transiting the fourth house. Jupiter (bhukti ruler) was transiting the sign of Cancer in the fourth house (vehicles) from the Moon.

"I graduated from chiropractic school in June of 1981."

Dasha/Bhukti: Sun Dasha/Mercury Bhukti

Sun Dasha: The Sun has already been discussed as giving him a drive to realize his career goals.

Mercury Bhukti: Mercury is the ruler of the fifth house (education) and it is placed in the seventh house, which is the eleventh house (finishing or completing things) from the ninth house (higher education).

Divisional Chart

Siddhamsha Chart: Mercury is the ruler of the eleventh house (finishing or completing projects and attainment of the fruits of labors) and is placed in the second house (another house of education). This also forms a Dhana Yoga, a combination for financial increase. Mercury is also the ruler of the eleventh house from the Sun (period ruler) and is placed in the fifth house (education) from the Sun. Hence, he completed his education during the Mercury bhukti, and this led to financial increase.

Transits

Both Jupiter and Saturn were transiting the fifth house, which is the house of education. The mutual influence of Jupiter and Saturn promotes positive results in a house. Jupiter was transiting the first drekkana of Virgo, which is symbolized by a girl who is carrying a pot of flowers to the home of her teacher. Saturn was in the second drekkana of Virgo, symbolized by a man with a pen working with his profits and losses. He graduated from college, which resulted in starting his own business as a healer.

"On August 24, 1982 my daughter was born."

Dasha/Bhukti: Sun Dasha/Venus Bhukti

Sun Dasha: The Sun is a planet of self-expression and procreativity. It rules fatherhood, so its period is typical for the birth of children.

Venus Bhukti: Venus is placed in the seventh house (one-to-one relationships). Venus is also in a conjunction with Mercury, which rules the fifth house (children).

Divisional Chart

Saptamsha Chart: The Sun is placed in the eleventh house in the Saptamsha chart. This eleventh house placement (achievement of desires) allows the person to achieve the desire of the divisional chart, which in the case of the Saptamsha chart is children. Venus (bhukti ruler) rules the fifth house (children) from the Sun (period ruler) in the Saptamsha chart. This makes it a strong contender for producing a child. It is placed in the ninth house from the Sun. The ninth house is the fifth house from the fifth house and therefore another important house for children. Venus is furthermore in a conjunction with Jupiter (karaka of children). Along with Jupiter, Venus aspects the lagna of the Saptamsha chart, which again makes it a very likely planet to produce a child.

Transits and Nakshatra Symbology

At the time of the birth of his child, Jupiter (karaka of children) was transiting the sign of Libra, and was forming a conjunction with his natal Sun (period ruler and karaka of fatherhood).

Saturn was transiting the fifth house (children) in a conjunction with natal Saturn. The natal placement of yogakaraka planet Saturn in the fifth house makes Saturn's transit more significant for events related to children.

The Sun (period ruler) was transiting the fifth house from the Moon in the constellation of Magha. Magha is related to the desire to give birth so that after death, one's offspring can pray for one's well being.

On the day of the birth, Mercury, ruler of the fifth house, moved into the fifth house in its own sign, Virgo. When a planet transits its own sign, then the house in which it is transiting tends to give its results.

"In August of 1983 I changed my residence, renting a house from my best friend's mother."

Dasha/Bhukti: Moon Dasha/Moon Bhukti

Moon Dasha/Moon Bhukti: The Moon dasha began August 26, 1983. The onset of a new major period frequently brings significant changes in life. The moon is one of the karakas of the home and the family. It is placed in a movable sign, Aries, in the twelfth house. The Moon is also in a conjunction with the eighth lord (changes), Jupiter.

Divisional Chart

Chaturtamsha Chart: In the Chaturtamsha chart, the Moon is placed in the sixth house (rental houses) in a conjunction with Ketu (change through letting go). It is also interesting that the Moon is a maternal planet and his new landlord was the mother of his best friend, who was like a second mother to him. The Moon is also in Aries in the Chaturtamsha chart, just as in the Rashi chart, which means it is vargottama. A planet that is vargottama behaves like an exalted planet in a divisional chart, usually bringing more significant events in the divisional chart's domain during its period.

Transits

At the time of the change of residence, Saturn was transiting Libra in a conjunction with his natal Sun. The Sun is the ruler of the fourth house (residence). It is neecha bhanga (producing problems which are overcome) in the sixth house (rentals), making the Sun predisposed to changes of residence. The Saturn transit, combined with the change of Mahadasha, triggered the move.

Also, at this time, Rahu had just changed signs, entering the sign of Taurus in mid-August. Taurus is the eighth house (change) from the Sun, which is the ruler of the fourth house (residence). Relative to the Sun in the Rashi chart, Rahu (change) is located in the fourth house (residence), giving it a predisposition to change of residence.

In the beginning of August, Mars began its transit into the sign of Cancer. Mars is the ruler of the Moon sign (a focal planet), the ruler of the eighth house from the Moon (change), and the karaka for real estate. In the natal chart, Mars is placed in the eighth house, giving it a predisposition to create change. The sign of Cancer is the fourth house (residence) from the Moon (the new Mahadasha ruler).

Venus (lagna lord) was transiting the sign of Leo, which is the fourth house (residence). It was retrograde giving it the tendency to produce restlessness and changes. In the natal chart, Venus is placed in the eighth house (change) from the Moon, in the sign of Scorpio (change), giving it a predisposition to produce changes.

"In October of 1983 I fell and hurt my knee. I had to have knee surgery in November of 1983."

Dasha/Bhukti: Moon Dasha/Moon Bhukti

Moon Dasha/Moon Bhukti: The Moon is the ruler of the third house, which is the eighth house (accidents) from the eighth house. It is placed in the twelfth house (a dusthana house). It is in a conjunction with Jupiter (the ruler of the eighth house from the lagna). It is also aspected by the Sun (a natural malefic). These configurations make the Moon predisposed to accidents. The Moon is also placed in the constellation of Ashwini, which represents the knees.

Divisional Chart

Shashtamsha Chart: The Moon is the ruler of the sixth house (accidents and injuries) and is placed in the third house (a minor dusthana house).

Transits

At the time of the accident, Saturn (karaka of physical problems) was transiting the sixth house (injuries) in the sign of Libra. It was moving towards the Sun (karaka of health and vitality). The surgery took place when transiting Saturn came to the exact degree of the natal Sun, in November 1983.

Mars (injuries and surgery) was in Cancer (debilitated). Cancer is the third house (a dusthana house). Transiting Mars was aspecting the natal Sun, which is placed in the sixth house.

Rahu (accidents) had just moved into the sign of Taurus, which is the first house (the physical body). The time when a transiting planet moves into a new sign frequently triggers events related to the house and sign that have just been entered.

"When I first got out of chiropractic school, I went to work as an associate chiropractor in the office of a successful chiropractor who had a charismatic personality. By the beginning of 1984, I was starting to feel very restless there. I felt eclipsed by his strong personality. I needed to go out on my own and make my own mark. I moved, opening my own clinic in July of 1984."

Dasha/Bhukti: Moon Dasha/Mars Bhukti

Moon Dasha: The Moon is placed in the sign of Aries (independence) in the Ashwini (healing) nakshatra.

Mars Bhukti: Mars is placed in the eighth house (change), giving it a general predisposition to create changes of various kinds during its period.

Divisional Chart

Dashamsha chart: The Moon (dasha lord) is exalted in the eleventh house (achievement of desires). A planet placed in the eleventh house of a divisional chart promotes the fulfillment of desires related to the divisional chart's domain during its period. In the case of the Dashamsha chart, this promoted the fulfillment of career desires. Hence, he got his own clinic.

Mars is placed in the Ascendant of the Dashamsha Chart. When a period planet is placed in the Ascendant of a divisional chart, it produces prominent events and new beginnings related to the domain of the chart. Mars is also neecha bhanga. Its debilitation is cancelled, both by the aspect of Jupiter and by Saturn's (exaltation sign ruler) placement in an angle from the Moon. When a planet is neecha bhanga in a divisional chart, it will first give a problem or a negative condition, and then it produces some kind of change that is a reaction to the problem. Neecha Bhanga Raja Yoga was covered in the chapter on yogas. The neecha bhanga effect will be related to career in this case because it occurs in the Dashamsha chart. Mars is placed in the sign of Cancer (residence and environment), which in the Dashamsha chart is related to the environment of work or the workplace. So he was fed up with his workplace and made a change to a new office. This is a clear example of Neecha Bhanga Raja Yoga.

Transits

At the time of the change of workplace, Saturn (work) was retrograding in an exact conjunction with the natal Sun. The Sun rules the fourth house (home or environment) and is placed in the sixth house (health), so this transit brought a change of work environment.

Jupiter, ruler of the eighth house (change), was transiting the eighth house over his natal Mars (bhukti ruler), furthering the tendency of

Mars to create change during its period. The Jupiter/Mars conjunction is also a conjunction that tends to produce new beginnings. Jupiter represents expansion and optimism. Mars represents action and new beginnings. Together they give confidence and the impulse to begin new enterprises.

"In January of 1984, I started getting the thought to call Dr. Berkebile. Dr. Berkebile was a great healer who lived in the mountains near North Bend, Washington. I had met him several years earlier and had always felt a desire to learn from him. He had been written about in Reader's Digest *in the 1950's because of a lawsuit that had been brought against him. What had happened was that the local authorities were miffed that he was practicing medicine and chiropractic care without a license. Dr. Berkebile was one of the old school chiropractors who learned chiropractic before there was formal training in that field. He was a full-body trance-channel as well, possessing a clarity about health issues on a level with Edgar Cayce. Anyway, during his trial, Dr. Berkebile protested that he could not be put on trial for practicing medicine or chiropractic therapies without a license. "I am not a chiropractor," he declared, "I am a cosmopractor!" This apparently motivated the judge to ask for an explanation. When Dr. Berkebile explained that his practice included many of the intuitive arts, including water witching, the judge ordered him to give the court a demonstration. A court date was set for the event. A schematic of the court building was acquired. Dr. Berkebile arrived, witching stick in hand. The judge asked him to find a water pipe somewhere in the building using his witching rod. Dr. Berkebile not only found a water pipe, he found every pipe in the building without a problem. Needless to say, the case was dropped, and Dr. Berkebile was never bothered by the local authorities again. He continued his "cosmopractic" practice until he died in 1985. I called him in July of 1984 and he invited me to become his student. I visited him each week at his home in the mountains. He gave me instructions by going into a trance, completely losing consciousness, and channeling various spiritual beings who had been great healers in the past. In this way, I gained knowledge of many unconventional healing methods that I have used effectively over the years with my own patients."*

Dasha/Bhukti: Moon Dasha/Mars Bhukti

Moon Dasha: The Moon is placed in Ashwini nakshatra. In mythology, the Ashwini Kumaras were healers, who learned the wisdom of immortality from a great yogi who was a disciple of Indra. (See *Path of Light, Volume I* for myths of Ashwini.) Dr. Berkebile had the presence of a great yogi and imparted what seemed to be magical knowledge.

Mars Bhukti: Mars is placed in the ninth house (teachers) from the Moon (the dasha ruler). It is placed in the third drekkana of Sagittarius that is symbolized by a man with a beard, sitting on a deerskin, holding a staff. This is an image of a guru or preceptor. Mars is placed in Purva Ashadha nakshatra. The shakti of this nakshatra is "the power to energize." From Dr. Berkebile, Mark learned how to channel healing energy through his hands in order to revitalize his patients.

Divisional Chart

Shashtamsha Chart (health): In the Shashtamsha chart the Moon is in Aries, vargottama, and placed in the third house (information, study, learning). Mars (sub-period ruler) is placed in the fifth house (education) from the Moon. It is in a conjunction with Jupiter (guru). These factors led Mark to study healing with a teacher.

Transits

In the Rashi chart, Jupiter (the guru) was transiting retrograde in the sign of Sagittarius in the ninth house (guru) from the Moon (period ruler). Jupiter was also in a conjunction with Mars (the sub-period ruler). A retrograde planet often brings a connection to the past. He had met Dr. Berkebile in the past and was reconnecting with him. Jupiter was transiting in the first drekkana of Sagittarius. The first drekkana of Sagittarius is symbolized by a man who lives in a hermitage and who protects the yogis and articles used for the ritual sacrifice. Mars in this drekkana gave him the inclination to visit Berkebile (the yogi) in his home in the mountains (the hermitage). The image is that of a devotee who serves his teacher.

"In August of 1984 I bought a gun at the prompting of a friend. It was a Colt 45. In the past, the neighborhood I was living in had been very peaceful. Recently, though, several drug addicts had moved into a house two blocks away. A wave of burglaries, plus my friend's encouragement, had convinced me to purchase the weapon. The opportunity to flirt with my "bad boy persona" again, along with the feeling of power I derived from owning a gun, also played a part in the decision. I had just purchased the gun and had gone to my friend's house to get some bullets. I was walking back to my house when a car pulled up in front of me. Four guys from the drug house got out of the car and started walking towards me in a way that

clearly meant I was about to be mugged. I pulled the gun out from under my coat and pointed it at the ground in front of them. They turned around, ran back into their car, and pulled away, tires screeching."

Dasha/Bhukti: Moon Dasha/Mars Bhukti

Moon Dasha: The Moon is placed in Aries, a martial sign ruled by Mars, the significator of war. It is placed in the first drekkana of Aries. The first drekkana of Aries is symbolized by a dark man with a white waistband. He has fiery red eyes and is holding an axe in the air, as if to protect. This is an ayudha (weapons) drekkana. The image is that of a man who is using a weapon for protection, making an angry face as if to scare off enemies.

Mars Bhukti: Mars is placed in the eighth house (death and violence). It is placed in the third drekkana of Sagittarius. This drekkana is also an ayudha drekkana, and depicts a man holding a staff (which can be described as a weapon).

Transits

Transiting Mars (bhukti ruler) and Ketu were passing through the sign of Scorpio. They were in a conjunction at the time of the event. Mars' conjunction with Ketu in Scorpio is a highly volatile combination. It occurred in the seventh house (one of the houses of warfare). Saturn was transiting the sixth house (enemies). A natural malefic transiting the sixth house causes the defeat of enemies.

"Over the next few months I got a few more guns. In the late fall of 1985, I caught someone stealing the wheels off my car. I was inside my house doing Tai Chi when I heard a noise outside. I looked out my window and saw a guy taking the wheels off my RX7. He looked at me with an expression that said, 'You won't shoot me.' He calmly gathered up his tools and left. He ended up getting two of my tires."

Dasha/Bhukti: Moon Dasha/Rahu Bhukti

Moon Dasha: The Moon dasha was discussed in the previous case regarding weapons.

Rahu Bhukti: Rahu is placed in the third drekkana of Capricorn, which is a weapons drekkana. It is symbolized by a man who is carrying a bow, arrows and a quiver. Rahu in mythology was a demon, who stole nectar from the gods, so its bhukti produced a theft.

Divisional Chart

Shodashamsha Chart (vehicles): In the Shodashamsha chart the Moon is placed in the first house, signifying prominent events connected to vehicles. Rahu is placed in the twelfth house (losses). The twelfth house is usually the house of the feet, but in the Shodashamsha chart it represents the tires. Rahu is aspected from the sixth house (theft) by Mars, so his tires were stolen by a thief in Rahu bhukti.

Transits

Rahu was transiting Bharani, the nakshatra ruled by Yama, the god of death. This indicated an event that could have potentially led to someone's death. Rahu was transiting the same sign (Aries) as the natal Moon (dasha ruler). When the bhukti ruler transits through the same sign as the natal placement of the dasha ruler or vice versa, it symbolizes pronounced events related to the disposition of the two planets.

"Acupuncture college started in September of 1985 and lasted three years."

Dasha/Bhukti: Moon Dasha/Rahu Bhukti

Moon Dasha: The Moon is placed in the constellation of Ashwini, which has previously been discussed regarding its proclivity for healing.

Rahu Bhukti: Rahu (unconventional values) is placed in the ninth house (higher education) from the lagna. It is also placed in the tenth house (career) from the Moon. Hence, he was motivated to further his professional education by studying an unconventional healing method.

Nakshatra and Drekkana Symbology

Rahu is placed in Dhanishtha nakshatra. This constellation is ruled by the eight Vasudevas, and symbolizes the attainment of high reputation and inclusion in elite circles. The desire of this nakshatra is "to revolve around the summit of the gods." It is interesting to note that this new venture in the field of acupuncture led him to become the President of the Washington State Acupuncture Association and the Chairman of the Board of the Northwest Institute of Oriental Medicine.

Rahu is placed in the third drekkana of Capricorn. The third drekkana of Capricorn is a man who is carrying a gem-studded water pot on his shoulder. He has a bow, arrows and a quiver. Arrows in a quiver could be symbolic of acupuncture needles.

Divisional Chart

Siddhamsha Chart: The Moon is placed in the first house in the Siddhamsha chart. The Moon is the ruler of the ninth house (higher education) in this chart and it is neecha bhanga in the first house of the chart. This gives the tendency to make new beginnings in education during the period. Rahu is placed in the fourth house (the educational institution) in a conjunction with Jupiter (teachers and knowledge).

Transits

At the time of returning to school, Rahu (sub-period ruler), was transiting the sign of Aries and in a conjunction with natal Jupiter. Rahu quickly entered Ashwini nakshatra and later conjoined with the natal Moon (period ruler). When the dasha ruler transits over the bhukti ruler or vice versa, the period will produce marked events related to what the two planets signify in the chart.

Jupiter was transiting the ninth house (education) where it was conjuncting natal Rahu. It is interesting to note that transiting Rahu was conjuncting natal Jupiter, while transiting Jupiter was conjuncting natal Rahu at the time of beginning school.

"In August of 1987, out of a desire to simplify my practice and to emulate the style of Dr. Berkebile, I bought a house and moved my clinic to my home."

Dasha/Bhukti: Moon Dasha/Jupiter Bhukti

Moon Dasha: The Moon is a general indicator of the home. Its predisposition to produce changes of residence and workplace has been discussed previously.

Jupiter Bhukti: Jupiter is the ruler of the eighth house (change) and is placed in a conjunction with the Moon (dasha lord), making the period predisposed to produce significant changes.

Divisional Chart

Chaturtamsha Chart: In the Chaturtamsha chart, Jupiter is neecha bhanga (its debilitation is cancelled due to the aspect of Mars, the planet which is exalted in Capricorn). A neecha bhanga planet usually suggests change due to discontent. The person frequently identifies a problem and then moves to correct it by making some sort of change. In this case, Jupiter (bhukti ruler) was placed in the tenth house (career) from the Moon (dasha ruler) in the Chaturtamsha chart. So the change of residence that took place, also affected the office.

Transits

Jupiter (the bhukti ruler) was transiting Ashwini nakshatra in an exact conjunction with the natal Moon (dasha ruler). When the dasha and bhukti ruler are conjunct by transit, the period produces more prominent events.

Saturn, which rules the tenth house (career) from the Moon (dasha ruler) was transiting Scorpio in the eighth house (change) from the Moon. This produced career changes. It was also passing over Venus, which rules the sixth house (healing).

"In the early part of 1994, I met a spiritual teacher from India who taught Kriya Yoga. I was initiated into that meditation and then went to Switzerland to study with the teacher."

Dasha /Bhukti: Mars Dasha/Rahu Bhukti

Mars Dasha: Mars is placed in the eighth house, which represents kundalini and the chakra system. Kriya Yoga is a technique that uses the chakras as a focus of the meditation. Mars is placed in the ninth house from the Moon (guru) in the third drekkana of Sagittarius. This drekkana is symbolized by a bearded man sitting on a deerskin, holding a staff. He is sitting in Varasana posture, which means "a majestic seat," and can symbolize both a yoga posture, as well as a seat of authority. The teacher was literally a bearded yogi. As part of the meditation practice, he was taught to practice the Mahamudra, a sitting yoga posture.

Rahu Bhukti: Rahu (change) is placed in the ninth house (guru and spiritual path) of the chart. Rahu is also a planet that is related to the astral plane, esoteric spiritual practices, and the chakra system. Hence, he changed his spiritual practice. The ninth house is also the house of long-distance travel. Rahu's (foreign places) placement in the ninth house produced foreign travel. Rahu is placed in the constellation of Dhanishtha. This nakshatra was discussed earlier as being related to the desire to be included in elite circles. He was invited to become part of a spiritual group and to become part of the inner circle close to the guru at this time. Due to Rahu's rebellious and independent nature, he declined the invitation and stayed on the periphery of the group.

Divisional Charts

Vimshamsha Chart (spirituality in general): Rahu is placed in the eighth house (change and also kundalini) in the Vimshamsha chart, suggesting a change taking place with his spiritual path.

Panchamsha Chart (spiritual practices): Mars (period ruler) is the ruler of the fifth house (spiritual practices) placed in the twelfth house (meditation) in Scorpio and conjunct Ketu, indicating that the period would be one of powerful changes and progress in meditation. The Mars/Ketu conjunction produces a connection to physical yoga postures.

Transits

Jupiter was transiting the sign of Libra over the natal Sun (the soul). Jupiter's conjunction with the Sun can increase spiritual expansion. Jupiter was also transiting the eleventh house (groups) from Mars (dasha ruler). Rahu (bhukti ruler) was transiting the twelfth house (meditation and distant places) from natal Mars (dasha ruler). Hence, he went to a foreign place and studied meditation.

"This was the beginning of a traveling phase of my life. I went to Egypt in late November of 1995. Before I left, I visited James Kelleher to get an astrological perspective on the trip. He told me that there was a lot of violence surrounding this trip, but that I could go anyway, because there would be no real threat to my life or well-being. He told me to watch my back, however, and to take things easy.

The trip was amazing. I had been dreaming about going to Egypt for years. I finally got my opportunity and went with a group led by the noted Egyptologist, John Anthony West. The trip turned out to be more exciting than I had imagined, however. While on the tour bus we were halted by an unexpected tragedy. We were traveling through the Nubian Desert, a vast expanse of sand and rock. This stretch of highway was known to be dangerous due to terrorist activities. We had armed guards with us, consisting of soldiers with AK 47's. All of a sudden, the truckload of soldiers in back of our bus passed us going 80 miles an hour. We knew the soldiers had left us for some important reason, assuming that terrorists were ahead. When we arrived on the scene, however, we saw that the bus in front of us had gotten into an accident. The injured passengers had just been taken away. All that remained was the damaged bus with several dead bodies lying around it. The bus stopped and waited there for about fifteen minutes. It was a shocking and horrifying experience to sit for fifteen minutes contemplating the harsh reality of death.

This was not the only event that was unexpected. While on a luxury riverboat, cruising on the Nile, I became friendly with an Egyptian woman. She became very interested in acupuncture and asked me for an acupuncture treatment. I got out my needles and gave her a treatment in her cabin. In the middle of the treatment, one of the workers on the boat entered the cabin. Although the situation was essentially innocent, all the man saw as he came in the door were the bare legs of the Egyptian lady on the bed and a strange western man hovering over her. The worker left the room before an explanation could be given. I was a little concerned because of the way in which Egyptian men view interactions between western men and Egyptian women, and I suspected that the worker might have gotten the wrong idea. Later that afternoon, I was walking through the lobby of the cruise ship when two large angry Egyptians accosted me, pushing me up against the wall next to the reception desk. In a confusing and emotional outburst, they claimed that I had taken advantage of the Egyptian woman. It was a tense situation that seemed to be headed in the direction of violence. I tried to remain calm, and explained that I was a doctor and that I was giving her a treatment. The man at the reception desk vouched for the fact that I was a doctor and the men apologized and let me go.

As if all this were not enough, two hours after our plane departed from Cairo International Airport, one of the two engines failed. The pilot turned back and headed towards Cairo. Being the son of a commercial pilot, I could tell that we had lost an engine. I knew that being two hours out to sea was a dangerous place to be in such a situation. As the plane entered the final approach to Cairo International Airport, I tightened my seatbelt. I was nervous about landing with only one engine, and hoped that the pilot knew what he was doing. As we touched down, there was an explosion, followed by a flash of smoke and fire. Several of the tires on the plane had blown out. The next thirty seconds were exciting as the plane rumbled to an undignified halt. No one was hurt, and everyone was relieved to have survived the incident.

As I exited the plane, I couldn't help but marvel at all of the unexpected mishaps during the trip. Egypt and I were not getting along, but in the end, *the trip turned out to be both thrilling and enjoyable."*

Dasha/Bhukti: Mars Dasha/Jupiter Bhukti

Mars Dasha: Mars is the ruler of the twelfth house (distant places). It is placed in the ninth house (long-distance travel) from the Moon. Mars' position in the eighth house (upheavals and changes) in a weapons drekkana (already discussed) gives it a tendency to produce upset and potential violence during travel in distant places.

Jupiter Bhukti: Jupiter is a natural significator of long-distance travel. It is placed in the twelfth house (distant places). It is involved in a Parivartana Yoga with Mars, which links the Moon's sign with the ninth house (long-distance travel) from the Moon. Jupiter is also involved in Gaja Kesari Yoga, which produces group events. He traveled with a group. Jupiter's rulership of the eighth house gives it a tendency to produce upset during travel. The placement of Jupiter (the king of the natural benefics) in the twelfth house, produces protection while traveling. In spite of the upsets, he was not harmed.

Transits

Transiting Ketu (foreign places) was transiting the twelfth house (distant places), so he traveled to a foreign country. Transiting Ketu was also in a close conjunction with the natal Moon. The natal Moon is the ruler of the third house (short-distance travel) placed in the twelfth house (long-distance travel), a combination for traveling.

Transiting Jupiter (bhukti ruler) was in a close conjunction with Venus (lagna lord). Jupiter/Venus conjunctions frequently cause self-indulgent expenditures and pleasureable experiences such as travel.

Transiting Mars (dasha lord) was passing through Mula nakshatra. Mula's shakti is "the power of destruction."

"In August of 1996, my dad got cancer. He died in early March of 1997."

Dasha/ Bhukti: Mars Dasha/Saturn Bhukti and Mercury Bhukti

Mars Dasha: Mars is placed in the eighth house (death) in the Rashi chart.

Saturn and Mercury Bhuktis: Saturn is the ruler of the ninth house (father) in the Rashi chart, suggesting prominent events connected with the father during its period. By itself, it does not indicate negative experiences because it is fairly well-placed. Both the dasha ruler and the bhukti ruler are first-rate natural malefics, however, which predisposes the sub-period to produce some negative results. His death actually took place in the Mercury bhukti. Mercury is placed in the twelfth house (loss) from Mars in the Rashi chart. It is conjunct the ruler of the sixth house (disease) and is aspected by Saturn.

Divisional Chart

Dwadashamsha Chart: Mars (dasha ruler) is placed in the eighth house (death) in the Dwadashamsha chart. Saturn (bhukti ruler at the time of diagnosis) is placed in the twelfth house (a dusthana house) from Mars. Mercury (bhukti ruler at the time of death) is placed in the sixth house (illness) from Mars in the Dwadashamsha chart and is in a conjunction with Jupiter, which is the debilitated ruler of the eighth house from Mars. Mercury is also placed in the first house of the Dwadashamsha chart, which indicates that a prominent event related to the father will take place during its period. It is also aspected by Saturn.

Transits

Saturn (bhukti ruler) was transiting in the sign of Pisces. Pisces is the sixth house (disease) from the natal Sun (father). Transiting Saturn was also casting a challenging aspect on natal Mars (period ruler). When a transiting malefic aspects a natal malefic, the results are usually negative. Saturn was transiting retrograde, which makes its energy more powerful and more malefic. It was also transiting the constellation of Uttara Bhadrapada, which is symbolized by a funeral cot.

At the time of the diagnosis of the disease, Mars (the Mahadasha ruler) was transiting in the sign of Gemini. Gemini is the sixth house (disease) from the ninth house (the father), indicating health problems for the father. From Gemini, Mars casts an aspect onto the ninth house and natal Rahu, further aggravating the situation. Mars was transiting through Ardra nakshatra, which is symbolized by a teardrop, indicating an emotional experience.

Rahu (a planet frequently associated with the disease, cancer) was transiting the sign of Virgo, and was in a conjunction with natal Saturn (bhukti ruler and ruler of the ninth house).

At the time of death, Mars (dasha lord) was transiting retrograde at 4 degrees of Virgo. Transiting Rahu was also at 4 degrees of Virgo. Both of these transiting and conjunct planets were in the same sign as Saturn, which is the ruler of the ninth house (father), indicating a negative event for the father.

Saturn was still in Pisces in Uttara Bhadrapada nakshatra, symbolized by a funeral cot, as described above.

Mercury (the bhukti ruler) had just entered Purva Bhadrapada nakshatra, which is also symbolized by a funeral cot.

"During the spring of 1998 I met a beautiful woman. She was into poetry and dancing, and we became immediate friends. I was very attracted to her and I guess you would say that I fell in love with her immediately. She was married, however, and so was I. The interesting thing about this experience was that even though I felt such a strong attraction, I did not feel the need to pursue this woman. I was simply enjoying the fact that I could feel very strong sexual and emotional energies without needing to get physically involved with her. On one hand, my heart, mind, and body totally enjoyed being in her presence. On the other, it was clear that if I pursued a relationship with her, the inevitable complications and pitfalls of all male-female relationships would inevitably follow. I opted for simply enjoying the sexual energy and avoiding the complications. This experience gave me a new realization about male-female energy, which gave me a great deal of freedom. The enjoyment of sexual attraction, love and intimacy are not dependent on coupling with a partner. They are internal experiences that can enrich and energize one's life if they are not suppressed. Yet the choice to make them permanent through bonding with a partner inevitably causes passion to fade."

Dasha/Bhukti: Mars Dasha/Ketu Bhukti

Mars Dasha: Mars is placed in the eighth house (sexual energy) of the Rashi chart. It is placed in a nakshatra ruled by Venus, which triggered Venus' results (love and affection) during its period.

Ketu Bhukti: Ketu is placed in the third house (a house related to information, and he was taking a class at the time of meeting the woman). Ketu is placed in the eighth house (sexual energy and transformation) relative to Mars (dasha ruler). Ketu is placed in the nakshatra of Ashlesha. Ashlesha is a nakshatra that is related to the passions and desires of the unconscious. It is ruled by the Nagas (serpents). In mythology, Shesha Naga, the king of the serpents, is depicted as sitting in Patala Loka, the abode of the serpents, while all around him serpent nymphs dance. They try to seduce him with their movements and smiles. He sits in completed detachment, enjoying the dance. In his detached state, his eyes roll back in his head. He experiences a state of inebriated bliss, while he holds the world on one of his thousand heads. This is a symbol of sublimated sexuality. As consciousness develops, the person gains the ability to witness and enjoy sexual energy without losing the awareness of self to another person. It is interesting to note the similarities between Mark's experience and the myth.

Divisional Chart

Navamsha Chart: Ketu is placed in the fifth house (romance and sexuality) from Mars. It is also placed in the eighth house (sexual energy and transformation) from the Navamsha lagna.

Transits and Nakshatra Symbology

Mars was transiting the constellation of Krittika at the time of the attraction. Krittika nakshatra is ruled by Agni, and is said to sometimes produce an attraction to the spouses of other people. In mythology Agni tried to seduce the wives of the seven sages. (See *Path of Light, Volume I* for stories related to Krittika nakshatra.)

Ketu, the bhukti ruler, was transiting Shatabhisha nakshatra. Shatabhisha challenges a person to let go of attachments. This nakshatra is ruled by Varuna. The myth of Varuna and the king who wanted to have a son is relevant here. Varuna told the king that he could have the son, but that he would have to sacrifice the son back to him. (See *Path of Light, Volume I* for the complete version of the story.)

"In September of 1998, my wife and I decided to take a dance class. This began an interest in dancing that has continued to the present time (2004). Dancing has provided me an outlet for my creative energy. It has also provided an avenue for interacting with women in a way that is both sexual and detached. It has given me a way of experiencing physical intimacy with women other than my wife, without the complications and entanglements of bonded relationships."

Dasha/Bhukti: Mars Dasha/Venus Bhukti

Mars Dasha: Mars is the planet of the physical body. It also rules the twelfth house (the feet). It is placed in the eighth house (therapies), where it symbolizes the therapeutic effect of physical movement.

Venus Bhukti: Venus is the planet of creativity. It is placed in the seventh house (partnership) in the constellation of Jyeshtha (sexual power and seduction), where it symbolized a sexually charged creative experience done with a partner. Venus is also placed in the twelfth house (the feet) from Mars. Hence, he took up dancing.

Transits and Nakshatra Symbology

Venus (bhukti ruler) was transiting the constellation of Purva Phalguni, which is symbolized by the conjugal bed. Its shakti is procreation. It is a nakshatra connected with both creative and sexual energy.

Mars (dasha ruler) was transiting the constellation of Ashlesha. It was conjunct Ketu at the time he began the dance class. Ketu was the sub-period that triggered the attraction to the married woman in the spring of 1998. All of the themes expressed at that time were being reiterated again. It was as if Mars was saying, "Remember what happened in your Ketu sub-period? I now have another level of Ashlesha's energy to reveal!"

Author's Journal:

Astrologer, Predict for Thyself

I once had an encounter with an astrologer who predicted his own death. This occurred in New Delhi, several years ago.

In astrology, one of the "toughest nuts to crack," as Dr. B.V. Raman once put it, is longevity. A good deal of astrological literature is devoted to this subject, and every novice astrologer at some point tries to work out his longevity and predict his time of death. One of the problems with making longevity predictions is the lack of good feedback in order to verify the usefulness of classical techniques. Normally clients come back to the astrologer and report, "I got married at the time you predicted," or "I got the job you predicted," or "Your prediction about my job failed." In any case, the astrologer gets needed feedback in order to refine his techniques of prediction. With longevity predictions, however, there is a pronounced lack of feedback. If the astrologer dares to enter into this touchy zone of prediction, then most of the predicted times of death are far in the future and can't be verified. And if he makes an accurate prediction for someone's time of death, the client can't come back to report! Mastering the prediction of longevity is, to say the least, an art, which comes only after many years and much experience practicing Jyotish.

Another problem that most astrologers struggle with is making predictions for themselves. There is a saying which goes, "A lawyer who defends himself, has a fool for a client." This thinking also applies to astrologers. Remaining objective, when it comes to one's own chart, makes it difficult to make accurate predictions. I have often had other good astrologers come to me and ask me to make a prediction for them, saying that they can predict for others, but not for themselves.

Anyway, because I travel to India so frequently, part of my role as a board member of the American College of Vedic Astrology (ACVA) has been to recruit good Indian astrologers to speak at the annual international Vedic astrology symposiums. On this occasion I was intending to drop in on R. Santhanam. The previous year, along with Dr. David Frawley and Dr. Dinesh Sharma, I had visited Mr. Santhanam at his home in New Delhi and he had accepted our invitation to be the keynote speaker at our next symposium. On this trip, however, I was feeling some doubts about Mr. Santhanam and felt the need to visit him again in order to firm up these plans. After phoning him to set up a meeting, I took a taxi across Delhi to Santhanam's house.

Mr. Santhanam greeted me at the door to his apartment building and led me up a couple of flights of stairs to his office, a small room attached to his apartment, filled with papers, notebooks, unfinished translations, and classical reference books. Mr. Santhanam had the bright face of an intellectual. He was a short, thin, wiry man, with a sharp intellect. He exuded mental energy, which he channeled into his many translations of classical works, as well as his magazine, The Times of Astrology. *After a brief conversation and accepting a mandatory cup of chai, I got to the point of my visit.*

"We are looking forward to your visit to the United States and are excited about having you as our keynote speaker next year," I said.

Santhanam looked away. He started talking about the conference and said he was also looking forward to it, but I sensed that he was being evasive.

I said, "I just wanted to get a final commitment from you about the conference. We have made many arrangements already, including advertising your lectures in our conference brochure, so I just wanted to be sure that everything is on track."

Again Mr. Santhanam seemed evasive. "Yes, I will be coming of course, but I can't give you a final commitment at this time," he said.

"Mr. Santhanam," I said in a somewhat irritated tone, "you gave us your final commitment last year. We have planned the symposium around you! How can you now say you are not sure? We've already spent a lot of money on advertising, based on what you told us last year!"

"Yes, yes," Mr. Santhanam chirped back, " I am going to Varanasi for a week. I will be able to give you a solid commitment after I get back. You can call me at that time and I will let you know if I can come."

Frustrated and annoyed, I left Mr. Santhanam's apartment. I knew something wasn't quite right. 'How could he be so flighty?' I thought.

I spent the next few days taking care of business in Delhi, and then board-

ed an overnight sleeper train for Vrindachal. Vrindachal is the home of the Deva Raha Hans Baba Ashram. Hans Baba is one of those yogis who moves around constantly. I had found out through one of his devotees in Delhi that he was in Vrindachal. This did not mean he would be there when I arrived, however. On the same sort of information, I had once traveled for two days by car, traveling on rough roads, deep into the interior of Gujarat, looking for him, only to find that he had left the day before I arrived. Hoping for better luck this time, I settled into my berth in the sleeper compartment and let the train rock me to sleep.

The approach to Hans Baba's ashram was very primitive. The red-dirt road had deep ruts. In the US, such roads are only recommended for 4-wheel drive vehicles. I had taken an auto-rickshaw, which is a rickety three-wheeled scooter with a small passenger compartment in the back. About halfway down the dirt road to the ashram, the auto-rickshaw got stuck, so I abandoned ship, put my small bag on my shoulder, paid the driver and walked the remaining mile to the ashram.

When Westerners think of India, they usually think of huge cities with dense crowds. That is the part of India I try to avoid. Most of India, however, is actually rural, and there are plenty of places that are very isolated and quiet. Hans Baba's ashram is in one of these places. Located several miles outside of the pilgrimage town of Vrindachal, it is set against a beautiful background of the most peaceful and isolated farmland. His ashram at that time was only beginning to be constructed, so I knew there would be no phones, toilets, and possibly no place for me to sleep. Nonetheless, as I walked along that dirt road, listening to the birds and enjoying the peace and tranquility of the farmland, I felt a wonderful sense of exhilaration.

As I entered the compound I could see Hans Baba's manch (hut on stilts) in the center. To the side was a temple that was being constructed. Men and women workers were carrying bricks on their heads and chatting quietly to each other as they worked. Hans Baba was inside his hut when I arrived, so I sat on the ground cross-legged below his deck waiting. After about an hour, he emerged, with bright eyes, long, gray, matted hair, and a bushy gray beard. His face emanated a luster, giving him a youthful, playful look. We spoke in Hindi. He said, "Hello child, you have come."

I reminded him of our meeting the previous year in Delhi. He said he remembered me and then began to chant loudly. I had experienced his chanting in my past meeting with Hans Baba. It is common for him to sit for hours singing a spontaneous song to God. He makes up the words as he goes, arranging the song to a simple melody comprised of just three or four notes. But he is very rhythmic, and his songs have very intricate and complex rhythms. I have often thought that with his long hair, beard and sense of rhythm, he would have made a great rock-n-roll drummer. Anyway, as he chanted he beckoned for me to come and stand under his foot, which he dangled over his porch. I did this and he rested his foot on my head and gave me shaktipat, channeling spiritual energy into my head. I listened to the words of his song and felt the energy run from the top of my head down to my toes. "I . . . I . . . I . . . I . . . am . . . am . . . am . . . am . . . in . . . in . . . in . . . in . . . you . . . you . . . you . . . you," he chanted rhythmically in Hindi. After about ten minutes of this the words suddenly changed. "I . . . I . . . I . . . I . . . am . . . am . . . am . . . am . . . giving . . . giving . . . giving . . . giving . . . you . . . you . . . you . . . you . . . Jyotish Vidya . . . Jyotish Vidya. . . ."

'Interesting,' I thought. I didn't know what it meant, but I didn't care because I was completely enjoying the shaktipat.

I ended up spending about four days at Hans Baba's ashram. He let me stay in an open-air hut with his assistant. I slept on a board and used my daypack for a pillow. I had brought a thin cotton cloth to use as a blanket and to cover my head at night to protect myself from mosquitoes. During the day, I purified water, using a water pump I had brought with me. There was no toilet, and no bathing facilities at the ashram. Being an avid backpacker and camper, however, I found all of this very familiar and adjusted to the accommodations quickly. It also reminded me of my days with my own guru, when sleeping in a car, on the floor, or on the roof of a temple was just part of "the training," as Gandhiji used to put it.

For some reason the days I picked for my visit to Hans Baba, were days when no one else was at the ashram. As a result, Hans Baba spent most of his time giving me shaktipat. After several hours of this I started to get a little restless. Once, in between shaktipat sessions, I was feeling like I needed a break, so I tried to sneak out for a walk. Hans Baba saw me walking away and shouted to me in Hindi, "Where are you going? Come back here!" He had caught me, and he laughed playfully as he began the shaktipat treatment all over again.

When I finally left him, my batteries were charged up, to say the least. I also noticed that my interest in astrology had increased. For about fifteen years previous to this visit I had been a practicing astrologer, with a completely packed schedule of clients. Although I am always interested in astrology, I was not doing very much "extra credit" studying of astrology outside of the charts I did for clients. After that visit, however, I noticed I was naturally much more absorbed in studying astrology. I also noticed a marked improvement in readings I gave to clients.

I returned to Delhi feeling totally energized. My first order of business was to visit Mr. Santhanam. Before calling him to set up the visit, however, I went to visit Mr. Sagar, a book publisher in Delhi. For astrologers visiting Delhi, no trip is complete without a visit to Sagar's little office in Janpath. He always has the latest translations of classics, as well as new books on astrology. He also knows most of the astrologers in Delhi and usually knows what each astrologer is up to. As I sat there in his shop going through new publications and assembling a pile of books to purchase, Sagar asked, "So, where will you go after this?"

I said, "I am going to call Mr. Santhanam to set up a visit."

Mr. Sagar's voice took on a serious tone, "I am sorry to tell you that Mr. Santhanam died in Varanasi just a few days ago."

"You're kidding!" I said. "What happened?"

Mr. Sagar then told me that he was not sure of the details, but that Santhanam had dropped dead in Varanasi. He said that he had talked to a neighbor of Mr. Santhanam's who told the following story.

The neighbor had come to see Mr. Santhanam the previous week (about the time that I had visited him) and asked him to do a reading. Mr. Santhanam refused. The neighbor pleaded with him, telling him that he was going through serious problems in his life and that he was desperate and needed to get Mr. Santhanam's advice. Mr. Santhanam again refused, telling him that he was about to go on a trip and could not do a reading. The man then begged Mr. Santhanam tearfully to give him the reading. Santhanam cut him off abruptly saying, "My dear sir, no matter how bad your chart is at the moment, it is nothing compared to mine!" He then left for Varanasi. A few days later he was dead.

Sagar said that Mr. Santhanam was having a yagya done in Varanasi in order to offset some very malefic planetary influences. He also reminded me that Varanasi is the place that all good Hindus visit when it is time to die. Apparently, Mr. Santhanam knew that his life could be ending.

I sat there in Sagar's office thinking about my visit with Mr. Santhanam. I suddenly understood his evasiveness as well as his inability to commit to our symposium plans. Whether he actually predicted his own death or not may remain a mystery. It is clear, however, that he knew that the period he was in was a critical one, and even knew the most critical week. This had allowed him to be prepared, and to end his life in a place that he revered. Ultimately, of course, astrologers can never be certain about the future. Even the best astrologer can only give his best-educated, intuitive guess about a future that only God knows for sure. Maybe this is why Mr. Santhanam left the possibility open for a visit to the United States. There is no question, however, that he was an accomplished astrologer, possibly one that had the ability to predict his own time of death down to the week. In any case, in analyzing his own chart, it is clear that he did not "have a fool for a client!"

Glossary

Aditi – mother of all the gods, primary mother goddess
Adhi Yoga – occurs when Jupiter, Mercury, and Venus are placed in the sixth, seventh, and eighth houses from the Moon in any order or combination
Agni – Hindu deity of fire
Amla Yoga – occurs when a benefic planet is placed in the tenth house from the Moon
Anapha Yoga – occurs when the Moon has planets (other than the Sun) placed in the twelfth house from itself
Anuradha – seventeenth Nakshatra
Aprarigrah – principle of non-attachment
Aquarius – eleventh sign of the zodiac
Ardra – sixth Nakshatra
Aries – first sign of the zodiac
Arishta Yogas – combinations that contribute to ill health
Arudha Lagna – astrological sign used as the Ascendant for the question chart
Ascendant – rising sign or first house, also called lagna
Ashlesha – ninth Nakshatra
Ashtamsha Chart – divisional chart that reveals upheavals, changes, accidents, surgeries, and even details regarding the person's death
Ashwini – first Nakshatra
Atmakaraka – planet with the highest degree in the natal chart
Avayogi – nakshatra ruler of the constellation occupied by the avayoga point that promotes expenditure, financial losses, or poverty
Ayudha Drekkanas – drekkanas that contain weapons as part of their image
Ayurveda – the Vedic medical system, used with Vedic astrology

Balarishta Yoga – classical combination yoga for early death
Bhadra Yoga – the Mahapurusha Yoga for Mercury
Bhakti Yoga – the path of devotion
Bharani – second Nakshatra
Bhukti – the sub-period in a major planetary period or dasha, and each bhukti is ruled by one of the nine planets
Brahma – the Vedic god of creation; part of the Hindu Trinity

Brihaspati – Jupiter

Cancer – fourth sign of the zodiac
Capricorn – tenth sign of the zodiac
Chaamara Yoga – (two types) 1. lagna lord is exalted and occupies a Kendra and is also aspected by Jupiter 2. two benefic planets are in a conjunction in the lagna, the seventh house, the ninth house, or the tenth house
Chandala – outcast
Chandradhi Yoga – when Adhi Yoga occurs from the Moon
Chandra Mangala Yoga – Mars in a conjunction with the Moon
Chaturtamsha Chart – divisional chart for information about the residence, as well as general happiness and well-being
Chatushpad Drekkanas – drekkanas in which animals appear as part of the image
Chitra – fourteenth Nakshatra
Combustion – planet closely conjunct the Sun
Constellations – a grouping of stars; another term for Nakshatras

Darshan – uplifting, radiant spiritual energy or blessing from being in the presence of an enlightened being or saint
Dashas – major planetary periods
Dashamsha Chart – divisional chart used for information about the career, hobbies, projects, and other ambitious pursuits
Debilitation – the weakest sign placement for a planet
Dhana Yogas – yogas or combinations that produce wealth or financial increase
Dharma – law, duty, or purpose; one of the four goals or aims of life
Dig Bala – directional strength of a planet; used in Shadbala
Divisional Charts – vargas, or special charts designed to reveal details about specific domains of life
Doshas – three bodily humors described in Ayurveda – vata (wind), pitta (bile), and Kapha (phlegm)
Drekkanas – one third of a sign
Drekkana Chart – divisional chart used to reveal details about siblings, and also used in medical astrology for insights into health problems
Duplicate Yogi – planetary ruler of the sign of the yoga point that promotes prosperity
Durga – form of the Divine Mother, female deity associated with the Moon and Rahu
Durudhara Yoga – occurs when the Moon has planets (other than the Sun) placed in both the second and twelfth houses from itself

Glossary

Dusthana – the challenging 6, 8, or 12 houses of the horoscope

Dwadashamsha Chart – divisional chart that gives information concerning the parents

Ekadashamsha Chart – divisional chart used to give information on financial matters, details on how we manifest what we desire, also used to predict cures in the case of health problems, and related to pets and animals in general with special emphasis on the pet's health

Ephemeris – reference book that lists the motions of the planets

Even Sign – signs 2, 4, 6, 8, 10, or 12

Exaltation – the best sign placement for a planet

Gaja Kesari Yoga – combination formed when Jupiter is placed in an angle (houses 1,4,7, and 10) from the Moon

Ganesha – elephant-headed god who removes obstacles; related to Jupiter

Garuda – half-bird/half-man ridden by Vishnu

Guru – Jupiter; or a spiritual guide

Guru Chandala Yoga – Jupiter in a conjunction with Ketu

Gyana Yoga – the path of the intellect

Hamsa Yoga – the Mahapurusha Yoga for Jupiter

Hasta – thirteenth Nakshatra

Hora Chart – divisional chart used for financial matters

Houses – twelve divisions of the zodiac

Indra – king of the gods, ruler of the heavens

Indu Lagna – important lagna that is used specifically to determine profits and losses, a focal point for financial matters

Ishta Devata – one's personal deity

Japa Yoga – the chanting of mantras

Jyeshtha – eighteenth Nakshatra

Jyotish – Vedic astrology, the science of light

Kaahla Yoga – (two types) 1. Fourth house lord and ninth house lord are in mutual kendras, and the lagna lord is strong 2. Fourth house lord is exalted or in its own house, conjunct, or aspected by the tenth house lord

Kagha Drekkanas – drekkanas in which birds appear as part of the image

Kala Sarpa Yoga – a combination in which all planets are hemmed in

between the lunar nodes Rahu and Ketu
Kali – dark form of the goddess; related to Saturn
Kapha – water dosha of Ayurveda
Karaka – significator
Karma Yoga – the path of action and service
Kartari Yoga – occurs when a planet is placed in both the twelfth house and the second house from the lagna
Karttikeya – war god, son of Shiva; related to Mars
Kemadruma Yoga – occurs when the Moon has no planets in the sign previous and after its placement, as well as no planets in a kendra to the lagna or Moon, and the Moon is not conjunct or aspected by a benefic planet
Kendra – angles of the horoscope
Kendra Houses – houses 1, 5, & 9
Ketu – south node of the Moon, considered a planet in Vedic astrology
Krittika – third Nakshatra

Labhamsha Chart – another name for the Ekadashamsha divisional chart, used for finances
Lagna – Ascendant or rising sign
Lagnadhi Yoga – when Adhi Yoga occurs from the Lagna or Ascendant
Lakshmi – Hindu goddess of prosperity and beauty; related to Venus
Lakshmi Yoga – combination occurs when lagna lord is very strong and the ninth lord is placed in a kendra, either in its own house, moolatrikona, or in exaltation
Leo – fifth sign of the zodiac
Libra – seventh sign of the zodiac
Lunar Yogas – combinations that involve the Moon

Maala Yoga – the seven planets each occupy one house in a wreath-like pattern, and the first planet can be in any house with the rest of the planets placed in consecutive houses from that house forward
Magha – tenth Nakshatra
Maha Bhagya Yoga – for a male, birth occurs in daytime and the lagna, Sun and Moon is in an odd sign; for a female, birth occurs at night and the lagna, Sun and Moon must be in an even sign
Maha Dasha – main planetary period
Mahamrityunjaya – the great mantra to Lord Shiva, often recited by devout Hindus for protection from disease and accidents
Mahapurusha Yoga – planetary combination that involves either Mercury, Venus, Mars, Jupiter or Saturn located in an angle house or its

exalted sign
Malavya Yoga – the Mahapurusha Yoga for Venus
Mantras – sacred sounds
Maraka Planets – rulers of houses 2 and 7 that can create death, provided the person has reached the appropriate phase of life
Moksha – liberation or spiritual freedom; one of the four goals or aims of life
Moolatrikona – portion of a sign in which a planet placed there is particularly strong
Moon – Chandra
Mrigashira – fifth Nakshatra
Muhurta – electional astrology; selecting an auspicious time to begin an undertaking
Mula – nineteenth Nakshatra

Nagas – deified serpents
Nakshatra – 27 lunar constellations, each a 13° 20" section
Natural Benefics – the planets Jupiter, Venus, Mercury, and a waxing Moon
Natural Malefics – the planets Saturn, Mars, Rahu, Ketu, and a waning Moon
Navamsha Chart – ninth divisional chart that gives information on life in general, and is used specifically for marriage as well as all types of relationships
Neecha Bhanga Raja Yoga – combination that cancels or reverses the debilitation of a planet
Nimitta – branch of Vedic astrology that works with omens

Odd Signs – signs 1, 3, 5, 7, 9, or 11
Omens – Nimitta

Panchamsha Chart – divisional chart used specifically to determine the style of the person's spiritual practices and rituals
Papa Kartari Yoga – combination formed by malefic planets hemming in the lagna
Parvata Yoga – (two types) 1. benefic planets occupy the kendras and the sixth and eighth houses are vacant or occupied by only benefic planets 2. lagna lord and the twelfth house lord are placed in mutual kendras and are aspected by a benefic planet
Parivartana Yoga – combination that occurs when two planets exchange signs
Parivritti Dwaya – method used to calculate the Hora chart popularized

by Iyer
Pisces – twelfth sign of the zodiac
Pitris – ancestral spirits; deities related to Magha Nakshatra
Pitta – fire dosha of Ayurveda
Prashna – horary astrology; creating a chart for the time a question is asked
Purnarvasu – seventh Nakshatra
Purva Ashadha – twentieth Nakshatra
Purva Bhadrapada – twenty-fifth Nakshatra
Purva Phalguni – eleventh Nakshatra
Pushan – deity of Revati nakshatra who is the caretaker of the animals and travelers
Pushya – eighth Nakshatra

Rahu – north node of the Moon, considered a planet in Vedic astrology
Raja Yoga – combination of planets that denotes a royal or kingly status
Rashi Chart – birth chart
Retrograde – the apparent backward movement of a planet, which gives a stronger dose of the planet's significations
Revati – twenty-seventh Nakshatra
Rohini – fourth Nakshatra
Ruchaka Yoga – the Mahapurusha Yoga for Mars
Rudra – fierce form of Shiva

Sagittarius – ninth sign of the zodiac
Saptamsha Chart – divisional chart used for information about children
Saraswati Yoga – Mercury, Jupiter, and Venus placed in kendras, trikonas, or the second house and Jupiter must be strong and in its own sign, a friendly sign, or exaltation sign
Sarpa Drekkanas – drekkanas in which serpents appear as part of the image
Scorpio – eighth sign of the zodiac
Seva – spiritual service
Shakata Yoga – combination occurs when Jupiter is in the sixth, eighth, or twelfth house from the Moon, and Jupiter is not placed in an angle of the chart
Shakti – energy or essence
Shaktipat – awakening of kundalini, energy transmission from an enlightened teacher

Shankha Yoga – (two types) 1. lords of the fifth and sixth houses are in mutual kendras and the lagna lord is strong 2. lagna lord and the tenth house lord occupy a movable sign, and the ninth house lord is in a position of strength

Shasha Yoga – the Mahapurusha Yoga for Saturn

Shashtamsha Chart – divisional chart used for information about the person's health

Shatabhisha – twenty-fourth Nakshatra

Shiva – the destroyer god; part of the Hindu trinity

Shodashamsha Chart – divisional chart used for detailed information about the person's vehicles

Shravana – twenty-second Nakshatra

Shrikanta Yoga – formed when the Sun, the Moon, and the lagna lord are placed in an angle or trine and in their own sign, exalted, or in a friendly sign

Shubha Kartari Yoga – combination formed by benefic planets hemming in the lagna

Shukra – Venus

Siddhamsha Chart – divisional chart for information on the person's education

Sunapha Yoga – occurs when the Moon has planets (other than the Sun) placed in the second house from itself

Swara – system of prediction based on which nostril is more clear at the time of asking the question

Swati – fifteenth Nakshatra

Tara – wife of Jupiter (Brihaspati)

Taurus – second sign of the zodiac

Trimshamsha Chart – divisional chart used to reveal difficulties in life, as well as insights about the person's character

Upachaya Houses – growing houses 3, 6, 10, & 11

Upasana – worship or devotion

Uttara Ashadha – twenty-first Nakshatra

Uttara Bhadrapada – twenty-sixth Nakshatra

Uttara Phalguni – twelfth Nakshatra

Varahamihira – one of most respected ancient authors of Jyotish literature, wrote the *Brihat Jataka*

Vargas – divisional charts

Vargottama – the same sign position of a planet in the natal chart and the Navamsha chart

Varshaphal – annual solar return chart
Varuna – god of the waters
Vasumat Yoga – occurs when benefic planets (Jupiter, Venus, and Mercury) occupy the upachaya houses (3, 6, 10, and 11) from the Moon
Vata – air dosha of Ayurveda
Vayu – deified wind, related to Swati Nakshatra
Vedic Astrology – Jyotish
Vidya – spiritual science
Vimshamsha Chart – main divisional chart for spirituality and gives details related to the Ishta Devata and the blessings that come from worshipping a deity
Vimshottari Dasha – most popular dasha system used in India, which is a planetary period system that takes 120 years to complete
Vishakha – sixteenth Nakshatra
Vishnu – the preserver of the universe; part of the Hindu trinity

Yagya – Vedic ceremony used as a remedy to improve certain conditions
Yama – god of death; related to Bharani Nakshatra
Yoga Point – a generally beneficial point in the horoscope that can be used for effectively predicting positive events, including financial gain or prosperity
Yogakaraka – planet that rules both an angle and a trine house at the same time; the planet of power for six of the Ascendants
Yoga – means "union" and refers to the joining or union of two planets which can occur in different ways
Yogi – planetary ruler of the nakshatra of the yoga point that promotes prosperity

Bibliography
Path of Light, Volumes I & II

CLASSICAL TEXTS

Burgess, Rev. Ebenezer. (trans.) *Surya Siddhanta* (Delhi, India: Motilal Banarsidass 1997)

Chidbhavananda, Swami (commentator). *The Bhagavad Gita* (Tirupparaitturai, Tiruchirappalli District, Tamil Nadu, India: Sri Ramakrishna Tapovanam, Secretary 1992)

Dhundiraj, Pt. *Jatakabharnam* Girish Chand Sharma (trans.) (New Delhi, India: Sagar Publications 1998)

Dikshita, Vaidyanatha. *Jataka Parijat, Volumes 1 - 3* V. Subramanya Sastri (trans.) (New Delhi, India: Ranjan Publications 1932)

Griffith, Ralph T. (trans.) *Rig Veda* (Delhi, India: Motilal Banarsidass 1992)

Kalidasa. *Uttara Kalamrita* P. S. Sastri (trans.) (New Delhi, India: Ranjan Publications 1994)

Mahadeva. *Jataka Tatva* S. S. Sareen (trans.) (New Delhi, India: Sagar Publications 1987)

Mantreswara. *Phala Deepika* S. S. Sareen (trans.) (New Delhi, India: Sagar Publications 1992)

Mukhopadhyaya, Satyamsu Mohan, et al. (trans.) *Vamana Purana* Anand Swarup Gupta (ed.) (Varanasi, India: All India Kashiraj Trust 1968)

Parasara, Maharishi. *Brihat Parasara Hora Sastra Volumes I & II* Girish Chand Sharma (trans.) (New Delhi, India: Sagar Publications 1995)

Parasara, Maharishi. *Brihat Parasara Hora Sastra, Volumes I & II* R. Santhanam (trans.) (New Delhi, India: Ranjan Publications, 1992)

Pargiter, F.E. (trans.) *Markandeya Purana* (Asiatic Society of Bengal & Shamsher Bahadur Singh 1995)

Raja, Punja. *Sambhu Hora Prakasha* R. Santhanam (trans.) (Delhi, India: R. Santhanam Associates 1995)

Rao, B. Suryanarain. *Sri Sarwarthachintamani* (Delhi, India: Motilal Banarsidass 1996)

Santhanam, R. (trans.) *Hora Ratna* (Delhi, India: R. Santhanam Associates 1995)

Sareen, S.S. (trans.) *Chamatkar Chintamani of Bhatt Narayana* (New Delhi, India: Sagar Publications, 1986)

Sattar, Arshia (trans.) *The Ramayana Valmiki* (Bombay, India: Penguin

Books 1996)

Satyacharya, Sage. *Satya Jatakam* (New Delhi, India: Ranjan Publications 1979)

Shastri, P.S. (trans.) *Brihat Jataka* (New Delhi, India: Ranjan Publications 1996)

Subramaniam, Kamala (trans.) *Mahabharata* (Bombay, India: Bharatiya Vidya Bhavan 1995)

Tagare, Ganesh Vasudeo (trans.) *Ancient Indian Tradition and Mythology (Volumes 1 - 62 of The Puranas)* (Delhi, India: Motilal Banarsidass 1970)

Bhagavata Purana, Part 2, Volume 8
Bhagavata Purana, Part 3, Volume 9
Bhagavata Purana, Part 4, Volume 10
Bhagavata Purana Part 4, Volume 11

Brahmanda Purana, Part 1, Volume 22
Brahmanda Purana, Part 2, Volume 23

Brahma Purana, Part 1, Volume 33

Siva Purana, Part 2, Volume 2
Siva Purana, Part 4, Volume 4

Agni Purana, Part 2, Volume 28
Agni Purana, Part 3, Volume 29

Kurma Purana, Part 2, Volume 20
Kurma Purana, Part 2, Volume 21

Narada Purana, Part 3, Volume 17
Narada Purana, Part 4, Volume 18

Skanda Purana, Part 1, Volume 49
Skanda Purana, Part 2, Volume 50
Skanda Purana, Part 3, Volume 51
Skanda Purana, Part 7, Volume 55
Skanda Purana, Part 11, Volume 59
Skanda Purana, Part 12, Volume 60

Padma Purana Part 7, Volume 45
Padma Purana, Part 9, Volume 47
Padma Purana, Part 10, Volume 48

Varaha Purana, Part 1, Volume 31
Varaha Purana, Part 2, Volume 32

Taluqdar of Oudh, A. (trans.) *The Matsya Puranam* (Delhi, India: Oriental Books Reprint Corp. 1980)

Varahamihira. *Brihat Jataka* B. Suryanarain Rao (trans.) (Delhi, India: Motilal Banarsidass 1996)

Varahamihira. *Brihat Jataka* Swami Vijnanananda (trans.) (Delhi, India: Oriental Books Reprint Corp. 1979)

Varma, Kalyana. *Saravali, Volumes 1 & 2* (New Delhi, India: Ranjan Publications 1996)

Vijnanananda, Swami (trans.) *Srimad Devi Bhagavatam* (India: Munshiram Manoharlal 1996)

CONTEMPORARY TEXTS

Bhat, M. Ramakrishna. *Fundamentals of Astrology* (Delhi, India: Motilal Banarsidass 1979)

Braha, James. *Ancient Hindu Astrology for the Modern Western Astrologer* (N. Miami, Florida: Hermetician Press, 1986)

Charak, Dr. K.S. *Elements of Vedic Astrology, Volumes 1 & 2* (New Delhi, India: Vision Wordtronic 1995)

Charak, Dr. K.S. *Essentials of Medical Astrology* (New Delhi, India: Vision Wordtronic 1994)

Danielou, Alain. *The Myths and Gods of India* (Rochester, Vermont: Inner Traditions 1991)

deFouw, Hart, and Robert Svoboda. *Light on Life* (London, England: Penguin Arkana, 1996)

Dowson, John. *A Classical Dictionary of Hindu Mythology* (London, England: Routledge & Kegan Paul Ltd. 1979)

Feuerstein, Georg, Subhash Kak, and David Frawley. *In Search of the Cradle of Civilization* (Madras, India: Quest Books 1995)

Frawley, David. *The Astrology of the Seers* (Salt Lake City, Utah: Passage Press 1990)

Gerson, Scott. *Ayurveda, The Ancient Indian Healing Art* (Rockport, MA: Element Books Limited 1997)

Gupta, Anima Sen. *Classical Samkhya: A Critical Study* (Delhi, India: Munishiriam Monoharlal Publishers Pvt. Ltd. 1982)

Gupta, Anima Sen. *The Evolution of the Samkhya School of Thought* (Delhi, India: Munishiriam Monoharlal Publishers Pvt. Ltd. 1986)

Hillebrandt, Alfred. *Vedic Mythology* (Delhi, India: Motilal Banarsidass 1981)

Iyer, H. R. Seshadri. *New Techniques of Prediction* (Bangalore, India: Janapriya Prakashana 1963)

O'Flaherty, Wendy Doniger. *Karma and Rebirth in Classical Indian Traditions* (Delhi, India: Motilal Banarsidass 1990)

Ojha, Pandit Gopesh Kumar. *Predictive Astrology of the Hindus* (Delhi,

India: D.B. Taraporevala and Sons 1990)

Rajaram, Navaratna S. and David Frawley. *Vedic Aryans and the Origins of Civilization* (New Delhi, India: Voice of India 2001)

Raman, B.V. *Graha and Bhava Balas* (Bangalore, India: P.N. Kamat 1979)

Raman, B.V. *How to Judge a Horoscope, Volumes 1 & 2* (Bangalore, India: P.N. Kamat 1980)

Raman, B.V. *A Manual of Hindu Astrology* (Bangalore, India: P.N. Kamat 1980)

Raman, B. V. (translator). *Prashna Marga, Volumes 1 & 2* (Delhi, India: Motilal Banarsidass 1994)

Rath, Sanjay. *The Crux of Vedic Astrology* (New Delhi, India: Sagar Publications 1998)

Rath, Sanjay. *Varga Chakra* (New Delhi, India: Sagar Publications 2002)

Reichenbach, Bruce R. *The Law of Karma* (Honolulu, Hawaii: University of Hawaii Press 1990)

Santhanam, R. *Practical Vedic Astrology* (Delhi, India: R. Santhanam Associates 1997)

Svoboda, Robert. *The Greatness of Saturn* (Tulsa, Oklahoma: Sadhana Publications 1997)

Index

A

Adhi Yoga 30, 31, 254, 497, 498, 500
Aditi 200, 296, 414, 464, 497
Agni 284, 352, 423, 443, 462, 490, 497, 506
Amala Yoga 38
Anapha Yoga 31, 497
Animal drekkana 58, 62, 66, 69-71, 77, 80, 81, 370, 371, 372
Anuradha 148, 349, 415, 442, 497
Aparigraha 418
Aquarius 28, 87-89, 146, 155, 171, 176, 180, 183, 196, 225, 238, 268, 347, 348, 350, 352, 359, 362, 373, 386, 441, 452, 461, 497
Ardra 121, 148, 270, 284, 360, 361, 370, 371, 373, 414, 489, 497
Aries 44, 57-59, 111, 121, 145, 146, 171, 173, 174, 180, 181, 196, 199, 201, 226, 227, 235, 271, 287, 343, 345, 358, 359, 360, 370, 380, 385, 433, 455, 458, 476, 478, 480-483, 497
Arishta Yogas 27, 497
Arudha lagna 111, 497
Ascendant 13, 23, 26-28, 47-50, 52, 55, 104, 105, 111-113, 121, 127, 142, 145, 150, 152, 153, 162, 164, 170, 172, 174, 178-183, 187, 198, 199, 201, 215, 218-220, 222, 225, 246, 247-249, 252, 255, 260, 261, 263, 265, 284, 287, 300, 307, 322, 331, 334, 335, 341, 350, 364, 370, 380, 385, 388, 397, 402, 422, 432, 434, 448, 452, 453, 454, 461, 462, 467, 471, 473, 478, 497, 500
Ashlesha 67, 68, 78, 79, 92, 93, 148, 162, 351, 352, 360, 361, 370, 415, 458, 469, 490, 491, 497
Ashtakavarga 54
Ashtamsha Chart 45, 53, 497
Ashwini 102, 148, 173, 179, 190, 191, 195, 268, 269, 271, 343, 345, 360, 370, 414, 454, 455, 456, 459, 466, 470, 473, 477, 478, 480, 482, 483, 484, 497
Ashwini Kumaras 268, 271, 370, 454, 455, 456, 466, 470, 473, 480
Avayogi 211, 212, 497
Ayudha Drekkanas 93, 94, 497
Ayurveda 149, 283, 497, 498, 500, 502, 504, 507
Ayurvedic 149, 150, 209

B

Baba, Beedi 408-411
Baba, Hans 167, 494, 495
Balarishta Yoga 121, 270, 296, 497
Benefics 18, 27, 38, 39, 50, 102, 105, 114, 152, 180, 181, 182, 216, 249, 251, 256, 281, 292, 301, 338, 367, 389, 390, 394, 396, 487, 501
Betz Ephemeris 1940-2040 113
Bhadra Yoga 32, 34, 173, 183, 385, 497
Bhagavad Gita 417, 505
Bhakti Yoga 413, 419, 497
Bharani 121, 148, 173, 269, 270, 297, 376, 414, 456, 457, 482, 497, 504
Bird drekkana 64, 69, 76, 87, 341, 370, 377, 378, 470
Brahma 260, 264, 347, 352, 423, 497, 506
Brighu 205
Brihaspati 108, 195, 198, 388, 434, 498, 503
Brihat Jataka 56, 96, 503, 506, 507
Brihat Samhita 210
Buddhism 254, 414

C

Cancer 13, 51, 66-68, 102, 104, 107-109, 145, 161, 171, 175, 178-180, 195, 197, 198, 199, 201, 202, 225, 236, 240, 345, 351, 358-361, 363, 370, 372, 374, 378, 385, 400, 432, 469, 472, 474, 477, 478, 498

Capricorn 21, 28, 37, 49, 51, 84-86, 109, 145, 163, 164, 171, 176, 180-183, 200, 201, 221, 238, 260, 266, 268, 272, 286, 287, 359, 362, 386, 451, 465, 472, 482-484, 498
Chaamara Yoga 39, 498
Chandala 136, 200, 202, 283, 284, 498, 499
Chandra Adhi Yoga 30
Chandra Mangala Yoga 40, 498
Chaturtamsha Chart 45, 49, 51, 52, 321, 322, 323, 324, 327, 448, 453, 472, 473, 476, 484, 498
Chatushpad Drekkanas 94, 498
Chitra 148, 179, 265, 312, 360, 361, 402, 415, 461, 466, 498
Combust 52, 239, 289
Constellation 121, 162, 173, 191, 192, 199, 211, 221, 254, 267-271, 284, 296, 312, 327, 341, 347, 348, 352, 363, 371, 400, 402, 442, 443, 450, 451, 453-459, 462-464, 469, 475, 477, 482, 483, 485, 488, 490, 491, 497
Converging Influence 24

D

Darshan 142, 143, 144, 498
Dasha 13, 22, 49, 94, 98-103, 106-108, 115, 118, 162-164, 184, 185, 191, 192, 196, 197-204, 258, 260, 264-272, 286, 290-292, 294, 296, 297, 303, 307, 314, 334, 337-339, 341-345, 347-352, 364, 371-378, 385, 389, 396-398, 405-407, 418, 429, 433, 434, 442, 448-478, 480-485, 487-491, 497, 500, 504
Dashamsha Chart 22, 45, 47-51, 174, 184-188, 191, 192, 196, 197-203, 252, 389, 442, 465, 478, 498
Dashas 13, 35, 98-100, 106, 145, 160, 184, 190, 194, 213, 257, 260, 263, 296, 307, 341, 347, 369, 396, 448, 498
Debilitated 28, 30, 35, 36, 37, 47, 48, 51, 101, 106-109, 151, 156, 160, 163, 185, 186, 188, 202, 226, 236, 248, 265, 266, 286, 296, 312, 313, 316, 345, 367, 370, 372, 375, 376, 378, 386, 387, 396, 400, 449-451, 472, 477, 488
Debilitation 34-37, 51, 52, 106, 108, 115, 188, 222, 236, 237, 248, 319, 407, 472, 478, 484, 498, 501
Dhana Yogas 26, 27, 219, 220, 222, 223, 250, 301, 396, 498
Dhanishtha 148, 183, 362, 416, 453-455, 483, 485
Dharma 33, 76, 176, 264, 413, 414, 416, 417, 432, 435, 457, 461, 465, 498
Divisional Charts 11, 18, 22, 25, 44, 47, 48, 103, 200, 222, 223, 225, 226, 250, 252, 270, 289, 300, 301, 314, 327, 335, 344, 367, 374, 376, 388, 389, 425, 426, 427, 448, 467, 472, 485, 498, 503
Domains of Life 13, 17, 18, 22, 44, 53, 140, 162, 251, 383, 498
Doshas 149, 498
Drekkana 18, 22, 44, 56-96, 101, 103, 108, 109, 190, 196, 198, 200, 312-319, 341, 344, 359-364, 367, 370-372, 377, 378, 389, 406, 424, 446, 461, 463, 465, 467, 468, 470-474, 480-484, 487, 498
Drekkana Chart 44, 313-317, 319, 367, 498
Drekkana Symbolism 18, 22, 344
Duplicate Yogi 211, 212, 216, 219, 220, 226, 498
Durga 422-424, 498
Durudhara Yoga 31, 498
Dusthana 26-30, 41, 47, 49, 104, 110, 115, 152, 154, 157, 160, 186, 202, 203, 212, 219, 222, 282, 343, 374, 376, 378, 389, 405, 450, 463, 477, 488, 499
Dusthanas 27, 49, 101, 104, 115, 151, 219, 223, 282, 393, 394
Dwadashamsha Chart 46, 103, 300, 301, 302-305, 307, 321, 448, 449, 488, 499

E

Eighth House 18, 19, 27, 30, 37, 50, 52, 53, 101, 107, 110, 115, 121, 146, 150, 154-157, 160, 162, 164, 167,

Index

175, 179-181, 186, 187, 190, 191, 195-197, 199, 200, 202, 203, 213-215, 220, 225, 226, 251, 252, 255, 264, 265, 270-272, 290, 292, 293, 296, 304, 307, 316, 322, 323, 324, 336, 338, 343-345, 347, 349, 351, 352, 366, 372-374, 376, 378, 380, 382, 390, 396, 397, 406, 407, 413, 419, 426, 429, 435, 442, 448, 449, 455, 459, 465, 466, 468, 471, 472, 476-79, 481, 484, 485, 487-491

Ekadashamsha Chart 46, 52, 222, 223, 225-227, 252, 366, 374-376, 378, 407, 499

Eleventh House 19, 21, 23, 120, 146, 151-154, 156, 157, 162, 163, 176, 180, 183, 188, 198, 199, 201, 204, 211-214, 220, 221, 222, 225, 256, 258, 263, 267-269, 287, 293, 301, 305, 307, 311-313, 316, 317, 322, 325, 337, 339, 342, 349, 364, 366, 370, 371, 373, 375, 377, 384, 390, 394, 395, 398, 405, 406, 419, 442, 459, 470, 473, 474, 475, 478, 485

Ephemeris 113, 125, 230, 380, 499

Essentials of Medical Astrology 151, 507

Even Sign 40, 499, 500

Exaltation 33, 40, 41, 195, 196, 222, 246, 478, 499, 500, 502

F

Fifth House 12, 16, 19, 21, 28, 50, 94, 113, 116, 120, 121, 146, 155, 175, 178-181, 187, 188, 190, 191, 195, 197, 198, 203, 211, 213-215, 221, 222, 225, 252, 255, 260, 264, 266, 267-269, 281-284, 286, 287-290, 292-294, 296, 304, 311, 313, 315, 323, 324, 327, 336, 338, 365, 373, 383, 384, 387-390, 397, 400, 405, 407, 413, 416, 417, 418, 422, 426, 429, 433, 435, 442, 456, 460, 461, 463, 465-468, 470, 473-476, 480, 485, 490

First House 19, 26-28, 47, 50, 53, 102, 104, 106, 112, 127, 146, 150, 151, 152, 154, 157, 160, 162, 164, 172, 174, 178, 181, 183, 184, 186, 192, 196, 197, 201, 212, 215, 219, 240, 246, 248, 249, 251, 252, 254-258, 286, 288, 291, 303, 312-314, 322, 323, 335-337, 342, 343, 365, 376, 396, 409, 416-418, 433, 452, 459, 462, 464, 478, 482, 483, 488, 497

Fourth House 17, 19, 21, 28, 37, 39, 40, 48, 49, 51, 94, 100, 101, 104, 107, 114, 118, 119, 128, 146, 154, 162, 163, 175, 178-180, 182, 186, 196, 197-199, 213, 214, 221, 225, 227, 251, 252, 260, 290, 291, 300-303, 307, 308, 315, 319, 321-324, 327, 331, 333-338, 341-345, 347-352, 365, 374, 383, 384, 388, 390-392, 397, 400, 402, 405-407, 418, 434, 442, 448, 449, 453, 459, 467, 469-474, 476, 477, 479, 483, 499

Frawley, Dr. David 7, 493, 507, 508

G

Gaja Kesari Yoga 28, 29, 103, 179, 181, 182, 183, 191, 192, 198, 203, 204, 302, 394, 430, 433, 456, 487, 499

Gandhiji 42, 43, 123-126, 408, 410, 495

Ganesh 62, 66, 382, 506

Ganesha 344, 423-425, 451, 499

Garuda 64, 359, 499

Gemini 35, 63, 64, 65, 114, 118, 120, 121, 128, 142, 145, 164, 171, 174, 179-181, 183, 200, 201, 234, 236, 241, 261, 265, 270, 342, 358, 359, 361, 371, 377, 385, 465, 488

Guru 83, 136, 200, 202, 229, 283, 388, 384, 195, 499, 408, 413, 419, 421, 429, 430, 434, 480, 484, 485, 495, 523

Guru Chandala Yoga 136, 200, 202, 283, 499

Gyana Yoga 413, 499

H

Hamsa Yoga 33, 34, 173, 195, 198, 430, 442, 499

Hasta 148, 190, 405, 406, 407, 415, 434, 499

Hemmed in 18, 38, 102, 297, 345, 378,

450, 452, 457, 499
Hindu Gods 422
Hora Chart 44, 222, 225, 226, 252, 407, 499, 501
House Rulers 17, 101, 113, 288
Houses 11, 13, 15-18, 21-23, 26-28, 30, 31, 35, 38-41, 47, 49, 101, 102, 110, 112-117, 128, 146, 151, 153, 157, 164, 172, 174, 180-183, 185, 186, 200, 207, 211-220, 222, 240, 246, 247, 249, 250-252, 254, 255, 257, 258, 266, 270, 282, 287-292, 300-303, 311-314, 321, 322, 323, 327, 334-337, 353, 364, 365, 373, 380, 383, 384, 388-390, 395, 396, 400, 402, 405, 407, 412, 416-418, 420, 424-427, 457, 458, 459, 466, 476, 481, 497, 498-501, 503, 504

I

Indra 341, 344, 423, 453, 454, 480, 499
Indu Lagna 219-221, 225, 226, 499
Ishta Devata 46, 422, 424, 499, 504

J

Jain 309
Jupiter 19, 21, 23, 26-30, 32, 33, 37, 38, 39, 41, 48, 49, 51, 52, 62, 99, 102-104, 112-120, 124, 126, 128, 129, 131, 132, 134-137, 139, 147, 149, 152, 153, 155, 156, 167, 172, 173, 178-183, 186, 188, 192, 194-198, 200-204, 210, 212-223, 225, 226, 241, 250, 254, 258, 260, 261, 264-268, 271, 272, 281-284, 286, 289, 290, 294, 296, 297, 302, 307, 319, 327, 335, 341-344, 347-352, 362-364, 370, 372, 373-378, 380, 386-388, 391-394, 406, 407, 413, 421, 423-427, 429, 430, 433, 435, 442, 452, 456-460, 468-480, 483, 484, 485, 487, 488, 497-504
Jyeshtha 148, 270, 341, 344, 415, 453, 455, 466, 491, 499
Jyotish 14, 15, 25, 42, 55, 96, 98, 99, 110, 114, 127, 166, 229, 230, 298, 337, 358, 408, 412, 418, 492, 495, 499, 503, 504, 519
Jyotishi 408

K

Kaahala Yoga 39
Kagha Drekkanas 94, 499
Kala Sarpa Yoga 297, 499
Kali 423, 500
Kapha 62, 66, 149, 498, 500
Karaka 18-21, 210, 384, 386, 500
Karma 13, 45, 169, 211, 213, 260, 310, 331, 395, 414, 465, 467, 500, 507, 508
Karma Yoga 414, 500
Kartari Yoga 38, 102, 152, 164, 308, 327, 345, 378, 449, 450, 462, 463, 500, 501, 503
Kartikeya 423, 443
Kemadruma Yoga 31, 500
Kendras 38, 39, 41, 101, 104, 499, 501-503
Ketu 19, 99, 102, 103, 106-109, 115, 129, 130, 131, 133-140, 147, 149, 157, 160, 162-164, 172, 178-180, 182, 183, 191, 199-201, 216, 218, 219, 226, 227, 238, 244, 245, 250, 254, 263, 265, 266, 270-272, 283, 284, 286, 287, 297, 301, 336, 350-352, 362-364, 372, 388, 391, 392, 405-407, 414, 422, 423, 425-427, 429, 436, 442, 448, 449, 451, 458, 465, 468, 469, 471, 472, 476, 481, 485, 487-491, 499-501
Krishna 99, 263, 271, 417, 420, 423, 424
Krittika 99, 148, 162, 260, 284, 349, 352, 414, 443, 462, 490, 500
Kundalini 93, 176, 413, 415, 416, 419, 421, 435, 484, 485, 502

L

Labhamsha Chart 222, 500
Lagna 21, 26-33, 35, 38, 39, 40, 47-50, 53, 94, 111, 113, 116, 118, 119, 151-153, 162, 163, 164, 167, 190, 195-199, 201, 202, 215, 216, 219-223, 225, 226, 234, 249, 251, 252, 254, 257, 258, 260, 263, 265-268, 270,

INDEX

287-290, 300, 307, 311, 313, 327, 334, 335, 342, 345, 347, 349, 350, 352, 364, 370, 371, 375, 380, 382, 389-395, 400, 426, 441, 442, 452, 463, 465, 467, 470, 473-475, 477, 482, 487, 490, 497-501, 503

Lakshmi 26, 40, 79, 423, 424, 500

Lakshmi Yoga 40, 500

Leo 23, 26, 69-71, 112, 128, 145, 170, 171, 175, 180, 181, 183, 197, 198, 236, 254, 271, 313, 350, 358, 359, 361, 363, 378, 381, 385, 413, 432, 433, 448, 450, 452, 471, 473, 474, 477, 500

Libra 17, 23, 28, 44, 53, 75-77, 101, 105, 116, 145, 151, 154, 164, 171, 175, 179-181, 183, 222, 237, 263, 265, 266, 312, 313, 327, 344, 349, 359, 361, 374, 375, 385, 454, 470, 471, 472, 473, 475, 476, 477, 485, 500

Longevity 19, 39, 146, 147, 155, 204, 270, 297, 492

Lunar Yogas 28, 500

M

Ma, Siddhi 141-143

Maala Yoga 40, 500

Magha 148, 198, 254, 319, 327, 378, 380, 388, 400, 415, 450, 463, 475, 500, 502

Maha Bhagya Yoga 40, 500

Mahabharata 57, 451, 506

Maha Dasha 99, 100, 103, 107, 108, 500

Mahamrityunjaya 229, 438, 500

Mahapurusha Yogas 31, 32, 34, 172

Maharaja, Teet 228, 229, 230

Malavaya Yoga 173, 178, 183, 246

Mantras 310, 413-415, 418, 422, 426, 429, 433, 467, 468, 499, 501

Mantra Siddhi 419

Maraka Planets 501

Mars 19-21, 26, 32, 37, 40, 59, 99, 100, 102, 105, 107, 118, 121, 128, 129, 132, 133, 135-137, 139, 147, 149, 151, 154, 155, 157, 160, 162-164, 172, 173, 179-181, 183, 185, 186, 188, 195-197, 199, 200, 201, 202, 204, 215-217, 219, 222, 225, 226, 240, 241, 248, 251, 260, 263, 264, 266, 268-272, 284, 286, 287, 296, 297, 302, 307, 308, 321, 322, 335, 342, 343, 347-352, 362-364, 370, 372, 374-378, 380, 382, 387, 391, 393, 400, 405-407, 413, 420, 423, 424, 432-434, 436, 441, 442, 448-452, 455, 456, 462, 468, 472, 473, 477-482, 484, 485, 487-491, 498, 500, 501, 502

Meditation 19, 141, 176, 229, 245, 254, 287, 325, 412, 413, 417-423, 429, 430, 433, 461-463, 465-468, 484, 485

Mercury 16, 17, 19, 30, 32, 35-38, 41, 43, 99, 102, 104, 106-108, 115, 118, 129, 131-135, 137, 139, 147, 149, 163, 167, 172, 173, 178, 179, 181-183, 190, 191, 195-197, 199, 200, 202, 203, 219, 221, 226, 241, 248, 254, 260, 264-266, 272, 297, 313, 331, 335, 343-345, 348, 349, 352, 362-364, 370, 371, 372, 374, 375, 380, 382, 384-388, 391, 405, 406, 413, 416, 421, 423, 424, 429, 430, 434, 435, 442, 449, 450, 467, 468, 474-476, 488, 489, 497, 500, 501, 502, 504

Moksha 19, 244, 414, 416, 417, 422, 430, 432-435, 467, 468, 501

Moolatrikona 40, 348, 461, 500, 501

Moon 19, 21, 28-35, 38, 40, 49, 50, 55, 94, 99, 102, 103, 109, 112-114, 119, 121, 127-133, 135, 137, 138, 147, 149, 150, 157, 162-164, 170, 172, 178-184, 190-192, 195, 196, 198-202, 204, 211, 215-219, 225-227, 234, 239, 240, 246, 254, 258, 260, 263, 265-272, 284, 286, 289, 290, 296, 300, 301, 302, 307, 321, 322, 327, 334, 335, 341, 342, 343, 345, 347, 349-354, 357, 362-364, 370, 372-377, 380, 381, 385, 387-394, 400, 405, 407, 413, 420, 422, 423, 424, 432-434, 441, 442, 448, 449, 454, 455, 456, 458-460, 465, 466, 468, 471, 473-478, 480-484, 487, 497-504

Mrigashira 148, 202, 204, 260, 264, 267, 268, 347, 352, 360, 361, 414, 442, 456, 457, 463, 501

Muhurtha 437, 438

Mula 102, 148, 179, 286, 296, 343, 415, 487, 501

Mythology 65, 101, 108, 173, 195, 199, 202, 343-345, 388, 413, 423, 438, 441, 450, 451, 453, 455-457, 459, 470, 480, 482, 490, 506, 507

N

Nagas 65, 67, 68, 78, 79, 92, 360, 490, 501

Nakshatra 18, 22, 23, 25, 34, 53, 65, 67, 68, 78, 79, 92, 93, 99, 101-103, 108, 119, 121, 127, 140, 147, 148, 151, 162-165, 172, 173, 190, 195, 196, 198-200, 202, 211, 212, 220, 258, 260, 263-265, 268-271, 284, 286, 296, 297, 312, 319, 327, 341, 343-345, 349, 351, 352, 364, 370, 371, 372, 373, 376, 377, 378, 388, 389, 400, 402, 405-407, 414, 416, 422, 429, 433-435, 441-443, 449, 450, 453-457, 459, 461-464, 466, 470, 473, 475, 478, 480, 482-485, 487, 489-491, 497-504

Nakshatras 7, 11, 22, 23, 56, 99, 102, 119, 147, 148, 150, 151, 179, 183, 216, 260, 284, 358, 360-362, 364, 365, 414, 498

Narasimha 62, 66, 80, 423

Natural Benefic 50, 105, 116, 152, 218, 241, 271, 373, 374, 377

Natural Malefic 105, 107, 108, 116, 147, 152-154, 162, 163, 178, 202, 203, 226, 301, 372, 374, 376, 388, 394, 406, 463, 477, 481

Navamsha 35, 44, 45, 48, 50, 53-55, 103, 182, 246, 249-255, 258-262, 264-270, 319, 367, 440, 442, 447, 456, 471, 472, 490, 501, 503

Navamsha Chart 35, 44, 45, 48, 50, 53, 55, 103, 246, 249-252, 254, 258, 260, 261, 264-270, 367, 442, 456, 471, 472, 490, 503

Navamsha in Astrology 55

Neecha Bhanga 34-37, 51, 52, 108, 188, 236, 237, 248, 249, 265, 286, 302, 319, 338, 387, 400, 407, 409, 432, 433, 434, 466, 472, 473, 476, 478, 479, 483, 484, 501

Neecha Bhanga Raja Yoga 34, 35, 36, 108, 265, 400, 478, 479, 501

Ninth House 19-21, 39, 51, 94, 104, 107, 114, 121, 146, 156, 157, 176, 178-181, 188, 195, 198, 200-202, 204, 211-214, 219, 221, 225, 251, 252, 255, 256, 260, 264, 267, 268, 272, 287-290, 293, 294, 296, 300, 301, 303, 305, 312, 316, 322, 324, 337, 338, 343, 366, 370, 371, 373, 374, 376, 380, 383, 384, 388-390, 392, 393, 396, 397, 407, 409, 413, 416, 417, 419, 432-435, 463, 467-469, 471, 474, 475, 480, 482-485, 487-489, 498, 499, 503

O

Odd sign 40, 500

Omenology 168

Omens 277, 309, 310, 320, 444, 501

P

Pakshi Drekkanas 344

Pancha Mahapurusha Yogas 31

Panchamsha Chart 45, 425, 426, 427, 429, 430, 433-435, 467, 485, 501

Papa Kartari Yoga 38, 102, 164, 308, 327, 345, 378, 449, 450, 462, 463, 501

Parivartana Yoga 28, 35, 240, 319, 400, 432, 487, 501

Parivritti Dwaya 501

Parvata Yoga 38, 501

Patel, Mr. C.S. 54

Path of Light, Volume I 14, 17-19, 23, 67, 68, 78, 79, 92, 93, 101, 102, 113, 114, 128, 151, 170, 174, 186, 216, 234, 235, 247, 249, 256, 260, 264, 282, 284, 290, 297, 311, 313, 314, 321, 345, 349, 351, 352, 392, 394, 396, 435, 441, 451, 454, 455, 457, 459, 463, 466, 473, 480, 490, 521

Phala Deepika 321, 363, 433, 505

Pisces 28, 36, 44, 90, 91, 92, 146, 171,

176, 178, 183, 202, 239, 248, 254, 271, 331, 342, 351, 359, 360, 362, 363, 386, 392, 406, 412, 430, 435, 463, 465, 488, 489, 502
Pitris 254, 342, 502
Pitta 149, 502
Planets 9, 11, 13, 15-19, 22, 23, 25-32, 35-37, 40, 47-50, 53, 61, 93, 94, 98-102, 104, 105, 107, 108, 110-120, 127-129, 140, 146, 147, 150-157, 162-164, 170-174, 178-188, 190, 195, 196, 198, 199, 201-203, 211-216, 219, 220, 223, 226, 235, 239, 241, 247-251, 256, 258, 264-266, 281, 282, 286, 288-290, 297, 301, 302, 311-315, 321-325, 327, 333, 335, 337, 341, 342, 344, 350, 355, 363, 364, 366, 367, 377, 383, 384, 387, 389-391, 393-396, 406, 413, 414, 416, 417, 420, 422, 424-427, 450, 462, 463, 466, 472, 482, 483, 489, 497-504
Prashna 309, 310, 424, 502, 508
Prashna Marga 310, 424, 508
Prediction 12-14, 24, 48, 97, 98, 100, 111, 113, 116, 118-120, 126, 147, 167, 186, 208, 251, 252, 290, 298, 309, 320, 334, 408, 492, 503, 507
Purnarvasu 502
Purva Ashadha 148, 202, 415, 480, 502
Purva Bhadrapada 121, 148, 351, 360, 416, 429, 489, 502
Purva Phalguni 101, 148, 164, 183, 260, 264, 269, 271, 415, 491, 502
Pushan 360, 362, 371, 441, 451, 502
Pushya 102, 108, 148, 162, 163, 195, 196, 267, 360, 361, 414, 433, 434, 502

Q

R

Rahu 99, 102, 103, 108, 109, 115, 121, 129, 130, 131, 133, 134, 136-140, 147, 149-151, 157, 160, 162, 163, 172, 179, 180, 183, 185, 191, 192, 201-204, 216, 218, 243, 244, 260, 261, 263, 268-270, 272, 283, 284, 286, 297, 307, 336, 343-345, 347, 348, 349, 351, 352, 362-364, 371, 377, 378, 388, 391, 392, 405-407, 414, 421, 423, 425, 430, 434, 435, 441, 442, 449, 452-455, 466, 469, 471-473, 476, 477, 482-485, 489, 498, 500-502
Raja Yogas 25, 26, 108, 183, 250, 268, 302, 395
Rama 57, 423
Raman, Dr. B.V. 11, 12, 96, 492, 508
Ramayana 76, 505
Rashi Chart 151-153, 157, 160, 162, 174, 184-187, 192, 195, 197, 222, 223, 225-227, 249, 251, 252, 260, 261, 264, 265, 267, 269, 270, 290, 296, 297, 301, 307, 308, 319, 321, 327, 334, 335, 343, 347-349, 352, 365, 367, 370, 374, 389, 390, 394, 395, 400, 402, 407, 426, 429, 430, 434, 442, 449, 457, 459, 460, 463, 465, 468, 471, 472, 476, 480, 488, 489, 502
Retrograde 35, 164, 202, 246, 247, 450, 457, 458, 462, 477, 480, 488, 489, 502
Revati 148, 192, 360, 362, 371, 372, 416, 441, 451, 502
Rohini 99, 148, 183, 199, 414, 453, 454, 456, 457, 502
Ruchaka Yoga 32, 34, 172, 173, 287, 382, 441, 502
Rudra 62, 66, 423, 451, 502

S

Sagittarius 17, 81-83, 104, 120, 145, 171, 176, 178-181, 200, 226, 237, 254, 267, 268, 296, 313, 331, 342, 352, 359, 361, 386, 392, 413, 470, 480, 481, 484, 502
Santhanam, Mr. R. 493, 495, 496, 505, 508
Saptamsha Chart 45, 48, 286, 289, 290, 291, 292, 293, 296, 297, 389, 442, 475, 502
Saraswati Yoga 41, 502
Sarpa Drekkanas 93, 502
Saturn 19, 21, 28, 29, 32-34, 49, 50, 53,

57, 73, 99-102, 104, 105, 107, 108, 115-121, 124, 126, 128, 129, 131, 132, 134, 136-139, 147, 149-151, 154, 155, 157, 160, 162-164, 172, 173, 179-183, 185, 186, 191, 195-198, 200-204, 216, 218, 219, 221, 226, 227, 236-238, 241-243, 248, 251, 258, 265-268, 270, 271, 272, 282, 283, 286, 294, 296, 297, 307, 308, 312, 319, 327, 331, 332, 336, 341-345, 348, 349, 350, 352-355, 357, 362-364, 371, 372, 374-376, 378, 391, 392, 402, 405-407, 414, 421, 423-425, 429, 434, 441, 442, 448-452, 458-469, 471, 473-479, 481, 484, 488, 489, 500, 501, 503, 508

Scorpio 78, 79, 80, 145, 160, 162, 163, 171, 175, 179, 180, 196, 203, 204, 225, 226, 234, 237, 270, 343, 348, 350, 352, 359-361, 363, 372, 386, 407, 413, 449, 450, 453, 455-457, 461, 464-468, 477, 481, 484, 485, 502

Second House 17, 19, 31, 37, 38, 41, 52, 95, 106, 107, 109, 113, 128, 146, 153, 154, 157, 160, 162, 174, 179, 182, 186, 198, 200, 211, 212, 214-217, 220, 222, 226, 240, 249, 251, 252, 255, 257, 290, 291, 296, 300, 301, 303, 314, 319, 323, 327, 336, 337, 341, 342, 348-350, 365, 374, 383, 384, 396, 407, 416, 418, 427, 429, 430, 434, 441, 461, 463-465, 472, 474, 500, 502, 503

Serpent Drekkana 78, 79, 92, 359, 370

Seva 502

Seventh House 18, 19, 21, 22, 30, 39, 40, 114, 118, 126, 131, 134, 146, 155, 160, 162-164, 175, 179-182, 187, 192, 213, 243-249, 251, 252, 254-258, 260, 261, 263-266, 268-272, 287, 288, 290, 292, 294, 301, 304, 307, 313, 316, 322, 324, 336, 338, 341, 343, 348-350, 352, 353, 365, 370, 371, 372, 390, 394, 397, 419, 434, 449, 454-456, 465-468, 470, 472, 474, 475, 481, 491, 498

Shakata Yoga 29, 30, 502
Shakti 229, 502
Shaktipat 502
Shankha Yoga 39, 503
Sharma, Mr. J.N. 166-168
Shasha Yoga 33, 34, 173, 180-182, 503
Shashtamsha Chart 45, 151-157, 160, 162-164, 252, 364-366, 371-374, 376, 378, 450, 452, 463, 464, 477, 480, 503
Shatabhisha 23, 148, 164, 179, 195, 284, 297, 344, 345, 348, 363, 416, 490, 503
Shiva 10, 57, 62, 66, 229, 344, 347, 420, 423, 424, 432, 433, 436, 438, 441, 443, 444, 500, 502, 503
Shiva Purana 62, 66
Shodashamsha Chart 46, 252, 321, 333, 334-339, 341, 343-345, 347-350, 352, 459, 460, 470, 473, 474, 482, 503
Shravana 148, 415, 429, 435, 503
Shrikanta Yoga 503
Shubha Kartari Yoga 38, 102, 152, 503
Shukra 195, 198, 202, 388, 413, 503
Siddhamsha Chart 46, 388-390, 392, 394-398, 400, 402, 406, 407, 469, 471, 472-474, 483, 503
Significator 18, 19, 21, 22, 48, 50, 108, 118, 119, 129, 164, 191, 212, 220, 221, 226, 246, 256, 284, 286, 355, 363, 370, 372, 388, 409, 413, 414, 433, 448-453, 455, 459, 466, 481, 487, 500
Signs 11, 16, 17, 23, 26, 28, 31, 40, 44, 46, 50, 56, 98, 101, 111, 114, 115, 145, 146, 150, 151, 170, 173, 174, 180, 216, 219, 222, 230, 234, 235, 239, 240, 254, 256, 287, 296, 302, 319, 327, 345, 349, 358, 360-365, 385, 392-394, 412, 424, 425, 444, 476, 499, 501
Sivananda, Swami 431
Sivanandamurthy, Swami 7, 205, 206, 209
Sixth House 19, 27, 28, 51, 94, 102, 104, 109, 146, 150-152, 154-157, 160, 162, 164, 173-175, 179-182, 187, 191, 198, 202, 213, 215, 226, 251,

252, 254, 255, 265, 266, 268-270, 292, 297, 300-302, 304, 307, 312, 315, 319, 324, 336, 338, 343, 345, 352, 364-367, 370-378, 397, 405, 407, 419, 429, 434, 449, 450, 452, 457, 460, 465, 466, 470, 472, 473, 476, 477, 479, 481, 482, 484, 488

Soma 79, 453, 454, 456

Sun 19, 21, 22, 31, 34, 40, 43, 49, 50, 55, 94, 99, 102, 103, 112-114, 118, 119, 121, 127-130, 132, 133, 135, 137, 138, 147, 149-151, 153, 157, 160, 162-164, 170, 172, 174, 178-181, 183, 184, 191, 195, 197, 198, 201-203, 211, 216, 217-219, 221, 222, 234, 239, 265-268, 270, 296-298, 300, 301, 307, 313, 334, 335, 341-343, 345, 347- 350, 352, 362-364, 370-377, 380, 382, 387, 390, 391, 413, 420, 423, 424, 432, 433, 441, 448-451, 453, 454, 462, 463, 466, 467, 469, 470-477, 479, 485, 488, 497, 498, 500, 503

Sunapha Yoga 31, 503

Swara 320, 503

Swati 148, 199, 284, 344, 360, 361, 388, 415, 470, 503, 504

T

Tajika System 313

Tara 423, 503

Taurus 60-62, 128, 145, 146, 163, 171, 174, 182, 183, 204, 222, 235, 254, 343, 349, 351, 358-360, 370, 371, 372, 385, 416, 441, 450, 452, 453, 462, 463, 464, 465, 476, 477, 503

Temporal Benefic 103, 105, 116, 152, 216

Temporal Malefic 23, 105, 107, 116, 222

Tenth House 17, 19, 22, 26, 29, 35, 37-39, 47, 49-51, 53, 93, 94, 107, 108, 114, 142, 146, 156, 157, 164, 169-171, 173, 174, 176, 178-184, 186, 188, 191, 195-199, 201, 203, 211, 213, 226, 249, 250, 252, 254, 255, 264, 267, 268, 287, 290, 292, 293, 301, 302, 305, 312, 316, 322, 323, 324, 325, 337, 339, 345, 347, 349, 352, 366, 380, 382, 385, 390, 394, 395, 398, 402, 405, 407, 419, 430, 433, 441, 442, 465-468, 471, 482, 484, 497-499, 503

Third House 17, 19, 20, 21, 26, 52, 94, 102, 128, 146, 154, 157, 160, 174, 179, 181-183, 186, 190, 191, 199, 200, 212, 240, 252, 254-256, 267, 270, 272, 287, 291, 300, 303, 311, 313, 314, 319, 322, 323, 336, 337, 344, 349, 365, 371, 373, 376, 384, 397, 406, 407, 418, 433, 451, 452, 469, 471, 472, 477, 480, 487, 489

Transits 9, 13, 30, 55, 112-115, 117-120, 123, 125, 126, 145, 163, 164, 197, 201-204, 257, 258, 260, 266, 270, 271, 272, 294, 308, 342, 343, 347-352, 371-375, 378, 449, 450, 452,-459, 462-465, 469, 471, 472-477, 479-485, 487, 488, 490, 491

Trimshamsha Chart 46, 503

Trinal Nakshatras 119

Twelfth House 19, 26, 29, 30, 31, 38, 39, 49, 51, 110, 111, 114, 115, 146, 156, 157, 176, 178, 179, 183, 188, 191, 196, 197, 214, 215, 226, 227, 238, 240, 251, 252, 265, 270, 271, 293, 297, 303, 305, 307, 316, 317, 322, 323, 324, 325, 337, 339, 345, 348, 351, 352, 366, 372, 374, 376, 378, 392, 398, 400, 402, 405, 406, 412, 417, 418, 420, 421, 422, 426, 429, 432-435, 441, 442, 448, 450, 453, 455-460, 463, 467, 468, 476, 477, 482, 485, 487, 488, 491, 497, 500-502

U

Upachaya 503

Upasana 503

Uttara Ashadha 148, 360, 361, 362, 382, 415, 451, 503

Uttara Bhadrapada 148, 360, 416, 435, 488, 489, 503

Uttara Phalguni 148, 179, 360, 415, 503

V

Varahamihira 9, 56, 96, 298, 503, 507

Varanasi 493, 496, 505
Vargas 9, 44, 46-48, 53, 252, 301, 314, 498, 503
Vargottama 48, 348, 476, 480, 503
Varshaphal 96, 97, 504
Varuna 23, 65, 297, 344, 345, 423, 490, 504
Vasudev, Mrs. Gayatri Devi 96, 298, 309
Vasudevas 483
Vasus 454
Vata 149, 504
Vayu 344, 360, 361, 470, 504
Vedha 112
Vedic Astrology 12, 15, 24, 53, 54, 149, 234, 493, 508, 504, 246, 256, 274, 277, 389, 408, 493, 497, 499, 500, 501, 502, 507
Venus 16, 17, 19, 21, 22, 28, 30, 32, 33, 35, 37, 38, 41, 48, 49, 50, 53, 99, 100, 102, 104, 108, 117-119, 128, 129, 131, 132, 134, 136-139, 142, 147, 149, 154, 156, 157, 163, 164, 172, 173, 178, 182, 183, 187, 190, 191, 195-198, 201-204, 214-216, 218, 219, 225, 226, 235-247, 251, 254-258, 260, 264-268, 270, 271, 272, 286, 297, 319, 321, 322, 327, 333-335, 341, 342, 343, 345, 348-350, 352, 362-364, 370-377, 380, 387, 388, 391, 392, 405, 413, 421, 423-425, 430, 433, 434, 441, 442, 449-469, 472-475, 477, 484, 487, 489, 491, 497, 500-504
Vidya 495, 504, 506
Vimshamsha Chart 46, 425, 426, 427, 433-435, 461, 462, 464, 467, 485, 504
Vimshottari Dasha 98-100, 504
Virgo 21, 22, 37, 44, 72-74, 93, 101, 113, 145, 164, 167, 171, 173-175, 179-182, 190, 199, 200, 236, 241, 261, 265, 271, 342, 348, 349, 358, 361, 385, 406, 449, 461, 463, 465, 466, 470, 473-476, 489
Vishakha 148, 263, 271, 406, 415, 504
Vishnu 57, 64, 79, 80, 423, 424, 429, 499, 504

W

Weapon Drekkana 57, 59, 64, 65, 70, 71, 73, 81, 83, 86

X

Y

Yagya 229, 462, 496, 504
Yama 69, 121, 173, 270, 376, 414, 457, 482, 504
Yantra 418
Yoga 22, 25-41, 53, 82, 83, 102, 103, 105, 108, 121, 133, 136, 142, 152, 154, 156, 157, 164, 167, 172, 173, 176, 178-183, 185, 186, 188, 191, 192, 195, 197-200, 202, 203, 204, 211-213, 220, 223, 225, 226, 229, 231, 240, 246, 250, 254, 265, 268, 270, 283, 286, 287, 296, 297, 301, 302, 303, 308, 319, 327, 345, 349, 350, 378, 382, 385, 394, 400, 405, 409, 412-414, 418-420, 423, 426, 430, 432, 433, 441, 442, 449, 450, 456, 462, 463, 466, 467, 468, 472-474, 478, 479, 484, 485, 487, 497-504
Yogakaraka 28, 504
Yoga Point 211, 212, 220, 225, 226, 498, 504
Yogas 11, 18, 22, 25, 26-28, 31, 32, 34, 38, 40, 53, 94, 108, 131, 154, 157, 172, 183, 215, 219, 220, 222, 223, 250, 268, 270, 286, 301, 302, 314, 319, 395, 396, 425, 426, 433, 466, 478, 497, 498, 500
Yogi 9, 52, 167, 195, 211, 212, 216, 219-221, 223, 225, 226, 228, 231, 233, 274, 280, 388, 413, 467, 480, 485, 498, 504

Z

252, 254, 255, 265, 266, 268-270, 292, 297, 300-302, 304, 307, 312, 315, 319, 324, 336, 338, 343, 345, 352, 364-367, 370-378, 397, 405, 407, 419, 429, 434, 449, 450, 452, 457, 460, 465, 466, 470, 472, 473, 476, 477, 479, 481, 482, 484, 488

Soma 79, 453, 454, 456

Sun 19, 21, 22, 31, 34, 40, 43, 49, 50, 55, 94, 99, 102, 103, 112-114, 118, 119, 121, 127-130, 132, 133, 135, 137, 138, 147, 149-151, 153, 157, 160, 162-164, 170, 172, 174, 178-181, 183, 184, 191, 195, 197, 198, 201-203, 211, 216, 217-219, 221, 222, 234, 239, 265-268, 270, 296-298, 300, 301, 307, 313, 334, 335, 341-343, 345, 347- 350, 352, 362-364, 370-377, 380, 382, 387, 390, 391, 413, 420, 423, 424, 432, 433, 441, 448-451, 453, 454, 462, 463, 466, 467, 469, 470-477, 479, 485, 488, 497, 498, 500, 503

Sunapha Yoga 31, 503

Swara 320, 503

Swati 148, 199, 284, 344, 360, 361, 388, 415, 470, 503, 504

T

Tajika System 313

Tara 423, 503

Taurus 60-62, 128, 145, 146, 163, 171, 174, 182, 183, 204, 222, 235, 254, 343, 349, 351, 358-360, 370, 371, 372, 385, 416, 441, 450, 452, 453, 462, 463, 464, 465, 476, 477, 503

Temporal Benefic 103, 105, 116, 152, 216

Temporal Malefic 23, 105, 107, 116, 222

Tenth House 17, 19, 22, 26, 29, 35, 37-39, 47, 49-51, 53, 93, 94, 107, 108, 114, 142, 146, 156, 157, 164, 169-171, 173, 174, 176, 178-184, 186, 188, 191, 195-199, 201, 203, 211, 213, 226, 249, 250, 252, 254, 255, 264, 267, 268, 287, 290, 292, 293, 301, 302, 305, 312, 316, 322, 323, 324, 325, 337, 339, 345, 347, 349, 352, 366, 380, 382, 385, 390, 394, 395, 398, 402, 405, 407, 419, 430, 433, 441, 442, 465-468, 471, 482, 484, 497-499, 503

Third House 17, 19, 20, 21, 26, 52, 94, 102, 128, 146, 154, 157, 160, 174, 179, 181-183, 186, 190, 191, 199, 200, 212, 240, 252, 254-256, 267, 270, 272, 287, 291, 300, 303, 311, 313, 314, 319, 322, 323, 336, 337, 344, 349, 365, 371, 373, 376, 384, 397, 406, 407, 418, 433, 451, 452, 469, 471, 472, 477, 480, 487, 489

Transits 9, 13, 30, 55, 112-115, 117-120, 123, 125, 126, 145, 163, 164, 197, 201-204, 257, 258, 260, 266, 270, 271, 272, 294, 308, 342, 343, 347-352, 371-375, 378, 449, 450, 452,- 459, 462-465, 469, 471, 472-477, 479-485, 487, 488, 490, 491

Trimshamsha Chart 46, 503

Trinal Nakshatras 119

Twelfth House 19, 26, 29, 30, 31, 38, 39, 49, 51, 110, 111, 114, 115, 146, 156, 157, 176, 178, 179, 183, 188, 191, 196, 197, 214, 215, 226, 227, 238, 240, 251, 252, 265, 270, 271, 293, 297, 303, 305, 307, 316, 317, 322, 323, 324, 325, 337, 339, 345, 348, 351, 352, 366, 372, 374, 376, 378, 392, 398, 400, 402, 405, 406, 412, 417, 418, 420, 421, 422, 426, 429, 432-435, 441, 442, 448, 450, 453, 455-460, 463, 467, 468, 476, 477, 482, 485, 487, 488, 491, 497, 500-502

U

Upachaya 503

Upasana 503

Uttara Ashadha 148, 360, 361, 362, 382, 415, 451, 503

Uttara Bhadrapada 148, 360, 416, 435, 488, 489, 503

Uttara Phalguni 148, 179, 360, 415, 503

V

Varahamihira 9, 56, 96, 298, 503, 507

Varanasi 493, 496, 505
Vargas 9, 44, 46-48, 53, 252, 301, 314, 498, 503
Vargottama 48, 348, 476, 480, 503
Varshaphal 96, 97, 504
Varuna 23, 65, 297, 344, 345, 423, 490, 504
Vasudev, Mrs. Gayatri Devi 96, 298, 309
Vasudevas 483
Vasus 454
Vata 149, 504
Vayu 344, 360, 361, 470, 504
Vedha 112
Vedic Astrology 12, 15, 24, 53, 54, 149, 234, 493, 508, 504, 246, 256, 274, 277, 389, 408, 493, 497, 499, 500, 501, 502, 507
Venus 16, 17, 19, 21, 22, 28, 30, 32, 33, 35, 37, 38, 41, 48, 49, 50, 53, 99, 100, 102, 104, 108, 117-119, 128, 129, 131, 132, 134, 136-139, 142, 147, 149, 154, 156, 157, 163, 164, 172, 173, 178, 182, 183, 187, 190, 191, 195-198, 201-204, 214-216, 218, 219, 225, 226, 235-247, 251, 254-258, 260, 264-268, 270, 271, 272, 286, 297, 319, 321, 322, 327, 333-335, 341, 342, 343, 345, 348-350, 352, 362-364, 370-377, 380, 387, 388, 391, 392, 405, 413, 421, 423-425, 430, 433, 434, 441, 442, 449-469, 472-475, 477, 484, 487, 489, 491, 497, 500-504
Vidya 495, 504, 506
Vimshamsha Chart 46, 425, 426, 427, 433-435, 461, 462, 464, 467, 485, 504
Vimshottari Dasha 98-100, 504
Virgo 21, 22, 37, 44, 72-74, 93, 101, 113, 145, 164, 167, 171, 173-175, 179-182, 190, 199, 200, 236, 241, 261, 265, 271, 342, 348, 349, 358, 361, 385, 406, 449, 461, 463, 465, 466, 470, 473-476, 489
Vishakha 148, 263, 271, 406, 415, 504
Vishnu 57, 64, 79, 80, 423, 424, 429, 499, 504

W

Weapon Drekkana 57, 59, 64, 65, 70, 71, 73, 81, 83, 86

X

Y

Yagya 229, 462, 496, 504
Yama 69, 121, 173, 270, 376, 414, 457, 482, 504
Yantra 418
Yoga 22, 25-41, 53, 82, 83, 102, 103, 105, 108, 121, 133, 136, 142, 152, 154, 156, 157, 164, 167, 172, 173, 176, 178-183, 185, 186, 188, 191, 192, 195, 197-200, 202, 203, 204, 211-213, 220, 223, 225, 226, 229, 231, 240, 246, 250, 254, 265, 268, 270, 283, 286, 287, 296, 297, 301, 302, 303, 308, 319, 327, 345, 349, 350, 378, 382, 385, 394, 400, 405, 409, 412-414, 418-420, 423, 426, 430, 432, 433, 441, 442, 449, 450, 456, 462, 463, 466, 467, 468, 472-474, 478, 479, 484, 485, 487, 497-504
Yogakaraka 28, 504
Yoga Point 211, 212, 220, 225, 226, 498, 504
Yogas 11, 18, 22, 25, 26-28, 31, 32, 34, 38, 40, 53, 94, 108, 131, 154, 157, 172, 183, 215, 219, 220, 222, 223, 250, 268, 270, 286, 301, 302, 314, 319, 395, 396, 425, 426, 433, 466, 478, 497, 498, 500
Yogi 9, 52, 167, 195, 211, 212, 216, 219-221, 223, 225, 226, 228, 231, 233, 274, 280, 388, 413, 467, 480, 485, 498, 504

Z

The Author

James Kelleher has been a full-time Vedic astrologer since 1980. He was introduced to Vedic astrology in 1975 by M. K. Gandhi, a world-renowned Vedic astrologer and spiritual adept. Gandhi gave Jim his first astrology reading in which he predicted that Jim would become an astrologer, and encouraged him to begin reading about the subject. Gandhi offered to train Jim in the Vedic system of astrology, and later invited him to become his personal assistant.

After studying astrology in India, Jim worked as a professional astrologer in London for five years, assisting Gandhi with his diverse international clientele. In 1984 he returned to the United States and quickly became one of the country's leading Vedic astrologers. He is the co-founder of the American Council of Vedic Astrology and the American College of Vedic Astrology. He is also an adjunct professor at Hindu University of America located in Orlando, Florida. He has been awarded the titles of *Jyotish Kovid* and *Jyotish Vachaspati* by the Indian Council of Astrological Sciences. Jim maintains a busy private practice in Los Gatos, California.

james@jameskelleher.com
www.jameskelleher.com

Path of Light
Volume I

Introduction
to
Vedic Astrology

Volume I of this remarkable set is available from
www.jameskelleher.com

Path of Light
Volume I

Introduction to Vedic Astrology

Volume I of this remarkable set is available from
www.jameskelleher.com

Nine Planets Mantra CD — $18

The Nine Planets Mantra CD provides a great resource for those wishing to benefit from the chanting of planetary bija mantras. These mantras were imparted to James Kelleher by his guru. Chanted by a traditional South Indian Vedic pundit, the mantras are beautifully recorded against the droning sound of a tambura. They can be easily learned and chanted by anyone. Listening to them and chanting them regularly will lead to greater prosperity, success and fulfillment in every domain of life.

"As part of a large-scale reorganization, my entire department at Boeing was laid off. On your recommendation, I began chanting the Venus mantra. After 3 days of chanting the mantra, I got a call from my boss. He said there had been a change. They had decided to lay off the entire department, except for me! This seemed to be more than a coincidence."
— S.M., Seattle, WA

"I have been chanting the Ketu mantra for the past year and have found that it makes me feel very smooth and seems to increase my intuition."
— T.S., New York, NY

Now available at www.jameskelleher.com

ABOUT THE TYPE

This book was set in Garamond, a typeface based on the types of the sixteenth-century printer, publisher, and type designer Claude Garamond, whose sixteenth-century types were modeled on those of Venetian printers from the end of the previous century. The italics are based on types by Robert Granjon, a contemporary of Garamond's. The Garamond typeface and its variations have been a standard among book designers and printers for four centuries.

Composed by JTC Imagineering, Santa Maria, CA
Designed by John Taylor-Convery

Maricopa County Hospital
(602) 344-5011